Holiness Through the Ages

First Fruits Press
The Academic Open Press of Asbury Theological Seminary
204 N. Lexington Ave., Wilmore, KY 40390
859-858-2236
first.fruits@asburyseminary.edu
asbury.to/firstfruits

Holiness through the Ages

An Historical Reader of Holiness Writers

Edited by
Robert E. Coleman
Robert A. Danielson
Faith E. Parry

First Fruits Press
Wilmore, Ky
c2014

Holiness Through the Ages: An Historic Reader of Christian Writers on Holiness,
edited by Robert E. Coleman, Robert A. Danielson, and Faith E. Parry

Published by First Fruits Press, © 2014

ISBN: 9781621711193 (Print)
9781621711599 (Digital), 9781621711605 (Kindle)

Digital version at http://place.asburyseminary.edu/

The author(s) has granted permission to First Fruits Press to electronically publish this item for academic use. Copyright of this item remains with the author(s). For any commercial or non-educational use of the material, please contact the author(s) directly. First Fruits Press is a digital imprint of the Asbury Theological Seminary, B.L. Fisher Library. Its publications are available for noncommercial and educational uses, such as research, teaching and private study. First Fruits Press has licensed the digital version of this work under the Creative Commons Attribution Noncommercial 3.0 United States License. To view a copy of this license, visit http://creativecommons.org/licenses/by-nc/3.0/us/.

For all other uses, contact First Fruits Press:
859-858-2236
first.fruits@asburyseminary.edu

Holiness through the ages : an historical reader of holiness writers / edited by Robert E. Coleman, Robert A. Danielson, Faith E. Parry
    ix, 683 pages ; 23 cm.
    Wilmore, Kentucky : First Fruits Press, ©2014.
    ISBN: 9781621711193 (pbk.)
    1. Holiness. I. Title. II. Coleman, Robert Emerson, 1928- III. Danielson, Robert A. (Robert Alden), 1969- IV. Parry, Faith E
    BT767 .H646 2014   234.8

Cover design by Kelli Dierdorf

Introduction

Holiness is living life, as God would have us live it. For flawed human beings, this is impossible without the power of the Holy Spirit and a strong commitment to prayer, studying scripture, and repentance with self-reflection, along with other spiritual disciplines. No Christian tradition has a monopoly on teaching holiness. In fact, it has been a part of the teachings of the Church from the very start.

This book brings together many Christian writers from many different traditions, but all with a common focus on how to live a holy life. From the Romafn Catholics, Brother Lawrence and Blaise Pascal to Puritans, Methodists, Baptists, and early Pentecostals, they all have some important lessons to teach those who desire to faithfully follow Christ today.

Dr. Robert "Clem" Coleman, who started printing small booklets of excerpts or abridged versions of spiritual classics when he was a professor at Asbury Theological Seminary, edited and wrote introductions for a number of these chapters. He continued this work with many others in producing booklets that were later published by the Billy Graham Center. Dr. Coleman wanted to use many of these writings for teaching a course in discipleship, but was frustrated by the difficulty of locating so many small booklets and reselling them to students. So we gathered permissions from all of the writers we could find, and are now publishing most of this material in one place.

Our hope is that this material, being made freely available online, will impact the lives of Christians all over the world. Holiness is what we are called to in the Christian journey. Conversion is just an important step on a much longer journey toward holiness. Never before have the needs of the world cried out for the People of God to live out their calling to be a light to the nations, as it has in this generation. Yet many believers still have not heard the message of living a holy life for a holy God.

Consumerism, materialism, individualism, rationalism, and the rejection of absolute truth have all led to a world desperately in need of the classical teachings of Christian holiness. This is just a small attempt to reintroduce these teachings once again. Read and reflect on these teachings and the lives of those who made such an impact in their own time. May their words inspire a new generation of Christians and light a fire in their hearts that will kindle a passion for holiness that will sweep over the earth!

By Robert Danielson,
Editor of First Fruits Press
and of The Asbury Journal

Using and Citing This Book

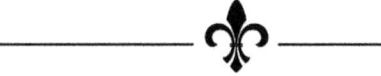

Because this book is a collection of books, the table of contents is marked accordingly. The Roman numerals are the books, while the Arabic numerals are the chapters within each book.. Each book has its own copyright page and citations. When citing the book, it is best to use the format of a chapter within a book. If using a digital version of this book, make the edition either PDF, Kindle, or ePub to reflect that it is a digital edition. For example:

MLA:

Lawrence, Brother. "Practicing the Presence of God." *Holiness Through the Ages: An Historical Reader of Christian Writers on Holiness.* Ed. Robert E. Coleman. Kindle Edition. Wilmore, Ky: First Fruits Press, 2014.

APA:

Lawrence, B. (2014). Practicing the Presence of God. In R. Coleman (Ed.), *Holiness Through the Ages: An Historical Reader of Christian Writers on Holiness* (Kindle Edition ed.). Wilmore, Ky: First Fruits Press.

Always refer to MLA or APA standards for the most updated citation format.

Books and Chapters

Introduction .... *i*
Using and Citing This Book .... *iii*

I. *Practicing the Presence of God*
Brother Lawrence 1611-1691   1

   1. Introduction
      By Robert E. Coleman 4
   2. Conversations 7
   3. Letters 16
   4. Notes 31

II. *The Saints' Everlasting Rest*
Richard Baxter 1615-1691   33

   1. Introduction
      By Timothy K. Beougher 36
   2. The Importance of Leading a Heavenly Life Upon Earth 39
   3. Directions on How to Lead a Heavenly Life Upon Earth 49
   4. The Nature of Heavenly Contemplation, with the Time, Place, and
      Frame of Mind Most Suited for It 62

III. *Aflame with Love*
Blaise Pascal 1623-1662   71

   1. Introduction
      By Robert E. Coleman 74
   2. Knowing God in Christ 81
   3. Proofs of Jesus 86
   4. Human Struggle 94
   5. The New Life 99

IV. Resolutions of a Saintly Scholar
Jonathan Edwards 1703-1758   107

1. Introduction
   By Robert E. Coleman 110
2. His Spiritual Delight 115
3. Personal Resolutions 120
4. Constant Review 127

V. The Scripture Way of Salvation
John Wesley 1703-1791   135

1. Introduction
   By Robert E. Coleman 138
2. The Scripture Way of Salvation 142
3. The Circumcision of the Heart 151
4. The Repentance of Believers 160
5. Notes 172

VI. Is Your Christian Faith Real?
George Whitefield 1714-1770   175

1. Introduction
   By Timothy K. Beougher 178
2. "The Almost Christian" 182
3. "Marks of a True Conversion" 192
4. Notes 203

VII. The Fruit of Revival
Charles G. Finney 1792-1875   205

1. Introduction
   By Robert E. Coleman 208
2. When a Revival is to Be Expected 213
3. How to Promote a Revival 218
4. The Way of Salvation 224
5. Christian Perfection 228
6. Love is the Whole of Religion 237
7. Notes 242

VIII. Faith in Action
George Müller 1805-1898   245

1. Introduction
   By David P. Setran 248
2. Faith 254

	3.	Stewardship	259
	4.	The Word of God	267
	5.	Prayer	274
	6.	The Deeper Life	277
	7.	The Christian in the Workplace	281
	8.	Working with Children	283
	9.	The Will of God	284
	10.	The Challenge	285
	11.	Notes	287

IX. *The Way of Holiness*
Phoebe Palmer 1807-1874   289

1. Introduction
   By Alathea Coleman Jones 292
2. The Way of Holiness 294

X. *Words to Winners of Souls*
Horatius Bonar 1808-1889   319

1. Introduction
   By Robert E. Coleman 322
2. The Importance of a Living Ministry 325
3. The Minister's True Life and Walk 330
4. Past Defects 334
5. Ministerial Confession 339
6. Revival in the Ministry 352
7. Notes 359

XI. *The Deeper Life*
Robert Murray McCheyne 1813-1843   361

1. Introduction
   By Lyle W. Dorsett and David P. Setran 365
2. Personal Renewal 368
3. Do What You Can 377
4. Reasons Why Children Should Fly to Christ Without Delay 383
5. Miscellaneous Quotes (Arranged by Topic) 390
6. Daily Bible Calendar 396
7. Notes 421

XII. *Holiness*
John Charles Ryle 1813-1900   423

1. Introduction
   By Tom Phillips 426

2.	Holiness	429
3.	Without Christ	437
4.	Thirst Relieved	442
5.	Christ is All	450

XIII. *Aggressive Christianity*
Catherine Booth 1829-1890 — 457

1.	Introduction By Lyle W. Dorsett	460
2.	Aggressive Christianity	463
3.	The World's Need	474
4.	Notes	483

XIV. *Preacher and Prayer*
E. M Bounds 1835-1913 — 485

1.	Introduction By Robert E. Coleman	488
2.	Men and Women of Prayer Needed	490
3.	Our Sufficiency Is of God	493
4.	The Letter Kills	496
5.	Tendencies to Be Avoided	499
6.	Prayer, the Great Essential	502
7.	Much Time Should Be Given to Prayer	505
8.	Heart Preparation Necessary	508
9.	Unction, the Mark of True Gospel Preaching	511
10.	Prayer Marks Spiritual Leadership	514
11.	A Praying Pulpit Gives Birth to a Praying Pew	517
12.	Notes	520

XV. *I Believe in the Holy Ghost*
D. L. Moody 1837-1899 — 521

1.	Introduction By Nathan L. Oates	525
2.	Honor the Holy Ghost	528
3.	Power—Its Source	530
4.	Power "In" and "Upon"	539
5.	Witnessing In Power	551
6.	Power Hindered	559

XVI. Say a Good Word for Jesus
John Watson (Ian Maclaren) 1850-1907 — 563

1. Introduction
   By Robert E. Coleman 566
2. His Mother's Sermon 570
3. The Transformation of Lachlan Campbell....................................577
4. Notes 592

XVII. Why God Used D.L. Moody
R.A. Torrey 1856-1928 — 593

1. Introduction
   By Robert E. Coleman 596
2. Why God Used D.L. Moody 599
3. A Fully Surrendered Man..601
4. A Man of Prayer...603
5. A Deep and Practical Student of the Bible....................................605
6. A Humble Man..609
7. His Entire Freedom from the Love of Money...............................612
8. A Consuming Passion for the Salvation of the Lost......................614
9. Definitely Endued with Power from on High 619

XVIII. Light on the Way
J. Wilbur Chapman 1859-1918 — 623

1. Introduction
   By K. Erik Thoennes...626
2. Light on the Way...631
3. My Covenant...654
4. Notes 655

XIX. The Laws of Revival
James Burns 1865-1945 — 657

1. Foreword
   By Tom Phillips 660
2. Introduction..661
3. Revivals...663

Practicing the Presence of God

*Conversations and Letters of
Nicholas Herman of Lorraine*

Brother Lawrence 1611-1691

*Translated, Edited, and Introduction
By Robert E. Coleman*

Abridged version of *Practicing the Presence of God*, Conversations and Letters of Nicholas Herman of Lorraine by Brother Lawrence. Abridged version originally published by the Institute of Evangelism Billy Graham Center, 1996, Wheaton, IL. Copyright of translated abridged version and introduction held by Robert Coleman, used with permission. Translated from the French. Artwork in the Public Domain.

Book Chapters

1. Introduction
   By Robert E. Coleman 4
2. Conversations 7
   First Conversation *7*
   Second Conversation *8*
   Third Conversation *11*
   Fourth Conversation *12*
   Other Accounts of Brother Lawrence *14*
3. Letters 16
   First Letter *16*
   Second Letter *17*
   Third Letter *20*
   Fourth Letter *20*
   Fifth Letter *22*
   Sixth Letter *23*
   Seventh Letter *24*
   Eighth Letter *24*
   Ninth Letter *25*
   Tenth Letter *26*
   Eleventh Letter *27*
   Twelfth Letter *28*
   Thirteenth Letter *28*
   Fourteenth Letter *29*
   Fifteenth Letter *30*
4. Notes 31

1. Introduction
By Robert E. Coleman

Truth is most beautiful when clothed with humility. And it is never so profound as when making simple the way of holiness.

Perhaps that is why this little book has been read by millions of people seeking the highest good. With captivating sweetness, it cuts through theological complexities and gets to the heart of Christian devotion. In an age of fierce turmoil, unconscious sainthood is seen in the daily, routine, menial tasks common to every man. There is no fanciful theory; no strutting with pious words. Just the gentle witness of one, unlearned in the esteem of the world, who found how every experience of life can be filled with the glory of God's Presence.

Sometimes called Lawrence of the Resurrection, Nicholas Herman was born of lowly parents at Herimesnil, Lorraine, France in 1611. Little is known of his early years, except that he was raised in poor circumstances with no formal education. As a youth, he served for a time in the army, fighting in the bloody church wars, that ravaged Europe during this period. A wound, which he received in battle, left him with a limp the rest of his life.

At the age of eighteen he experienced a remarkable awakening while gazing upon a barren tree standing dormant against the snow on a mid-winter day. The sight stirred thoughts of the change coming in the spring when the tree would bring forth leaves and fruit. Gripped by the fact of God's power and providence, he set about to free himself from this world, and so to live each day that "he might perform all his actions for the love of God."[1]

In the following years he worked as a domestic servant and for a while was an aid to the treasurer of the King of France. He described himself as "a great awkward fellow who broke everything,"[2] suggesting a cumbersome manner about his work, which makes us even more aware of our affinity with his humanness.

Moved by a desire to renounce all for Christ's sake, in 1666, perhaps earlier,[3] he became a lay brother of the barefooted Carmelites, and entered the monastery at Paris. He was assigned to the kitchen, where for the next thirty or more years he was the cook, being relieved of this duty only because of blindness before his death. It was while serving in this capacity that he became known as Brother Lawrence.

Though the love that was kindled in his heart at his conversion never left him, for years he experienced periods of vacillation and doubt. There were seasons when temptations overwhelmed him, and he even despaired of his salvation. Despite all his efforts to concentrate upon God, he could not seem to maintain the constancy of worship his spirit so earnestly sought.[4]

Out of this soul-searching came a deeper illumination and trust. As he put it, "When I thought of nothing but to end my days in these troubles, I found myself changed all at once."[5] The struggle was gone. Relying entirely upon the faithfulness of God, he "felt a profound inward peace," as if he were in the "center and place of rest."[6]

Thereafter Brother Lawrence walked "before God simply, in faith, with humility and with love," applying himself "diligently to do nothing and think nothing" which might displease his Lord.[7] He was so resigned to the will of God that he "would not take up a straw from the ground against His order, or from any other motive than purely that love to Him."[8] His one desire was for God to form His perfect image in his soul.

This was not a passive resignation to the divine will, but rather an active perseverance in the Presence of God, wherein he kept himself by constant attention. When he saw his faults, he freely confessed them to God, and then returned immediately to his accustomed adoration. Sanctification involved for him an earnest growth in truth, because, as he put it, "not to advance in the spiritual life is to go back."[9]

In this pursuit, he made his work an occasion of praise, "The time of business," he said, "does not with me differ from the time of prayer, and in the noise and clatter of my kitchen, while several persons are at the same time calling for different things, I possess God in as great tranquility as if I were upon my knees at the blessed sacrament."[10]

Physical infirmities, which came to Brother Lawrence in his last years, did not diminish his joy. Sufferings were regarded as a paradise so long as they could be shared with his Lord, while "the greatest pleasures would be hell" if he had to "relish them without Him."[11] He knew that God's love was in everything and thus could accept "the sweet and the biter" as from the same loving hand.[12] On February 12, 1691, in perfect peace, this humble servant of the Lord quietly left his earthly tabernacle to enter into another dimension of the Presence he knew so well. Shortly before the transition came, he was asked by another brother, what was on his mind. The dying saint replied characteristically, "I am doing that which I shall be doing through eternity, thanking God, praising God, adoring God, offering Him the love that fills my heart."[13]

It was never his intention that what he said would be published. However, Joseph du Beaufont, vicar-general of the Diocese of Paris under Cardinal Noailles, recognized the need to preserve the lay brother's words. Accordingly, he wrote *The Conversations* he had with him in 1666 and 1667, endeavoring to record as closely as possible Lawrence's own manner of speech. Upon Beaufont's recommendation, some letters were also gathered, all written during the final decade of his life. The first edition of the combined collection was published in 1692, which is the basis for the translation reproduced here.

Nearly three centuries have passed since his writings first appeared, but they have lost neither their freshness nor their practical wisdom. Spiritual pilgrims still sit at the feet of this natural teacher who "all his life studied to avoid the gaze of men." It is my hope that the truth, which he taught, may help us know more fully that Holy Presence in which is fullness of joy.

Robert E. Coleman

2. Conversations

First Conversation

The first time I saw Brother Lawrence was upon the third of August 1666. He told me that God had done him a singular favor in his conversion at the age of eighteen.

That in the winter, seeing a tree stripped of its leaves, and considering that within a little time the leaves would be renewed, and after that the flowers and fruit would appear, he received a high view of the providence and power of God, which has never since been effaced from his soul. That this view had perfectly set him loose from the world, and kindled in him such a love for God that he could not tell whether it has increased during the more than forty years he had lived since.

That he had been footman to M. Fieubert, the treasurer, and that he was a great awkward fellow who broke everything.

That he had desired to be received into a monastery, thinking that he would there be made to smart for his awkwardness and the faults he should commit, and so he should sacrifice to God his life, with its pleasures; but that God had disappointed him, he having met with nothing but satisfaction in that state.

That we should establish ourselves in a sense of God's presence by continually conversing with Him. That it was a shameful thing to quit His conversation to think of trifles and fooleries.

That we should feel and nourish our souls with high notions of God; which yield us great joy in being devoted to Him.

That we ought to quicken—i.e., to enliven—our faith. That it was lamentable we had so little; and that instead of taking faith for the rule of their conduct, men amused themselves with trivial devotions, which changed daily. That the way of faith was the spirit of the church, and that it was sufficient to bring us to a high degree of perfection.

That we ought to give ourselves up to God, with regard both to things temporal and spiritual, and seek our satisfaction only in the fulfilling of His will, whether He lead us by suffering or by consolation, for all would be equal to a soul truly resigned. That there needed fidelity in those drynesses or insensibilities and irksomenesses in prayer by which God tries our love to Him; that then was the time for us to make good and effectual acts of resignation, whereof one alone would oftentimes very much promote our spiritual advancement.

That as for the miseries and sins he heard of daily in the world, he was so far from wondering at them that, on the contrary, he was surprised that there were not more, considering the malice sinners were capable of: that, for his part, he prayed for them; but knowing that God could remedy the mischiefs they did when He pleased, he gave himself no further trouble.

That to arrive at such resignation as God requires, we should watch attentively over all the passions which mingle as well in spiritual things as in those of a grosser nature; that God would give light concerning those passions to those who truly desire to serve Him. That if this was my design, sincerely to serve God, I might come to him (Brother Lawrence) as often as I pleased, without any fear of being troublesome, but if not, that I ought no more visit him.

Second Conversation

That he had always been governed by love, without selfish views, and that having resolved to make the love of God the end of all his actions, he had found reasons to be well satisfied with his method. That he was pleased when he could take up a straw, from the ground for the love of God, seeking Him only, and nothing else, not even His gifts.

That he had been long troubled in mind from a certain belief that he should be damned: that all the men in the world could not have persuaded him to the contrary; but that he had thus reasoned with himself about it. *I engaged in a religious life only for the love of God, and I have endeavored to act only for Him, whatever becomes of me, whether I be lost or saved. I will always continue to act purely for the love of God. I shall have this good at least; that till death I shall have done all that is in me to love Him.* That this trouble of mind has lasted four years, during which time he had suffered much, but that at last he had seen that this trouble arose from want of faiths and that since he had passed his life in perfect liberty and continual joy. That he had placed his sins betwixt him and God, as it were, to tell Him that he did not deserve His favors, but that God still continued to bestow them in abundance.

That in order to form a habit of conversing with God continually, and referring all we do to Him, we must first apply to Him with some diligence: but that after a little care we should find His love inwardly excite us to it without any difficulty.

That he expected, after the pleasant days God had given him, he should have his turn of pain and suffering; but that he was not uneasy about it, knowing very well that as he could do nothing of himself, God would not fail to give him the strength to bear it.

That when an occasion of practicing some virtue offered, he addressed himself to God, saying, *Lord, I cannot do this unless Thou enablest me:* and that then he received strength more than sufficient.

That when he had failed in his duty, he only confessed his fault, saying to God, *I shall never do otherwise leave me to myself; it is You who must hinder my falling and mend what is amiss.* That after this he gave himself no further uneasiness about it.

That we ought to act with God in the greatest simplicity, speaking to Him frankly and plainly, and imploring His assistance in our affairs, just as they happen. That God never failed to grant it, as he had often experienced.

That he had been lately sent into Burgundy, to buy the provision of wine for the society, which was a very unwelcome task for him, because he had no turn for business, and because he was lame and could not go about the boat but by rolling himself over the casks. That, however, he gave himself no uneasiness about it, or about the purchase of wine. That he said to God it was His business he was about, and that he afterward found it very well performed. That he had been sent into Auvergne, the year before, upon the same account; that he could not tell how the matter passed, but that it proved very well.

So, likewise, in his business in the kitchen (to which he had naturally a great aversion), having accustomed himself to do everything there for the love of God, and with prayer, upon all occasions, for His grace to do his work well, he had found everything easy, during fifteen years that he had been employed there.

That he was very well pleased with the post he was now in: but that he was as ready to quit that as the former, he was always pleasing to himself in every condition by doing little things for the love of God.

That with him the set times of prayer were not different from other times, that he retired to pray, according to the directions of his superior, but that he did not want such retirement, nor ask for it, because his greatest business did not divert him from God.

That he knew his obligation to love God in all things, and as he endeavored so to do, he had no need of a director to advise him, but that he needed much a confessor to absolve him. That he was very sensible of his faults, but not discouraged by them; that he confessed them to God, but did not plead against Him to excuse them. When he had so done, he peaceably resumed his usual practice of love and adoration.

That in his trouble of mind he had consulted nobody, but knowing only by the light of faith that God was present, he contented himself with directing all his actions to Him, i.e., doing them with a desire to please Him, let what would come of it.

That useless thoughts spoil all; that the mischief began there; but that we ought to reject them as soon as we perceive their impertinence to the matter in hand, or our salvation, and return to our communion with God.

That at the beginning he had often passed his time appointed for prayer in rejecting wandering thoughts and falling back into them. That he could never regulate his devotion by certain methods as some do. That, nevertheless, at first he had meditated for some time, but afterward that went off, in a manner he could give no account of.

That all bodily mortifications and other exercises are useless, except as they serve to arrive at the union with God by love: that he had well considered this, and found it the shortest way to go straight to Him by a continual exercise of love and doing all things for His sake.

That we ought to make a great difference between the acts of the understanding and those of the will that the first were comparatively of little value, and the others, all. That our only business was to love and delight ourselves in God.

That all possible kinds of mortification, if they were void of the love of God, could not efface a single sin. That we ought, without anxiety, to expect the pardon of our sins from the blood of Jesus Christ, only endeavoring to love Him with all our hearts. That God seemed to have granted the greatest favors to the greatest sinners, as more signal monuments of His mercy.

That the greatest pains or pleasures of this world were not to be compared with what he had experienced of both kinds in a spiritual state;

so that he was careful for nothing and feared nothing, desiring only one thing of God, viz., that he might not offend Him.

That he had no scruples; for, said he, when I fail in my duty, I readily acknowledge it, saying, *I am used to do so; I shall never do otherwise I am left to myself.* If I fail not, then I give God thanks, acknowledging that the strength comes from Him.

Third Conversation

He told me that the foundation of the spiritual life in him had been a high notion and esteem of God in faith, which when he had once well conceived, he had no other care at first but faithfully to reject every other thought, *that he might perform all his actions for the love God.* That when sometimes he had not thought of God for a good while, he did not disquiet himself for it; but after having acknowledged his wretchedness to God, he returned to Him with so much the greater trust in Him as he had found himself wretched through forgetting Him.

That the trust we put in God honors Him much and draws down great graces.

That it was impossible not only that God should deceive, but also that He should long let a soul suffer which is perfectly resigned to Him, and resolved to endure everything for His sake.

That he had so often experienced the ready succors of divine grace upon all occasions, that from the same experience when he had business to do, he did not think of it beforehand: but when it was time to do it, he found in God, as in a clear mirror, all that was fit for him to do. That of late he had acted thus, without anticipating care: but before the experience mentioned above, he had used it in his affairs.

When outward business diverted him a little from the thought of God, a fresh remembrance coming from God invested his soul, and so inflamed and transported him that it was difficult for him to contain himself.

That he was more united to God in his outward employments than when he left them for devotion and retirement.

That he expected hereafter some great pain of body or mind; that the worst that could happen to him was to lose that sense of God which he had enjoyed so long; but that the goodness of God assured him He would not forsake him utterly, and that He would give him strength to bear whatever evil He permitted to happen to him; and therefore that he feared nothing, and had no occasion to consult with anybody about his state. That when he had attempted to do it, he had always come away more perplexed; and that, as he was conscious of his readiness to lay down his life for the love of God, he had no apprehension of danger. That perfect resignation to God was a sure way to heaven, a way in which he had always-sufficient light for conduct.

That in the beginning of the spiritual life we ought to be faithful in doing our duty and denying ourselves; but after that, unspeakable pleasures followed. That in difficulties we need only to have recourse to Jesus Christ, and beg His grace: with that everything became easy.

That many do not advance in the Christian progress because they stick in penances and particular exercises, while they neglect the love of God, which is the end. That this appeared plainly in their works, and was the reason why we see so little solid virtue.

That there needed neither art nor science for going to God, but only a heart resolutely determined to apply itself to nothing but Him, or for His sake, and to love Him only.

Fourth Conversation

He discoursed with me frequently, and with great openness of heart, concerning his manner of going to God, whereof some part is related already.

He told me that all consists in one hearty renunciation of everything, which we are sensible does not lead to God. That we might accustom ourselves to a continual conversation with Him, with freedom and in simplicity. That we need only to recognize God intimately present with us, to address ourselves to Him every moment, that we may beg His assistance for knowing His will in things doubtful, and for rightly performing those which 'we plainly see He requires of us, offering them to Him before we do them, and giving Him thanks when we have done.

That in this conversation with God we are also employed in praising, adoring, and loving Him incessantly, for His infinite goodness and perfection.

That, without being discouraged on account of our sins, we should pray for His grace with a perfect confidence, as relying upon the infinite merits of our Lord Jesus Christ. That God never failed offering us His grace at each action: that he distinctly perceived it, and never failed of it unless when his thoughts had wandered from a sense of God's presence, or he had forgotten to ask His assistance.

That God always gave us light in our doubts when we had no other design but to please Him.

That our sanctification did not depend upon changing our works, but in doing that for God's sake which we commonly do for our own. That it was lamentable to see how many people mistook the means for the end, addicting themselves to certain works, which they performed very imperfectly by reason of their human or selfish regards.

That the most excellent method he had found of going to God was that of doing our common business without any view of pleasing men, (Galatians 1:10, Ephesians 65:6), and (as far as we are capable) purely for the love of God.

That it was a great delusion to think that the times of prayer ought to differ from other times; that we are as strictly obliged to adhere to God by action in the time of action as by prayer in the season of prayer.

That his prayer was nothing else but a sense of the presence of God, his soul being at that time insensible to everything but divine love; and that when the appointed times of prayer were past, he found no difference because he still continued with God, praising and blessing Him with all his might, so that he passed his life in continual joy: hoped that God would give him somewhat to suffer when he should grow stronger.

That we ought, once for all heartily to put our whole trust in God, and make a total surrender of ourselves to Him, secure that He would not deceive us.

That we ought not to be weary of doing little things for the love of God, who regards not the greatness of the work, but the love with which it is performed. That we should not wonder if, in the beginning, we often failed in our endeavors, but that at last we should gain a habit, which will naturally produce its acts in us, without our care, and to our exceeding great delight

That the whole substance of religion was faith, hope, and charity, by the practice of which we become united to the will of God: that all besides is indifferent, and to be used as a means that we may arrive at our end, and be swallowed up therein, by faith and charity.

That all things are possible to him who *believes*, that they are less difficult to him who *hopes*, that they are more easy to him who *loves*, and still more easy to him who *perseveres* in the practice of these three virtues.

That the end we ought to propose to ourselves is to become in this life, the most perfect worshippers of God we can possibly be, as we hope to be through all eternity.

That when we enter upon the spiritual life, we should consider and examine to the bottom what we are. And then we should find ourselves worthy of all contempt, and not deserving indeed the name of Christians; subject to all kinds of misery and numberless accidents, which trouble us and cause perpetual vicissitudes in our health, in our humors, in our internal and external dispositions; in fine, persons whom God would humble by many pains and labors, as well within as without. After this we should not wonder what troubles, temptations, oppositions, and contradictions happen to us from men. We ought, on the contrary, to submit ourselves to them, and bear them as long as God pleases, as things highly advantageous to us.

That the greater perfection a soul aspires after, the more dependent it is upon divine grace.

Other Accounts of Brother Lawrence

Being questioned by one of his own society (to whom he was obliged to open himself) by what means he had attained such an habitual sense of God, he told him that since his first coming to the monastery, he had considered God as the end of all his thoughts and desires, as the mark to which they should tend, and in which they should terminate.

That in the beginning of his novitiate he spent the hours appointed for private prayer in thinking of God, so as to convince his mind of, and to impress deeply upon his heart, the divine existence, rather by devout sentiments, and submission to the lights of faith, than by studied reasoning and elaborate meditations. That by this short and sure method he exercised himself in the knowledge and love of God, resolving to use his utmost endeavor to live in a continual sense of His presence, and, if possible never to forget Him more.

That when he had thus in prayer filled his mind with great sentiments of that infinite Being, he went to his work appointed in the kitchen (for he was cook to the society). There having first considered severally the things his office required, and when and how each thing was to be done, he spent all the intervals of his time, before, as well as after his work, in prayer.

That when he began his business, he said to God, with a filial trust in Him: *O my God, since Thou art with me, and I must now, in obedience to Thy commands, apply my mind to these outward things, I beseech Thee to grant me the grace to continue in Thy presence; and to this end do Thou prosper me with Thy assistance, receive all my works, and possess all my affections.*

As he proceeded in his work he continued his familiar conversation with his Maker, imploring His grace, and offering to Him all his actions.

When he had finished he examined himself how he had discharged his duty; if he found well, he returned thanks to God; if other wise, he asked pardon, and without being discouraged, he set his mind right again, and continued his exercise of the presence of God as if he had never deviated from it. "Thus," said he, "by rising after my falls, and by frequently renewed acts of faith and love, I am come to a state wherein it would be as difficult for me not to think of God as it was at first to accustom myself to it."

As Brother Lawrence had found such an advantage in walking in the presence of God, it was natural for him to recommend it earnestly to others; but his example was a stronger inducement than any arguments he could propose. His very countenance was edifying, such a sweet and calm devotion appearing in it as could not but affect the beholders. And it was observed that in the greatest hurry of business in the kitchen he still preserved his recollection and heavenly-mindedness. He was never hasty nor loitering, but did each thing in its season, with an even, uninterrupted composure and tranquility of spirit. "The time of business," said he, "does not with me differ from the time of prayer; and in the noise and clatter of my kitchen, while several persons are at the same time calling for different things, I possess God in as great tranquility as if I were upon my knees at the Blessed Sacrament."

3. Letters

First Letter

Since you desire so earnestly that I should communicate with you the method by which I arrived at that *habitual sense of God's presence,* which our Lord, of His mercy, has been pleased to vouchsafe to me, I must tell you that it is with great difficulty that I am prevailed on by your importunities; and now I do it only upon the terms that you show my letter to nobody. If I knew that you would let it be seen, all the desire that I have for your advancement would not be able to determine me to it. The account I can give you is:

Having found in many books different methods of going to God, and diverse practices of the spiritual life, I thought this would serve rather to puzzle me than facilitate what I sought after, which was nothing but how to become wholly God's. This made me resolve to give the all for the all; so after having given myself wholly to God, that He might take away my sin, I renounced, for the love of Him, everything that was not He, and I began to live as if there was none but He and I in the world. Sometimes I considered myself before Him as a poor criminal at the feet of his Judge; at other times I beheld Him in my heart as my Father, as my God. I worshipped Him the oftenest that I could, keeping my mind in His holy presence, and recalling it as often as I found it wandering from Him. I found no small pain in this exercise, and yet I continued it, notwithstanding all the difficulties that occurred, without troubling or disquieting myself when my mind had wandered involuntarily. I made this my business as much all the day long as at the appointed times of prayer, for at all times, every hour, every minute, even in the height of my business, I drove away from my mind everything that was capable of interrupting my thought of God.

Such has been my common practice ever since I entered in religion; and though I have done it very imperfectly, yet I have found great advantages by it. These, I well know, are to be imputed to the mere mercy and goodness of God, because we can do nothing without Him, and I still less than any. But when we are faithful to keep ourselves in His holy presence, and set Him always before us, this not only hinders our offending Him and doing anything that may displease Him, at least willfully, but it also begets in us a holy freedom, and, if I may so speak, a familiarity with God, wherewith we ask, and that successfully, the graces we stand in need of. In fine, by often repeating these acts, they become habitual, and the presence of God rendered as it were natural to us. Give Him thanks, if you please, with me, for His great goodness toward me, which I can never sufficiently admire, for the many favors He has done to so miserable a sinner as I am. May all things praise Him, Amen.

I am, in our Lord, yours…

Second Letter

To the Reverend
Not finding my manner of life in books, although I have no difficulty about it, yet, for greater security, I shall be glad to know your thoughts concerning it.

In a conversation some days since with a person of piety, he told me the spiritual life was a life of grace, which begins with servile fear, which is increased by hope of eternal life, and which is consummated by pure love; that each of these states had its different stages, by which one arrives at last at that blessed consummation.

I have not followed all these methods. On the contrary, from I know not what instincts, I found they discouraged me; this was the reason why, at my entrance into religion, I took a resolution to give myself up to God, as the best return I could make for His love, and, for the love of Him, to renounce all besides. For the first year I commonly employed myself during the time set apart for devotion with the thought of death, judgment, heaven, hell, and my sins. Thus I continued some years, applying my mind carefully the rest of the day, and even in the midst of my business, to the presence of God, whom I considered always as with me, often as in me.

At length I came insensibly to do the same thing during my set time of prayer, which caused in me great delight and consolation. This practice produced in me so high an esteem for God that faith alone was capable to satisfy me in that point.[14]

Such was my beginning, and yet I must tell you that for the first ten years I suffered much. The apprehension that I was not devoted to God as I wished to be, my past sins always present to my mind, and the great-unmerited favors, which God did me, were the matter and source of my sufferings. During this time I fell often, and rose again presently. It seemed to me that all creatures, and God Himself were against me, and faith alone for me. I was troubled sometimes with thoughts that to believe I had received such favor was an effect of my presumption, which pretended to be at once where others arrive with at other times, that it was a willful delusion, and that there was no salvation for me.

When I thought of nothing but to end my days in these troubles (which did not at all diminish the trust I had in God, and which served only to increase my faith), I found myself changed all at once; and my soul, which till that time was in trouble, felt a profound inward peace, as if she were in her center and place of rest.

Ever since that time I walked before God, simply, in faith, with humility and with love, and I apply myself diligently to do nothing and think nothing, which may displease Him. I hope that when I have done what I can, He will do with me what He pleases.

As for what passes in me at present, I cannot express it. I have no pain or difficulty about my state, because I have no will but that of God, which I endeavor to accomplish in all things, and to which I am so resigned that I would not take up a straw from the ground against His order, or from any other motive than purely that of love to Him.

I have quitted all forms of devotion and set prayers but those to which my state obliges me. And I make it my business only to persevere in His holy presence, wherein I keep myself by a simple attention, and a general fond regard to God, which I may call an actual presence of God; or, to speak better, an habitual, silent, and secret conversation of the soul with God, which often causes me joys and raptures inwardly, and sometimes also outwardly, so great that I am forced to use means to moderate them and prevent their appearance to others.

In short, I am assured beyond all doubt that my soul has been with God above these thirty years. I pass over many things that I may not be tedious to you, yet I think it proper to inform you after what manner I consider myself before God, whom I behold as my King.

I consider myself as the most wretched of men, full of sores and corruption, and who has committed all sorts of crimes against his King. Touched with sensible regret, I confess to Him all my wickedness, I ask

His forgiveness, I abandon myself in His hands that He may do what He pleases with me. The King, full of mercy and goodness, very far from chastising me, embraces me with love, makes me eat at His table, serves me with His own hands, gives me the key of His treasures; He converses and delights Himself with me incessantly, in a thousand and a thousand ways, and treats me in all respects as His favorite. It is thus I consider myself from time to time in His holy presence.

My most useful method is this simple attention, and such a general passionate regard to God, to whom I find myself often attached with greater sweetness and delight than that of an infant at the mother's breast: so that, if I dare use the expression, I should choose to call this state the bosom of God, for the inexpressible sweetness, which I taste, and experience there.

If sometimes my thoughts wander from it by necessity or infirmity, I am presently recalled by inward motions so charming and delicious that I am ashamed to mention them. I desire your reverence to reflect upon my great wretchedness, of which you are fully informed, than upon the great favors which God does me, all unworthy and ungrateful as I am.

As for my set hours of prayer, they are only a continuation of the same exercise. Sometimes I consider myself there as a stone before a carver, whereof he is to make a statue: presenting myself thus before God, I desire Him to form His perfect image in my soul, and make me entirely like Himself.

At other times, when I apply myself to prayer, I feel all my spirit and all my soul lift itself up without any care or effort of mine, and it continues as it were suspended and firmly fixed in God, as in its center and place of rest.

I know that some charge this state with inactivity, delusion, and self-love. I confess that it is a holy inactivity, and would be a happy self-love if the soul in that state were capable of it, because, in effect, while she is in this repose, she cannot be disturbed by such acts as she was formerly accustomed to, and which were then her support, but which now rather hinder than assist her.

Yet I cannot bear that this should be called delusion, because the soul, which thus enjoys God, desires herein nothing but Him. If this were delusion in me, it belongs to God to remedy it. Let Him do what He pleases with me; I desire only Him, and to be wholly devoted to Him. You will, however, oblige me in sending me your opinion, to which I always pay a great deference, for I have a singular esteem for your reverence, and am in our Lord.

Yours...

Third Letter

We have a God who is infinitely gracious and knows all about our wants. I always thought that He would reduce you to extremity. He will come in His own time, and when you least expect it. Hope in Him more than ever; thank Him with me for the favors He does you, particularly for the fortitude and patience which He gives you in your afflictions. It is a plain mark of the care He takes of you. Comfort yourself, then, with Him, and give thanks for all.

I admire also the fortitude and bravery of Mr.— God has given him a good disposition and a good will; but there is in him still a little of the world and a great deal of youth. I hope the affliction which God has sent him will prove a wholesome remedy to him `, and make him enter into himself. It is an accident, which should engage him to put all his trust in Him who accompanies him everywhere. Let him think of Him as often as he can, especially in the greatest dangers. A little lifting up of the heart suffices. A little remembrance of God, one act of inward worship, though upon a march, and a sword in hand, are prayers, which however short, are nevertheless very acceptable to God; and far from lessening a soldier's courage in occasions of danger, they best serve to fortify it.

Let him then think of God the most he can. Let him accustom himself, by degrees, to this small but holy exercise. No one will notice it, and nothing is easier than to repeat often in the day these little internal adorations. Recommend to him, if you please, that he thinks of God the most he can, in the manner here directed. It is very fit and most necessary for a soldier who is daily exposed to the dangers of life. I hope that God will assist him and all the family, to whom I present my service, being theirs and

Yours...

Fourth Letter

I have taken this opportunity to communicate to you the sentiments of one of our society, concerning the admirable effects and continual assistances, which he receives from *the presence of God*. Let you and me both profit by them.

You must know his continual care has been, for about forty years past that he has spent in religion, to be always with God, and to do nothing which may displease Him, and this without any other view than purely for the love of Him, and because He deserves infinitely more.

He is now so accustomed to that divine presence that he receives from it continual succors upon all occasions. For about thirty years his soul has been filled with joys so continual, and sometimes so great, that he is forced to use means to moderate them, and to hinder their appearing outwardly.

If sometimes he is a little too much absent from that divine presence, God presently makes Himself to be felt in his soul to recall him, which often happens when he is most engaged in his outward business. He answers with exact fidelity to these inward drawings, either by an elevation of his heart toward God, or by a meek and fond regard to Him: or by such words as love forms upon these occasions, as, for instance, *My God, here I am all devoted to Thee. Lord, make me according to Thy heart.* And then it seems to him (as in effect he feels it) that this God of love, satisfied with such few words, reposes again, and rests in the fund and center of his soul. The experience of these things gives him such an assurance that God is always in the fund or bottom of his soul that it renders him incapable of doubting it upon any account whatever.

Judge by this what content and satisfaction he enjoys while he continually finds in him so great a treasure. He is no longer in an anxious search after it, but has it open before him, and may take what he pleases of it.

He complains much of our blindness, and cries often that we are to be pitied who content ourselves with so little. God, said he, has infinite treasure to bestow, and we take up with little sensible devotion, which passes in a moment. Blind as we are, we hinder God and stop the current of His graces. But when He finds a soul penetrated with a lively faith, He pours into it His graces and favors there they flow like a torrent, which, after being forcibly stopped against its ordinary course, when it has found a passage, spreads itself with impetuosity and abundance.

Yes, we often stop this torrent by the little value we set upon it. But let us stop it no more; let us enter into ourselves and break down the bank, which hinders it. Let us make way for grace; let us redeem the lost time, for perhaps we have but little left. Death follows us close; let us be well prepared for it, for we die but once, and a miscarriage there is irretrievable.

I say again, let us enter into ourselves. The time presses, there is no room for delay; our souls are at stake. I believe you have taken such effectual measures that you will not be surprised I commend you for it; it is the one thing necessary. We must, nevertheless, always work at it because not to advance in the spiritual life is to go back But those who have the gale of the Holy Spirit go forward even in sleep. If the vessel of our soul is still tossed with winds and storms, let us awake the Lord, who reposes in it, and He will quickly calm the sea.

I have taken the liberty to impart to you these good sentiments, that you may compare them with your own. It will serve again to kindle and inflame them, if by misfortune (which God forbid, for it would be indeed a great misfortune) they should be, though never so little, cooled. Let us then both recall our first fervors. Let us profit by the example and the sentiments of this brother, who is little known of the world, but known of God, and extremely caressed by Him. I will pray for you, do you pray instantly for me, who am, in our Lord,

Yours...

Fifth Letter

I received this day two books and a letter from Sister—, who is preparing to make her profession, and upon that account desires the prayers of your holy society, and yours in particular. I perceive that she reckons much upon them; pray do not disappoint her. Beg of God that she may make her sacrifice in the view of His love alone, and with firm resolution to be wholly devoted to Him. I will send you one of these books, which treat of the presence of God, a subject which, in my opinion, contains the whole spiritual life; and it seems to me that whoever duly practices it will soon become spiritual.

I know that for the right practice of it the heart must be empty of all other things, because God will possess the heart alone; and as He cannot possess it alone without emptying it of all besides, so neither can He act there, and do in it what He pleases, unless it be left vacant to Him.

There is not in the world a kind of life more sweet and delightful than that of a continual conversation with God. Those only can comprehend it who practice and experience it; yet I do not advise you to do it from that motive. It is not pleasure which we ought to seek in this exercise; but let us do it from a principle of love, and because God would have us.

Were I a preacher, I should, above all other things, preach the practice of the presence of God; and were I a director, I should advise all the world to do it, so necessary do I think it, and so easy, too.

Ah! Knew we but the want we have of the grace and assistance of God, we should never lose sight of Him-no, not for a moment. Believe me; make immediately a holy and firm resolution nevermore willfully to forget Him, and to spend the rest of your days in His sacred presence, deprived, for the love of Him, if He thinks fit, of all consolations.

Set heartily about this work, and if you do it, as you ought, be assured that you will find the effects of it. I will assist you with my prayers, poor as they are. I recommend myself earnestly to yours and those of your holy society, being theirs, and more particularly,

Yours…

Sixth Letter

To the same

I have received from Mrs.—the things which you gave her for me. I wonder that you have not given me your thoughts of the little book I sent you, and which you must have received. Pray set heartily about the practice of it in your old age; it is better late than never.

I cannot imagine how religious persons can live satisfied without the practice of the presence of God. For my part, I keep myself retired with Him in the fund or center of my soul as much as I can; and while I am so with Him I fear nothing, but the least turning from Him is insupportable.

This exercise does not much fatigue the body; it is, however, proper to deprive it sometimes, nay, often, of many little pleasures which are innocent and lawful, for God will not permit that a soul which desires to be devoted entirely to Him should take other pleasures than with Him that is more than reasonable.

I do not say therefore we must put any violent constraints upon ourselves. No, we must serve God in a holy freedom; we must do our business faithfully, without trouble or disquiet, recalling our minds to God mildly, and with tranquility, as often as we find it wandering from Him.

It is, however, necessary to put our whole trust in God, laying aside all other cares, and even some particular forms of devotion, though very good in themselves, yet such as one often engages in unreasonably, because these devotions are only means to attain to the end. So when by this exercise of the presence of God we are *with Him* who is our end, it is then useless to return to the means; but we may continue with Him our commerce of love, persevering in His holy presence, one while by an act of praise, of adoration, or of desire; one while by an act of resignation or thanksgiving; and in all ways which our spirit can invent.

Be not discouraged by the repugnance, which you may find in it from nature: you must do yourself violence. At the first one often thinks it lost time, but you must go on, and resolve to persevere in it to death, notwithstanding all the difficulties that may occur. I recommend myself to the prayers of your holy society, and yours in particular I am, in our Lord,

Yours...

Seventh Letter

I pity you much. It will be of great importance if you can leave the care of your affairs to—, and spend the remainder of your life only in worshipping God. He requires no great matters of us: a little remembrance of Him from time to time; a little adoration; sometimes to pray for His grace, sometimes to offer Him your sufferings, and sometimes to return to Him thanks for the favors He has given you, and still gives you, in the midst of your troubles, and to console yourself with Him the oftenest you can. Lift up your heart to Him, sometimes even at your meals, and when you are in company; the least little remembrance will always be acceptable to Him. You need not cry very loud; He is nearer to us than we are aware of.

It is not necessary for being with God to be always at church. We may make an oratory of our heart wherein to retire from time to time to converse with Him in meekness, humility, and love. Every one is capable of such familiar conversations with God, some more, some less. He knows what we can do. Let us begin, then. Perhaps He expects but one generous resolution on our part. Have courage. We have but little time to live; you are near sixty-four, and I am almost eighty. Let us live and die with God. Sufferings will be sweet and pleasant to us while we are with Him, and the greatest pleasures will be, without Him, a cruel punishment to us. May He be blessed for all? Amen.

Accustom yourself, then, by degrees thus to worship Him, to beg His grace, to offer Him your heart from time to time in the midst of your business, even every moment, if you can. Do not always scrupulously confine yourself to certain rules, or particular forms of devotion, but act with a general confidence in God, with love and humility. You may assure—of my poor prayers, and that I am their servant, and particularly.

Yours in our Lord...

Eighth Letter

Concerning Wandering Thoughts in Prayer

You tell me nothing new; you are not the only one that is troubled with wandering thoughts. Our mind is extremely roving; but as the will is mistress of all our faculties, she must recall them, and carry them to God as their last end.

When the mind, for want of being, sufficiently reduced by recollection at our first engaging in devotion, has contracted certain bad habits of wandering and dissipation, they are difficult to overcome, and commonly draw us, even against our wills, to the things of the earth.

I believe one remedy for this is to confess our faults and to humble ourselves before God. I do not advise you to use multiplicity of words in prayer, many words, and long discourses being often the occasions of wandering. Hold yourself in prayer before God like a dumb or paralytic beggar at a rich man's gate. Let it be your business to keep your mind in the presence of the Lord. If it sometimes wander and withdraw itself from Him, do not much disquiet yourself for that: trouble and disquiet serve rather to distract the mind than to recollect it: the will must bring it back in tranquility. If you persevere in this manner, God will have pity on you.

One way to recollect the mind easily in the time of prayer, and preserve it more in tranquility, is not to let it wander too far at other times. You should keep it strictly in the presence of God: and being accustomed to think of Him often, you will find it easy to keep your mind calm in the time of prayer, or at least to recall it from its wanderings.

I have told you already at large, in my former letters, of the advantages we may draw from this practice of the presence of God. Let us set about seriously, and pray for one another.

Yours...

Ninth Letter

The enclosed is an answer to that which I received from—: pray deliver it to her. She seems to me full of good will but she would go faster than grace. One does not become holy all at once. I recommend her to you: we ought to help one another by our advice, and yet more by our good examples. You will oblige me to let me hear of her from time to time, and whether she be very fervent and very obedient.

Let us think often that our only business in this life is to please God, and that all besides is but folly and vanity. You and I have lived about forty years in religion (i.e., a monastic life). Have we employed them in loving and serving God, who by His mercy has called us to this state, and for that very end? I am filled with shame and confusion when I reflect, on one hand, upon the great favors, which God has done, and incessantly continues to do me; and on the other upon the ill use I have made of them, and my small advancement in the way of perfection.

Since by His mercy He gives us still a little time, let us begin in earnest: let us repair the lost time: let us return with a full assurance to that Father of mercies, who is always ready to receive us affectionately. Let us renounce, let us generously renounce, for the love of Him, all that is not Himself; He deserves infinitely more. Let us think of Him perpetually. Let us put all our trust in Him. I doubt not but we shall soon find the effects of it in receiving the abundance of His grace, with which we can do all things, and without which we can do nothing but sin.

We cannot escape the dangers which abound in life without the actual and continual help of God. Let us, then, pray to Him for it continually. How can we pray to Him without being with Him? How can we be with Him but in thinking of Him often? And how can we often think of Him but by a holy habit, which we should form of it? You will tell me that I am always saying the same thing. It is true, for this is the best and easiest method I know: and as I use no other. I advise all the world to do it we must know before we can love. In order to know God, we must often think of Him: and when we come to love Him, we shall also think of Him often, for our hearts will be with our treasure. This is an argument which well deserves your consideration.

I am, Yours...

Tenth Letter

I have had a good deal of difficulty to bring myself to write to Mr.—, and I do it now purely because you and Madam—desire me. Pray write the directions and send it to him, I am very well pleased with the trust which you have in God; I wish that He may increase it in you more and more. We cannot have too much in so good and faithful a Friend, who will never fail us in this world nor the next.

If Mr.—makes his advantage of the loss he has had, and puts all his confidence in God, he will soon give him another friend, more powerful and more inclined to serve him. He disposes of hearts as He pleases. Perhaps Mr.—was too much attached to him he has lost. We ought to love our friends, but without encroaching upon the love due to God, which must be the principal.

Pray remember what I have recommended to you, which is, to think often on God, by day, by night, in your business, and even in your diversions. He is always near you and with you; leave Him not alone. You would think it rude to leave a friend alone who came to visit you; why, then, must God be neglected? Do not, then, forget Him, but think on Him often, adore Him continually, live and die with Him; this is the glorious employment of a Christian. In a word, this is our profession: if we do not know it we must learn it. I will endeavor to help you with my prayers, and am, in our Lord,

Yours...

Eleventh Letter

I do not pray that you may be delivered from your pains, but I pray God earnestly that He would give you strength and patience to bear them as long as He pleases. Comfort yourself with Him who holds you fastened to the cross. He will loose you when He thinks fit. Happy those who suffer with Him. Accustom yourself to suffer in that manner, and seek from Him the strength to endure as much, and as long, as He shall judge to be necessary for you. The men of the world do not comprehend these truths, nor is it to be wondered at, since they suffer like what they are, and not like Christians. They consider sickness as a pain to nature, and not as a favor from God: and seeing it only in that light, they find nothing in it but grief and distress. But those who consider sickness as coming from the hand of God, as the effect of His mercy, and the means which He employs for their salvation—such commonly find in it great sweetness and sensible consolation.

I wish you could convince yourself that God is often (in some sense) nearer to us, and more effectually present with us, in sickness than in health. Rely upon no other physician for, according to my apprehension, he reserves your cure to Himself. Put, then, all your trust in Him, and you will soon find the effects of it in your recovery, which we often retard by putting greater confidence in physic than in God.

Whatever remedies you make use of, they will succeed only as far as He permits. When pains come from God, He only can cure them. He often sends diseases of the body to cure those of the soul. Comfort yourself with the sovereign Physician both of the soul and body.

Be satisfied with the condition in which God places you: however happy you may think me, I envy you. Pains and suffering would be a paradise to me while I should suffer with my God, and the greatest pleasures would be hell to me if I could relish them without Him. All my consolation would be to suffer something for His sake.

I must, in a little time, go to God. What comforts me in this life is that I now see Him by faith, and I see Him in such a manner as might make me say sometimes, I believe no more, but I see. I feel what faith teaches us, and in that assurance and that practice of faith I will live and die with Him.

Continue, then, always with God: it is the only support and comfort for your affliction. I shall beseech Him to be with you. I present my service.

I am, Yours...

Twelfth Letter

If we were well accustomed to the exercise of the presence of God, all bodily diseases would be much alleviated thereby. God often permits that we should suffer a little to purify our souls and oblige us to continue with Him. Take courage: offer Him your pains incessantly; pray to Him for strength to endure them. Above all, get a habit of entertaining yourself often with God, and forget Him the least you can. Adore Him in your infinities, offer yourself to Him from time to time, and in the height of your sufferings beseech Him humbly and affectionately (as a child his father) to make you conformable to His holy will. I shall endeavor to assist you with my poor prayers.

God has many ways of drawing us to Himself. He sometimes hides Himself from us: but faith alone, which will not fail us in time of need, ought to be our support, and the foundation of our confidence, which must be all in God.

I know not how God will dispose of me. I am always happy. All the world suffers: and I, who deserve the severest discipline, feel joys so continual and so great that I can scarce contain them.

I would willingly ask of God a part of your sufferings, but that I know my weakness, which is so great that if He left me one moment to myself I should be the most wretched man alive. And yet I know not how He can leave me alone, because faith gives me as strong a conviction as sense can do that He never forsakes us until we have first forsaken Him. Let us fear to leave Him. Let us be always with Him. Let us live and die in His presence. Do you pray for me as I for you.

I am, Yours...

Thirteenth Letter

To the Same

I am in pain to see you suffer so long. What gives me some ease and sweetens the feelings I have for your grief is that they are proofs of God's love toward you. See them in that view and you will bear them more easily. As your case is, it is my opinion that you should leave off human remedies, and resign yourself entirely to the providence of God. Perhaps He stays only for that resignation and a perfect trust in Him to cure you. Since, notwithstanding all your cares, physic has hitherto proved unsuccessful, and your malady still increases, it will not be tempting God to abandon yourself in His hands and expect all from Him.

I told you in my last letter that He sometimes permits bodily diseases to cure the distempers of the soul. Have courage, then; make a virtue of necessity. Ask of God, not deliverance from your pains, but strength to bear resolutely, for the love of Him, all that He should please, and as long as He shall please.

Such prayers, indeed, are a little hard to nature, but most acceptable to God, and sweet to those that love Him. Love sweetens pains; and when one loves God, one suffers for His sake with joy and courage. Do you so, I beseech you: comfort yourself with Him, who is the only Physician of all our maladies. He is the Father of the afflicted, always ready to help us. He loves us infinitely, more than we imagine. Love Him, then, and seek no consolation elsewhere. I hope you will soon receive it. Adieu. I will help you with my prayers, poor as they are, and shall always be, in our Lord,

Yours...

Fourteenth Letter

To the Same

I render thanks to our Lord for having relieved you a little, according to your desire. I have been often near expiring, but I never was so much satisfied as then. Accordingly, I did not pray for relief, but I prayed for strength to suffer with courage, humility, and love. Ah, how sweet it is to suffer with God! However great the sufferings may be, receive them with love. It is paradise to suffer and be with Him so that if in this life we would enjoy the peace of paradise we must accustom ourselves to a familiar, humble, affectionate conversation with Him. We must hinder our spirits' wandering from Him upon any occasion. We must make our heart a spiritual temple, wherein to adore Him incessantly. We must watch continually over ourselves, that we may not do nor say nor think anything that may displease Him. When our minds are thus employed about God, suffering will become full of unction and consolation.

I know that to arrive at this state and beginning is very difficult, for we must act purely in faith. But though it is difficult, we know also that we can do all things with the grace of God, which He never refuses to them who ask for it earnestly. Knock, persevere in knocking, and I answer for it that He will open to you all at once what He has deferred during many years. Adieu. Pray to Him for me as I pray to Him for you. I hope to see Him quickly.

I am, yours...

Fifteenth Letter

To the Same

God knows best what is needful for us, and all that He does is for our good. If we knew how much He loves us, we should always be ready to receive equally and with indifference from His hand the sweet and the bitter. All would please that came from Him. That sorest afflictions never appear intolerable, except when we see them as dispensed by the hand of God, when we know that it is our loving Father who abases and distresses us, our sufferings will lose their bitterness and become even matter of consolation.

Let all our employment be to know God; the more one knows Him, the more one desires to know Him. And as knowledge is commonly the measure of love, the deeper and more extensive our knowledge shall be, the greater will be our love; and if our love of God were great, we should love Him equally in pains and pleasures.

Let us not content ourselves with loving God for the mere sensible favors, how elevated soever, which He has done or may do us. Such favors, though never so great, cannot bring us so near to Him as faith does in one simple act. Let us seek Him often by faith. He is within us: seek Him not elsewhere. If we do love Him alone, are we not rude, and do we not deserve blame, if we busy ourselves about trifles, which do not please and perhaps offend Him? It is to be feared these trifles will one day cost us dear.

Let us begin to be devoted to Him in good earnest. Let us cast everything besides out of our hearts. He would possess them alone. Beg this favor of Him. If we do what we can on our parts, we shall soon see that change wrought in us, which we aspire after. I cannot thank Him sufficiently for the relaxation He has vouchsafed you. I hope from His mercy the favor to see Him with a few days.[15] Let us pray for one another.

I am, in our Lord, yours…

4. Notes

1. His Third *Conversion* (see page 11); Compare First *Conversion* (see page 7).

2. First *Conversions* (see page 7).

3. In the First *Conversion* (see page 7) M. Beaufont mentions August 3, 1666 as the date when he first met with Brother Lawrence at the monastery. But in a Letter written March 3, 1689, the author states that he had "lived about forty years in religion," that is, in a monastic order. This would imply that he entered the monastery around 1649 (Ninth *Letter*, see page 27.)

4. This period of spiritual inconsistency and suffering seems to have extended over at least ten years. In his Second *Conversion* (see page 8) reference is made to four years in which he suffered much, which led him to the realization that his "trouble arose from want of faith." Even so, in his Second *Letter* (see page 18), he speaks of suffering still after ten years. The exact number of years is not important, but it is interesting that an interval of time passed between his conversion and the point of his complete rest and inward confidence.

5. Second *Letter* (see page 18).

6. Ibid.

7. Ibid.

8. Ibid.

9. Forth *Letter* (see page 22).

10. Fourth *Conversion* (see page 13).

11 Eleventh *Letter* (see page 29). Compare Seventh *Letter* (see p. 37).

12 Fifteenth *Letter* (see page 33).

13 Quoted in Sheldon Cherry, *Men Who Have Walked With God* (New York: Alfred A. Knoph, 1945), p 302.

14 I suppose he means that all distinct notions he could form of God were unsatisfactory, because he perceived them to be unworthy of God; and therefore his mind was not to be satisfied but by the views of faith, which apprehend God as infinite and incomprehensible, as He is in Himself, and not as He can be conceived by human ideas.

15 Unfortunately, he took to his bed days after, and died within the week.

The Saints' Everlasting Rest

Richard Baxter 1615-1691

*Edited with an Introduction
By Timothy K. Beougher*

Abridged version of *The Saints' Everlasting Rest* by Richard Baxter. Abridged version originally published by the Institute of Evangelism Billy Graham Center, 1994, Wheaton, IL. Copyright of abridged version and introduction held by Timothy K. Beougher, used with permission. Scripture quotations are taken from the Holy Bible, New International Version (NIV) © 1973, 1978, 1984, International Bible Society. Used by permission of Zondervan Bible Publishers. Artwork in the Public Domain.

Book Chapters

1. Introduction
   By Timothy K. Beougher 36
2. The Importance of Leading a Heavenly Life Upon Earth 39
3. Directions on How to Lead a Heavenly Life Upon Earth......................49
4. The Nature of Heavenly Contemplation, with the Time, Place, and Frame of Mind Most Suited for It..62

1. Introduction
By Timothy K. Beougher

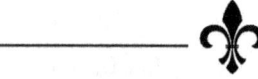

A tourist travelling through Kidderminster, England will find in the city center a statue of a man with the following inscription:

> Between the years 1641 and 1660
>
> This Town was the scene of the labors of
>
> RICHARD BAXTER
>
> renowned equally for his Christian learning and his pastoral fidelity. In a stormy divided age he advocated unity and comprehension pointing the way to
> "The Everlasting Rest"
> Churchmen and Nonconformists united to raise this memorial.
>
> A.D. 1875

Born in 1615, Baxter lived and ministered throughout most of the seventeenth century, a watershed in English history. Before his death in 1691, he would witness the Civil War, the beheading of Charles I, the Commonwealth under Oliver Cromwell, the Restoration of the monarchy under Charles II, the persecution of Nonconformity, the Great Ejection, and the struggle for toleration, which culminated in the Act of Toleration of 1689. Baxter was no passive observer of these events, no idle bystander. As a prominent religious leader, he actively participated in the numerous political and ecclesiastical struggles of his day.

Baxter exercised the most fruitful Puritan pastorate anywhere recorded, converting almost the entire population of Kidderminster (2,000 persons). His motto for ministry was to preach "as a dying man to dying men." After being forced from his pulpit with some two thousand other Puritan ministers in the Great Ejection of 1660, he continued his writing ministry, authoring more than 140 books before his death in 1691.

He wrote numerous works on conversion, among them *Treatise on Conversion, Now or Never, Directions and Persuasions to a Sound Conversion*, and *Call to the Unconverted*. His *Call* was the most popular book of its day in all of England, selling over 20,000 copies the first year. He received letters virtually every week from those converted by his books.

His best known work, *The Reformed Pastor* (today we would say Revived), has remained a classic for pastors around the world since its writing. Its contemporary influence is reflected in the extant correspondence of Baxter. A Swiss pastor tells Baxter that he bought the book in London, and goes on to speak of the gratitude of his brethren and himself for such discovery. Numerous New England Puritan pastors testified as to the impact it made on their lives. The book greatly impacted Philip Jacob Spener, the founder of German pietism. Wesley, Rutherford, Asbury, and Spurgeon all spoke in glowing terms of the book's effect on their lives and ministries.

Baxter's literary accomplishments are even more impressive when one considers his continual battle against poor health. For anyone to have produced the writings he did would be staggering, but for a near invalid it is nothing short of remarkable! His entire life was spent battling sickness. He was harassed by a constant cough, frequent nosebleeds, migraine headaches, digestive ailments, kidney stones, and gallstones; he was a virtual museum of diseases. Living in an era before painkillers, Baxter remarked that from the age of 21 onwards there was "seldom an hour free from pain."

In fact, it was his poor health that provided the context for the writing of *The Saints' Everlasting Rest*. Baxter wrote this treatise to help prepare him for death during a life-threatening illness at the age of thirty-five. As he began to meditate on the joys of heaven, which he soon expected to enter, he wrote down his thoughts. He eventually recovered and published his reflections in book form. The work was a runaway best seller, selling thousands of copies and going through eight editions within eight years.

In this classic work, Baxter makes the gateway to heaven ring with the notes of the awaiting triumph. Working from the text of Hebrews 4:9, "There remained a Rest to the people of God," he deals with believers' responsibility to focus attention on their future glory. He emphasized that meditation was not a mindless activity but a focused one. Baxter's meditation filled him with joy and proved to be a source of seemingly boundless energy! His long ministry is a vibrant example of "the joy of the Lord is your strength," (Nehemiah 8:10).

A popular expression in our day is "he's too heavenly-minded to be of any earthly good." Baxter would take great exception to that expression. He would argue that it is only when persons are heavenly-minded that they can be of any earthly good! Focused meditation upon heaven will supply believers with energy and direction for living in the present.

Baxter's original work, published in 1649, contained some eight hundred thousand words spread throughout forty-six chapters and covering 844 pages. Benjamin Fawcett abridged the work in 1758, condensing it to sixteen chapters. I have edited Chapters 11-13 from Fawcett's edition for the current booklet.

These three chapters are filled with Scripture. Baxter utilizes not only direct quotations, but also makes numerous allusions to biblical passages. Some of these are in italics, some are not. Where Baxter quotes a verse and reference, I have cited the verse in the New International Version. Where he merely makes allusions to biblical passages, I have modernized the language as I have with the remaining material. The italicized material has been left as it was in the original. *The Saints' Everlasting Rest* has inspired Christians for centuries to lift their eyes above this world to the place where they will spend eternity. May it do the same for you.

Timothy K. Beougher

2. The Importance of Leading a Heavenly Life Upon Earth

Is a heavenly rest available to us? Why then are our thoughts no more upon it? Why are not our hearts continually there? Has the eternal God provided us such a glory, and promised to take us up to dwell with Himself, and is not this worth thinking on? Should not the strongest desires of our hearts be after it? Do we believe this, and yet forget and neglect it? How freely, how frequently can we think of our pleasures, our friends, our labors, our flesh and its lusts, our miseries, our fears and sufferings? But where is the Christian whose heart is on his rest? What is the matter? Are we so full of joy that we need no more? Or is there nothing in heaven for our joyous thoughts? Or rather, are not our hearts carnal and stupid? Let us humble these sensual hearts that have in them no more of Christ and glory. If this world were the only subject of our discourse, all would consider us ungodly; why then may we not call our hearts ungodly that have so little delight in Christ and heaven?

I require you, Reader, as ever you hope for a part in this glory, that you presently take your heart to task, chide it for its willful strangeness to God, turn your thoughts from the pursuit of vanity, bend your soul to study eternity, and busy it about the life to come. Habituate yourself to such contemplations, and let not those thoughts be seldom and cursory, but bathe your soul in heaven's delights. If your backward soul begins to languish, and your thoughts to scatter, call them back, hold them to their work, and bear not with their laziness. And when you have, in obedience to God, tried this work, got acquainted with it, and kept a guard on your thoughts till they are accustomed to obey, you will then find yourself in the suburbs of heaven, and that there is, indeed, a sweetness in the work and way of God, and that the life of Christianity is a life of joy. You will meet with those abundant consolations which you have prayed for and groaned after, and which so few Christians do ever here obtain, because they know not the way to them, or else make no effort towards them. Do not say, "We are unable to set our own hearts on heaven; this must be the work of God only." Though God be the chief disposer of your hearts, yet next under Him you have the greatest command of them yourselves. Though without Christ you can do nothing, yet under Him you may do much, and must, or else it will be undone, and yourselves undone, through your neglect.

Christians, if your souls were healthful and vigorous, they would perceive incomparably more delight and sweetness in the believing joyful thoughts of your future blessedness, than the soundest stomach finds in its food, or the strongest senses in the enjoyment of their objects; so little painful would this work be to you. But because I know while we have flesh about us, and any remains of that *sinful mind, which is hostile to God*, and to this noble work, that all motives are little enough. I will here lay down some considerations, which, if you will deliberately weigh, with an impartial judgment. I doubt not, but they will prove effectual with your hearts, and make you resolve on this excellent duty.

Consider, a heart set upon heaven will be one of the most unquestionable evidences of your sincerity, and a clear discovery of a true work of saving grace upon your souls. You are often asking, "How shall we know that we are truly saved?" Here you have a sign, infallible from the mouth of Jesus Christ Himself: *where your treasure is, there your heart will be also* (Matthew 6:21). God is the saints' treasure and happiness; heaven is the place where they must fully enjoy Him. A heart therefore set upon heaven, is no more but a heart set upon God: and surely, a heart set upon God through Christ is the truest evidence of saving grace. When learning will be no proof of grace; when knowledge, duties, and gifts will fail; when arguments from your tongue may be refuted; yet then will this from the intent of your heart prove you sincere.

Take a poor Christian, of a weak understanding, a feeble memory, and a stammering tongue; yet his heart is set on God, he has chosen Him for his portion, his thoughts are on eternity, his desires there, and he cries out, "O that I were there!" He takes that day for a time of imprisonment, in which he has not had one refreshing view of eternity. I would rather die in this man's condition, than in the case of him who has the most eminent gifts, and is most admired for his performances, while his heart is not thus taken up with God. Christians, as you would have a proof of your title to glory, labor to get your hearts above. If sin and Satan keep not your affections from there, they never will be able to keep away your persons.

A heart in heaven is the highest excellence of your Christian disposition. As there is a common excellence by which Christians differ from the world, so there is this peculiar dignity of spirit, by which the more excellent differ from the rest. The noblest of Christians are they whose faces are set most direct for heaven. Such a heavenly saint, who has been immersed with God in his contemplations, and is newly come down from the views of Christ, what discoveries will he make of those superior regions! How high and sacred is his discourse! Enough to convince an understanding hearer that he had seen the Lord, and that no man could speak such words, except he had been with God. This, this is the noble Christian. The most famous mountains and trees are those that reach nearest to heaven; and he is the choicest Christian, whose heart is most frequently and most delightfully there. If a man lives near the king, he will be thought a step higher than his neighbors. What then shall we judge of him that daily travels as far as heaven, and there has seen the *King of kings*, has frequent admittance into the divine presence, and feasts his soul upon the tree of life? For my part, I value this man before the noblest, the richest, and the most learned in the world.

A heavenly mind is the nearest and truest way to a life of comfort. The countries far north are cold and frozen, because they are distant from the sun. What makes such frozen uncomfortable Christians, but their living so far from heaven? And what makes others so warm in comforts, but their living higher, and having nearer access to God? When the sun in the spring draws near our part of the earth, how do all things congratulate its approach? The earth looks green, the trees shoot forth, the plants revive, the birds sing, and all things smile upon us. If we would but try this life with God, and keep these hearts above, what a spring of joy would be within us? How should we forget our winter sorrows? How early should we rise to sing the praise of our great Creator? O Christian, get above! Those that have been there have found it warmer, and I doubt not but you have sometime tried it yourself. When have you largest comforts? Is it not when you have conversed with God and filled you soul with the forethoughts of glory? If you know by experience what this practice is, I dare say you know what spiritual joy is. If, as David professes, *the light of God's countenance brings more joy than grain and new wine*; then surely they that draw nearest, and most behold it, must be fullest of these joys.

Whom should we blame then, that we are so void of consolation, but our own negligent hearts? God has provided us a crown of glory and praise to set it shortly on our heads, and we will not so much as think of it. He bids us behold and rejoice, and we will not so much as look at it, and yet we complain for lack of comfort. It is by believing that we are filled with joy and peace, and no longer than we continue our believing. It is in hope the saints rejoice, and no longer than they continue hoping. God's Spirit produces our comforts, by setting our own spirits at work upon the promises, and raising our thoughts to the place of our comforts. As you would delight a covetous man by showing him gold, so God delights His people by leading them, as it were, into heaven, and showing them Himself, and their rest with Him. He does not fill us with joy while we are idle or taken up with other things. He gives the fruits of the earth while we plow, and sow, and weed, and water, and fertilize, and with patience expect His blessing; so does He give the joys of the soul.

I entreat you, Reader, in the name of the Lord, and as you value the life of constant joy, and that good conscience, which is a continual feast, to set upon this work seriously, and learn the art of heavenly-mindedness, and you shall find the increase an hundred-fold, and the benefit abundantly exceed your labor. But this is the misery of man's nature; though every man naturally hates sorrow, and loves the most merry and joyful life, yet few love the way to joy, or will endure the pains by which it is obtained. They will take what comes the easiest, and content themselves with earthly pleasures, rather than ascending to heaven to seek it.

A heart in heaven will be a most excellent preservative against temptations to sin. It will keep the heart well employed. When we are idle, we tempt the devil to tempt us, as careless persons make thieves. A heart in heaven can reply to the tempter, as Nehemiah did, *I am doing a great work, so that I cannot come.* It has no leisure to be lustful and wanton, ambitious or worldly. If you were but busy in your lawful callings, you would not be so ready to respond to temptations, much less if you were also busy above with God. Would a judge be persuaded to rise from the bench, when he is sitting upon life and death, to go and play with children in the streets? No more will a Christian; when he is taking a survey of his eternal rest, give ear to the alluring charms of Satan. The children of that kingdom should never have time for trifles, especially when they are employed in the affairs of the kingdom. This employment is one of the saint's chief preservatives from temptations.

A heavenly mind is the freest from sin, because it has truer and lively apprehensions of spiritual things. It has so deep an insight into the evil of sin, the vanity of the creature, the brutishness of fleshly sensual delights, that temptations have little power over it. *In vain the net is spread, says Solomon, in the sight of any bird.* And usually in vain does Satan lay his snares to entrap the soul that plainly sees them. Earth is the place for his temptations, and earth's the ordinary bait. How shall these ensnare the Christian who has left the earth and walks with God?

Is converse with wise and learned men the way to make one wise? Much more is converse with God. If travelers return home with wisdom and experience, how much more he that travels to heaven? If our bodies become suited to the air and climate we live in, then his understanding must be fuller of light, who lives with the Father of lights.

The men of the world that dwell below and know no other conversation but earthly, no wonder if their *understanding be darkened*, and Satan *takes them captive at his will*. How can worms and moles see, whose dwelling is always in the earth? While this dust is in their eyes, no wonder they mistake gain for godliness, sin for grace, the world for God, their own wills for the law of Christ, and as a result, hell for heaven. But when a Christian withdraws himself from his worldly thoughts, and begins to converse with God in heaven, he is, as Nebuchadnezzar, taken from the beasts of the field to the throne, and *his reason returns to him*. When he has had a glimpse of eternity and looks down on the world again, how does he charge with folly his neglect of Christ, his fleshly pleasures, and his earthly cares? How does he think there is no man so truly insane, as willful sinners, and unworthy slighters of Christ and glory?

This makes a dying man usually wiser than others, because he looks on eternity as near, and has more heart-piercing thoughts of it than he ever had in health and prosperity. Then many of the most bitter enemies of the saints have their eyes opened and, like Balaam, cry out, *O that I might die the death of the righteous, and that my last end might be like his!* Yet let the same men recover, and lose their apprehensions of the life to come, and how quickly do they lose their understandings with it? Tell a dying sinner of the riches, honors, or pleasures of the world, and would he not answer, "What is all this to me, who must presently appear before God, and give account of all my life?" Christian, if the apprehended nearness of eternity will work such strange effects upon the ungodly, and make them so much wiser than before, then what rare effects would it produce in you, if you could always dwell in the views of God and in lively thoughts of your everlasting state! Surely a believer should ordinarily have more quickening apprehensions of the life to come in the time of his health, than an unbeliever has at the hour of his death.

A heavenly mind is also fortified against temptations because the affections are thoroughly possessed with the high delights of another world. He that loves most, and not he that only knows most, will most easily resist the motions of sin. The will relishes goodness as the understanding does truth; and here lies much of a Christian's strength. When you have had a fresh delightful taste of heaven you will not be so easily persuaded from it. You cannot persuade a child to part with his candy while he has the taste in his mouth. O that you would be much in feeding on *the hidden manna*, and be frequently tasting the delights of heaven! How would this make you despise the foolish things of the world!

If the Devil had set upon Peter in the Mount of Transfiguration, when he saw Moses and Elijah talking with Christ, would he so easily have been drawn to deny his Lord? What, with all that glory in his eye? No! So if he should set upon a believing soul, when he is taken up in fellowship with Christ, what would such a soul say? "Get thee behind me, Satan; would you persuade me here with trifling pleasures, and steal my heart from this my rest? Would you have me sell these joys for nothing? Is there any honor or delight like this? Or can that be profit, for which I must lose this?" But Satan stays till we are come down, and the taste of heaven is out of our mouths, and the glory we saw is even forgotten, and then he easily deceives our hearts. Though the Israelites below eat, drink, and rise up to play before their idol, Moses on the mountain will not do so. If we could keep the taste of our souls continually delighted with the sweetness above, with what disdain should we spit out the baits of sin.

The diligent keeping your hearts in heaven, will maintain the vigor of all your graces, and put life into all your duties. The heavenly Christian is the lively Christian. It is our strangeness to heaven that makes us so dull. Observe but the man who is much in heaven, and you shall see he is not like other Christians. There is something of what he has seen above which appears in all his duty and conversation. Set upon this employment, and others will see *the face* of your lifestyle *shine*, and say, surely he has been *with God in the mount*. But if you lie complaining of deadness and dullness, that you cannot love Christ, nor rejoice in His love, that you have no life in prayer, nor any other duty, and yet neglect this quickening employment, you are the cause of **your** own complaints. Is not your life hid with Christ in God? Where must you go, but to Christ for it? And where is that, but to heaven, *where Christ is? You will not come to Christ, that you may have life.*

If you would have light and heat, why are you no more in the sunshine? For want of this recourse to heaven, your soul is as a lamp that is not lighted, and your duties as a sacrifice, which has no fire. Fetch one coal daily from this altar, and see if your offering will not burn. Light your lamp at the flame, feed it daily with oil from there, and see if it will not gloriously shine. Keep close to this reviving fire and see if your affections will not be warm. In your want of love to God, lift up your eye of faith to heaven, behold His beauty, contemplate His excellences, and see whether His amiableness and perfect goodness will not ravish your heart. As exercise maintains appetite, strength, and vigor to the body; so these heavenly exercises will quickly cause the increase of grace and spiritual life.

Besides, it is not false or strange fire, which you fetch from heaven for your sacrifices. The zeal, which is kindled by your meditations on heaven, is most likely to be a heavenly zeal. Some men's fervency is only drawn from their books, and some from their sharpness of affliction, and some from the mouth of an inspiring minister; but he that knows this way to heaven, and derives it daily from the true fountain, shall have his soul revived with the water of life, and enjoy that quickening which is peculiar to the saints. When others are ready, like Baal's priests, to *cut themselves*, because their sacrifice will not burn, you may breathe the spirit of Elijah, and in the chariot of contemplation soar aloft, till your soul and sacrifice gloriously flame, though the flesh and the world should cast upon them all the water of their opposing enmity. Say not, "how can mortals ascend to heaven?" Faith has wings, and meditation is its chariot. Faith is a burning-glass to your sacrifice, and meditation sets it to the face of the sun. Only take it not away too soon, but hold it there awhile, and your soul will feel the happy effect.

Reader, are you not thinking, when you see a lively Christian and hear his lively fervent prayers, and edifying discourse, "O how happy a man is this! O that my soul were in this blessed condition!" I here advise you from God, set your soul conscientiously to this work, wash frequently in this Jordan, and your leprous dead soul will revive, *and you shall know that there is a God in Israel*, and that you may live a vigorous and joyful life, if you do not willfully neglect your own mercies.

The frequent believing views of glory are the most precious motivations in all afflictions. Having our heart in heaven cheers our spirits, renders our sufferings far more easy, enables us to bear them with patience and joy, and so strengthens our resolutions that we forsake not Christ for fear of trouble. If the way be ever so rough, can it be tedious if it leads to heaven? O sweet sickness, reproaches, imprisonments, or death, accompanied with these tastes of our future rest! This keeps the sufferings from the soul, so that it can only touch the flesh. Had not it been for that little (alas, too little) taste which I had of rest, my sufferings would have been grievous, and death more terrible. Unless *this promised rest* had been my delight, I would have perished in my affliction. One thing I ask of the Lord, this is what I seek: that I may dwell in the house of the Lord all the days of my life, to gaze upon the beauty of the Lord and to seek Him in His temple. For in the day of trouble He will keep me safe in His dwelling; He will hide me in the shelter of His tabernacle and set me high upon a rock. Then my head will be exalted above the enemies who surround me; at His tabernacle will I sacrifice with shouts of joy; I will sing and make music to the Lord (Psalm 119:92; 27:4-6).

All sufferings are nothing to us, so far as we have these supporting joys. When persecution and fear have shut the doors. *Christ can come in.*

and stand in the midst, and say to his disciples, *Peace be unto you.* Paul and Silas can be in heaven, even when they are thrust into the inner prison, their bodies scourged with *many stripes, and their feet fast in the stocks.* The martyrs find more rest in their flames than their persecutors in their pomp and tyranny; because they foresee the flames they escape, and the rest, which their fiery chariot is conveying them to. If *the Son of God* will *walk with us*, we are *safe in the midst of* those *flames*, which shall devour them that cast us in. *Abraham went out of his country not knowing where he was going*, because *he looked for a city, which had foundations, whose builder and Maker, is God.* "Moses esteemed the reproach of Christ greater riches than the treasures in Egypt, because he looked to the reward. He forsook Egypt, not fearing the wrath of the king, because he endured as seeing Him who is invisible. Others were tortured, not accepting deliverance, that they might obtain a better resurrection. *Even* Jesus, the Author and finisher of our faith, for the joy that was set before Him, endured the cross, despising the shame, and is set down at the right hand of the throne of God."

This is the noble advantage of faith; it can look on the means and end together. This is the great reason of our impatience and censuring of God, because we gaze on the evil itself, but fix not our thoughts on what is beyond it. They that saw Christ only on the cross, or in the grave, do *shake their heads*, and think Him lost. But God saw Him dying, buried, rising, glorified, and all this at one view. Faith will in this imitate God, so far as it has a promise to help it. We see God burying us under ground, but we foresee not the spring, when we shall all revive. Could we but clearly see heaven as the end of all God's dealings with us, surely none of His dealings could be grievous. But as *Abraham saw Christ's day and rejoiced*, so we, in our most forlorn state, might see that day when Christ shall give us rest, and therein rejoice.

I beseech you, Christian, for the honor of the gospel, and for your soul's comfort, be not slow to learn this heavenly art, when in your greatest extremity you have most need to use it. He that, with Stephen, *sees the glory of God, and Jesus standing on the right hand of God*, will comfortably bear the showers of stones. The joy of the Lord is our strength, and that joy must be fetched from the place of our joy! If we walk without our strength, how long are we likely to endure?

Our hearts should be on God because the heart of God is so much on us. If the Lord of glory can stoop so low as to set His heart on sinful dust, we should easily be persuaded to set our hearts on Christ and glory, and ascend to Him in our daily affections, who so much condescends to us. Christian, do you not perceive that the heart of God is set upon you and that He is still watching over you with tender love, even when you forget both yourself and Him? Is He not following you with daily mercies, moving upon your soul, providing for your body, preserving both? Does He not bear you continually in the arms of love, and promise that *all shall work together for your good,* and suit all His dealings to your greatest advantage, and *give His angels charge over you?*

And can you be taken up with the joys below and forget your Lord, who forgets not you? Unkind ingratitude! When He speaks o f His own kindness for us, hear what He says: "Zion said, 'The Lord has forsaken me, the Lord has forgotten me.' Can a mother forget the baby at her breast and have no compassion on the child she has borne? Though she may forget, I will not forget you! See, I have engraved you on the palms of my hands; your walls are ever before me" (Isaiah 49: 14-16). But when He speaks of our regards to Him, the case is otherwise. *Does a maiden forget her jewelry, a bride her wedding ornaments? Yet my people have forgotten me, days without number* (Jeremiah 2:32). Give not God cause to say this about us. Rather let our souls get up to God, and visit Him every morning, and our hearts be towards Him every moment.

Moreover, our house and home is above. Now we know that if the earthly tent we live in is destroyed, we have a building from God, an eternal house in heaven, not built by human hands. Why do we then look no more often towards it, and groan, longing to be clothed with our heavenly dwelling? (2 Corinthians 5:1-2). If you were but banished into a strange land, how frequently would your thoughts be at home? And why is it not thus with us in respect to heaven? Is not that more truly and properly our home, where we must take up our everlasting abode, than this, which we are every hour expecting to be separated from, and to see no more? We are strangers here—heaven is our true country. We are heirs, and that is our inheritance; even an inheritance that can never perish, spoil or fade—kept in heaven for you (1 Peter 1:4). The very hope of our souls is there: all our hope of relief from our distresses; all our hope of happiness, when here we are miserable; all this hope is stored up for you in heaven (Colossians 1:5). Why, beloved Christians, have we so much interest and so few thoughts there?

Does it speak well of us to be so delighted in the company of strangers, so as to forget our Father and our Lord? Or to be so well pleased with those that hates and grieves us, as to forget our best and dearest friends? Or to be so fond of borrowed trifles as to forget our own possession and treasure? Or to be so much impressed with fears and wants as to forget our eternal joy and rest? Men commonly over love and overvalue their own things, and mind them too much. O that we could mind our own inheritance and value it half as much as it deserves!

Once more consider, there is nothing but heaven worth setting our hearts upon. Have you found out some other God? Or something that will serve you instead of rest? Have you found on earth an eternal happiness? Where is it? What is it made of? Who was the man that found it out? Who was he that last enjoyed it? Where dwelt he? What was his name? If Satan should *take you up the mountain of temptation, and show you all the kingdoms of the world, and the glory of them*, he could show you nothing that is worthy of your thoughts, much less to be preferred before your rest. Indeed, so far as duty and necessity require it, we must be content to mind the things below; but who is he that contains himself within the compass of those limits? And yet if we ever so diligently constrain our cares and thoughts we shall find the least to be bitter and burdensome.

Christian, focus on the emptiness of all these things and the preciousness of the things above! If your thoughts should, like the laborious bee, go over the world from flower to flower, from creature to creature, they would bring no honey or sweetness home, save what they gathered from their relations to eternity. Though every truth of God is precious, and ought to be defended; yet even all our study of truth should be still in reference to our rest. The observation is too true, "that the lovers of controversies in religion, have never been warmed with one spark of the love of God." Even all our dealings in the world, our buying and selling, our eating and drinking, our building and marrying, our peace and war, so far as they relate not to the life to come, but tend only to the pleasing of the flesh, are not worthy the frequent thoughts of a Christian. And now does not your conscience say, that there is nothing but heaven and the way to it, that is worth your contemplation?

Now, Reader, are these considerations weighty or not? Have I proved it your duty to keep your heart on things above or have I not? If you say not, I am confident you contradict your own conscience. If you acknowledge yourself convinced of the duty, then every word of yours shall condemn you, if you willfully neglected such a confessed duty. Be thoroughly willing and the work is more than half done. I have now a few plain directions to give you for your help in this great work. But it is in vain to mention them, except you be willing to put them in practice. However, I will propose them to you, and may the Lord persuade your heart to the work!

3. Directions on How to Lead a Heavenly Life Upon Earth

As you value the comforts of a heavenly lifestyle, I must here charge you from God to avoid carefully some dangerous hindrances, and then, faithfully and diligently to practice such duties as will especially assist you in attaining to a heavenly life. The hindrances to be avoided with all possible care are: living in any known sin; an earthly mind; the company of the ungodly; a proud and lofty spirit; a slothful spirit; and resting in mere preparations for this heavenly life, without any acquaintance with the thing itself.

Continuing in any known sin is a grand impediment to a heavenly lifestyle. What havoc will this make in your soul! O the joys that this has destroyed! And the ruin it has made among men's graces! The soul-strengthening duties it has hindered! Christian Reader, are you one that has ignored your conscience? Are you a willful neglecter of known duties, public, private, or secret? Are you a slave to your appetites? Are you a proud seeker of your own esteem? Are you a person who is easily angered, ready to take offense at every word, or look, or supposed slight? Are you a deceiver of others in your dealings, or one that will be rich, right, or wrong? If this be your case, I dare say heaven and your soul are very great strangers. These beams in your eyes will not allow you to look to heaven; they will be a cloud between you and your God. When you attempt to study eternity, and gather comforts from the life to come, your sin will presently look you in the face and say, "These things belong not to you. Why should you take comfort from heaven, who takes so much pleasure in the lusts of the flesh?" How long will this dampen your joys and make the thoughts of that day become a burden and not your delight?

Every willful sin will be to your comforts, as water to the fire; when you think to quicken them, this will quench them. It will utterly indispose and disable you that you can no more ascend in divine meditation than a bird can fly when its wings are clipped. Sin cuts the very sinews of this heavenly life. O man! What a life do you lose? What daily delights do you sell for a vile lust? If heaven and hell can meet together, and God become a lover of sin; then may you live in your sin, and in the tastes of glory, and have communion in heaven, though you cherish your corruption. Watch therefore; especially resolve to keep from the occasions of sin, and out of the way of temptations. What need have we daily to pray, *Lead us not into temptation, but deliver us from evil!*

An earthly mind is another hindrance to be carefully avoided. *God and Mammon*, earth and heaven, cannot both have the delight of your heart. When the heavenly believer is blessing himself in his God, and rejoicing in hope of the glory to come, perhaps you are blessing yourself in your worldly prosperity, and rejoicing in hope of your thriving here. When he is comforting his soul in the views of Christ, whom he shall live with forever; then you are comforting yourself with your wealth, in looking over your possessions, and in thinking of the favor of prominent people, of the pleasure of a large estate, of larger provision for your children after you, of the advancement of your family, or the increase of your dependents. If Christ pronounced him a fool, that said, *Soul, take it easy, you have enough laid up for many years;* how much more so are you, who knowingly speaks in your heart the same words? Tell me, what difference between this fool's expressions and your affections? Remember, you must bear the scrutiny of the Searcher of Hearts.

Certainly, so much as you delight and take up your rest on earth; so much of your delight in God is abated. Your earthly mind may consist with your outward profession and common duties, but it cannot consist with this heavenly duty. You yourself know how seldom and cold, how cursory, and reserved, your thoughts have been of the joys above ever since you did trade so eagerly for the world. O the cursed madness of many that seems to be religious! They thrust themselves into a multitude of employments, till they are so loaded with labors, and clogged with cares, that their souls are as unfit to converse with God as a man to walk with a mountain on his back, and as unable to soar in meditation, as their bodies to leap above the sun! And when they have lost that heaven upon earth, which they might have had, they take up with a few rotten arguments to prove it lawful; though indeed, they cannot.

I advise you, Christian, who has tasted the pleasures of a heavenly life; as ever you would taste of them any more, avoid this devouring gulf of an earthly mind. If once you come to this, *that you want to get rich, you fall into temptation and a trap and into many foolish and harmful desires* (1 Timothy 6:9). Keep these things loose about you, like a sweater or coat that you may lay them aside whenever there is need; but let God and glory be next to your heart. Ever remember, "that friendship with the world is hatred toward God. Anyone who chooses to be a friend of the world becomes the enemy of God" (James 4:4). "Do not love the world or anything in the world. If anyone loves the world, the love of the Father is not in him" (1 John 2:15). This is quite clear instruction, and happy is he that faithfully receives it!

Beware of the company of the ungodly. Not that I would dissuade you from necessary contact, or from doing them any good possible; especially, not from laboring for the good of their souls, as long as you have any opportunity. But it is the unnecessary companionship of ungodly men and too much familiarity with unprofitable companions that I dissuade you from. Not only the openly profane, the swearer, the drunkard, and the enemies of godliness, will prove hurtful companions to us, though these indeed are chiefly to be avoided; but too frequent companionship with persons merely civil and moral, whose lifestyle is empty and unedifying, may much divert our thoughts from heaven.

Our backwardness is such that we need the most constant and powerful helps. A stone, or a clod, is as fit to arise and fly in the air, as our hearts are naturally to move toward heaven. You need not hinder the rocks from flying up to the sky; it is sufficient that you do not help them.

And surely if our spirits have not great assistance, they may easily be kept from soaring upward, though they never should meet with the least impediment. O think of this in the choice of your companions! When your spirits are so disposed for heaven that you need no help to lift them up, but, as flames, you are always climbing higher and carrying with you all that is in your way, then you may, indeed, be less careful of your companions; but till then, as you love the delights of a heavenly life, be careful herein.

Men cannot talk of one thing and focus their hearts on another, especially things of such different natures. You *young men*, who are most liable to this temptation, think seriously of what I say; can you have your hearts in heaven while among your roaring companions in a tavern? Or when you work in your shops with those whose common language is oaths, *filthiness, or foolish talking, or jesting?* No, if you choose such company when you might have better, and find your delight in such, you are very far from a heavenly conversation. If your treasure was there, your heart could not be on things so distant. In a word, our company will be part of our happiness in heaven, and it is a singular part of our furtherance to it, or hindrance from it.

Take heed of a proud and lofty spirit. There is such an antipathy between this sin and God that you will never get your heart near Him, nor get Him near your heart, as long as this prevails in it. If it cast the angels out of heaven, it will keep your heart from heaven. If it cast our first parents out of paradise, and brought separation between the Lord and us, and brought His curse on all the creatures here below, it will certainly keep our hearts from paradise, and increase the cursed separation from our God. Communion with God will keep men low, and that lowliness will promote their communion. When a man spends much time in fellowship with God, and is taken up in the study of His glorious attributes, he *abhors himself in dust and ashes*; and that self-abhorrence is his best preparative to obtain admittance to God again. Therefore after a soul-humbling day, or in times of trouble, when the soul is lowest, it normally has freest access to God, and savors most of the life above. The delight of God is in him that *is humble, and contrite in spirit, and trembles at* His word (Isaiah 66:2). And the delight of such a soul is in God, and where there is mutual delight, there will be freest admittance, heartiest welcome, and most frequent fellowship. But God is so far from dwelling in the soul that is proud, that He will not admit it to any near access: *the proud he knows from afar* (Psalm 138:6). *God opposes the proud but gives grace to the humble* (1 Peter 5:5).

A proud mind is high in conceit, self-esteem, and carnal aspiring; a humble mind is high, indeed, in God's esteem, and in holy aspiring. These two sorts of high mindedness are most of all opposite to each other. Well then, are you a man of worth in your own eyes? Are you delighted when you hear of your esteem with men, and much dejected when you hear that they slight you? Do you love those best that honor you, and think poorly of them that do not, though they be otherwise men of godliness and honesty? Must you have your judgment be a rule, and your word a law to all about you? Are your passions kindled if your word or will be crossed? Are you ready to judge humility to be worthless, and know not how to submit to humble confession when you have sinned against God or injured your brother? Are you one that looks strange at the godly poor, and are almost ashamed to be their companion? Can you not serve God in a low place as well as a high? Are your boastings restrained more by prudence than humility? Do you desire to have all men's eyes upon you, and to hear them say, *"This is he?"* Are you unacquainted with the deceitfulness and wickedness of your heart? Are you more ready to defend your innocence than accuse yourself, or confess your fault? Can you hardly bear a close reproof or digest plain dealing from others?

If these symptoms be undeniable in your heart, you are a proud person. There is too much of hell abiding in you to have any acquaintance with heaven; your soul is too like the devil to have any familiarity with God. A proud man makes himself his god, and sets up himself as his idol: how then can his affections be set on God? How can he possibly have his heart in heaven? Invention and memory may possibly furnish his tongue with humble and heavenly expressions, but in his spirit there is no more heaven than there is humility.

I speak the more of it, because it is the most common and dangerous sin and most promotes the great sin of infidelity O Christian! If you would live continually in the presence of your Lord, lie in the dust, and He will then take you up. Learn of Him who is *gentle and humble in heart, and you will find rest for your souls* (Matthew 11:29). Otherwise your soul will be *like the tossing sea, which cannot rest, whose waves cast up mire and mud* (Isaiah 57:20); and instead of these sweet delights in God, your pride will fill you with perpetual disquiet. As he that *humbles himself like this child is the greatest in the kingdom of heaven* (Matthew 18:4); so shall he now be greatest in the foretastes of that kingdom. God dwells "with him who is contrite and lowly in spirit, to revive the spirit of the lowly, and to revive the heart of the contrite" (Isaiah 57:15). Therefore, "humble yourselves before the Lord, and he will lift you up" (James 4:10).

A slothful spirit is another impediment to this heavenly life. And I truly think, there is nothing that hinders it more than this in men of a good understanding. If it were only the exercise of the body, the moving of the lips, and bending of the knee, men would as commonly travel to heaven as they go to visit a friend. But to separate our thoughts and affections from the world, to draw forth all our graces, and increase each in its proper object, and hold them to it till the work prospers in our hands; this, this is the difficulty.

Reader, heaven is above you, and do you think to travel this steep ascent without labor and resolution? Can you get that earthly heart to heaven, and bring that backward mind to God, while you lie still and take your ease? If lying down at the foot of a hill and looking toward the top and wishing we were there would accomplish anything, then we should have daily travellers for heaven. But *the kingdom of heaven has been forcefully advancing, and forceful men lay hold of it* (Matthew 11:12). There must be great effort used to get these first fruits, as well as to get the full possession.

Do you not feel it so, though I should not tell you? Will your heart get upwards except you drive it? You know that heaven is all your hopes, that nothing below can yield you rest, that a heart seldom thinking of heaven can fetch but little comfort here; and yet do you not lose your opportunities and lie below, when you should walk above and live with God? Do you not commend the sweetness of a heavenly life, and judge those best Christians that use it, and yet never try it yourself? As the sluggard that stretches himself on his bed, and cries, "O that this were working!" So do you talk, and trifle, and live at your ease, and say, "O that I could get my heart to heaven!" How many read books and hear sermons expecting to hear of some easier way, or to meet with a shorter course to comfort, than they are ever going to find in Scripture? Or they ask for directions for a heavenly life, and if the hearing of them will accomplish it, they will be heavenly Christians. But if we show them their work and tell them they cannot have these delights on easier terms, then they leave us, as *the young man* left Christ *sorrowful*.

    If you are convinced, Reader, that this work is necessary to your comfort, set upon it resolutely. If your heart draws back, force it on with the command of reason. If your reason begins to dispute, produce the command of God and urge your own necessity. Let not such an incomparable treasure lie before you with your hand in your bosom. Let not your life be a continual famine when it might be a continual feast, only because you will not exert yourself. Sit not still with a disconsolate spirit, while comforts grow before your eyes, like a man in the midst of a garden of flowers, that will not rise to get them and partake of their sweetness. Christ is the fountain; but the well is deep, and you must bring forth this water before you can be refreshed with it. I know, so far as you are spiritual, you need not all this striving and violence; but in part you are carnal, and as long as it is so, there is need of labor. It was a custom of the Parthians not to give their children any meat in the morning before they saw the sweat on their faces with some labor. And you shall find this to be God's usual course, not to give His children the taste of His delights till they begin to sweat in seeking after them.

    Judge therefore whether a heavenly life or your carnal ease be better, and as a wise man make your choice accordingly. Then let me add for your encouragement, you need not meditate more than you do now; it is only to fix your thoughts upon better and more proper objects. Employ but as many serious thoughts every day upon the excellent glory of the life to come as you now do on worldly affairs, yea, on vanities and trifles, and your heart will soon be at heaven. On the whole, it is *the field of the sluggard, where thorns had come up everywhere, the ground was covered with weeds; the sluggard's craving will be the death of him, because his hands refuse to work; and it is* the sluggard who says, *there is a lion in the road, a fierce lion roaming the streets.* "As a door turns on its hinges, so a sluggard turns on his bed. The sluggard buries his hand in the dish;

he is too lazy to bring it back to his mouth" (Proverbs 24:30-31, 21:25, 26:13-15), though it be to feed himself with the food of life. What is this but throwing away our consolations, and consequently the precious blood that bought them? *For he that is slothful in his work is brother to him that is a great waste.* Apply this to your spiritual work, and study well the meaning of it.

Contentment with the mere preparative to this heavenly life, while we are utter strangers to the life itself, is also a dangerous and secret hindrance. We are deceived when we take up with the mere study of heavenly things, or the talking with one another about them, as if this were enough to make us heavenly. None are in more danger of this snare than those that are employed in leading the devotions of others, especially preachers of the gospel. O how easily may such be deceived! While they do nothing so much as read and study of heaven; preach, and pray, and talk of heaven; is not this the heavenly life? Alas! All this is but mere preparation! This is but collecting the materials, not erecting the building itself. It is but gathering the manna of others, and not eating and digesting ourselves. As he that sits at home may draw exact maps of countries, and yet never see them, nor travel toward them; so may you describe to others the joys of heaven and yet never come near it in your own hearts. A blind man, by learning, may speak of light and colors; so may you set forth to others that heavenly light which never enlightened your own souls, and bring that fire from the hearts of your people which never warmed your own hearts. What heavenly passages had Balaam in his prophecies, yet how little of it in his spirit? Ministers are under a more subtle temptation than any other men to draw us from this heavenly life. Studying and preaching of heaven more resembles a heavenly life than thinking and talking of the world does; and the resemblance is apt to deceive us. This is to die the most miserable death, even to famish ourselves, because we have bread on our tables; and to die for thirst while we draw water for others, thinking it enough that we have daily to do with it, though we never drink for the refreshment of our souls.

Having thus shown you what hindrances will resist you in the work, I expect you to resolve against them and avoid them faithfully, or else your labor will be in vain. I must also tell you that I here expect your promise, as you value the delights of these foretastes of heaven, to make certain of performing the following duties. Merely knowing them without practicing them will not bring heaven into your heart. Particularly, be convinced that: heaven is the only treasure and happiness, and labor to know that it is your own; and how near it is; frequently and seriously talk of it; endeavor to raise your affections nearer to it in every duty; to the same purpose improve every object and event; be much in the angelical work of praise; possess your soul with believing thoughts of the infinite love of God; carefully observe and cherish the motions of the Spirit of God; and do not neglect your bodily health.

Be convinced that heaven is the only treasure and happiness, and labor to know what a treasure and happiness it is. If you do not believe it to be the chief good you will never set your heart upon it; and this conviction must sink into your affections. If it be only a notion, it will have little efficacy. If Eve once supposes she sees more worth in the forbidden fruit than in the love and enjoyment of God, no wonder if it have more of her heart than God. If your judgment once prefers the delights of the flesh before the delights in the presence of God, it is impossible your heart should be in heaven. As it is ignorance of the emptiness of things below that makes men so overvalue them; so it is ignorance of the high delights above which is the cause that men so little mind them. If you see a purse of gold and believe it to be but rocks, it will not entice your affections to it. It is not the real excellence of a thing itself, but its believed excellence that excites desire. If an ignorant man sees a book, containing the secrets of arts or sciences, he values it no more than a common piece, because he knows not what is in it; but he that knows it, highly values it, and can even forbear his meat, drink, and sleep to read it. The world cries out for rest, and busily seeks for delight and happiness, because they know it not; for did they thoroughly know what it is, they could not so slight the everlasting treasure.

Labor also to know that heaven is your own happiness. We may confess heaven to be the best condition, though we despair of enjoying it; and we may desire and seek it, if we see the attainment but probable. But we can never delightfully rejoice in it till we are in some measure persuaded of our title to it. What comfort is it to a man that is naked to see the rich attire of others? Would not all this rather increase his anguish and make him more sensible of his own misery? So for a man to know the excellences of heaven and not to know whether he shall ever enjoy them, may raise desire and urge pursuit, but he will have little joy. Who will set his heart on another man's possessions? If your houses, your goods, your cattle, and your children were not your own, you would less mind them and less delight in them.

O Christian! Rest not therefore till you can call this rest your own. Bring your heart to the bar of trial. Set the qualifications of the saints on one side, and of your soul on the other, and then judge how near they resemble. You have the same Word to judge yourself by now as you will be judged by at the great day. Mistake not the Scripture's description of a saint, that you neither acquit, nor condemn yourself upon mistakes. For as groundless hopes tend to confusion, and are the greatest causes of most men's damnation; so groundless doubts tend to, and are the great cause of the saints' perplexity and distress. Therefore lay your foundation for trial carefully, and proceed in the work deliberately and resolutely, nor give over till you can say, either you have, or have not yet, a title to this rest. If men did truly know that God is their own Father, and Christ their own Redeemer and Head, and that heaven is their own everlasting habitation, and that there they must abide and be happy forever, how could they choose but be transported with the forethoughts thereof? If a Christian could but look upon sun, moon, and stars, and reckon all his own in Christ, and say, "These are the blessings that my Lord has procured me, and things incomparably greater than these," what holy raptures would his spirit feel?

Labor to understand how near your rest is. What we think near at hand we are more sensible of, than that which we behold at a distance. When judgments or mercies are far off, we talk of them with little concern; but when they draw close to us, we tremble at, or rejoice in, them. This makes men think on heaven so insensibly, because they think it is at a great distance; they look on it as twenty, thirty, or forty years off. How much better is it to receive the *sentence of death* (2 Corinthians 1:9) and to look on eternity as near at hand. While I am thinking and writing of it, it hastens near, and I am even entering into it before I am aware. While you are reading this, whoever you are, time flies, and your life soon will be gone. If you truly believed you should die tomorrow, how seriously would you think of heaven tonight? If Christ should say to a believing soul, tomorrow shall you be with Me; this would bring him in spirit to heaven beforehand. Do but suppose that you are soon entering into heaven, and it will greatly help you more seriously to meditate upon it.

Let your eternal rest be the subject of your frequent serious discourse, especially with those that can speak from their hearts and are seasoned themselves with a heavenly nature. It is pity Christians should ever meet together without some talk of their meeting in heaven, or of the way to it, before they part. It is a pity so much time is spent in vain conversation and useless disputes, and not a serious word of heaven among them. I think we should meet together on purpose to warm our spirits with discoursing of our rest. To hear a Christian set forth that blessed, glorious state, with life and power, from the promises of the gospel, should make us say, *Were not our hearts burning within us while he talked with us on the road and opened the Scriptures to us* (Luke 24:32)? If a Felix will *tremble* when he hears his judgment powerfully represented, why should not the believer be revived when he hears his eternal rest described? Wicked men can be delighted in talking together of their wickedness; should not Christians then be delighted in talking of Christ? And the heirs of heaven in talking of their inheritance? This may make our hearts revive, as it did Jacob's to hear the message that called him to

Goshen, and to see the chariots that should bring him to Joseph. O that we were furnished with skill and resolution to turn the stream of men's common discourse to these more sublime and precious things! Had it not been to deter us from unprofitable conversation, Christ would not have talked of our having to give account on the Day of Judgment for every careless word they have spoken (Matthew 12:36). Say then, as the Psalmist, when you are in company, *May my tongue cling to the roof of my mouth, if I do not…consider Jerusalem my highest joy* (Psalm 137:6). Then you shall find it true, that *the tongue that brings healing is a tree of life* (Proverbs 15:4).

Endeavor in every duty to raise your affections nearer to heaven. God's end in the institution of His ordinances was that they should be as so many steps to advance us to our rest, and by which, in subordination to Christ, we might daily ascend in our affections. Let this be your end in using them and doubtless they will not be unsuccessful. When you open your Bible or other book, hope to meet with some passage of divine truth and such blessing of the Spirit with it as will give you a fuller taste of heaven. When you are going to the house of God, say, "I hope to meet with God to raise my affections before I return. I hope the Spirit will give me the meeting, and sweeten my heart with those celestial delights. I hope Christ will *appear to me in that way, and shine about me with light from heaven*, let me hear His instructing and reviving voice, and cause the *scales to fall from my eyes*, that I may see more of that glory than I ever yet saw. I hope, before I return, my Lord will bring my heart within the view of rest, and set before His Father's presence, that I may return as the shepherds, from the heavenly vision, *"glorifying and praising God for all the things I have heard and seen."* Certainly God would not fail us in our duties if we did not fail ourselves. Remember, therefore, always to pray for your minister, that God would put some divine message into his mouth, which may leave a heavenly relish on your spirit.

Improve every object and every event to remind your soul of its approaching rest. As all providences and creatures are means to our rest, so they point us to that as their end. God's sweetest dealings with us at the present would not be half as sweet as they are, if they did not intimate some further sweetness. You take but the bare interest and overlook the main sum, when you receive your mercies, and forget your crown. O that Christians were skillful in this art! You can open your Bibles; learn to open also the volumes of creation and providences, to read there also of God and glory. Thus we might have a fuller taste of Christ and heaven in every common meal than most men have in a sacrament.

If you prosper in the world, let it make you more sensible of your perpetual prosperity. If you are weary with labor, let it make the thoughts of your eternal rest more sweet. If things go poorly, let your desires be more earnest to have sorrows and sufferings forever cease. Is your body refreshed with food or sleep? Remember the inconceivable refreshment with Christ. Do you hear any good news? Remember what glad tidings it will be to hear the trumpet of God and the applauding sentence of Christ. Are you delighted with the society of the saints? Remember what the perfect society in heaven will be. Is God communicating Himself to your spirit? Remember the time of your highest advancement, when both your communion and joy shall be full. Do you hear the raging noise of the wicked and the confusion of the world? Think of the blessed harmony in heaven. Do you hear the tempest of war? Remember the day when you shall be in perfect peace, under the wings of the Prince of Peace forever. Thus every condition and creature affords us advantages for a heavenly life, if we had but hearts to improve them.

Little do we know how we wrong ourselves by shutting out of our prayers the praises of God, or allowing them so narrow a room as we usually do, while we are plentiful in our confessions and petitions. Reader, I entreat you, let praises have a larger room in your duties; keep material ready at hand to feed your praise, as well as material for confession and petition. To this end, study the excellences and goodness of the Lord as frequently as your own wants and unworthiness; the mercies you have received and those, which are promised as often as the sins, you have committed. "It is fitting for the upright to praise him. He who sacrifices thank offerings honors me. Praise the Lord, for the Lord is good; sing praise to his name, for that is pleasant" (Psalms 33:1; 50:23; 135:3). "Let us continually offer to God a sacrifice of praise-the fruit of lips that confess his name" (Hebrews 13:15). Had not David a most heavenly spirit, who was so much in this heavenly work? Does it not sometimes raise our hearts when we only read the Psalms of David? How much more would it raise and refresh us to be skillful and frequent in the work ourselves!

O the madness of youth that layout their vigor of body and mind upon vain delights and fleshly lusts, which is so unfit for the noblest work of man! And O, the sinful folly of many of the saints, who drench their spirits in continual sadness, and waste their days in complaints and groans, and so make themselves both in body and mind unfit for this sweet and heavenly work! Instead of joining with the people of God in His praises, they are questioning their worthiness and studying their miseries; and so rob God of His glory and themselves of their consolation. But the greatest destroyer of our comfort *in* this duty is our taking up with the tune and melody, and suffering the heart to be idle, which ought to perform the principal part of the work, and use the melody to revive and exhilarate itself.

Ever keep your soul possessed with believing thoughts of the infinite love of God. Love is the attraction of love. Who will not love those that love them? No doubt it is the death of our heavenly life to have hard thoughts of God, to conceive of Him as one that would rather damn than save us. This is to put the blessed God into the similitude of Satan. When our ignorance and unbelief have drawn the most deformed picture of God in our imaginations, then we complain that we cannot love Him, nor delight in Him. This is the case of many thousand Christians. Alas, that we should thus blaspheme God, and blast our own joys! Scripture assures us that God is love (1 John 4:16); and that he *takes no pleasure in the death of the wicked, but rather that they turn from their ways and live* (Ezekiel 33:11). Much more has He testified His love to His chosen and His full resolution effectually to save them.

O that we could always think of God as we do of a friend; as of one that unfeignedly loves us, even more than we do ourselves; whose very heart is set upon us to do us good, and has therefore provided for us an everlasting dwelling with Himself. It would not then be so hard to have our hearts ever with Him! Where we love most heartily, we shall think most sweetly, and most freely. I fear most Christians think higher of the love of a hearty friend than of the love of God; and what wonder then if they love their friends better than God, and trust them more confidently than God, and had rather live with them than with God?

Carefully observe and cherish the promptings of the Spirit of God. If ever your soul will rise above this earth, and get acquainted with this heavenly life, the Spirit of God must be to you as the chariot to Elijah, by which you must move and ascend. O then, grieve not your guide, quench not your life, knock not off your chariot-wheels! You little think how much the life of all your graces and the happiness of your souls depend upon your ready and sincere obedience to the Spirit. When the Spirit urges you to secret prayer, or forbids you your known transgressions, or points out to you the way in which you should go, and you will not obey, no wonder if heaven and your soul be strange. If you will not follow the Spirit while He would draw you to Christ and your duty, how should He lead you to heaven and bring your heart into the presence of God?

What supernatural help, what bold access, shall the soul find in its approaches to the Almighty, that constantly obeys the Spirit? And how backward, how dull, how ashamed, will he be in these addresses, who have often broken away from the Spirit that would have guided him? Christian Reader, do you not feel sometimes a strong impression to retire from the world and draw near to God? Do not disobey, but take the offer and hoist up your sails while this blessed wind may be had. The more we obey, the speedier will be our pace.

I advise you as an additional help to this heavenly life not to neglect the due care of your bodily health. Your body is a useful servant if you give it its due, and no more than its due; but it is a most devouring tyrant if you allow it to have what it unreasonably desires. When we consider how few use their bodies correctly, we cannot wonder if they be much hindered in their converse with heaven. Most men are slaves to their appetite and can scarce deny anything to the flesh, and are therefore willingly carried by it to their sports, or profits, or vain companions, when they should raise their minds to God and heaven. As you love your *souls, do not think about how to gratify the desires of the sinful nature* (Romans 13:14); but remember, "the mind of sinful man is death...because the sinful mind is hostile to God. It does not submit to God's law, nor can it do so. Those controlled by the sinful nature cannot please God. Therefore, brothers, we have an obligation-but it is not to the sinful nature, to live according to it. For if you live according to the sinful nature, you will die; but if by the Spirit you put to death the misdeeds of the body, you will live" (Romans 8:6-8, 12, 13).

There are a few who much hinder their heavenly joy by denying the body its necessities, and so making it unable to serve them. If such wronged their flesh only, it would be no great matter; but they wrong their souls also, as he that spoils the house injures the inhabitants. When the body is sick and the spirits languish, how slowly do we move in the thoughts and joys of heaven?

4. The Nature of Heavenly Contemplation, with the Time, Place, and Frame of Mind Most Suited for It

Once more I entreat you, Reader, as you dare not willfully resist the Spirit, as you value the high delights of a saint and the soul ravishing exercise of heavenly contemplation, that you diligently study and speedily and faithfully practice the following directions. If, by this means you do not find an increase of all your graces and do not grow beyond the stature of common Christians, and are not made more effective in your service for Christ, and more precious in the eyes of all discerning persons, and if your soul does not enjoy more communion with God and your life is not fuller of comfort, then cast away these directions, and exclaim against me forever as a deceiver.

The duty, which I press upon you so earnestly, and in the practice of which I am now to direct you, is, "The set and solemn acting of all the powers of your soul in meditation upon your everlasting rest. Many that faithfully perform other duties easily neglect this. They are troubled if they miss a sermon or a prayer meeting. Yet they are not troubled that they have omitted meditation perhaps all their life, though it is that duty by which all other duties are improved, and by which the soul digests truths for its nourishment and comfort. It was God's command to Joshua, *Do not let his Book of the Law depart from your mouth; meditate on it day and night, so that you may be careful to do everything written in it* (Joshua 1:8). As digestion turns food into nourishment for the body, so meditation turns the truths received and remembered into warm affection, firm resolution, and a holy lifestyle.

This meditation is the acting of all the powers of the soul. It is the most spiritual and sublime work we can engage in. It therefore cannot be performed by a heart that is carnal and earthly. You must necessarily have some relation to heaven before you can familiarly converse there. I suppose them to be such as having a title to rest when I persuade them to rejoice in the meditations of rest. And supposing you to be a Christian, I am now exhorting you to be an active Christian. And it is the work of the soul I am setting you to, for bodily exercise profits but little.

And it must have **all** the powers of the soul to distinguish it from the common meditation of students; for the understanding is not the whole soul, and therefore cannot do the whole work. The understanding must take in truths, and prepare them for the will, and that for the affections. Christ and heaven have various excellences, and therefore God has formed the soul with different powers for apprehending those excellences. What good would fragrant flowers be if we had no smell? Or what good would language or music have done us if we could not hear? Or what pleasure should we have found in food without the sense of taste? So, what good could all the glory of heaven have done us, or what pleasure should we have had in the perfections of God Himself, if we had been without the affections of love and joy? And what strength or sweetness can you possibly receive by your meditations on eternity, while you do not exercise those affections of the soul by which you must be sensible of this sweetness and strength?

It is the mistake of Christians to think that meditation is only the work of the understanding and memory. Even a child can use his understanding and memory, as can persons that hate the things, which they think on. So you see there is more to be done than merely to remember and think of heaven. Some exercise stirs only a hand or a foot, while some utilizes the entire body. Genuine meditation must engage the whole soul. As the affections of sinners are set on the world, turned to idols, and fallen from God, as well as their understanding; so must their affections be returned to God, as well as the understanding. As their whole soul was filled with sin before, so the whole must be filled with God now. See David's description of the blessed man, *his delight is in the law of the Lord, and on his law he meditates day and night* (Psalm 1:2).

This meditation is set and solemn. As there is solemn prayer, when we set ourselves wholly to that duty, and *ejaculatory prayer*, when in the midst of other business we send some short requests to God; so also there is solemn meditation, when we apply ourselves wholly to that work, and transient meditation, when in the midst of other business we have some good thoughts of God in our minds. Now, though I would persuade you to that meditation which is mixed with your common labors, and also that which special occasions direct you to; yet I would have you likewise make it a constant standing duty, as you do by hearing, praying, and reading the scriptures; and no more intermix other matters with it, than you would with prayer, or other stated solemnities.

This meditation is upon your everlasting rest. As heaven has the pre-eminence in perfection, it should have it also in our meditation. That which will make us most happy when we possess it will make us most joyful when we meditate upon it. Other meditations are as numerous as there are lines in Scripture or particular providences in the world. But this is a walk to mount Zion: from the kingdoms of this world to the kingdom of saints; from earth to heaven: from time to eternity; it is walking upon sun, moon, and stars, in the garden and paradise of God. It may seem far off, but spirits are quick. Whether in the body or out of the body, their motion is swift.

You need not fear, like the men of the world, lest these thoughts should make you insane. It is heaven and not hell that I persuade you to walk in. It is joy and not sorrow that I persuade you to exercise. I urge you to look on no deformed objects, but only upon the ravishing glory of saints and the unspeakable excellences of the God of glory and the beams that stream from the face of His Son. Will it distract a man to think of his only happiness? Will it distract the miserable to think of mercy, or the prisoner to foresee deliverance, or the poor to think of approaching riches and honor? I think it should rather make a man insane to think of living in a world of woe and abiding in poverty and sickness, among the rage of wicked men, than to think of living with Christ in bliss. Knowledge has no enemy but the ignorant. This heavenly course was never spoken against by any but those that never knew it or never used it. I fear more the neglect of men that approve it, than the opposition or arguments of any against it.

As to the best time for this heavenly contemplation, give it a stated time. Having a predetermined time is a hedge to duty, and defends it against many temptations to omission. Let it be frequent, as well as stated. How often it should be, I cannot determine, because men's circumstances differ. But in general, scripture requires it to be frequent when it mentions *meditating day and night*. I advise that it be once a day at least. Frequency in heavenly contemplation is particularly important to prevent a shyness between God and your soul. Frequent society breeds familiarity, and familiarity increases love, delight, and makes us bold in our addresses. The chief end of this duty is to have acquaintance and fellowship with God, and therefore if you come but seldom to it, you will keep yourself a stranger still. Therefore I persuade to frequency in this duty.

You will also prevent the loss of that heat and life you have obtained. If you eat but once in two or three days, you will lose your strength as fast as it comes. If in holy meditation you get near to Christ, and warm your heart with the fire of love, and then come but seldom, your former coldness will soon return, especially as the work is so spiritual and against the bent of depraved nature.

Choose also the most seasonable time. All things are beautiful and excellent in their season. The same hour may be seasonable to one and unseasonable to another. You should observe when you find your spirits most active and fit for contemplation, and fix upon that as the stated time. I have always found that the best time for myself is the evening. I also mention this, because it was the experience of a better and wiser man, for it is expressly said of Isaac, *He went out to the field one evening to meditate* (Genesis 24:63).

The Lord's Day is exceeding seasonable for this exercise. When should we more seasonably contemplate on rest than on that day of rest, which typifies it to us? It being a day appropriated to spiritual duties, we should never exclude this duty, which is so eminently spiritual. I truly think this is the chief work of a Christian Sabbath. What better time to converse with our Lord than on the Lord's Day? What better day to ascend to heaven than that on which He arose from earth and fully triumphed over death and hell. The best disposition for a true Christian is, like John, to say *On the Lord's Day I was in the Spirit* (Revelations 1:10). And what can bring us to this joy in the Spirit but the spiritual beholding of our approaching glory?

Besides the constant seasonableness of every day, and particularly every Lord's Day, there are also more peculiar seasons for heavenly contemplation. One excellent time is when God has more abundantly warmed your spirit with fire from above. Then you may soar with greater freedom. A little labor will set your heart soaring at such a time as this whereas at another time you may strive with little result. Observe the wind of the Spirit, and how the Spirit of Christ moves your spirit. *Without Christ we can do nothing*, and therefore let us be doing, while He is doing. Be sure not to be out of the way nor asleep when He comes. When the Spirit finds your heart, like Peter, in prison, and in irons, and smites you, and says, *Rise up quickly, and follow me;* be sure you then arise, and follow, and you shall find your *chains fall off*, and all *doors will open*, and you will be at heaven before you are aware.

Another peculiar season for this duty is when you are in a suffering, distressed, or tempted state. When do we need encouragement but in times of fainting? When is it more seasonable to walk to heaven then when we know not in what corner of earth to live with comfort? Or when should our thoughts converse more above then when they have nothing but grief below? Where should Noah's dove be but in the ark, when the waters cover all the earth, and she cannot find rest for the sole of her foot? What should we think on but our *Father's house*, when we have not even the husks of the world to feed upon? Surely God sends your afflictions to this very purpose. Happy are you, poor man, if you make this use of your poverty! And you that are sick, if you so improve your sickness! It is seasonable to go to the Promised Land when our burdens are increased in Egypt, and our troubles in the wilderness.

Reader, if you knew what sweet medicine to your grieves the serious views of glory are, you would less fear these harmless troubles, and more use that preserving, reviving remedy. When anxiety was great within me, said David, *your consolation brought joy to my soul* (Psalm 94:19). I consider, said Paul, that *our present sufferings are not worth comparing with the glory that will be revealed in us* (Romans 8: 18). "Therefore we do not lose heart. Though outwardly we are wasting away, yet inwardly we are being renewed day by day. For our light and momentary troubles are achieving for us an eternal glory that far outweighs them all. So we fix our eyes not on what is seen, but on what is unseen. For what is seen is temporary, but what is unseen is eternal," (2 Corinthians 4:16-18).

Another season peculiarly fit for this heavenly duty is when God summons us to die. When should we most frequently sweeten our souls with the believing thoughts of another life than when we find that this life is almost ended? No men have greater need of supporting joys than dying men; and those joys must be fetched from our eternal joy. As heavenly delights are sweetest when nothing earthly is joined with them; so the delights of dying Christians are oftentimes the sweetest they ever had. With what a heavenly song and divine benediction did Moses conclude his life? What heavenly advice and prayer had the disciples from their Lord when He was about to leave them? When Paul *was ready to be offered up*, what heavenly exhortation and advice did he give the Philippians, Timothy, and the elders of Ephesus? How near to heaven was John in Patmos but a little before his translation there? It is the general inclination of the saints to be then most heavenly when they are nearest heaven.

If it be your case, Reader, to perceive your dying time drawing near, O where should your heart now be but with Christ! I think you should even behold Him standing by you, and should behold Him as your physician and your friend. Look upon your pain and sickness as

Jacob did on Joseph's chariots, and let your spirit revive within you, and hear Christ's words, *"Because I live, you also will live,"* (John 14:19). Do you need the choicest encouragements? Here are choicer than the world can afford! Here are all the joys of heaven, even the vision of God, and Christ, and whatsoever the blessed here possess. These dainties are offered you by the hand of Christ. He has written the receipt in the promises of the gospel and has prepared the ingredients in heaven. Only put forth the hand of faith, feed upon them, rejoice, and live!

Concerning the best place for heavenly contemplation, it is sufficient to say that the most convenient is some private place. Our spirits need every help, and to be freed from every hindrance in the work. If in private prayer, Christ directs you to go *into your room, close the door and pray to your Father* (Matthew 6), so should you do in this meditation. How often did Christ Himself retire to some mountain, or wilderness, or other solitary place? I give not this advice for occasional meditation, but for that which is set and solemn. Therefore withdraw yourself from all society, even the society of godly men, that you may a while enjoy the society of your Lord. If a student cannot study in a crowd, who exercises only his memory; much less should you be in a crowd, who are to exercise all the powers of your soul, and upon an object so far above nature. We seldom read of God's appearing by Himself, or by His angels, to any of His prophets or saints in a crowd, but frequently when they were alone.

But observe for yourself what place best agrees with your spirit; whether within doors, or without. Isaac's example in *going out to meditate in the field*, will, I believe, best suit with most. Our Lord so much used a solitary garden that even Judas, when he came to betray Him, knew where to find Him. And though Christ took His disciples there with Him, *yet He withdrew about a stone's throw beyond them* for more secret devotions (John 18:1-2; Luke 22:41). So that as Christ had His accustomed place, so must we. Only there is a wide difference in the object: Christ meditates on the sufferings that our sins had deserved, so that the wrath of his Father passed through all His soul; but we are to meditate on the glory He has purchased, that the love of the Father and the joy of the Spirit may enter at our thoughts, and revive our affections, and overflow our souls.

I am next to advise you concerning the preparations of your heart for this heavenly contemplation. The success of the work much depends on the frame of your heart. When man's heart had nothing in it to grieve the Spirit, it was then the delightful habitation of His Maker. God did not quit His residence there till man expelled Him by unworthy provocations. There was no shyness or reserve till the heart grew sinful, and too loathsome a dungeon for God to delight in. And was this soul reduced to its former innocence, God would quickly return to His former habitations; yea, so far as it is renewed and repaired by the Spirit, and purged from its lusts, and beautified with his image, the Lord will yet acknowledge it his own. Christ will manifest Himself unto it, and the Spirit will take it for His temple and residence. So far as the heart is qualified for conversing with God, so far it usually enjoys Him. Therefore, with *above all else, guard your heart, for it is the wellspring of life* (Proverbs 4:23).

More particularly, get your heart as clear from the world as you can. Wholly lay aside the thoughts of your business, troubles, enjoyments, and everything that may take up any room in your soul. Get it as empty of the world as you possibly can, that it be the more capable of being filled with God. When you shall go into the mount of contemplation you will be like the covetous man at the heap of gold, who, when he might take as much as he could, lamented that he was able to carry no more. So you will find as much of God and glory as your narrow heart is able to contain, and almost nothing to hinder your full possession but the incapacity of your own spirit. Then you will think, "O that this understanding and these affections could contain more! It is more my unfitness than anything else that even this place is not my heaven. O, the words of love Christ has to speak, and the wonders of love He has to show, but I cannot bear them yet! Heaven is ready for me, but my heart is unready for heaven."

Therefore, Reader, seeing your enjoyment of God in this contemplation much depends on the capacity and disposition of your heart, seek Him with all your soul. Thrust not Christ into the stable and the manger, as if you had better guests for the chief rooms. Say to all your worldly business and thoughts, as Christ to His disciples, *Stay here, while I go and pray.* Or as Abraham to his servants, when he went to offer Isaac, *Stay here, and I will go and worship, and come again to you.* Even as the priests *thrust king Uzziah out of the temple*, where he presumed to burn incense, when they saw *the leprosy* upon him; so do you thrust those thoughts from the temple of your heart, which have the badge of God's prohibition upon them.

Be sure to set upon this work with the greatest solemnity of heart and mind. There is no trifling in holy things. God says, *"Among those who approach me I will show myself holy,"* (Leviticus 10:3). These spiritual, excellent, soul-raising duties, are, if well used, most profitable; but when used unfaithfully, most dangerous. Labor therefore to have the deepest apprehensions of the presence of God and his incomprehensible greatness. If queen Esther must not draw near, till *the king held out the scepter*, think, then, with what reverence you should approach Him who made the worlds with the word of His mouth, who upholds the earth as in the palm of His hands, who keeps the sun, moon, and stars in their courses, and who sets bounds to the raging sea. You are going to converse with Him, before whom the earth will quake, and devils do tremble, and at whose bar you and all the world must shortly stand, and be finally judged. O think, "I shall then have lively apprehensions of His majesty. My drowsy spirits will then be awakened, and my irreverence be laid aside; and why should I not now be roused with the sense of His greatness, and the dread of His name possess my soul?"

Labor also to apprehend the greatness of the work, which you attempt, and to be deeply sensible both of its importance and excellence. If you were pleading for your life at the bar of an earthly judge, you would be serious; and yet that would be a trifle to this. If you were engaged in such a work as David against Goliath, on which the welfare of a kingdom depended; in itself considered, it is nothing to this. Suppose you were going to such a wrestling as Jacob's, or to see the sight, which the three disciples saw in the mount; how seriously, how reverently, would you, both approach and behold! If but an angel from heaven should appoint to meet you, at the same time and place of your contemplations; with what dread would you be filled? Consider then, with what a spirit you should meet the Lord, and with what seriousness and awe you should daily converse with Him!

Consider also the blessed result of the work. It will be your admission into the presence of God, and the beginning of your eternal glory on earth; a means to make you live above the level of other men, and be in the next room to the angels themselves, that you may both live and die joyfully. The prize being so great, your preparations should be of the same magnitude. There is none on earth who live such a life of joy and blessedness as those that are acquainted with this heavenly conversation. The joys of all other men are but like a child's play, a fool's laughter, or a sick man's dream of health. He that trades for heaven is the only gainer, and he that neglects it is the only loser. How heartily, therefore, should this work be done!

Aflame with Love

Selections from Writings
Blaise Pascal 1623-1662

Compiled with an Introduction
By Robert E. Coleman

Abridged version of *Pensées* by Blaise Pascal. Abridged version originally published by the Institute of Evangelism Billy Graham Center, 1974, Wheaton, IL. Copyright of translated abridged version and introduction held by Robert Coleman, used with permission. Translated from the French. Artwork in the Public Domain.

Book Chapters

1. Introduction
   By Robert E. Coleman 74
2. Knowing God in Christ 81
3. Proofs of Jesus 86
   The Mystery of Jesus 88
   The Sepulcher of Jesus Christ 92
4. Human Struggle 94
   External Works 95
5. The New Life 99
   On the Miracle 105

1. Introduction
By Robert E. Coleman

In the year of Grace, 1654,

On Monday, 23rd of November, Feast of St. Clement, Pope and Martyr, and of others in the Martyrology,

Vigil of St. Chrysogonus, Martyr, and others, From about half past ten in the evening until about half past twelve,

FIRE

God of Abraham, God of Isaac, God of Jacob, not of the philosophers and scholars.
Certitude. Certitude. Feeling. Joy. Peace. God of Jesus Christ.
"Thy God shall be my God."
Forgetfulness of the world and of everything, except God.

> He is to be found only by the ways taught in the Gospel.
> Greatness of the Human Soul.
> "Righteous Father, the world hath not known Thee. But I have known Thee."
> Joy, joy, joy, tears of joy.
> I have separated myself from Him.

"My God, wilt Thou leave me?" Let me not be separated from Him eternally.

"This is the eternal life, that they might know Thee, the only true God, and the one whom Thou hast sent, Jesus Christ."
Jesus Christ.

JESUS CHRIST

I have separated myself from Him: I have fled from Him, denied Him, and crucified Him.

Let me never be separate from Him.

We keep hold of Him only by the ways taught in the Gospel.

Renunciation, total and sweet.

Total submission to Jesus Christ and to my director.

Eternally in joy for a day's training on earth. Amen.

Seldom has one expressed with such precision and feeling his confrontation with Jesus Christ. The terse stenographic account was written on a parchment, at the top of which was etched a cross-surrounded by rays. As a constant reminder of this experience, the paper was sewed by the author inside the lining of his coat. One can imagine him during times of temptation and suffering slipping his hand over the hidden treasure and pressing its hallowed message to his heart. Not until after his death was the document discovered. The reality, which it describes, changed the life of Blaise Pascal, universally acclaimed scientist, inventor, psychologist, philosopher, and Christian apologist; by any comparison one of the greatest thinkers of all time.

He was born in Clennont-Terand in France, June 19, 1623. His mother, a godly woman, died when he was three, leaving his father to care for Blaise and his two sisters. The elder Pascal, Etienne, was a man of genuine devotion and ability, and he eagerly sought to stimulate the minds of his children. In order to improve their educational opportunities, he gave up his post as magistrate, and moved with his family to Paris in 1631.

The extraordinary gifts of the son began to appear very early. By the time he was twelve, having mastered Greek and Latin, his compulsive desire to find things out for himself led him to work through, on his own, the thirty-two geometric theorems of Euclid's *First Book*. When this almost unbelievable feat became known, he was invited to accompany his father to the weekly meetings of the Academy of Science, where he mingled freely with the greatest intellectuals of his day. Before he was sixteen, the young genius had unraveled the mystery of conic sections, composing a treatise, which anticipated projective geometry. Thereafter, he discovered the famous lemma in mathematics, which came to be called the Pascal theorem. Just as an aside, while still in his teens, he invented and constructed the first calculating machine, showing himself as skilled in applied science as in pure thought.

The Pascal household observed a nominal Catholic religious practice until 1646 when they came into contact with Jansenism. This group within the Roman Church, somewhat comparable to Protestant Puritans, stressed divine grace and election in redemption. Blaise embraced their teaching, and soon won over to his new faith the other members of his family. From this time on, he became a diligent student of the Bible and generally tried to follow a life of personal piety.

His resolution to "live only for God" did not keep him from continuing his scientific research. In the course of his experiments, he demonstrated the fact of atmospheric pressure, the vacuum and the weight of air. These findings, published in 1647, led to his investigation of the equilibrium of liquids, establishing the principle of hydrodynamics. From these discoveries came the barometer, the vacuum pump, the air compressor, the syringe, and the hydraulic press. Not stopping with these practical applications of his thinking, he later explored the concept of universal, physical relativity and developed the theory of probability, from which emerged infinitesimal calculus. During this time, he advanced the axiom, which was to become the guiding dictum of modern science—"that experiments are the true masters to follow in physics."

Interestingly, this passion for objective proof comes through in his treatment of theology. Not in the sense that religious truth can be demonstrated through the human sciences or metaphysical reasoning, for it is of a supernatural order. But in its own order of knowledge, spiritual reality can be validated through the testimony of Scripture, which Pascal believed to be "the Word of God infallible in the facts which it records." In this position, he came to reject the speculative approach of scholasticism, and maintained that the Bible alone is our basis for the Christian faith. He recognized the importance of Church Councils and tradition in defining the proper interpretation, but insisted that no authoritative view can be contrary to the Bible. For, as he said, "he who will give the meaning of Scripture, and does not take it from Scripture, is an enemy of Scripture."

Pascal's father died in 1651, and soon afterward, his younger sister, Jacqueline, entered the Jansenist convent at Port-Royal (his older sister had married earlier). Bereft of family companionship, Blaise unwisely turned to some of his aristocratic friends to fill the void, and with them sought diversion in the pleasures of fashionable society. After a year or more of this attachment to the "world," he was left disillusioned, and became more convinced than ever of the vanity of man. Neither the delight of idle amusement nor the renown of great achievement could satisfy his yearning soul. He was brought to the point of despair.

It was in this state that he was reading the Scripture on that eventful evening in 1654 when God appeared to him in Fire. He had opened to the seventeenth chapter of John's Gospel where Jesus is seen in prayer before giving Himself over to be crucified. As he read, suddenly the room was filled with the flaming Presence of Him who is perfect Holiness and Love. The Word written in the Book was confirmed by the Word present in the Son. Here was certitude. Before such experiential Truth he could only bow in "total submission to Jesus Christ."

After this experience, called his "second conversion," the broken and penitent scholar saw even more clearly the futility of living for self. He renounced every resource of the fleshly nature, and gave himself completely to the message of Scripture. All his worldly endeavors were abandoned. He sold his coach and horses, his fine furniture and silverware, and gave the money to the poor. Even his extensive library was discarded, keeping only a few devotional books and his Bible. The glory of his Savior became his only concern. Never again would he ever sign his name to his own writings, nor let his name be mentioned in praise. Taking the guise of Monsieur de Mons, he left Paris and went to live among the Jansenist "solitaries" of Port-Royal.

The views of this holiness sect were not popular in the more easygoing establishment of the Sorbonne and among the Jesuits. Eventually the Pope was persuaded to condemn them. Amid the controversy. Pascal came forth to defend their cause. His vindication, appearing as *The Provincial Letters*, began in 1656, and established him as the most articulate polemist of his generation. The dialogues cast the whole dispute in simple logic, showing by withering irony and wit that the real issue was one of morality, not dogma. He did not deprecate official church doctrine, but decried the way clever maneuvering with words was being used to subvert the intent of Scripture. Such casuistry he saw as a form of self-esteem, and therefore leads to concupiscence or creature love. To Pascal, the love of God alone motivates the body of Christ, and this love is evidenced by obedience to His Word.

His *Letters* suddenly broke off in 1657, for his attention had focused on the larger task of constructing an *Apology for the Christian Religion*. It was designed to be a demonstration of Christianity, setting forth reasons which would convince the unbeliever. He planned to spend ten years on the work, but as it turned out, there was time only to prepare his notes for the final draft. Ranging from a few cryptic words to short essays, the "thoughts" were collected by the Port-Royalists and published as the *Pensees* eight years after his death. The more than seven hundred fragments have come to be regarded as his greatest masterpiece.

Beginning with the human dilemma, he draws a picture of natural man's misery on the one hand and his glory on the other. There would be no meaning nor purpose in life apart from God's disclosure of His Word. Indifference of the skeptic is overcome by means of a "wager," based on his law of probability, whereby everyone is confronted with an all-encompassing choice. God is or is not. One who responds in the affirmative has everything to gain and nothing to lose; whereas the person who denies God has nothing permanently to gain and everything to lose. Though it is self-interest, which provokes the reasonable decision, still it causes one to move from a habit of disbelief, and invites a new direction toward truth.

God's saving Revelation, however, comes only through divine illumination in the believer's soul. "It is the heart which experiences God, and not the reason. This, then, is faith: God felt by the heart." By this Pascal does not mean mystical emotion, but rather, an intuitive love for God Himself. Those awakened by grace will have this perception. Moreover, God has so constructed the universe that He will be found of those who search for Him with all their heart.

The focus is Jesus Christ, the object of all Scripture, for He alone incarnated the Infinite Word in our human estate. In His Person is revealed both the Truth of God and the Truth of man. Yet only persons who renounce self-love will know what this means. Herein is exposed the error of those who do not find the Truth. A genuine Christian does not squabble over signs; he humbly bows in adoration before his majestic Lord.

He was still working on his *Pensees* when urged by some friends to solve a geometric problem, which had baffled mathematicians for centuries. Thinking that it would give his Christian apology a greater hearing, and also to distract his mind from an incessant headache, he analyzed the nature of cycloid curves. His findings, published in 1658, laid the foundations for differential and integral calculus. In another moment of this inventive genius, noticing the numbers of people walking long distances in Paris, he designed an omnibus carriage for public transport, which brought into being the world's first bus service. However, such scientific exploits were mere pastimes. His attention now was fixed on something far more profound. So engrossed was he in thought on spiritual things that he wrote in 1660, "I would not take two steps for geometry...I am engaged in studies so remote from such preoccupations that I can scarcely remember that they actually exist."

But the terrible pain, which had punished him through most of his life, grew worse, and finally he was unable to continue any mental exercise. One of the last things he wrote was "A Prayer Asking God to Use His Illness for a Good End." The following excerpt beautifully reflects his trust in the perfect will of God.

> Lord, whose Spirit is so good and so gentle, and who is so compassionate that not only all prosperity but even all afflictions that come to thine elect are the results of Thy compassion...
>
> Grant that I may conform to Thy will, just as I am, that, being sick as I am, I may glorify Thee in my sufferings. Without them I cannot attain to glory; without them, my Savior, even Thou would not not have risen to glory. By the marks of Thy sufferings Thou dost recognize those who are Thy disciples. Therefore recognize me as Thy disciple by the ills that I endure, in my body and in my spirit, for the offenses, which I have committed. And since nothing is pleasing to God unless it be offered to Him by Thee, unite my will with Thine and my sufferings with those that Thou hast suffered; grant that mine may become Thine. Unite me with Thee; fill me with Thee and Thy Holy Spirit. Enter into my heart and into my soul, there to bear my sufferings and to continue in me that part of the suffering of Thy passion which yet remains to be endured, which Thou art yet completing in Thy members until the perfect consummation of Thy Body, so that it shall no longer be I who live and suffer but that it shall be Thou who dost live and suffer in me, O my Savior. And thus, having some small part in Thy suffering, I shall be filled wholly by Thee with the glory which it has brought to Thee, the glory in which Thou dost dwell with the Father and the Holy Spirit, forever and ever. Amen.

On August 19, 1662, his intense bodily suffering ended. The awe-inspiring saint, with faith "simple as a child," died at the home of his brother-in-law, having turned his house over to an impoverished family. He was thirty-nine years old.

Few men have ever lived who thought more deeply upon the nature of reality. "At an age when others have hardly begun to see the light, he had completed the cycle of human knowledge," and seeing its emptiness, directed his remaining energies to know Him in whom is hidden all the wisdom and the glory of God. Here Pascal found the answer to his heart's desire, and in that assurance, he discovered the Truth that sets men free—the Truth that every man can know by faith in Jesus Christ.

Some of his reflections appear on the following pages. Though space permits only a few to be cited, it is my hope that reading these thoughts will bring one to feel something of his passion for God, and thereby, to experience more fully the Word aflame with Love.

2. Knowing God in Christ

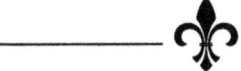

"It is in vain, O men, that you seek within yourselves the remedy for your ills. All your light can only reach the knowledge that not in yourselves will you find truth or good. The philosophers have promised you that, and have been unable to do it. They neither know what is your true good, nor what is your true state. How could they have given remedies for your ills, when they did not even know them? Your chief maladies are pride, which takes you away from God, and lust, which binds you to earth; and they have done nothing else but cherish one or other of these diseases. If they gave you God as an end, it was only to administer to your pride; they made you think that you are by nature like Him, and conformed to Him. And those who saw the absurdity of this claim put you on another precipice, by making you understand that your nature was like that of the brutes, and led you to seek your good in the lusts which are shared by the animals. This is not the way to cure you of your unrighteousness, which these wise men never knew. I alone can make you understand who you are..."

Adam, Jesus Christ...

—Incredible that God should unite Himself to us. —This consideration is drawn only from the sight of our vileness. But if you are quite sincere over it, follow it as far as I have done, and recognize that we are indeed so vile that we are incapable in ourselves of knowing if His mercy cannot make us capable of Him. For I would know how this animal, who knows himself to be so weak, has the right to measure the mercy of God, and set limits to it, suggested by his own fancy. He has so little knowledge of what God is, that he does not know what he himself is, and, completely disturbed at the sight of his own state, dares to say that God cannot make him capable of communion with Him.

But I would ask him if God demands anything else from him than the knowledge and love of Him, and why, since his nature is capable of love and knowledge, he believes that God cannot make Himself known and loved by him. Doubtless he knows at least that he exists, and that he loves something. Therefore, if he set's anything in the darkness wherein he is, and if he finds some object of his love among the things on earth, why, if God impart to him some ray of His essence will he not be capable of knowing and of loving Him in the manner in which it shall please Him to communicate Himself to us? There must then be certainly an intolerable presumption in arguments of this sort, although they seem founded on an apparent humility, which is neither sincere nor reasonable, if it does not make us admit that, not knowing of ourselves what we are, we can only learn it from God.

I do not mean that you should submit your belief to me without reason, and I do not aspire to overcome you by tyranny. In fact, I do not claim to give you a reason for everything. And to reconcile these contradictions, I intend to make you see clearly, by convincing proofs, those divine signs in me, which may convince you of what I am, and may gain authority for me by wonders and proofs which you cannot reject; so that you may then believe without...the things which I teach you, since you will find no other ground for rejecting them, except that you cannot know of yourselves if they are true or not.

God has willed to redeem men, and to open salvation to those who seek it. But men render themselves so unworthy of it, that it is right that God should refuse to some, because of their obduracy, what He grants to others from a compassion which is not due to them. If He had willed to overcome the obstinacy of the most hardened, He could have done so by revealing Himself so manifestly to them that they could not have doubted of the truth of His essence; as it will appear at the last day, with such thunders and such a convulsion of nature, that the dead will rise again, and the blindest will see Him.

It is not in this manner that He has willed to appear in His advent of mercy, because, as so many make themselves unworthy of His mercy, He has willed to leave them in the loss of the good which they do not want. It was not then right that He should appear in a manner manifestly divine, and completely capable of convincing all men; but it was also not right that He should come in so hidden a manner that He could not be known by those who should sincerely seek Him. He has willed to make Himself quite recognizable by those; and thus, willing to appear openly to those who seek Him with all their heart, and to be hidden from those who flee from Him with all their heart. He so regulates the knowledge of Himself that He has given signs of Himself, visible to those who seek Him, and not to those who seek Him not. There is enough light for those who only desire to see and enough obscurity for those who have a contrary disposition.

(Pensees, 430)

Had Epictetus seen the way perfectly, he would have said to men, "You follow a wrong road"; he shows that there is another but he does not lead to it. It is the way of willing what God wills. Jesus Christ alone leads to it.

(Pensees, 466)

If the compassion of God is so great that He instructs us to our benefit, even when He hides Himself, what light ought we not to expect from Him when He reveals Himself?

(Pensees, 847)

The God of the Christians is a God who makes the soul feel that He is her only good, that her only rest is in Him, that her only delight is in loving Him; and who makes her at the same time abhor the obstacles which keep her back, and prevent her from loving God with all her strength. Self-love and lust, which hinder us, are unbearable to her. Thus God makes her feel that she has this root of self-love which destroys her, and which He alone can cure.

(Pensees, 543)

Jesus Christ did nothing but teach men that they loved themselves, that they were slaves, blind, sick, wretched, and sinners; that He must deliver them, enlighten, bless, and heal them; that this would be effected by hating self, and by following Him through suffering and the death on the cross.

(Pensees, 544)

Without Jesus Christ man must be in vice and misery; with Jesus Christ man is free from vice and misery; in Him all our virtue and all our happiness. Apart from Him there is but vice, misery, darkness, death, despair.

(Pensees, 545)

We know God only by Jesus Christ. Without this mediator all communion with God is taken away; through Jesus Christ we know God. All those who have claimed to know God, and to prove Him without Jesus Christ, have had only weak proofs. But in proof of Jesus Christ we have the prophecies, which are solid and palpable proofs. And these prophecies, being accomplished and proved true by the event, mark the certainty of these truths, and therefore the divinity of Christ. In

Him then, and through Him, we know God. Apart from Him, and without the Scripture, without original sin, without a necessary Mediator promised and come, we cannot absolutely prove God, nor teach right doctrine and right morality. But through Jesus Christ, and in Jesus Christ, we prove God, and teach morality and doctrine. Jesus Christ is then the true God of men.

But we know at the same time our wretchedness; for this God is none other than the Savior of our wretchedness. So we can only know God well by knowing our iniquities. Therefore those who have known God, without knowing their wretchedness, have not glorified Him, but have glorified themselves.

(*Pensees*, 546)

Not only do we know God by Jesus Christ alone, but we know ourselves only by Jesus Christ. We know life and death only through Jesus Christ. Apart from Jesus Christ, we do not know what is our life, nor our death, nor God, nor ourselves.

Thus without the Scripture, which has Jesus Christ alone for its object, we know nothing, and see only darkness and confusion in the nature of God, and in our own nature.

(*Pensees*, 547)

The Word, which was from all eternity, God in God, the Word through which all things, even the visible things were made, made itself man. And thus, in order to save the world. He came in the fullness of time into the world, which He had created. He was not received by the world, but only by those to whom He gave the power to become children of God, inasmuch as they were reborn of the Holy Spirit by the will of God, and not born of flesh and blood by the will of men. And He conversed among men, bereft of His glory, and clothed in the form of a slave, and He underwent many sufferings unto death on the cross, on which He bore our weariness and our infirmities. He destroyed our death through His death, and, after having voluntarily given up His life which He had power to give up and to resume, He raised Himself from the dead on the third day. By His new life He communicated life to all those who are reborn in Him, just as Adam had communicated death to all those who were born of him. And finally, after having ascended from the realm of the dead above all the heavens in order that He might fill all things. He is seated at the right of the Father from where He will come to judge the quick and the dead, and to bring back the Elect, who are incorporated in Him, to the bosom of God, with whom He is united and will remain united in substance forever. When the graciousness of God appeared and when these great things were accomplished on earth, there were many who offered to put in writing the history of His life. But since so holy a life, whose slightest acts and deeds merited narrative, could be written only by the same Spirit which had brought about its birth, they did not succeed, for they followed their own spirit. And this is why God raised up four consecrated men, contemporaries of Jesus Christ, who, being divinely inspired, did write the things which He said and which He did. Not that they wrote everything, for that would require more volumes than the world could possibly contain; because there is not a move, act or thought which does not merit being expressed in all its particulars, as all of them were bent on glorifying the Father and were controlled by the intimate working of the Holy Spirit. But the aim of all that has been written is that we shall believe that Jesus is the Son of God and that, by believing, we shall have eternal life through His name.

(from the Preface to *Pascal's Short Life of Christ*)

3. Proofs of Jesus

What do the prophets say of Jesus Christ? That He will be clearly God? No; but that He will be slighted; that none will think that it is He; that He will be a stone of stumbling, upon which many will stumble, etc. Let people then reproach us no longer for want of clearness, since we make profession of it.

(Pensees, 750)

The time of the first advent was foretold; the time of the second is not so; because the first was to be obscure, and the second is to be brilliant, and so manifest that even His enemies will recognize it. But, as He was first to come only in obscurity, and to be known only of those who searched the Scriptures...

(Pensees, 756)

The prophets foretold and were not foretold. The saints again were foretold, but did not foretell. Jesus Christ both foretold and was foretold.

(Pensees, 738)

Jesus Christ, whom the two Testaments regard, the Old as its hope, the New as its model, and both as their center.

(Pensees, 739)

The Jews reject Him, but not all. The saints receive Him, and not the carnal-minded. And so far is this from being against His glory, that it is the last touch, which crowns it. For their argument the only one found in all their writings, in the Talmud and in the Rabbinical writings, amounts only to this, that Jesus Christ has not subdued the nations with sword in hand. (Is this all they have to say? Jesus Christ has been slain, say they. He has failed. He has not bestowed upon us their spoil. He does not give riches. Is this all they have to say? It is in this respect that He is lovable to me. I would not desire Him whom they fancy.) It is evident that it is only His life, which has prevented them from accepting Him; and through this rejection they are irreproachable witnesses, and, what is more, they thereby accomplish the prophecies.

(*Pensees*, 759)

Those who have a difficulty in believing seek a reason in the fact that the Jews do not believe. "Were this so clear," say they, "why did the Jews not believe?" And they almost wish that they had believed, so as not to be kept back by the example of their refusal. But it is their very refusal that is the foundation of our faith. We should be much less disposed to the faith, if they were on our side. We should then have a more ample pretext. The wonderful thing is to have made the Jews great lovers of the things foretold, and great enemies of their fulfillment.

(*Pensees*, 744)

Jesus Christ typified by Joseph, the beloved of his father, sent by his father to see his brethren, etc., innocent, sold by his brethren for twenty pieces of silver, and thereby becoming their lord, their savior, the savior of strangers, and the savior of the world; which had not been but for their plot to destroy Him, and their rejection of Him.

In prison Joseph innocent between two criminals; Jesus Christ on the cross between two thieves. Joseph foretells freedom to the one and death to the other, from the same omens. Jesus Christ saves the elect, and condemns the outcast for the same sins. Joseph foretells only; Jesus Christ acts. Joseph asks him who will be saved to remember him, when he comes into his glory, and he whom Jesus Christ saves asks that He will remember him when He comes into His Kingdom.

(*Pensees*, 767)

What man ever had renown? The whole Jewish people foretell Him before His coming. The Gentile people worship Him after His coming. The two peoples, Gentile and Jewish, regard Him as their center.

And yet what man enjoys this renown less? Of thirty-three years, He lives thirty without appearing. For three years He passes as an impostor; the priests and the chief people reject Him; His friends and His nearest relatives despise Him. Finally, He dies, betrayed by one of His own disciples, denied by another, and abandoned by all.

What part, then, has He in this renown? Never had man so much renown; never had man more ignominy. All that renown has served only for us, to render us capable of recognizing Him; and He had none of it for Himself.

(Pensees, 791)

Of all that is on earth, He partakes only of the sorrows, not of the joys. He loves His neighbors, but His love does not confine itself within these bounds, and overflows to His own enemies, and then to those of God.

(Pensees, 766)

Jesus Christ said great things so simply, that it seems as though He had not thought them great; and yet so clearly that we easily see what He thought of them. This clearness joined to this simplicity is wonderful.

(Pensees, 796)

I consider Jesus Christ in all persons and all ourselves: Jesus Christ as a Father in His Father, Jesus Christ as a Brother in His brethren, Jesus Christ as poor in the poor, Jesus Christ as rich in the rich, Jesus Christ as Doctor and Priest in priests, Jesus Christ as Sovereign in princes, etc. For by His glory He is all that is great, being God; and by His mortal life He is all that is poor and abject. Therefore He has taken this unhappy condition so that He could be in all persons, and the model of all conditions.

(Pensees, 784)

The Mystery of Jesus

Jesus suffers in His passions the torments, which men inflict upon Him, but in His agony He suffers the torments, which He inflicts upon Himself. This is a suffering from no human, but an almighty hand, for He must be almighty to bear it.

Jesus seeks some comfort at least in His three dearest friends, and they are asleep. He prays them to bear with Him for a little, and they leave Him with entire indifference, having so little compassion that it could not prevent their sleeping even for a moment. And thus Jesus was left alone to the wrath of God.

Jesus is alone on the earth, without anyone not only to feel and share His suffering, but even to know of it; He and Heaven were alone in that knowledge.

Jesus is in a garden, not of delight as the first Adam, where he lost himself and the whole human race, but in one of agony, where He saved Himself and the whole human race.

He suffers this affliction and this desertion in the horror of night.

I believe that Jesus never complained but on this single occasion; but then He complained as if He could no longer bear His extreme suffering. "My soul is sorrowful, even unto death."

Jesus seeks companionship and comfort from men. This is the sole occasion in all His life, as it seems to me. But He receives it not, for His disciples are asleep.

Jesus will be in agony even to the end of the world. We must not sleep during that time.

Jesus, in the midst of this universal desertion, including that of His own friends chosen to watch with Him, finding them asleep, is vexed because of the danger to which they expose, not Him, but themselves; He cautions them for their own safety and their own good, with a sincere tenderness for them during their ingratitude, and warns them that the spirit is willing and the flesh weak.

Jesus, finding them still asleep, without being restrained by any consideration for themselves or for Him, has the kindness not to waken them, and leaves them in repose.

Jesus prays, uncertain of the will of His Father, and fears death; but, when He knows it, He goes forward to offer Himself to death.

Jesus asked of men and was not heard.

Jesus, while His disciples slept, wrought their salvation. He has wrought that of each of the righteous while they slept, both in their nothingness before their birth, and in their sins after their birth.

He prays only once that the cup pass away, and then with submission; and twice that it come if necessary.

Jesus is weary.

Jesus, seeing all His friends asleep and all His enemies wakeful, commits Himself entirely to His Father.

Jesus does not regard in Judas his enmity, but the order of God, which He loves and admits, since He calls him friend.

Jesus tears Himself away from His disciples to enter into His agony; we must tear ourselves away from our nearest and dearest to imitate Him.

Jesus being in agony and in the greatest affliction, let us pray longer.

We implore the mercy of God, not that He may leave us at peace in our vices, but that He may deliver us from them.

If God gave us masters by His own hand, oh! how necessary for us to obey them with a good heart! Necessity and events follow infallibly.

—"Console thyself, thou wouldst not seek Me, if thou hast not found Me.

I thought of thee in Mine agony, I have sweated such drops of blood for thee.

It is tempting Me rather than proving thyself, to think if thou wouldst do such and such a thing on an occasion which has not happened; I shall act in thee if it occur.

Let thyself be guided by My rules; see how well I have led the Virgin and the saints who have let Me act in them.

The Father loves all that I do.

Dost thou wish that it always cost Me the blood of My humanity, without thy shedding tears?

Thy conversion is My affair: fear not, and pray with confidence as for Me.

I am present with thee by My Word in Scripture, by My Spirit in the Church and by inspiration, by My power in the priests, by My prayer in the faithful.

Physicians will not heal thee, for thou wilt die at last. But it is I who heal thee and make the body immortal.

Suffer bodily chains and servitude, I deliver thee at present only from spiritual servitude.

I am more a friend to thee than such and such an one, for I have done for thee more than they, they would not have suffered what I have suffered from thee, and they would not have died for thee as I have done in the time of thine infidelities and cruelties, and as I am ready to do, and do, among my elect and at the Holy Sacrament."

If thow knewest thy sins, thou wouldst lose heart."

—I shall lose it then, Lord, for on Thy assurance I believe their malice.

—"No, for I, by whom thou learnest, can heal thee of them, and what I say to thee is a sign that I will heal thee. In proportion to thy expiation of them, thou wilt know them, and it will be said to thee:

'Behold, thy sins are forgiven thee.' Repent, then, for thy hidden sins, and for the secret malice of those which thou knowest."

—Lord, I give Thee all.

—"I love thee more ardently than thou hast loved thine abominations.

To Me be the glory, not to thee, worm of the earth.

Ask thy confessor, when My own words are to thee occasion of evil, vanity, or curiosity."

—I see in me depths of pride, curiosity, and lust. There is no relation between me and God, nor Jesus Christ the Righteous. But He has been made sin for me; all Thy scourges are fallen upon Him. He is more abominable than I, and, far from abhorring me, He holds Himself honored that I go to Him and succor Him.

But He has healed Himself, and still more so will He heal me.

I must add my wounds to His, and join myself to Him; and He will save me in saving Himself. But this must not be postponed to the future.

Each one creates his god, when judging, "This is good or bad"; and men mourn or rejoice too much at events.

Do little things as though they were great, because of the majesty of Jesus Christ who does them in us, and who lives our life; and do the greatest things as though they were little and easy, because of His omnipotence.

(Pensees, 552)

It seems to me that Jesus Christ only allowed His wounds to be touched after His resurrection. We must unite ourselves only to His sufferings.

At the Last Supper He gave Himself in communion as about to die; to the disciples at Emmaus as risen from the dead; to the whole Church as ascended into Heaven.

(Pensees, 553)

"Compare not thyself with others, but with Me. If thou dost not find Me in those with whom thou compare thyself, thou compare thyself to one who is abominable. If thou finds Me in them, compare thyself to Me. But whom wilt thou compare? Thyself, or Me in thee? If it is thyself, it is one who is abominable. If it is I, thou comparest Me to Myself. Now I am God in all.

    I speak to thee, and often counsel thee, because thy director cannot speak to thee, for I do not want thee to lack a guide.

    And perhaps I do so at his prayers, and thus he leads thee without my seeing it. Thou would not seek Me, if thou didst not possess Me.

    Be not therefore troubled."

(Pensees, 554)

The Sepulcher of Jesus Christ

Jesus Christ was dead, but seen on the Cross. He was dead, and hidden in the Sepulcher.

Jesus Christ was buried by the saints alone.

.Jesus Christ wrought no miracle at the Sepulcher.

Only the saints entered it. It is there, not on the Cross, that Jesus Christ takes a new life.

It is the last mystery of the Passion and the Redemption.

Jesus Christ had nowhere to rest on earth but in the Sepulcher.

His enemies only ceased to persecute Him at the Sepulcher.

(Pensees, 551)

I love poverty because He loved it. I love riches because they afford me the means of helping the very poor. I keep faith with everybody; I do not render evil to those who wrong me, but I wish them a lot like mine, in which I receive neither evil nor good from men. I try to be just, true, sincere, and faithful to all men; I have a tender heart for those to whom God has more closely united me; and whether I am alone, or seen of men, I do all my actions in the sight of God, who must judge of them, and to whom I have consecrated them all.

These are my sentiments; and every day of my life I bless my Redeemer, who has implanted them in me, and who, of a man full of weakness, of miseries, of lust, of pride, and of ambition, has made a man free from all these evils by the power of His grace, to which all the glory of it is due, as of myself I have only misery and error.

(Pensees, 549)

Jesus Christ came to blind those who saw clearly, and to give sight to the blind; to heal the sick, and leave the healthy to die; to call to repentance, and to justify sinners, and to leave the righteous in their sins; to fill the needy, and leave the rich empty.

(*Pensees*, 770)

...Therefore, I reject all other religions. In that way I find an answer to all objections. It is right that a God so pure should only reveal Himself to those whose hearts are purified. Hence this religion is lovable to me, and I find it now sufficiently justified by so divine a mortality. But I find more in it.

I find it convincing that, since the memory of man has lasted, it was constantly announced to men that they were universally corrupt, but that a Redeemer should come; that it was not one man who said it, but innumerable men, and a whole nation expressly made for the purpose, and prophesying for four thousand years. This is a nation, which is more ancient than every other nation. Their books, scattered abroad, and four thousand years old.

The more I examine them, the more truths I find in them....

I find this succession, this religion, wholly divine in its authority, in its duration, in its perpetuity, all its morality, in its conduct, in its doctrine, in its effects.

So I hold out my arms to my Redeemer, who, having been foretold for four thousand years, has come to suffer and to die for me on earth, at the time and under all the circumstances foretold. By His grace, I await death in peace, in the hope of being eternally united to Him. Yet I live with joy, whether in the prosperity, which it pleases Him to bestow upon me, or in the adversity, which He sends for my good, and which He has taught me to bear by His example.

(*Pensees*, 736)

4. Human Struggle

Every religion is false, which as to its faith does not worship one God as the origin of everything, and which as to its morality does not love one only God as the object of everything.

(*Pensees*, 487)

...But it is impossible that God should ever be the end, if He is not the beginning. We lift our eyes on high, but lean upon the sand; and the earth will dissolve, and we shall fall whilst looking at the heavens.

(*Pensees*, 488)

If there is one sole source of everything, there is one sole end of everything; everything through Him, everything for Him. The true religion, then, must teach us to worship Him only, and to love Him only. But as we find ourselves unable to worship what we know not, and to love any other object but ourselves, the religion which instructs us in these duties must instruct us also of this inability, and teach us also the remedies for it. It teaches us that by one man all was lost, and the bond broken between God and us, and that by one man the bond is renewed.

We are born so averse to this love of God, and it is so necessary that we must be born guilty, or God would be unjust.

(*Pensees*, 489)

"Had I seen a miracle," say men, "I should become converted." How can they be sure they would do a thing of the nature of which they are ignorant? They imagine that this conversion consists in a worship of God, which is like commerce, and in a communion such as they picture to themselves. True religion consists in annihilating self before that Universal Being, whom we have so often provoked, and who can justly destroy us at any time: in recognizing that we can do nothing without Him, and have deserved nothing from Him but His displeasure. It consists in knowing that there is an unconquerable opposition between us and God, and that without a mediator there can be no communion with Him.

(Pensces, 470)

Self-will will never be satisfied, though it should have command of all it would: but we are satisfied from the moment we renounce it. Without it we cannot be discontented; with it we cannot be content.

(Pensees, 472)

When we want to think of God, is there nothing, which turns us away, and tempts us to think of something else? All this is bad, and is born in us.

(Pensees, 478)

It is true there is difficulty in entering into godliness. But this difficulty does not arise from the religion, which begins in us, but from the religion, which is still there. If our senses were not opposed to penitence, and if our corruption were not opposed to the purity of God, there would be nothing in this painful to us. We suffer only in proportion as the vice, which is natural to us, resists supernatural grace. Our heart feels torn asunder between these opposed efforts. But it would be very unfair to impute this violence to God, who is drawing us on, instead of to the world, which is holding us back. It is as a child, which a mother tears from the arms of robbers, in the pain it suffers, should love the loving and legitimate violence of her who procures its liberty, and detest only the impetuous and tyrannical violence of those who detain it unjustly. The most cruel war, which God can make with men in this life, is to leave them without that war which He came to bring. "I came to send war," He says, "and to teach them of this war. I came to bring fire and the sword." Before Him the world lived in this false peace.

(Pensees, 498)

External Works

There is nothing so perilous as what pleases God and man. For those states, which please God and man, have one property which pleases God, and another which pleases men; as the greatness of Saint Teresa. What pleased God was her deep humility in the midst of her revelations; what pleased men was her light. And so we torment ourselves to imitate her discourse, thinking to imitate her conditions, and not so much to love what God loves, and to put ourselves in the state, which God loves.

It is better not to fast, and be thereby humbled, than to fast and be self-satisfied therewith. The Pharisee and the Publican.

What use will memory be to me, if it can alike hurt and help me, and all depends upon the blessing of God, who gives only to things done for Him, according to His rules and in His ways, the manner being thus as important as the thing, and perhaps more; since God can bring forth good out of evil, and without God we bring forth evil out of good?

(Pensees, 499)

Abraham took nothing for himself, but only for his servants. So the righteous man takes for himself nothing of the world, nor of the applause of the world, but only for his passions, which he uses as their master, saying to the one, "Go," and to another, "Come." The passions thus subdued are virtues. Even God attributes to Himself avarice, jealousy, anger; and these are virtues as well as kindness, pity, constancy, which are also passions. We must employ them as slaves, and leaving to them their food, prevent the soul from taking any of it. For, when the passions become masters, they are vices; and they give their nutriment to the soul, and the soul nourishes itself upon it, and is poisoned.

(Pensees, 502)

We must consider ourselves as criminals in a prison completely filled with images of their liberator and with instructions necessary to be released from servitude. But we must confess that we cannot behold these holy images without a supernatural light. For just as all things speak of God to those that know Him, and just as they are revealed to those who love Him, so these same things are hidden from those who do not know Him. Accordingly we see that in the darkness of this world people follow them with brutish blindness, we see them become attached to them and make them the final goal of their desires; this cannot be done without sacrilege, for God alone must be the final goal as well as the sole and the true principle. To be sure, created nature has some resemblance with its Creator, and at least by their union with the rest of nature even the least things and the smallest and vilest parts of the world represent the perfect unity, which is found only in God. Nevertheless, we cannot rightfully pay them sovereign respect because there is nothing so abominable in the eyes of God and men as idolatry, for idolatry renders to the creature the honor which is due solely to the Creator. Scripture is full of the vengeance of God on those who were guilty of idolatry, and the first commandment of the Decalogue, which embraces all the others, forbids adoration of the images of all things. But since He is far more jealous of our affections than of our respect, it is obvious that there is no crime, which would be more injurious or more detestable than supreme love of created things even though they represent Him.

That is why those, to whom God has made these great verities known, must use these images in order to possess Him whom they represent, so that they may not remain forever in that carnal and Judaic blindness which leads men to take the shadow for reality.

(Excerpt from *a Letter to Madame Perier*, April 1, 1648)

I try as much as possible to let nothing trouble me and to make the best of everything that happens. I believe this to be a duty, and that we sin in doing otherwise. For, after all, the reason why sins are sins is that they are contrary to the will of God; and so, since the essence of sin consists in having a will which is opposed to what we know to be God's will, it seems obvious to me that when He discloses His will to us through events, it would be a sin not to adjust oneself to them.

(Excerpt from *a Letter to Monsieur and Mlle. de Rouannez*, October, 1656)

We owe a great debt to those who point out our faults. For they mortify us. They teach us that we have been despised. They do not prevent our being so in the future; for we have many other faults for which we may be despised. They prepare for us the exercise of correction and freedom from fault.

(*Pensees*, 534)

It is undeniable that we never break ties without pain. We are unaware of a bond when we voluntarily follow him who leads us on, as Saint Augustine says. But when we begin to resist and to withdraw, we suffer greatly; the bond is stretched and undergoes heavy strain, and this strain is our own body, which is broken by death. Our Lord said that since the coming of John the Baptist, that is to say since His own advent into the world, and consequently since His advent in all the faithful, the Kingdom of God has been suffering violence, and that the violent take it by force. Before being reached [by the message of election], we have but the weight of our lust, which bears us down to earth. When God draws us upward, the two opposing forces cause this violence, which God alone can overcome. But we can do all things, says Saint Leo, with Him, without whose aid we can do nothing. Therefore we must resolve to suffer this warfare all our life, for there is no peace here below, Jesus Christ came to send not peace but a sword. Nevertheless, one must admit with the Scriptures that the wisdom of this world is but folly before God. Moreover, we may say that this struggle, which seems so hard to mankind, is peace with God, for it is this peace also which Jesus Christ has brought. Yet it will be perfect peace only when the body shall be destroyed. It is this that makes us long for death, while nevertheless we willingly suffer for the love of Him who suffered life and death for us, and who is able to do exceedingly abundantly above all that we ask or think.

(Excerpt from a Letter to Monsieur and
Mlle. de Rouannez, September 24, 1656)

Misery induces despair, pride induces presumption. The Incarnation shows man the greatness of his misery by the greatness of the remedy, which he required.

(*Pensees*, 525)

The knowledge of God without that of man's misery causes pride. The knowledge of man's misery without that of God causes despair. The knowledge of Jesus Christ constitutes the middle course, because in Him we find both God and our misery.

(*Pensees*, 526)

Jesus Christ is a God whom we approach without pride, and before whom we humble ourselves without despair.

(*Pensees*, 527)

We love ourselves, because we are members of Jesus Christ. We love Jesus Christ, because he is the body of which we are members. All is one, one is in the other, like the Three Persons.

(*Pensees*, 483)

5. The New Life

The first thing which God inspires in the soul, which He truly deigns to touch, is an understanding and a quite extraordinary insight by means of which the soul considers things and itself in an entirely new manner.

This new light brings fear to the soul and an agitation, which disturbs the repose, which it found in the things that delighted it.

The soul can no longer tranquilly enjoy the things, which charmed it. Constant scruples assail it in this enjoyment and because of this introspection it no longer finds the accustomed sweetness in the things to which it abandoned itself freely with an overflowing heart.

But the soul finds even more bitterness in the practice of holiness than in the vanities of the world. On the one hand, the presence of visible things touches it more than the hope of things unseen; on the other hand, the stability of things unseen touches it more than does the vanity of visible things. And thus the presence of the one and the stability of the other contend for its affection; the vanity of the one and the absence of the other arouse its aversion.

The soul considers perishable things as perishing and even as already perished. In the definite prospect of the annihilation of all that it loves, it is frightened by this consideration, when it sees every moment snatch away the enjoyment of its endowment: when that which is dearest to it slips away every moment, and when finally a certain day will come when it will find itself destitute of all the things on which it had set its hopes. And so it understands perfectly that since its heart is attached only to fragile and vain things, the soul must find itself alone and abandoned on leaving this life, since it has not taken care to unite itself with a good which is genuine, which exists independently, and which may sustain it during and after this life.

As a result, the soul begins to regard as nothing all that must return to nothingness, the sky, the earth, its mind, its body, its relatives, its friends, its enemies, its goods, its poverty, disgrace, prosperity, honor, ignominy, esteem, scorn, authority, indigence, health, illness, and life itself; in short, everything which is less enduring than the soul is incapable of satisfying the design of this soul which seriously seeks to establish itself in a felicity as enduring as it is itself.

It begins to wonder at the blindness in which it has lived; and when it considers on the one hand how long it has lived without such reflections and how many people live in this manner, and on the other hand how certain it is that the soul, being immortal, can never find its happiness among perishable things which are taken from it at least in death, it then enters into a holy state of confusion and of wonder which bring to it a wholly salutary agitation.

For it considers that no matter how great may be the number of those who grow old in the maxims of this world, and no matter what authority may reside in this multitude of examples of those who see their happiness in the world, nevertheless this is certain: If the things of this world afforded substantial pleasure—which is recognized as false through an infinite number of deadening and continual experiences, it is inevitable that the loss of these things or that death will ultimately deprive us of these things. As a result, since the soul has amassed treasures of temporal goods of whatever kind they may be, either gold or science or reputation, it is inevitable that it will ultimately find itself denuded of all the objects of its happiness. And so, even if they were capable of satisfying it, they will be unable to satisfy it forever; moreover, if this means producing genuine happiness, it does not offer a very enduring happiness, since it must be limited by the course of this life. Thus through a holy humility which again elevates God above vainglory, the soul begins to rise above the generality of men, it condemns their conduct, it detests their maxims, it mourns their blindness, it inclines to seek the true good. It understands that it must have these two Qualities: one, which endures as long as it does and which can be taken from it only by its consent, and the other, than which there is nothing more lovable.

It sees that in the love, which it had for the world, it found this second quality in its blindness, for it recognized nothing more lovable; but since it does not see the first, it knows that it is not the sovereign good. Hence the soul seeks this elsewhere—it begins to seek above.

This elevation is so eminent and so transcendent that it does not stop at the sky. The heart can stop beating only when it has surrendered itself at the very throne of God where it begins to find its repose. For it understands that creatures cannot be more lovable than their Creator; there is nothing more lovable than God, and that He can be taken only from those who reject Him, since to possess Him is to desire Him, and to refuse Him is to lose Him.

Thus it rejoices at having found a good which cannot be taken from it so long as it desires this good, and which is transcended by nothing. And amid these new reflections it comes to see the greatness of its Creator both in humiliations and deep adoration. In consequence it annihilates itself. It makes new efforts to humble itself to the very depth of nothingness, while considering God in the boundlessness, which it multiplies incessantly. Finally, it adores Him in silence, it considers itself as His vile and useless creature, it adores Him and blesses Him. Then it recognizes the grace He has bestowed upon it by manifesting His infinite majesty to so feeble a worm; it blushes at having preferred so much vanity to this divine Master.

It raises ardent prayers to God to obtain from His mercy that, having deigned to reveal Himself, He may be pleased to guide the soul and make known the means of coming to God. It desires God alone to be its path, its object, and its ultimate end.

It is resolved to conform to His will for the rest of its life; but since its natural weakness, together with the habit it has of sinning wherever it has lived, have reduced it to the impossibility of attaining such happiness, it implores of His mercy the means of coming to Him, of attaching itself to Him and of adhering to Him eternally...

Thus the soul recognizes that as a creature it must adore God, as a debtor it must render Him thanks, being culpable it must make amends, and being needy it must implore Him.

(Writing on the *Conversion of the Sinner*, November-December, 1654)

We must not believe that the life of Christians is a life of sadness. We give up pleasures only for greater pleasures. Pray without ceasing, says St. Paul, in everything give thanks, and rejoice evermore. It is the joy of having found God. The people of the world do not have this joy, which *the world can neither give nor take*, as Jesus Christ Himself said. The blessed have this joy without any sadness; the people of the world have their sadness without this joy, and the Christians have this joy mingled with the sadness of having followed other pleasures and with the fear of losing it by the attraction of those other pleasures, which tempt us without any respite. Remember the good in the days of thine affliction, and remember thine affliction in the days of rejoicing, says the Scripture.

Let us not be cast down by sadness, nor believe that piety consists only in bitterness without consolation.

> (Excerpt from a Letter to Monsieur and Mlle. de Rouannez, November, 1656)

The infinite distance between body and mind is a symbol of the infinitely more infinite distance between mind and charity; for charity is supernatural.

All the glory of greatness has no luster for people who are in search of understanding.

The greatness of clever men is invisible to kings, to the rich, to chiefs, and to all the worldly great.

The greatness of wisdom, which is nothing if not of God, is invisible to the carnal-minded and to the clever. These and three orders differing in kind.

Great geniuses have their power, their glory, their greatness, their victory, their luster, and have no need of worldly greatness, with which they are not in keeping. They are seen, not by the eye, but by the mind; this is sufficient.

The saints have their power, their glory, their victory, their luster, and need no worldly or intellectual greatness, with which they have no affinity; for these neither add anything to them, nor take away anything from them. They are seen of God and the angels, and not of the curious mind. God is enough for them.

Archimedes, apart from his rank, would have the same veneration. He fought no battles for the eyes to feast upon; but he has given his discoveries to all men. Oh! how brilliant he was to the mind!

Jesus Christ, without riches, and without any external exhibition of knowledge, is in His own order of holiness. He did not invent; He did not reign. But He was humble, patient, holy, holy to God, terrible to devils, without any sin. Oh! in what great pomp, and in what wonderful splendor, He is come to the eyes of the heart, which perceive wisdom!

It would have been useless for Archimedes to have acted the prince in his books on geometry, although he was a prince.

It would have been useless for our Lord Jesus Christ to come like a king, in order to shine forth in His kingdom of holiness. But He came there appropriately in the glory of His own order.

It is most absurd to take offence at the lowliness of Jesus Christ, as if His lowliness were in the same order as the greatness, which He came to manifest. If we consider this greatness in His life, in His passion, in His obscurity, in His death, in the choice of His disciples, in their desertion, in His secret resurrection, and the rest, we shall see it to be so immense, that we shall have no reason for being offended at a lowliness which is not of that order.

But there are some who can only admire worldly greatness, as though there were no intellectual greatness; and others who only admire intellectual greatness, as though there were not infinitely higher things in wisdom.

All bodies, the firmament, the stars, the earth and its kingdoms, are not equal to the lowest mind; for mind knows all these and itself; and these bodies nothing.

All bodies together, and all minds together, and all their products are not equal to the least feeling of charity. This is of an order infinitely more exalted.

From all bodies together, we cannot obtain one little thought; this is impossible, and of another order. From all bodies and minds, we cannot produce a feeling of true charity; this is impossible, and of another and supernatural order.

(*Pensees*, 792)

Grace is indeed needed to turn a man into a saint; and he who doubts it does not know what a saint or a man is.

(*Pensees*, 508)

Man is not worthy of God, but he is not incapable of being made worthy.

It is unworthy of God to unite Himself to wretched man; but it is not unworthy of God to pull him out of his misery.

(*Pensees*, 510)

If we would say that man is too insignificant to deserve communion with God, we must indeed be very great to judge of it.

(*Pensees*, 511)

The elect will be ignorant of their virtues, and the outcast of the greatness of their sins: "Lord, when saw we Thee an hungered, thirsty?" etc.

(*Pensees*, 514)

Comfort yourselves. It is not from yourselves that you should expect grace; but, on the contrary, it is in expecting nothing from yourselves, that you must hope for it.

(*Pensees*, 516)

There is no doctrine more appropriate to man than this, which teaches him his double capacity of receiving and of losing grace, because of the double peril to which he is exposed, of despair or of pride.

(*Pensees*, 523)

The continuation of the justice of the faithful is nothing but the continuation of the infusion of grace and not through one single grace, which lives forever. It is this, which teaches us perfectly our perpetual dependence on the mercy of God, since if He interrupts its flow ever so little, drought will necessarily set in. In view of this necessity, it is easy to see that we must continually make new efforts to acquire this continued renewal of spirit. For we can preserve the old grace only by our acquiring a new grace, otherwise we will lose that which we think we retain, like those, who, wishing to shut in the light, merely shut in darkness. Thus we must unceasingly watch over the purification of our inner being, which is ever sullied by new stains while at the same time retaining the old ones, since without constant renewal we are incapable of receiving this new wine which will not be put into old bottles.

Now the creatures who make up the world acquit themselves of this obligation by remaining in a limited perfection, inasmuch as the perfection of the world is also limited. But the children of God must impose no limits on their purity and their perfection because they are part of a body, which is wholly divine and infinite in its perfection. So we see that Jesus Christ does not limit the commandment of perfection, and that He proposes a model of infinite perfection when He says: "Be ye therefore perfect, even as your Father which is in heaven is perfect." Moreover, a harmful and common error among Christians and even among those who profess piety lies in persuading themselves that there is a certain degree of perfection in which one is secure, and that it is unnecessary to go beyond this, since there is no wrong in stopping there, and since one may risk falling by ascending higher.

(Excerpt from a *Letter to Madame Perier*, April 1. 1648)

None is so happy as a true Christian, nor so reasonable, virtuous, or amiable.

(*Pensees*, 540)

On the Miracle

As God has made no family more happy, let it also be the case that He find none more thankful.

(*Pensees*, 855)

Resolutions of a Saintly Scholar

Selections from the Writings

Jonathan Edwards 1703-1758

*With an Introduction
By Robert E. Coleman*

Abridged version of *Resolutions of a Saintly Scholar* by Jonathan Edwards. Abridged version originally published by World Wide Publications and the Institute of Evangelism Billy Graham Center, 1974, Wheaton, IL. Copyright of abridged version and introduction held by Robert Coleman, used with permission. Scripture quotations are taken from the Holy Bible, King James Version (KJV), in the Public Domain. Artwork in the Public Domain.

Book Chapters

1. Introduction
   By Robert E. Coleman..110
2. His Spiritual Delight 115
3. Personal Resolutions 120
   Remember to Read over These Resolutions Once a Week....................120
4. Constant Review..127
   December, 1722 127
   1722-1723..128

1. Introduction
By Robert E. Coleman

Among the shapers of American intellectual and religious history, no man stands out more brilliantly than Jonathan Edwards. His vigorous thought and exemplary life gave leadership to the Great Awakening of the eighteenth century, and laid the foundation for a new rationale of transforming personal experience of far-reaching consequence. Though the Puritan cause he espoused largely has been rejected, the voice of Edwards still can be heard through the pretense of human sufficiency, reminding us that only God is great, and that finally before Him every knee shall bow. Hurried students today, especially those engaged in theological pursuits, could well afford to spend some time with this saintly sage—one of the world's most renowned Christian scholars.

He was born at East Windsor, Connecticut, October 5, 1703, the fifth child and only son of Reverend and Mrs. Timothy Edwards' eleven children. His unusual mental and spiritual aptitude began appearing very early. He was studying Latin under his father by the time he was six. When he was ten he composed a tract on the immaterial nature of the soul. At eleven, he was writing scientific observations on insects, followed by an essay on the rainbow. Soon he was contemplating the philosophic significance of atomic physics, and grappling with such weighty problems as the meaning of personal identity, mind-body relationship, causation, and the limits of knowledge.

Just before his thirteenth birthday, the fledgling genius entered Yale College. He graduated at the head of his class of ten members in 1720; then continued studies in theology for two more years, preparing for ordination to the ministry. Licensed to preach in 1722, he went to

New York City and pastored a small Presbyterian church. His work was well received, but after eight months he returned home to give himself more fully to serious study. The following year he received the Master of Arts from Yale, and was elected as a tutor.

In 1726 he accepted a call as pastoral assistant to his aging maternal grandfather, the Reverend Solomon Stoddard, at Northampton, Massachusetts. Three years later, Stoddard died, and his grandson assumed full responsibility for the large, wealthy congregation, at the time the most influential parish in New England.

Shortly after beginning his new office Edwards married Sarah Pierpont of New Haven. She was a lady of rare piety and prudence. Her ability to assume most of the domestic cares of the house enabled her husband to pursue his work without undue interruptions. They shared a common sense of mission. During their beautiful married life of thirty years, they prayed together at least once a day, unless something extraordinary happened.

Into their home eleven children were born. Early the ten girls and one son were taught the meaning of reverence. Family prayers always preceded the business of the day, and after supper each evening; Edwards took an hour with his family to converse on the things of God. Probably the highest tribute that can be paid to Jonathan and Sarah Edwards is that all their children followed in the way of their godly parents.

The loving father and pastor lived an exacting example of personal discipline. Every waking moment was regimented to his holy calling. Periods were established for eating, physical exercise, and sleep, but only as they were necessary to assure alertness of mind. It was not uncommon for him to spend thirteen hours a day in his study, beginning at four o'clock in the morning. When making calls by horseback, he continued his meditations and would jot fleeting ideas down on paper. Though never strong in body, he constantly practiced self-denial. On occasion, he set aside whole days for fasting and self-examination. With a consuming thirst for knowledge, he read all the books he could obtain on a wide range of subjects. Supremely, though, he fixed his attention upon the Bible, the sole authority for his faith and ministry.

Out of this consecrated devotion he prepared his masterful sermons. Seldom have more profound messages been delivered. His words were precise, set in simple speech, and fell with such solemn weight upon the hearers that few could turn away unmoved. Even more significant were the literary works, which flowed from his pen. His published writings eventually developed into a small theological library.

In 1731 he was first brought into national prominence by the publication of a formal theological lecture entitled *God Glorified in Man's Dependence*. This reasoned discourse established the quiet scholar as a worthy defender of Calvinism against the challenge of a decadent Arminianism rising in his day. Edwards' message was unequivocal. God is sovereign. He owes man nothing, nor can man add anything to God's perfection by good works. Divine grace alone offers any hope or meaning to human existence. All man can do is receive God's love through Jesus Christ.

Nourished by such teaching, Northampton experienced a gracious revival in 1734 and 1735. It extended to every part of town, and someone in nearly every household was touched. More than 300 persons were converted within a few months. The whole character of the community was changed. Responding to many inquiries, an account of the work of grace was published by Edwards under the title *A Faithful Narrative of the Surprising Work of God in the Conversion of Many Hundred Souls* (1736).

Again, in 1740, his parish was the scene of mighty spiritual renewal. George Whitefield, the famous evangelist, visited Northampton at its height and became a close friend of Edwards. Fanned by the preaching of these and other men, revival fires spread throughout New England. Hundreds of cold churches and thousands of people were quickened by the Spirit of God. The famous Enfield sermon, *Sinners in the Hands of an Angry God*, belongs to this period.

But as is true of all movements among men, there were some abuses, which caused controversy. To counteract some of the misunderstandings, Edwards wrote *Distinguishing Marks of a Work of God* (1741), showing the difference between genuine and false experience. Another defense of the revival against the objections of its opponents was *Thoughts Concerning the Present Revival of Religion in New England* (1742). *A Treatise Concerning Religious Affections* (1746) also came out of this era, his classic treatment of subjective spiritual experience, in which he concludes: "The essence of all true religion lies in holy love."

Tension in the church began to surface when Edwards reprimanded some young people from prominent families for reading clean books. It reached a climax when the pastor reversed a policy of his predecessor by insisting that only persons professing a living faith in Jesus Christ be admitted to Holy Communion. Finally, the matter went before a church council, which in 1750 requested that Edwards leave. Such is the fickleness of human nature. Sometimes people that have known the greatest privilege have become the most ungrateful.

The faithful pastor received his rejection with resignation to the will of God. There was no bitterness or rancor toward his antagonists.

His *Farewell Sermon* is one of the purest examples of a loving shepherd's concern ever written.

Of the places of service offered to him, Edwards accepted a call to Stockbridge, a mission post on the frontier. There he assumed the care of a small congregation, while ministering to the Housatonic and Mohawk Indians of the area. Demands of the wilderness life, learning a new language, and frequent sickness were no deterrent to his faith. However, all was not peaceful. Quarrels among the settlers and shameless exploitation of the Indians by unscrupulous whites made his work difficult. Yet he patiently held up the Word of Life, and sought to lead his people in a more excellent way.

In this remote setting he was able to bring to completion many of his major works. His greatest, *Freedom of the Will*, was finished in 1754. Endeavoring to make the eternal decrees of God accord more with the prevailing notions of human freedom, he emphasized that man has the natural power to serve God if he chooses; but he will not be so inclined unless God reveals Himself as man's highest good. Still the choice belongs to man. The idea was further clarified in *Original Sin Defended* (1758). Other notable works of this period, published posthumously, were *The Nature of True Virtue* (1765), *The End for Which God Created the World* (1765), and the monumental *History of the Work of Redemption* (1774).

In 1757 Edwards was elected to the presidency of the College of New Jersey. It seemed at last that he would be in an environment congenial to his academic talents. But soon after arriving at Princeton, before he could be joined by his wife, complications developed from smallpox inoculation, and he died on March 22, 1758. He was fifty-four years of age.

When he knew that the end was near, he said to his daughter with him:

> Dear Lucy, it seems to me to be the will of God that I must shortly leave you; therefore give my kindest love to my dear wife. Tell her that the uncommon union, which has so long subsisted between us, has been of such a nature as, I trust, is spiritual, and therefore will continue forever; and I hope she will be supported under so great a trial, and submit cheerfully to the will of God. And as to my children, you are now like to be left fatherless; which I hope will be an inducement to you all to seek a Father who will never fail you.

The last he was heard to say, addressing some friends at his bedside, was: "Trust in God, and you need not fear."

These words reflect the spirit by which Jonathan Edwards lived. He was a man "swallowed up" in his Father's will. Whatever happened, he knew that God never made a mistake.

2. His Spiritual Delight

This explicit trust in the providence of God seems to have come into focus toward the latter part of his college course. Reflecting upon it years later, he recounts in his own *Personal Narrative* how "not only a conviction, but a delightful conviction" of God's absolute sovereignty broke upon his consciousness.

The first that I remember that ever I found anything of that sort of inward, sweet delight in God and divine things, that I have lived much in since, was on reading those words: *"Now unto the King eternal, immortal, invisible, the only wise God, be honor and glory for ever and ever. Amen"* (1 Timothy 1:17). As I read the words, there came into my soul, and was as it were diffused through it, a sense of the glory of the divine Being; a new sense, quite different from anything I ever experienced before. Never any words of Scripture seemed to me as these words did. I thought with myself, how excellent a being that was; and how happy I should be, if I might enjoy that God, and be wrapped up to God in heaven, and be as it were swallowed up in Him. I kept saying, and as it were singing over these words of Scripture to myself; and went to prayer, to pray to God that I might enjoy Him; and prayed in a manner quite different from what I used to do; with a new sort of affection. But it never came into my thought, that there was anything spiritual, or of a saving nature in this.

From about that time, I began to have a new kind of apprehensions and ideas of Christ, and the work of redemption, and the glorious way of salvation by Him. I had an inward, sweet sense of these things, that at times came into my heart; and my soul was led away in pleasant views and contemplations of them. And my mind was greatly engaged, to spend my time in reading and meditating on Christ: and the beauty and excellency of His person, and the lovely way of salvation, by free grace in Him. I found no books so delightful to me, as those that treated of these subjects...

Not long after I first began to experience these things, I gave an account to my father, of some things that had passed in my mind. I was pretty much affected by the discourse we had together. And when the discourse was ended, I walked abroad alone, in a solitary place in my father's pasture, for contemplation. And as I was walking there, and looked up on the sky and clouds, there came into my mind a sweet sense of the glorious majesty and grace of God that I know not how to express. I seemed to see them both in a sweet conjunction: majesty and meekness joined together: it was sweet and gentle, and holy majesty; and also a majestic meekness; an awful sweetness; a high, and great, and holy gentleness.

After this my sense of divine things gradually increased, and became more and more lively, and had more of that inward sweetness. The appearance of everything was altered; there seemed to be, as it were, a calm, sweet cast, or appearance of divine glory, in almost everything. God's excellency, His wisdom, His purity and love, seemed to appear in everything; in the sun, moon and stars; in the clouds, and blue sky; in the grass, flowers, trees; in the water, and all nature; which used greatly to fix my mind. I often used to sit and view the moon, for a long time; and so in the daytime, spent much time in viewing the clouds and sky, to behold the sweet glory of God in these things: in the meantime, singing forth with a low voice, my contemplations of the Creator and Redeemer. And scarce anything, among all the works of nature, was so sweet to me as thunder and lightning. Formerly, nothing had been so terrible to me. I used to be a person uncommonly terrified with thunder; and it used to strike me with terror when I saw a thunderstorm rising. But now, on the contrary, it rejoiced me. I felt God at the first appearance of a thunderstorm. And used to take the opportunity at such times to fix myself to view the clouds, and see the lightning play, and hear the majestic and awful voice of God's thunder: which oftentimes was exceeding entertaining, leading me to sweet contemplations of my great and glorious God. And while I viewed, used to spend my time, as it always seemed natural to me, to sing or chant forth my meditations; to speak my thoughts in soliloquies, and speak with a singing voice.

I felt then a great satisfaction as to my good estate. But that did not content me. I had vehement longings of soul after God and

Christ, and after more holiness; wherewith my heart seemed to be full, and ready to break: which often brought to my mind, the words of the psalmist: *"My soul breaketh for the longing it hath"* (Psalm 119:20). I often felt a mourning and lamenting in my heart that I had not turned to God sooner, that I might have had more time to grow in grace. My mind was greatly fixed on divine things; I was almost perpetually in the contemplation of them. I spent most of my time in thinking of divine things, year after year. And used to spend abundance of my time, in walking alone in the woods, and solitary places, for meditation, soliloquy and prayer, and converse with God. And it was always my manner, at such times, to sing forth my contemplations. And was almost constantly in ejaculatory prayer, wherever I was. Prayer seemed to be natural to me; as the breath, by which the inward burnings of my heart had vent…

My sense of divine things seemed gradually to increase, till I went to preach at New York; which was about a year and a half after they began. While I was there, I felt them, very sensibly, in a much higher degree, than I had done before. My longings after God and holiness, were much increased. Pure and humble, holy and heavenly Christianity, appeared exceeding amiable to me. I felt in me a burning desire to be in everything a complete Christian; and conformed to the blessed image of Christ: and that I might live in all things, according to the pure, sweet and blessed rules of the gospel. I had an eager thirsting after progress in these things. My longings after it, put me upon pursuing and pressing after them. It was my continual strife day and night, and constant inquiry, how I should be more holy, and live more holily, and more becoming a child of God, and disciple of Christ. I sought an increase of grace and holiness, and that I might live an holy life, with vastly more earnestness, than ever I sought grace, before I had it. I used to be continually examining myself, and studying and contriving for likely ways and means, how I should live holily, with far greater diligence and earnestness, than ever I pursued anything in my life. But with too great a dependence on my own strength; which afterwards proved a great damage to me. My experience had not then taught me, as it has done since, my extreme feebleness and impotence, every manner of way; and the innumerable and bottomless depths of secret corruption and deceit, that there was in my heart. However, I went on with my eager pursuit after more holiness; and sweet conformity to Christ.

The heaven I desired was a heaven of holiness; to be with God, and to spend my eternity in divine love, and holy communion with Christ. My mind was very much taken up with contemplations on heaven, and the enjoyments of those there: and living there in perfect holiness, humility, and love. And it used at that time to appear a great part of the happiness of heaven, that there the saints could express their love to

Christ. It appeared to me a great clog and hindrance and burden to me, that what I felt within, I could not express to God, and give vent to, as I desired. The inward ardor of my soul, seemed to be hindered and pent up, and could not freely flame out as it would. I used often to think, how in heaven, this sweet principle should freely and fully vent and express itself. Heaven appeared to me exceeding delightful as a world of love. It appeared to me, that all happiness consisted in living in pure, humble, heavenly, divine love.

I remember the thoughts I used then to have of holiness. I remember I then said sometimes to myself, I do certainly know that I love holiness, such as the gospel prescribes. It appeared to me, there was nothing in it but what was ravishingly lovely. It appeared to me, to be the highest beauty and amiableness, above all other beauties: that it was a divine beauty; far purer than anything here upon earth; and that everything else, was like mire, filth and defilement, in comparison of it.

Holiness, as I then wrote down some of my contemplations on it, appeared to me to be of a sweet, pleasant, charming, serene, calm nature. It seemed to me, it brought an inexpressible purity, brightness, peacefulness and ravishment to the soul: and that it made the soul like a field or garden of God, with all manner of pleasant flowers; that is all pleasant, delightful and undisturbed; enjoying a sweet calm, and the gently vivifying beams of the sun. The soul of a true Christian, as I then wrote my meditations, appeared like such a little white flower, as we see in the spring of the year; low and humble on the ground, opening its bosom, to receive the pleasant beams of the sun's glory; rejoicing as it were, in a calm rapture; diffusing around a sweet flagrancy; standing peacefully and lovingly, in the midst of other flowers round about; all in like manner opening their bosoms, to drink in the light of the sun…

It has often appeared sweet to me, to be united to Christ; to have Him for my Head, and to be a member of His body: and also to have Christ for my Teacher and Prophet. I very often think with sweetness and longings and panting of soul, of being a little child, taking hold of Christ, to be led by Him through the wilderness of this world. That text, Matthew 18, near at the beginning, has often been sweet to me, *"Except ye be converted, and become as little children…"* I love to think of coming to Christ, to receive salvation of Him, poor in spirit, and quite empty of self; humbly exalting Him alone; cut entirely off from my own root, and to grow into, and out of Christ: to have God in Christ to be all in all: and to live by faith on the Son of God, a life of humble, unfeigned confidence in Him. That Scripture has often been sweet to me. *"Not unto us, O Lord, not unto us, but unto thy name give glory, for thy mercy, and for thy truth's sake"* (Psalm 115:1). And those words of Christ: *"In that hour Jesus rejoiced in spirit, and said, I thank thee, O Father, Lord of heaven and earth, that thou hast hid these things from the wise and prudent, and hast revealed them unto babes: even so, Father, for so it seemed good in thy sight"* (Luke 10:21). That sovereignty of God that Christ rejoiced in, seemed to me to be worthy to be rejoiced in; and that rejoicing of Christ, seemed to me to show the excellency of Christ, and the Spirit that He was of…

The sweetest joys and delights I have experienced have not been those that have arisen from a hope of my own good estate; but in a direct view of the glorious things of the gospel. When I enjoy this sweetness, it seems to carry me above the thoughts of my own safe estate. It seems at such times a loss that I cannot bear, to take off my eye from the glorious, pleasant object I behold without me, to turn my eye in upon myself, and my own good estate…

3. Personal Resolutions

The description of his experience, like that of many others, expresses a rapturous desire to sit with Christ in heavenly places. But it would be wrong to conclude that it was only an ecstatic feeling. There was a methodical discipline of will, which undergirded his devotion and directed his life. This comes through clearly in his *Resolutions*.

These seventy intentions were drawn up during his graduate study and before his settlement at Northampton. It was not unusual for sensitive young people of that day to define for themselves goals of life, and to set standards of conduct by which their aspirations might be realized. Because these resolves express so earnestly a heart panting after God, they are cited here in full.

Being sensible that I am unable to do anything without God's help, I do humbly entreat Him by His grace, to enable me to keep these Resolutions, so far as they are agreeable to His will, for Christ's sake.

Remember to Read over These Resolutions Once a Week

1. *Resolved*, That I *will do whatsoever* I think to be most to the glory of God and my own good, profit and pleasure, in the whole of my duration; without any consideration of the time, whether now, or never so many myriads of ages hence. Resolved to do whatever I think to be

my *duty*, and most for the good and advantage of mankind in general. Resolved, so to do, whatever *difficulties* I meet with, how many soever, and how great soever.

2. *Resolved*, To be continually endeavoring to find out some *new contrivance*, and invention, to promote the fore mentioned things.

3. *Resolved*, If ever I shall fall and grow dull, so as to neglect to keep any part of these Resolutions, to repent of all I can remember, when I come to myself again.

4. *Resolved*, Never to do any manner of thing, whether in soul or body, less or more, but what tends to the glory of God, nor be, nor suffer it, if I can possibly avoid it.

5. *Resolved*, Never to lose one moment of time, but to improve it in the most profitable way I possibly can.

6. *Resolved*, To live with all my might, while I do live.

7. *Resolved*, Never to do anything, which I should be afraid to do, if it were the last hour of my life.

8. *Resolved*, To act, in all respects, both speaking and doing, as if nobody had been so vile as I, and as if I had committed the same sins, or had the same infirmities or failings as others; and that I will let the knowledge of their failings promote nothing but shame in myself, and prove only an occasion of my confessing my own sins and misery to God. *Vid. July 30.*

9. *Resolved*, To think much, on all occasions, of my own dying, and of the common circumstances, which attend death.

10. *Resolved*, When I feel pain, to think of the pains of martyrdom, and of hell.

11. *Resolved*, When I think of any theorem in divinity to be solved, immediately to do what I can towards solving it, if circumstances do not hinder.

12. *Resolved*, If I take delight in it as a gratification of pride, or vanity, or on any such account, immediately to throw it by.

13. *Resolved*, To be endeavoring to find out fit objects of charity and liberality.

14. *Resolved*, Never to do anything out of revenge.

15. *Resolved*, Never to suffer the least motions of anger towards irrational beings.

16. *Resolved*, Never to speak evil of anyone, so that it shall tend to his dishonor, more or less, upon no account except for some real good.

17. *Resolved*, That I will live so, as I shall wish I had done when I come to die.

18. *Resolved*, To live so, at all times, as I think is best in my most devout frames, and when I have the clearest notions of the things of the gospel, and another world.

19. *Resolved*, Never to do anything, which I should be afraid to do, if I expected it would not be above an hour. before I should hear the last trumpet.

20. *Resolved*, To maintain the strictest temperance, in eating and drinking.

21. *Resolved*, Never to do anything, which if I should see in another, I should count a just occasion to despise him for, or to think any way the more meanly of him.

22. *Resolved*. To endeavor. to obtain for myself as much happiness, in the other world, as I possibly can, with all the power, might, vigor, and vehemence , yea violence, I am capable of, or can bring myself to exert, in any way that can be thought of.

23. *Resolved*, Frequently to take some deliberate action, which seems most unlikely to be done, for the glory of God, and trace it back to the original intention, designs and ends of it; and if I find it not to be for God's glory, to repute it as a breach of the fourth Resolution .

24. *Resolved*, Whenever I do any conspicuously evil action, to trace it back, till I come to the original cause; and then, both carefully endeavor to do so no more, and to fight and pray with all my might against the original of it.

25. *Resolved*, To examine carefully, and constantly, what that one thing in me is, which causes me in the least to doubt of the love of God; and to direct all my forces against it.

26. *Resolved*, To cast away such things, as I find do abate my assurance.

27. *Resolved*, Never willfully to omit anything, except the omission be for glory of God; and frequently to examine my omissions.

28. *Resolved*, To study the Scriptures so steadily, constantly and frequently, so that I may find, and plainly perceive myself to grow in the knowledge of the same.

29. *Resolved*, Never to count that a prayer nor to let that pass as a prayer, nor that as a petition of a prayer, which is so made, that I cannot hope that God will answer it; nor that as a confession, which I cannot hope God will accept.

30. *Resolved*, To strive, every week, to be brought higher in religion, and to a higher exercise of grace, than I was the week before.

31. *Resolved*, Never to say anything at all against anybody, but when it is perfectly agreeable to the highest degree of Christian honor, and of love to mankind, agreeable to the lowest humility, and sense of my own faults and failings, and agreeable to the Golden Rule; often, when I have said anything against anyone, to bring it to, and try it strictly by the test of this Resolution.

32. *Resolved*, To be strictly and firmly faithful to my trust, that, in Proverbs 20:6, "*A faithful man, who can find?*" may not be partly fulfilled in me.

33. *Resolved*, To do, always, what I can towards making, maintaining, and preserving peace, when it can be done without an overbalancing detriment in other respects. *Dec. 26, 1722.*

34. *Resolved*, In narrations, never to speak anything but the pure and simple verity.

35. *Resolved*, Whenever I so much question whether I have done my duty, as that my quiet and calm is thereby disturbed, to set it down, and also how the question was resolved. *Dec. 18, 1722*

36. *Resolved*, Never to speak evil of any, except I have some particular good call to it. *Dec. 19, 1722*

37. *Resolved*, To inquire every night, as I am going to bed: Wherein I have been negligent? What sin I have committed? and Wherein I have denied myself? Also, at the end of every week, month, and year. *Dec. 22 and 26, 1722.*

38. *Resolved*, Never to utter anything that is sportive, or matter of laughter, on a Lord's day. *Sabbath evening. Dec. 23, 1722.*

39. *Resolved*, Never to do anything, of which I so much question the lawfulness, as that I intend, at the same time, to consider and examine afterwards, whether it be lawful or not; unless I as much question the lawfulness of the omission.

40. *Resolved*, To inquire every night, before I go to bed, whether I have acted in the best way I possibly could, with respect to eating and drinking. *Jan. 7, 1723.*

41. *Resolved*, To ask myself, at the end of every clay, week, month, and year, wherein I could possibly, in any respect, have done better. *Jan. 11, 1723.*

42. *Resolved*, Frequently to renew the dedication of myself to God, which was made at my baptism, which I solemnly renewed, when I was received into the communion of the church, and which I have solemnly remade this 12th day of January, 1723.

43. *Resolved*, Never, henceforward, till I die, to act as if I were any way my own, but entirely and altogether God's; agreeably to what is to be found in Saturday, January 12th. *Jan. 12th, 1723.*

44. *Resolved*, That no other end but religion, shall have any influence at all on any of my actions; and that no action shall be, in the least circumstance, any otherwise than the religious end will carry it. *Jan. 12, 1723.*

45. Resolved, Never to allow any pleasure or grief, joy or sorrow, nor any affection at all, nor any degree of affection, nor any circumstance relating to it, but what helps Religion. *Jan. 12 and 13, 1723.*

46. *Resolved*, Never to allow the least measure of any fretting or uneasiness at my father or mother. *Resolved*, To suffer no effects of it, so much as in the least alteration of speech, or motion of my eye; and to be especially careful of it with respect to any of our family.

47. *Resolved*, To endeavor, to my utmost, to deny whatever is not most agreeable to a good and universally sweet and benevolent quiet, peaceable, contented and easy, compassionate and generous, humble and meek, submissive and obliging, diligent and industrious, charitable and even, patient, moderate, forgiving and sincere, temper; and to do, at all times, what such a temper would lead me to; and to examine strictly, at the end of every week, whether I have so done. *Sabbath morning, May 5, 1723.*

48. *Resolved*, Constantly, with the utmost niceness and diligence, and the strictest scrutiny, to be looking into the state of my soul, that I may know whether I have truly an interest in Christ or not; that when I come to die, I may not have any negligence respecting this, to repent of. *May 26, 1723.*

49. *Resolved*, That this never shall be, if I can help it.

50. *Resolved*, That I will act so, as I think I shall judge would have been best, and most prudent, when I come into the future world. *July 5, 1723.*

51. *Resolved*, That I will act so, in every respect, as I think I shall wish I had done. If I should at last be damned. *July 8, 1723.*

52. I frequently hear persons in old age, say how they would live, if they were to live their lives over again: *Resolved*, That I will live just so as I can think I shall wish I had done, supposing I live to old age. *July 8, 1723.*

53. *Resolved*, To improve every opportunity, when I am in the best and happiest frame of mind, to cast and venture my soul on the Lord Jesus Christ, to trust and confide in Him, and consecrate myself wholly to Him; that from this I may have assurance of my safety, knowing that I confide in my Redeemer. *July 8, 1723.*

54. *Resolved*, Whenever I hear anything spoken in commendation of any person, if I think it would be praiseworthy in me that I will endeavor to imitate it. *July 8, 1723.*

55. *Resolved*, To endeavor, to my utmost, so to act, as I can think I should do, if I had already seen the happiness of heaven, and hell torments. *July 8, 1723.*

56. *Resolved*, Never to give over, nor in the least to slacken, my fight with my corruptions, however unsuccessful I may be.

57. *Resolved*, When I fear misfortunes and adversity, to examine whether I have done my duty, and resolve to do it, and let the event be just as Providence orders it. I will, as far as I can, be concerned about nothing but my duty, and my sin. *June 9 and July 13, 1723.*

58. *Resolved*, Not only to refrain from an air of dislike, fretfulness, and anger in conversation, but to exhibit an air of love, cheerfulness, and benignity. *May 27 and July 13, 1723.*

59. *Resolved*, When I am most conscious of provocations to ill nature and anger, that I will strive most to feel and act good-naturedly; yea, at such times, to manifest good nature, though I think that in other respects it would be disadvantageous, and so as would be imprudent at other times. *May 12, July 11, and July 13.*

60. *Resolved*, Whenever my feelings begin to appear in the least out of order, when I am conscious of the least uneasiness within, or the least irregularity without, I will then subject myself to the strictest examination. *July 4 and 13, 1723.*

61. *Resolved*, That I will not give way to that listlessness which I find unbends and relaxes my mind from being fully and fixedly set on religion, whatever excuse I may have for it—that what my listlessness inclines me to do, is best to be done, etc. *May 21 and July 13, 1723.*

62. *Resolved*, Never to do anything but my duty, and then according to Ephesians 6:6-8, to do it willingly and cheerfully, as unto the Lord, and not to man: knowing that whatever good thing any man doth, the same shall he receive of the Lord. *June 25 and July 13, 1723.*

63. On the supposition, that there never was to be but one individual in the world, at anyone time, who was properly a complete Christian, in all respects of a right stamp, having Christianity always shining in its luster, and appearing excellent and lovely, from whatever part and under whatever character viewed: *Resolved*, To act just as I would do, if I strove with all my might to be that one, who should live in my time. *Jan. 14 and July 13, 1723.*

64. *Resolved*, When I find those *"groaning which cannot be uttered,"* of which the apostle speaks, and those *"breakings of soul* for the longing it hath," of which the psalmist speaks (Psalm 119), that I will promote them to the utmost of my power, and that I will not be weary of earnestly endeavoring to vent my desires, nor of the repetitions of such earnestness. *July 23 and Aug. 10, 1723.*

65. *Resolved*, very much to exercise myself in this, all my life long, *viz.*, with the greatest openness, of which I am capable, to declare my ways to God, and lay open my soul to Him, all my sins, temptations, difficulties, sorrows, fears, hopes, desires, and everything, and every circumstance, according to Dr. Manton's sermon on Psalm 119. *July 26 and Aug. 10, 1723.*

66. *Resolved*, That I will endeavor always to keep a benign aspect, and air of acting and speaking in all places, and in all companies, except it should so happen that duty requires otherwise.

67. *Resolved*, After afflictions, to inquire, What I am the better for them? What good I have got by them? and What I might have got by them?

68. *Resolved*, To confess frankly to myself all that which I find in myself, either infirmity or sin; and, if it be what concerns religion, also to confess the whole case to God, and implore needed help. *July 23 and Aug. 10, 1723.*

69. *Resolved*, Always to do that, which I shall wish I had done when I see others do it. *Aug. 11, 1723.*

70. Let there be something of benevolence, in all that I speak. *Aug. 17, 1723.*

4. Constant Review

The fidelity with which Edwards sought to keep these commitments may be seen in his *Diary*. He began to make these notations about the same time as his *Resolutions*, and continued with interruptions until 1735. A check upon his accomplishments in fulfilling the resolves, the journal shows a conscious Quest in spiritual self-discipline. There is no attempt to build up himself in his own eyes. Rather he tells it like it is—his joy and his despair, his success and his failure. Here is revealed a man's burning desire to bring his soul under the refining light of God's holiness. The following excerpts are representative:

December, 1722

Dec. 18. This day made the 35th Resolution. The reason why I, in the least, question my interest in God's love and favor, is 1. Because I cannot speak so fully to my experience of that preparatory work, of which divines speak. 2. I do not remember that I experienced regeneration, exactly in those steps, in which divines say it is generally wrought. 3. I do not feel the Christian graces sensibly enough, particularly faith. I fear they are only such hypocritical outside affections, which wicked men may feel, as well as others. They do not seem to be sufficiently inward, full, sincere, entire, and hearty. They do not seem so substantial, and so wrought into my very nature, as I could wish. 4. Because I am sometimes guilty of sins of omission and commission. Lately I have doubted, whether I do not transgress in evil speaking. This day, resolved.

Dec. 21, Friday. This day, and yesterday. I was exceedingly, dull, dry and dead.

Dec. 22, Saturday. This day, revived by God's Holy Spirit; affected with the sense of the excellency of holiness, felt more exercise of love to Christ, than usual. Have, also, felt sensible repentance for sin, because it was committed against so merciful and good a God. This night made the 37th Resolution.

Dec. 24, Monday. Higher thoughts than usual of the excellency of Christ and His kingdom. Concluded to observe, at the end of every month, the number of breaches of Resolutions, to see whether they increase or diminish, to begin from this day, and to compute from that weekly account, my monthly increase and, out of the whole, my yearly increase, beginning from new year days.

1722-1723

Jan. 1, Tuesday. Have been dull for several days. Examined whether I have not been guilty of negligence today; and resolved.

Wednesday, Jan. 2. Dull. I find, by experience, that, let me make Resolutions, and do what I will, with never so many inventions, it is all nothing, and to no purpose at all, without the motions of the Spirit of God; for if the Spirit of God should be as much withdrawn from me always, as for the week past, not withstanding all I do, I should not grow, but should languish, and miserably fade away. I perceive, if God should withdraw His Spirit a little more, I should not hesitate to break my Resolutions, and should soon arrive at my old state. There is no dependence on myself. Our resolutions may be the highest one day, and yet, the next day, we may be in a miserable dead condition, not at all like the same person who resolved. So that it is to no purpose to resolve, except we depend on the grace of God. For, if it were not for His mere grace, one might be a very good man one day, and a very wicked one the next. I find also by experience, that there is no guessing on the ends of Providence, in particular dispensations towards me—any otherwise than as afflictions come as corrections for sin, and God intends when we meet with them, to desire us to look back on our ways, and see wherein we have done amiss, and lament that particular sin, and all our sins, before Him—knowing this, also, that all things shall work together for our good; not knowing in what way, indeed, but trusting in God.

Jan. 6, Sabbath. At night. Much concerned about the improvement of precious time. Intend to live in continual mortification, without ceasing, and even to weary myself thereby, as long as I am in this world, and never to expect or desire any worldly ease or pleasure.

Jan. 12, Saturday. In the morning. I have this day, solemnly renewed my baptismal covenant and self-dedication, which I renewed, when I was taken into the communion of the church. I have been before God, and have given myself, all that I am, and have, to God; so that I am not, in any respect, my own. I can challenge no right in this understanding, this will, and these affections, which are in me. Neither have I any right to this body, or any of its members-no right to this tongue, these hands, these feet; no right to these senses, these eyes, these ears, this smell, or this taste. I have given myself clear away, and have not retained anything, as my own. I gave myself to God, in my baptism, and I have been this morning to Him, and told Him, that I gave myself *wholly* to Him. I have given every power to Him; so that for the future, I'll challenge no right in myself, in no respect whatever, I have expressly promised Him, and I do now promise Almighty God, that by His grace, I will not. I have this morning told Him that I did take Him for my whole portion and felicity, looking on nothing else, as any part of my happiness, nor acting as if it were; and His law, for the constant rule of my obedience; and would fight, with all my might, against the world, the flesh and the devil, to the end of my life; and that I did believe in Jesus Christ, and did receive Him as a Prince and Savior; and that I would adhere to the faith and obedience of the gospel, however hazardous and difficult, the confession and practice of it may be; and that I did receive the blessed Spirit, as my Teacher, Sanctifier, and only Comforter, and cherish all His motions to enlighten, purify, confirm, comfort and assist me. This, I have done; and I pray God, for the sake of Christ, to look upon it as a self-dedication, and to receive me now, as entirely His own, and to deal with me, in all respects, as such, whether He afflicts me, or prospers me, or whatever He pleases to do with me, who am His. Now, henceforth, I am not to act, in any respect, as my own. I shall act as my own, if I ever make use of any of my powers, to anything, that is not to the glory of God, and do not make the glorifying of Him, my whole and entire business—if I murmur in the least at affliction; if I grieve at the prosperity of others; if I am in any way uncharitable; if I am angry, because of injuries; if I revenge them; if I do anything, purely to please myself, or if I avoid anything, for the sake of my own ease; if I omit anything, because it is great self-denial; if I trust to myself; if I take any of the praise of any good that I do, or that God doth by me; or if I am in any way proud. This day, made the 42nd and 43rd Resolutions.

Feb. 16, Saturday. I do certainly know that I love holiness, such as the gospel prescribes. *At night.* For the time past of my life, I have been negligent, in that I have not sufficiently kept up that part of divine worship, singing the praise of God in secret, and with company. I have been negligent the month past, in these three things. I have not been watchful enough over my appetites, in eating and drinking; in rising too late in the morning; and in not applying myself with sufficient application to the duty of secret prayer.

Feb. 17, Sabbath day. Near sunset. Renewably promised, that I will accept of God for my whole portion, and that I will be contented, whatever else I am denied. I will not murmur nor be grieved, whatever prosperity upon any account I see others enjoy, and I am denied. To this I have lately acted contrary.

April 1, Monday morning. I think it best not to allow myself to laugh at the faults, follies and infirmities, of others.

May 1, Wednesday forenoon. I have always, in every different state of life I have hitherto been in, thought that the troubles and difficulties of that state were greater than those of any other state that I proposed to be in; and when I have altered, with assurance of mending myself, I have still thought the same, yea that the difficulties of that state are greater than those of that I left last. Lord, grant that from hence I may learn to withdraw my thoughts, affections, desires and expectations entirely from the world, and may fix them upon the heavenly state, where there is fullness of joy; where reigns heavenly, sweet, calm and delightful love without alloy; where there are continually the dearest expressions of this love: where there is the enjoyment of this love without ever parting; and where those persons, who appear so lovely in this world, will be inexpressibly more lovely, and full of love to us. How sweetly will those, who thus mutually love, join together in singing the praises of God and the Lamb. How full will it fill us with joy, to think that this enjoyment, these sweet exercises, will never cease or come to an end, but will last to all eternity.

May 4, Saturday night. Although I have, in some measure, subdued a disposition to chide and fret, yet I find a certain inclination, which is not agreeable to Christian sweetness of temper and conversation: either too much dogmaticalness or too much egotism, a disposition to manifest my own dislike and scorn, and my own freedom from those which are innocent, sinless, yea common infirmities of men, and many other such like things. O that God would help me to discover all the flaws and defects of my temper and conversation, and help me in the difficult work of amending them; and that He would grant me so full a measure of vital Christianity, that the foundation of all these disagreeable irregularities may be destroyed, and the contrary sweetness and beauties may of themselves naturally follow.

July 23, Tuesday afternoon. When I find those *groaning which cannot be uttered*, of which the apostle speaks, and those *soul-breakings for the longing it hath*, of which the psalmist speaks (Psalm 119:20), *Resolved*, to favor and promote them to the utmost of my power, and not to be weary of earnestly endeavoring to vent my desires, and not to be weary of the repetitions of such earnestness.

To count it all joy, when I have occasions of great self-denial; because, then, I have a glorious opportunity of giving deadly wounds to the body of sin, and of greatly confirming, and establishing the new creature. I seek to mortify sin, and increase in holiness.

July 30, Tuesday night. Have concluded to endeavor to work myself into duties by searching and tracing back all the real reasons why I do them not, and narrowly searching out all the subtle subterfuge of my thoughts, and answering them to the utmost of my power, that I may know what are the very first originals of my defect, as with respect to want of repentance, love to God, loathing of myself-to do this sometimes in sermons. *Vid. Resolution 8.* Especially, to take occasion therefrom, to bewail those sins of which I have been guilty, that are akin to them; as for instance, from pride in others, to take occasion to bewail my pride; from their malice, to take occasion to bewail the same in myself: when I am evil-spoken of, to take occasion to bewail my evil speaking: and so of other sins. *Mem.* To receive slanders and reproaches, as glorious opportunities of doing this.

Aug. 9, Friday afternoon. With respect to the important business which I have now on hand, *Resolved*, to do whatever I think to be duty, prudence and diligence in the matter, and to avoid ostentation; and if I succeed not, and how many disappointments so ever I meet with, to be entirely easy; only to take occasion to acknowledge my unworthiness; and if it should actually not succeed, and should not find acceptance, as I expected, yet not to afflict myself about it, according to the 57th Resolution. *At night.* One thing that may be a good help towards thinking profitably in times of vacation, is, when I find a profitable thought that I can fix my mind on, to follow it as far as I possibly can to advantage. —I missed it, when a graduate at college, both in point of duty and prudence, in going against a universal benevolence and good nature.

Aug. 24, Saturday morning. Have not practiced quite right about revenge; though I have not done anything directly out of revenge, yet, I have perhaps, omitted some things, that I should otherwise have done, or have altered the circumstances and manner of my actions, hoping for a secret sort of revenge thereby. I have felt a little sort of satisfaction, when I thought that such an evil would happen to them by my actions, as would make them repent what they have done. To be satisfied for their repenting, when they repent from a sense of their error, is right. But a satisfaction in their repentance, because of the evil that is brought upon them, is revenge. This is in some measure, a taking the matter out of God's hands when He was about to manage it, who is better able to plead it for me. Well, therefore, may He leave me to boggle at it.

Aug. 28, Wednesday night. When I want books to read; yea, when I have not very good books, not to spend time in reading them, but in reading the Scriptures, in perusing Resolutions, Reflections, etc., in writing on types of the Scripture, and other things, in studying the languages, and in spending more time in private duties. To do this, when there is a prospect of wanting time for the purpose. Remember as soon as I can, to get a piece of *slate*, or something, whereon I can make short memorandums while traveling.

Aug. 29, Thursday. Two great *Quaerenda* with me now are: How shall I take advantage of all the time I spend in journeys? And how shall I make a glorious improvement of afflictions?

Sept. 23, Monday. I observe that old men seldom have any advantage of new discoveries, because they are beside the way of thinking, to which they have been so long used. *Resolved*, if ever I live to years, that I will be impartial to hear the reasons of all pretended discoveries, and receive them if rational, how long so ever I have been used to another way of thinking. My time is so short, that I have not time to perfect myself in all studies: Wherefore resolved, to omit and put off, all but the most important and needful studies.

Nov. 26, Tuesday forenoon. It is a most evil and pernicious practice, in meditations on afflictions, to sit ruminating on the aggravations of the affliction, and reckoning up the evil, dark circumstances thereof, and dwelling long on the dark side: it doubles and trebles the affliction. And so, when speaking of them to others, to make them as bad as we can, and use our eloquence to set forth our own troubles, is to be all the while making new trouble, and feeding and pampering the old; whereas, the contrary practice, would starve our affliction. If we dwelt on the bright side of things in our thoughts, and extenuated them all that we possibly could, when speaking of them, we should think little of them ourselves, and the affliction would, really, in a great measure, vanish away.

Dec. 27, Friday morning. At the end of every month, to examine my behavior strictly, by some chapter in the New Testament, more especially made up of rules of life. At the end of the year, to examine my behavior by the rules of the New Testament in general, reading many chapters. It would also be convenient, some time at the end of the year, to read, for this purpose, in the Book of Proverbs.

Feb. 22, Saturday. I observe that there are some evil habits, which do increase and grow stronger, even in some good people, as they grow older; habits that much obscure the beauty of Christianity: some things which are according to their natural tempers, which, in some measure, prevails when they are young in Christ, and the evil disposition, having an unobserved control, the habit at last grows very strong, and commonly regulates the practice until death. By this means, old Christians are very commonly, in some respects, more unreasonable than those who are young. I am afraid of contracting such habits, particularly of grudging to give, and to do, and of procrastinating.

Feb. 23, Sabbath. I must be contented, where I have anything strange or remarkable to tell, not to make it appear so remarkable as it is indeed; lest through the fear of this, and the desire of making a thing appear very remarkable, I should exceed the bounds of simple verity.

Nov. 22, Sabbath. Considering that bystanders always copy some faults, which we do not see, ourselves, or of which, at least, we are not so fully sensible; and that there are many secret workings of corruption, which escape our sight, and of which, others only are sensible: *Resolved*, therefore, that I will, if I can by any convenient means, learn what faults others find in me, or what things they see in me, that appear any way blameworthy, unlovely, or unbecoming.

April 4, 1735. When at any time, I have a sense of any divine thing, then to turn it in my thoughts, to a practical improvement. As for instance, when I am in my mind on some argument for the truth of religion, the reality of a future state, and the like, then to think with myself, how safely I may venture to sell all, for a future good. So when, at any time, I have a more than ordinary sense of the glory of the saints, in another world; to think how well it is worth my while, to deny myself, and to sell all that I have for this glory, etc.

So beat the heart of Jonathan Edwards, truly an extraordinary man by any measure. His penetrating insights into the reality of things have justly earned him a place in America's Hall of Fame. But however one may view his legacy, he must be regarded as a saintly scholar. It was his simple faith and childlike piety which gave distinction to his other gifts. He could not tolerate the sham of human self-sufficiency, most of all when it masqueraded under the guise of intelligence. To him the fear of God was the beginning of wisdom. Yet it was a holy fear founded upon an implicit trust in the grace of a loving Savior. Jesus commanded his obedience. As few men of his age, he resolved to dedicate all his mind, all his soul, all his strength to the praise of his majestic Lord.

Should we not make the same resolution?

The Scripture Way of Salvation

Sermons of

John Wesley 1703-1791

*With an Introduction
By Robert E. Coleman*

Abridged version of *The Scripture Way of Salvation*, Sermons by John Wesley. Abridged version originally published by the Institute of Evangelism Billy Graham Center, 1994, Wheaton, IL. Copyright of abridged version and introduction held by Robert Coleman, used with permission. Scripture quotations are taken from the Holy Bible, King James Version (KJV), in the Public Domain. Artwork in the Public Domain.

Book Chapters

1. Introduction
   By Robert E. Coleman 138
2. The Scripture Way of Salvation...142
   Section 1 142
   Section 2 144
   Section 3 145
3. The Circumcision of the Heart 151
   Section 1 152
   Section 2. 156
4. The Repentance of Believers 160
5. Notes..172

1. Introduction
By Robert E. Coleman

Few persons have ever lived who exerted more positive influence on their time than John Wesley. His prodigious life and work, spanning most of the Eighteenth Century, epitomized and gave direction to an evangelical revival that changed the face of England.

Born at Epworth, June 17, 1703, he was the second surviving son of Samuel and Susanna Wesley, and the fifteenth of nineteen children. In the Anglican vicar's home where he grew up, he learned early the importance of sound doctrine and vigorous piety.

At the age of ten, John went to London to attend the Charterhouse School, and seven years later, he entered Christ Church College, Oxford. After graduation he offered himself to become a priest of the Church of England, and was ordained a deacon in 1725. For a while he assisted his father in pastoral work, but meeting with meager success, he returned to his scholarly pursuits at the University, where he had been made a teaching fellow at Lincoln College.

Here Wesley joined his brother, Charles, along with a few other students, in a closely knit fellowship of earnest souls seeking God's will. The group met regularly for study and worship, practiced fasting twice a week, and engaged themselves in a number of benevolent services to the poor. Because of their vigorous discipline they were dubbed in derision "The Holy Club" or "Methodists."

Following his father's death in 1735, John accepted an appointment as a missionary to the colonists and Indians in Georgia. However, his strict adherence to order did not set well with the more easy-going frontiersmen of the new world. A courtship rejection by one of the ladies of the colony added to his difficulties. Finally, after nearly two years of frustration, the broken Wesley returned to England. Typifying his anguish, on shipboard he wrote in his *Journal*. "I went to America to convert the Indians; but O! Who shall convert me?"[1]

Back in London, his longing for spiritual reality eventually led to a little Moravian prayer meeting on Aldersgate Street. There on May 24, 1738, about a quarter before nine, while a layman was reading from Luther's Preface to the Book of Romans, "describing the change which God works in the heart through faith in Christ," Wesley laid hold on the promise of grace, and received assurance that he was delivered from the law of sin and death.[2] This experience kindled a fire in his life, which was to set a nation aflame.

England was in desperate circumstances. Centuries of turmoil had left the people bitter and restless. Poverty was everywhere. Society reeked with moral decay. Making the situation more tragic, the apathetic, established church was completely discredited and out of touch with the working masses.

Into this generation of despair, seething on the verge of revolution, John Wesley began to herald a Gospel of free and full salvation—a deliverance, which any person can know through simple faith in the finished work of Jesus Christ. Sophisticated churchmen closed their doors to his preaching. But Wesley, seeing all the world as his parish, following the example of George Whitfield, "submitted to be more vile," and began to proclaim in the streets and fields the glad tiding of salvation.[3]

Soon the soft-spoken Oxford don in clerical garb, standing scarcely five feet four inches tall, with his long, silken hair blowing in the wind, became a familiar sight across the land. Multitudes were arrested by his message, especially the poor, the outcasts of society, and those disenchanted with the cold religious institutions of the day.

For fifty years Wesley carried his ministry to the people. Hazardous conditions never deterred him from his mission to reform the nation and to spread Scriptural holiness over the land. It is estimated that he traveled 250,000 miles on horseback. During this period he preached 42,000 sermons, an average of more than 15 a week. Still, shortly before his death on March 2, 1791, his eyes dim, his right hand shaking with a lingering fever almost every day, he wrote in his *Journal*: "Blessed be God, I do not slack my labor."[4]

Part of his energy was given to reading and study, particularly the Bible which he revered as the inerrant Word of God. Out of this came a profusion of writings on a wide variety of subjects, including Gospel tracts, letters, appeals, hymns, textbooks, histories, Bible commentaries, and a well-kept personal journal.

It was in his written sermons, however, that his message comes through most fully. Though most of the illustration material was edited out before publication, the keen reasoning of his theology cannot be missed. Whatever the theme, at its heart will be seen the need and provision for heart purity. "Our main doctrines," wrote Wesley, "which include all the rest are repentance, faith and holiness. The first of these we account, as it were, the porch of religion: the next, the door; the third, religion itself."[5]

The three sermons reproduced in this book typify this preaching—the kind of preaching that uncovers the depths of sin while exalting the heights of redeeming grace. The first sermon is a message on Ephesians 2:8. Its genesis goes back to Wesley's early ministry, probably the substance being preached on May 14, ten days before his conversion. When proclaimed again on June 11, at Oxford, now eighteen days after his conversion at Aldersgate, it must have had a different ring. The manifesto, "Salvation by Faith," announced a new day in religion. Apparently it was one of Wesley's favorites, for it was placed first in his collection of sermons and there are numerous references to it throughout his *Journal*, up to 1760. Sometime after this, the sermon was entirely rewritten, and published in 1765 as "The Scripture Way of Salvation."

The revised message gives more attention to the place of prevenient grace in God's saving work, while also treating more adequately his position on faith and sanctification. The concise exposition affords an excellent overview of basic Wesleyan thought. From this standpoint, one eminent scholar has said that the sermon "is of more practical value than all the sermons put together.[6]" Be that as it may, it summarizes great truth, and befitting its evangelist-author, leaves one with a challenge for decision. The instructions of the 1766 *Minutes*, that this message be distributed to all Methodist Societies, has lost none of its urgency in the subsequent more than two hundred years.

The second sermon, "The Circumcision of the Heart," again one of Wesley's earliest preserved discourses, was preached first at Oxford at St. Mary's Oxford on New Year's Day, 1733. It reflects the aspirations of that little group of earnest souls in the University banded together to seek the holy life. Delivered more than five years before Wesley's heartwarming experience at Aldersgate, the sermon describes his concept of holiness worked out intellectually by honestly searching the Scriptures. Though later his views of sanctification were given more refinement, writing to a friend in May of 1765, he said: "This sermon...contains all that I now teach concerning salvation from all sin, and loving God with an undivided heart."[7] Interestingly, when the message was published in his *Second Volume of Sermons* in 1748, Wesley mentions in a footnote that he had added to the original manuscript a more complete definition of saving faith as he had come to experience it in 1738.[8]

The selection concludes with his message, "The Repentance of Believers," written on April 24, 1767, and published in pamphlet form the following year. It was included in the 1771 edition of his *Works* to further elucidate his message, "On Sin in Believers" (1763). Getting at the true spirituality, the sermon stresses the necessity of dealing with man's self-nature contrary to the mind of Christ. Though not as definitive as his *Plain Account on Christian Perfection* (1766), it underscores the all sufficiency of God's grace enabling one to live under the complete lordship of the King, while showing how repentance and faith answer each other. No one can read this message without being moved. To me it is the most searching of all Wesley's preaching.

These sermons are reprinted unabridged as published in the 1771 Edition of Wesley's *Works*. At a time when many spokesmen of the church seem intent upon entertaining our self-centered generation, lest people take offense, we would do well to listen again to the probing voice of John Wesley. One may take exception to his views, but there can be no dispute that under such preaching forces of righteousness were set in motion that still have reverberations across the earth.

Robert E. Coleman

2. The Scripture Way of Salvation

Ye are saved through faith. -Ephesians 2:8b

Section 1

Nothing can be more intricate, complex, and hard to be understood, than religion, as it has been often described. And this is not only true concerning the religion of the Heathens, even many of the wisest of them, but concerning the religion of those also who were, in some sense, Christians; yea, and men of great name in the Christian world; men who seemed to be pillars thereof. Yet how easy to be understood, how plain and simple a thing, is the genuine religion of Jesus Christ; provided only that we take it in its native form, just as it is described in the oracles of God! It is exactly suited, by the wise Creator and Governor of the world, to the weak understanding and narrow capacity of man in his present state. How observable is this, both with regard to the end it proposes, and the means to attain that end! The end is, in one word, salvation; the means to attain it, faith.

It is easily discerned, that these two little words, I mean faith and salvation, include the substance of all the Bible, the marrow, as it were, of the whole Scripture. So much the more should we take all possible care to avoid all by the power of God. We feel "the love of God shed abroad in our heart by the Holy Ghost which is given unto us;" producing love to all mankind, and more especially to the children of God: expelling the love of the world, the love of pleasure, of ease, of honor, of money, together with pride, anger, self-will, and every other evil temper: in a word, changing the earthly, sensual devilish mind, "into the mind which was in Christ Jesus."

How naturally do those who experience such a change imagine that all sin is gone; that it is utterly rooted out of their heart, and has no more any place therein! How easily do they draw that inference. "I *feel* no sin: therefore, I have none; it does not stir: therefore, it does not *exist*; it has no *motion*; therefore, it has no *being*!"

But it is seldom long before they are undeceived, finding sin was only suspended, not destroyed. Temptations return, and sin revives; showing it was but stunned before, not dead. They now feel two principles in themselves, plainly contrary to each other: "the flesh lusting against the Spirit;" nature opposing the grace of God. They cannot deny, that although they still feel power to believe in Christ, and to love God; and although His "Spirit" still "witnesses with their spirits, that they are children of God:" yet they feel in themselves sometimes pride or self-will, sometimes anger or unbelief. They find one or more of these frequently *stirring* in their heart, though not *conquering*; yea, perhaps, "thrusting sore at them that they may fall"; but the Lord is their help.

How exactly did Macarius, fourteen hundred years ago, describe the present experience of the children of God: "The unskillful," or unexperienced, "when grace operates, presently imagine they have no more sin. Whereas they that have discretion cannot deny, that even we who have the grace of God may be molested again. For we have often had instances of some among the brethren, who have experienced such grace as to affirm that they had no sin in them: and yet, after all, when they thought themselves entirely freed from it, the corruption that lurked within was stirred up anew, and they were well nigh burned up."

From the time of our being born again, the gradual work of sanctification takes place. We are enabled "by the Spirit" to "mortify the deeds of the body," of our evil nature: and as we are more and more dead to sin, we are more and more alive to God. We go on from grace to grace, while we are careful to "abstain from all appearance of evil," and are "zealous of good works," as we have opportunity, doing good to all men; while we walk in all His ordinances blameless, therein worshipping Him in spirit and truth; while we take up our cross, and deny ourselves every pleasure that does not lead us to God.

It is thus that we wait for entire sanctification; for a full salvation from all our sins—from pride, self-will, anger, unbelief: or, as the Apostle expresses it, "go on unto perfection." But what is perfection: The word has various senses; here it means perfect love. It is love excluding sin: love filling the heart, taking up the whole capacity of the soul. It is love "rejoicing evermore, praying without ceasing, in everything giving thanks."

Section 2

But what is that faith through which we are saved? This is the second point to be considered.

Faith, in general, is defined by the Apostle πραγματῶγ ελεγχος ου βλεπομενῶν – an *evidence*, a divine *evidence and conviction* (the word means both) *of things not seen;* not visible, not perceivable either by sight, or by any other of the external senses. It implies both a supernatural *evidence* of God, and of the things of God; a kind of spiritual *light* exhibited to the soul, and a supernatural *sight* or perception thereof. Accordingly, the Scripture speaks of God's giving sometimes light, sometimes a power of discerning it. So St. Paul: "God, who commanded light to shine out of darkness, hath shined in our hearts, to give us the light of the knowledge of the glory of God in the face of Jesus Christ." And elsewhere the same Apostle speaks of "the eyes of our "understanding being opened." By this two-fold operation of the Holy Spirit, having the eyes of our soul both *opened and enlightened*, we see the things which the natural "eye hath not seen, neither ear heard." We have a prospect of the invisible things of God: we see the *spiritual world*, which is all round about us, and yet no more discerned by our natural faculties than if it had no being. And we see the *eternal world*; piercing through the veil, which hangs between time and eternity. Clouds and darkness then rest upon it no more, but we already see the glory, which shall be revealed. Taking the word in a more particular sense, faith is a divine *evidence* and *conviction* not only that "God was in Christ, reconciling the world unto Himself," but also that, Christ loved me, and gave Himself for *me.* It is by this faith (whether we term it the *essence*, or rather a *property* thereof) that we *receive Christ*; that we receive Him in all His offices, as our Prophet, Priest, and King. It is by this that He is "made of God unto us wisdom, and righteousness, and sanctification, and redemption."

But is this the *faith of assurance, or faith of adherence*? The Scripture mentions no such distinction. The Apostle says, "There is one faith, and one hope of our calling"; one Christian, saving faith; "as there is one Lord," in whom we believe, and "one God and Father of us all." And it is certain, this faith necessarily implies an *assurance* (which is here only another word for *evidence*, it being hard to tell the difference between them) that Christ loved me, and gave Himself for me. For "he that believeth" with the true living faith "hath the witness in himself; "the Spirit witnessed with his spirit that he is a child of God." "Because he is a son, God hath sent forth the Spirit of His Son into his heart, crying,

Abba, Father"; giving him an assurance that he is so, and a childlike confidence in Him. But let it be observed, that, in the very nature of the thing, the assurance goes before the confidence. For a man cannot have a childlike confidence in God till he knows he is a child of God. Therefore, confidence, trust, reliance, adherence, or whatever else it be called, is not the first, as some have supposed, but the second, branch or act of faith.

It is by this faith we are saved, justified, and sanctified; taking that word in its highest sense. But how are we justified and sanctified by faith? This is our third head of inquiry. And this being the main point in question, and a point of no ordinary importance, it will not be improper to give it more distinct and particular consideration.

Section 3

And, first, how are we justified by faith? In what sense is this to be understood? I answer. Faith is the condition, and the only condition, of justification. It is the *condition*; none is justified but he that believes; without faith no man is justified. And it is the *only condition*; this alone is sufficient for justification. Everyone that believes is justified, whatever else he has or has not. In other words: no man is justified till he believes: every man when he believes is justified.

"But does not God command us to repent also? Yea, and to "bring forth fruits meet for repentance"—to cease, for instance, from doing evil, and learn to do well? And is not both the one and the other of the utmost necessity, insomuch that if we willingly neglect either, we cannot reasonably expect to be justified at all? But if this be so, how can it be said that faith is the only condition of justification?"

God does undoubtedly command us both to repent, and to bring forth fruits meet for repentance; which if we willingly neglect, we cannot reasonably expect to be justified at all; therefore both repentance, and fruits meet for repentance, are, in some sense, necessary to justification. But they are not necessary in the *same sense* with faith, nor in the *same degree*. Not in the same degree: for those fruits are only necessary *conditionally*; if there be time and opportunity for them. Otherwise a man may be justified without them, as was the *thief* upon the cross (if we may call him so; for a late writer has discovered that he was not thief, but a very honest and respectable person!); but he cannot be justified without faith; this is impossible. Likewise, let a man have ever so much repentance, or ever so many of the fruits meet for repentance, yet all this does not at all avail. He is not justified till he believes. But the moment he believes, with or without those fruits, yea, with more or less repentance, he is justified. —Not in the *same sense*; for repentance and its fruits are only *remotely* necessary; necessary in order to faith whereas faith is *immediately* and *directly* necessary to justification. It remains, that faith is the only condition which is immediately and *proximately* necessary to justification.

"But do you believe we are sanctified by faith? We know you believe that we are justified by faith; but do not you believe, and accordingly teach, that we are sanctified by our works?" So it has been roundly and vehemently affirmed for these five-and-twenty years; but I have constantly declared just the contrary: and that in all manner of ways I have continually testified in private and in public, that we are sanctified as well as justified by faith. And indeed the one of those great truths does exceedingly illustrate the other. Exactly as we are justified by faith, so are we sanctified by faith. Faith is the condition, and the only condition, of sanctification, exactly as it is of justification. It is the *condition*: none is sanctified but he that believes: without faith no man is sanctified. And it is the *only condition*: this alone is sufficient for sanctification. Everyone that believes is sanctified, whatever else he has or has not. In other words, no man is sanctified till he believes; every man when he believes is sanctified.

"But is there not repentance consequent upon, as well as a repentance previous to, justification? And is it not incumbent on all that are justified to be 'zealous of good works'? Yea, are not these so necessary, that if a man willingly neglect them he cannot reasonably expect that he shall ever be sanctified in the full sense; that is, perfected in love? Nay, can he grow at all in grace, in the loving knowledge of our Lord Jesus Christ? Yea, can he retain the grace, which God has already given him? Can he continue in the faith, which he has received, or in the favor of God? Do not you yourself allow all this, and continually assert it? But, if this be so, how can it be said that faith is the only condition of sanctification?"

I do allow all this, and continually maintain it as the truth of God. I allow there is a repentance consequent upon, as well as a repentance previous to, justification. It is incumbent on all that are justified to be zealous of good works. And these are so necessary, that if a man willingly neglect them, he cannot reasonably expect that he shall ever be sanctified; he cannot grow in grace, in the image of God, the mind, which was in Christ Jesus; nay, he cannot retain the grace he has received; he cannot continue in faith, or in the favor of God.

What is the inference we must draw here from? Why, that both repentance, rightly understood, and the practice of all good works— works of piety, as well as works of mercy (now properly so called, since they spring from faith), are, in some sense, necessary to sanctification.

I say, "repentance rightly understood"; for this must not be confounded with the former repentance. The repentance consequent upon justification is widely different from that which is antecedent to it. This implies no guilt, no sense of condemnation, and no consciousness of the wrath of God. It does not suppose any doubt of the favor of God, or any "fear that hath torment." It is properly a conviction, wrought by the Holy Ghost, of the *sin* which still *remains* in our heart: of the θρονημα ο αρκος the: carnal mind, which "does still *remain*" (as our Church speaks) "even in them that are regenerate": although it does no long *reign*; it has not now dominion over them. It is a conviction of our proneness to evil, of an heart bent to backsliding, of the still continuing tendency of the flesh to lust against the spirit. Sometimes, unless we continually watch and pray, it lusted to pride, sometimes to anger, sometimes to love of the world, love of case, love of honor, or love of pleasure more than of God. It is a conviction of the tendency of our heart to self-will, to atheism, or idolatry: and above all, to unbelief: whereby, in a thousand ways, and under a thousand pretenses, we are ever departing, more or less, from the living God.

With this conviction of the sin remaining in our hearts, there is joined a clear conviction of the sin remaining in our lives: still *cleaving* to all our words and actions. In the best of these we now discern a mixture of evil, either in the spirit, the matter, or the manner of them; something that could not endure the righteous judgment of God, were He extreme to mark what is done amiss. Where we least suspected it, wie find a taint of pride or self-will, of unbelief or idolatry: so that we are now more ashamed of our best duties than formerly of our worst sins: and hence we cannot but feel that these are so far from having anything meritorious in them, yea, so far from being able to stand in sight of the divine justice, that for those also we should be guilty before God, were it not for the blood of the covenant.

Experience shows that, together with this conviction of sin *remaining* in our hearts, and *cleaving* to all our words and as well as the guilt which on account thereof we should incur, were we not continually sprinkled with the atoning blood; one thing more is implied in this repentance; namely, a conviction of our helplessness, of our utter inability to think one good thought, or to form one good and much more to speak one word aright, or to perform one good action, but through His free, almighty grace, first preventing us, and then accompanying us every moment.

"But what good works are those, the practice of which you affirm to be necessary to sanctification?" First, all works of piety; such as public prayer, family prayer, and praying in our closet; receiving the supper of the Lord; searching the Scriptures, by hearing, reading, meditation; and using such a measure of fasting or abstinence as our bodily health allows.

Secondly, all works of mercy; whether they relate to the bodies or souls of men; such as feeding the hungry, clothing the naked, entertaining the stranger, visiting those that are in prison, or sick, or variously afflicted; such as the endeavoring to instruct the ignorant, to awaken the stupid sinner, to quicken the lukewarm, to confirm the wavering, to comfort the feebleminded, to succor the tempted, or contribute in any manner to the saving of souls from death. This is the repentance, and these the "fruits meet for repentance," which are necessary to full sanctification. This is the way wherein God hath appointed His children to wait for complete salvation.

Hence may appear the extreme mischievousness of that seemingly innocent opinion, that there is no sin in a believer: that all sin is destroyed, root and branch, the moment a man is justified. By totally preventing that repentance, it quite blocks up the way to sanctification. There is no place for repentance in him who believes there is no sin either in his life or heart: consequently, there is no place for his being perfected in love, to which that repentance is indispensably necessary.

Hence, it may likewise appear, that there is no possible danger in *thus* expecting full salvation. For suppose we were mistaken, suppose no such blessing ever was or can be attained, yet we lose nothing: nay, that very expectation quickens us in using all the talents which God has given us: yea, in improving them all so that when our Lord cometh, He will receive His own with increase.

But to return. Though it be allowed, that both this repentance and its fruits are necessary to full salvation: yet they are not necessary either in the same sense with faith, or in the same degree. —Not in the *same degree*: for these fruits are only necessary *conditionally*, if there be time and opportunity for them; otherwise a man may be sanctified without them. But he cannot be sanctified without faith. Likewise, let a man have ever so much of this repentance, or ever so many good works, yet all this does not at all avail; he is not sanctified till he believes. But the moment he believes, with or without those fruits, yea, with more or less of this repentance, he is sanctified. —Not in the *same sense* for this repentance and these fruits are only *remotely* necessary—necessary in order to the continuance of his faith, as well as the increase of it whereas faith is *immediately* and *directly* necessary to sanctification. It remains, that faith is the only condition, which is *immediately* and *proximately* necessary to sanctification.

"But what is that faith whereby we are sanctified,—saved from sin, and perfected in love?" It is a divine evidence and conviction, first, that God hath promised it in the holy Scripture. Till we are thoroughly satisfied of this, there is no moving one step further. And one would imagine there needed not one word more to satisfy a reasonable man of this, than the ancient promise, "Then will I circumcise thy heart, and the heart of thy seed, to love the Lord thy God with all thy heart, and with all thy soul, and with all thy mind." How clearly does this express the being perfected in love! —How strongly imply the being saved from all sin! For as long as love takes up the whole heart, what room is there for sin therein?

It is a divine evidence and conviction, secondly that what God hath promised He is able to perform. Admitting, therefore, that "with men it is impossible: to 'bring a clean thing out of an unclean,' to purify the heart from all sin, and to fill it with all holiness: yet this creates no difficulty in the case, seeing 'with God all things are possible.'" And surely no one ever imagined it was possible to any power less than that of the Almighty! But if God speaks, it shall be done. God said, "Let there be light: and there" is "light"!

It is, thirdly, a divine evidence and conviction that He is able and willing to do it now. And why not? Is not a moment to Him the same as a thousand years? He cannot want more time to accomplish whatever is His will. And He cannot want to stay for any more *worthiness* or *fitness* in the persons life is pleased to honor. We may therefore boldly say, at any point of time, "Now is the day of salvation!" "Today, if we will hear His voice, harden not your hearts!" "Behold, all things are now ready: come unto the marriage!"

To this confidence, that God is both able and willing to sanctify us now, there needs to be added one thing more, —a divine evidence and conviction that He doeth it. In that hour it is done: God says to the inmost soul, "According to thy faith be it unto thee!" Then the soul is pure from every spot of sin: it is clean "from all unrighteousness." The believer then experiences the deep meaning of those solemn words, "If we walk in the light as He is in the light, we have fellowship one with another, and the blood of Jesus Christ His Son cleanse us from all sin."

"But does God work this great work in the soul gradually or instantaneously,?" Perhaps it may be gradually wrought in some: I mean in this sense-they do not advert to the particular moment wherein sin ceases to be. But it is infinitely desirable, were it the will of God, that it should be done instantaneously: that the Lord should destroy sin "by the breath of His mouth," in a moment, in the twinkling of an eye. And so He generally does; a plain fact, of which there is evidence enough to satisfy any unprejudiced person. *Thou* therefore look for it every moment! Look for it in the way above described: in all those *good works* whereunto thou art "created anew in Christ Jesus." There is then no danger; you can be no worse, if you are no better, for that expectation. For were you to be disappointed of your hope, still you lose nothing. But you shall not be disappointed of your hope: it will come, and will not tarry. Look for it then every day, every hour, every moment. Why not this hour, this moment? Certainly you may look for it *now*, if you believe it is by faith. And by this token you may surely know whether you seek it by faith or by works. If by works, you want something to be done *first*, *before* you are sanctified. You think, I must first *be* or *do* thus or thus. Then you are seeking it by works unto this day. If you seek it by faith, you may expect it as you are; and if as you are, then expect it now. It is of importance to observe, that there is an inseparable connexion between these three points,—expect it by *faith*; expect it as you *are*; and expect it *now*. To deny one of them, is to deny them all; to allow one, is to allow them all. Do *you* believe we are sanctified by faith? Be true then to your principle: and look for this blessing just as you are, neither better nor worse: as a poor sinner that has still nothing to pay, nothing to plead, but "Christ died." And if you look for it as you are, then expect it *now*. Stay for nothing: why should you? Christ is ready: and He is all you want. He is waiting for you: He is at the door' Let your inmost soul cry out.

> *Come in, come in. Thou heavenly Guest!*
>   *Nor hence again remove;*
> *But sup with me, and let the feast*
>   *Be everlasting love.*

3. The Circumcision of the Heart

Circumcision is that of the heart, in the spirit, and not the letter.
—Romans 2:29b

It is the melancholy remark of an excellent man, that he who now preaches the most essential duties of Christianity runs the hazard of being esteemed, by a great part of his hearers, "a setter forth of new doctrines." Most men have so *lived away* the substance of that religion, the profession whereof they still retain, that no sooner are any of those truths proposed which difference the Spirit of Christ from the spirit of the world, than they cry out, "Thou bringest strange things to our ears; we would know what these things mean": though he is only preaching to them "Jesus and the resurrection," with the necessary consequence of it.—If Christ be risen, ye ought then to die unto the world, and to live wholly unto God.

A hard saying this to the natural man, who is alive unto the world, and dead unto God: and one that he will not readily be persuaded to receive as the truth of God, unless it be so qualified in the interpretation, as to have neither use or significance left. He "receiveth not the" words "of the Spirit of God," taken in their plain and obvious meaning; "they are foolishness unto him, neither" indeed "can he know them, because they are spiritually discerned"; they are perceivable only by that spiritual sense, which in him was never yet awakened; for want of which he must reject, as idle fancies of men, what are both the wisdom and the power of God.

That "circumcision is that of the heart, in the spirit, and not in the letter"—that the distinguishing mark of a true follower of Christ of one who is in a state of acceptance with God, is not either outward circumcision, or baptism, or any other outward form, but a right state of soul, a mind and spirit renewed after the image of Him that created it— is one of those important truths that can only be spiritually discerned. And this the Apostle himself intimates in the next words: "Whose praise is not of men, but of God." As if he had said, "Expect not, whoever thou art, who thus followest thy great Master, that the world, the men who follow Him not," will say, "Well done, good and faithful servant!" Know that the circumcision of the heart, the seal of thy calling, is foolishness with the world. Be content to wait for thy applause till the day of thy Lord's appearing. In that day shalt thou have praise of God, in the great assembly of men and angels."

I design, first, particularly to inquire, wherein this circumcision of the heart consists; and, secondly, to mention some reflections that naturally arise from such an inquiry.

Section 1

I am, first, to inquire, wherein that circumcision of the heart consists, which will receive the praise of God. In general we may observe, it is that habitual disposition of soul which, in the sacred writings, is termed holiness; and which directly implies, the being cleansed from sin, "from all filthiness both of flesh and spirit"; and, by consequence, the being endured with those virtues which were also in Christ Jesus; the being so "renewed in the spirit of our mind," as to be "perfect as our Father in heaven is perfect."

To be more particular: circumcision of heart implies humility, faith, hope, and charity. Humility, a right judgment of ourselves, cleanses our minds from those high conceits of our own perfections, from that undue opinion of our own abilities and attainments, which are the genuine fruit of a corrupted nature. This entirely cuts off that vain thought, "I am rich, and wise, and have need of nothing"; and convinces us that we are by nature "wretched, and poor, and miserable, and blind, and naked." It convinces us, that in our best estate we are, of ourselves, all sin and vanity; that confusion, and ignorance, and error reign over our understanding; that unreasonable, earthly, sensual, devilish passions usurp authority over our will in a word, that there is no whole part in our soul, that all the foundations of our nature are out of course.

At the same time we are convinced, that we are not sufficient of ourselves to help ourselves; that, without the Spirit of God, we can do nothing but add sin to sin; that it is He alone who worketh in us by His almighty power, either to will or do that which is good; it being as impossible for us even to think a good thought, without the supernatural assistance of His Spirit, as to create ourselves, or to renew our whole souls in righteousness and true holiness.

A sure effect of our having formed this right judgment of the sinfulness and helplessness of our nature, is a disregard of that "honor which cometh of man," which is usually paid to some supposed in us. He who knows himself neither desires nor values the applause which he knows he deserves not. It is therefore "a very small thing with him, to be judged by man's judgment." He has all reason to think, by comparing what it has said, either for or against him, with what he feels in his own breast, that the world, as well as the god of this world, was "a liar from the beginning." And even as to those who are not of the world; thought he would choose, if it were the will of God, that they should account of him as of one desirous to be found a faithful steward of his Lord's goods, if haply this might be a means of enabling him to be of more use to his fellow servants, yet as this is the one end of his wishing for their approbation, so he does not at all rest upon it; for he is assured, that whatever God wills, he can never want instruments to perform; since He is able, even of these stones, to raise up servants to do His pleasure.

This is that lowliness of mind, which they have learned of Christ, who follow His example and tread in His steps. And this knowledge of their disease, whereby they are more and more cleansed from one part of it, pride and vanity, disposes them to embrace, with a willing mind, the second thing implied in circumcision of the heart, —that faith which alone is able to make them whole, which is the one medicine given under heaven to heal their sickness.

The best guide of the blind, the surest light of them that are in darkness, the most perfect instructor of the foolish, is faith. But it must be such a faith as is "mighty through God, to the pulling down of strongholds"—to the overturning all the prejudices of corrupt reason, all the false maxims revered among men, all evil customs and habits, all that "wisdom of the world which is foolishness with God"; as "casteth down imaginations," reasonings, "and every high thing that exalteth itself against the knowledge of God, and bringeth into captivity every thought to the obedience of Christ."

"All things are possible to him that thus believeth." "The eyes of his understanding being enlightened," he sees what is his calling: even to glorify God, who hath bought him with so high a price, in his body and in his spirit, which now are God's by redemption, as well as by creation. He feels what is "the exceeding greatness of His power," who, as He raised up Christ from the dead, so is able to quicken us, dead in sin, "by His Spirit which dwelleth in us." "This is the victory which overcometh the world, even our faith"; that faith, which is not only an unshaken assent to all that God hath revealed in Scripture—and in particular to those important truths. "Jesus Christ came into the world to save sinners." "He bare our sins in His own body on the tree." "He is the propitiation for our sins, and not for ours only, but also for the sins of the whole world,"—but likewise the revelation of Christ in our hearts: a divine evidence or conviction of His love. His free, unmerited love to me a sinner: a sure confidence in His pardoning mercy, wrought in us by the Holy Ghost: a confidence, whereby every true believer is enabled to bear witness, "I know that my Redeemer liveth," that I have an "Advocate with Father," and that "Jesus Christ the righteous" is my Lord, and "the propitiation for my sins"—I know He hath "loved me, and given Himself for me"—He hath reconciled me, even me, to God: and I "have redemption through His blood, even the forgiveness of sins."

Such a faith as this cannot fail to show evidently the power of Him that inspires it, by delivering His children from the yoke of sin, and "purging their consciences from dead works": by strengthening them so, that they are no longer constrained to obey sin in the desires thereof: but instead of "yielding their members unto it, as instruments of unrighteousness," they now "yield themselves" entirely "unto God, as those that are alive from the dead."

Those who are thus by faith born of God have also strong consolation through hope. This is the next thing which the circumcision of the heart implies; even the testimony of their own spirit with the Spirit which witnesses in their hearts that they are the children of God. Indeed it is the same Spirit who works in them that clear and cheerful confidence that their heart is upright toward God; that good assurance, that they now do, through His grace, the things which are acceptable in His sight; that they are now in the path which leadeth to life, and shall, by the mercy of God, endure therein to the end. It is He who giveth them a lively expectation of receiving all good things at God's hand; a joyous prospect of that crown of glory which is reserved in heaven for them. By this anchor a Christian is kept steady in the midst of the waves of this troublesome world, and preserved from striking upon either of those fatal rocks,—presumption or despair. He is neither discouraged by the misconceived severity of his Lord, nor does he "despise the riches of His goodness." He neither apprehends the difficulties of the race set before him to be greater than he has strength to conquer, nor expects them to be so little as to yield in the conquest till he has put forth all his strength. The experience he already has in the Christian warfare, as it assured him his "labor is not in vain," if whatever his hand findeth to do, he doeth it with his might"; so it forbids his entertaining so vain a thought as that he can otherwise gain any advantage; as that any virtue can be shown, any praise attained, by faint hearts and feeble hands; or, indeed, by any but those who pursue the same course with the great Apostle of the Gentiles; "I" says he, "so run, not as uncertainly; so fight I, not as one that beateth the air: but I keep under my body, and bring it unto subjection, lest, by any means, when I have preached to others, I myself should be castaway."

By the same discipline is every good soldier of Christ to inure himself to endure hardship. Confirmed and strengthened by this, he will be able not only to renounce the works of darkness, but every appetite too, and every affection, which is not subject to the law of God. For "everyone," saith St. John, "who hath this hope, purifieth himself even as He is pure." It is his daily care, by the grace of God in Christ, and through the blood of the covenant, to purge the inmost recesses of his soul from the lusts that before possessed and defiled it: from uncleanness, and envy, and malice, and wrath: from every passion and temper that is after the flesh, that either springs from or cherishes his native corruption: as well knowing, that he whose very body is the temple of God, ought to admit into it nothing common or unclean; and that holiness becometh that house for ever, where the Spirit of holiness vouchsafes to dwell.

Yet lackest thou one thing, whosoever thou art, that to a deep humility, and a steadfast faith, hast joined a lively hope, and thereby in a good measure cleansed thy heart from its inbred pollution. If thou wilt be perfect, add to all these, charity: add love, and thou hast the circumcision of the heart. "Love is the fulfilling of the law, the end of the commandment." Very excellent things are spoken of love; it is the essence, the spirit, the life of all virtue. It is not only the first and great command, but it is all the commandments in one. "Whatsoever things are just, whatsoever things are pure, whatsoever things are amiable," or honorable; "if there be any virtue, if there be any praise," they are all comprised in this one word,—love. In this is perfection, and glory, and happiness. The royal law of heaven and earth is this. "Thou shalt love the Lord thy God with all thy heart, and with all thy soul, and with all thy mind, and with all thy strength."

Not that this forbids us to love anything besides God; it implies that we love our brother also. Nor yet does it forbid us (as some have strangely imagined) to take pleasure in anything but God. To suppose this, is to suppose the Fountain of holiness is directly the author of sin; since He has inseparably annexed pleasure to the use of those creatures which are necessary to sustain the life He has given us. This, therefore, can never be the meaning of His command. What the real sense of it is, both our blessed Lord and His Apostles tell us too frequently, and too plainly, to be misunderstood. They all with one mouth bear witness, that the true meaning of those several declarations, "The Lord thy God is one Lord"; "Thou shalt have no other gods but Me"; "Thou shalt love the Lord thy God with all thy strength"; "Thou shalt cleave unto Him"; "The desire of thy soul shall be to His name," is no other than this: The one perfect God shall be your one ultimate end. One thing shall ye desire for its own sake,—the fruition of Him that is All in all. One happiness shall ye propose to your souls, even as union with Him that made them; the having "fellowship with the Father and the Son": the being joined to the Lord in one Spirit. One design you are to pursue to the end of time,— the enjoyment of God in time and in eternity. Desire other things, so far as they tend to this. Love the creature, as it leads to the Creator. But in every step you take, be this the glorious point that terminates your view. Let every affection, and thought, and word, and work, be subordinate to this. Whatever ye desire or fear, whatever ye seek or shun, whatever ye think, speak or do, be it in order by your happiness in God, the sole End, as well as Source, of your being.

Have no end, no ultimate end, but God. Thus our Lord; "One thing is needful"; and if thine eye be singly fixed on this one thing, "thy whole body shall be full of light." Thus St. Paul: "This one thing I do: I press toward the mark, for the prize of the high calling in Christ Jesus." Thus St. James: "Cleanse your hands, ye sinners: and purify your hearts, ye double-minded." Thus St. John: "Love not the world, neither the things that are in the world. For all that is in the world, the lust of the flesh, the lust of the eye, and the pride of life, is not of the Father, but is of the world." The seeking happiness in what gratifies either the desire of the flesh, by agreeably striking upon the outward senses; the desire of the eye, of the imagination, by its novelty, greatness, or beauty; or the pride of life. Whether by pomp, grandeur, power, or, the usual consequence of them, applause and admiration,—"is not of the Father," cometh not from, neither is approved by, the Father of spirits: "but of the world": it is the distinguishing mark of those who will not have Him to reign over them.

Section 2.

Thus have I particularly inquired, what that circumcision of heart is, which will obtain the praise of God. I am, in the second place, to mention some reflections that naturally arise from such an inquiry, as a plain rule whereby every man may judge of himself, whether he be of the world or of God.

And, first. it is clear from what has been said, that no man has a title to the praise of God, unless his heart is circumcised by humility; unless he is little, and base, and vile in his own eyes; unless he is deeply convinced of that inbred "corruption of his nature," "whereby he is very far gone from original righteousness," being prone to all evil, averse to all good, corrupt and abominable; having a "carnal mind which is enmity against God, and is not subject to the law of God, nor indeed can be";

unless he continually feels in his inmost soul, that without the Spirit of God resting upon him, he can neither think, nor desire, nor speak, nor act anything good, or well-pleasing in His sight.

No man, I say, has a title to the praise of God, till he feels his want of God; not indeed, till he seeketh that "honour which cometh of God" only; and neither desires nor pursues that which cometh of man, unless so far only as it tends to this.

Another truth, which naturally follows from what has been said, is, that none shall obtain the honor that cometh of God, unless his heart be circumcised by faith: even a "faith of the operation of God"; unless, refusing to be any longer led by his senses, appetites, or passions, or even by that blind leader of the blind, so idolized by the world, natural reason, he lives and walks by faith: directs every step, as "seeing Him that is invisible": "looks not at the things that are seen, which are temporal, but at the things that are not seen, which are eternal"; and governs all his desires, designs, and thoughts, all his actions and conversations, as one who is entered in within the veil, where Jesus sits at the right hand of God.

It were to be wished, that they were better acquainted with this who employ much of their time and pains in laying another foundation: in grounding religion on the eternal *fitness* of things, on the intrinsic *excellence* of virtue, and the *beauty* of actions flowing from it: on the *reasons*, as they term them, of good and evil, and the *relations*, of beings to each other. Either these accounts of the grounds of Christian duty coincide with the scriptural, or not. If they do, why are well-meaning men perplexed, and drawn from the weightier matters of the law, by a cloud of terms, whereby the easiest truths are explained into obscurity? If they are not, then it behoves them to consider who is the author of this new doctrine; whether he is likely to be an angel from heaven, who preacheth another gospel than that of Christ Jesus; though, if he were, God, not we, hath pronounced his sentence: "Let him be accursed."

Our gospel, as it knows no other foundation of good works than faith, or of faith than Christ, so it clearly informs us, we are not His disciples while we either deny Him to be the Author, or His Spirit to be the Inspirer and Perfecter, both of our faith and works. "If any man have not the Spirit of Christ, he is none of his." He alone can quicken those who are dead unto God, can breathe into them the breath of Christian life, and so prevent, accompany, and follow them with His grace, as to bring their good desires to good effect. And, "as many as are thus led by the Spirit of God, they are the sons of God." This is God's short and plain account of true religion and virtue; and "other foundation can no man lay."

From what has been said, we may, thirdly, learn, that none is truly "led by the Spirit," unless that "Spirit bear witness with his spirit, that he is a child of God"; unless he see the prize and the crown before him, and "rejoice in hope of the glory of God." So greatly have they erred who have taught that in serving God, we ought not to have a view to our own happiness! Nay, but we often and expressly taught of God, to have "respect unto the recompense of reward"; to balance the toil with the "joy set before us," these "light afflictions" with that "exceeding weight of glory." Yea, we are "aliens to the covenant of promise," we are "without God in the world," until God, "of His abundant mercy, hath begotten us again unto a living hope of the inheritance incorruptible, undefiled, and that fadeth not away."

But if these things are so, it is high time for those persons to deal faithfully with their own souls, who are so far from finding in themselves this joyful assurance that they fulfill the terms, and shall obtain the promises, of that covenant, as to quarrel with the covenant itself, and blaspheme the terms of it: to complain, they are too severe; and that no man ever did or shall live up to them. What is this but to reproach God, as if He were an hard Master, requiring of His servants more than He enables them to perform?—as if He had mocked the helpless works of His hands, by binding them to impossibilities; by commanding them to overcome, where neither their own strength nor His grace was sufficient for them?

These blasphemers might almost persuade those to imagine themselves guiltless, who, in the contrary extreme, hope to fulfill the commands of God without taking any pains at all. Vain hope! that a child of Adam should ever expect to see the kingdom of Christ and of God without striving, without *agonizing*, first "to enter in at the strait gate"; that one who was "conceived and born in sin," and whose "inward parts are very wickedness," should once entertain a thought of being "purified as his Lord is pure," unless he tread in His steps, and "take up his cross daily," unless he "cut off his right hand," and "pluck out the right eye, and cast it from him"; that he should ever dream of shaking off his old opinions, passions, tempers, of being "sanctified throughout in spirit, soul, and body," without a constant and continued course of general self-denial!

What less than this can we possibly infer from the above-cited words of St. Paul, who, living "in infirmities, in reproaches, in necessities, in persecutions, in distresses" for Christ's sake; who, being full of "signs and wonders, and mighty deeds," who, having been "caught up into the third heaven,"—yet reckoned, as a late author strongly expresses it, that all his virtues would be insecure, and even his salvation in danger, without this constant self-denial? So run I, says he, "not as uncertainly; so fight

I, not as one that beateth the air": by which he plainly teaches us, that he who does not thus run, who does not thus deny himself daily, does run uncertainly, and fighteth to as little purpose as he that "beateth the air."

To as little purpose does he talk of "fighting the fight of faith," as vainly hope to attain the crown of incorruption (as we may, lastly, infer from the preceding observations), whose heart is not circumcised by love. Love, cutting off both the lust of the flesh, the lust of the eye, and the pride of life—engaging the whole man, body, soul, and spirit, in the ardent pursuit of that one so essential to a child of God, that without it, whosoever liveth is counteth dead before Him. "Thought I speak with the tongues of men and of angels, and have not love, I am as sounding brass, or a tinkling cymbal. Though I have the gift of prophecy, and understand all mysteries, and all knowledge: and though I have all faith, so as to remove mountains, and have not love, I am nothing." Nay, "though I give all my goods to feed the poor, and my body to be burned, and have not love, it profiteth me nothing."

Here, then, is the sum of the perfect law: this is the true circumcision of the heart. Let the spirit return to God that gave it, with the whole train of its affections. "Unto the place from whence all the rivers came," thither let them flow again. Other sacrifices from us He would not; but the living sacrifice of the heart He hath chosen. Let it be continually offered up to God through Christ, in flames of holy love. And let no creature be suffered to share with Him; for He is a jealous God. His throne will He not divide with another. He will reign without a rival. Be no design, no desire admitted there, but what has Him for its ultimate object. This is the way wherein those children of God once walked, who, being dead, still speak to us: "Desire not to live but to praise His name: let all your thoughts, words, and works tend to His glory. Set your heart firm on Him, and on other things only as they are in and from Him. Let your soul be filled with so entire a love of Him that you may love nothing but for His sake." "Have a pure intention of heart, a steadfast regard to His glory in all your actions," "Fix your eye upon the blessed hope of your calling, and make all the things of the world minister unto it." For then, and not till then, is that "mind in us which was also in Christ Jesus"; when, in every motion of our heart, in every word of our tongue, in every work of our hands, we "pursue nothing but in relation to Him, and in subordination to His pleasure": when we, too, neither think, nor speak, nor act, to fulfill our "own will, but the will of Him that sent us"; when, whether we "eat or drink, or whatever we do, we do all to the glory of God."

4. The Repentance of Believers

It is generally supposed, that repentance and faith are only the gate of religion; that they are necessary only at the beginning of our Christian course, when we are setting out in the way to the kingdom. And this may seem to be confirmed by the great Apostle, where, exhorting the Hebrew Christians to "go on to perfection," he teaches them to *leave* these first "principles of the doctrine of Christ"; "not laying again the foundation of repentance from dead works, and of faith towards God"; which must at least mean, that they should comparatively leave these, that at first took up all their thoughts, in order to "press forward toward the prize of the high calling of God in Christ Jesus."

And this is undoubtedly true, that there is a repentance and a faith, which are, more especially, necessary at the beginning: a repentance, which is a conviction of our utter sinfulness, and guiltiness, and helplessness; and which precedes our receiving that kingdom of God, which, our Lord observes , is "within us"; and a faith, whereby we receive that kingdom, even "righteousness, and peace, and joy in the Holy Ghost."

But, notwithstanding this, there is also a repentance and a faith (taking the words in another sense, a sense not quite the same, nor yet entirely different) which are requisite after we have "believed the gospel"; yea, and in every subsequent stage of our Christian course, or we cannot "run the race which is set before us." And this repentance and faith are as full as necessary, in order to our *continuance* and *growth* in grace, as the former faith and repentance were, in order to our entering into the kingdom of God.

But in what sense are we to repent and believe, after we are justified? This is an important question, and worthy of being considered with the utmost attention.

And, first, in what sense are we to repent?

Repentance frequently means an inward change, a change of mind from sin to holiness. But we now speak of it in a quite different sense, as it is one kind of self-knowledge, and knowing ourselves sinners, yea, guilty, helpless sinners, even though we know we are children of God.

Indeed when we first know this; when we first find redemption in the blood of Jesus; when the love of God is first shed abroad in our hearts, and His kingdom set up therein; it is natural to suppose that we are no longer sinners, that all our sins are not only covered but destroyed.

As we do not then feel any evil in our hearts, we readily imagine none is there. Nay, some well-meaning men have imagined this not only at that time, but ever after; having persuaded themselves, that when they were justified, they were entirely sanctified: yea, they have laid it down as a general rule, in spite of Scripture, reason, and experience. These sincerely believe, and earnestly maintain, that all sin is destroyed when we are justified; and that there is no sin in the heart of a believer; but that it is altogether clean from that moment. But though we readily acknowledge, "he that believeth is born of God," and "he that is born of God doth not commit sin"; yet we cannot allow that he does not feel it within: it does not reign, but it does remain. And a conviction of the sin which *remains* in our heart, is one great branch of the repentance we are now speaking of.

For it is seldom long before he who imagined all sin was gone, feels there is still pride in his heart. He is convinced both that in many respects he has thought of himself more highly than he ought to think, and that he has taken to himself the praise of something he had received, and gloried in it as though he had not received it; and yet he knows he is in the favor of God. He cannot, and ought not to, "cast away his confidence." "The Spirit" still "witnesses with" his "spirit, that he is a child of God."

Nor is it long before he feels self-will in his heart; even a will contrary to the will of God. A will every man must inevitably have, as long as he has an understanding. This is an essential part of human nature, indeed of the nature of every intelligent being. Our blessed Lord Himself had a will as a man; otherwise He had not been a man. But His human will was invariably subject to the will of His Father. At all times, and on all occasions, even in the deepest affliction. He could say, "Not as I will, but as Thou wilt." But this is not the case at all times, even with a true believer in Christ. He frequently finds his will more or less exalting itself against the will of God. He wills something, because it is pleasing to nature, which is not pleasing to God: and he nills (is averse from) something, because it is painful to nature, which is the will of God concerning him. Indeed, suppose he continues in the faith, he fights against it with all his might: but his very thing implies that it really exists, and that he is conscious of it.

Now self-will, as well as pride, is a species of *idolatry*; and both are directly contrary to the love of God. The same observation may be made concerning *the love of the world*. But this likewise even true believers are liable to feel in themselves: and everyone of them does feel it, more or less, sooner or later, in one branch or another. It is true, when he first "passes from death unto life," he desires nothing more but God, He can truly say, "All my desire is unto Thee, and unto the remembrance of Thy name": "Whom have I in heaven but Thee? and there is none upon earth that I desire beside Thee." But it is not so always. In process of time he will feel again, though perhaps only for a few moments, either "the desire of the flesh," or "the desire of the eye," or "the pride of life". Nay, if he does not continually watch and pray, he may find *lust* reviving; yea, and thrusting sore at him that he may fall, till he has scarce any strength left in him. He may feel the assaults of *inordinate affection*; yea, a strong propensity to "love the creature more than the Creator": whether it be a child, a parent, a husband, or wife, or "the friend that is as his own soul." He may feel, in a thousand various ways, a desire of earthly things or pleasures. In the same proportion he will forget God, not seeking his happiness in Him, and consequently being a "lover of pleasure more than a lover of God."

If he does not keep himself every moment, he will again feel *the desire of the eye*; the desire of gratifying his imagination with something great, or beautiful, or uncommon. In how many ways does this desire assault the soul! Perhaps with regard to the poorest trifles, such as dress, or furniture: things never designed to satisfy the appetite of an immortal spirit. Yet, how natural is it for us, even after we have "tasted of the powers of the world to come," to sink again into these foolish, low desires of things that perish in the using! How hard is it, even for those who know in whom they have believed, to conquer but one branch of the desire of the eye, curiosity; constantly to trample it under their feet; to desire nothing merely because it is new!

And how hard is it even for the children of God wholly to conquer the *pride of life*! St. John seems to mean by this nearly the same with what the world terms "the sense of honor." This is no other than a desire of, and delight in, "the honor that cometh of men": a desire and love of praise: and, which is always joined with it, a proportionable *fear of dispraise*. Nearly allied to this is evil shame; the being ashamed of that wherein we ought to glory. And this is seldom divided from the *fear of man*, which brings a thousand snares upon the soul. Now where is he, even among those that seem strong in the faith, who does not find in himself a degree of all these evil tempers? So that even these are but in part "crucified to the world'; for the evil root still remains in their heart.

And do we not feel other tempers, which are as contrary to the love of our neighbor as these are to the love of God? The love of our neighbor "thinketh no evil." Do not we find anything of the kind? Do we never find any *jealousies*, any evil *surmising*, any groundless or unreasonable suspicions? He that is clear in these respects, let him cast the first stone at his neighbor. Who does not sometimes feel other tempers or inward motions, which he knows are contrary to brotherly love? If nothing of *malice*, *hatred*, or *bitterness*, is there no touch of *envy*: particularly toward those who enjoy some real or supposed good, which we desire, but cannot attain? Do we never find any degree of *resentment*, when we are injured or affronted: especially by those whom we peculiarly loved, and whom we had most labored to help or oblige? Does injustice or ingratitude never excite in us any desire of *revenge*? any desire of returning evil for evil, instead of "overcoming evil with good?" This also shows, how much is still in our heart, which is contrary to the love of our neighbor.

Covetousness, in every kind and degree, is certainly as contrary to this as to the love of God; whether φιλαργυρια, the love of money, which is too frequently "the root of all evil": πλεονεξια literally, a desire of *having more*, or increasing in substance. And how few, even of the real children of God, are entirely free from both! Indeed one great man, Martin Luther, used to say, he "never had any covetousness in him"(not only in his converted state, but) "ever since he was born." But, if so, I would scruple to say, he was the only man born of a woman (except Him that was God as well as man), who had not, who was born without it. Nay, I believe never was anyone born of God, that lived any considerable time after, who did not feel more or less of it many times, especially in the latter sense. We may therefore set it down as an undoubted truth, that covetousness, together with pride, and self-will, and anger, remain in the hearts even of them that are justified.

It is their experiencing this, which has inclined so many serious persons to understand the latter part of the seventh chapter to the Romans, not of them that are "under the law," that are convinced of sin, which is undoubtedly the meaning of the Apostle, but of them that are "under grace"; that are "justified freely through the redemption that is in Christ." And it is most certain, they are thus far right,—there does still *remain*, even in them that are justified, a *mind* which is in some measure *carnal* (so the Apostle tells even the believers at Corinth, "Ye are carnal") an *heart bent to backsliding*, still ever ready to "depart from the living God"; a propensity to pride, self-will, anger, revenge, love of the world, yea, and all evil: a root of bitterness, which, if the restraint were taken off for a moment, would instantly spring yea, such a depth of corruption, as, without clear light from God, we cannot possibly conceive. And a conviction of all this sin *remaining* in *their hearts* is the repentance which belongs to them that are justified,

But we should likewise be convinced, that as sin remains in our hearts, so it cleaves to all our words and actions. Indeed it is to be feared, that many of our words are more than mixed with sin; that they are sinful for such undoubtedly is all *uncharitable conversation;* all which does not spring from brotherly love; all which does not agree with that golden rule. "What ye would that others should do to you, even so do unto them, "Of this kind is all backbiting, all tale-bearing, all whispering, all evil speaking, that is, repeating the faults of absent persons; for none would have others repeat his faults when he is absent. Now how few are there, even among believers, who are in no degree guilty of who steadily observe the good old rule, "Of the dead and the absent, nothing but good." And suppose they do, do they likewise abstain from *unprofitable conversation?* Yet all this is unquestionably sinful, and "grieves the Holy Spirit yea, and for every idle word that men shall speak, they shall give an account in the Day of Judgment."

But let it be supposed, that they continually "watch and pray," and so do "not enter into" this "temptation"; that they constantly set a watch before their mouth, and keep the door of their lips; suppose they exercise themselves herein, that *all* their "conversation may be in grace, seasoned with salt, and meet to minister grace to the hearers": yet do they not daily slide into useless discourse, not withstanding all their caution? And even when they endeavor to speak for God, are their words pure, free from unholy mixtures? Do they find nothing wrong in their very *intention*? Do they speak merely to please God, and not partly to please themselves? Is it wholly to do the will of God, and not their own will also? Or, if they being with a single eye, do they go on "looking unto Jesus," and talking with Him all the time they are talking with their neighbor? When they are reproving sin, do they feel no anger or unkind temper to the sinner? When they are instructing the ignorant, do they not find any pride, any self-preference? When they are comforting the afflicted, or provoking one another to love and to good works, do they never perceive any inward self-commendation: "*Now you have spoke well*"? Or any vanity—a desire that others should think so, and esteem them on the account? In some or all of these respects, how much sin cleaves to the best conversation even of believers! The *conviction* of which is another branch of the repentance which belongs to them that are justified.

And how much sin, if their conscience is thoroughly awake, may they find cleaving to *their actions* also! Nay, are there not many of these, which, though they are such as the world would not condemn, yet cannot be commended, no, nor excused, if we judge by the Word of God? Are there not many of their actions which, they themselves know, are not to the glory of God? many, wherein they did not even aim at this: which were not undertaken with an eye to God? And of those that were, are there not many, wherein their eye is not singly fixed on God—wherein they are doing their own will, at least as much as His: and seeking to please themselves as much, if not more, than to please God? And while they are endeavoring to do good to their neighbor, do they not feel wrong tempers of various kinds? Hence their good actions, so called, are far from being strictly such: being polluted with such a mixture of evil: such are their works of *mercy*. And is there not the same mixture: in their works of *piety*? While they are hearing the word, which is able to save their souls, do they not frequently find such thoughts as make them afraid lest it should turn to their condemnation, rather than their salvation? Is it not often the same case, while they are endeavoring to offer up their prayers to God, whether in public or private? Nay, while they are engaged in the most solemn service, even while they are at the table of the Lord, what manner of thoughts arise in them! Are not their hearts sometimes wandering to the ends of the earth; sometimes filled with such imaginations, as make them fear lest all their sacrifice should be an abomination to the Lord? So that they are now more ashamed of their best duties, than they were once of their worst sins.

Again: how many *sins of omission* are they chargeable with! We know the words of the Apostle: "To him that knoweth to do good, and doeth it not, to him it is sin." But do they not know a thousand instances, wherein they might have done good, to enemies, to strangers, to their brethren, either with regard to their bodies or their souls, and they did it not? How many omissions have they been guilty of, in their duty toward God! How many opportunities of communicating, of hearing His word, of public or private prayer, have they neglected! So great reason had even that holy man, Archbishop Usher, after all his labors for God, to cry out almost with his dying breath, "Lord, forgive me my sins of omission!"

But besides these outward omissions, may they not find in themselves *inward defects* without number? defects of every kind: they have not the love, the fear, the confidence they ought to have, toward God. They have not the love which is due to their neighbor, to every child of man; no, nor even that which is due to their brethren, to every child of God, whether those that are at a distance from them, or those with whom they are immediately connected. They have no holy temper in the degree they ought: they are defective in everything—in a deep consciousness of which they are ready to cry out, with M. De Renty, "I am a ground all overrun with thorns"; or, with Job, "I am vile: I abhor myself, and repent as in dust and ashes."

A conviction of their *guiltiness* is another branch of that repentance which belongs to the children of God. But this is cautiously to be understood, and in a peculiar sense. For it is certain, "there is no condemnation to them that are in Christ Jesus," that believe in Him, and, in the power of that "walk not after the flesh, but after the Spirit." Yet can they no more bear the *strict justice* of God now, than before they believed. This pronounces them to be still *worthy of death*, on all the preceding accounts. And it would absolutely condemn them thereto, were it not for the atoning blood. Therefore they are thoroughly convinced, that they still *deserve* punishment, although it is hereby turned aside from them. But here there are extremes on one hand and on the other, and few steer clear of them. Most men strike on one or the other, either thinking themselves condemned when they are not, or thinking they *deserve* to be acquitted. Nay the truth lies between: they still *deserve*, strictly speaking only the damnation of hell. But what they deserve docs not come upon them, because they "have an Advocate with the Father." His life, and death, and intercession still interpose between them and condemnation.

A conviction of their *utter helplessness* is yet another branch of this repentance. I mean hereby two things: first, that they are no more able now of *themselves* to think one good thought, to form one good desire, to speak one good word, or do one good work, than before they were justified; that they have still no kind or degree of strength of *their own*; no power either to do good, or resist evil; no ability to conquer or even withstand the world, the devil, or their own evil nature. They can, it is certain, do all these things: but it is not by their own strength. They have power to overcome all these enemies: for "sin hath no more dominion over them"; but it is not from nature, either in whole or in part; it is the *mere* gift of God: not is it given all at once, as if they had a stock laid up for many years: but from moment to moment.

By this helplessness I mean, secondly, an absolute inability to deliver ourselves from that guiltiness or desert of punishment whereof we are still conscious; yea, and an inability to remove, by all the grace we have (to say nothing of our natural powers), either the pride, self-will, love of the world, anger, and general proneness to depart from God, which we experimentally know to *remain* in the heart, even of them that are regenerate; or the evil which, in spite of all our endeavors, cleaves to all our words and actions. Add to this, an utter inability wholly to avoid uncharitable, and, much more, unprofitable, conversation: and an inability to avoid sins of omission, or to supply the numberless defects we are convinced of; especially the want of love, and other right tempers both to God and man.

If any man is not satisfied of this, if any believes that whoever is justified is able to remove these sins out of his heart and life, let him make the experiment. Let him try whether, by the grace he has already received, he can expel pride, self-will, or inbred sin in general. Let him try whether he can cleanse his words and actions from all mixture of evil: whether he can avoid all uncharitable and unprofitable conversation, with all the sins of omission: and, lastly, whether he can supply the numberless defects which he still finds in himself. Let him not be discouraged by one or two experiments, but repeat the trial again and again: and the longer he tries, the more deeply will he be convinced of his utter helplessness in all these respects.

Indeed this is so evident a truth, that well-nigh all the children of God, scattered abroad, however they differ in other points, yet generally agree in this that although we may, "by the Spirit, mortify the deeds of the body," resist and conquer both outward and inward sin: although we may *weaken* our enemies day by day: yet we cannot *drive them out*. By all the grace which is given at justification we cannot extirpate them. Though we watch and pray ever so much, we cannot wholly cleanse either our hearts or hands. Most sure we cannot, till it shall please our Lord to speak to our hearts again: to speak the second tune, "Be clean"; and then only the leprosy is cleansed. Then only, the evil root, the carnal mind, is destroyed; and inbred sin subsists no more. But if there be no such second change, if there be no instantaneous deliverance after justification, if there be *none but* a gradual work of God (that there is a gradual work none denies), then we must be content, as well as we can, to remain full of sin till death: and, if so, we must remain guilty till death, continually *deserving* punishment. For it is impossible the guilt, or desert of punishment, should be removed from us, as long as all this sin remains in our heart, and cleaves to our words and actions. Nay, in rigorous justice, all we think, and speak, and act, continually increases it.

In this sense we are to *repent*, after we are justified. And till we do so, we can go no farther. For, till we are sensible of our disease, it admits of no cure. But, supposing we do thus repent, then are we called to "believe the gospel."

And this also is to be understood in a peculiar sense, different from that wherein we believed in order to justification. Believe the glad tidings of great salvation, which God hath prepared for all people. Believe that He who is "the brightness of His Father's glory, the express image of His person," is "able to save unto the uttermost all that come unto God through Him." He is able to save you from all the sin that still remains in your heart. He is able to save you from all the sin that cleaves to all your words and actions. He is able to save you from sins of omission, and to supply whatever is wanting in you. It is true, this is impossible with man: but with God-Man all things are possible. For what can be too hard for Him who hath "all power in heaven and earth"? Indeed, His bare power to do this is not a sufficient foundation for our faith that He will do it, that He will thus exert His power, unless He hath promised it. But this He has done: He has promised it over and over in the strongest terms. He has given us these "exceeding great and precious promises," both in the Old and the New Testaments. So we read in the law, in the most ancient part of the oracles of God. "The Lord thy God will circumcise thy heart, and the heart of thy seed, to love the Lord thy God with all thy heart, and with all thy soul" (Deuteronomy 30:6). So in the Psalms. "He shall redeem Israel," the Israel of God, "from all his sins." So in the Prophet, "Then will I sprinkle clean water upon you, and ye shall be clean: from all your filthiness, and from all your idols, will I cleanse you. And I will put My Spirit within you, and ye shall keep My judgments, and do them. I will also save you from all your uncleanness's (Ezekiel 36:25, &c.). So likewise in the New Testament, "Blessed be the Lord God of Israel: for He hath visited and redeemed His people, and hath raised up an horn of salvation for us…to perform the oath which He swear to our father Abraham, that He would grant unto us, that we being delivered out of the hands of our enemies should serve Him without fear, in holiness and righteousness before Him, all the days of our life"(Luke 1:68, &c.).

You have therefore good reason to believe, He is not only able, but willing to do this: to cleanse you from all your filthiness of flesh and spirit; to "save you from all your uncleanness." This is the thing which you now long for: this is the faith which you now particularly need, namely, that the Great Physician, the Lover of my soul, is willing to make me clean, But is He willing to do this to-morrow, or to-day? Let Him answer for Himself: "To-day, if ye will hear" My "voice, harden not your hearts." If you put it off till tomorrow, you harden your hearts; you refuse to hear His voice, Believe, therefore, that He is willing to save you *to-day*, He is willing to save you *now*. "Behold, now is the accepted time." He now saith, "Be thou clean!" Only believe, and you also will immediately find, "all things are possible to him that believeth."

Continue to believe in Him that loved thee, and gave Himself for thee; that bore all thy sins in His own body on the tree: and He saves thee from all condemnation, by His blood continually applied. Thus it is that we continue in a justified state, And when we go on "from faith to faith," when we have faith to be cleansed from indwelling sin, to be saved from all our un-cleanesses, we are likewise saved from all that *guilt*, that *desert* of punishment, which we felt before. So that then we may say, not only:

> *Every moment, Lord, I want*
> *The merit of Thy death!*

but, likewise, in the full assurance of faith,

> *Every moment, Lord, I have*
> *the merit of Thy death!*

For, by that in His life, death, and intercession for us, renewed from moment to moment, we are every whit clean, and there is not only now no condemnation for us, but no such desert of punishment as was before, the Lord cleansing both our hearts and lives.

By the same faith we feel the power of Christ every moment resting upon us, whereby alone we are what we are: whereby we are enabled to continue in spiritual life, and without which, notwithstanding all our present holiness, we should be devils the next moment. But as long as we retain our faith in Him, we "draw water out of the wells of salvation." Leaning on our Beloved, even Christ in us the hope of glory, who dwelled in our hearts by faith, who likewise is ever interceding for us at the right hand of God. We receive heir from Him, to think, and speak, and act, what is acceptable in His sight. Thus does He "prevent" them that believe, in all their "doings, and further them with His continual help": so that all their designs, conversations, and actions are "begun, continued, and ended in Him." Thus doth He "cleanse the thoughts or their hearts, by the inspiration of His Holy Spirit, that they may perfectly love Him, and worthily magnify His holy name."

Thus it is, that in the children of God, repentance and faith exactly answer each other. By repentance we feel the sin remaining in our hearts, and cleaving to our words and actions: by faith, we receive the power of God in Christ, purifying our hearts, and cleansing our hands. By repentance, we are still sensible that we deserve punishment for all our tempers, and words, and actions; by faith, we are conscious that our Advocate with the Father is continually pleading for us, and thereby continually turning aside all condemnation and punishment from us. By repentance we have an abiding conviction that there is no help in us: by faith we receive not only mercy, "but grace to help in" *every* "time of need." Repentance disclaims the very possibility of any other help: faith accepts all the help we stand in need of, from Him that hath all power in heaven and earth. Repentance says, "Without Him I can do nothing": faith says, "I can do all things through Christ strengthening me." Through Him "I cannot only overcome, but expel, all the enemies of my soul. Through Him I can "love the Lord my God with all my heart, mind, soul, and strength"; yea, and "walk in holiness and righteousness before Him all the days of my life."

From what has been said we may easily learn the mischievousness of that opinion—that we are *wholly* sanctified when we are justified: that our hearts are then cleansed from all sin. It is true, we are then delivered, as was observed before, from the dominion of outward sin: and, at the same time, the power of inward sin is so broken, that we need no longer follow, or be led by it: but it is by no means true, that inward sin is then totally destroyed: that the root of pride, self-will, anger, love of the world, is then taken out of the heart: or that the carnal mind, the heart bent to backsliding, are entirely extirpated. And to suppose the contrary is not, as some may think, an innocent harmless mistake. No: it does immense harm: it entirely blocks up the way to any farther change: for it is manifest, "they that are whole need not a physician, but they that are sick." *If*, therefore, we think we are quite made whole already, there is no room to seek any further healing. On this supposition it is absurd to expect a father deliverance from sin, whether gradual or instantaneous.

On the contrary, a deep conviction that we are not yet whole: that our hearts are not fully purified: that there is yet in us a "carnal mind," which is still in its nature "enmity against God": that a whole body of sin remains in our heart, weakened indeed, but not destroyed: shows, beyond all possibility of doubt, the absolute necessity of a father change. We allow, that at the very moment of justification, we are *born again*: in that instant we experience that inward change from "darkness into marvelous light": from the image of the brute and the devil, into the image of God; from the earthly, sensual, devilish mind, to the mind which was in Christ Jesus. But are we then *entirely* changed? Are we *wholly* transformed into the image of Him that created us? Far from it: we still retain a depth of sin; and it is the consciousness of this, which constrains us to groan. for a full deliverance, to Him that is mighty to save. Hence it is, that those believers who are not convinced of the deep corruption of their hearts, or but slightly, and, as it were, notionally convinced, have little concern about entire sanctification. They may possibly hold the opinion that such a thing is to be; either at death, or some time they know not when, before it. But they have no great uneasiness for the want of it, and no great hunger or thirst after it. They cannot, until they know themselves better, until they repent in the sense above described, until God unveils the inbred monster's face, and shows them the real state of their souls. Then only, when they feel the burden, will they groan for deliverance from it. Then, and not till then, will they cry out, in the agony of their soul,

> Break off the yoke of inbred sin,
> And full set my spirit free!

> I cannot rest till pure within,
> *Till I am wholly lost in Thee.*

We may learn from hence, secondly, that a deep conviction of our demerit, after we are accepted (which in one sense may be termed guilt), is absolutely necessary, in order to our seeing the true value of the atoning blood; in order to our feeling that we need this as much, after we are justified, as ever we did before. Without this conviction, we cannot but account the blood of the covenant as a common thing, something of which we have not now any great need, seeing all our past sins are blotted out. Yea, but if both our hearts and lives are thus unclean, it is a kind of guilt which we are contracting every moment, and which, of consequence, would every moment expose us to fresh condemnation, but that:

> *He ever lives above,*
> For us to intercede,
> His all atoning love,
> *His precious blood, to plead.*

It is this repentance, and the faith intimately connected with it, which are expressed in those strong lines:

> *I sin in every breath I draw,*
> Nor do Thy will, nor keep Thy law
> On earth, as angels do above;
> But still the fountain open stands,
> Washes my feet, my heart, my hands,
> *Till I am perfected in love.*

We may observe, thirdly, a deep conviction of our utter *helplessness*, of our total inability to retain anything we have received, much more to deliver ourselves from the world of iniquity remaining both in our hearts and lives, teaches us truly to live upon Christ by faith, not only as our Priest, but as our King. Hereby we are brought to "magnify Him," indeed: to "give Him all the glory of His grace"; to "make Him a whole Christ, an entire Savior; and truly to set the crown upon His head." These excellent words, as they have frequently been used, have little or no meaning; but they are fulfilled in a strong and deep sense, when we thus, as it were, go out of ourselves, in order to be swallowed up in Him; when we sink into nothing, that He may be all in all. Then, His almighty grace having abolished "every high thing which exalted itself against Him; every temper, and thought, and word, and work is brought to the obedience of Christ."

5. Notes

1   John Wesley, written in his *Journal*, Tuesday, January 24, 1738, *The Heart of John Wesley's Journal* (New Canaan, CT: Keats Publishing, 1979), p. 29.

2   John Wesley, *Journal*, May 24, 1738, *Ibid*, p. 43.

3   John Wesley, *Journal*, April 2, 1739, *Ibid*, p. 47.

4   John Wesley, *Journal*, January 17, 1790, *Ibid*, p. 481.

5   Letter to Thomas Church, written June 17, 1746, in *The Letters of the Reverend John Wesley, A.M.*, ed. By John Telford, II (London: The Epworth Press, 1931), p. 268.

6   Dr. J.A. Beet, *London Quarterly Review*, January, 1920, as quoted in Edward H. Sugden, *Wesley's Standard Sermons*, II (London: The Epworth Press, 1968), p. 443).

7   Letter to John Newton, Written at Londonberry, May 14, 1765, in Telford, *Letters,* IV, p. 299. An entry in his *Journal,* September 1, 1778, also is significant. He says: "I know not that I can write a better sermon on the circumcision of the heart than I did five and forty years ago, than I did then, and may know a little more History or Natural Philosophy than I did; but I am not sensible that this has made any essential addition to my knowledge in Divinity. Forty years ago I knew and preached every Christian doctrine which I preach now," in *The Works of John Wesley,* 1872 Edition, IV, reproduction (Grand Rapids: Zondervan Publishing House), p. 1350. It is interesting that the later reference to forty years, as distinguished from the former mention of forty-five years, would go back to 1738, when Wesley personally received by faith the consciousness of a new heart.

8   Sugden, *Wesley's Standard Sermons,* I, op. cit, p. 265.

Is Your Christian Faith Real?

George Whitefield 1714-1770

*With an Introduction
By Timothy K. Beougher*

Abridged version of *Is Your Christian Faith Real?*, Sermons by George Whitefield. Abridged version originally published by the Institute of Evangelism Billy Graham Center, 1999, Wheaton, IL. Reprinted with permission by Timothy K. Beougher. Scripture quotations are taken from the King James Version (KJV), in the Public Domain. Artwork in the Public Domain.

Book Chapters

1. Introduction
   By Timothy K. Beougher 178
2. "The Almost Christian"..182
   I. And, FIRST, I am to Consider What is Meant by an Almost Christian 183
   II. I Proceed to the Second General Thing Proposed; to Consider the Reasons Why so Many are No More than Almost Christians ..186
   III. Proceed We Now to the General Thing Proposed, Namely, to Consider the Folly of Being No More Than an Almost Christian .. 189
3. "Marks of a True Conversion"..192
4. Notes..203

1. Introduction
By Timothy K. Beougher

> "Have we read or heard of any person since the Apostles, who testified the gospel of the grace of God...through so large a part of the habitable world? Have we read or heard of any person who called so many thousands, so many myriads, of sinners to repentance? Above all, have we read or heard of any who has been a blessed instrument in his [God's] hand of bringing so many sinners from 'darkness to light, and from the power of Satan unto God?'"
>
> —excerpted from John Wesley's funeral sermon for George Whitefield, November 18, 1770

The early life of George Whitefield (pronounced WIT-field) betrayed nothing of his future worldwide impact for the cause of Christ. The son of an innkeeper, Whitefield was born in Gloucester, England, on December 16, 1714. His father died when he was young and he and six siblings were raised by their mother at the Bell Inn.

He was able to attend Oxford as a "servitor," one who earned tuition by serving wealthier students. It was there he met John and Charles Wesley and became a part of the "Holy Club," a group devoted to the strict practice of religious duties. Whitefield experienced the joy of a new birth in Christ while at Oxford.

Following his ordination as a preaching deacon in the Church of England in 1737, Whitefield began a dynamic preaching ministry that emphasized the necessity of the New Birth. When churches began to close their doors to his "enthusiastic" style, he took to the open fields of England to preach to whoever would gather to listen. He said, "I believe

I was never more acceptable to my Master than when I was standing to teach those hearers in the open fields."

In 1739 he wrote of the response of coal miners to the gospel message:

> "Having no righteousness of their own to renounce, they were glad to hear of a Jesus who was a friend to publicans, and came not to call the righteous but sinners to repentance. The first discovery of their being affected was the sight of the white gutters made by their tears, which plentifully fell down their black cheeks as they came out of their coal pits. Hundreds of them were soon brought under deep conviction, which, as the event proved, happily ended in a sound and thorough conversion."

His preaching style was direct and passionate. Benjamin Franklin, who greatly admired Whitefield, once estimated that he could be heard by up to thirty thousand people at one gathering. Franklin was a lifelong friend of Whitefield's and published many of his sermons.

Whitefield's communication skills were truly legendary. Lord Bolingbroke and Lord Chesterfield both proclaimed Whitefield the greatest orator they had ever heard, and David Garrick, the premier British actor of the day, reputedly claimed he would give a hundred guineas if he could just say "oh" like Whitefield.

Whitefield made seven trips to America by sea, no easy voyage in that age. He also traveled more than a dozen times to Scotland, and made trips to Wales, Ireland, Bermuda, and Holland as well.

Whitefield faced opposition from some within the established church, and at times faced mob violence when he preached. On one occasion he remarked, "I was honored with having a few stones, dirt, rotten eggs, and pieces of dead cats thrown at me." Yet he kept on preaching and three hundred souls were "awakened."

Whitefield was a Calvinist in his theology, believing in the doctrines of grace. His ministry is a powerful apologetic against those who argue that Calvinistic theology discourages evangelism. Whitefield maintained that the doctrines of grace were an immense encouragement to him and others for reaching out with the gospel to the unregenerate.

Whitefield was also sensitive to the plight of the destitute. In 1738 he began work on an orphanage in Savannah, Georgia, which he would name Bethesda, meaning "House of Mercy." In the years to come he tirelessly raised funds for its operation.

Whitefield married a widow, Elizabeth James, in 1741. The couple had a son who died in infancy. Elizabeth died shortly before Whitefield embarked on his final voyage to the colonies. Shortly after preaching his last sermon, Whitefield died in 1770 in Newburyport, Massachusetts.

It has been estimated that during his ministry he preached to over ten million people, and that eighty percent of the people in the American colonies heard him preach at least once. The First Great Awakening in the American colonies was sparked in large part by Whitefield's preaching tour of 1739-1740. Though John Wesley is considered the founder of the Methodist movement, Whitefield formed the first Methodist society.

Whitefield preached at least 18,000 times during his ministry in Great Britain and the American Colonies, and if you count informal opportunities, it is probable that he proclaimed God's Word on over 30,000 occasions. While he repeated some of his sermons numerous times, the sheer number of his different messages was staggering. Unfortunately, we do not know exactly how many different sermons he developed, as a lifetime listing of Whitefield's sermons does not exist. Collections of Whitefield's messages available today generally have either fifty-seven sermons (the number found in the first collected edition of Whitefield's works, edited by John Gillies in 1771), or fifty-nine sermons (adding two other messages published in *Select Sermons of George Whitefield*, London: Banner of Truth, 1958).

The title for this booklet, "Is Your Christian Faith Real?" reflects my desire to represent the heart of Whitefield's burden — that people experience the new birth. For this purpose, I have edited and brought together two of his sermons: *"The Almost Christian"* and *"Marks of a True Conversion."* I have italicized the text when Whitefield directly quotes from Scripture as well as when he makes an allusion to a biblical passage.

In these two sermons we can see that George Whitefield clearly realized, as we certainly must today, that all individuals must be "born from above" to experience God's forgiveness and eternal life. It was not to a total pagan that Jesus directed the words "You must be born again," but to Nicodemus, a Jewish Pharisee, who was one of the most religious persons of his day. In his sermons, Whitefield set forth the clear teaching of the New Testament: religion does not save; only a personal relationship with Jesus Christ brings salvation. May all of us who read his sermons understand this central truth.

I would like to thank a former student, Tom Johnston, whose Master's level work at Wheaton Graduate School first encouraged me to read Whitefield's sermons, and a current Ph.D. student, Tim McKnight, whose deep interest in Whitefield's theology and evangelistic ministry has led me to keep material on Whitefield close at hand. Both of you men encourage me with your passion to follow the Scottish theologian James Denney's famous dictum, "If our evangelists were theologians and our theologians evangelists, we would be nearer the ideal church."

You have discovered a wonderful role model in George Whitefield (as you know, he was C. H. Spurgeon's role model also!). May you both, and may all who read this booklet, be encouraged to follow Whitefield's passion and zeal in sharing the glorious gospel of grace.[1]

Timothy K. Beougher
Billy Graham Professor of Evangelism
The Southern Baptist Theological Seminary
Louisville, Kentucky, 1999

2. "The Almost Christian"

"Almost thou persuadest me to be a Christian." —Acts 26:28b

 The chapter, out of which the text is taken, contains an admirable account, which the great St. Paul gave of his wonderful conversion from Judaism to Christianity, when he was called to make his defense before Festus, a Gentile governor, and king Agrippa. Our blessed Lord had long since foretold, that when the Son of man should be lifted up, *"his disciples should be brought before kings and rulers, for his name's sake, for a testimony unto them."* And very good was the design of infinite wisdom in thus ordaining it; for Christianity being, from the beginning, a doctrine of the Cross, the princes and rulers of the earth thought themselves too high to be instructed by such ordinary teachers, or too happy to be disturbed by such unwelcome truths; and therefore would have always continued strangers to Jesus Christ, and him crucified, had not the apostles, by being arraigned before them, gained opportunities of preaching to them *"Jesus and the resurrection."*

 St. Paul knew full well that this was the main reason, why his blessed Master permitted his enemies at this time to arraign him at a public trial; and therefore, in compliance with the divine will, thinks it not sufficient, barely to make his defense, but endeavors at the same time to convert his judges. And this he did with such demonstration of the spirit, and of power, that Festus, unwilling to be convinced by the strongest evidence, cries out with a loud voice, *"Paul, much earning doth make thee mad."* To which the brave apostle (like a true follower of the holy Jesus) meekly replies, *"I am not mad, most noble Festus, but speak forth the words of truth and soberness."* But in all probability, seeing king Agrippa more affected with his discourse, and observing in him an inclination to know the truth, he applies himself more particularly to him *"The king knows of these things, before whom also I speak freely, for I am persuaded that none of these things are hidden from him."* And then, that if possible he might complete his wished-for conversion, he with an inimitable strain of oratory, addresses himself still more closely, *"King Agrippa, believes thou the prophets? I know that thou believe them."* At which the passions of the king began to work so strongly, that he was obliged in open court, to own himself affected by the prisoner's preaching, and ingenuously to cry out, *"Paul, almost thou persuades me to be a Christian."*

Which words, taken with the context, afford us a lively representation of the different reception, which the doctrine of Christ's ministers, who come in the power and spirit of St. Paul, meets with now-a-days in the minds of men. For not-withstanding they, like this great apostle, *"speak forth the words of truth and soberness;"* and with such energy and power, that all their adversaries cannot justly gainsay or resist; yet, too many, with the noble Festus before-mentioned, being like him, either too proud to be taught, or too sensual, too careless, or too worldly-minded to live up to the doctrine, in order to excuse themselves, cry out, that *"much learning, much study, or, what is more unaccountable, much piety, hath made them mad."* And though, blessed be God! All do not thus disbelieve our report; yet amongst those who gladly receive the word, and confess that we speak the words of truth and soberness, there are so few, who arrive at any higher degree of piety than that of Agrippa, or are any farther persuaded than to be almost Christians, that I cannot but think it highly necessary to warn my dear hearers of the danger of such a state. And therefore, from the words of the text, shall endeavor to show these three things:

FIRST, What is meant by an almost-Christian.

SECONDLY, What are the chief reasons, why so many are no more than almost Christians.

THIRDLY, I shall consider the ineffectualness, danger, absurdity, and uneasiness which attends those who are but almost Christians; and then conclude with a general exhortation, to set all upon striving not only to be almost, but altogether Christians.

I. And, FIRST, I am to Consider What is Meant by an Almost Christian

An almost Christian, if we consider him in respect to his duty to God, is one that halts between two opinions; that wavers between Christ and the world; that would reconcile God and Mammon, light and darkness, Christ and Belial. It is true, he has an inclination to religion, but then he is very cautious how he goes too far in it: his false heart is always crying out, "*Spare thyself, do thyself no harm.*" He prays indeed, that "*God's will may be done on earth, as it is in heaven.*" But notwithstanding, he is very partial in his obedience, and fondly hopes that God will not be extreme to mark everything that he willfully does amiss; though an inspired apostle has told him, that "*he who offends in one point is guilty of all.*" But chiefly, he is one that depends much on outward ordinances, and on that account looks upon himself as righteous, and despises others; though at the same time he is as great a stranger to the divine life as any other person whatsoever. In short, he is fond of the form, but never experiences the power of godliness in his heart. He goes on year after year, attending on the means of grace, but then, like Pharaoh's lean cows, he is never the better, but rather the worse for them.

If you consider him in respect to his neighbor, he is one that is strictly just to all but then this does not proceed from any love to God or regard to man, but only through a principle of self-love because he knows dishonesty will spoil his reputation, and consequently hinder his thriving in the world.

He is one that depends much upon being negatively good, and contents himself with the consciousness of having done no one any harm; though he reads in the gospel, that "*the unprofitable servant was cast into outer darkness,*" and the barren fig-tree was cursed and dried up from the roots, not for bearing bad, but no fruit.

He is no enemy to charitable contributions in public, if not too frequently recommended: but then he is unacquainted with the kind offices of visiting the sick and imprisoned, clothing the naked, and relieving the hungry in a private manner. He thinks that these things belong only to the clergy, though his own false heart tells him, that nothing but pride keeps him from exercising these acts of humility; and that Jesus Christ, in the 25th chapter of St. Matthew, condemns persons to everlasting punishment, not merely for being fornicators, drunkards, or extortioners, but for neglecting these charitable offices,

> "When the Son of man shall come in his glory, he shall set the sheep on his right-hand, and the goats on his left. And then shall he say unto them on his left hand, depart from me, ye cursed, into everlasting fire, prepared for the devil and his angels: for I was an hungered, and ye gave me no meat; I was thirsty, and ye gave me no drink. I was a stranger, and ye took me not in; naked, and ye clothed me not, sick and in prison, and ye visited me not. Then shall they also say, Lord, when saw we thee a hungered, or athirst, or a stranger,

or naked, or sick, or in prison, and did not minister unto thee? Then shall he answer them, Verily I say unto you, inasmuch as ye have not done it unto one of the least of these my brethren, ye did it not unto me, and these shall go away into everlasting punishment."

I thought proper to give you this whole passage of scripture at large, because our Savior lays such a particular stress upon it; and yet it is so little regarded, that were we to judge by the practice of Christians, one should be tempted to think there were no such verses in the Bible.

But to proceed in the character of an ALMOST CHRISTIAN: If we consider him in respect of himself, as we said he was strictly honest to his neighbor, so he is likewise strictly sober in himself: but then both his honesty and sobriety proceed from the same principle of a false self-love. It is true, he runs not into the same excess of riot with other men; but then it is not out of obedience to the laws of God, but either because his constitution will not allow intemperance: or rather because he is cautious of forfeiting his reputation, or unfitting himself for temporal business. But though he is so prudent as to avoid intemperance and excess, for the reasons before mentioned; yet he always goes to the extremity of what is lawful. It is true, he is no drunkard: but then he has no CHRISTIAN SELF-DENIAL. He cannot think our Savior to be so austere a Master, as to deny us to indulge ourselves in some particulars: and so by this means he is destitute of a sense of true religion, as much as if he lived in debauchery, or any other crime whatever. As to settling his principles as well as practice, he is guided more by the world, than by the word of God: for his part, he cannot think the way to heaven so narrow as some would make it; and therefore considers not so much what scripture requires, as what such and such a good man does, or what will best suit his own corrupt inclinations. Upon this account, he is not only very cautious himself, but likewise very careful of young converts, whose faces are set heavenward; and therefore is always acting the devil's part, and bidding them spare themselves, though they are doing no more than what the scripture strictly requires them to do. The consequence of which is, that *"he suffers not himself to enter into the kingdom of God, and those that are entering in he hinders."*

Thus lives the almost Christian: not that I can say, I have fully described him to you; but from these outlines and sketches of his character, if your consciences have done their proper office, and made a particular application of what has been said to your own hearts, I cannot but fear that some of you may observe some features in his picture, odious as it is, to near resembling your own; and therefore I cannot but hope, that you will join with the apostle in the words immediately following the text, and wish yourselves "to be not only almost, but altogether Christians."

II. I Proceed to the Second General Thing Proposed; to Consider the Reasons Why so Many are No More than Almost Christians

1. And the first reason I shall mention is, because so many set out with false notions of religion; though they live in a Christian country, yet they know not what Christianity is. This perhaps may be esteemed a hard saying, but experience sadly proves the truth of it; for some place religion in being of this or that communion; more in morality; most in a round of duties, and a model of performances; and few, very few acknowledge it to be, what it really is, a thorough inward change of nature, a divine life, a vital participation of Jesus Christ, an union of the soul with God; which the apostle expresses by saying, *"He that is joined to the Lord is one spirit."* Hence it happens, that so many, even of the most knowing professing believers, when you come to converse with them concerning the essence, the life, the soul of religion, I mean our new birth in Jesus Christ, confess themselves quite ignorant of the matter, and cry out with Nicodemus, *"How can this thing be?"* And no wonder then, that so many are only almost Christians, when so many know not what Christianity is: no marvel, that so many take up with the form, when they are quite strangers to the power of godliness; or content themselves with the shadow, when they know so little about the substance of it. And this is one cause why so many are almost, and so few are altogether Christians.

2. A second reason that may be assigned why so many are no more than almost Christians, is a servile fear of man: multitudes there are and have been, who, though awakened to a sense of the divine life, and have tasted and felt the powers of the world to come; yet out of a base sinful fear of being counted singular, or despised by men, have suffered all those good impressions to wear off It is true, they have some esteem for Jesus Christ; but then, like Nicodemus, they would come to him only by night: they are willing to serve him; but then they would do it secretly, for fear of the Jews they have a mind to see Jesus, but then they cannot come to him because of the crowd, and for fear of being laughed at, and ridiculed by those with whom they used to sit at meat. But well did our Savior prophesy of such persons, *"How can ye love me, who receive honor one of another?"* Alas! have they never read, that *"the friendship of this world is enmity with God;"* and that our Lord himself has threatened, *"Whosoever shall be ashamed of me or of my words, in this wicked and adulterous generation, of him shall the Son of man be ashamed, when he cometh in the glory of his Father and of his holy angels?"* No wonder that so many are no more than almost Christians, since so many *"love the praise of men more than the honor which cometh of God."*

3. A third reason why so many are no more than almost Christians, is a reigning love of money. This was the pitiable case of that presumptuous young man in the gospel, who came running to our blessed Lord, and kneeling before him, inquired *"what he must do to inherit eternal life;"* to whom our blessed Master replied, *"Thou knowest the commandments. Do not kill. Do not commit adultery, Do not steal."* To which the young man replied, *"All these have I kept from my youth."* But when our Lord proceeded to tell him, *"Yet lackest thou one thing: Go sell all that thou hast, and give to the poor, he was grieved at that saying, and went away sorrowful, for he had great possessions!"* Poor youth! He had a good mind to be a Christian, and to inherit eternal life, but thought it too dear, if it could be purchased at no less an expense than of his estate! And thus many, both young and old, now a days, come running to worship our blessed Lord in public, and kneel before him in private, and inquire at his gospel, what they must do to inherit eternal life but when they find they must renounce the self-enjoyment of riches, and forsake all in affection to follow him, they cry, *"The Lord pardon us in this thing! We pray thee, have us excused."*

But is heaven so small a trifle in men's esteem, as not to be worth a little gilded earth? Is eternal life so ordinary a purchase, as not to deserve the temporary renunciation of a few transitory riches? Surely it is. But however inconsistent such a behavior may be, this inordinate love of money is too evidently the common and fatal cause, why so many are no more than almost Christians.

4. Nor is the love of pleasure a less uncommon, or a less fatal cause why so many are no more than almost Christians. Thousands and ten thousands there are, who despise riches, and would willingly be true disciples of Jesus Christ, if parting with their money would make them so; but when they are told that our blessed Lord has said, "Whosoever will come after him must deny himself;" like the pitiable young man before-mentioned, "they go away sorrowful" for they have too great a love for sensual pleasures. They will perhaps send for the ministers of Christ, as Herod did for John, and hear them gladly: but touch them in their Herodias, tell them they must part with such or such a darling pleasure; and with wicked Ahab they cry out, *"Hast thou found us, O our enemy?"* Tell them of the necessity of mortification and self-denial, and it is as difficult for them to hear, as if you was to bid them *"cut off a right-hand, or pluck out a right-eye."*

They cannot think our blessed Lord requires so much at their hands, though an inspired apostle has commanded us to "mortify our members which are upon the earth." And who himself, even after he had converted thousands, and was very near arrived to the end of his race, yet professed that it was his daily practice to *"keep under his body, and bring* it into subjection, lest after he had preached to others, he himself should be a cast-away!"

But some men would be wiser than this great apostle, and chalk out to us what they falsely imagine an easier way to happiness. They would flatter us, we may go to heaven without offering violence to our sensual appetites; and enter into the strait gate without striving against our carnal inclinations. And this is another reason why so many are only almost, and not altogether Christians.

5. The fifth and last reason I shall assign why so many are only almost Christians, is a fickleness and instability of disposition.

It has been, no doubt, a misfortune that many a minister and sincere Christian has met with, to weep and wail over numbers of promising converts, who seemingly began in the Spirit, but after a while fell away, and basely ended in the flesh; and this not for want of right notions in religion, nor out of a servile fear of man, nor from the love of money, or of sensual pleasure, but through an instability and fickleness of disposition.

They looked upon religion merely for novelty, as something, which pleased them for a while; but after their curiosity was satisfied, they laid it aside again like the young man that came to see Jesus with a linen cloth about his naked body, they have followed him for a season, but when temptations came to take hold on them, for want of a little more resolution, they have been stripped of all their good intentions, and fled away naked. They at first, like a tree planted by the waterside, grew up and flourished for a while; but having no root in themselves, no inward principle of holiness and piety, like Jonah's gourd, they were soon dried up and withered. Their good intentions are too like the violent motions of the animal spirits of a body newly beheaded, which, though impetuous, are not lasting. In short, they set out well in their journey to heaven, but finding the way either narrower or longer than they expected, through an unsteadiness of disposition, they have made an eternal halt, and so *"returned like the dog to his vomit, or like the sow that was washed to her wallowing in the mire!"*

But I tremble to pronounce the fate of such unstable professing believers, who having put their hands to the plough, for want of a little more resolution, shamefully look back. How shall I repeat to them that dreadful threatening, *"If any man draw back, my soul shall have no pleasure in him;"* And again, *"It is impossible* (that is, exceeding difficult at least) *for those that have been once enlightened, and have tasted of the heavenly gift, and the powers of the world to come, if they should fall away, to be renewed again unto repentance."* But not withstanding the gospel is so severe against apostates, yet many that begun well, through a fickleness of disposition,

(O that none of us here present may ever be such) have been by this means of the number of those that turn back unto perdition. And this is the fifth, and the last reason I shall give, why so many are only almost, and not altogether Christians.

III. Proceed We Now to the General Thing Proposed, Namely, to Consider the Folly of Being No More Than an Almost Christian

1. And the FIRST proof I shall give of the folly of such a proceeding is, that it is ineffectual to salvation. It is true, such men are almost good: but almost to hit the mark, is really to miss it. God requires us *"to love him with all our hearts, with all our souls, and with all our strength."* He loves us too well to admit any rival; because, so far as our hearts are empty of God, so far must they be unhappy. The devil, indeed, like the false mother that came before Solomon, would have our hearts divided, as she would have had the child; but God, like the true mother, will have all or none. *"My Son, give me thy heart,"* thy whole heart, is the general call to all: and if this be not done, we never can expect the divine mercy.

Persons may play the hypocrite; but God at the great day will strike them dead, (as he did Ananias and Sapphira by the mouth of his servant Peter) for pretending to offer him all their hearts, when they keep back from him the greatest part. They may perhaps impose upon their fellow-creatures for a while; but he that enabled Elijah to cry out, *"Come in thou wife of Jeroboam,"* when she came disguised to inquire about her sick son, will also discover them through their most artful dissimulations; and if their hearts are not wholly with him, appoint them their portion with hypocrites and unbelievers.

2. But, SECONDLY, What renders a halfway-piety more inexcusable is, that it is not only insufficient to our own salvation, but also very prejudicial to that of others.

An almost Christian is one of the most hurtful creatures in the world; he is a wolf in shee's clothing: he is one of those false prophets, our blessed Lord bids us beware of in his sermon on the mount, who would persuade men, that the way to heaven is broader than it really is; and thereby, as it was observed before, *"enter not into the kingdom of God themselves, and those that are entering in they hinder."* These, these are the men that turn the world into a lukewarm Laodicean spirit; that hang out false lights, and so shipwreck unthinking benighted souls in their voyage to the haven of eternity. These are they who are greater enemies to the cross of Christ, than infidels themselves: for of an unbeliever every one will be aware; but an almost Christian, through his subtle hypocrisy, draws away many after him; and therefore must expect to receive the greater damnation.

3. But, THIRDLY, As it is most prejudicial to ourselves and hurtful to others, so it is the greatest instance of ingratitude we can express towards our Lord and Master Jesus Christ. For did he come down from heaven, and shed his precious blood, to purchase these hearts of ours, and shall we only give him half of them? O how can we say we love him, when our hearts are not wholly with him? How can we call him our Savior, when we will not endeavor sincerely to approve ourselves to him, and so let him see the travail of his soul, and be satisfied!

Suffer me to add a word or two of exhortation to you, to excite you to be not only almost, but altogether Christians. O let us scorn all base and treacherous treatment of our King and Savior, of our God and Creator. Let us not take some pains all our lives to go to heaven, and yet plunge ourselves into hell as last. Let us give to God our whole hearts, and no longer halt between two opinions: if the world be God, let us serve that; if pleasure be a God, let us serve that; but if the Lord he be God, let us, O let us serve him alone. Alas! why, why should we stand out any longer? Why should we be so in love with slavery, as not wholly to renounce the world, the flesh, and the devil, which, like so many spiritual chains, bind down our souls, and hinder them from flying up to God? Alas! what are we afraid of? Is not God able to reward our entire obedience? If he is, as the almost Christian's lame way of serving him seems to grant, why then will we not serve him entirely? For the same reason we do so much, why do we not do more? Or do you think that being only half religious will make you happy, but that going farther will render you miserable and uneasy? Alas! this, my brethren, is delusion all over: for what is it but this half piety, this wavering between God and the world, that makes so many, that are seemingly well disposed, such utter strangers to the comforts of religion? They choose just so much of religion as will disturb them in their lusts, and follow their lusts so far as to deprive themselves of the comforts of religion. Whereas on the contrary, would they sincerely leave all in affection, and give their hearts wholly to God, they would then (and they cannot till then) experience the unspeakable pleasure of having a mind at unity with itself, and enjoy such a peace of God, which even in this life passes all understanding, and which they were entire strangers to before. It is true, if we will devote ourselves entirely to God, we must meet with contempt: but then it is because contempt is necessary to heal our pride. We must renounce some sensual pleasures, but then it is because those unfit us for spiritual ones, which are infinitely better. We must renounce the love of the world; but then it is that we may be filled with the love of God and when that has once enlarged our hearts, we shall, like Jacob when he served for his beloved Rachel, think nothing too difficult to undergo, no hardships too tedious to endure, because of the love we shall then have for our dear Redeemer. Thus easy, thus delightful will be the ways of God even in this life: but when once we throw off these bodies, and our souls are filled with all the fullness of God. O! what heart can conceive, what tongue can express, with what unspeakable joy and consolation shall we then look back on our past sincere and hearty services. Think you then, my dear hearers, we shall repent we had done too much: or rather think you not, we shall be ashamed that we did no more; and blush we were so backward to give up all to God; when he intended hereafter to give us himself?

Let me therefore, to conclude, exhort you, my brethren, to have always before you the unspeakable happiness of enjoying God. And think also, that every degree of holiness you neglect every act of piety you omit, is a jewel taken out of your crown, a degree of blessedness lost in the vision of God. O! do but always think and act thus, and you will no longer be laboring to compound matters between God and the world; but, on the contrary, be daily endeavoring to give up yourselves more and more unto him; you will be always watching, always praying, always aspiring after farther degrees of purity and love, and consequently always preparing yourselves for a fuller sight and enjoyment of that God, in whose presence there is fullness of joy, and at whose right-hand there are pleasures for ever more. Amen! Amen!

3. "Marks of a True Conversion"

"Verily, I say unto you, except ye be converted, and become as little children, ye shall not enter into the kingdom of heaven."—Matthew 18:3

I suppose I may take it for granted, that all of you, among whom I am now about to preach the kingdom of God, are fully convinced, that it is appointed for all men once to die, and that ye all really believe that after death comes the judgment, and that the consequences of that judgment will be, that ye must be doomed to dwell in the blackness of darkness, or ascend to dwell with the blessed God, for ever and ever. I may take it for granted also, that whatever your practice in common life may be, there is not one, though ever so profligate and abandoned, but hopes to go to that place, which the scriptures call Heaven, when he dies. And, I think, if I know anything of mine own heart, my heart's desire, as well as my prayer to God, for you all, is, that I may see you sitting down in the kingdom of our heavenly Father. But then, though we all hope to go to heaven when we die, yet, if we may judge by people's lives, and our Lord says, *"that by their fruits we may know them,"* I am afraid it will be found, that thousands, and ten thousands, who hope to go to this blessed place after death, are not now in the way to it while they live. Though we call ourselves Christians, and would consider it as an affront put upon us, for anyone to doubt whether we were Christians or not; yet there are a great many, who bear the name of Christ, that yet do not so much as know what real Christianity is. Hence it is, that if you ask a great many, upon what their hopes of heaven are founded, they will tell you, that they belong to this, or that, or the other denomination, and part of Christians, into which Christendom is now unhappily divided.

If you ask others, upon what foundation they have built their hope of heaven, they will tell you, that they have been baptized, that their fathers and mothers, presented them to the Lord Jesus Christ in their infancy; and though, instead of fighting under Christ's banner, they have been fighting against him, almost ever since they were baptized, yet because they have been admitted to church, and their names are in the Register book of the parish, therefore they will make us believe, that their names are also written in the book of life. But a great many, who will not build their hopes of salvation upon such a sorry rotten foundation as this, yet if they are, what we generally call, negatively good people; if they live so as their neighbors cannot say that they do anybody harm, they do not doubt but they shall be happy when they die; nay, I have found many such die, as the scripture speaks, *"without any hands in their death."* And if a person is what the world calls an honest moral man, if he does justly, and…reach out his hand to the poor, receives the sacrament once or twice a year, and is outwardly sober and honest; the world looks upon such an one as a Christian indeed, and doubtless we are to judge charitably of every such person. There are many likewise, who go on in a round of duties, a model of performances, that think they shall go to heaven; but if you examine them, though they have a Christ in their heads, they have no Christ in their hearts.

The Lord Jesus Christ knew this full well; he knew how desperately wicked and deceitful men's hearts were; he knew very well how many would go to hell even by the very gates of heaven, how many would climb up even to the door, and go so near as to knock at it, and yet after all be dismissed with a *"verily I know you not."* The Lord, therefore, plainly tells us, what great change must be wrought in us, and what must be done for us, before we can have any well grounded hopes of entering into the kingdom of heaven. Hence, he tells Nicodemus, *"that unless a man be born again, and from above, and unless a man be born of water and of the Spirit, he cannot enter into the kingdom of God."* And of all the solemn declarations of our Lord, I mean with respect to this, perhaps the words of the text are one of the most solemn, *"except, (says Christ) ye be converted, and become as little children, ye shall not enter into the kingdom of heaven."*

FIRST, I shall endeavor to show you in what respects we are to understand this assertion of our Lord's, *"that we must be converted and become like little children."* I shall then,

SECONDLY, Speak to those who profess a little of this childlike disposition,

And LASTLY, shall speak to you, who have no reason to think that this change has ever past upon your souls. And

FIRST, I shall endeavor to show you, what we are to understand by our Lord's saying, *"Except ye be converted and become as little children."*

The Evangelist tell us, *"that the disciples at this time came unto Jesus, saying, Who is the greatest in the kingdom of heaven?"* These disciples had imbibed the common prevailing notion, that the Lord Jesus Christ was to be a temporal prince; they dreamed of nothing but being ministers of state, of sitting on Christ's right hand in his kingdom, and lording it over God's people; they thought themselves qualified for state offices, as generally ignorant people are apt to conceive of themselves. Well, say they, *"Who is the greatest in the kingdom of heaven?"* Which of us shall have the chief management of public affairs? A pretty question for a few poor fishermen, who scarcely knew how to drag their nets to shore, much less how to govern a kingdom. Our Lord, therefore, in the 2nd verse, to mortify them, calls a little child, and sets him in the midst of them. This action was as much as if our Lord had said,

> "Poor creatures in Your imaginations are very towering; you dispute who shall be greatest in the kingdom of heaven; I will make this little child preach to you, or I will preach to you by him. Verily I say unto you, (I who am truth itself, I know in what manner my subjects are to enter into my kingdom; I say unto you, ye are so far from being in a right disposition for my kingdom, that) except ye be converted, and become as this little child, ye shall not enter into the kingdom of heaven, (unless ye are, comparatively speaking, as loose to the world, as loose to crowns, scepters, and kingdoms, and earthly things, as this poor little child I have in my hand) ye shall not enter into my kingdom."

So that what our Lord is speaking of, is not the innocence of little children, if you consider the relation they stand in to God, and as they are in themselves, when brought into the world; but what our Lord means is, that as to ambition and lust after the world, we must in this sense become as little children. Is there never a little boy or girl in this congregation? Ask a poor little child, that can just speak, about a crown, scepter, or kingdom; the poor creature has no notion about it. Give a little boy or girl a small thing to play with; it will leave the world to other people. Now in this sense we must be converted, and become as little children; that is, we must be as loose to the world, comparatively speaking, as a little child.

Do not mistake me, I am not going to persuade you to shut up your shops, or leave your business; I am not going to persuade you, that if ye will be Christians, ye must turn hermits, and retire out of the world; ye cannot leave your wicked hearts behind you, when you leave the world; for I find when I am alone, my wicked heart has followed me, go where I will. No, the religion of Jesus is a social religion. But though Jesus Christ does not call us to go out of the world, shut up our shops, and leave our children to be provided for by miracles; yet this must be said to the honor of Christianity, if we are really converted, we shall be loose from the world though we are engaged in it, and are obliged to work for our children; though we are obliged to follow trades and merchandise, and to be serviceable to the commonwealth, yet if we are real Christians, we shall be loose to the world; though I will not pretend to say that all real Christians have attained to the same degree of spiritual mindedness. This is the primary meaning of these words, that we must be converted and become as little children; nevertheless, I suppose the words are to be understood in other senses.

When our Lord says, we must be converted and become as little children, I suppose he means also, that we must be sensible of our weakness, comparatively speaking, as a little child. Every one looks upon a little child, as a poor weak creature; as one that ought to go to school and learn some new lesson every day; and as simple and artless; one without guile, having not learned the abominable art, called deceit. Now in all these senses, I believe we are to understand the words of the text.

Are little children sensible of their weakness? Must they be led by the hand? Must we take hold of them or they will fall? So, if we are converted, if the grace of God be really in our hearts, my dear friends, however we may have thought of ourselves once, whatever were our former high exalted imaginations; yet we shall now be sensible of our weakness; we shall no more say, *"We are rich and increased with goods, and lack nothing;"* we shall be inwardly poor; we shall feel *"that we are poor, miserable, blind, and naked."* And as a little child gives up its hand to be guided by a parent or a nurse, so those who are truly converted, and are real Christians, will give up the heart, their understandings, their wills, their affections, to be guided by the word, providence, and the Spirit of the Lord. Hence it is, that the Apostle, speaking of the sons of God, says, *"As many as are led by the Spirit of God, they are* (and to be sure he means they only are) *the sons of God."*

And as little children look upon themselves to be ignorant creatures, so those that are converted, do look upon themselves as ignorant too. Hence it is, that John, speaking to Christians, calls them little children; *"I have written unto you, little children."* And Christ's flock is called a little flock, not only because it is little in number, but also because those who are members of his flock, are indeed little in their own eyes. Hence that great man, that great apostle of the Gentiles, that spiritual father of so many thousands of souls, that chosen vessel, the Apostle Paul, when he speaks of himself, says, "Unto me, who am less than the least of all saints, is this grace given, that I should preach among the Gentiles the unsearchable riches of Christ." Perhaps some of you, when you read these words, will be apt to think that Paul did not speak true, that he did not really feel what he said; because you judge Paul's heart by your own proud hearts: but the more ye get of the grace of God, and the more ye are partakers of the divine life, the more will ye see your own meanness and vileness, and be less in your own eyes. Hence it is, that Mr. Flavel, in his book called, HUSBANDRY SPIRITUALIZED, compares young Christians to green corn; which before it is ripe, shoots up very high, but there is little solidity in it: whereas, an old Christian is like ripe corn; it doth not lift up its head so much, but then it is more weighty, and fit to be cut down, and put into the farmer's barn. Young Christians are also like little rivulets; ye know rivulets are shallow, yet make great noise; but an old Christian, he makes not much noise, he goes on sweetly, like a deep river sliding into the ocean.

And as a little child is looked upon as an harmless creature, and generally speaks true: so, if we are converted, and become as little children, we shall be guileless as well as harmless. What said the dear Redeemer when he saw Nathaniel? As though it was a rare sight he gazed upon, and would have others gaze upon it: "Behold an Israelite indeed;" Why so? "In whom is no guile." Do not mistake me; I am not saying, that Christians ought not to be prudent: they ought exceedingly to pray to God for prudence, otherwise they may follow the delusions of the devil, and by their imprudence give wrong touches to the ark of God. It was the lamentation of a great man, *"God has given me many gifts, but God has not given me prudence."* Therefore, when I say, a Christian must be guileless, I do not mean, he should expose himself, and lie open to everyone's assault: we should pray for the wisdom of the serpent, though we shall generally learn this wisdom by our blunders and imprudence and we must make some advance in Christianity, before we know our imprudence. A person really converted, can say, as it is reported of a philosopher, *"I wish there was a Window in my breast, that everyone may see the uprightness of my heart and intentions."* And though there is too much of the old man in us, yet, if we are really converted, there will be in us no allowed guile, we shall be harmless. And that is the reason why the poor Christian is too often imposed upon; he judges other people by himself; having an honest heart, he thinks every one as honest as himself, and therefore is a prey to everyone. I might enlarge upon each of these points, it is a copious and important truth; but I do not intend to multiply many marks and headings.

And therefore, as I have something to say by way of personal application, give me leave therefore, with the utmost tenderness, and at the same time with faithfulness, to call upon you, my dear friends. My text is introduced in an awful manner, *"Verily I say unto you;"* and what Jesus said then, he says now to you, to me, and to as many as sit under a preached gospel, and to as many as the Lord our God shall call. Let me exhort you to see whether ye are converted; whether such a great and almighty change has passed upon any of your souls. As I told you before, so I tell you again, ye all hope to go to heaven, and I pray God Almighty ye may be all there: when I see such a congregation as this, if my heart is in a proper frame, I feel myself ready to lay down my life, to be instrumental only to save one soul. It makes my heart bleed within me, it makes me sometimes most unwilling to preach, lest that word that I hope will do good, may increase the damnation of any, and perhaps of a great part of the auditory, through their own unbelief. Give me leave to deal faithfully with your souls. I have your death warrant in my hand: Christ has said it, Jesus will stand to it, it is like the laws of the Medes and Persians, it alter not. Hark, O man! Hark, O woman! He that hath ears to hear, let him hear what the Lord Jesus Christ says, *"Verily I say unto you, except ye be converted, and become as little children, ye shall not enter into the kingdom of heaven."* Though this is Saturday night, and ye are now preparing for the Sabbath, for what you know, you may yet never live to see the Sabbath. You have had awful proofs of this lately; a woman died but yesterday, a man died the day before, another was killed by something that fell from a house, and it may be in twenty-four hours more, many of you may be carried into an unalterable state. Now then, for God's sake, for your own souls sake, if ye have a mind to dwell with God, and cannot bear the thought of dwelling in everlasting burning, before I go any further, silently put up one prayer, or say Amen to the prayer I would put in your mouths; *"Lord, search me and try me, Lord, examine my heart, and let my conscience speak: O let me know whether I am converted or not!"* What say ye, my dear hearers? What say ye, my fellow-sinners? What say ye, my guilty brethren? Has God by his blessed Spirit wrought such a change in your hearts? I do not ask you, whether God has made you angels? That I know will never be; I only ask you, Whether ye have any well-grounded hope to think that God has made you new creatures in Christ Jesus? So renewed and changed your natures, that you can say, I humbly hope, that as to the habitual disposition and tendency of my mind, that my heart is free from wickedness; I have a husband, I have a wife, I have also children, I keep a shop, I mind my business; but I love these creatures for God's sake, and do everything for Christ: and if God was now to call me away, according to the habitual disposition of my mind, I can say, Lord, I am ready; and however I love the creatures, I hope I can say, Whom have I in heaven but thee? Whom have I in heaven, O my God and my dear Redeemer, that I desire in comparison of thee? Can you thank God for the creatures, and say at the same time, these are not my Christ? I speak in plain language, you know my way of preaching I do not want to play the orator, I do not want to be counted a scholar; I want to speak so as I may reach poor people's hearts. What say ye, my dear hearers? Are ye sensible of your weakness? Do ye feel that ye are poor, miserable, blind, and naked by nature? Do ye give up your hearts, your affections, your wills, your understanding to be guided by the Spirit of God, as a little child gives up its hand to be guided by its parent? Are ye little in your own eyes? Do ye think humbly of yourselves? And do you want to learn something new every day? I mention these marks, because I am apt to believe they are more adapted to a great many of your capacities. A great many of you have not that showing of affection ye sometimes had, therefore ye are for giving up all your evidences, and making way for the devil's coming into your heart. You are not brought up to the mount as ye used to be, therefore ye conclude ye have no grace at all. But if the Lord Jesus Christ has emptied thee, and humbled thee, if he is giving thee to see and know that thou art nothing; though thou are not growing upward, thou art growing downward; and though thou hast not so much joy, yet thy heart is emptying to be more abundantly replenished by and by. Can any of you follow me? Then, give God thanks, and take the comfort of it.

If thou art thus converted, and become a little child, I welcome thee, in the name of the Lord Jesus, into God's dear family; I welcome thee, in the name of the dear Redeemer, into the company of God's children. O ye dear souls, though the world sees nothing in you, though there be no outward difference between you and others, yet I look upon you in another light, even as so many king's sons and daughters: all hail! In the name of God, I wish every one of you joy from my soul, ye sons and daughters of the King of kings. Will not you henceforth exercise a childlike disposition? Will not such a thought melt down your hearts, when I tell you, that the great God, who might have frowned you to hell for your secret sins, that nobody knew of but God and your own souls, and who might have damned you times without number, hath cast the mantle of his love over you; his voice hath been, Let that man, that woman live, for I have found a ransom. O will ye not cry out, Why me, Lord? Was King George to send for any of your children, and were you to hear they were to be his adopted sons, how highly honored would you think your children to be? What great condescension was it for Pharaoh's daughter to take up Moses, a poor child exposed in an ark of bulrushes, and bring him up for her child? But what is that happiness in comparison of thine, who was the other day a child of the devil, but now by converting grace art become a child of God? Are ye converted? Are ye become like little children? Then what must ye do? My dear hearers, be obedient to God, remember God is your father; and as every one of you must know what a dreadful cross it is to have a wicked, disobedient child:

if ye do not want your children to be disobedient to you, for Christ's sake be not disobedient to your heavenly parent. If God be your father, obey him: if God be your father, serve him; love him with all your heart, love him with all your might, with all your soul, and with all your strength. If God be your father, fly from everything that may displease him; and walk worthy of that God, who has called you to his kingdom and glory. If ye are converted and become like little children, then behave as little children: they long for the breast, and with it will be contented. Are ye new-born babes? Then desire the sincere milk of the word, that ye may grow thereby.

Are ye children? Then grow in grace, and in the knowledge of your Lord and Savior Jesus Christ Have any of you children that do not grow? Do not ye lament these children, and cry over them; do not ye say, my child will never be fit for anything in the world? Well, doth it grieve you to see a child that will not grow; how much must it grieve the heart of Christ to see you grow so little? Will ye be always children? Will ye be always learning the first principles of Christianity, and never press forward toward the mark, for the prize of the high calling of God in Christ Jesus? God forbid. Let the language of your heart be, *"Lord Jesus help me to grow, help me to learn more, learn me to live so as my progress may be known to all!"*

Are ye God's children? Are ye converted, and become like little children? Then deal with God as your little children do with you; as soon as ever they want anything, or if anybody hurt them, I appeal to yourselves if they do not directly run to their parent. Well, are ye God's children? Doth the devil trouble you? Doth the world trouble you? Go tell your father of it, go directly and complain to God. Perhaps you may say, I cannot utter fine words; but do any of you expect fine words from your children? If they come crying, and can speak but half words, do not your hearts yearn over them? And has not God unspeakably more pity to you? If ye can only make signs to him; *"As a father pitieth his children, so will the Lord pity them that fear him."*

Are ye converted, and become as little children, have ye entered into God's family? Then assure yourselves, that your heavenly father will chasten you now and then: *"for what son is there whom the father chasteneth not: if ye are without chastisement, of which all are partakers, then are ye bastards and not sons."* It is recorded of bishop Latimer, that in the house where he came to lodge, he overheard the master of the house say, *"I thank God I never had a cross in my life"*: O said he, *"then I will not stay here."*

I believe there is not a child of God, when in a good frame, but has prayed for great humility; they have prayed for great faith, they have prayed for great love, they have prayed for all the graces of the Spirit: Do ye know, when ye put us these prayers, that ye did also say, Lord send us great trials: for how is it possible to know ye have great faith, humility and love, unless God put you into great trials, that ye may know whether ye have them or not. I mention this, because a great many of the children of God (I am sure it has been a temptation to me many times, when I have been under God's smarting rod) when they have great trials, think God is giving them over. If therefore ye are God's children; if ye are converted and become as little children; do not expect that God will be like a foolish parent; no, he is a jealous God, he loves his child too well to spare his rod. How did he correct Miriam? How did he correct Moses? How hath God in all ages corrected his dearest children?...

Are ye God's children? Are ye converted and become as little children? Then will ye not long to go home and see your Father? O happy they that have gotten home before you; happy they that are up yonder, happy they who have ascended above this field of conflict. I know not what you may think of it, but since I heard that some, whose hearts God was pleased to work upon, are gone to glory, I am sometimes filled with grief, that God is not pleased to let me go home too. How can you see so much coldness among God's people? How can ye see God's people like the moon, waxing and waning? Who can but desire to be forever with the Lord? Thanks be to God, the time is soon coming; thanks be to God, he will come and will not tarry. Do not be impatient, God in his own time will fetch you home. And though ye may be brought to short allowance now, though some of you may be narrow in your circumstances, yet do not repine; a God, and the gospel of Christ, with brown bread, are great riches. In thy Father's house there is bread enough and to spare; though thou are now tormented, yet by and by thou shalt be comforted; the angels will look upon it as an honor to convey thee to Abraham's bosom, though thou are but a Lazarus here. By the frame of my heart, I am much inclined to speak comfortably to God's people.

But I only mention one thing more, and that is, if ye are converted, and become as little children, then for God's sake take care of doing what children often do; they are too apt to quarrel one with another. O love one another; *"he that dwells in love dwells in God, and God in him."* Joseph knew that his brethren were in danger of falling out, therefore when he left them, says he, *"fall not out by the way."* Ye are all children of the same Father, ye are all going to the same place; why should ye differ? The world has enough against us, the devil has enough against us, without our quarreling with each other; O walk in love. If I could preach no more, if I was not able to hold out to the end of my sermon, I would say as John did, when he was grown old and could not preach, *"Little children, love one another;"* if ye are God's children, then love one another. There is nothing grieves me more, than the differences amongst God's people. O hasten that time, when we shall either go to heaven, or never quarrel any more!

Would to God I could speak to all of you in this comfortable language; but my master tells me, I must *"not give that which is holy to dogs. I must not cast pearls before swine;"* therefore, though I have been speaking comfortably, yet what I have been saying, especially in this latter part of the discourse, belongs to children; it is children's bread, it belongs to God's people. If any of you are graceless, Christless, unconverted creatures, I charge you not to touch it, I fence it in the name of God; here is a flaming sword turning every way to keep you from this bread of life, till ye are turned to Jesus Christ. And therefore, as I suppose many of you are unconverted, and graceless, go home! And away to your closets, and down with your stubborn hearts before God; if ye have not done it before, let this be the night. Or, do not stay till ye go home; begin now, while standing here; pray to God, and let the language of thy heart be, Lord convert me! Lord make me a little child, Lord Jesus let me not be banished from thy kingdom! My dear friends, there is a great deal more implied in the words, than is expressed: when Christ says, *"Ye shall not enter into the kingdom of heaven,"* it is as much to say, *"ye shall certainly go to hell, ye shall certainly be damned, and dwell in the blackness of darkness for ever, ye shall go where the worm dies not, and where the fire is not quenched."* The Lord God impress it upon your souls! May an arrow (as one lately wrote me in a letter) dipped in the blood of Christ, reach every unconverted sinner's heart! May God fulfill the text to every one of your souls. It is he alone that can do it. If ye confess your sins, and leave them, and lay hold on the Lord Jesus Christ, the Spirit of God shall be given you; if you will go and say, turn me, O my God! Thou know not, O man, what the return of God may be to thee. Did I think that preaching would be to the purpose, did I think that arguments would induce you to come, I would continue my discourse till midnight. And however some of you may hate me without a cause, would to God every one in this congregation was as much concerned for himself, as at present (blessed be God) I feel myself concerned for him. O that my head were waters, O that mine eyes were a fountain of tears, that I might weep over an unconverted, graceless, wicked, and adulterous generation. Precious souls, for God's sake think what will become of you when ye die, if you die without being converted: if ye go hence without the wedding garment, God will strike you speechless, and ye shall be banished from his presence for ever and ever. I know ye cannot dwell with everlasting burnings: behold then I show you a way of escape; Jesus is the way, Jesus is the truth, the Lord Jesus Christ is the resurrection and the life. It is his Spirit who must convert you. Come to Christ, and ye shall have it;

and may God for Christ's sake give it to you all, and convert you, that we may all meet, never to part again, in his heavenly kingdom; even so Lord Jesus, Amen and Amen.

4. Notes

1   For further study on the life and ministry of George Whitefield see: Arnold Dallimore, *George Whitefield: The Life and Times of the Great Evangelist of the Eighteenth-Century Revival*. 2 vol. (London: Banner of Truth, 1970,1979); Richard Owen Roberts, *Whitefield in Print: A Bibliographic Record* (Wheaton, Ill. Richard Owen Roberts, 1988); and *George Whitefield's Journals* (London Banner of Truth, 1960).

The Fruit of Revival

Charles G. Finney 1792-1875

*With an Introduction
By Robert E. Coleman*

Abridged version of *The Fruit of Revival* by Charles G. Finney.
Abridged version originally published by the Institute of Evangelism
Billy Graham Center, 1991, Wheaton, IL. Copyright of abridged
version and introduction held by Robert Coleman, used with
permission. Scripture quotations are taken from the King James
Version (KJV), in the Public Domain. Artwork in the Public Domain.

Book Chapters

1. Introduction
   By Robert E. Coleman..208

2. When a Revival is to Be Expected.......................................213
   I. When a Revival of Religion Is Needed............................213
   II. The Importance of Revival in Such Circumstances........214
   III. When a Revival May Be Expected 215

3. How to Promote a Revival...218
   What is It to Break Up the Fallow Ground? 218
   How is the Fallow Ground to Be Broken Up?...................219
   Sins of Omission..219
   Sins of Commission 220
   Remarks 223

4. The Way of Salvation 224
   Remarks 226

5. Christian Perfection...228
   Objections..233
   Remarks 234

6. Love is the Whole of Religion..237
   What is essential to perfect love? 239
   Remarks 240

7. Notes..242

1. Introduction
By Robert E. Coleman

Few men have had a more pervasive influence for holiness and revival in America than Charles Grandison Finney. His anointed ministry, spanning half the nineteenth century, is said to have brought no less than 500,000 persons into the Kingdom of God[1] and introduced multiplied thousands more into what he called an experience of "perfect love."

He was born in Warren, Connecticut in 1792, and was the seventh child of a revolutionary war soldier. The family moved to the frontier in western New York, where Finney attended school and later did some teaching. In 1818 he became an apprentice in the law office of Judge Benjamin Wright in Adams.

Up to this time Finney had never given much attention to religious matters, but now finding frequent references to the Mosaic institutions in his study of jurisprudence, he began to read the Bible. He also started attending the Presbyterian Church. Though not impressed by the hyper Calvinism of the pastor, his own searching of the Scripture brought conviction to his restless soul.

On Sunday night, October 7, 1821, Finney made up his mind to "settle the question,"[2] but it was not until Wednesday that he found peace. That morning he went out into a nearby woods and made a Bethel for himself under some trees that had fallen against each other. "I will give my heart to God," he resolved, "or I will never come down from here."[3] As he sought the Lord on his knees, finally the realization carne that "faith was a voluntary trust instead of an intellectual state,"[4] and without more argumentation, like a little child, he took God at His Word.

The sun was setting when Finney returned to his office, and there, alone, a sense of the presence of Christ overwhelmed him. As he described it: "The Holy Spirit descended upon me in a manner that seemed to go through me, body and soul...Indeed, it seemed to come in waves of liquid love."[5] A member of the church later happened to come by, and finding the lawyer praising God, asked, "Are you in pain?" To which he replied, "No, but so happy I cannot live."[6]

With his newfound faith came an irresistible desire to preach. When asked by a client to take his case to court, he told him, "I have a retainer from the Lord Jesus Christ to plead His cause, and I cannot plead yours."[7]

Finney offered himself as a candidate for the Gospel ministry. Not having any formal Seminary training, some Presbyterians urged him to go to Princeton, but he declined, saying that the graduates he had seen from that school did not meet his "ideal of what a minister of Christ should be."[8] Quite a rebuke to those who pressed him for a reason, but it shows something of the forthright, independent spirit of this young preacher.

Grudgingly the St. Lawrence Presbytery placed Finney under the care of his pastor for the study of theology. Their views always conflicted, but the differences did not prevent them from recognizing his call to preach. When called upon to speak at his ordination service, the text he chose clearly reflected the focus of his ministry: "Without holiness no man shall see the Lord."[9]

Not long after being appointed as a missionary to a rural area in upstate New York, in October of 1824, Finney married Lydia Andrews, a young lady who had prayed for him during his law days at Adams. A couple of days after the wedding he set out for Evans Mills to make arrangements for moving their goods. On the way he was met by a man who begged him to preach in the community, which Finney agreed to do. So great was the response to his preaching that he stayed on for another day, then another, and finally gave up returning that week to get his wife.

Revival spread to neighboring towns, and continued through the winter. Finney wrote his wife that such were the circumstances he would have to delay his coming for her. When at last he started to get her in the spring, his horse lost a shoe, and he had to stop to have it reset. When people learned who he was, they entreated him to preach to them that afternoon in the schoolhouse. The Spirit of God fell in such power upon the audience that he consented to their pleas to spend the night and preach the next day. Again it was the same story. Constrained not to leave the harvest, he finally sent a man to take his horse and go to get his wife.

On first reading, six months separation during a honeymoon might suggest an indifference of feeling, even lack of affection. Such was not the case, however. Those who have followed Finney most closely say, "throughout his life he was passionately devoted to his family" (which eventually included eight children).[10] What happened following his marriage is but another insight into his passion for souls.

Finney's wife shared the burden for revival with her husband, and for several years accompanied him in his meetings as an intercessor and co-worker. Another companion was "Father" David Nash, an old Presbyterian minister who went along to pray while the evangelist preached. Finney, too, spent hours each day on his knees.

Bathed in prayer and the Scripture, Finney preached with power, addressing people much as he would speak to a jury. With relentless logic and simplicity, it was said, "Such a view of the holiness of God was presented" that resistance to the Gospel was "swept away."[11]

His very appearance seemed to convey a solemnity. On one occasion, while visiting a cotton mill during a revival meeting, some girls who had laughed at Finney burst into tears when he looked at them, and soon the feeling moved through the whole factory. "Stop the mill," cried the owner, "and let the people attend to religion."[12] It was not long before nearly everyone was crying out to God for mercy.

Revival spread from rural towns to urban centers like Philadelphia, Boston, and New York City. During six months of protracted meetings in Rochester, from September 1830 to March 1831, the city was shaken to its foundations, and most of the leading lawyers, doctors, and businessmen of the city were converted. One hundred thousand people, it is reported by Lyman Beecher, connected themselves with churches as a result of the revival,[13] an effect in so short a time probably unparalleled in American church history.

Finney's itinerant ministry of evangelism continued throughout his life, even occasioning two trips to England. But a recurrent respiratory illness forced him to curtail his travels in 1832. He accepted the Presbyterian pastorate of the Chatham Street Chapel, a renovated theater in New York City. Two years later he went to the newly built Broadway Tabernacle and became a Congregationalist.

While pastoring the church, he was asked by the editor of *The New York Evangelist* to give some lectures on revival. The publication of these

Friday evening discourses in 1835 probably has impacted serious believers more than any other book ever written on this subject. Two abridged excerpts from this volume are reproduced in the following pages.

Revival is seen as "the return of the church from her backslidings," resulting in "a new beginning of obedience to God."[14] This renewed faith finds expression in "a longing desire for the salvation of the whole world," even as it "breaks the power of sin over Christians."[15] Such a state, he believed, was "not a miracle, nor dependent on a miracle," but purely "the result of the right use of the appropriate means."[16] Finney was not minimizing divine sovereignty in sending revival, but simply asserting our human responsibility to respond fully to God's Word. He believed in the depravity of mankind, and a consequent natural inclination to sin, but insisted that God's grace enabled every person through the Holy Spirit to lay hold upon the provisions of salvation.

In the same year his *Lectures on Revival* were released, Finney accepted a professorship at Oberlin College, a small abolitionist school in Ohio. There he taught theology for the next 40 years, while still going out from time to time in revival meetings. He served as pastor of the Congregational Church in town from 1836 to 1872, and during part of this period, President of the College.

Under his leadership and that of a colleague, Asa Mohan, Oberlin became the nation's center of evangelical revival theology, emphasizing especially the perfectibility of the Christian life. This concern for sanctification, always present in his holiness ethic, increasingly captivated Finney's attention, as is evident in his Lectures on Systematic Theology, published in 1846, as well as many other printed lectures and sermons.

The selections from this literature condensed here are taken from sermons preached in New York during 1836 and 1837, and later published under the title, Lectures to Professing Christians.[17] These messages came after observing that many believers "were making very little progress in grace" and "would fall back from a revival state."[18] He was led to inquire from the Scripture whether there was something better, and came to the conclusion that "an altogether higher and more stable form of Christian life was attainable, and was the privilege of all Christians."[19] Teaching this "higher" way became the hallmark of his mature ministry.

Early on Monday morning, August 16, 1875, Finney died at his home in Oberlin. The evening before, hearing the church choir lifting their voices in the distance, he and his wife quietly joined in the singing, "Jesus lover of my soul, let me to Thy bosom fly." A few hours later he fell asleep, and when he awoke it was in the arms of Jesus.[20]

Today in the church where he preached one can read this inscription: "From this pulpit for many years Charles G. Finney presented to this community and to the world the unsearchable riches of Christ." I trust that the following excerpts from his teaching will make us ponder again some of those "unsearchable riches."

Robert E. Coleman
Wheaton, IL

2. When a Revival is to Be Expected

> Wilt Thou not revive us again: that Thy people may rejoice in Thee?
> —Psalms 85:6

The Psalmist felt that God had been very favorable to the people, and while contemplating the goodness of the Lord in bringing them back from the land whither they had been carried away captive, and while looking at the prospects before them, he breaks out into a prayer for a revival of religion: "Wilt Thou not revive us again, that Thy people may rejoice in Thee?"

I. When a Revival of Religion Is Needed

1. When there is a want of brotherly love and Christian confidence among professors of religion, then a revival is needed. Then there is a loud call for God. When Christians have sunk down into a low and backslidden state, they neither have, nor can have, the same love and confidence toward each other, as when they are all alive, and active, and living holy lives.

2. When there are dissensions, and jealousies, and evil speaking among professors of religion, then there is a great need of a revival.

3. When there is a worldly spirit in the Church. It is manifest that the Church has sunk down into a low and backslidden state.

4. When the Church finds its members falling into gross and scandalous sins, then it is time to awake and cry to God for a revival of religion.

5. When there is a spirit of controversy in the Church or in the land, a revival is needful.

6. When the wicked triumph over the Churches, and revile them, it is time to seek for a revival of religion.

7. When sinners are careless and stupid, it is time Christians should bestir themselves. It is as much their duty to awake as it is for the firemen to do so when a fire breaks out in the night in a great city. Should the firemen sleep and let the whole city burn down, what would be thought of such firemen? And yet their guilt would not compare with the guilt of Christians who sleep while sinners around them are sinking stupidly into the fires of hell.

II. The Importance of Revival in Such Circumstances

1. A revival of religion is the only possible thing that can wipe away the reproach which covers the Church, and restore religion to the place it ought to have in the estimation of the public. There must be a waking up of energy on the part of Christians, and an outpouring of God's Spirit, or the world will laugh at the Church.

2. Nothing else will restore Christian love and confidence among Church members.

3. At such a time a revival of religion is indispensable to avert the judgments of God from the Church. The fact is Christians are more to blame for not being revived, than sinners are for not being converted. And if they are not awakened, they may know assuredly that God will visit them with His judgments. How often God visited the Jewish Church with judgments because they would not repent and be revived at the call of His prophets! How often have we seen Churches, and even whole denominations, cursed with a curse, because they would not wake up and seek the Lord, and pray: "Wilt Thou not revive us again, that Thy people may rejoice in Thee?"

4. Nothing but a revival of religion can preserve such a Church from annihilation.

5. Nothing but a revival of religion can present the means of grace from doing a great injury to the ungodly. Without a revival they will grow harder and harder under preaching, and will experience a more horrible damnation than they would if they had never heard the Gospel.

The Gospel is the savor of death unto death, if it is not made a savor of life unto life.

6. There is no other way in which a Church can be sanctified, grow in grace, and be fitted for heaven.

III. When a Revival May Be Expected

1. When the providence of God indicates that a revival is at hand. There is a conspiring of events to open the way, a preparation of circumstances to favor a revival, so that those who are looking out can see that a revival is at hand.

2. When the wickedness of the wicked grieves and humbles and distresses Christians. Sometimes Christians do not seem to mind anything about the wickedness around them. Or, if they do talk about it, it is in a cold, and callus, and unfeeling way, as if they despaired of a reformation: they are disposed to scold sinners – not to feel the compassion of the Son of God for them. But sometimes the conduct of the wicked drives Christians to prayer, breaks them down, and makes them sorrowful and tenderhearted, so that they can weep day and night, and instead of scolding the wicked they pray earnestly for them. Then you may expect a revival. Indeed, it is begun already.

Often the first indication of a revival is that the devil gets up something new in opposition. This will invariably have one of two effects. It will either drive Christians to God, or it will drive them farther away from God, to some carnal policy or other that will only make things worse. Frequently the most outrageous wickedness of the ungodly is followed by a revival. If Christians are made to feel that they have no hope but in God, and if they have sufficient feeling left to care for the honor of God and the salvation of the souls of the impenitent, there will certainly be a revival. Let hell boil over if it will, and spew out as many devils as there are stones in the pavement, if it only drives Christians to God in prayer – It cannot hinder a revival.

3. A revival may be expected when Christians have a spirit of prayer for a revival. That is, when they pray as if their hearts were set upon it. Sometimes Christians are not engaged in definite prayer for a revival, not even when they are warm in prayer. Their minds are upon something else; they are praying for something else – the salvation of the heathen and the like – and not for a revival among themselves. But when they feel the want of a revival, they pray for it; they feel for their own families and neighborhoods; they pray for them as if they could not be denied. What constitutes a spirit of prayer? Is it many prayers and warm

words? No. Prayer is the state of the heart. The spirit of prayer is a state of continual desire and anxiety of mind for the salvation of sinners. This travail of soul is that deep agony which persons feel when they lay hold on God for such a blessing, and will not let Him go till they receive it. I do not mean to be understood that it is essential to a spirit of prayer that the distress should be so great as this. But this deep, continual, earnest desire for the salvation of sinners is what constitutes the spirit of prayer for a revival. Generally there are but few professors of religion who know anything about this spirit of prayer which prevails with God.

Now mark me. Go and inquire among the obscure members of the Church and you will always find that somebody had been praying for a revival, and was expecting it – some man or woman had been agonizing in prayer for the salvation of sinners, until the blessing was gained. It may have found the minister and the body of the Church fast asleep, and they would wake up all of a sudden, like a man just rubbing his eyes open, running round the room, pushing things over, and wondering where all the excitement comes from. But though few knew it, you may be sure there had been somebody on the watchtower; constant in prayer till the blessing came. Generally, a revival is more or less extensive, as there are more or less persons who have the spirit of prayer.

4. Another sign that a revival may be expected is when the attention of ministers is especially directed to this particular object, and when their preaching and other efforts are aimed particularly at the conversion of sinners.

I believe a man may enter on the work of promoting a revival with as reasonable an expectation of success as he can enter on any other work with an expectation of success – with the same expectation as the farmer has of a crop when he sows his grain. I have sometimes seen this tried and succeed under circumstances the most forbidding that can be conceived. The great revival at Rochester began under the most disadvantageous circumstances that could well be imagined. It seemed as though Satan had interposed every possible obstacle to a revival. The three Churches were at variance. One had no minister: one was divided and was about to dismiss its minister. An elder of the third Presbyterian Church had brought a charge against the pastor of the first Church. After the work began, one of the first things was, the great stone Church gave way and created a panic. Then one of the Churches went on and dismissed their minister right in the midst of it. Many other things occurred, so that it seemed as if the devil were determined to divert public attention from the subject of religion. But there were a few remarkable cases of the spirit of prayer, which assured us that God was there, and we went on; and the more Satan opposed, the Spirit of the Lord lifted up the standard higher and higher, till finally a wave of salvation rolled over the place.

5. A revival of religion may be expected when Christians begin to confess their sins to one another. At other times they confess in a general manner, as if they are only half in earnest. But when there is an ingenuous breaking down, and a pouring out of the heart in confession of sin, the floodgates will soon burst open, and salvation will flow over the place.

A revival may be expected whenever Christians are found willing to make the sacrifices necessary to carry it on. They must be willing to sacrifice their feelings, their business, their time to help forward the work. Ministers must be willing to lay out their strength, and to jeopardize their health and life. They must be willing to offend the impenitent by plain and faithful dealing, and perhaps offend many members of the Church who will not come up to the work. They must take a decided stand with the revival, be the consequences what they may.

6. A revival may be expected when ministers and professors are willing to have God promote it by whatsoever instruments He pleases. Sometimes ministers are not willing to have a revival unless they can have the management of it. They wish to prescribe to God what He shall direct and bless, and what men He shall put forward. They have a good deal to say about God being a Sovereign, and that He will have revivals come in His own way and time. But then He must choose to have it just in their way or they will have nothing to do with it. Such men will sleep on until they are awakened by the judgment trumpet, without a revival, unless they are willing that God should come in His own way – unless they are willing to have anything or anybody employed that will do the most good.

7. Strictly I should say that when the foregoing things occur, a revival, to some extent, already exists. In truth a revival should be expected whenever it is needed. If we need to be revived it is our duty to be revived. If it is duty it is possible, and we should set about being revived ourselves.

3. How to Promote a Revival

> Break up your fallow ground: for it is time to seek the Lord, till He come and rain righteousness upon you. —Hosea 10:12b

The Jews were a nation of farmers, and it is therefore a common thing in the Scriptures to refer for illustrations to their occupation, and to the scenes with which farmers and shepherds are familiar. The prophet Hosea addresses them as a nation of backsliders; he reproves them for their idolatry, and threatens them with the judgments of God. Fallow ground is ground which has once been tilled, but which now lies waste, and needs to be broken up and mellowed, before it is suited to receive grain.

What is It to Break Up the Fallow Ground?

To break up the fallow ground, is to break up your hearts, to prepare your minds to bring forth fruit unto God. The mind of man is often compared in the Bible to ground, and the Word of God to seed sown therein, the fruit representing the actions and affections of those who receive it. To break up the fallow ground, therefore, is to bring the mind into such a state that it is fitted to receive the Word of God. Sometimes your hearts get matted down, hard and dry, till there is no such thing as getting fruit from them till they are broken up, and mellowed down, and fitted to receive the Word. It is this softening of the heart, so as to make it feel the truth, which the prophet calls breaking up your fallow ground.

How is the Fallow Ground to Be Broken Up?

If you mean to break up the fallow ground of your hearts, you must begin by looking at your hearts: examine and note the state of your minds, and see where you are. Many never seem to think about this. They pay no attention to their own hearts, and never know whether they are doing well in religion or not; whether they are gaining ground or going back; whether they are fruitful, or lying waste. Now you must draw off your attention from other things, and look into this. Make a business of it. Do not be in a hurry. Examine thoroughly the state of your hearts, and see where you are: whether you are walking with God every day, or with the devil; whether you are serving God or serving the devil most; whether you are under the dominion of the prince of darkness, or of the Lord Jesus Christ. To do this, you must set yourself to work to consider your sins.

Self-examination consists in looking at your lives, in considering your actions, in calling up the past, and learning its true character. Look back over your past history. Take up your individual sins one by one, and look at them. I do not mean that you should just cast a glance at your past life, and see that it has been full of sins, and then go to God and make a sort of general confession, and ask for pardon. That is not the way. You must take them up one by one. It will be a good thing to take a pen and paper, as you go over them, and write them down as they occur to you. Go over them as carefully as a merchant goes over his books; and as often as a sin comes before your memory, add it to the list. General confessions of sins will never do. Your sins were committed one by one; and as far as you can come at them, they ought to be reviewed and repented of one by one. Now begin, and take up first what are commonly, but improperly, called

Sins of Omission

1. Ingratitude. Take this sin, for instance, and write down under that head all the instances you can remember wherein you have received favors from God for which you have never exercised gratitude.

2. Want of love to God. Think how grieved and alarmed you would be if you discovered any flagging of affection for you in your wife, husband, or children; if you saw another engrossing their hearts, and thoughts, and time. Perhaps in such a case you would well nigh die with a just and virtuous jealousy. Now, God calls Himself a jealous God; and have you not given your heart to other loves and infinitely offended Him?

3. Neglect of the Bible. Put down the cases when for perhaps weeks, or longer, God's Word was not a pleasure.

4. Unbelief. Recall the instances in which you have virtually charged the God of truth with lying, by your unbelief of His express promises and declarations. God has promised to give the Holy Spirit to them that ask Him. Now, have you believed this? If you have not believed nor expected to receive the blessing which God has expressly promised, you have charged Him with lying.

5. Neglect of prayer.

6. Neglect of the means of grace.

7. Want of love for the souls of your fellowmen. Look round upon your friends and relatives, and remember how little compassion you have felt for them. You have stood by and seen them going right to hell, and it seems as though you did not care if they did go.

8. Want of care for the heathen. Perhaps you have not cared enough for them to attempt to learn their condition. Measure your desire for their salvation by the self-denial you practice, in giving of your substance to send them the Gospel.

9. Neglect of family duties. Think how you have lived before your family, how you have prayed, what an example you have set before them.

10. Neglect of watchfulness over your own life. In how many instances you have hurried over your private duties, and have neither taken yourself to task, nor honestly made up your accounts with God?

11. Neglect to watch over your brethren. How often have you broken your covenant that you would watch over them in the Lord! How many times have you seen your brethren growing cold in religion, and have not spoken to them about it? And yet you pretend to love them.

12. Neglect of self-denial. Oh, how soon such professors will be in hell! Some are giving of their abundance, and are giving much, and are ready to complain that others do not give more; when, in truth, they do not themselves give anything that they need, anything that they could enjoy if they kept it.

From these we now turn to

Sins of Commission

1. Worldly mindedness. What has been the state of your heart in regard to your worldly possessions? Have you looked at them, as really yours – as if you had a right to dispose of them as your own, according to your own will?

2. Pride. Recollect all the instances you can, in which you have detected yourself in the exercise of pride. You have gone caring more as to how you appeared outwardly in the sight of mortal man, than how your soul appeared in the sight of the heart-searching God. You have, in fact, set up yourself to be worshipped by them, rather than prepared to worship God yourself.

3. Envy. Look at the cases in which you were envious of those whom you thought were above you in any respect. Or perhaps you have envied those who have been more talented or more useful than yourself. Have you not so envied some, that you have been pained to hear them praised? Be honest with yourself; and if you have harbored this spirit of hell, repent deeply before God.

4. Censoriousness. Instances in which you have had a bitter spirit, and spoken of Christians in a manner devoid of charity and love; of charity, which requires you always to hope the best the case will admit, and to put the best construction upon any ambiguous conduct.

5. Slander. The times you have spoken behind people's backs of the faults, real or supposed, of members of the Church or others, unnecessarily, or without good reason.

6. Levity. How often have you trifled before God, as you would not have dared to trifle in the presence of an earthly sovereign?

7. Lying. Understand now what lying is. Any species of designed deception. If you design to make an impression contrary to the naked truth, you lie.

8. Cheating. Set down all the cases in which you have dealt with an individual, and done to him that which you would not like to have done to you.

9. Hypocrisy. For instance, in your prayers and confessions to God. How many times have you confessed sins that you did not mean to break off, and when you had no solemn purpose not to repeat them?

10. Robbing God. Think of the instances in which you have misspent your time, squandering the hours which God gave you to serve Him and save souls, in vain amusements or foolish conversation, cases where you have misapplied your talents and powers of mind. Perhaps some of you have laid out God's money for tobacco. I will not speak of intoxicating drink, for I presume there is no professor of religion here that would drink it, and I hope there is not one that uses that filthy poison, tobacco. Think of a professor of religion using God's money to poison himself with tobacco!

11. Bad temper. Perhaps you have abused your wife, or your children, or your family, or servants, or neighbors.

12. Hindering others from being useful. Perhaps you have weakened their influence by insinuations against them. You have not only robbed God of your own talents, but tied the hands of somebody else.

If you find you have committed a fault against an individual, and that individual is within your reach, go and confess it immediately, and get that out of the way. If the individual you have injured is too far off for you to go and see him, sit down and write him a letter and confess the injury. If you have defrauded anybody, send the money, the full amount and the interest.

Go thoroughly to work in all this. Go now. Confess to God those sins that have been committed against God, and to man those sins that have been committed against man. In breaking up your fallow ground, you must remove every obstruction. Things may be left that you think little things, and you may wonder why you do not feel as you wish to feel in religion, when the reason is that your proud and carnal mind has covered up something which God required you to confess and remove. Break up all the ground and turn it over. Do not "balk" it, as the farmers say; do not turn aside for little difficulties; drive the plough right through them, beam deep, and turn the ground up, so that it may all be mellow and soft, and fit to receive the seed and bear fruit "an hundred-fold."

When you have gone over your whole history in this way, thoroughly, if you will then go over the ground the second time, and give your solemn and fixed attention to it, you will find that the things you have put down will suggest other things of which you have been guilty, connected with them, or near them. Then go over it a third time, and you will recollect other things connected with these. And you will find in the end that you can remember an amount of history, and particular actions, even in this life, which you did not think you, would remember in eternity. Unless you take up your sins in this way, and consider them in detail, one by one, you can form no idea of the amount of them. You should go over the list as thoroughly, and as carefully, and as solemnly, as you would if you were just preparing yourself for the Judgment.

As you go over the catalogue of your sins, be sure to resolve upon present and entire reformation. Wherever you find anything wrong, resolve at once, in the strength of God, to sin no more in that way. It will be of no benefit to examine yourself, unless you determine to amend in every particular that which you find wrong in heart, temper, or conduct.

Remarks

1. It will do no good to preach to you while your hearts are in this hardened, waste, and fallow state. The farmer might just as well sow his grain on the rock. It will bring forth no fruit. This is the reason why there are so many fruitless professors in the Church, and why there is so much outside machinery and so little deepened feeling.

2. Professors of religion should never satisfy themselves, or expect a revival, just by starting out of their slumbers, and blustering about, and talking to sinners. They must get their fallow ground broken up. You may get into an excitement without this breaking up; you may show a kind of zeal, but it will not last long, and it will not take hold of sinners, unless your hearts are broken up.

3. Will you break up your fallow ground? Will you enter upon the course now pointed out and persevere till you are thoroughly awake?

4. The Way of Salvation

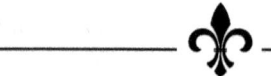

> Sirs, what must I do to be saved? And they said, "Believe on the Lord Jesus Christ." Who of God is made unto us wisdom and righteousness, and sanctification, and redemption. —Acts 16:30b-31a, with 1 Corinthians 1:30b

There can be no objection to putting these texts together in this manner as only a clause in the first of them is omitted, which is not essential to the sense, and which is irrelevant to my present purpose.

In the passage first quoted, the apostle tells the inquiring jailer, who wished to know what he must do to be saved, "Believe on the Lord Jesus Christ and thou shalt be saved." And in the other he adds the explanatory remark, telling what a Savior Jesus Christ is, "Who of God is made unto us wisdom, and righteousness, and sanctification, and redemption."

Christ is the covenant head of those that believe. He is not the natural head, as Adam was, but our covenant relation to him is such, that whatever is given to him is given to us. Whatever he is, both in his divine and human nature; whatever he has done, either as God or man, is given to us by covenant, or promise, and is absolutely ours.

And here let me say, that we receive this grace by faith. It is not by works; by anything we do, more or less, previous to the exercise of faith, that we become interested in this righteousness. But as soon as we exercise faith, all that Christ has done, all there is of Christ, all that is contained in the covenant of grace, becomes ours by faith. The soul becomes actually possessed of all that is embraced in that act of faith. If there is not enough received to break the bonds of sin and set the soul at once at liberty, it is because the act has not embraced enough of what Christ is, and what he has done.

I have read the verse from Corinthians, for the purpose of remarking on some of the fundamental things contained in this covenant of grace. "Of him are ye in Christ Jesus, who of God is made unto us wisdom, and righteousness, and sanctification, and redemption." When Christ is received and believed on, he is "made to us" what is meant by these several particulars.

In what sense is Christ our wisdom?

These two things are contained in the idea of wisdom. First, as Christ is our representative, we are interested in all his wisdom, and all the wisdom he has is exercised for us. His infinite wisdom is actually employed for our benefit. Second, that his wisdom, just as much as is needed, is guaranteed to be always ready to be imparted to us, whenever we exercise faith in him for wisdom. From his infinite fullness, in this respect, we may receive all we need.

He is made unto us righteousness. What is the meaning of this?

It is, that Christ's righteousness becomes ours by gift. God has so united us to Christ, as on his account to treat us with favor. It is just like a case, where a father had done some signal service to his country, and the government thinks it proper to reward such signal service with signal reward; and not only is the individual himself rewarded, but all his family receive favors on his account, because they are the children of a father who had greatly benefitted his country. It is just so in the divine government. Christ's disciples are in such a sense considered one with him, and God is so highly delighted with the signal service he has done the kingdom, from the circumstances under which he became a Savior, that God accounts his righteousness to them as if it were their own; or in other words, treats them just as he would treat Christ himself.

In what sense is Christ made unto us sanctification?

Sanctification is inward purity. And the meaning is, that he is our inward purity. The control which Christ himself exercises over us, his Spirit working in us, to will and to do, his shedding his love abroad in our hearts, so controlling us that we are ourselves, through the faith which is of the operation of God, made actually holy. By faith Christ is received and enthroned as king in our hearts; when the mind, from confidence in Christ, just yields itself up to him, to be led by his Spirit, and guided and controlled by his hand.

It is said Christ is made of God unto us redemption. What are we to understand by that?

Here the apostle plainly refers to the Jewish practice of redeeming estates, or redeeming relatives that had been sold for debt. When an estate had been sold out of the family, or an individual had been deprived of liberty for debt, they could be redeemed, by paying the price of redemption. There are very frequent allusions in the Bible to this practice of redemption. And where Christ is spoken of as our redemption, I suppose it means just what it says. While we are in our sins, under the law, we are sold as slaves, in the hand of public justice, bound over to death, and have no possible way to redeem ourselves from the curse of the law. Now, Christ makes himself the price of our redemption. In other words, he is our redemption money; he buys us out from under the law, by paying himself as a ransom.

Under this covenant of grace, our own works, or any thing that we do, or can do, as works of law, have no more to do with our salvation, than if we had never existed. I wish your minds to separate entirely between salvation by works, and salvation by grace. Our salvation by grace is founded on a reason entirely separate from and out of ourselves. Whether we love God or do not love God so far as it is a ground of our salvation, is of no account. The whole is entirely a matter of grace, through Jesus Christ. However perfect and holy we may become, in this life, or to all eternity, Jesus Christ will forever be the sole reason in the universe why we are not in hell.

Remarks

There is no such thing as spiritual life in us, or anything acceptable to God, until we actually believe in Christ.

We are nothing, as Christians, any farther than we believe in Christ.

Many seem to be waiting to do something first, before they receive Christ.

Some wait to become more dead to the world. Some to get a broken heart. Some to get their doubts cleared up before they come to Christ. This is a grand mistake. It is expecting to do that first, before faith, which is only the result of faith. Your heart will not be broken, your doubts will not be cleared up, and you will never die to the world, until you believe. The moment you grasp the things of Christ, your mind will see, as in the light of eternity, the emptiness of the world, of reputation, riches, honor, and pleasure. To expect this first, preparatory to the exercise of faith, is beginning at the wrong end. It is seeking that as a preparation for faith, which is always the result of faith.

Perfect faith will produce perfect love.

When the mind duly recognizes Christ, and receives him, in his various relations; when the faith is unwavering and the views clear, there will be nothing left in the mind contrary to the law of God.

Abiding faith would produce abiding love.

Faith increasing would produce increasing love. And here you ought to observe, that love may be perfect at all times, and yet be in different degrees at different times. An individual may love God perfectly and eternally, and yet his love may increase in vigor to all eternity, as I suppose it will. As the saints in glory see more and more of God's excellences, they will love him more and more, and yet will have perfect love all the time. That is, there will be nothing inconsistent with love in the mind, while the degrees of love will be different as their views of the character of God unfold. As God opens to their view the wonders of his glorious benevolence, they will have their souls thrilled with new love to God. In this life, the exercises of love vary greatly in degree. Sometimes God unfolds to his saints the wonders of his government, and gives them such views as well nigh prostrate the body, and then love is greatly raised in degree. And yet the love may have been perfect before; that is, the love of God was supreme and single, without any mixture of inconsistent affections.

You see, beloved, from this subject, the way in which you can be made holy, and when you can be sanctified.

Whenever you come to Christ, and receive him for all that he is, and accept a whole salvation by grace, you will have all that Christ is to you, wisdom, and righteousness, and sanctification, and redemption. There is nothing but unbelief to hinder you from now enjoying it all. You need not wait for any preparation. There is no preparation that is of any avail. You must receive a whole salvation, as a free gift. When will you thus lay hold on Christ? When will you believe? Faith, true faith, always works by love, and purifies the heart, and overcomes the world. Whenever you find any difficulty in your way, you may know what is the matter. It is a want of faith. No matter what may befall you outwardly: if you find yourself thrown back in religion, or your mind thrown all into confusion, unbelief is the cause, and faith the remedy. If you lay hold on Christ, and keep hold, all the devils in hell can never drive you away from God, or put out your light. But if you let unbelief prevail, you may go on in this miserable, halting way, talking about sanctification, using words without knowledge, and dishonoring God, till you die.

5. Christian Perfection

> Be ye therefore perfect, even as your Father which
> is in heaven is perfect. —Matthew 5:48

In the 43rd verse, the Savior says, "Ye have heard that it hath been said, 'Thou shalt love thy neighbor, and hate thine enemy;' but I say unto you, 'Love your enemies, bless them that curse you, do good to them that hate you, and pray for them which despitefully use you and persecute you, that ye may be the children of your Father which is in heaven:' for he maketh his sun to rise on the evil and on the good, and sendeth rain on the just and on the unjust. For if ye love them which love you, what reward have ye? Do not even the publicans the same: And if ye salute your brethren only, what do ye more than others? Do not even the publicans so? Be ye therefore perfect, even as your Father which is in heaven is perfect," (Matthew 5:43-48).

I am to show you what Christian Perfection is not. It is not required that we should have the same natural perfections that God has. The perfection required in the text is not perfection of knowledge, even according to our limited faculties.

Christian Perfection, as here required, is not freedom from temptation, either from our constitution or from things that are about us. The mind may be ever so sorely tried with the animal appetites, and yet not sin. The apostle James says, "Every man is tempted, when he is drawn away of his own lust, and enticed," (1:14). The sin is not in the temptations, but in yielding to them. A person may be tempted by Satan, as well as by the appetites, or by the world, and yet not have sin. All sin consists in voluntary consenting to the desires.

Neither does Christian perfection imply a freedom from what ought to be understood by the Christian warfare.

The perfection required is not the infinite moral perfection, which God has, because man, being a finite creature, is not capable of infinite affections. God being infinite in himself for him to be perfect is to be infinitely perfect. But this is not required of us.

I am to show what Christian perfection is; or what is the duty actually required in the text. It is perfect obedience to the law of God. The law of God requires perfect, disinterested, impartial benevolence, love to God and love to our neighbor. Christianity requires that we should do neither more nor less than the law of God prescribes.

I am to show that Christian Perfection is a duty.

This is evident from the fact that God requires it, both under the law and under the gospel.

The command in the text, "Be ye perfect, even as your Father which is in heaven is perfect," (Matthew 5:48) is given under the gospel. Christ here commands the very same thing that the law requires. Some suppose that much less is required of us under the gospel, than was required under the law. It is true that the gospel does not require perfection, as the condition of salvation. But no part of the obligation of the law is discharged. The gospel holds those who are under it to the same holiness as those under the law.

I argue that Christian Perfection is a duty, because God has no right to require anything less.

God cannot discharge us from the obligation to be perfect, as I have defined perfection. If he were to attempt it, he would just so far give a license to sin. He has no right to give any such license. While we are moral beings, there is no power in the universe that can discharge us from the obligation to be perfect. Can God discharge us from the obligation to love him with all our heart, and soul, and mind, and strength? That would be saying that God does not deserve such love. And if he cannot discharge us from the whole law, he cannot discharge from any part of it, for the same reason.

Should anyone contend that the gospel requires less holiness than the law, I would ask him to say just how much less it requires.

If we are allowed to stop short of perfect obedience, where shall we stop? How perfect are we required to be? Where will you find a rule in the Bible, to determine how much less holy you are allowed to be under the gospel, than you would be under the law? Shall we say each one must judge for himself? Then I ask if you think it is your duty to be any more perfect than you are now? Probably all would say, yes. Can you lay down any point at which, when you have arrived, you can say, "Now I am perfect enough; it is true. I have some sin left, but I have gone as far as it is my duty to go in this world?" Where do you get your authority for any such notion? No, the truth is that all who are truly pious, the more pious they are, the more strongly they feel the obligation to be perfect, as God is perfect.

I will now show that Christian Perfection is attainable, or practicable, in this life.

Here let me observe, that so much has been said within a few years about Christian Perfection, and individuals who have entertained the doctrine of Perfection have run into so many wild notions, that it seems as if the devil had anticipated the movements of the church, and created such a state of feeling. But I will say, notwithstanding the errors into which some of those called Perfectionists have fallen, there is such a thing held forth in the Bible as Christian Perfection, and that the Bible doctrine on the subject is what nobody needed to fear, but what everybody needs to know.

1. God wills it. The law of God is itself as strong as expression as he can give of his will on the subject, and it is backed up by an infinite sanction. The gospel is but a republication of the same will in another form. How can God express his will more strongly on this point than he has in the text? "Be ye therefore perfect, even as your Father which is in heaven is perfect," (Matthew 5:48). In 1 Thessalonians 4:3, we are told expressly, "for this is the will of God, even your sanctification." If you examine the Bible carefully, from one end to another, you will find that it is everywhere just as plainly taught that God wills the sanctification of Christians in this world, as it is that he wills sinners should repent in this world. And if we go by the Bible, we might just as readily question whether he wills that men should repent, as whether he wills that Christians should be holy. Why should he not reasonably expect it? He requires it. What does he require? When he requires men to repent, he requires that they should love God with all the heart, soul, mind, and strength. What reason have we to believe that he wills they should repent at all, or love him at all, which is not a reason for believing that he wills they should love him perfectly? Strange logic, indeed! to teach that he wills it in one case, because he requires it, and not admit the same inference in the other. No man can show, from the Bible, that God does not require perfect sanctification in this world, nor that he does not will it, nor that it is not just as attainable as any degree of sanctification.

If you have never looked into the Bible with this view, you will be astonished to see how many more passages there are that speak of deliverance from the commission of sin, than there are that speak of deliverance from the punishment of sin.

2. All the promises and prophecies of God, that respect the sanctification of believers in this world, are to be understood of course, of their perfect sanctification.

What is sanctification, but holiness? When a prophecy speaks of the sanctification of the church, are we to understand that it is to be sanctified only partially? When God requires holiness, are we to understand that of partial holiness? Surely not. By what principle, then, will you understand it of partial holiness when he promises holiness. We have been so long in the way of understanding the scriptures with reference to the existing state of things, that we lose sight of the real meaning. But if we look only at the language of the Bible, I defy any man to prove that the promises and prophecies of holiness mean anything short of perfect sanctification, unless the requirements of both the law and gospel are to be understood of partial obedience, which is absurd.

3. Perfect sanctification is the great blessing promised, throughout the Bible.

The apostle says we have exceeding great and precious promises, and what are they, and what is their use? "Whereby are given unto us exceeding great and precious promises, that by these ye might be partakers of the divine nature, having escaped the corruption that is in the world through lust," 2 Peter 1:4. If that is not perfect sanctification, I beg to know what is. It is a plain declaration that these "exceeding great and precious promises" are given for this object, that by believing, appropriating, and using them, we might become partakers of the divine nature. And if we will use them for the purposes for which they were put in the Bible, we may become perfectly holy.

Look at some of these promises in particular. In Ezekiel 36:25, this blessing is expressly promised, as the great blessing of the gospel: "Then will I sprinkle clean water upon you, and ye shall be clean: from all your filthiness, and from all your idols, will I cleanse you. A new heart also will I give you, and a new spirit will I put within you: and I will take away the stony heart out of your flesh, and I will give you a heart of flesh. And I will put my Spirit within you: and cause you to walk in my statutes, and you shall keep my judgments, and do them."

So it is in Jeremiah 33:8: "And I will cleanse them from all their iniquity, whereby they have sinned against me; and I will pardon all their iniquities, whereby they have sinned, and whereby they have transgressed against me." But it would take up too much time to quote all the passages in the Old Testament prophecies that represent holiness to be the great blessing of the covenant. I desire you all to search the Bible for yourselves, and you will be astonished to find how uniformly the blessing of sanctification is held up as the principal blessing promised to the world through the Messiah.

In the New Testament, the first account we have of the Savior, tells us that he was called "Jesus, for he shall save his people from their sins." So it is said, "He was manifested to take away our sins," and "to destroy the works of the devil." In Titus 2:13, the apostle Paul speaks of the grace of God, or the gospel, as teaching us to deny ungodliness. "Looking for that blessed hope, and the glorious appearing of the great God, and our Savior Jesus Christ, who gave himself for us, that he might redeem us from all iniquity, and purify unto himself a peculiar people, zealous of good works." And in Ephesians 5:26, we learn that "Christ loved the church, and gave himself for it; that he might sanctify and cleanse it with the washing of water by the word, that he might present it to himself a glorious church, not having spot or wrinkle, or any such thing; but that it should be holy and without blemish." I only quote these few passages by way of illustration, to show that the object for which Christ came is to sanctify the church to such a degree that it should be absolutely "holy and without blemish."

In 1 Thessalonians 5:23, the apostle Paul prays a very remarkable prayer: "And the very God of peace sanctify you wholly; and I pray God your whole spirit, and soul, and body, be preserved blameless unto the coming of our Lord Jesus Christ." What is that? "Sanctify you wholly." Could an inspired apostle make such a prayer, if he did not believe the blessing prayed for to be possible? But he goes on to say, in the very next verse, "Faithful is he that calleth you, who also will do it." Is that true, or is it false?

4. The perfect sanctification of believers is the very object for which the Holy Spirit is promised.

To quote the passages that show this, would take up too much time. The whole tenor of scripture respecting the Holy Spirit proves it. The whole array of gospel means through which the Holy Spirit works, is aimed at this, and adapted to the end of sanctifying the church. All the commands to be holy, all the promises, all the prophecies, all the ordinances, all the providences, the blessings and the judgments, all the duties of religion, are the means which the Holy Ghost is to employ for sanctifying the church.

5. If it is not a practicable duty to be perfectly holy in this world, then it will follow that the devil has so completely accomplished his design in corrupting mankind, that Jesus Christ is at fault, and has no way to sanctify his people but by taking them out of the world.

6. If perfect sanctification is not attainable in this world, it must be either from a want of motives in the gospel, or a want of sufficient power in the Spirit of God.

It is said that in another life we may be like God, for we shall see him as he is. But why not here, if we have that faith which is the "substance of things hoped for, and the evidence of things not seen?" There is a promise to those who "hunger and thirst after righteousness" that "they shall be filled." What is it to be "filled" with righteousness, but to be perfectly holy? And are we never to be filled with righteousness until we die? Are we to go through life hungry, and thirsty and unsatisfied? So the Bible has been understood, but it does not read so.

Objections

1. "The power of habit is so great, that we ought not to expect to be perfectly sanctified in this life."

Answer. If the power of habit can be so far encroached upon that an impenitent sinner can be converted, why can it not be absolutely broken, so that a converted person may be wholly sanctified? The greatest difficulty, surely, is when selfishness has the entire control of the mind, and when the habits of sin are wholly unbroken. This obstacle is so great, in all cases, that no power but that of the Holy Ghost can overcome it: and so great, in many instances, that God himself cannot, consistently with his wisdom, use the means necessary to convert the soul. But is it possible to suppose, that after he has begun to overcome it, after he has broken the power of selfishness and the obstinacy of habit, and actually converted the individual, that after this God has not resources sufficient to sanctify the soul altogether!

2. "But so many profess to be perfect, who are not so, that I cannot believe in perfection in this life."

Answer. How many people profess to be rich, who are not. Will you therefore say you cannot believe anybody is rich? Fine logic!

3. "So many who profess perfection have run into error and fanaticism, that I am afraid to think of it."

Answer. I find in history, that a sect of Perfectionists has grown out of every great and general revival that ever took place. And this is exactly one of the devil's masterpieces, to counteract the effects of a revival. He knows that if the church were brought to the proper standard of holiness, it would be a speedy deathblow to his power on earth, and he takes this course to defeat the efforts of the church for elevating the standard of piety, by frightening Christians from marching right up to the point, and aiming at living perfectly conformed to the will of God.

And so successful has he been, that the moment you begin to crowd the church up to be holy, and give up all their sins, somebody will cry out, "Why, this leads to Perfectionism;" and thus give it a bad name and put it down.

4. "But do you really think anybody ever has been perfectly holy in this world?"

Answer. I have reason to believe there have been many. It is highly probable that Enoch and Elijah were free from sin, before they were taken out of the world. And in different ages of the church there have been numbers of Christians who were intelligent and upright, and had nothing that could be said against them, who have testified that they themselves lived free from sin.

People have the strangest notions on this subject. Sometimes you will hear them argue against Christian Perfection on this ground, that a man who was perfectly holy could not live, could not exist in this world. I believe I have talked just so myself, in time past. I know I have talked like a fool on this subject. Why, a saint who was perfect would be more alive than ever, to the good of his fellow men.

Remarks

We can see now the reasons why there is no more perfection in the world.

1. Christians do not believe that it is the will of God, or that God is willing they should be perfectly sanctified in this world.

They know he commands them to be perfect, as he is perfect, but they think that he is secretly unwilling, and does not really wish them to be so; "Otherwise," say they, "why does he not do more for us, to make us perfect?" Sinners reason just as these professors reason. They say, "I don't believe he wills my repentance; if he did, he would make me repent." Sinner, God may prefer your continued impenitence, and your damnation, to using any other influences than he does use to make you repent. But for you to infer from this, that he does not wish you to yield to the influences he does use is strange logic!

2. They do not expect it themselves.

The great part of the church does not really expect to be any more pious than they are.

3. Much of the time, they do not even desire perfect sanctification.

4. They overlook the great design of the gospel.

Too long has the church been in the habit of thinking that the great design of the gospel is, to save men from the punishment of sin, whereas its real design and object is to deliver men from sin. But Christians have taken the other ground, and think of nothing but that they are to go on in sin, and all they hope for is to be forgiven, and when they die made holy in heaven. Oh, if they only realized that the whole framework of the gospel is designed to break the power of sin, and fill men on earth with all the fullness of God, how soon there would be one steady blaze of love in the hearts of God's people all over the world!

5. The promises are not understood, and not appropriated by faith.

If the church would read the Bible, and lay hold of every promise there, they would find them exceeding great and precious. But now the church loses its inheritance, and remains ignorant of the extent of the blessings she may receive.

6. They seek it by the law, and not by faith.

How many are seeking sanctification by their own resolutions and works, their fasting and prayers, their endeavors and activity, instead of taking right hold of Christ, by faith, for sanctification, as they do for justification. It is all work, work, work, when it should be by faith in "Christ Jesus, who of God is made unto us wisdom, and righteousness, and sanctification, and redemption." When they go and take right hold of the strength of God, they will be sanctified. Faith will bring Christ right into the soul, and fill it with the same spirit that breathes through himself. These dead works are nothing. It is faith that must sanctify, it is faith that purifies the heart; that faith which is the substance of things hoped for, takes hold of Christ and brings him into the soul, to dwell there the hope of glory; that the life which we live here should be by the faith of the Son of God. It is from not knowing, or not regarding this, that there is so little holiness in the church.

7. From the want of the right kind of dependence.

Instead of taking scriptural views of their dependence and seeing where their strength is, they sit down, in unbelief and sin, to wait God's time, and call this depending on God. Alas, how little is felt, after all this talk about dependence on the Holy Spirit; how little is really felt of it; and how little is there of the giving up of the whole soul to his control and guidance, with faith in his power to enlighten, to lead, to sanctify, to kindle the affections, and fill the soul continually with all the fullness of God!

8. The fact is Christians do not really believe much that is in the Bible. Now, suppose you were to meet God, and you knew it was God himself, speaking to you, and he should reach out a book in his hand,

and tell you to take that book, and that the book contains exceeding great and precious promises, of all that you need, or ever can need, to resist temptation, to overcome sin, and to make you perfectly holy, and fit you for heaven; and then he tells you that whenever you are in want of anything for this end, you need only take the appropriate promise, and present it to him at any time, and he will do it. Now, if you were to receive such a book, directly from the hand of God, and knew that God had written it for you, with his own hand, would you not believe it? And would you not read it a great deal more than you now read the Bible? How eager you would be to know all that was in it? And how ready to apply the promises in time of need! You would want to get it all by heart, and often repeat it all through, that you might keep your mind familiar with its contents, and be always ready to apply the promises you read! Now, the truth is, the Bible is that book. It is written just so, and filled with just such promises; so that the Christian, by laying hold of the right promise, and pleading it, can always find all that he needs for his spiritual benefit.

Christ is a complete Savior. All the promises of God are in him Yea, and in Him Amen, to the glory of God the Father.

6. Love is the Whole of Religion

> Love worketh no ill to his neighbor; therefore, love is the fulfilling of the law. —Romans 13:10

I will mention some things that are not essential to perfect love.

1. The highest degree of emotion is not essential to perfect love.

It is manifest that the Lord Jesus Christ very seldom had the highest degree of emotion of love, and yet he always had perfect love. He generally manifested very little emotion, or excitement. Excitement is always proportioned to the strength of the emotions as it consists in them. The Savior seemed generally remarkably calm. Sometimes his indignation was strong, or his grief for the hardness of men's hearts; and sometimes we read that he rejoiced in spirit. But he was commonly calm, and manifested no high degree of emotion. And it is plainly not essential to perfect love that the emotion of love should exist in a high degree.

2. Perfect love does not exclude the idea of increase in love or growth in grace.

I suppose the growth of the mind in knowledge, to all eternity, naturally implies growth in love to all eternity. The Lord Jesus Christ, in his human nature, grew in stature, and in favor with God and man. Doubtless, as a child, he grew in knowledge, and as he grew in knowledge, he grew in love toward God, as well as in favor with God. His love was perfect when he was a child, but it was greater when he became a man. As a human being, he probably always continued to increase in love to God as long as he lived. From the nature of mind, we see that it may be so with all the saints in glory that their love will increase to all eternity, and yet it is always perfect love.

3. It is not essential to perfect love, that love should always be exercised towards all individuals alike.

We cannot think of all individuals at once. You cannot even think of every individual of your acquaintance at once. The degree of love towards an individual depends on the fact that the individual is present to the thoughts.

4. It is not essential to perfect love, that there should be the same degree of the spirit of prayer for every individual, or for the same individual at all times.

The spirit of prayer is not always essential to pure and perfect love. The saints in heaven have pure and perfect love for all beings, yet we know not that they have the spirit of prayer for any. You may love any individual with a very strong degree of love, and yet not have the spirit of prayer for that individual. That is, the Spirit of God may not lead you to pray for the salvation of that individual. You do not pray for the wicked in hell. The spirit of prayer depends on the influences of the Holy Ghost, leading the mind to pray for things agreeable to the will of God. You cannot pray in the Spirit, with the same degree of fervor and faith, for all mankind. Jesus Christ said expressly, he did not pray for all mankind: "I pray not for the world." Here has been a great mistake in regard to the spirit of prayer. Some suppose that Christians have not done all their duty when they have not prayed in faith for every individual, as long as there is a sinner on the earth. Then Jesus Christ never did all his duty, for he never did this. God has never told us he will save all mankind, and never gave us any reason to believe he will do it. How then can we pray in faith for the salvation of all? What has that faith to rest on?

What is essential to perfect love?

It implies:

1. That there is nothing in the mind inconsistent with love, no hatred, malice, wrath, envy, or any other malignant emotion that is inconsistent with pure and perfect love.

2. That there is nothing in the life inconsistent with love. All the actions, words, and thoughts, continually under the entire and perfect control of love.

3. That the love to God is supreme. The love to God is completely supreme, and so entirely above all other objects, that nothing else is loved in comparison with God.

4. That love to God is disinterested. God is loved for what he is not for his relation to us, but for the excellence of his character.

5. That love to our neighbor should be equal, i.e. that his interest and happiness should be regarded by us of equal value with our own, and he and his interests are to be treated accordingly by us.

I am to mention some of the effects of perfect love.

1. One effect of perfect love to God and man will certainly be, delight in self-denial for the sake of promoting the interests of God's kingdom and the salvation of sinners.

See affectionate parents, how they delight in self-denial for the sake of promoting the happiness of their children. There is a father; he gives himself up to exhausting labor, day by day, and from year to year, through the whole of a long life, rising early, and eating the bread of carefulness continually, to promote the welfare of his family. And he counts all this self-denial and toil not a grief or a burden, but a delight, because of the love he bears to his family. See that mother; she wishes to educate her son at college. And now, instead of finding it painful it is a joy to her to sit up late and labor incessantly to help him. That is because she really loves her son. Such parents rejoice more in conferring gifts on their children, than they would in enjoying the same things themselves. What parent does not enjoy a piece of fruit more in giving it to his little child, than in eating it himself? The Lord Jesus Christ enjoyed more solid satisfaction in working out salvation for mankind than any of his saints can ever enjoy in receiving favors at his hands. He testified that it is more blessed to give than to receive. This was the joy set before him, for which he endured the cross and despised the shame. His love was so great for mankind, that it constrained him to undertake this work, and sustained him triumphantly through it. – The apostle Paul did not count it a grief and a hardship to be hunted from place to place, imprisoned, scourged, stoned, and counted the offscouring of all things, for the sake of spreading the gospel and saving souls. It was his joy. The love of Christ so constrained him, he had such a desire to do good, that it was his highest delight to lay himself on that altar as a sacrifice to the cause. Other individuals have had the same mind with the apostle. They have been known who would be willing to live a thousand years, or to the end of time, if they could be employed in doing good, in promoting the kingdom of God, and saving the souls of men, and willing to forego even sleep and food to benefit objects they so greatly love.

2. It delivers the soul from the power of legal motives.

Perfect love leads a person to obey God, not because he fears the wrath of God, or hopes to be rewarded for doing this or that, but because he loves God and loves to do the will of God. There are two extremes on this subject. One class make virtue to consist in doing right, simply because it is right, without any reference to the will of God, or any influence from God. Another class makes virtue to consist in acting from love to the employment, but without reference to God's authority, as a Ruler and Lawgiver. Both of these are in error. To do a thing simply because he thinks it right, and not out of love to God is not virtue. Neither is it virtue to do a thing because he loves to do it, with no regard to God's will. A woman might do certain things because she knew it would please her husband, but if she did the same thing merely because she loved to do it, and with no regard to her husband, it would be no virtue as it respects her husband. If a person loves God, as soon as he knows what is God's will, he will do it because it is God's will. Perfect love will lead to universal obedience; to do God's will in all things, because it is the will of God.

3. The individual who exercises perfect love will be dead to the world.

I mean by this that he will be cut loose from the influence of worldly considerations. Perfect love will so annihilate selfishness, that he will have no will but the will of God, and no interest but God's glory.

4. It is hardly necessary to say that perfect joy and peace are the natural results of perfect love.

Remarks

1. How much that is called religion has no love.

How much of what passes for works of religion is constrained by outward causes and influences, and not by the inward power of love. It ought to be better understood than it is, that unless love is the mainspring, no matter what the outward action may be, whether praying, praising, giving, or anything else, there is no religion in it.

2. Those religious excitements, which do not consist in the spirit of love, are not revivals of religion.

3. The thing on which the Lord Jesus Christ is bent is to bring all mankind under the influence of love.

Is it not a worthy object? He came to destroy the works of the devil; and this is the way to do it. Suppose the world was full of such men as Jesus Christ was in his human nature – compare it with what it is now. Would not such a change be worthy of the Son of God? What a glorious end, to fill the earth with love.

4. It is easy to see what makes heaven. It is love – perfect love. And it is easy to see what makes heaven begun on earth, in those who are full of love. How sweet their temper; what delightful companions; how blessed to live near them: so full of candor, so kind, so gentle, and so careful to avoid offence, so divinely amiable in all things!

And is this to be attained by men? Can we love God, in this world with all the heart, and soul, and strength, and mind? Is it our privilege and our duty to possess the Spirit of Christ – and shall we exhibit the spirit of the devil? Beloved, let our hearts be set on perfect love, and let us give God no rest till we feel our hearts full of love, and till all our thoughts and all our lives are full of love to God and love to man. O, when will the church come up to this ground? Only let the church be full of love, and she will be fair as the moon, clear as the sun, and terrible to all wickedness, in high places and low places, as an army with banners.

7. Notes

1   This estimate is commonly mentioned by reputable historians, e.g. Earle E. Cairns, *An Endless Line of Splendor* (Wheaton: Tyndale House, 1986), p. 135; John Mark Terry, *Evangelism: A Concise History* (Nashville: Broadman and Holman, 1994), p. 146.

2   Charles G. Finney, *The Memoirs of Charles G. Finney, The Complete Restored Text*, edited by Garth M. Rosell and Richard A. G. Dupius (Grand Rapids: Zondervan Publishing House, 1989), p. 16. This edition with its extensive footnotes and supplementary information is by far the best-printed resource on the life and work of Finney. The first edition of the Memoirs, edited by James Harris Fairchild, was published in 1876 under the title, *Memoirs of Rev. Charles G. Finney*, Written by himself (New York: A. S Barnes & Co.), but considerable portions of the original manuscript were edited out of the published text.

3   *Ibid.,* p. 19.

4   *Ibid.,* p. 20.

5   *Ibid.,* p. 23.

6   *Ibid.,* p. 24.

7   *Ibid.,* p. 27.

8   *Ibid.,* p. 47. This comment interested me since I am a graduate of Princeton Theological Seminary.

9   Hebrew 12:14, *Ibid., p. 83.*

10 Prof. G. Fedrick Wright, quoted by Basil Miller, *Charles G. Finney* (Grand Rapids: Zondervan, 1912), p. 46. Similarly Garth Rosell, eminent Finney authority, calls him a "devoted father and husband," *Great Leaders of the Christian Church*, John Woodbridge, Gen. Ed. (Chicago: Moody Press, 1988), p. 319.

11 *Memoirs,* op. cit., p. 67.

12 *Ibid.,* pp. 182-183.

13 *Ibid.,* pp. 325-326. This figure may have been too high, unless allowance is made for the revival outreach in other areas. However, some estimates of the converted at Rochester reach 200,000. A discussion of this number is in footnote 115, *Ibid.*, p. 326.

14 Charles G. Finney, *Revivals of Religion* (Westwood, N.J., Fleming H. Revell, n.d.), p. 7.

15 *Ibid.,* p. 8.

16 *Ibid.,* p. 5.

17 Notes of the messages were taken by the editor of *The New York Evangelist*, revised by Finney, and printed in book form in 1837. The selections quoted here are from the 1878 edition prepared by E.J. Goodrich, and reprinted by Fleming H. Revell (New York).

18 *Memoirs,* op. cit., p. 390.

19 *Ibid.,* p. 392. In this position, Finney came to the same conclusion as John Wesley. Their views on entire sanctification or perfect love are in substantial agreement. See notes in *Ibid.*, pp. 391-392.

20 For a beautiful account of Finney's last hours, see Lewish A. Drummond, *Charles Grandison Finney and the Birth of Modern Evangelism* (London: Hodder and Stoughton, 1983), pp. 258-261.

Faith in Action

George Müller 1805-1898

With an Introduction
By David P. Setran

Abridged version of *Faith in Action* by George Müller. Abridged version originally published by The Institute of Evangelism Billy Graham Center, 1994, Wheaton, Il. Copyright of abridged version and introduction held by David P. Setran, used with permission. Scripture quotations are taken from the Holy Bible, King James Version (KJV), in the Public Domain. Artwork in the Public Domain.

Book Chapters

1. Introduction
   By David P. Setran 290
2. Faith..296
   Have My Faith Strengthened 297
3. Stewardship...301
   Passages on Stewardship 301
   Steward for God 307
4. The Word of God..309
5. Prayer...316
6. The Deeper Life 319
7. The Christian in the Workplace 323
   Am I in a Calling in Which I Can Abide with God? 323
   Why Do I Carry on This Business?..324
8. Working with Children...325
9. The Will of God 326
10. The Challenge 327
11. Notes..329

1. Introduction
By David P. Setran

George Müller will forever be remembered as a man of extraordinary faith. In his 92 years on this earth, Müller accomplished a great deal for the Kingdom of God. He supported more than 10,000 orphans in five separate orphanages, built under his own supervision. He traveled more than 200,000 miles in 42 countries, preaching the Gospel of Jesus Christ and the need for a more radical trust in His provision. He established an institution dedicated to the promulgation of the Gospel through Sunday schools, day schools, Bible distribution and missionary assistance. Nearly 260,000 pounds were raised for worldwide missionary ventures. For these vast and diverse projects, Müller raised a total of nearly 1.5 million pounds, an exorbitant amount, especially by 19th century stands. Even more remarkable, however, he received this large sum solely through prayer and faith without a single incident of personal solicitation.

The first twenty years of George Müller's life belied his future role as a Christian leader. Born on September 27, 1805 in Kroppenstaedt, Prussia, Müller spent his early years in profligate revelry, borrowing large sums of money to support his own indulgences. He stole regularly from stores and from his father, who was the collector of taxes for the region of Heimersleben. At the age of sixteen, he was arrested and spent four weeks in prison for his inability to make payments at two hotels which had afforded him luxurious accommodations at their own expense.

Despite his reckless living, Müller desired to honor his father's dream for him to go into the ministry, a request based in monetary rather than spiritual concerns. With this in mind, in 1825, Müller applied and was accepted at Halle University to study under the learned professor of Theology, Dr. Friedrich Tholuck. Although his rebellious and sullied lifestyle continued unremitted, a close friend soon invited him to a Christian meeting where, for the first time, he heard the true meaning of salvation through Jesus Christ. After excitedly attending these studies for a short time, Müller committed his life to Christ:

> That evening was the turning point in my life...What all the exhortations and precepts of my father and others could not effect; what all my resolutions could not bring about...I was enabled to do, constrained by the love of Jesus.[1]

In the wake of his conversion, Müller's life changed drastically and immediately. With his new desire for moral purity came an equally potent longing for ministry. After completing his coursework at Halle and being exempted from military service on account of poor health, he rejected his father's pecuniary interests and began evangelistic work among the Jews in London. However, after a short time in this work, a rather serious illness forced him to move to the more healthful climate of nearby Teignmouth. There, Müller came into contact with a nascent Brethren movement, particularly the form espoused by his later soul mate and co-worker, Henry Craik. His tendencies towards premillenial and Calvinistic theology were shaped by these early encounters, as was his high views of Scripture and personal holiness. After these important meetings, Müller felt compelled to terminate his association with the missionary society in London. Although he had profited greatly through his work among the Jews, he purposed in his heart to be guided, from that time on, solely by the Holy Spirit and the Word of God. He also desired a ministry that would enable him to minister to both Jews and Gentiles alike.

With this connection officially severed, Müller was asked to become pastor of Ebenezer Chapel in Teignmouth, a congregation of only eighteen members at the time. After several speaking engagements here and in the surrounding regions, he married Miss Mary Groves of Exeter, the sister of a prominent Brethren layman. Soon after their union, the couple jointly decided to forsake Müller's set salary in favor of a life lived completely by faith in the Lord's provision. This decision began a life-long adventure of faith for the couple, as each resolved to reveal their financial and material needs only to the Lord.

Müller's friend, Henry Craik, soon implored him to move to Bristol to assist him in the work at Gideon Chapel. Feeling this to be the Lord's will, Müller and his wife left Teignmouth and the congregation of Ebenezer Chapel in May of 1832, roughly two and a half years after he had arrived.

Within a few months, Müller and Craik had also assumed leadership of a struggling congregation at Bethesda Chapel in Bristol. Their joint ministry at these two churches consumed much of Müller's time in the first two years of this new ministry. However, in 1834, about two years after their first child, Lydia, was born, the Müllers also established the Scriptural Knowledge Institution for Home and Abroad. This organization was set up to promote day schools, Bible distribution, and missionary assistance to the foreign field. Despite its rather lengthy and pedantic title, this Institution flourished under Müller's leadership. During his lifetime, nearly 115,000 pounds was spent on school work, 90,000 on the dissemination of Bibles and tracts and 260,000 pounds on missionary support.

In spite of these enormous responsibilities, Müller still found time to respond to the disturbing plight of the orphans in Bristol and the surrounding regions. He initiated plans, in December of 1835, to open house on Wilson Street that would assuage the situation of the urban poor, while also preventing street children from being forced into the iniquitous workhouses in the area. Philanthropy was not Müller's only concern, however. In fact, while this was a major factor in his decision to embark on this project, it was clearly not the primary motive:

> I certainly did from my heart desire to be used by God to benefit the bodies of poor children bereaved of both parents, and seek, in other respects, with the help of God, to do them good for this life...but still, the first and primary object of the work was that God might be magnified by the fact, that the orphans under my care are provided, with all they need, only by *prayer* and *faith*, without anyone being asked by me or my fellow-laborers, whereby, it may be seen, that God is FAITHFUL STILL and HEARS PRAYER STILL.[2]

In each of these purposes, Müller was remarkably successful. Without solicitation, monetary and material gifts began arriving in response to his prayers. By June of 1836, three houses were operational, one for girls, one for boys, and one for infants of both sexes.

The life of faith, though rewarding, was not always easy or straightforward. The vast responsibilities of the work often taxed Müller's weak physical constitution, and he suffered numerous recurring illnesses. Funds were often depleted until the very hour before a specific need arose. But, despite these hardships, God always provided physical health and material resources at precisely the right time. Müller's response to hardship was in keeping with his overall purpose:

> The chief end for which the Institution was established is, that the Church of Christ at large might be benefited by seeing manifestly the hand of God stretched out on our behalf in the hour of need, in answer to prayer. Our desire...is not that we may be without trials of faith, but that the Lord graciously would be pleased to support us in the trial, that we may not dishonor Him by distrust.[3]

As the work progressed, the Wilson Street location became problematic. Space limitations left Müller with no choice but to reject hundreds of applications, and there was little room for the orphans to play without disturbing neighbors in close proximity. After much prayer, Müller felt that the Lord wanted him to enlarge his vision for the project. In faith, he purchased a large plot of land as Ashley Down, on the northern outskirts of Bristol. God's gracious hand was seen, not only in the location, but also in the fact that the owner felt strangely led to reduce his asking price considerably. By 1870, five new homes had been constructed at the new site. These homes now included more than two hundred paid staff and approximately 2000 orphans to feed and clothe.

Despite these exacting financial pressures, Müller was able to give generous support to more than two hundred missionaries during the 1870s. In fact, for a time he almost singlehandedly supported the 21 missionary families of the China Inland Mission, including Mr. and Mrs. Hudson Taylor. All in all, this decade saw George Müller send more than 10,000 pounds annually to overseas missions projects throughout the world. As with the orphan work, these funds were miraculously raised through prayer and faith, without prior announcement or solicitation.

After the death of Müller's wife in 1870, he remarried in 1871 and began a worldwide preaching tour that, with some interruption, lasted seventeen years. He and his new wife, Susannah, began with a stint in Britain, Scotland, and Ireland; following up the tremendous Moody and Sankey revivals with disciplined biblical exposition and discipleship. A larger European tour saw Müller preach in France, Switzerland, Germany, and Holland, with extended speaking engagements in each country. In 1877, Müller traveled to the United States, speaking more than three hundred times and traveling in excess of 19,000 miles during his nine-month stay. Highlights of this trip included preaching stints in Moody's tabernacles in Chicago and Boston, as well as a guided tour of the White House from President and Mrs. Hayes. Other tours over the next fifteen years included stops in Spain, Egypt, Palestine, Syria, Austria, India,

China, Japan, and New Zealand, to name a few. By the time his tours had ended in 1892, Müller had traveled approximately 200,000 miles in 42 countries, giving evangelistic meetings and imploring believers to live a life of implicit trust in the Lord.

George Müller went to be with the Lord on March 10, 1898 at the age of 92. He had outlived two wives and his daughter by that time, and had seen God's gracious provision even in his own physical longevity. Müller did not own a great deal at the time of his death. It has been estimated that 81,000 of the 934,000 pounds he received for personal expenses were given away, either to missionaries on the foreign field or to the work of the orphanage and the Scriptural Knowledge Institution. At the time of his death, his entire estate was valued at a mere one hundred sixty pounds, including furniture and other personal items. By worldly standards, Müller died a poor man. But he had accomplished what he held as the goal for all Christians: "he was rich towards God." Müller himself stated the purpose of his life with great clarity:

> My chief object was the glory of God, by giving a practical demonstration as to what could be accomplished simply through the instrumentality of prayer and faith, in order thus to benefit the Church of Christ at large and to lead a careless world to see the reality of the things of God, by showing them, in the work, that the Living God is still, as 4,000 years ago, the Living God. This my aim has been abundantly honored.[4]

Indeed, this desire has been, and continues to be, realized among God's people who are acquainted with his work.

Müller's legacy has been furthered chiefly through the influence of his one written work, *A Narrative of Some of the Lord's Dealings with George Müller*. Müller himself claims that more prayer went into this one work than all other endeavors. His purpose in writing was simple. He saw, in his many years of ministry, that the greatest problem among Christians was a lack of faith in the Lord's provision. He desired to show, then, through is own personal example, that the Lord was still able to meet the needs of his servants. He wanted to show that his extraordinary faith was really a very ordinary response to God's tremendous faithfulness.

It is said that George Müller knew of more than 50,000 specific answers to prayer in his lifetime. These *Narratives* continue to be one in that number.

The following excerpts have been selected chiefly from the writings of George Müller in *A Narrative of Some of the Lord's Dealings with George Müller:* parts 1-3 (London: J. Nisbet and co., 1860, sixth ed.), *A Narrative of Some of the Lord's Dealings with George Müller:* part 4 (London, J. Nisbet and Co., 1873, third ed.), *Counsel to Christians* (London: J. Nisbet and CO., 1878, third ed.) and the *Autobiography of George Müller* (London: J. Nisbet and Co., 1905).

David P. Setran
Wheaton, Illinois, 1994

2. Faith

Faith is above circumstances. No war, no fire, no water, no mercantile panic, no loss of friends, no death can touch it. It goes on its own steady course. It triumphs over all difficulties. It works most easily in the greatest difficulties. Those who really confide in God, because they know the power of His arm, and the love of His heart, as shown most in the death and resurrection of His only begotten Son, are helped, whatever their trials and difficulties might be (*Autobiography of George Müller*, p. 353).

The natural mind is ever prone to *reason*, when we ought to *believe*; and to be *at work*, we ought to be *quiet*; to go our own way, when we ought steadily to walk on in God's ways, however trying to nature. When first converted, I should have said, "What harm can there be to take some of the money, which has been put by for the Building Fund? God will help me again after some time with means for the Orphans, and then I can replace it" …I know that many would act thus. But how does it work, when we thus anticipate God, by going our own way? We bring, in many instances, guilt on our conscience; but if not, we certainly weaken faith, instead of increasing it; and each time we work thus a deliverance of our own, we find it more and more difficult to trust in God, till at last we give way entirely to our natural fallen reasons, and unbelief prevails. How different, if one is enabled to wait for God's own time, and to look alone to Him for help and deliverance! When at last help comes, after many seasons of prayer it may be, and after much exercise of faith and patience it may be, how sweet it is, and what present recompense does the soul at once receive for trusting in God, and waiting patiently for His deliverance! Dear Christian reader, if you have never walked in this path of obedience before, do so now, and you will then know experimentally the sweetness of the joy which results from it (*A Narrative of Some of the Lord's Dealings with George Müller*, part 4, p. 295).

Have My Faith Strengthened

You ask, "How may I, a true believer, have my faith strengthened?" The answer is this:

"Every good gift and every perfect gift is from above, and cometh down from the Father of lights with whom there is no variableness, neither shadow of turning, "(James 1:17).

The following means, however, ought to be used:

Carefully Read and Meditate on the Word of God

Through the reading of the Word of God, and especially through meditation on the Word of God, the believer becomes more and more acquainted with the nature and character of God, and thus sees more and more, besides His holiness and justice, what a kind, loving, gracious, merciful, mighty, wise, and faithful Being He is, and therefore in poverty, affliction of body, bereavement in his family, difficulty in his service, want of a situation of employment, he will repose on the *ability* of God to help him, because he has not only learned from His Word that He is of almighty power and infinite wisdom, but he has also seen instance upon instance in the Holy Scriptures in which His almighty power and infinite wisdom have been actually exercised in helping and delivering His people; and he will repose upon the *willingness* of God to help him, because he has not only learned from the Scriptures what a kind, good, merciful, gracious, and faithful Being God is, but because he has also seen in the Word of God, how in a great variety of instances He has proved Himself to be so. And the consideration of this, if *God has become known to us through prayer and meditation on His own word*, will lead us, in general at least, with a measure of confidence to rely upon Him: and thus the reading on the Word of God, together with meditation on it, will be one special means to strengthen our faith.

Maintain an Upright Heart and a Good Conscience

As with reference to the growth of every grace of the Spirit, it is of the utmost importance that we seek to maintain an upright heart and a good conscience, and therefore, do not knowingly and habitually indulge in those things which are contrary to the mind of God, so it is also particularly the case with reference to the *growth in faith*. How can I possibly continue to act in faith upon God, concerning anything, if I am habitually grieving Him, and seek to detract from the glory upon whom I profess to depend? All my confidence towards God, all my leaning upon Him in the hour of trial, will be gone, if I have a guilty conscience, and do not seek to put away this guilty conscience, but still continue to do things which are contrary to the mind of God.

And if, in any particular instance, I cannot trust in God, because of the guilty conscience, then my faith is weakened by that instance of distrust; for faith with every fresh trial of it, either increases by trusting God, and thus obtains help, or it decreases by not trusting Him; and then there is less and less power of looking simply and directly to Him, and a habit of self dependence is begotten or encouraged. One or the other of these will always be the case in each particular instance. Either we trust God, and in that case we neither trust in ourselves nor in our fellowmen nor in circumstances nor in anything besides; or *do* trust in one or more of these, and in that case we do NOT trust in God.

Shrink Not From Opportunities Where Our Faith May be Tried

If we, indeed, desire our faith to be strengthened, we should not shrink from opportunities where our faith may be tried, and therefore, through the trials be strengthened. In our natural state we dislike dealing with God alone. Through our natural alienation from God we shrink from Him, and from eternal realities. This cleaves to us, more or less, even after our regeneration. Hence it is, that more or less, even as believers, we have the same shrinking from standing with God alone—from depending upon Him alone—and yet this is the very position in which we ought to be, if we wish to have our faith strengthened.

The more I am in a position to be tried in faith with reference to my body, my family, my service for the Lord, my business, etc., the more shall I have opportunity of seeing God's help and deliverance; and every fresh instance, in which He helps and delivers me, will tend towards the increase of my faith. On this account, therefore, the believer should not shrink from situations, positions, circumstances, in which his faith may be tried; but should cheerfully embrace them as opportunities where he may see the hand of God stretched out on his behalf, to help and deliver him, and whereby he may thus have his faith strengthened.

Let God Work for Us

The last important point for the strengthening of our faith is that we let God work for us, when the hour of the trial of our faith comes, and do not work a deliverance of our own. Wherever God has given faith, it is given, among other reasons, for the very purpose of being tried. Yea, however weak our faith may be, God will try it; only with this restriction, that as in every way, He leads on gently, gradually, patiently, so also with reference to the trial of our faith. At first our faith will be tried very little in comparison with what it may be afterwards; for God never lays more upon us than He is willing to enable us to bear. Now when the trial of faith comes, we are naturally inclined to distrust God, and to trust rather in ourselves, or in our friends, or in circumstances. We will father work a deliverance of our own somehow or other than simply look to God and wait for His help. But if we do not patiently wait for God's help, if we work a deliverance of our own, then at the next trial of our faith it will be thus again, we shall be again included to deliver ourselves; and thus, with every fresh instance of that kind, our faith will decrease; whilst, on the contrary, were we to stand still, in order to see the salvation of God, to see His hand stretched out on our behalf, trusting in Him alone, then our faith would be increased, and, with every fresh case in which the hand of God is stretched out on our behalf in another hour of the trial of our faith, our faith would be increased yet more. Would the believer, therefore, have his faith strengthened, he must, especially, give time to God, who tried this faith in order to prove His child, in the end, how willing He is to help and deliver him, the moment it is good for him (*Narrative*, pt 3, pp. 453-456).

From my inmost soul I do ascribe it to God alone that He has enabled me to trust in Him, and that He has not suffered my confidence in Him to fail. But I thought it needful to make these remarks, lest anyone should think that my depending upon God was a particular gift given to me, which other saints have no right to look for; or lest it should be thought that this my depending upon Him had *only to do with the obtaining of MONEY by prayer and faith*. By the grace of God I desire that my faith in God should extend towards EVERY thing, the smallest of my own temporal and spiritual concerns, and the smallest of the temporal and spiritual concerns of my family, towards the saints among whom I labor, the church at large…Dear reader, do not think that I have attained in faith (and how much less in other respects!) to that degree to which I might and ought to attain; but thank God for the faith which he has given me, and ask him to uphold and increase it.

And lastly, once more, let not Satan deceive you in making you think that you could not have the same faith, but that it is only for persons who are situated as I am. When I lose such a thing as a key, I ask the Lord to direct me to it, and I look for an answer to my prayer; when a person with who I have made an appointment does not come at the fixed time, and I begin to be inconvenienced by it, I ask the Lord to be pleased to hasten him to me, and I look for an answer; when I do not understand a passage from the Word of God, I lift up my heart to the Lord that He would be pleased by His Holy Spirit, to instruct me, and I expect to be taught though I do not fix the time when, and the manner how it should be; when I am going to minister in the Word, I seek help from the Lord, and while I, in the consciousness of natural inability as well as utter unworthiness, begin this His service, I'm not cast down, but of good cheer, because I look for His assistance, and believe that He for His dear Son's sake will help me. And thus in other of my temporal and spiritual concerns I pray to the Lord, and expect an answer to my request; and may not you do the same, dear believing reader?

Oh! I beseech you, do not think me an extraordinary believer, having privileges above other of God's dear children, which they cannot have; nor look on my way of acting as something that would not do for other believers…Do see the help of God, if you trust in Him. But there is so often a forsaking the ways of the Lord in the hour of trial, and thus the *food of faith*, the means whereby our faith may be increased, is lost (*Narrative*, pt 3, pp. 452-453).

3. Stewardship

Passages on Stewardship

I now add some hints on a few passages of the Word of God, both because I have so very frequently found them little regarded by Christians, and also because I have proved their preciousness, in some measure, in my own experience:

Matthew 6:19-21

In Matthew 6:19-21, it is written:

> "Lay not up for yourselves treasures upon earth, where moth and rust doth corrupt, and where thieves break through and steal; but lay up for yourselves treasures in heaven, where neither moth nor rust doth corrupt, and where thieves do not break through nor steal: for where your treasure is, there will your heart be also."

—Observe, dear reader, the following points concerning this part of the divine testimony:

I. It is the Lord Jesus, our Lord and Master, who speaks this as the lawgiver of His people. He who has infinite wisdom and unfathomable love for us, who therefore both knows what is for our real welfare and happiness, and who cannot exact from us any requirement inconsistent with that love which led Him to lay down His life for us. Remembering then, who it is who speaks to us in these verses, let us consider them.

II. His counsel, His affectionate entreaty, and His commandment to us His disciples is: "Lay not up for yourselves treasures upon earth." The meaning obviously is, that the disciples of the Lord Jesus, being strangers and pilgrims on the earth, i.e. neither belonging to the earth nor expecting to remain in it, should not seek to increase their earthly possessions, in whatever these possessions may consist. This is a word for poor believers as well as for rich believers; it has as much a reference to putting shillings into the savings' bank as to putting thousands of pounds into the funds, or purchasing one house, or one farm after another.

It may be said, but does not every prudent and provident person seek to increase his means, that he may have a goodly portion to leave to his children, or have something for old age, or for the time of sickness, etc.? My reply is, it is quite true that this is the custom of the world. It was thus in the days of our Lord, and Paul refers to this custom of the world when he says, "The children ought not to lay up for the parents, but the parents for the children," (2 Corinthians 12:14).

But whilst thus it is in the world and we have every reason to believe ever will be so among those that are of the world, and who therefore have their partion on earth, we disciples of the Lord Jesus, being born again, being the children of God not nominally, but really, being truly partakers of the divine nature, being in fellowship with the Father and the Son, and having in prospect "an inheritance incorruptible, and undefiled, and that fadeth not away," (1 Peter 2:4), ought in every respect to act differently from the word, and so in this particular also. If we disciples of the Lord Jesus seek, like the people of the world, after an increase of our possessions, may not those who are of the world justly question whether we believe what we say, when we speak about our inheritance, our heavenly calling, our being the children of God, etc.? Often it must be a sad stumbling block to the unbeliever to see a professed believer in the Lord Jesus acting in this particular just like himself.

Consider this, dear brethren in the Lord, should this remark apply to you—I have more than once had the following passage quoted to me as a proof that parents ought to lay up money for their children, or husbands for their wives: "But if any provide not for his own, and especially for those of his own house (or kindred), he hath denied the faith, and is worse than an infidel," (1 Timothy 5:8). It is, however, concerning this verse, only needful, in childlike simplicity to read the connection from verse 3 to 5, and it will be obvious that the meaning is this, that while the poor widows of the church are to be cared for by the church, yet if any such needy believing widow had children or grandchildren (not nephews), these children or grandchildren should provide for the widow, that the church might not be charged; but that, if a believer's child, or grandchild, in such a case did not do so, such a one did not act according to the obligations laid upon him by his holy faith, and was worse than an unbeliever. Not a word, then, is there in this passage to favor the laying up treasures upon earth for our children or our wives.

III. Our Lord says concerning the earth that it is a place "where moth and rust doth corrupt, and where thieves break through and steal." All that is of the earth, and in any way connected with it, is subject to corruption, to change, to dissolution. There is no reality, or substance, in anything else but in heavenly things. Often the careful amassing of earthly possessions ends in losing them in a moment by fire, by robbery, by a change of mercantile concerns, or by loss of work, etc.; but suppose all this was not the case still, yet a little while, and your soul shall be required of you; or, yet a little while, and the Lord Jesus will return; and what profit shall thou then have, dear reader, if thou hast carefully sought to increase your earthly possessions?

My brother, if there were one particle of real benefit to be derived from it, would not He, whose love to us has been proved to the uttermost, have wished that you and I should have it? If, in the least degree, it could tend to the increase of our peace, or joy in the Holy Ghost, or heavenly mindedness, He who laid down His life for us, would have commanded us to LAY UP treasure upon earth.

IV. Our Lord, however, does not merely bid us not to lay up treasure upon earth; for if He had said no one, this commandment might be abused, and persons might find it in an encouragement for their extravagant habits, for their love of pleasure, for their habit of spending everything they have, or can obtain, *upon themselves*. It does not mean, then, as is the common phrase, that we should live up to our income; for, He adds: "But lay up for yourselves treasures in heaven." There is such a thing as laying up as truly in Heaven as there is laying up on earth; if it were not so, our Lord would not have said so.

Just as persons put one sum after another into the bank, and it is put down to their credit, and they may use the money afterwards: so truly the penny, the shilling, the pound, the hundred pounds, the ten thousand pounds, *given for the Lord's sake, and constrained by the love of Jesus*, to poor brethren, or in any way spent in the work of God, He marks down in the book of remembrance, He considers as laid up in Heaven. *The money is not lost, it is laid up in the bank of Heaven*; yet so, that, whilst an earthly bank may break, or through earthly circumstances we may lose our earthly possessions, the money, which is thus secured in Heaven, *cannot be lost.*

But this is by no means the only difference. I notice a few more points. Treasures laid up on earth bring along with them many cares; treasures laid up in Heaven never give care. Treasures laid up on earth never can afford spiritual joy; treasures laid up in Heaven bring along with them peace and joy in the Holy Ghost even now. Treasures laid up on earth, in a dying hour cannot afford peace and comfort, and when life is over, they are taken from us; treasures laid up in Heaven draw forth thanksgiving that we were permitted and counted worthy to serve the Lord with the means with which He was pleased to entrust us as stewards; and when this life is over we are not deprived of what was laid up there, but when we go to Heaven we go to the place where our treasures are, and we shall find them there.

Often we hear it said when a person has died: "he died worth so much." But whatever be the phrases common in the world, it is certain that a person may die worth fifty thousand pounds sterling, as the world reckons, and yet that individual may not posses, in the sight of God, one thousand pounds, because *he was not rich towards God*, he did not lay up treasure in Heaven. And so on the other hand, we can suppose a man of God falling asleep in Jesus, and his surviving widow finding scarcely enough left behind to suffice for the funeral, who was nevertheless *rich towards God*; in the sight of God he may posses five thousand pounds, he may have laid up that sum in Heaven...

Dear reader, does your soul long to be rich towards God, to lay up treasures in Heaven? The world passes away and the lust thereof! Yet a little while, and our stewardship will be taken from us. At present we have the opportunity of serving the Lord, with our time, our talents, our bodily strength, our gifts, and also with our property; but shortly this opportunity may cease. Oh! how shortly may it cease. Before ever this is read by any one, I may have fallen asleep and the very next day after you have read this, dear Reader, you may fall asleep, and therefore, whilst we have the opportunity, let us serve the Lord—I believe, and therefore I speak.

My own soul is so fully assured of the wisdom and love of the Lord toward us His disciples as expressed in this Word, that by His grace I do most heartily set my seal to the preciousness of the command, and I do from my inmost soul not only desire not to lay up treasures upon earth, but, believing as I do what the Lord says, I do desire to have grace to lay up treasures in heaven. And then, suppose after a little while you should fall asleep, someone may say, your wife and child will be unprovied for, because you did not make a provision for them. My reply is, the Lord will take care of them. The Lord will abundantly provide for them, as He now abundantly provides for us.

V. The Lord lastly adds: "For where your treasure is, there will your heart be also." Where should the heart of the disciple of the Lord Jesus be, but in Heaven? Our calling is a heavenly calling; our inheritance is a heavenly inheritance, and reserved for us in Heaven; our citizenship is in Heaven; but if we believers in the Lord Jesus lay up treasures on earth, the necessary result of it is that our hearts will be upon earth; nay, the very fact of our doing so proves that they are there! Nor will it be otherwise till there is a ceasing to lay up treasures upon earth.

The believer who lays up treasures upon earth may, at first, not live openly in sin; he is a measure may yet bring some honor to the Lord in certain things; but the injurious tendencies of this habit will show themselves more and more, while the habit of laying up treasures in Heaven would draw the heart more and more heavenward; would be continually strengthening his new, his divine nature, his spiritual faculties, because it would be strengthened; and he would more and more, while yet in the body, have his heart in Heaven, and set upon heavenly things; and thus the laying up treasures in Heaven would bring along with it, even in this life, precious spiritual blessings as a reward of obedience to the commandment of our Lord (*Narrative*, pt 3, pp. 575-579).

Matthew 6:33

The next passage, on which I desire to make a few remarks, is Matthew 6:33,

"But seek ye first the kingdom of God, and his righteousness; and all these things shall be added unto you."

After our Lord, in the previous verses, had been pointing His disciples to the "fowls of the air," and "the lilies of the field," in order that they should be without carefulness about the necessaries of life, He adds: "Therefore take no thought, (literally, be not anxious) saying, What shall we eat? Or, What shall we drink? Or, Wherewithal shall we be clothed? (for after all these things do the Gentiles seek), for your heavenly Father knoweth that ye have need of all these things."

Observe here particularly that we, the children of God, should be different from the nations of the earth, from those who have no Father in heaven, and who therefore make it their great business, their first anxious concern, what they shall eat, and what they shall drink, and wherewithal they shall be clothed. We, the children of God, should, as in every other respect, so in this particular also, be different from the world, and prove to the world that we believe that we have a Father in heaven, who knows that we have need of all these things. The fact that our Almighty Father, who is full of infinite love for us His children, (and who has proved to us His love in the gift of His only begotten Son, and His almighty power in raising Him from the dead), knows that we have need of these things, should remove all anxiety from our minds.

There is, however, one thing that we have to attend to, with reference to our temporal necessities; it's mentioned in our verse: "But seek ye first the kingdom of God and His righteousness." The great business which the disciples of the Lord Jesus has to be concerned about (for this word was spoken to disciples, to professed believers) is to seek the Kingdom of God, i.e. to seek, as I view it, after the external and internal prosperity of the Church of Christ. If, according to our ability, and according to the opportunity which the Lord gives us, we seek to win souls for the Lord Jesus, that appears to me to be seeking the *external prosperity* of the Kingdom of God; and if we, as members of the body of Christ, seek to benefit our fellow members in the body, helping them on in grace and truth, or caring for them in any way to their edification, that would be seeking the *internal prosperity* of the Kingdom of God.

But in connection with this we have also "to seek His righteousness," which means, (as it was spoken to disciples, to those who have a Father in Heaven, and not to those who were without), to seek to be more and more like God, to seek to be inwardly conformed to the mind of God. If these two things are attended to, (and they imply also that we are not slothful in business), then do we come under that precious promise: "And all these things (that is food, raiment, or anything else that is needful for this present life) shall be added unto you." It is not *for* attending to these two things that we obtain the blessing, but *in* attending to them.

I now ask you, my dear reader, a few questions in all love, because I do seek your welfare, and I do not wish to put these questions to you, without putting them first to my own heart. Do you make it your primary business, your first great concern to seek the Kingdom of God and His righteousness? Are the things of God, the honor of His name, the welfare of his Church, the conversion of sinners, and the profit of your own soul, your chief aim? Or does your business, or your family, or your own temporal concerns, in some shape or other *primarily* occupy your attention? If the latter be the case, then, though you may have all the necessaries of life, yet could you be surprised if you had them not? Remember that the world passes away, but that the things of God can endure forever.

I never knew a child of God who acted according to the above passage, in whose experience the Lord did not fulfill His word of promise "All these things will be added to you as well" (*Narrative*, pt 3, pp 579-581).

Steward for God

The child of God has been bought with the "precious blood of the Christ," and is altogether His property, with all that he possesses: his bodily strength, his mental strength, his ability of every kind, his trade, business, art, or profession, his property, etc.; for it is written: "Ye are not your own; for ye are bought with a price," (1 Corinthians 6:19-20). The proceeds of our calling are therefore not our own in the sense of using them as our natural heart wishes to do, whether to spend them on the gratification of our pride, or our love of pleasure, or sensual indulgences, or to lay by the money for ourselves or our children or use it in any way as we *naturally* like; but we have to stand before our Lord and Master, whose stewards we are, to seek to ascertain his will, how He will have us use the proceeds of our calling.

But is this indeed the spirit in which the children of God generally are engaged in their calling? It is but too well known that it is not the case! Can we then wonder at it, that even God's own dear children should so often be found greatly in difficulty with regard to their calling, and be found so often complaining about stagnation or competition in trade, and the difficulties of the times, though there have been given to them such precious promises as: "Seek ye first the kingdom of God and His righteousness; and all these things shall be added unto you," (Matthew 6:33) or, "Let your conversation (disposition or turn of mind) be without covetousness; and be content with such things as ye have: for He hath said, I will never leave thee, nor forsake thee," (Hebrews 8:5)?

Is it not obvious enough, that, when our Heavenly Father sees that we His children do, or would, use the proceeds of our calling, as our *natural mind* would desire, that He either cannot at all entrust us with means, or will be obliged to decrease them. No wise and really affectionate mother will permit her infant to play with a razor, or with fire, however much the child may desire to have them; and so the love and wisdom of our Heavenly Father will not, cannot, entrust us with pecuniary means (*except it be in the way of chastisement, or to show us finally their utter vanity*), if He sees that we do not desire to possess them as *stewards* for Him, in order that we may spend them as He may point out to us by His Holy Spirit, through His Word (*Narrative*, pt 3, pp. 585-587 589).

We cannot limit the extent to which God may use us as instruments in communicating blessing, both temporal and spiritual, if we are willing to yield ourselves as instruments to the loving God, and are content to be only instruments, and to give him all the glory. But with regard to temporal things it will be thus, that if indeed we walk according to the mind of God in these things, while more and more we become instruments of blessings to others, we shall not seek to enrich ourselves, but be content when the last day of another year finds us still in the body, to possess no more than on the last day of the previous year, or even considerably less, while we have been, however, in the course of the year the instruments of communicating largely to others, through the means of which the Lord had intrusted us. As to my own soul, by the grace of God it would be a burden to me to find, that however much my income in the course of a year might have been, I was increasing in earthly possession; for it would be a plain proof to me, that I had not been acting as a *steward* for God, and had not been yielding myself as a channel for the waters of God's bounty to pass through (*Narrative*, pt 3, pp. 595-596).

4. The Word of God

If anyone should ask me how he may read the Scriptures most profitably, I would advise him that:

I. Above all he should seek to have it settled in his own mind, that God alone, by His Spirit, can teach him, and that therefore, as God will be enquired of for blessings, it becomes him to seek God's blessing previous to reading, and also while reading.

II. He should have it, moreover, settled in his mind, that although the Holy Spirit is the *best* and *sufficient* teacher, this teacher does not always teach immediately when we desire it, and that, therefore, we may have to entreat Him again and again for the explanation of certain passages; but that He will surely teach us at last, if indeed we are seeking for light prayerfully, patiently, and with a view to the glory of God.

III. It is of immense importance for the understanding of the Word of God, to read it in course, so that we may read everyday a portion of the Old and a portion of the New Testament, going on where we previously left off. This is important.

1. Because it throws light upon the connection; and a different course, according to which one habitually selects particular chapters, will make it utterly impossible ever to understand much of the Scriptures.

2. While we are in the body, we need a change even in spiritual things, and this change the Lord has graciously provided in the great variety which is to be found in His word.

3. It tends to the glory of God; for the leaving out some chapters here and there, is practically saying that certain portions are better than

others; or, that there are certain parts of revealed truth unprofitable or unnecessary.

4. It may keep us, by the blessing of God, from erroneous views, as in reading thus regularly through the Scriptures we are led to see the meaning of the whole, and also kept from laying too much stress upon certain favorite views.

5. The Scriptures contain the whole revealed will of God, and therefore we ought to seek to read from time to time through the whole of that revealed will. There are many believers, I fear, in our day, who have not read even once through the whole of Scripture; and yet in a few months, by reading only a few chapters everyday, they might accomplish it.

IV. It is also of the greatest importance to meditate on what we read, so that perhaps a small portion of that which we have read, or, if we have time, the whole, may be meditated upon in the course of the day. Or a small portion of a book, or an epistle, or a gospel, through which we go regularly for meditation, may be considered everyday, without, however, suffering oneself to be brought into bondage by this plan.

Learned *commentaries* I have found to store the *head* with many notions, and often also with the truth of God; but when the *Spirit* teaches, through the instrumentality of prayer and mediation, the heart is affected. The former kind of knowledge generally puffs up, and is often renounced, when another commentary gives a different opinion, and often also is found to be good for nothing, when it is to be carried out into practice. The latter kind of knowledge generally humbles, gives joy, leads us nearer to God, and is not easily reasoned away; and having been obtained from God, and thus having entered into the heart, and become our own, is also generally carried out...

V. The last and most important means of grace, namely, prayer, was comparatively but little improved by me. I prayed, and I prayed often. I also prayed, in general, by the grace of God, with sincerity; but had I been more earnestly praying, or even only as much as I have prayed of late years, I should have made much more rapid progresses (*Narrative*, pt 1, pp. 30-32).

I am aware that it is a common temptation of Satan to make us give up the reading of the Word and prayer when our enjoyment is gone; as if it were no use to read the Scriptures when we do not enjoy them, and as if it were no use to pray when we have no spirit of prayer; whilst the truth is, in order to enjoy the Word, we ought to continue to read it, and the way to obtain a spirit of prayer is to continue prayer; for the less we read the Word of God, the less we desire to read it, and the less we pray, the less we desire to pray (*Narrative*, pt 1, p. 53).

I fell into the snare, into which so many young believers fall, the reading of religious books in preference to the Scriptures. I could now no longer read French and German novels, as I had formerly done, to feed my carnal mind; but still I did not put in the room of those books the best of all books. I read tracts, missionary papers, sermons, and biographies of godly persons. The last kind of books found more profitable than the others, and had they been well selected or had I not read too much of such writings, or had any of them tended particularly to endear the Scriptures to me, they might have done me much good. I never had been, at any time in my life, in the habit of reading the Holy Scriptures. When under fifteen years of age, I occasionally read a little of them at school; afterwards God's precious book was entirely laid aside so that I never read one single chapter of it, as far as I remember, till it pleased God to begin a work of grace in my heart.

Now the scriptural way of reasoning would have been: God Himself has condescended to become an author, and I am ignorant about that precious book, which His Holy Spirit has caused to be written through the instrumentality of His servants, and it contains that which I ought to know, and the knowledge of which will lead me to true happiness; therefore I ought to read again and again this most precious book, this book of books, most earnestly, most prayerfully, and with much meditation and in this practice I ought to continue all the days of my life. For I was aware, though I read it but little, that I knew scarcely anything of it. But instead of acting thus, and being led by my ignorance of the Word of God to study it more, my difficulty in understanding it, and the little enjoyment I had in it, made me careless of reading it (for much prayerful reading of the Word gives not merely more knowledge, but increases the delight we have in reading it); and thus, like many believers, I practically preferred, for the first four years of my divine life, the works of uninspired men to the oracles of the living God.

The consequence was, that I remained a babe, both in knowledge and in grace. In knowledge I say; for all *true* knowledge must be derived, by the Spirit, from the Word. And as I neglected the Word, I was for nearly four years so ignorant, that I did not *clearly* know even the *fundamental* points of our holy faith. And this lack of knowledge most sadly kept me back from walking steadily in the ways of God. For it is the truth that makes us free (John 8:31, 32) by delivering us from the slavery of the lusts of the flesh, the lusts of the eyes, and the pride of life. The Word proves it. The experience of the saints proves it; and also my own experience most decidedly proves it. For when it pleased the Lord in August 1829, to bring me really to the Scriptures, my life and walk became very different. And though even since then I have very much fallen short of what I might and ought to be, yet, by the grace of God, I have been enabled to live much nearer to Him than before.

If any believers read this, who practically prefer other books to the Holy Scriptures, and who enjoy the writings of men much more than the Word of God, may they be warned by my loss. I shall consider this book to have been the means of doing much good, should it please the Lord, through its instrumentality, to lead some of His people no longer to neglect the Holy Scriptures, but to give them that preference, which they have hitherto bestowed on the writings of men...

Before I leave this subject I would only add: if the reader understands very little of the Word of God, he ought to read it very much; for the Spirit explains the Word by the Word. And if he enjoys the reading of the Word little, that is just the reason why he should read it much; for the frequent reading of the Scripture creates a delight in them, so that the more we read them, the more we desire to do so. And if the reader should be an unbeliever, I would likewise entreat him to read the Scriptures earnestly, but to ask God previously to give him a blessing. For in doing so, God may make him wise for salvation (2 Timothy 3:16) (*Narrative*, pt 1, pp. 28-30).

When I was staying at Nailsworth, it pleased the Lord to teach me a truth, irrespective of human instrumentality...The point is this: I saw more clearly than ever, that the first great and primary business to which I ought to attend every day was to have my soul happy in the Lord. The first thing to be concerned about was not, how much I might serve the Lord...but how I might get my soul into a happy sate, and how my inner man might be nourished. For I might seek to set the truth before the unconverted, I might seek to benefit believers, I might seek to relieve the distressed, I might in other ways seek to behave myself as it becomes a child of God in this world; and yet, not being happy in the Lord, and not being nourished and strengthened in my inner man day by day, all this might now be attended to in a right spirit. Before this time my practice had been, at least for ten years previously, as an habitual thing, to give myself to prayer, after having dressed in the morning. Now I saw that the most important thing I had to do was to give myself to the reading of the Word of God and to meditation on it, that thus my heat might be comforted, encouraged, warned, reproved, instructed; and that thus, whilst meditating, my heart might be brought into experimental communion with the Lord. I began therefore to meditate on the New Testament, from the beginning, early in the morning. The first thing I did, after having asked in a few words the Lord's blessing upon His precious Word, was to begin to meditate on the Word of God, searching as it were into every verse, to get blessing out of it; not for the sake of the public ministry of the Word; not for the sake of preaching on what I had meditated upon, but for the sake of obtaining food for my own soul.

The result I had found to be almost invariably this, that after a very few minutes my soul has been led to confession, or to thanksgiving, or to intercession, or to supplication; so that, though I did not, as it were, give myself to *prayer*, but to *meditation*, yet it turned almost immediately more or less into prayer. When thus I have been for a while making confession, or intercession, or supplication, or have given thanks, I go on to the next words or verse, turning all, as I go on, into prayer for myself or others, as the Word may lead to it; but still continually keeping before me, that food for my own soul is the object of my meditation.

The result of this is, that there is always a good deal of confession, thanksgiving, supplication, or intercession mingled with my meditation, and that my inner man almost invariably is even sensibly nourished and strengthened, and that by breakfast time, with rare exceptions, I am in a peaceful if not happy state of heart. Thus also the Lord is pleased to communicate unto me that which either very soon after, or at a later time, I have found to become food for other believers, though it was not for sake of the public ministry of the Word that I gave myself to meditation, but for the profit of my own inner man...

The difference then between my former practice and my present one is this. Formerly, when I rose, I began to pray as soon as possible, and generally spent all my time till breakfast in prayer, or almost all the time. At all events, I almost invariably began with prayer, except when I felt my soul to be m`ore than usually barren, in which case I read the word of God for food, or for refreshment, or for a revival and renewal of my inner man, before I gave myself to prayer.

But what was the result? I often spent a quarter of an hour, or half an hour, or even an hour on my knees, before being conscious to myself of having derived comfort, encouragement, humbling of soul, etc.; and often, after having suffered much from wandering of mind for the first ten minutes, or a quarter of an hour, or even half an hour, I only then began *really to pray*. I scarcely even suffer now in this way. For my heart being nourished by the truth, being brought into *experimental* fellowship with God, I speak to my Father, and to my Friend (vile though I am, and unworthy of it!) about the things that He has brought before me in His precious Word.

It often now astonishes me that I did not sooner see this point. In no book did I ever read about it. No public ministry ever brought the matter before me. No private intercourse with a brother stirred me up to his matter. And yet now, since God has taught me this point, it is as plain to me as anything that the first thing the child of God has to do morning-by-morning is to *obtain food for his inner man*. As the outward man is not fit for work for any length of time, except we take food, and this is one of the first things we do in the morning, so it should be with the inner man. We should take food for that, as everyone must allow. Now what is the food for the inner man? Not prayer, but the *Word of God*; and here again not the simple reading of the Word of God, so that it only passes through our minds just as water runs through a pipe, but considering what we read, pondering over it, and applying it to our hearts.

When we pray we speak to God. Now, prayer, in order to be continued for any length of time in any other than a formal manner, requires, generally speaking, a measure of strength or godly desire, and the season, therefore, when this exercise of the soul can be most effectually performed, is after the inner man has been nourished by meditation on the Word of God, where we find our Father speaking to us, to encourage us, to comfort us, to instruct us, to humble us, or to reprove us. We may therefore profitably meditate, with God's blessing, though we are ever so weak spiritually; nay, the weaker we are, the more we need meditation for the strengthening of our inner man. There is thus far less to be feared from wandering of mind than if we give ourselves to prayer without having had previously time for meditation.

I dwell so particularly on this point because of the immense spiritual profit and refreshment I am conscious of having derived from it myself, and I affectionately and solemnly beseech all my fellow-believers to ponder this matter. By the blessing of God I ascribe to this mode the help and strength which I have had from God to pass in peace through deeper trials in various ways than I had ever had before; and after having now above eighteen years tried this way, I can most fully, in the fear of God, commend it...How different when the soul is refreshed and made happy early in the morning, from what it is when, without spiritual preparation, the service, the trials, and the temptations of the day come upon one (*Narrative*, pt 3, pp. 440-408).

5. Prayer

In order to have your prayers answered, you need to make your requests unto God on the ground of the merits and worthiness of the Lord Jesus. You must not depend upon your own worthiness and merits, but solely on the Lord Jesus, as the ground of acceptance before God, for your person, for your prayers, for your labors, and for everything else. Do you really believe in Jesus? Do you verily depend upon Him alone for the salvation of your soul? See to it well, that not the least degree of your own righteousness is presented unto God as a ground of acceptance.

But then, if you believe in the Lord Jesus, it is further necessary, in order that your prayers may be answered, that the things which you ask of God should be of such a kind, that God can give them to you, because they are for His honor and your real good. If the obtaining of your requests were not for your real good, or were not tending to the honor of God, you might pray for a long time, without obtaining what you desire. The glory of God should be always before the children of God, in what they desire at His hands; and their own spiritual profit, being so intimately connected with the honor of God, should never be lost sight of, in their petitions.

But now, suppose we are believers in the Lord Jesus, and make our request unto God, depending alone on the Lord Jesus as the ground of having them granted; suppose also, that, so far as we are able honestly and uprightly to judge, the obtaining of our requests would be for our real spiritual good and for the honor of God; we yet need, lastly, to *continue* in prayer, until the blessing is granted unto us. It is not enough to begin to pray, nor to pray aright; nor is it enough to continue *for a time* to pray; but we must patiently, believingly continue in prayer, until we obtain an answer; and further, we have not only *to continue* in prayer unto the end, but we have also *to believe* that God does hear us, and will answer our prayers. Most frequently we fail in not continuing in prayer until the blessing is obtained and *in not expecting the blessing*. As assuredly as in any individual these various points are found united, so assuredly answers will be granted to his requests (*Narrative*, pt 4, pp. 289).

The next point on which I will speak for a few moments, has been more or less referred to already; it is that of prayer. You might read the word and seem to understand it very fully, yet, if you are not in the habit of waiting continually upon God, you will make little progress in the divine life. We have not naturally in us any good thing, and cannot expect, save by the help of God, to please Him. Therefore, it is the will of the Lord, that we should always throw our dependence upon Him, and it becomes us to follow in prayer the earnestness of the Lord Jesus Christ.

That blessed One gave us an example in this particular. He gave whole nights to prayer, and we find Him on the lonely mountain engaged by night in prayer. And as in every way He is to be an example to us, so, in particular, on this point, He is also an example to us. The old evil, corrupt nature is still in us, though we are born again; therefore we have to come in prayer to God for help. We have to cling to the power of the Mighty One. Concerning everything we have to pray. Not simply when great troubles come, when our home is on fire, or our beloved wife is on the point of death, or our dear children are laid down in sickness, not simply at such times, but also in little things. From the very early morning, let us make everything a matter of prayer, and let it be so throughout the day, and throughout our whole life.

A Christian lady said, lately, that thirty-five years ago she heard me speak on this subject in Devonshire; and that then I referred to praying about little things. I had said, that suppose a parcel came to us, and it should prove difficult to untie the knot, and you cannot cut it; then you should ask God to help you, even to untie the knot. I myself had forgotten the words, but she had remembered them, and the remembrance has been a great help to her again and again. So I would say to you, my beloved friends, there is nothing too small for prayer. In the simplest things connected with our daily life and walk, we should give ourselves to prayer; and we shall have the living, loving Lord Jesus to help us. Even in the most trifling matters I give myself to prayer, and often in the morning, even ere I leave my room; I have two or three answers to prayer in this way.

Young believers, in the very outset of the Divine life, learn, in childlike simplicity, to wait upon God for everything! Treat the Lord Jesus Christ as your personal friend, able and willing to help you in everything. How blessed it is to be carried in His loving arms all the daylong! I would say, that the divine life of the believers is made up of a vast number of little circumstances and little things. Every day there comes before us a variety of little trials, and if we seek to put them aside in our own strength and wisdom, we shall quickly find that we are confounded. But if on the contrary, we take everything to God, we shall be helped and our way shall be made plain. Thus our life will be a happy life (*Counsel to Christians*, pp. 29-31).

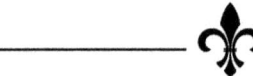

The disciples of the Lord Jesus should labor with all their might in the work of God, as if everything depends upon their own exertions; and yet, having done so, they should not in the least trust in their labors and efforts, and in the means which they use for the spread of the truth, but in God; and they should with all earnestness seek the blessing of God, in preserving, patient, and believing prayer.

Here is the great secret of success, my Christian reader. Work with all your might; but trust not in the least in your work. Pray with all your might for the blessing of God; but work, at the same time, with all diligence, with all patience, with all perseverance. Pray then, and work. Work and pray. And still again pray, and then work. And so on all the days of your life. The blessing, however, should be sought by us *habitually* and *perseveringly* in prayer. It should also be fully *expected* (*Narrative*, pt 4, p. 301).

6. The Deeper Life

On September 28th we left Teignmouth for Plymouth. During my stay at Plymouth I was stirred up afresh to early rising, a blessing, the results of which I have not lost since. That which led me to it was the example of the brother in whose house I was staying, and a remark which he made in speaking on the sacrifices in Leviticus, "That as not the refuse of the animals was to be offered up, *so the best part of our time should be especially given to communion with the Lord.*" I had been, on the whole, rather an early riser during former years. But since my head had been so weak, I thought that, as the day was long enough for my strength, it would be best for me not to rise early, in order that thus my head might have the longer quiet. On this account I rose only between six and seven, and sometimes after seven… In this way, however, my soul suffered more or less everyday, and sometimes considerably, as now and then unavoidable work came upon me before I had had sufficient time for prayer and the reading of the Word. After I had heard the remark to which I had alluded, I determined, that whatever my body might suffer, I would no longer let the most precious part of the day pass away, while I was in bed. By the grace of God I was enabled to begin the very next day to rise earlier, and have continued to rise early since that time.

Any one need but make the experiment of spending one, two, or three hours in prayer and mediation before breakfast, either in his room, or with his Bible in his hand in the fields, and he will soon find out the beneficial effect which early rising has upon the outward and inward man. I beseech all my brethren and sisters into whose hands this may fall, and who are not in the habit of rising early, to make the trial, and they will praise the Lord for having done so…How much more important still is it to retire early and then rise early, in order to *make sure of time for prayer and meditation before the business of the day commences,* and to devote to those exercises that part of our time, when the mind and the body are most fresh, in order thus to obtain spiritual strength for the conflict, the trials, and the work of the day (*Narrative*, pt 2, pp. 294-297).

Everything that is a mere form, a mere habit, and custom in divine things, is to be dreaded exceedingly: *life*, *power*, *reality*, this is what we have to aim after. Things should not result from without, but from within. The sort of clothes I wear, the kind of house I live in, the quality of the furniture I use, all such like things should not result from other persons doing so and so, or because it is customary among those brethren with whom I associate to live in such and such a simple, inexpensive, self-denying way; but whatever be done in these things, in the way of giving up, or self-denial, or deadness to the world, should result from the joy we have in God, from the knowledge of our being children of God, from the entering into the preciousness of our future inheritance, etc.

Far better that for the time being we stand still, and do not take the steps which we see others take, than that it is merely the force of example that leads us to do a thing, and afterwards it be regretted. Not that I mean in the least by this to imply we should continue to live in luxury, self-indulgence, and the like, while others are in great need; but we should begin the thing in a right way, i.e. aim after the right state of heart; being *inwardly* instead of *outwardly*. In otherwise, it will not last. We shall look back, or even get into a worse state than we were before.

But oh! how different if joy in God leads us to any little act of self-denial. How gladly do we do it then! How great an honor then do we esteem it to be! How much does the heart then long to be able to do more for him who has done so much for us! We are far then from looking down in proud self-complacency upon those who do not go as far as we do, both rather pray to the Lord that He would be pleased to help our dear brethren and sisters forward who may seem to us weak in any particular point; and we we also conscious to ourselves, that if we have a little more light or strength with reference to one point, other brethren may have more light of grace in other respects (*Narrative*, pt 3, pp. 529-530).

So, my beloved younger brethren and sisters in Christ, at the very outset of your spiritual life, say boldly,

> "I will be, by the grace of God, an out-and-out Christian, living for God. I will, by His grace, seek to bear fruit to His glory and honor. I will, by His grace, seek to have done with this sinful world. I will, by His grace, strive so to live, that a line of demarcation shall be clearly seen between me and the world, and that the people of the world shall seek to have no intercourse with me, seeing that I do not belong to them, but that I belong to the kingdom of Heaven."

That is what we have to aim after; and what would be the result? Not only should we be holy men and women, but also happy men and women, in whom God delights; and we should also be useful men and women. The world ought to say of each of us, "If ever there was a Christian, it is surely that man or that women. Surely that man or woman has been with Jesus." If the world does not say that of us, there is something wanting. We ought to be ashamed, if anyone is able to live three of four days in the house with us, without finding out that we are not of the world, but are born again (*Counsel to Christians*, pp. 8-9).

At the very outset of the divine life we must make a plain, bold confession of the Lord Jesus Christ. Very few things are of greater importance than this. The temptation will be to keep your new life to yourself: I can get to heaven without telling. Well, if you do so, you are weak, and will remain weak. It is of great importance, even for the vigor of your own Christian life, to make confession, and come out boldly for Christ at once. The reason is this—people will know that you are the Lord's, and see the line of demarcation between you and the world; they will not seek your company. I remember when I was converted; I was a student in a large university, where there were twelve hundred and sixty students. Amongst all these there were only three who were known as disciples of the Lord Jesus Christ; but it was well known what they were; they were "marked men." ...

Again, in doing so, we stand by the side of Christ. He comes forward, and takes His stand by our side, saying, "In weakness thou hast stood for Me; now I will stand by thee;" and thus we reap the benefit in our own souls. We can never have grace and strength by keeping our religion to ourselves. You will never be out-and-out Christians—never be a happy Christina—without this confession.

The will of the Lord is that we should be as cities set on a hill, which cannot be hid; or as lights, not placed under a bushel, but set on a lamp-stand, so as to be seen. And let us aim after this, if it is not the case with us now; and let us be assured, that, when any man aims at keeping his religion to himself, he is going the wrong road. People must know that we are the Lord's, and on His side; and we should not rest satisfied without this. Our duty, remember, is to win souls for Him; and how can we do this, if we hide our light? Although we are neither evangelists, missionaries, Sunday-school teachers, nor visitors, yet God will help us to win souls; therefore, we have to come out boldly for Him (*Counsel to Christians*, pp. 12-14).

7. The Christian in the Workplace

The children of God, who are strangers and pilgrims on earth, have at all times had difficulty in the world, for they are not *at* home but *from* home; nor should they, until the return of the Lord Jesus, expect it to be otherwise with them. All difficulties may be overcome by acting according to the Word of God. At this time I more especially desire to point out the means whereby the children of God who are engaged in any earthly calling may be able to overcome the difficulties, which arise from competition in business...

Am I in a Calling in Which I Can Abide with God?

The first thing which the believer, who is in such difficulties, has to ask himself is, "Am I in a calling in which I can abide with God?" If our occupation be of that kind, that we cannot ask God's blessing upon it, or that we should be ashamed to be found in it at the appearing of the Lord Jesus, or that it *of necessity* hinders our spiritual progress, then we must give it up and be engaged in something else; but in few cases only this is needful. Far the greater part to the occupations in which believers are engaged are not of such a nature, as that they need to give them up in order to maintain a good conscience, and in order to be able to walk with God though, perhaps, certain alterations may need to be made in the manner of conducting their trade, business, or profession. About those parts of our calling, which may need alteration, we shall receive instruction from the Lord, if we indeed desire it, and wait upon him for it, and expect it from him.

Why Do I Carry on This Business?

Now suppose the believer is in a calling in which he can abide with God, the next point to be settled is: "Why do I carry on this business, or why am I engaged in this trade or profession?" In most instances, so far as my experience goes, which I have gathered in my service among the saints during the last fifteen years and a half, I believe the answer would be: "I am engaged in my earthly calling, that I may earn the means of obtaining the necessaries of life for myself and family." Here is the chief error from which almost all the rest of the errors, which are entertained by children of God, relative to their calling, spring. It is no right and Scriptural motive, to be engaged in a trade, or business, or profession, *merely* in order to earn the means for the obtaining of the necessaries of life for ourselves and family, *but we should work because it is the Lord's will concerning us*. This is plain from the following passages: 1 Thessalonians 4:11, 12; 2 Thessalonians 3:10-12; Ephesians 4:28.

It is quite true that, in general, the Lord provides the necessaries of life by means of our ordinary calling; but that that is not THE REASON why we should work is plain enough from the consideration, that if our possessing the necessaries of life depend upon our ability of working, we could never have *freedom from anxiety*, for we should always have to say to ourselves, "and what shall I do when I am too old to work? or when by reason of sickness I am unable to earn my bread?"

But if, on the other hand, we are engaged in our earthly calling because *it is the will of the Lord concerning us that we should work*, and that thus laboring we may provide for our families and also be able to support the weak, the sick, the aged, and the needy, then we have good and scriptural reasons to say to ourselves: should it please the Lord to lay me on a bed of sickness, or keep me otherwise by reason of infirmity, or old age, or want of employment, from earning my bread by means of the labor of my hands, or my business, or my profession, he will yet provide for me.

Because we who believe are servants of Jesus Christ, who has bought us with his own precious blood, and are not our own, and because this, our precious Lord and Master, has commanded us to work, therefore we work; and *in doing so* our Lord will provide for us, but whether in this way or any other way, he is sure to provide for us; for we labor in obedience to him; and if even a just earthly master gives wages to his servants, the Lord will surely see to it that we have our wages, if in obedience to him we are engaged in our calling, and not for our own sake (*Narrative*, pt 3, pp. 585-587).

8. Working with Children

As far as my experience goes, it appears to me that believers generally have expected far too little of *present* fruit upon their labors among children. There has been a hoping that the Lord some day or other would own the instruction which they give to children, and would answer at sometime or another, though after many years only, the prayers which they offer up on their behalf. Now, while such passages as Proverbs 22:6, Ecclesiastes 11:1, Galatians 6:9, 1 Corinthians 15:58, give to us assurance not merely respecting everything which we do for the Lord, in general, but also respecting bringing up children in the fear of the Lord, in particular, that our labor is not in vain in the Lord; yet we have to guard against abusing such passages, by thinking it a matter of little moment whether we see *present* fruit or not; but, on the contrary, present fruit, and therefore in preserving, yet submissive, prayer, we should make known our request unto God.

I add, as an encouragement to believers who labor among children, that, during the last two years, seventeen other young persons or children, from the age of eleven and a half to seventeen, have been received into fellowship among us, and that I am looking out now for many more to be converted, and that not merely of the orphans, but of the Sunday and day school children. As in so many respects will live in remarkable times, so in this respect also, that the Lord is working greatly among the children in many places (*Narrative*, pt 2, pp. 372-373).

9. The Will of God

[In a leaflet entitled, *How To Ascertain The Will of God*, Müller penned the following:]

I seek at the beginning to get my heart in such a state that it has no will of its own in regard to a given matter. Nine tenths of a trouble with people generally is just here. Nine tenths of the difficulties are overcome when our hearts are ready to do the Lord's will, whatever it may be. When one is truly in this state, it is usually but a little way to the knowledge of what His will is.

Having done this, I do not leave the result to feeling or simple impression. If so, I make myself liable to great delusions.

I seek the will of the Spirit of God through, or in connection with, the Word of God. The Spirit and the Word must be combined. If I look to the Spirit alone without the Word, I lay myself open to great delusions also. If the Holy Spirit guides us at all, He will do it according to the Scriptures and never contrary to them.

Next I take into account providential circumstances. These often plainly indicate God's will in connection with His Word and Spirit.

I ask God in prayer to reveal His will to me aright.

Thus through prayer to God, the study of the Word, and reflection, I come to a deliberate judgment according to the best of my ability and knowledge; and if my mind is thus at peace, and continues so after two or three more petitions, I proceed accordingly. In trivial matters, and in transactions involving most important issues, I have found this method always effective (*How To Ascertain The Will of God*, 1895, ECL Leaflet).

10. The Challenge

[George Müller did not seek to elevate himself by listing the various ways in which God dealt with him in his pilgrimage. In fact, he desired to communicate with intensity the message that all Christians serve the same living God and are equally responsible to live the life of faith before Him. Müller's life should serve as an example to follow, but, more importantly, it should bring us to our knees before the same God that provided so abundantly for his needs. His words set forth the challenge:]

My dear Christian reader, will you not try this way? Will you not know for yourself, if as yet you have not known it, the preciousness and the happiness of this way of casting all your cares and burdens and necessities upon God? This way is as open to you as to me. Everyone of the children of God is not called by Him to be engaged in such a service as that to which He has condescended to call me; but everyone is invited and commanded to trust in the Lord, to trust in Him with all his heart, and to cast his burden upon Him, and to call upon Him in the day of trouble. Will you not do this, my dear brethren in Christ? I long that you may do so. I desire that you may taste the sweetness of that state of heart, in which, while surrounded by difficulties, you can yet be at peace, because you know that the Living God, your Father in Heaven, cares for you.

Should, however, anyone read this, who is not reconciled to God, but is still going on in the ways of sin and carelessness, unbelief and self-righteousness, then let me say to such, that it is impossible that you should have confidence to come boldly to God in such a state, and I therefore ask you to make confession of your sins to Him, and to put your trust for eternity entirely in the merits of the Lord Jesus, that you may obtain forgiveness of your sins.

Again, should anyone read this, who has believed in the Lord Jesus, but who is not again living in sin, who is again regarding iniquity in his heart, let no such a one be surprised that he has no confidence toward God, and that he does not know the blessedness of having answers to his prayers; for it is written: *"If I regard iniquity in my heart, the Lord will not hear me: but verily God hath heard me; He hath attended to the voice of my prayer,"* (Psalms 66:18-19). The first thing such a one has to do is, to forsake his evil course, to make confession of it, and to know afresh the power of the blood of the Lord Jesus on his conscience, by putting his trust in that precious blood, in order that he may obtain confidence toward God (*Autobiography*, pp. 315-316).

11. Notes

1 *A Narrative of Some of the Lord's Dealings with George Müller* (London: J. Nisbet & Co., 1860, sixth ed.), p. 13.

2 *Ibid.*, p. 146.

3 *Ibid.*, pp. 367-368.

4 *Autobiography of George Müller* (London: J. Nisbit & Co., 1905), pp. 292-293.

For more information on the life and ministry of George Müller, see:

Müller, George. *A Narrative of Some of the Lord's Dealings with George Müller*, published in four parts (1860, 1873, 1874, 1886).

_____. *Counsel to Christians* (1878).

_____. *Autobiography of George Müller* (1905).

Steer, Roger. *George Müller: Delighted in God* (1975).

The Way of Holiness

Phoebe Palmer 1807-1874

With an Introduction
By Alathea Coleman Jones

Abridged version of *The Way of Holiness* by Phoebe Palmer. Abridged version originally published by Christian Outreach, Asbury Theological Seminary, 1981, Wilmore, Ky. Reprinted with permission from Asbury Theological Seminary. Scripture quotations are taken from the Holy Bible, King James Version (KJV), in the Public Domain. Artwork in the Public Domain.

Book Chapters

1. Introduction
   By Alathea Coleman Jones 334
2. The Way of Holiness 336
   Section I 336
   Section II 338
   Section III 339
   Section IV 341
   Section V 343
   Section VI 346
   Section VII 348
   Section VIII 352
   Section IX 354

1. Introduction
By Alathea
Coleman Jones

Phoebe Palmer excelled in leading Christian pilgrims into the experience of perfect love. It is estimated that 25,000 persons came to know the way of God more perfectly through her influence, including Bishops Hamline, Janes, and Olin of the Methodist Church; John Dempster, founder of Concord (later Boston) and Garrett seminaries; Randolf S. Foster, eminent theologian; and Thomas C. Upham, distinguished professor of Bowdoin College. Probably no other woman of the 19th century exerted a more formidable influence on the holiness movement in America.

This modern day Priscilla was born in New York, December 18, 1807. With her nine brothers and sisters, Phoebe learned from her godly parents the beauty of worship and discipline. When 19 she married Walter Clark Palmer, a physician, who, like his wife, had been "powerfully converted." Six children were born of this union, though only three lived to maturity. Frail in body but dauntless in spirit, Mrs. Palmer never tired in serving others, until her death on November 2, 1874.

Early in their marriage the doctor and his wife dedicated their house to the promotion of holiness. It became a center of spiritual quest, especially on Tuesday afternoons, when leaders from all over the city gathered to explore the deeper riches of grace. In their later years, supported by his medical practice, the Palmers traveled extensively across the Eastern States, Canada, and England, speaking at churches and camp meetings, with mighty revivals attending their labors.

The witness of the preached Word was amplified by corresponding deeds of compassion. Among their many benevolent projects was the establishment of a city mission and settlement house for the poor. Phoebe also helped organize the Ladies Christian Union, a fellowship on the order of the later YWCA. Though she sought to avoid public acclaim, and eschewed feminist rights, her example did much in her day to popularize the role of women in religious work.

Phoebe said that she wanted only to be a "Bible Christian." This desire came to a climax in 1837, when in obedience to the command of Scripture; she laid herself completely on the altar of God, and by faith rested upon the promises of His Word. "O! into what a region of light, glory and purity, was my soul at this moment ushered," she said. "I felt that I was but as a drop in the ocean of infinite LOVE, and Christ was ALL and ALL."

Yet it had taken her many years of needless struggle to know this certainty. When asked if there was a shorter way one could enter the promised blessing, Phoebe replied, "Yes, there is a shorter way." Then, with solemn feeling, she added, "But there is only one way."

The steps of that pilgrimage are recounted in *The Way of Holiness*. Many other books were written by Mrs. Palmer, but none received as wide a circulation as this small volume. First published in 1845, it went through 50 editions before going out of print.

To make the book once again easily accessible, it is reproduced here in this inexpensive format. Though abridged and edited, none of the original meaning has been lost. Pilgrims today will still find its counsel helpful in pursuing the way to that holiness of life, which God has called His people to follow.

2. The Way of Holiness

Section I

> An highway shall be there, and a way, and it shall be called the way of holiness —Isaiah 35:8a.

"I have thought," said one of the children of Zion to the other, as in love they journeyed onward in the way cast up for the ransomed of the Lord to walk in; "I have thought," said he, "whether there is not a shorter way of getting into this way of holiness than some of our brethren apprehend?"

"Yes," said the sister addressed, whom was a member of the denomination alluded to; "Yes, brother, THERE IS A SHORTER WAY! Oh! I am sure this long waiting and struggling with the powers of darkness is not necessary. There is a shorter way." And then, with a solemn feeling of responsibility, and with a realizing conviction of the truth uttered, she added, "But, brother, there is but one way."

Days and even weeks elapsed; and yet the question, with solemn bearing, rested upon the mind of that sister. She thought of the affirmative given in answer to the inquiry of the brother, then examined yet more closely the scriptural foundation upon which the truth of the affirmative rested, and the result of the investigation tended to add still greater confirmation to the belief, that many sincere disciples of Jesus, by various needless perplexities, consume much time in endeavoring to get into this way, which might, more advantageously to themselves and others, be employed in making progress in it, and testifying, from experimental knowledge, of its blessedness.

How many, whom Infinite Love would long since have brought into this state, instead of seeking to be brought into the possession of the blessing at once, are seeking a preparation for the reception of it! They feel that their convictions are not deep enough to warrant an approach to the throne of grace, with the confident expectation of receiving the blessing now. Just at this point some may have been lingering months and years, as did the sister who so confidently affirmed, "There is a shorter way."

On looking at the requirements of the Word of God, she beheld the command "Be ye holy" (1 Peter 116). She then began to say in her heart, "Whatever my former deficiencies may have been, God requires that I should now be holy whether *convicted*, or otherwise, *duty* is *plain*. God requires present holiness. On coming to this point, she at once apprehended a simple truth before unthought-of, that is, *knowledge is conviction*. She well knew that for a long time she had been assured that God required holiness. But she had never deemed this knowledge a sufficient plea to take to God—and because of present need, to ask a present bestowment of the gift.

Another difficulty by which her course had been delayed she found to be here. She had been accustomed to look at the blessing of holiness as such a high attainment, that her general habit of soul inclined her to think it almost beyond her reach. This erroneous impression rather influenced her to rest the matter thus: "I will let every high state of grace in name alone, and seek only to be *fully conformed to the will of God, as recorded in His written Word*. My chief endeavors shall be centered in the aim to be a humble *Bible Christian*. By the grace of God, all my energies shall be directed to this one point. With this single aim, I will journey onward, even though my faith may be tried to the uttermost by those manifestations being withheld, which have previously been regarded as essential for the establishment of faith."

On arriving at this point, she gained clearer insight into the simplicity of the way and took the Bible as the Rule of life, instead of the opinions and experiences of professors. She found, on taking the blessed Word more closely to the companionship of her heart, that no one declaration spoke more appealingly to her understanding than this: "Ye are not your own. For ye are bought with a price therefore glorify God in your body, and in your spirit, which are God's" (1 Corinthians 6: 19-20).

By this she perceived the duty of entire consecration in a stronger light, and as more sacredly binding than ever before. Here she saw God as her Redeemer, claiming, by virtue of the great price paid for the redemption of body, soul, and spirit, the *present and entire service* of all these redeemed powers.

By this she saw that if she lived constantly in the entire surrender of all that had been thus dearly purchased unto God, she was but an unprofitable servant; and that, if less than all was rendered, she was worse than unprofitable, inasmuch as she would be guilty of keeping back part of the price which had been purchased unto God: "Not...with corruptible things, as silver and gold,...but with the precious blood of Christ" (1 Peter 1:18-19). And after so clearly discerning the will of God concerning her, she felt that the sin of Ananias and Sapphira would be less culpable in the sight of heaven than her own, should she not at once resolve to live in the entire consecration of all her redeemed powers to God.

Deeply conscious of past unfaithfulness, she now determined that the time past would suffice; and with a humility of spirit, induced by a consciousness of not having lived in the performance of such a "reasonable service" (Romans 12:1), she was enabled, through grace, to resolve, with firmness of purpose, that entire devotion of heart and life to God should be the absorbing subject of the succeeding pilgrimage of life.

Section II

<blockquote>
We by His spirit prove,
And know the things of God,
The things which freely of His love
He hath on us bestow'd.
</blockquote>

After hewing thus resolved on devoting the entire service of her heart and life to God, the following questions occasioned much serious solicitude: How shall I know *when* I have consecrated all to God? And how ascertain whether God accepts the sacrifice? And how know the manner of its acceptance? Here again the blessed Bible, which she had now taken as her Counselor, said to her heart, "We have received, not the spirit of the world, but the spirit which is of God; that we might know the things that die freely given to us of God" (1 Corinthians 2:12).

It was thus she became assured that it was her privilege to *know when she* had consecrated all to God and also to know that the sacrifice was *accepted*, and the resolve was solemnly made that the subject would not cease to be absorbing until this knowledge was obtained.

She felt it a matter of no small importance to stand thus solemnly pledged to God, conscious that sacred responsibilities were included in these engagements. Realizing that neither body, soul, spirit, time, talent, nor influence were, even for one moment, at her own disposal, consecration began to assume the tangibility of living truth to her mind in a manner not before apprehended.

From a sense of responsibility thus imposed, she began to be more abundant in labors "instant in season and out of season" (2 Timothy 4:2).

While thus engaged, another difficulty presented itself: "How much of self was in these performances?" her accuser demanded. Bewildered, her heart began to sink, and she felt more keenly that she had no certain standard to rise against this accusation.

It was here again that the blessed Word sweetly communed with her heart, presenting the marks of the way, by a reference to the admonition of Paul: "Therefore, my beloved brethren, be ye steadfast, unmovable, always abounding in the work of the Lord, forasmuch as ye know that your labor is not in vain in the lord" (1 Corinthians 15:58).

These blessed communings continued thus: If the primitive Christians had the assurance that their labors were in the Lord, and thus enjoyed the heart inspiring *confidence* that their labors were *not in vain*, because performed in the might of the Spirit, then it is also your privilege to know that your labor is in the Lord. It was at this point in her experience that she first perceived the *necessity*, and also the *attainableness* of the witness of *purity of intention*.

It was by the Word of the Lord she became fully convinced that she needed this heart-encouraging confidence in order to insure success in her labors of love. The next step taken was to resolve, as in the presence of the Lord, not to cease importuning the throne of grace until the witness was given "that the spring of every motive was pure."

On coming to this decision, the blessed Word, most encouragingly, yea, and also assuring, said to her heart, "Stand still, and see the salvation of God."

Section III

Here, in Thine own appointed way,
I wait to learn Thy will;
Silent I stand before Thy face,
And hear Thee say, "Be still!"
Be still! and know that I am God:"
'Tis all I wish to know,
to feel the virtue of Thy blood,
And spread its praise below.

Thus admonished, she began to anticipate with longings unutterable, the fulfillment of the WORD upon which she had been enabled to rest her hope. These exercises powerfully and permanently assured her heart that "the word of God is quick, and powerful and sharper than any two edged sword, piercing even to the dividing asunder of soul and spirit, and of the joints and marrow, and is a discerner of the thoughts and intents of the heart" (Hebrews 4:12). But they were not of that distressing character which, according to her preconceived opinions, was necessary, preparatory to entering into a state of holiness.

So far from having overwhelming perceptions of guilt on which she had relied, she was constantly and consciously growing in grace daily; even hourly her heavenward progress seemed marked by the finger of God.

No gloomy fears that she was *not* a child of God, which had presented fearful anticipations of impending wrath, dimmed her spiritual horizon. There had been a period in her past experience during which she was delivered from any *lingering doubt of her acceptance with God, as a member of the household of faith*. But, conscious that she had *not the* witness of entire consecration to God, nor the assurance that her heart was pure, she was impelled onward by such an intense desire to be *fruitful in every good work*, that the emotions of her spirit could not perhaps be more clearly expressed than in the nervous language of the poet:

> My heartstrings groan with deep complaint,
> My flesh lies panting, Lord, for Thee;
> And every limb, and every joint
> Stretches for perfect purity.

And yet, to continue poetic language, it was a "sweet distress," for the Word of the Lord continually said to her heart, "The Spirit also helpeth our infirmities," (Romans 8:26); and conscious that she had submitted herself to the dictations of the Spirit, a sacred conviction took possession of her mind that she was being led into all truth.

"Stand still, and see the salvation of the Lord," was now the listening attitude, in which her soul eagerly waited before the Lord, and it was but a few hours later that she set apart a season to wait before the Lord for the bestowment of the object, or rather the two distinct objects previously stated.

On first kneeling, she thought of resolving that she would continue to wait before the Lord until the desire of her heart was granted. But the adversary, who had stood ready to withstand every progressive step, suggested, "Be careful, God may disappoint your expectations, and suppose you should be left to wrestle all night; ay, and all the morrow too?"

She had ever felt it a matter of momentous import to say, (either with the language of the heart or lip) "I have lifted my hand to God." For a moment she hesitated whether she should continue in a waiting attitude until the desire of her heart was fulfilled, but finally decided to rest the matter thus: One duty can never, in the order of God, interfere with another; and, unless necessarily called away by surrounding circumstances, I will in the strength of grace, wait till my heart is assured, though it may be all night, and all the morrow too.

And here most emphatically could she say, she was led by a way she knew not so simple, so clearly described, and urged by the Word of the Lord, and yet so often overlooked, for want of that childlike simplicity which, without reasoning, takes God at His Word. It was just while engaged in the act of preparing the way, as she deemed, to some great and indefinable exercise, that the Lord, through the medium of faith in His written Word, led her astonished soul directly into the "way of holiness," where, with unutterable delight, she found the comprehensive desires of her soul blended and satisfied in the fulfillment of the command, "Be ye holy."

Section IV

> Thou message from the skies!
> Ray for the Rayless heart!
> Thou fount of wisdom for the wise,
> A balm for all though art.
>
> Man of my counsel, thou,
> Blessing untold rejoice
> The heart of those who meekly bow,
> To listen to thy voice.

It was in this way that the *Word of the Lord*, the "Book of Books," as a "mighty counselor," urged her onward, and by unerring precept directed every step of the way. She progressed through each step of this blessed state of experience, as distinctly marked by its holy teachings as those already given. And so, to assist one, to rest more confidently in the assurance that "the word of the Lord is tried" (Psalm 18:30), and is the same in its immutable nature as the Faithful and True, she described the steps by which she entered into discipleship with Jesus.

Many times previous to the time mentioned, she had endeavored to give herself away in covenant to God. But she had never, till this hour, deliberately resolved in counting the cost, with the solemn intention to reckon herself "dead *indeed* unto sin, but alive unto God through Jesus Christ our Lord," (Romans 6:11). She determined to account herself permanently the Lord's, and in truth no more at *her own* disposal, but *irrevocably the Lord's property*, for time and eternity. Now, in the name of the Lord Jehovah, after having deliberately counted the cost, she resolved to enter into the bonds of an everlasting covenant, with the fixed purpose of *count all things loss* for the excellency of the knowledge of Jesus. Her purpose was to know Him and the power of His resurrection, by being made conformable to His death, and raised to an entire newness of life.

Apart from any excitement of feeling other than the sacred awe inspired by the solemnity of the act, she now *did* lay hold upon the terms of the covenant by which God has condescended to bind himself to His people. She made herself willing, yea, even desirous, of bringing down the responsibility of a perpetual engagement upon herself in the sight of heaven. She asked that the solemn act might be recorded before the eternal throne, so that the "host of the Lord that encamp round about them that fear him" might bear witness. She also desired that the redeemed, blood-washed spirits should behold yet another added to their choir in spirit and in song; and though still a resident of earth, she wanted them to witness the ceaseless return of all her redeemed powers, *through Christ*, ascending as an acceptable sacrifice. The obligation to take the service of God as the absorbing business of life, and to regard heaven as her native home, and the accumulation of treasure in heaven the chief object of ambition, was at this solemn moment entered upon.

On doing this, a hallowed sense of consecration took possession of her soul and she had a divine conviction that the covenant was recognized in heaven and that the seal, proclaiming her wholly the Lord's, was set. She had a deep and abiding consciousness that she had been but a co-worker with God in this matter, and this added still greater confirmation to her conception of the mighty work that had been wrought in and for her soul, which she felt assured would tell on her eternal destiny. She did not at the moment regard the state into which she had been brought as the "way of holiness," nor had the word *holiness* been the most prominent topic during this solemn transaction. Conformity to the will of God in all things was the absorbing desire of her heart. Yet after having passed through these exercises she began to give expression to her full soul thus: "I am wholly Thine!—Thou dost reign unrivaled in my heart! There is not a tie that binds me to earth; every tie has been severed, and now I am wholly, wholly Thine!"

While lingering on the last words, the Holy Spirit appealingly repeated the confident expressions to her heart, saying: What! wholly the Lord's? Is not this the holiness that God requires? What have you more to render? Does God require more than all hath He issued the command, "Be ye holy," and not given the ability, with the command, for the performance of it? Is He a hard master, unreasonable in His requirements? She realized her error in regarding holiness as an attainment beyond her reach, and stood reproved, though consciously shielded by the Atonement from condemnation.

Now the eyes of her understanding were more fully opened, and she knew that "if any man will do his will, he shall know of the doctrine" (John 7:17).

Section V

> Let us, to perfect love restored,
> Thine image here retrieve,
> And in the presence of our Lord
> The life of angels live.
>
> But is it possible that I
> Should live and sin no more?
> Lord, if on Thee I dare rely,
> The faith shall bring the power.

She now saw that holiness, instead of being an attainment beyond her reach, was a state of grace in which everyone of the Lord's redeemed ones should live—that the service was indeed a "reasonable service," in as much as the command "Be ye holy" is founded upon the absolute right which God, as our Creator, Preserver, and Redeemer, has upon the *entire* service of His creatures.

Instead of perceiving anything meritorious in what she had been enabled, through grace, to do, by laying all upon the altar, she saw that she had but tendered back to God that which was already His own.

She looked upon family, influence, and earthly possessions, and chided herself with "What hast thou that thou didst not receive? Now if thou didst receive it, why dost thou glory, as if thou hadst not received it?" (2 Corinthians 4:7). And though with Abraham in the sacrifice of his beloved Isaac, she was called seemingly to sacrifice what was of all earthly objects surpassingly dear, yet so truly did she now see that the Giver of every good gift but rightfully required His own in His own time, that she could only repeat, "The Lord gave, and the Lord hath taken away; blessed be the name of the Lord" (Job 1:21).

And O, what cause for abasement before God did she now perceive, in that she had so long kept back part of that price which, by the requirement of that blessed word, and she now so clearly discerned infinite love had demanded." And when she inquired of herself, "Is God unreasonable in His requirement of holiness?" her inmost soul, penetrated with a sense of past unfaithfulness, acknowledge not only the reasonableness of the obligation, but also the unreasonableness of not having lived in obedience to such a plain scriptural requirement.

With a depth of feeling not before experienced, she could now respond heartily to the sentiment:

> I loathe myself when Christ I see,
> And into nothing fall,
> Content if God exalted be,
> And Christ be all in all.

Never before did she so deeply realize the truth of the words, "We had the sentence of death in ourselves, that we should not trust in ourselves, but in God which raiseth the dead" (2 Cor. 1:9). With poverty of spirit her heart was constantly giving utterance to its emotions with the poet:

> Thou all our works in us hast wrought,
> Our good is all divine;
> The praise of every virtuous thought
> And righteous act is Thine.

As she continued in a waiting attitude before the Lord, the Spirit appealed to her understanding in this way: "Through what power have you been enabled thus to present yourself a living sacrifice to God?" Her heart replied. "Through the power of God. I could no more have brought myself, but through faith in God, believing it to be His requirement, than I could have created a world!" Immediately the Spirit suggested, "If God has enabled you to bring it, will He not, now that you bring it and lay it on His altar, accept it at your hands?" She now, indeed, began to feel that all things were ready! and, in thrilling anticipation, began to say, "Thou *wilt* receive me! Yes, Thou *wilt receive me!*"

And still she felt that something was wanting. "But *when* and *how* shall I *know* that Thou *dost* receive me?" said the importunate language of her heart. The Spirit presented the declaration of the written Word in reply. "Now is the accepted time," (2 Corinthians 6:2). Still her insatiable desires were unsatisfied, and yet she continued to wait with unutterable importunity of desire and longing expectation, looking upward for the coming of the Lord. The Spirit continued to urge the scriptural declarations. "'*Now is the accepted time*,' *I will receive you. Only believe!* Trust all *now* and *forever,* upon the faithfulness of the IMMUTABLE WORD, and you are *now* and *forever* the *saved* of the Lord!"

An increase of light in reference to the sacredness and immutability of the Word of God burst upon her soul! An assurance that the Holy Scripture is, in verity the WORD OF THE LORD, and as immutable in its nature as the *throne of the Eternal,* assumed the vividness and vitality of TRUTH, in a manner that she had never before realized.

These views were given in answer to an inquiry that rose in her mind; Shall I *venture* upon these declarations without *previously* realizing a change sufficient to warrant such conclusions? Venture *now*, merely because they stand thus recorded in the *written Word?*

She here perceived that the declaration of Scripture were as truly the WORD OF THE LORD to her soul, as though they were proclaimed from the holy mount in the voice of thunder, or blazoned across the vault of heaven in characters of flame. She now saw into the simplicity of faith in a manner that astonished and humbled her soul. She was astonished she had not before perceived it, and humbled because she had been so slow of heart to believe God. Her perception of faith and its effect were these: *Faith is taking God at His Word,* relying unwavering upon His truth. The nature of the truth believed, whether joyous or otherwise, will necessarily produce corresponding feeling. Yet, *faith* and *feeling* are two distinct objects, though so nearly allied.

Here she saw an error, which, during the whole of her former pilgrimage in the heavenly way, had been detrimental to her progress. She now perceived that she had been much more solicitous about *feeling,* than *faith*—requiring feeling, the *fruit* of faith, previous to having exercised faith.

Now, on discerning the way more clearly, she was enabled by the heir of the Spirit to resolve that she *would take God at His Word,* whatever her emotions might be. She lingered at counting the cost of living, a life of faith on the Son of God. The question was presented, "Suppose after you have ventured upon the bare declaration of God—resolved to believe that *as you venture upon His Word, He doth receive you just because* He hath said, 'I will receive you,'—and then should perceive no chance, no extraordinary evidence, or emotion, to confirm your faith, would you still believe?" The answer from the WORD was, "The just shall live by faith" (Romans 1:17).

She now came to the decision that if called to live *peculiarly* the life of faith, and denied all outward or inward manifestations to an extent before unheard of, with the exception of him who journeyed onward in obedience to the command of God, "not knowing whither he went" (Hebrews 11:8), she would still, through the power of the Almighty, who has said, "Walk before me, and be thou perfect," (Genesis 17:1), journey onward through the pilgrimage of life—walking by faith. She resolved that the shield of faith should never be relinquished, but retained even with the unyielding grasp of death. Never can the important step that followed be forgotten in time or in eternity.

Section VI

Faith in Thy power Thou seest I have,
For Thou this faith hast wrought,
Dead souls Thou call'st from the grave,
and speakest worlds from naught.
In hope against all human hope,
Self desperate, I believe;
Thy quickening word shall raise me up,
Thou shalt Thy Spirit give.
The thing surpasses all my thought,
But faithful is my Lord;
Through unbelief I stagger not,
For God hath spoke the word.

From the preceding views she discerned clear that *one* more step must be taken before she could fully test the faithfulness of God. "Faithful is he that calleth you, who also will do it," (1 Thessalonians 5:24), was not no longer a matter of opinion, but a truth confidently believed. She saw that she must relinquish the confident expression before indulged in, as promising something in the *future*, "Thou *wilt* receive me!" for the yet more confident expression, implying *present* assurance, "Though *dost* receive!" It is perhaps, almost needless to say that the enemy, who had heretofore endeavored to withstand every step of the Spirit's leadings, now confronted her, with much greater energy. The suggestion that it was strangely presumptuous to believe in such a way, was presented to her mind with plausibility which only satanic subtlety could invent. But the resolution to believe was fixed; and then the Spirit most inspiringly said to her heart, "The kingdom of heaven suffereth violence, and the violence take it by force, "(Matthew 11:12).

And now, realizing that she was engaged in a transaction eternal in its consequences, she said, with the strength and the presence of the Father, Son, and Holy Spirit, and those spirits that minister to the heirs of salvation, "O Lord, I call heaven and earth to witness that I *now lay body, soul, and spirit,* with *all these redeemed powers, upon Thine altar, to be forever* THINE! "Tis DONE! Thou hast promised to receive me! Thou canst not be unfaithful! *Thou dost receive me now!* From this time henceforth I *am thine—wholly thine!*"

The enemy suggested, "'Tis but the work of your own understanding—the effort of your own understanding—the effort of your own will." But the Spirit of the Lord raised up a standard, which Satan, with his combined forces, could not overthrow. It was by the following presentation of truth that the Spirit helped her infirmities: "Do not your perceptions of right—even your *own understanding*—assure you that it is a matter of *thanksgiving to God* that you have been thus enabled to present your all to Him?" "Yes," responded her whole heart, "it has all been the work of the Spirit. I will praise Him! Glory be to God in the highest! Worthy is the Lamb to receive glory, honor, and blessing! Hallelujah! the Lord God omnipotent reigneth! Yes, Thou dost reign unrivaled in my heart! Though hast subdued all things to thyself, and now Thou dost reign throughout the empire of my soul, the Lord God of every motion!"

The SPIRIT now bore full testimony to her spirit, of the TRUTH *of* THE WORD! She felt that it was not in vain she had believed; her very existence seemed lost and swallowed up in God; she plunged, as it were, into a immeasurable ocean of love, light, and power, and realized that she was encompassed with the "favor of the Almighty as with a shield." She felt assured that while she rested her entire being on the faithfulness of God, she might confidently stand "rejoicing in hope," and exultingly sing with the poet—

> My steadfast soul from falling free
> Shall now no longer rove,
> But Christ be all in all to me,
> And all my soul be love.

She now saw infinite propriety, comprehensiveness, and beauty, in those words of DIVINE origin, from which she had before shrunk, as implying a state too high and sacred for ordinary attainment or expectation.

Holiness, sanctification, and *perfect love* were words no longer so incomprehensible, or indefinite in nature or bearing, in relation to the individual experience of the Lord's redeemed ones. She wondered not that it should be said in reference to the "way of holiness." "The ransomed of the Lord shall walk there," (Isaiah 35:8-10). She perceived that these terms were most significantly expressive of a state of soul in which *every* believer should live, and felt that no words of mere earthly origin could embody to her own perceptions, or convey to the understanding of others, half the comprehensiveness of meaning contained in them. These terms stand forth so prominently in the Word of God, assuring men that they are given by the express dictation of the Holy Spirit.

She now thought of her former peculiar scruples in reference to the *use* of these words of divine origin, as in a degree partaking of the sin of Uzzah. She had been implying an unwarrantable carefulness about the ark of God, as though infinite wisdom had not devised the most proper mode of expression. She well remembered how often her heart had risen against these expressions, as objectionable, when she had heard other travelers in the "way of holiness" use the terms as expressive of the state of grace into which the Lord had brought them, the very same words which she now saw were beautifully expressive of the state into which the Lord had brought *her* own soul.

She felt such a mighty increase of confidence in God, that she hesitated not to trust the entire management of His own cause—her life—in His hands. She was desirous to become an instrument through which He might show forth His power to save unto the uttermost—to be accounted of no reputation—to be but as a "*voice*" sounding forth the praise of the "Almighty to save." She was willing that the instrument should be despised and rejected, so that the voice of God should alone be heard, and the Savior honored and accepted.

Section VII

"'Tis done! Thou dost this moment save,
With full salvation bless;
Redemption through Thy blood I have,
And spotless love and peace.

Now that she was so powerfully and experimentally assured of the blessedness of this "shorter way," how she longed to say to every redeemed one, "You have been fully redeemed—redeemed from all iniquity—that you should be unto God a peculiar people zealous of good works!"

It did appear so reasonable that all the Lord's ransomed ones, who had been so fully *redeemed*, and *chosen out of the world*, should be sanctified and set apart for holy service, as chosen vessels unto God. It also seemed so reasonable that they had been chosen to bear His hallowed name before an opposing world, by having the seal legibly stamped upon the forehead, proclaiming them as "not of the world," a "peculiar people" to "show forth His praise," (John 17:14, Titus 2:14, cf. 1 Peter 2:9). All the energies of her mind were now absorbed in the desire to communicate the living intensity of her soul on this subject to the heart of every professed disciple.

Her now newly inspired spirit could scarcely conceive of a higher ambition in the present state of existence, than to be endued with the unction of the Holy One, and then permitted, by the power of the Spirit, to say to every lover of Jesus, "this is the will of God, even *your* sanctification," (1 Thessalonians 4:3). Jesus, *your* Redeemer, *your* Savior, waits even now to sanctify your wholly; "and I pray God your *whole spirit* and *soul* and *body* be preserved blameless unto the coming of our Lord Jesus Christ. Faithful is he that calleth you, who also will do it," (5:23-24).

It was in that same hallowed hour when she was first, through the Blood of the everlasting covenant, permitted to enter within the veil and *prove* the blessedness of the "way of holiness." The weighty responsibilities and inconceivably glorious destination of the believer were unfolded to her spiritual vision in a manner inexpressibly surpassing her former perceptions.

She seemed permitted to look down through the vista of the future, to behold her as having begun a race. She was luminously lit up by the rays of the Son of righteousness, with the gaze of myriads of interested spectators—yes, even the gaze of the upper, as also the lower world—intensely fixed upon her. The spectators were watching her progress in a course that seemed to admit of no respite or turning to the right or to the left, and where consequences, inconceivably momentous and eternal in duration, were pending.

She was now confronted by questions! Have you brought yourself into this state of blessedness? Is it through your own exertion that this light has been kindled in your heart? As her heart responded to these interrogatories, she deeply felt that it was *all* the work of the Spirit. Never before did such a piercing sense of her own demerit and helplessness penetrate her mind as at that hour, while her inmost soul replied, 'Tis from the "father of lights," the Giver of "every good gift and every perfect gift" (James 1:17), that I have received this precious *gift*. Yes, it is a gift from God, and to His name be all the glory!

The Spirit then suggested: If it is a gift from God, you will be required to declare it as His gift, through our Lord Jesus Christ, ready for the acceptance of all, and this, if you would retain the blessing, will not be left to your own choice. You will be called to profess this blessing before thousands! Can you do it?

And here she was permitted again to count the cost. She had been saying: Rather let me die than lose the blessing, for Satan had suggested that she would ever be vacillating in her experience, one day professing the blessing, and another not. Satan also suggested that she was so constitutionally prone to reason, that it would require an extraordinary miracle to sustain her amid the array of unpropitious circumstances, which, like a mighty phalanx, crowded before the vision of her mind.

But the Spirit brought to her remembrance the continuous miracle of the Israelite nation, fed daily with bread directly from heaven. And though assured that a miracle equal in magnitude would be constantly requisite for her support, yet she gloried in the assurance that the same almighty power stood continuously pledged for its performance. And now that she was called to count the cost of coming out in the profession of this blessing before thousands, the enemy directed her mind most powerfully to what her former failures had been, in reference to making confession with the mouth.

In few duties had she more frequently brought condemnation of her soul than in this; and the suggestion from the adversary that a failure in this requirement was precisely the ground on which she should lose the blessing, assumed more plausibility than former temptations. But with the Spirit's assistance, she was enabled to resolve to be a worker together with God, so that the onward pilgrimage of more than five succeeding years had tested the happy consequences of the decision, and proved that it was indeed the Spirit of the Lord that raised the standard—the Spirit that taught!

The matter was decided thus: Some settled principles must be established in the soul, by which it may be known what shall constitute duty in reference to this subject. Duty must be determined by a reference to the requirements of the Word; and it would be settled thus; the voice of duty is literally the *voice of God to the soul*.

She was then enabled to decide the matter of testifying to the work of the Spirit in this way: The Church is represented as Christ's Body. I am one of the members of that Body. If I, by testifying of the Spirit's operation in my heart, am individually benefited, the whole Body is advantaged; while if I neglect to testify and, in consequence, suffer loss, my relation to the Body will of necessity cause it to participate in that loss. It is plain, therefore, and beyond all contradiction, my duty is to declare the work of God. The health of my own soul and that of the previous Body of Christ, of which I am a member, demands its performance.

The inquiry then arose: But am I by my own power of reasoning to determine in matters so momentous? The answer was: If you have power to reason above an idiot, or the beast that perish, God has given that power; it is a talent entrusted, for which you will be called to render an account of stewardship. *Natural* abilities are as truly *gifts from God* as those termed by men *gracious* abilities. Grace does not render natural endowments in any degree useless; it only turns them into a *sanctified* channel.

Having received a confirmed sense of duty and an assurance that the voice of duty was a voice of God, she resolved that however formidable the circumstances were, even if it literally cost her life in the effort to go forward, she would still proceed. Though she might be a martyr to the cause, it would be enough that the Almighty had said, "Go forward."

On coming to this point, a yet more glorious increase of light burst upon her way. The Spirit brought to her remembrance the words she had most solemnly uttered but a few moments before, when making the sacred dedication of all her power forever to God. She had used the dedicatory words of David, "Into thine hand I commit my spirit; thou hast redeemed me, O Lord God of truth," (Psalm 31:5). She had *realized* and acknowledged the offering accepted. And now the Spirit said: If your spirit actually had left the body and mingled with the spirits before the throne, when you thus solemnly committed it into the hands of God, and if the Father of spirits had permitted you to return and again actuate that body for the special purpose of declaring before thousands that Jesus is a full Savior, able to save to the uttermost, could you do it?

She thought of the Blood-washed spirits as messengers of love, surrounding the eternal throne, and waiting to communicate tidings of grace to whatever sphere commissioned. She thought of one sent to the earth with a special embassy, charged to communicate it to the greatest possible number of its inhabitants. She conjectured about the zeal he would manifest in giving publicity to the tidings, and of the expedients he would use to convey the ideas to his auditors of the importance of his mission. She also thought about their probable indifference and scorn, pronouncing him overzealous and charging him with carrying matters too far. Perchance *fanatic* or *monomaniac* might be the epithets that would serve to distinguish him from the mass of mankind, and be the only reward of his labors of love during the performance of his earthly mission.

Yet the thought of the manner in which these considerations would affect him tended to instruct and admonish her. She contemplated that a contemptuous reception of his message would have little weight on his personal feelings, and affect him only so far as the honor of his Sovereign was concerned. She also thought of his slight association and attachments to earth, except as the place for the completion of his work, and of his thoughts of heaven as the end of his operations, as the home of his heart, and as his native country.

It was now that the scriptural meaning of many words became clear to her. "The very God of peace sanctify you wholly...spirit and soul and body," (1 Thessalonians 5:23); "Thy will be done in earth, as it is in heaven," (Matthew 6:10); "They are not of the world," (John 17:16); "redeemed us from all iniquity...a peculiar people," (Titus 2:14); "strangers and pilgrims," "sojourning," (1 Peter 2:11; 1:17); "fellow citizens with the saints," (Ephesians 2:19); and more verses poured torrent after torrent of light upon the peculiar nature, responsibilities, and infinite blessedness of the way upon which she had newly entered. And in answer to the Sovereign's inquiry, Can you declare this great salvation to others? her heart responded, Yea, Lord, to an assembled world at once, if it be at Thy bidding! Her only request was to "arm me with Thy Spirit's might." "Into thy hands I commit my spirit;" let it but actuate this body for the performance of Thy good will and pleasure in all things. If at any time

Thou seest me about the department from Thee, cut short the work in righteousness, and take me home to thyself.

Section VIII

>Light from the enteral hills!
>Thou lamp of life divine!
>River of God, of many rills,
>Reaching to all mankind.
>
>Laden with previous freight,
>Fresh from the courts above;
>Alike to all, both small and great,
>Thine embassy of love.
>
>Gold were a thing of naught,
>Rubies of priceless worth,
>Compared with treasures thou hast brought
>To fallen sons of earth.

Oh, how precious, precious beyond all computation, was the blessed Word of God now to her soul! She had valued it before, but now, as she retraced the way by which the Lord had brought her, she saw that each progressive step had been distinctly marked by a reference to its requirements.

Though she loved the assembling of fellow travelers to the heavenly city and was greatly assisted by hearing of their experiences, she found, on looking back, that former perplexities in experience had too frequently arisen from a proneness to follow the traditions of men, instead of the oracles of God.

She now found that *"there is but one way"*—and this way far better and "shorter" also—by bringing every diversified state of experience, however specious or complex, to compare "to the law and to the testimony," (Isaiah 8:20). If the experience could not be tested against these, she was sure that the true light had not been followed. From this period, therefore, it became an immovable axiom with her never to deem an experience satisfactory that could not be substantiated with an emphatic "*Thus saith the Lord.*"

On getting into the "way of holiness," she found much clearer light beaming upon her path. Never in former experience did she so sweetly apprehend the truth of the words, "Thy sun shall no more go down; neither shall thy moon withdraw itself; for the Lord shall be thine everlasting light, and the days of thy mourning shall be ended," (Isaiah 60:20).

It was while walking in this light that the subtlety, maliciousness, and power of the arch deceiver became much more apparent. This would have caused more dread had she not also discovered, with the prophet's servant when his eyes were opened, that more were they that were for her than all that were against her. And then the knowledge that she was, in experimental truth, *resting upon Christ*, the Anointed of God, imparted such an increase of holy energy that she was enabled to obey the command to "Rejoice evermore," (1 Thessalonians 5:16). She sought Jesus, her Savior and Redeemer, for the full supply of all her wants, under every variety of circumstance, and became so divinely assured that the trial of her faith was *previous* that it was not hard to "glory in tribulations," (Romans 5:3).

Her perceptions of the absolute need of the Atonement were never so vivid as while journeying onward in this way. She felt she could not take one progressive step, or for one moment present an acceptable sacrifice, but through the merits of her Savior. She deeply realized the truth of her Savior's words, "Without me ye can do nothing," (John 15:5), and felt that it would not be to the honor of His real name should she not live in the enjoyment of that state of salvation in which she should be enabled to say, "I can do all things through Christ which strengthened me," (Philippians 4:13).

In reference to temptation, she learned from experience that "the disciple is not above his master," (Matthew 10:24). She ever found that trials, well circumstanced in fiendish subtlety, beset her way. But by the increase of light which beamed upon her path as she entered the highway of holiness, she could now, with much stronger confidence, exclaim, "We are not ignorant of his devices," (2 Corinthians 2:11). Her soul was encouraged when she remembered that the Savior "was in all points tempted like as we are, yet without sin," (Hebrews 4:15); and her heart rejoiced that she had the same potent Sword of the Spirit.

Yet she did not find the "highway of holiness" a place for inglorious ease. It was indeed, as significantly implied in the scriptural phrase, "a way," and required *interminable progression!*

Still she loved to call it the "rest of faith" and joyously quoted the writer of Hebrews, "For we which have believed *do* enter into rest," (4:3). Yet she could not conceive of a rest sweeter to the follower of Jesus than to *do the will of God*.

The standard for Christian imitation she deemed to be established by inspiration—"Let this mind be in you, which was also in Christ," (Philippians 2:5). She felt that the most conclusive way of coming to the knowledge of duty was through the Spirit and the example of Christ. In conformity with these principles, she regarded that state of soul which would constrain the disciple of Jesus to copy his Lord's words, "The zeal of thine house hath eaten me up," (John 2:17), as compatible with the assurance of having entered into this state of rest. The proportion in which this conformity to Christ was realized she described as the rest of faith—"the way of holiness."

The standard of Christian excellence being thus fixed by the ratio of approximation to the image of Christ, wherever she saw the characteristics of His loveliness most clearly described, her love was more abundant.

She well knew that in the present imperfect state of existence, we can know only in part, and perfection only can exist in the gospel sense, which ordains that "love is the fulfilling of the law," (Romans 13:10). There is need for that constant exercise that the "charity [that] suffereth long, and is kind," (1 Corinthians 13:4); and wherever she saw this spirit with corresponding action, her heart was most enduringly united. She was most endearingly attached to the division of Christ's Body where from infancy she had been graciously cherished, yet the point of attraction was centered in the nearest resemblance to the image of the Savior. The most uniform exhibition of the mind that was in Christ, inducing conformity to His will, was recognized here; and her heart exclaimed with her Lord, "The same is my brother, and sister, and mother," (Matthew 12:50).

It was thus, from what she deemed the requirement and spirit of the blessed Bible, that a foundation was laid for a characteristic in her experience which was a source of much satisfaction to herself and others; and she did not wonder that one of the blessed memory, while walking in this highway, should declare that here

> Names and sects and parties fall,
> And Christ alone is All in All.

Section IX

> Having therefore, brethren, boldness to enter into the holiest by the blood of Jesus, by a new and living way, which he hath consecrated for us, through the veil, that is to say, his flesh; and having a high priest over the house of God; let us draw near with a true heart in full assurance of faith, having our hearts sprinkled from an evil conscience, and our bodies washed with pure water (Hebrews 10:19-22).

It may be asked: How did the process described in the preceding sections cause that disciple to be brought into the holiest by the blood of Jesus? Did the resolution to be a Bible Christian—the determination to consecrate all to God by laying all upon the altar of sacrifice—or the act of entering into the bonds of an everlasting covenant to be wholly the Lord's—bring about this entrance into the new and living way? How could these purposes, however well intentioned, result in having the heart sprinkled from an evil conscience, and the body washed with pure water? Can aught but the blood of Christ do this?

> Jesus, my Lord, Thy blood alone
> Hath power sufficient to atone

were the confirmed sentiments of her heart. "Not by works of righteousness which we have done, but according to his mercy he saved us, by the washing of regeneration, and renewing of the Holy Ghost," (Titus 3:5), was the response ever uppermost in her heart in answer to such inquiries. She realized that it was these pious resolves that enabled her to be a worker together with God. That God cannot be unfaithful rested with weight upon her mind as an absorbing truth; and some principles founded on the faithfulness of God following that, by testing, assured her that "it is a good thing that the heart be established with grace," (Hebrews 13:9).

God, in His infinite love, has provided a way by which lost, guilty men, may be redeemed, justified, cleansed, and saved, with the power of an endless life. Provision has thus been made for the restoration of man, by availing himself of which, in the way designated in the Scriptures, he may regain that which was lost in Adam—even the image of God reenstamped upon the soul.

To bring about this restoration, the Father so loved the world that He gave His only begotten Son, who from eternity had dwelt in His bosom. At the appointed time, Christ, the Anointed of God, was revealed, and, as our Example, lived a life of disinterested devotion to the interests of mankind. As the Lamb slain from the foundation of the world, He laid himself upon the altar: He did "taste death for every man," (Hebrews 2:9) and "bare our sings in his own body," (1 Peter 2:24). As an assurance of the amplitude of His grace, and that He is no respecter of persons, He said, "And I, if I be lifted up from the earth, will draw all men unto me," (John 12:32). "The Spirit of truth, which proceeded from the Father, he shall testify of me," (15:26). The Spirit, true to His appointed office, reproves of sin, righteousness, and judgment. And now the entire voice of divine revelation proclaims, "All things are ready," (Matthew 22:4). "The Spirit and the bride say, Come," (Revelations 22:17).

The altar, thus provided by the conjoint testimony of the Father, Son, and Holy Spirit, is Christ. His sacrificial death and sufferings are the sinner's plea; the immutable promises of the Lord Jehovah are the ground of claim. If, true to the Spirit's operations on the heart, men, as workers together with God, "confess" their sins. The faithfulness and justice of God stand pledge not only to "forgive," but also to "cleanse... from all unrighteousness," (1 John 1:9).

By her resolve to be a "Bible Christian," this traveler in the "way of holiness" placed herself in a position to receive the direct teaching of the Spirit. It was the one and the *only* way for the attainment of the salvation promised in the gospel of Christ, inasmuch as it is written, "He became the author of eternal salvation unto all them that obey him," (Hebrews 5:9).

She determined to consecrate all upon the altar of sacrifice to God and resolved to "enter into the bonds of an everlasting covenant to be wholly the Lord's for time and eternity." She then resolved to act in conformity with this decision, *actually laying all upon the altar*, by the most unequivocal Scripture testimony. Her resolution placed her under the most solemn obligation to *believe that the sacrifice became the Lord's property, and by virtue of the altar upon which the offering was laid, became "holy" and "acceptable."*

The written testimony of the Old and New Testament Scriptures upon which, to her mind, the *obligation* for this belief rested, was brought out by comparing the design and learning of the old and new covenant dispensations. Thus, the old ordained that an altar be erected (see Exodus 27:1). This altar, before being eligible for the reception of offerings, was to be "atoned for," cleansed, and sanctified. (See Exodus 29:36-37). This being done, it was ordained by God to be "an altar most holy;" and having been proclaimed that by the Holy One, whatever *touched* the altar became holy, virtually the *Lord's property, sanctified to His service.* The sacredness and perpetuity of this ordnance were recognized by "God... manifest in the flesh," centuries afterward (1 Timothy 3:16). It is "the *altar* that sanctified the gift," (Matthew 23:19).

As the old dispensation but shadowed forth good things to come, so under the new, Christ is apprehended as the Bringer-in of a better hope. "For their sakes I *sanctify* myself, that *they* also might be *sanctified* through the truth," (John 17:10), declared the blessed Savior, in praying for His disciples. "Neither pray I for *these* alone, but for them also which shall *believe on me* through *their* word," (v. 20). Here she beheld the *Christian altar*, so exultingly recognized by the writer to the Hebrews, in contradistinction to the Jewish altar: "We have an altar, whereof they have no right to eat which serve the tabernacle. ...Wherefore Jesus also, that he might sanctify the people with his own blood, suffered without the gate. Let us go forth therefore unto him," (13:10, 12-13). "He taketh away the first, that he may establish the *second*," (10:9). And here she beheld "an altar most holy." If, under the old covenant, it was ordained that "whatsoever toucheth the altar shall be holy," (Exodus 29:37), her heart, in its confident exultations, said, "How much more shall the blood of Christ, who through the eternal Spirit offered himself without spot to God, purge your conscience from dead works to serve the living God?" (Hebrews 9:14). Here she did "behold the Lamb of God, which taketh away the sin of the world," (John 1:29).

It was by "laying all upon this altar" that she, by the most unequivocal Scripture testimony, laid herself under the most sacred obligation to *believe*. The sacrifice became "holy and acceptable" and virtually the *Lord's property*, even by virtue of the sanctity of the *altar* upon which it was laid. It continued "holy and acceptable," so long as kept inviolably upon this hallowed altar. At an early stage of her experience in the "way of holiness," the Holy Spirit powerfully opened to her understanding the following passage, as corroborative of this view of the subject: "I beseech you therefore, brethren, by the mercies of God, that ye present your bodies a living sacrifice, holy, acceptable unto God, which is your reasonable service," (Romans 12:1).

From these important considerations, she perceived that it was indeed by the Spirit's teachings she had been led to "enter into the bonds of an everlasting covenant to be wholly the Lord's." By removing this offering from the *hallowing* altar, she should cease to be holy, as it is "that altar the sanctified the gift," (Matthew 23:19).

In this light, she also saw why it is that *all* is so imperatively required, inasmuch as it is the Redeemer who makes the demand for the "living sacrifice." The Redeemer has purchased *all*—body, soul, and spirit—unto himself. And she did not wonder that an offering *consciously* not entire—known by the offerer to be *less* than *all*—is not acceptable, inasmuch as God has pronounced such offerings unacceptable (see Malachi 1:8, 13-14). She also thought it scriptural that such an offering is not received, even though the reception of it be greatly desired by the offerer (see Malachi 2:13). That such a one *could not believe* while still halting between the world and an *entire surrender*, she thought fully explained by the words of the Savior, "How can ye believe, which receive honor one of another, and seek not the honor that cometh from God only?" (John 5:44). This she believed to be the hindrance with thousands of professed disciples who hear the sayings of Jesus, and desire holiness, and yet, by refusing to come to His terms, affirm that His sayings are hard. Many go back altogether, and follow the Savior no more—even though He so confidently and persuasively affirms, "If any man *will do* his will, he shall *know* of the doctrine," (John 7:17).

It was on coming to *this altar* she realized that the devotions of the believer, while resting here, are "unto God a sweet savor of Christ," (2

Corinthians 2:15), inasmuch as no service can be "holy, acceptable" unto God, unless presented through this medium. The duty of believing, and also of having a scriptural foundation for faith to rest upon, she regarded as most important. She felt assured that God has so explicitly given, in His written Word, a thorough foundation for our faith that the sin of unbelief is *dishonoring to God*. She was not surprised that he "fearful, and unbelieving" should be excluded from the believer's test, and numbered by the Revelation in such revolting company (Revelations 21:8).

And thus she found the "*shorter*, the *one*, and the *only way*," of which it is said that the redeemed of the Lord shall walk there. She surrendered all to the Redeemer and believingly ventured her entire being upon *Jesus*! Resting here, she proved experimentally the truth of His declaration, "I am the way," (John 14:6); she was enabled to realize continually the purifying virtue of His atoning blood, and to testify that it was not in vain He had offered himself up "that he might sanctify the people with his own blood," (Hebrews 13:12).

And though she apprehended that nothing *but the blood of Jesus* could *sanctify* and *cleanse* from sin, yet she was so scripturally assured that it was needful for the recipient of this grace as a worker together with God, to place himself believingly *upon* "the altar that sanctified the gift." He must do this before he could prove all-cleansing Blood. Gracious intentions and strong desires, she was convinced, are not sufficient to bring about these important results; corresponding *action* is also necessary. The offering must be *brought* and believingly *laid upon the altar* before the acceptance of it can be realized. In this crucifixion of nature, the Spirit helps our infirmities and works mightily to *will*—but *man must act*.

As illustrative, in a degree, of her views of responsibility, she would refer to a would-be offerer at the Jewish altar. For months, he graciously intended to present the sacrifices required by the law, yet deferred from a variety of causes, seemingly plausible, to *comply* with the requirement of handing over his gift. Finally the laws, which he had ever, acknowledged "just, and good," (Romans 7:12), cut him off from the community of his people. She was apprehensive that many who graciously *intend* to be holy by laying all upon the Christian altar are delaying from seemingly plausible causes to comply with the requirement, "Be ye holy." And finally, at an unlooked-for hour, the law, which they have ever pronounced "just, and good," excludes them from the community of the redeemed, Blood-washed company in heaven.

She also found one act of faith not sufficient to insure a continuance in the "way of holiness," but that a *continuous* act was requisite. "As ye have therefore received Christ Jesus the Lord, so walk ye in him," (Colossians 2:6) was an admonition greatly blessed in her soul. Assured that there was no other way of retaining this state of grace but by the exercise of the same resoluteness of character, presenting *all* and *keeping* all upon the hallowed altar, and also in the exercise of the same faith, she was enabled, through the teaching of the Spirit, to "walk by the same rule, [and] mind the same thing," (Philippians 3:16). For years afterward she continued an onward walk in the "way of holiness."

She was impelled by a divine constraint to test every progressive step by the powerful persuasive, "Thus it is written." She became so increasingly confident in her rejoicings, that her faith did not stand in the wisdom of being vacillating in her experience, as had been so painfully suggested by the tempter; and she was enabled daily to become more firmly rooted and grounded in the faith, abounding therein with thanksgiving.

It was thus that, through the Spirit's teachings, she was ready to give an answer to those that asked a reason of her hope, and these teachings were communicated most peculiarly through the medium of the *written Word*. Through each succeeding year of her pilgrimage in the heavenly way she learned to place a yet higher estimate upon its truths. The nearer she drew to the city of her God, the clearer was the light that shone upon its sacred pages, proclaiming it to be the Word of the Lord. And as she continued to pass down through time, leaning on its sacred declarations, she verily believed herself to be as divinely sustained as though to her *outward perceptions* she *knew* and could *feel* herself leaning for support upon the "Faithful and True," "with a vesture dipped in blood," called, by the Revelator, "The Word of God," (Revelations 19:13)!

Thy statutes have been my song in the house of my pilgrimage (Psalm 119:54).

Blessed Bible! How I love it!
How it doth my bosom cheer.
What hath earth like this to covet?
Oh, what stores of wealth are here!
Man was lost, and doom'd to sorrow,
Not one ray of light or bliss
Could he from earth's treasures borrow,
Till his way was cheer'd by this.

Yes, I'll to my bosom press thee,
Precious Word, I'll hide thee here;
Sure my very heart will bless thee,
For thou ever sayest, "Good cheer!"
Speak, my heart, and tell thy ponderings,
Tell how far thy rovings led,

When this Book brought back thy wanderings,
　Speaking life as from the daed.

Yes, sweet Bible! I will hide thee
　Deep, yes, deeper in this heart;
Thou through all my life wilt guilde me,
　And in death we will not part.
Part in death? No! never! Never!
　Through death's vale I'll lean on thee;
Then, in worlds above, forever,
　Sweeter still thy truths shall be!

Words to Winners of Souls

Horatius Bonar 1808-1889

With an Introduction
By Robert E. Coleman

Abridged version of *Words to Winners of Souls* by Horatius Bonar. Abridged version originally published by World Wide Publications, Billy Graham Evangelistic Association, 1994, Wheaton, Il. Copyright of abridged version and introduction held by Robert Coleman, used with permission. Scripture quotations are taken from the Holy Bible, King James Version (KJV), in the Public Domain. The image was in the Public Domain.

Book Chapters

1. Introduction
   By Robert E. Coleman 364
2. The Importance of a Living Ministry 367
   Two Classes of Preachers 368
   The Object of Ministry 369
   Christ the Answer 370
3. The Minister's True Life and Walk 372
   Walking with God 373
   Faithfulness and Success 374
4. Past Defects 376
   Going Through the Motions 377
   True Submission 378
   Weep Over the Lost 379
5. Ministerial Confession 381
   Making Excuses 382
   Self-Centered 383
   Scornful of Opponents 385
   We Have Failed God 386
6. Revival in the Ministry 394
   Our Need Today 395
   Learning from Myconius 396
   Preaching to the Dying 397
   Should We Be Less Earnest? 398
7. Notes 401

1. Introduction
By Robert E. Coleman

Feeling deeply the plight of persons without Christ, and the urgency of getting the saving Gospel to them, Horatius Bonar wrote:

> Go, labor on, while it is day;
> The world's dark night is hastening on;
> Speed, speed thy work, cast sloth away,
> It is not thus that souls are won![1]

The words reflect the compelling love of this serious winner of souls, said to be "one of the most Christ-like" and "radiant" persons of his day.[2]

He was born in Edinburgh, Scotland, December 19, 1808. After completing his education, the young scholar worked in a mission at Leith. In 1837 he accepted appointment to the Presbyterian Church at Kelso, and later became parish minister of the newly formed Free Church in the city, where he served for nearly thirty years. Going then to the famous Chalmers Memorial Church at Edinburgh, he faithfully proclaimed the Word until his death on July 31, 1889. Though I suspect it was of little consequence to Bonar, as an indication of the esteem in which he was held by his peers, he received the D.D. degree from the University of Aberdeen, and in 1883 was elected Moderator of the General Assembly of his Church.

Not only was Dr. Bonar recognized as a powerful preacher: he was also revered as a gifted writer. Among the numerous books, which came from his pen, are: *The Night of Weeping* (1846), *Looking to the Cross* (1851), *God's Way of Peace* (1862), *God's Way of Holiness* (1865), and *The Eternal*

Way (1869). Many of his sermons, too, found their way into print, and are still being read in various publications. In addition he edited several journals, including *The Christian Treasury*, *The Presbyterian Review*, and *The Quarterly Journal of Prophecy*.

Probably, though, this remarkable man is best known for his poetry and hymns. Nearly every modern hymnal contains some of his songs, like "I Heard the Voice of Jesus Say"; "Here, O My Lord, I See Thee Face to Face'"; "When the Weary, Seeking Soul"; and "What a Friend We Have in Jesus."

Running through all his work, whether preaching or writing, is a fervent yet loving call to holiness of life, and work, which meant to him simply Christ-likeness. Any ministry without this authenticating mark of discipleship, he believed, is wasted energy: indeed, it may do more harm than good. God is calling us, Bonar pleads, to the obedience of the cross.

A slumbering church indifferent to perishing men and women must hear this message, especially the preachers. It summons us to repentance and renewal of our first love. Significantly, at the time *Words to Winners of Souls* was written in 1859, great revivals were sweeping across many parts of the British Isles and America, and the book captures that concern. While focusing the need for evangelism, the underlying theme is getting right with God and walking every day in fellowship with Christ.

One seeking entertainment or some new and fascinating technique of witnessing will find the book unappealing. These words of Bonar are not about methods, but the messengers of the Gospel-broken and contrite lovers of Jesus whose lips have been touched with a coal of fire from the altar of God.

Though first published more than 130 years ago, the message has lost none of its pungency and directness. In this slightly abridged edition, the words still speak to persons who yearn to be winners of souls, sanctified, fitted for the Master's use. That is why again and again I read the book. And perhaps, too, it will bring you, as it does me, to a place of renewed dedication and prayer.

Robert E. Coleman

'Tis not for man to trifle. Life is brief,
And sin is here.
Our age is but the falling of a leaf—
A dropping tear.
We have no time to sport away the hours;
All must be earnest in a world like ours.

Not many lives, but only one have we,—
One, only one;
How sacred should that one life ever be—
That narrow span!
Day after day filled up with blessed toil,
Hour after hour still bringing in new spoil.

2. The Importance of a Living Ministry

"How much more would a few good and fervent men effect in the ministry than a multitude of lukewarm ones!"

Such was the remark of Oecolampadius, the Swiss Reformer, a man who had been taught by experience, and who has recorded that experience for the benefit of other churches and other days. It is a remark, however, the truth of which has been but little acknowledged and acted on; nay, whose importance is to this day unappreciated even where its truth is not denied.

The mere multiplying of men calling themselves ministers of Christ will avail little. They may be like Achans, troubling the camp; or perhaps Jonahs, raising the tempest. Even when sound in faith, yet, through unbelief, lukewarmness, and slothful formality, they may do irreparable injury to the cause of Christ; freezing and withering up all spiritual life around them. The lukewarm ministry of one who is theoretically orthodox, is often more extensively and fatally ruinous to souls than that of one grossly inconsistent or flagrantly heretical. "What man on earth is so pernicious a drone as an idle minister?" said Cecil. And Fletcher remarked as well, "lukewarm pastors made careless Christians." Can the multiplication of such ministers, to whatever amount, be counted a blessing to a people? The fathers of the Scottish Church, acting upon this principle, preferred keeping a parish vacant to appointing over it an unsuitable pastor. And when the church of Christ, in all her denominations, returns to primitive example, and, walking in apostolic footsteps, seeks to be conformed more closely to inspired models, allowing nothing that pertains to earth to come between her and her living Head, then will she give more careful heed to see that the men to whom she entrusts the care of souls, however learned and able, should be yet more distinguished by their spirituality and zeal and faith and love.

Two Classes of Preachers

In comparing Baxter and Orton together, the biographer of the former remarks that "Baxter would have set the world on fire while Orton was lighting a match." How true! Yet not true alone of Baxter or of Orton. These two individuals are representations of two classes in the church of Christ in every age, and of every denomination. The latter classes are far the more numerous: the Ortons you may count by hundreds, the Baxters by tens; yet who would not prefer a solitary specimen of the one to a thousand of the other? "When he spoke of weighty soul concerns," says one of his contemporaries of Baxter, "*you might find his very spirit drenched therein.*"[3]

No wonder that he was blessed with such amazing success! Men felt that in listening to him they were in contact with one who was dealing with realities, and these of infinite moment.

This is one of the secrets of ministerial strength and ministerial success. And who can say how much of the overflowing infidelity of the present day is owing not only to the lack of spiritual instructors, not merely to the existence of grossly unfaithful and inconsistent ones, but to the *coldness* of many who are reputed sound and faithful. Men cannot but feel that if religion is worth anything, it is worth everything; that if it calls for any measure of zeal and warmth, it will justify the utmost degrees of these; and that there is no consistent medium between reckless atheism and the intensest warmth of religious zeal. Men may dislike, detest, scoff at, persecute the latter, yet their consciences are all the while silently reminding them that, if there be a God and a Savior, a heaven and a hell, anything short of such life and love is hypocrisy, dishonesty, perjury!

And thus the lesson they learn from the lifeless discourses of the class we are alluding to, is, that as the men do not believe the doctrines they are preaching, there is no need for their hearers believing them; if ministers only believe them because they make their living by them, why should those who make nothing by them scruple about denying them?

"*Rash* preaching," said Rowland Hill, "disgusts; *timid* preaching leaves poor souls fast asleep; *bold* preaching is the only preaching that is owned of God."

It is not merely unsoundness in faith, nor negligence in duty, nor open inconsistency of life that mars the ministerial work and ruins souls. A man may be free from all scandal either in creed or conduct, and yet may be a most grievous obstruction in the way of all spiritual good to his people. He may be a dry and empty cistern, notwithstanding his orthodoxy. He may be freezing up or blasting life, at the very time that he is speaking of the way of life. He may be repelling men from the cross even when he is in words proclaiming it. He may be standing between his flock and the blessing even when he is, in outward form, lifting up his hands to bless them. How many souls have been lost for want of earnestness, want of solemnity, want of love in the preacher, even when the words uttered were precious and true!

The Object of Ministry

We take for granted that the object of the Christian ministry is to *convert sinners and to edify the body of Christ*. No faithful minister can possibly rest short of this. Applause, fame, popularity, honor, and wealth—all these are vain. If souls are not won, if saints are not matured, our ministry itself is vain.

The question, therefore, which each of us has to answer to his own conscience is, "Has it been the end of my ministry, has it been the desire of my heart to save the lost and guide the saved? Is this my aim in every sermon I preach, in every visit I pay? Is it under the influence of this feeling that I continually live and walk and speak? Is it for this I pray, toil, fast, and weep? Is it for this I spend and am spent, counting it, next to the salvation of my own soul, my chief joy to be the instrument of saving others? Is it for this that I exist? and to accomplish this would I gladly die? Have I seen the pleasure of the Lord prospering in my hand? Have I seen souls converted under my ministry? Have God's people found refreshment from my lips, and gone upon their way rejoicing? or have I seen no fruit of my labors, and yet am I content to remain un-blest? Am I satisfied to preach, and yet not know of one saving impression made, one sinner awakened? Can I go contentedly through the routine of ministerial labor, and never think of asking how God is prospering the work of my hands and the words of my lips?"

Nothing short of positive success can satisfy a true minister of Christ. His plans may proceed smoothly, and his external machinery may work steadily; but without actual fruit in the saving of souls, he counts all these as nothing. His feeling is. "My little children, of whom I travail in birth again, until Christ be formed in you." And it is this feeling, which makes him successful.

"Ministers," said Owen, "are seldom honored with success, unless they are continually aiming at the conversion of sinners." The resolution that in the strength and with the blessing of God he will never rest without success will insure it. It is the man who has made up his mind to confront every difficulty, who has counted the cost, and, fixing his eye upon the prize, has determined to fight his way to it—it is such a man that conquers.

The dull apathy of other days is gone. Satan has taken the field actively, and it is best to meet him front to front. Besides, men's consciences are really on edge. God seems extensively striving with them, as before the flood. A breath of the Divine Spirit has passed over the earth, and hence the momentous character of the time, as well as the necessity for improving it so long as it lasts.

The one true goal or resting-place, where doubt and weariness, and the strings of a pricking conscience, and the longings of an unsatisfied soul would all be quieted, is *Christ Himself*. Not the church, but Christ. No doctrine, but Christ. Not forms, but Christ. Not ceremonies, but Christ; Christ the God-man, giving His life for ours; sealing the everlasting covenant, and making peace for us through the blood of His cross; Christ the divine storehouse of all light and truth, "in whom are hid all the treasures of wisdom and knowledge;" Christ the infinite vessel, filled with the Holy Spirit, the lightener, the teacher, the quickener, the comforter, so that "out of his fullness we may receive, and grace for grace." This, this alone is the vexed soul's refuge, its rock to build on, its home to abide in till the great tempter be bound, and every conflict ended in victory.

Christ the Answer

Let us, then, meet this "earnestness," which is now the boast, but may ere long be the bane of the age, with that which alone can bring down its feverish pulse, and soothe it into blessed calm, "the gospel of the grace of God." All other things are but opiates, drugs, quackeries; this is the divine medicine; this is the sale, the speedy, the eternal cure. It is not by "opinion" that we are to meet "opinion"; it is the TRUTH OF GOD that we are to wield; and, applying the *edge* of the "sword of the Spirit" to the theories of man (which he proudly calls his "opinions"), make him feel what a web of sophistry and folly he has been weaving for his own entanglement and ruin.

It is not opinions that man needs: it is TRUTH. It is not theology: it is GOD. It is not religion: it is CHRIST. It is not literature and science; but the knowledge of the free love of God in the gift of His only-begotten Son.

"I know not," says Richard Baxter, "what others think, but, for my own part, I am ashamed of my stupidity, and wonder at myself that ideal not with my own and others' souls as one that looks for the great day of the Lord; and that I can have room for almost any other thoughts and words; and that such astonishing matters do not wholly absorb my mind. I marvel how I can preach of them slightly and coldly; and how I can let men alone in their sins; and that I do not go to them, and beseech them, for the Lord's sake, to repent, however they may take it, and whatever pain and trouble it should cost me. I seldom come out of the pulpit but my conscience-smitten me that I have been no more serious and fervent in such a case. It accuses me not so much for want of ornaments and elegancy, nor for letting fall an unhandsome word; but it asks me, 'How could thou speak of life and death with such a heart? How could thou preach of heaven and hell in such a careless, sleepy manner? Dost thou believe what thou say? Art thou in earnest, or in jest? How canst thou tell people that sin is such a thing, and that so much misery is upon them and before them, and be no more affected with it? Should thou not weep over such a people, and should not thy tears interrupt thy words? Should thou not cry aloud, and show them their transgressions; and entreat and beseech them as for life and death? Truly this is the peal that conscience doth ring in my ears, and yet my drowsy soul will not be awakened. Oh, what a thing is a senseless, hardened heart! O Lord, save us from the plague of infidelity and hard-heartedness ourselves, or else how shall we be fit instruments of saving others from it?

3. The Minister's True Life and Walk

The *true* minister must be a *true* Christian. He must be called by God, before he can call others to God. The Apostle Paul thus states the matter: "God hath reconciled us to himself by Jesus Christ, and hath given to us the ministry of reconciliation." They were first reconciled, and then they had given to them the ministry of reconciliation. Are we reconciled? It is but reasonable that a man who is to act as a spiritual guide to others should himself know the way of salvation. It has been frequently said that "the way to heaven is blocked up with dead professors"; but is it not also true that the melancholy obstruction is not composed of members of churches only? Let us take heed unto ourselves! As the minister's life is in more than one respect the life of a ministry, let us speak a few words on ministerial holy living.

Let us seek the Lord *early*. "If my heart be early seasoned with His presence, it will savor of Him all day after," (Bishop Hall: Psalm 5:4. *vide* Hebrew). Let us see God before man everyday.

"I ought to pray before seeing anyone. Often when I sleep long, or meet with others early, and then have family-prayer and breakfast and forenoon callers, it is eleven or twelve o'clock before I begin secret prayer. This is a wretched system. It is unscriptural. Christ rose before day, and went into a solitary place… Family-prayer loses much of its power and sweetness; and I can do no good to those who come to seek for me. The conscience feels guilty, the soul unfed, the lamp not trimmed. Then, when secret prayer comes, the soul is often out of tune. I feel it far better to begin with God, to see His face first, to get my soul near Him before it is near another… It is best to have at least one hour *alone with God*, before engaging in anything else. At the same time, I must be careful not to reckon communion with God by minutes, or hours, or by solitude," (McCheyne).

Hear this true servant of Christ exhorting a beloved brother: "Take heed to *thyself*. Your own soul is your first and greatest care. You know a sound body alone can work with power, much more a *healthy soul*. Keep a clear conscience through the blood of the Lamb. Keep up close communion with God. Study likeness to Him in all things. Read the Bible for your own growth first, then for your people."

"With him," says his biographer, "the commencement of all labor invariably consisted in the preparation of his own soul. The forerunner of each day's visitations was a calm season of private devotion during morning hours. The walls of his chamber were witnesses of his prayerfulness—I believe of his tears as well as of his cries. The pleasant sound of psalms often issued from his room at an early hour; then followed the reading of the Word for his own sanctification: and few have so fully realized the blessing of the first psalm." Would that it were so with us all! "Devotion," said Bishop Hall, "is the life of religion, the very soul of piety, the highest employment of grace."

Walking with God

It is said of the energetic, pious, and successful John Berridge, that "communion with God was what he enforced in the latter stages of his ministry. It was, indeed, his own meat and drink, and the banquet from which he never appeared to rise." This shows us the source of his great strength. If we were always sitting at this banquet, then it might be recorded of us ere long, as of him, "He was in the first year visited by about a thousand persons under serious impressions."

To the *men* even more than to their doctrine we would point the eye of the inquirer who asks, Whence came their success? and why may not the same success be ours? We may take the sermons of Whitefield or Berridge or Edwards for our study or our pattern, but it is the individuals themselves that we must mainly set before us; it is with the spirit of the men, more than of their works, that we are to be imbued. They were spiritual men, and walked with God. It is living fellowship with a living Savior, which, transforming us into His image, fits us for being able and successful ministers of the gospel.

Without this nothing else will avail. Neither orthodoxy, nor learning, nor eloquence, nor power of argument, nor zeal, nor fervor, will accomplish aught without this. It is this that gives power to our words, and persuasiveness to our arguments; making them either as the balm of Gilead to the wounded spirit, or as sharp arrows of the mighty to the conscience of the stouthearted rebel. From them that walk with Him in holy, happy fellowship, a virtue seems to go forth, a blessed fragrance seems to compass them whithersoever they go. Nearness to Him, intimacy with Him, assimilation to His character—these are the elements of a ministry of power.

When we can tell our people, "We beheld His glory, and therefore we speak of it; it is not from report we speak, but we have seen the King in His beauty"—how lofty the position we occupy! Our power in drawing men to Christ springs chiefly from the fullness of our personal joy in Him, and the nearness of our personal communion with Him. The countenance that reflects most of Christ, and shines most with His love and grace, is most fitted to attract the gaze of a careless, giddy world, and win their restless souls from the fascinations of creature-love and creature-beauty. A ministry of power must be the fruit of a holy, peaceful, loving intimacy with the Lord.

Faithfulness and Success

"The law of truth was in his mouth, and iniquity was not found in his lips: He walked with me in peace and equity, and did turn many away from iniquity," (Malachi 2:6). Let us observe the connection here declared to subsist between faithfulness and success in the work of the ministry; between a godly life and the "turning away many from iniquity." The end for which we first took office, as we declared at ordination, was the saving of souls; the end for which we still live and labor is the same; the means to this end are a holy life and a faithful fulfillment of our ministry.

The connection between these two things is close and sure. We are entitled to calculate upon it. We are called upon to pray and labor with the confident expectation of its being realized; and where it is not, to examine ourselves with all diligence, lest the cause of the failure be found in ourselves; in our want of faith, our want of love, our want of prayer, our want of zeal and warmth, our want of spirituality and holiness of life; for it is by these that the Holy Spirit is grieved away. Success is attainable; success is desirable; success is promised by God; and nothing on earth can be bitterer to the soul of a faithful minister than the want of it. To walk with God, and to be faithful to our trust, is declared to be the certain way of attaining it. Oh, how much depends on the holiness of our life, the consistency of our character, the heavenliness of our walk and conversation!

Our position is such that we cannot remain neutral. Our life cannot be one of harmless obscurity. We must either repel or attract—save or ruin souls! How loud, then, the call, how strong the motive, to spirituality of soul and circumspectness of life! How solemn the warning against worldly-mindedness and vanity—against levity and frivolity—against negligence and sloth and cold formality!

Of all men, a minister of Christ is especially called to walk with God. Everything depends on this; his own peace and joy, his own future reward at the coming of the Lord. But especially does God point to this as the true and sure way of securing the blessing. This is the grand secret of ministerial success. One who walks with God reflects the light of His countenance upon a benighted world; and the closer he walks, the more of this light does he reflect. One who walks with God carries in his very air and countenance a sweet serenity and holy joy that diffuses tranquility around. One who walks with God receives and imparts life whithersoever he goes; as it is written, "Out of him shall flow rivers of living water." He is not merely the world's light, but the world's fountain; dispensing the water of life on every side, and making the barren wastes to blossom as the rose. He waters the world's wilderness as he moves along his peaceful course. His life is blessed; his example is blessed; his fellowship is blessed; his words are blessed; his ministry is.

4. Past Defects

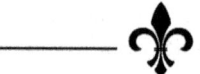

"O my God, I am ashamed and blush to lift up my face to Thee, my God: O our God, what shall we say after this?" —Ezra 9:6, 10

    To deliver sermons on each returning Sabbath; to administer the Lord's Supper statedly; to pay an occasional visit to those who request it; to attend religious meetings; this, we fear, sums up the ministerial life of multitudes who are, by profession, overseers of the flock of Christ. An incumbency of thirty, forty, or fifty years, often yields no more than this. So many sermons, so many baptisms, so many sacraments, so many visits, so many meetings of various kinds—these are all the pastoral annals, the parish records, the ALL of a lifetime's ministry to many! Of SOULS that have been saved, such a record could make no mention.

    Multitudes have perished under such a ministry; the judgment only will disclose whether so much as one has been saved. There might be learning, but there was no "tongue of the learned to speak a word in season to him that is weary." There might be wisdom, but it certainly was not the wisdom that "wins souls." There might even be the sound of the gospel, but it seemed to contain no glad tidings at all; it was not sounded forth from warm lips into startled ears as the message of eternal life—"the glorious gospel of the blessed God." Men live, and it was never asked of them by their minister whether they were born again! Men sickened, sent for the minister, and received a prayer upon their deathbeds as their passport into heaven. Men died, and were buried where all their fathers had been laid; there was a prayer at their funeral, and decent respects to their remains; but their souls went up to the judgment-seat unthought of, uncared for; no man, not even the minister who had vowed to watch for them, having said to them, "Are you ready?"—or warned them to flee from the wrath to come.

Is not this description too true of many a district and many a minister in our land? We do not speak in anger; we do not speak in scorn: we ask the question solemnly and earnestly. It needs an answer. If ever there was a time when there should be "great searching of heart," and frank acknowledgment of unfaithfulness, it is now when God is visiting us—visiting us both in judgment and mercy. We speak in brotherly-kindness; surely the answer should not be of wrath and bitterness. And if this description were true, what sin must there be in ministers and people! How great must be the spiritual desolation that prevails! Surely there is something in such a case grievously wrong: something which calls for solemn self-examination in every minister: something which requires deep repentance.

Going Through the Motions

Fields plowed and sown; yet yielding no fruit! Machinery constantly in motion, yet all without one particle of produce! Nets cast into the sea, and spread wide, yet no fishes enclosed! All this for years-for a lifetime! How strange! Yet it is true. There is neither fancy nor exaggeration in the matter. Question some ministers, and what other account can they give? They can tell you of sermons *preached*, but of sermons blest they can say nothing. They can speak of discourses that were admired and praised, but of discourses that have been made effectual by the Holy Spirit, they cannot speak. They can tell you how many have been baptized, how many communicants admitted; but of souls awakened, converted, ripening in grace, they can give no account. They can enumerate the sacraments they have dispensed; but as to whether any of them have been "times of refreshing," or times of awakening, they cannot say. They can tell you what and how many cases of discipline have passed through their hands: but whether any of these have issued in godly sorrow for sin, whether the professed penitents, who were absolved by them, gave evidence of being "washing and sanctified and justified," they can give no information; they never thought of such an issue!

They can tell what is the attendance at school, and what are the abilities of the teacher: but how many of these precious little ones, whom they have vowed to feed, are seeking the Lord, they know not: or whether their teacher be a man of prayer and piety, they cannot say. They can tell you the population of their parish, or the number of their congregation, or the temporal condition of their flocks; but as to their spiritual state, how many have been awakened from the sleep of death, how many are followers of God as dear children, they cannot pretend to say. Perhaps they would deem it rashness and presumption, if not fanaticism, to inquire. And yet they have sworn, before men and angels, to *watch for their souls* as they that must give account! But oh, of what use are sermons, sacraments, schools, if *souls* are left to perish; if living religion be lost sight of; if the Holy Spirit be not sought; if men are left to grow up and die unpitied, unprayed for, unwarned!

It was not so in other days. Our fathers really watched and preached for souls. They asked and they expected a blessing. Nor were they denied it. They were blessed in turning many to righteousness. Their lives record their successful labors. How refreshing the lives of those who lived only for glory of God and the good of souls! There is something in their history that compels us to feel that they were ministers of Christ—true watchman.

How cheering to read of Baxter, and his labors at Kidderminster! How solemn to hear of Venn and his preaching, in regard to which it is said that men "fell before him like slaked lime!" And in the much-blessed labors of that man of God, the apostolic Whitefield, is there not much to humble us, as well as to stimulate? Of Tanner, who was himself awakened under Whitefield, we read that he "seldom preached one sermon in vain." Of Berridge and Hicks we are told that, in their missionary tours throughout England they were blessed in one year to awaken four thousand souls. Oh for these days again! Oh for one day of Whitefield again!

Thus one has written—"The language we have been accustomed to adopt is this; "we must use the means, and leave the event to God; we can do no more than employ the means; this is our duty, and, having done this, we must leave the rest to Him who is the disposer of all things." Such language sounds well, for it seems to be an acknowledgment of our own nothingness, and to savor of submission to God's sovereignty; but it is only sound: it has not really any substance in it, for though there is truth stamped on *the face* of it, there is falsehood at *the root* of it. To talk of submission to God's sovereignty is one thing; but really to submit to it is another and quite a different thing."

True Submission

"Really to submit to God's sovereign disposal, does always necessarily involve the deep renunciation of our own will in the matter concerned; and such a renunciation of the will can never be effected without a soul being brought through very severe and trying exercises of an inward and most humbling nature. Therefore, if whilst we are quietly satisfied in using means without obtaining the end, and this cost us no such painful inward exercises and deep humbling as that alluded to, we think that we are leaving the affair to God's disposal—we deceive ourselves, and the truth in this matter is not in us.

"No; really to give anything to God, implies that *the will*, which is emphatically *the heart*, has been *set on that thing*; and if *the heart* has indeed been *set* on the salvation of sinners, as the end to be answered by the means we use, we cannot possibly give up that end, without, as was before observed, the heart being severely exercised and deeply pained by the renunciation of the will involved in it. When, therefore, we can be quietly content to use the means for saving souls, without seeing them saved thereby, it is, no real giving up to God in the affair. The fact is, the will—that is, *the heart*—had never really been set upon this end; if it had, it could not possibly give up such an end without being *broken* by the sacrifice.

"When we can thus be satisfied to use the means without obtaining the end, and speak of it as though we were submitting to the Lord's disposal, we use a truth to hide a falsehood, exactly in the same way that those formalists in religion do, who continue in forms and duties without going beyond them, though they know they will not save them, and who, when they are warned of their danger, and earnestly entreated to seek the Lord with all the heart, reply by telling us they know they must repent and believe, but that they cannot do either the one or the other of themselves, and that they must wait till God gives them grace to do so. Now, this is a truth, absolutely considered; yet most of us can see that they are using it as a falsehood to cover and excuse a great insincerity of heart. We can readily perceive that if their hearts were really set upon salvation, they could not rest satisfied without it. Their contentedness is the result, not of heart-submission to God, but in reality of *heart-indifference to the salvation of their own souls.*"

Weep Over the Lost

"Exactly so it is with us as ministers: when we can rest satisfied with using the means for saving souls without seeing them really saved, or we ourselves being broken-hearted by it, and at the same time quietly talk of leaving the event to God's disposal, we make us of a truth to cover and excuse a falsehood; for our ability to leave the matter thus is not, as we imagine, the result of heart-submission to God, but of heart-indifference to the salvation of the souls we deal with. No, truly; if the heart is really set on such an end, it must gain that end or break in loosing it."

It is told of Archbishop Usher that, at one period of his life, he used on Saturday afternoon to go alone to a riverside, and there sorrowfully recount his sins, and confess and bewail them to the Lord with floods of tears. Is this not fitting to reprove many, many of us? And even where we lament our sins, how many of us go apart oftentimes to weep over lost souls, to cry to the Lord for them, to implore, to beseech, to agonize with

Him in their behalf? Where is the waterside beside which our eyes have poured out streams in our intense compassion for the perishing?

Do we believe there is an *everlasting hell!*—and *everlasting hell* for every Christless soul? And yet we are languid, formal, easy in dealing with and for the multitudes that are near the gate of that tremendous furnace of wrath! Our families, our schools, our congregations, not to speak of our cities at large, our land, our world, might well send us daily to our knees; for the loss of even *one soul* is terrible beyond conception. Eye has not seen, nor ear heard, nor has entered the heart of man, what a soul in hell must suffer forever. Lord, give us bowels of mercies! "What a mystery? The soul and eternity of one man depends upon the voice of another!"

5. Ministerial Confession

"Remember therefore from whence thou art fallen, and repent, and do the first works; or else I will come unto thee quickly, and will remove thy candlestick out of his place, except thou repent"—Revelations 2:5

In the year 1651, the Church of Scotland, feeling in regard to her ministers "how deep their hand was in the transgression, and that ministers had no small accession to the drawing on the judgments that were upon the land," drew up what they called a humble acknowledgment of the sins of the ministry. This document is a striking and searching one. It is perhaps one of the fullest, most faithful, and most impartial confessions of ministerial sin ever made. A few extracts from it will suitably introduce this chapter on ministerial confession. It begins with confessing sins before entrance on the ministry:—

Lightness and profanity in conversation, unsuitable to that holy calling which they did intend, not thoroughly repented of. Not studying to be in Christ, before they be in the ministry; not to have the practical knowledge and experience of the mystery of the gospel in themselves, before they preach it to others. Neglecting to fit themselves for the work of the ministry, in not improving prayer and fellowship with God, and opportunities of a lively ministry, and other means; and not mourning for these neglects. Not studying self-denial, nor resolving to take up the cross of Christ. Negligence to entertain a sight and sense of sin and misery; not wrestling against corruption, nor studying of mortification and subduedness of spirit (Romans 7:14, 15).

Of entrance on the ministry it thus speaks: Entering to the ministry without respect to a commission from Jesus Christ; by which it hath come to pass, that many have run unsent. Entering to the ministry not from the love of Christ, nor from a desire to honor God in gaining of souls, but for by-ends, for a name, and for a livelihood in the world, notwithstanding a solemn declaration to the contrary at admission. Too much weighed with inclination to be called to the ministry in a place where we have carnal [family] relations (Romans 1:8-16).

Of the sins after entrance on the ministry, it thus searchingly enumerates:

> Ignorance of God; want of nearness with Him, and taking up little of God in reading, meditating, and speaking of Him. Exceeding great selfishness in all that we do; acting from ourselves, for ourselves, and to ourselves. Not caring how unfaithful and negligent others were, so being it might contribute a testimony to our faithfulness and diligence, but being rather content, if not rejoicing at their faults. Least delight in those things werein lies our nearest communion with God; great inconstancy in our walk with God, and neglect of acknowledging Him in all our ways. In going about duties, least careful of those things, which are most remote from the eyes of men. Seldom in secret prayer with God, except to fit for public performance; and even that much neglected, or gone about very superficially.

Making Excuses

Glad to find excuses for the neglect of duties. Neglecting the reading of Scriptures in secret, for edifying ourselves as Christians; only reading them in so far as may fit us for our duty as ministers, and oft times neglecting that. Not given to reflect upon our own ways, not suffering conviction to have a thorough work upon us; deceiving ourselves, by resting upon absence from, and abhorrence of evils, from the light of a natural conscience, and looking upon the same as an evidence of a real change of state and nature. Evil guarding of, and watching over the heart, and carelessness in self-searching; which makes much unacquaintedness with ourselves, and estrangedness from God. Not guarding or wrestling against seen and known evils, especially our predominant. A facility to be drawn away with the temptations of the time, and other particular temptations, according to our inclinations and fellowship.

Instability and wavering in the ways of God, through the fears of persecutions, hazard, or loss of esteem; and declining duties because of the fear of jealousies and reproaches. Not esteeming the cross of Christ, and sufferings for His name, honorable, but rather shifting sufferings, from self-love. Deadness of spirit, after all the sore strokes of God upon the land. Little conscience made of secret humiliation and fasting, by ourselves apart, and in our families, that we might mourn for our own and the land's guiltiness and great backslidings; and little applying of public humiliation to our own hearts. Finding of our own pleasure, when the Lord calls for our humiliation.

Not laying to heart the sad and heavy sufferings of the people of God abroad, and the not thriving of the kingdom of Jesus Christ, and the power of godliness among them. Refined hypocrisy; desiring to appear what, indeed, we are not. Studying more to learn the language of God's people than their exercise. Artificial confessing of sin, without repentance; professing to declare iniquity, and not resolving to be sorry for sin. Confession in secret much slighted, even of those things whereof we are convinced. No reformation, after solemn acknowledgements and private vows; thinking ourselves exonerated after confession. Readier to search out and ensure faults in others than to see or take with them in ourselves. Accounting of our estate and way according to the estimation that others have of us. Estimation of men, as they agree with or disagree from us. Not fearing to meet with trials, but presuming, in our own strength, to go through them unshaken. Not learning to fear, by the falls of gracious men; nor mourning and praying for them. Not observing particular deliverances and rods; not improving of them, for the honor of God, and the edification of others and ourselves. Little or no mourning for the corruption of our nature, and less groaning under, and longing to be delivered from, that body of death, the bitter root of all our other evils.

Fruitless conversing ordinarily with others, for the worse rather than for the better. Foolish jesting away of time with impertinent and useless discourse, very unbecoming the ministers of the gospel. Spiritual purposes often dying in our hands, when they are begun by others. Carnal familiarity with natural, wicked, and malignant men, whereby they are hardened, the people of God stumbled, and we ourselves blunted.

Self-Centered

Slighting of fellowship with those by whom we might profit. Desiring more to converse with those that might better us by their parts than the such as might edify us by their graces. Not studying opportunities of doing good to others. Shifting of prayer and other duties, when called thereto choosing rather to omit the same than that we should be put to them ourselves. Abusing of time in frequent recreation and pastimes, and loving our pleasures more than God. Taking little or no time in Christian discourse with young men trained up for the ministry. Common and ordinary discourse on the Lord's Day. Sighting Christian admonition from any of our flocks or others, as being below us; and ashamed to take light and warning from private Christians. Dislike of, or bitterness against, such as deal freely with us by admonition or reproof, and not dealing faithfully with others who would welcome it off our hands. Neglecting admonition to friends and others in an evil course. Reservedness in laying out our condition to others. Not praying for men of a contrary judgment, but using reservedness and distance from them; being more ready to speak of them than to them or to God for them. Not weighed with the failings and miscarriages of others, but rather taking advantage thereof for justifying ourselves. Talking of and sporting at the faults of others, rather than compassionating of them. No due painstaking in religious ordering of our families, nor studying to be patterns to other families in the government of ours. Hasty anger and passion in our families and conversation with others. Covetousness, worldly-mindedness, and an inordinate desire after the things of this life, upon which followed a neglect of the duties of our calling, and our being taken up for the most part with the things of the world. Want of hospitality and charity to the members of Christ. Not cherishing godliness in the people; and some being afraid of it and hating the people of God for piety, and studying to bear down and quench the work of the Spirit amongst them (2 Corinthians 1:6-12, 14, 24).

It next takes up ministerial duties more especially, and then solemnly proceeds: Not entertaining that edge of spirit in ministerial duties, which we found at the first entry to the ministry. Great neglect of reading, and other preparation; or preparation merely liberal and bookish, making an idol of a book, which hindered communion with God, or presuming on bygone assistance, and praying little. Careless in employing Christ, and drawing virtue out of Him, for enabling us to preach in the Spirit and in power.

In praying for assistance we pray more for assistance to the messenger than to the message which we carry; not caring what becomes of the Word, if we be with some measure of assistance carried on in the duty. The matter we bring forth is not seriously, recommended to God by prayer, to be quickened to His people. Neglect of prayer after the Word is preached, that I may receive the first and latter rain; and that the Lord would put in the hearts of His people what we speak to them in His name.

Neglect to warn, in preaching, of snares and sins in public affairs by some; and too much, too frequent, and unnecessary speaking by others of public business and transaction. Exceeding great neglect and unskillfulness to set forth the excellences and usefulness and [and the necessity of an interest in] Jesus Christ, and the new covenant, which ought to be the great subject of a minister's study and preaching. Speaking of Christ more by hearsay than from knowledge and experience, or any real impression of Him upon the heart. The way of most ministers' preaching too legal. Want of sobriety in preaching the gospel; not savoring anything but what is new; so that the substantials of religion bear but little bulk.

Not preaching Christ in the simplicity of the gospel, nor ourselves the people's servants, for Christ's sake. Preaching of Christ, not that the people may know Him. Not preaching with bowels of compassion to them that are in hazard to perish. Preaching against public sins, neither in such a way, nor for such an end, as we ought, for the gaining of souls, and drawing men out of their sins; but rather because it is our concernment to say something of these evils.

Scornful of Opponents

Bitterness, instead of zeal, in speaking against malignant, sectaries, and other scandalous persons; and unfaithfulness therein. Not studying to know the particular condition of the souls of the people, that we may speak to them accordingly; nor keeping a particular record thereof, though convinced of the usefulness of this. Not carefully choosing what may be most profitable and edifying; and want of wisdom in application to the several conditions of souls; not so careful to bring home the point by application as to find out the doctrine, nor speaking the same with that reverence which becomes His word and message.

Choosing texts whereon we have something to say, rather than suiting to the condition of souls and times, and frequent preaching of the same things, that we may not be put to the pains of new study. Such a way of reading, preaching, and prayer as puts us in these duties farther from God. Too soon satisfied in the discharge of duties, and holding off challenges of conscience with excuses. Indulging the body, and wasting much time idly. Too much eyeing our own credit and applause; and being taken with it when we get it, and unsatisfied when it is wanting. Timorousness in delivering God's message; letting people die in reigning sins without warning. Studying the discharge of duties, rather to free us from censure than to approve ourselves to God.

Not making all the counsel of God known; to His people; and particularly, not giving testimony in times of defection. Not studying to profit by our own doctrine, nor the doctrine of others. For most part, preaching as if we ourselves were not concerned in the message, which we carry to the people. Not rejoicing at the conversion of sinners; but content with the unthriving of the Lord's work amongst His people, as suiting best with our minds; fearing, if they should thrive better, we should be more put to it, and less esteemed of by them. We preach not as before God, but as to men; as doth appear by the different pains in our preparation to speak to our ordinary hearers, and to others to whom we would approve ourselves.

Negligent, lazy, and partial visiting of the sick. If they be poor, we go once, and only when sent for; if they be rich, and of better note, we go oftener, and unsent for. Not knowing how to speak with the tongue of the learned a word in season to the weary, and exercise in conscience; nor to such as are under the loss of husband, wife, children, friends, or goods, for the improving of these trials to their spiritual advantage; nor to dying persons. In visiting, wearying or shunning to go to such as we esteem graceless. Not visiting the people from house to house; nor praying with them at fit opportunities (2 Timothy 4:1-5).

Lazy and negligent in catechizing. Not preparing our hearts before, nor wrestling with God for a blessing to it, because of the ordinariness and apprehended easiness of it; whereby the Lord's name is much taken in vain, and the people little profited. Looking on that exercise as a work below us, and not condescending to study a right and profitable way of instructing the Lord's people. Partial in catechizing, passing by those that are rich, and of better quality, though many of such stand ordinarily in great need of instruction. Not waiting upon, and following the ignorant; but often passionately upbraiding them (Galatians 4:11-20).

These are solemn confessions, the confessions of men who knew the nature of that ministry on which they had entered, and who were desirous of approving themselves to Him who had called them, that they might give in their account with joy and not with grief.

We Have Failed God

Let us, as they did, deal honestly with ourselves. Our confessions ought to be no less ample and searching.

1. We Have Been Unfaithful

The fear of man and the love of his applause have often made us afraid. We have been unfaithful to our own souls, to our flocks, and to our brethren; unfaithful in the pulpit, in visiting, in discipline, in the church. In the discharge of every one of the duties of our stewardship there has been grievous unfaithfulness. Instead of the special particularization of the sin reproved, there has been the vague allusion. Instead of the bold reproof, there has been the feeble disapproval. Instead of the unswerving consistency of a holy life whose uniform tenor should be a protest against the world and a rebuke of sin, there has been such an amount of unfaithfulness in our walk and conversation, in our daily deportment and conversation with others, that any degree of faithfulness we have been enabled to manifest on the Lord's Day is almost neutralized by the want of circumspection with our weekday life exhibits.

Few men ever lived a life so busy, and so devoted to God, as Usher, Archbishop of Armagh. His learning, habits of business, station, and friends, all contributed to keep his hands every moment full; and then his was a soul that seemed continually to hear a voice saying: "redeem the time, for the days are evil." Early, too, did he begin, for at ten years of age he was hopefully converted by a sermon preached on Romans 12:1, "I beseech you, therefore, by the mercies of God, that ye present your bodies a living sacrifice." He was a painstaking, laborious preacher of the Word for fifty-five years.

Yet hear him on his deathbed! How he clings to Christ's righteousness alone, and seems to himself, even after such a life, only sin and want. The last words he was heard to utter were about one o'clock in the afternoon, and these words were uttered in a loud voice, *"But, Lord, in special forgive me my sins of OMISSION."* It was omissions, says his biographer; he begged forgiveness of with his most fervent last breath! —he who was never known to omit an hour, but who employed the shred ends of his life for his great Lord and Master! The very day he took his last sickness, he rose up from writing one of his great works, and went out to visit a sick woman, to whom he spoke of fitly and fully, that you would have taken him to have spoken of heaven before he came there. Yet this man was oppressed with a sense of his OMISSIONS!

Reader, what think you of yourself, --your undone duties; your unimproved hours; times of prayer omitted; your shrinking from unpleasant work, and putting it on others; your being content to sit under your vine and fig tree without using all efforts for the souls of others? Oh, sins of omission! *"Lord, in special forgive me my sins of omission!"*

Hear the confession of Edwards, in regard both to personal and ministerial sins:

> "Often I have had very affecting views of my own sinfulness and vileness; very frequently to such a degree as to hold me in considerable time together, so that I have often been forced to shut myself up. I have had a vastly greater sense of my own wickedness, and the badness of my heart, than ever I had before my conversion. My wickedness, as I am in myself, has long appeared to me perfectly ineffable, swallowing up all thought and imagination. I know not how to express better what my sins appear to me to be, than by heaping infinite upon infinite, and multiplying infinite by infinite. When I look into my heart, and take a view of my wickedness, it looks like an abyss infinitely deeper than hell. And yet it seems to me that my conviction of sin is exceedingly small and faint; it is enough to amaze me that I have no more sense of

my sin. I have greatly longed of late for a broken heart, and to lie low before God."

2. We Have Been Carnal and Unspiritual

The tone of our life as been low and earthly. Associating too much and too infinitely with the world, we have in a great measure become assimilated to its ways. Hence our tastes have been vitiated, our consciences blunted, and that sensitive tenderness of feeling which, while it turns not back from suffering yet shrinks form the remotest contact with sin, has worn of, and given place to an amount of callousness of which we once, in fresher days, believe ourselves incapable.

Perhaps we can call to mind a time when our views and aims were fixed upon a standard of almost unearthly elevation; and, contrasting these with our present state, we are startled at the painful change. And besides intimacy with the world, other causes have operated in producing this deterioration in the spirituality of our minds. The study of truth in its dogmatical more than in its devotional form, has robbed it of its freshness and power; daily, hourly occupation in the routine of ministerial labor has engendered formality and coldness; continual employment in the most solemn duties of our office, such as dealing with souls in private about their immortal welfare, or guiding the meditations and devotions of God's assembled people, or handling the sacramental symbols—this, gone about often with so little prayer and mixed with so little faith, has tended grievously to divest us of that profound reverence and godly fear which ever ought to posses and pervade us. How truly, and with what emphasis we may say: "I am carnal, sold under sin," (Romans 7:14). The world has not been crucified to us, or we unto the world; the flesh, with its members, has not been mortified. What a sad effect all this has had, not only upon our peace of soul, on our growth in grace, but upon the success of our ministry!

3. We Have Been Selfish

We have shrunk from toil, from difficulty, from endurance, counting not only our lives dear unto temporal ease, but even our comfort and us. "We have sought to please ourselves," instead of "pleasing every one his neighbor, for his good to edification." We have not "borne one another's burdens; so fulfilling the law of Christ." We have been worldly and covetous. We have not presented ourselves unto God as "living sacrifices," laying ourselves, our lives, our substance, our time, our strength, our faculties, our all, upon His altar. We seem altogether to have lost sight of this self-sacrificing principle on which even as Christians, but much more as ministers, we are called upon to act. We have had little idea of anything like *sacrifice* at all. Up to the point where a sacrifice was demanded, we may have been willing to go, but there we stood; counting it unnecessary, perhaps calling it impudent and unadvised, to proceed further. Yet, ought not the life of every Christian, especially of every minister, to be a life of self-sacrifice of self-denial throughout, even as was the life of Him who "pleased not Himself"?

4. We Have Been Slothful

We have been sparing of our toil. We have not endured hardness as good soldiers of Jesus Christ. Even when we have been instant *in* season, we have not been so *out* of season; neither have we sought to gather up the fragments of our time, that not a moment might be thrown idly or unprofitably away. Precious hours and days be wasted in sloth, in company, in pleasure, in idle or desultory reading, that might have been devoted to the closet, the study, the pulpit, or the meeting! Indolence, self-indulgence, fickleness, flesh pleasing, have eaten like a canker into our ministry, arresting the blessing, and marring our success. It cannot be said of us, "For my name's sake thou has labored, and has not fainted," (Revelations 2:3). Alas! We have fainted, or at least grown "weary in well doing." We have not made conscience of our work. We have not dealt honestly with the church to which we pledged the vows of ordination. We have dealt deceitfully with God, whose servants we profess to be. We have manifested but little of the unwearied, self-denying love with which, as shepherds, we ought to have watched over the flocks committed to our care. We have fed ourselves, and not the flock.

5. We Have Been Cold

Even when diligent, how little warmth and glow! The whole soul is not poured into the duty, and hence it wears too often the repulsive air of routine and form. We do not speak and act like men in earnest. Our words are feeble, even when sound and true; our looks are careless, even when our words are weighty; and our tones betray the apathy, which both words and looks disguise. Love is wanting, deep love, love strong as death, love such as made Jeremiah weep in secret places for the pride of Israel, and Paul speak, "even weeping," of the enemies of the cross of Christ. In preaching and visiting, in counseling and reprove, what formality, what coldness, how little tenderness and affection! "Oh that I was all heart," said Rowland Hill, "and soul, and spirit, to tell the glorious gospel of Christ to perishing multitudes!"

6. We Have Been Timid

Fear has often led us to smooth down or generalize truths, which, if broadly stated, must have brought hatred and reproach upon us. We have thus often failed to declare to our people the whole counsel of God. We have shrunk from reproving, rebuking, and exhorting with all long-suffering and doctrine. We have feared to alienate friends, or to awaken the wrath of enemies. Hence our preaching of the law has been feeble and straitened; and hence our preaching of a free gospel has been yet more vague, uncertain, and timorous. We are greatly deficient in that majestic boldness and nobility of spirit which peculiarly marked Luther and Calvin and Knox, and the mighty men of the Reformation. Of Luther it was said, "every word was a thunderbolt."

7. We Have Been Wanting in Solemnity

In reading the lives of Howe or Baxter, of Brainerd or Edwards, we are in company with men who, in solemnity of deportment, and gravity of demeanor, were truly of the apostolic school. We feel that these men must have carried weight with them, both in their words and lives. We see also the contrast between them and ourselves in respect of that deep solemnity of air and tone, which made men feel that they walked with God. How deeply ought we to be abased at our levity, frivolity, flippancy, vain mirth, foolish talking and jesting, by which grievous injury has been done to souls, the progress of the saints retarded, and the world countenanced in its wretched vanities.

8. We Have Preached Ourselves, Not Christ

We have sought applause, courted honor, been avaricious of fame, and jealous of our reputation. We have preached too often so as to exalt ourselves instead of magnifying Christ; so as to draw men's eyes to ourselves instead of fixing them on Him and His cross. Nay, and have we not often preached Christ for the very purpose of getting honor to ourselves? Christ, in the sufferings of His first coming and the glory of His second, has not been the Alpha and Omega, the first and the last, of all our sermons.

9. We Have Used Words of Man's Wisdom

We have forgotten Paul's resolution to avoid the enticing words of man's wisdom, lest he should make the cross of Christ of none effect. We have reversed his reasoning as well as his resolution, and acted as if by well-studied, well-polished, well-reasoned discourses, we could so gild and beatify the cross as to make it no longer repulsive, but irresistibly attractive to the carnal eye! Hence we have often sent men home well satisfied with themselves, convinced that they were religious because affected by our eloquence, touched by our appeals, or persuaded by our arguments. In this way we have made the cross of Christ of none effect, and sent souls to hell with a lie in their right hand. Thus, by avoiding the offense of the cross and the foolishness of preaching, we have had to labor in vain, and mourn over an unblest, unfruitful ministry.

10. We Have Not Fully Preached a Free Gospel

We have been afraid of making it *too free*, lest men should be led into licentiousness; as if it were possible to preach too free a gospel, or as if its *freeness* could lead men into sin. It is only a free gospel that can bring men peace, and it is only a free gospel that can make men holy. Luther's preaching was summed up in these two points, --"That we are justified by faith alone, and that we must be assured that we are justified"; and it was this that he urged on his brother Brentius to preach *usque ad fastidium*; and it was by such free, full, bold preaching of the glorious gospel, untrammeled by works, merits, terms, conditions, and unclouded by the fancied humility of doubts, fears, uncertainties, that such blessed success accompanied his labors. Let us go and do likewise. Allied to this is the necessity of insisting on the sinner's *immediate* turning to God, and demanding in the Master's name the sinner's *immediate* surrender of heart to Christ. Strange that sudden conversion should be so much disliked by some ministers. They are the most scriptural of all conversions.

11. We Have Not Duly Studied and Honored the Word of God

We have given a greater prominence to man's writings, man's opinions, and man's systems in our studies than to the WORD. We have drunk more out of human cisterns than divine. We have held more communions with man than God. Hence the mold and fashion of our spirits, our lives, our words, have been derived more from man than God. We must study the Bible more. We must steep our souls in it. We must not only lay it up within us, but also transfuse it through the whole texture of the soul.

12. We Have Not Been Men of Prayer

The spirit of prayer has slumbered amongst us. The closet has been too little frequented and delighted in. We have allowed business, or study, or active labor to interfere with our closet-hours. And how much has the feverish atmosphere in which, for some years past, both the church and nation have been enveloped, found its way into our closet, disturbing the sweet calm of its blessed solitude. Sleep, company, idly visiting, foolish talk and jesting, idle reading, unprofitable occupations, engross time that might have been redeemed for prayer.

Why is there so little anxiety to get time to pray? Why is there so little forethought in the laying out of time and employments, so as to secure a large portion of each day for prayer? Why is there so much speaking, yet so little prayer? Why is there so much running to and fro, yet so little prayer? Why so much bustle and business, yet so little prayer? Why so many meetings with our fellow men, yet so few meetings with God? Why so little being alone, so little thirsting of the soul for the calm, sweet hours of unbroken solitude, when God and His child hold fellowship together, as if they could never part? It is the want of the solitary hours that not only injures our own growth in grace, but also makes us such unprofitable members of the church of Christ; that renders our lives useless. In order to grow in grace, we must be much *alone*. It is not in society—even Christian society—that the soul grows most rapidly and vigorously. In *one single* quiet hour of prayer it will often make more progress than in days of company with others. It is in the desert that the dew falls freshest, and the air is purest. So with the soul. It is when none but God is nigh; when His presence alone, like the desert air in which there is mingled no noxious breath of man, surrounds and pervades the soul; it is then that the eye gets the clearest, simplest view of eternal certainties; it is then that the soul gathers in wondrous refreshment and power and energy.

And so it is also in this way that we become truly useful to others. It is when coming out fresh from communion with God that we go forth to do His work successfully. It is in the closet that we get our vessels so filled with blessing, that, when we come forth, we cannot contain it to ourselves, but must, as by a blessed necessity, pour it out withersoever we go. "We have not stood continually upon our watchtower in the daytime, nor have we been set in our ward whole nights." Our life has not been a lying-in-wait for the voice of God. "Speak, Lord, for Thy servant heareth," hath not been the attitude of our souls, the guiding principle of our lives. Nearness to God, fellowship with God, waiting upon God, resting in God, has been too little the characteristic either of our private or our ministerial walk. Hence our example has been so powerless, our labors so unsuccessful, our sermons so meager, and our whole ministry so fruitless and feeble.

13. We Have Not Honored the Spirit of God

It may be that in words we have recognized His agency, but we have not kept this continually before our eyes, and the eyes of the people. We have not given Him the glory that is due unto His name. We have not sought His teaching, "His anointing,"—the "unction from the Holy One, whereby we know all things." Neither in the study of the Word, nor the preaching of it to others, have we duly acknowledged His officer, as the enlightener of the understanding, the revealer of the truth, the testifier and glorifier of Christ. We have grieved Him by the dishonor done to His person as the third person of the glorious Trinity; and we have grieved Him by the slight put upon His office as the teacher, the convincer, the comforter, and the sanctifier. Hence, He has almost departed from us, and left us to reap the fruit of our own perversity and unbelief. Besides, we have grieved Him by our inconsistent walk, by our want of circumspection, by our worldly-mindedness, by our unholiness, by our prayerlessness, by our unfaithfulness, or want of solemnity, by a life and conversation so little in conformity with the character of a disciple, or the office of ambassador.

14. We Have Had Little of the Mind of Christ

We have come far short of the example of the apostles, much more of Christ; we are far behind the servants, much father behind the Master. We have had little of the grace, the compassion, the meekness, the lowliness, the love of God's eternal Son. His weeping over Jerusalem is a feeling in which we have but little heartfelt sympathy. His "seeking of the lost" is little imitated by us. His unwearied "teaching of the multitudes" we shrink from, as too much for flesh and blood. His days of fasting, His nights of watchfulness and prayer, are not fully realized as models for us to copy. His counting not His life dear unto Him that He might glorify the Father, and finish the work given Him to do, is but little remembered by us as the principle on which we are to act. Yet surely we are to follow His steps; the servant is to walk where his Master has led the way; the under shepherd is to be what the Chief Shepherd was. We must not seek rest or ease in a world where He whom we love had none.

6. Revival in the Ministry

"Take heed unto thyself." –1 Timothy 4:16

It is easier to speak or write about revival than to set about it. There is so much rubbish to be swept out; so many self-raised hindrances to be dealt with; so many old habits to be overcome; so many old habits to be overcome; so much sloth and easy-mindedness to be contended with; so much of ministerial routine to be broken through; and so much crucifixion, both of self and of the world, to be undergone. As Christ said of the unclean spirit which the disciples could not cast out, so we may say of these: "These kind goeth not out but by prayer and fasting."

So thought a minister in the seventeenth century; for, after lamenting the evils both of his life and his ministry, he thus resolved to set about their renewal.

    1. "In imitation of Christ and his apostles, and to get good done. I purpose to rise timely every morning. Job 1:5, 2 Chronicles 36:15.

    2. To prepare as soon as I am up some work to be done, and how that when to do it; to engage my heart to it. 1 Timothy 4:7, and at even to call myself to account, and to mourn over my failings.

    3. To spend a compent portion of time every day in prayer, reading, meditating, spiritual exercises; morning, mid-day, evening, and ere I go to bed.

4. Once in the month, either the end or middle of it, I keep a day of humiliation for the public condition; for the Lord's people and their sad condition; for the raising up of the work and people of God.

5. I spend, besides this, one day for my own private condition, in conflicting with spiritual evils, and to get my heart more holy, or to get some special exercise accomplished, once in six months.

6. I spend every week, once four hours over and above my daily portion in private, for some special causes relating either to myself or others.

7. To spend some time on Saturday, towards night, for preparation for the Sabbath.

8. To spend six or seven days together, once a year, when I have greatest conveniency, wholly and only on spiritual accounts."

Our Need Today

Such was the way in which he set about personal and ministerial revival. Let us take an example from him. If he needed it much, we need it more.

In the fifth and sixth centuries. Gildas and Salvia arose to alarm and arouse a careless church and a formal ministry. In the sixteenth, such was the task, which devolved on the Reformers. In the seventeenth, Baxter, among others, took a prominent part in stimulating the languid piety and dormant energies of his fellow-ministers. In the eighteenth, God raised up some choice and noble men to awaken the church, and lead the way to a higher and bolder career of ministerial duty. The nineteenth stands no less in need of some such stimulating influence. We have experienced many symptoms of life, but still the mass is not quickened. We require some new Baxter to arouse us by his voice and his example. It is melancholy to see the amount of ministerial languor and inefficiency that still overspreads our land. How long, O Lord, how long!

The infusion of new life into the ministry ought to be the object of more direct and special effort, as well as of more united and fervent prayer. To the students, the preachers, the ministers of the Christian church, the prayers of the Christians ought more largely to be directed. It is a LIVING ministry that our country needs; and without such a ministry it cannot long expect to escape the judgments of God. WE NEED MEN THAT WILL SPEND AND BE SPENT—THAT

354 | Words to Winners of Souls

WILL LABOR AND PRAY—THAT WILL WATCH AND WEEP FOR SOULS.

Learning from Myconius

In the life of Myconius, the friend of Luther, as given by Melchior Adam, we have the following beautiful and striking account of an event which proved the turning point in his history, and led him to devote his energies to the cause of Christ. The first night that he entered the monastery, intending to become a monk, he dreamed; and it seemed as if he was ranging a vast wilderness alone. Suddenly a guide appeared, and led him onwards to a most lovely vale, watered by a pleasant stream; but of that he was not permitted to taste; then to a marble fountain of pure water. He tried to kneel and drink; when, lo! a crucified Savior stood forth to view, from whose wounds gushed the copious stream. In a moment his guide flung him into the fountain. His mouth met the flowing wounds, and he drank most sweetly, never to thirst again.

No sooner was he refreshed himself than he was led away by his guide to be taught what great things he was yet to do for the crucified One whose precious wounds had poured the living water into his soul. He came to a wide stretching plain covered with waving grain. His guide orders him to reap. He excuses himself by saying that he is wholly unskilled in such labor. "What you know not you shall learn," was the reply. They came nearer, and he saw a solitary reaper toiling at the sickle with such prodigious effort, as if he were determined to reap the whole field himself. The guide orders him to join this laborer, and, seizing a sickle, shows him how to proceed.

Again, the guide led him to a hill. He surveys the vast plain beneath him, and, wondering, asks how long it will take to reap such a field with so few laborers? "Before winter the last sickle must be thrust in," replied his guide. "Proceed with all your might. The Lord of the harvest will send more reapers soon." Wearied with his labor, Myconius rested for a little. Again the crucified One was at his side, wasted and marred in form. The guide laid his hand on Myconius, saying, "You must be conformed to Him."

With these words the dreamer awake. But he awoke to a life of zeal and love. He found the Savior for his own soul, and he went forth to preach of Him to others. He took his place by the side of that noble reaper, Martin Luther. He was stimulated by his example, and toiled with him in the vast field, till laborers arose on every side, and the harvest was reaped before the winter came. The lesson to us is, trust in your sickles. The fields are white, and they are wide in compass; the laborers are few, but there are some devoted ones toiling there already. In other years we have seen Whitefield and Hill putting forth their enormous efforts, as if they would reap the whole field alone.

"When do you intend to stop?" was the question once put by a friend to Rowland Hill. "Not till we have carried all before us," was the prompt reply. Such is our answer too. The fields are vast, the grain whitens, the harvest waves; and through grace we shall go forth with our sickles, never to rest till we shall lie down where the Lamb Himself shall lead us, by the living fountains of waters, and where God shall wipe off the sweat of toil from our weary foreheads, and dry up all the tears of earth from our weeping eyes. Some of us are young and fresh; many days may yet be, in the providence of God, before us. These must be days of strenuous, ceaseless, persevering, and, if God bless us, successful toil. We shall labor till we are worn out and laid to rest.

Preaching to the Dying

Vincent, the Non-conformist minister, in his volume on the great plague and fire in London, entitled *God's Terrible Voice in the City*, gives a description of the manner in which the faithful ministers who remained amid the danger discharged their solemn duties to the dying inhabitants, and of the manner in which the terror stricken multitudes hung with breathless eagerness upon their lips, to drink in salvation ere the dreaded pestilence had swept them away to the tomb. Churches were flung open, but the pulpits were silent, for there was none to occupy them; the hirelings had fled.

Then did God's faithful band of persecuted ones come forth from their hiding-places to fill the forsaken pulpits. Then did they stand up in the midst of the dying and the dead, to proclaim eternal life to men who were expecting death before the morrow. They preached in season and out of season. Weekday or Sabbath was the same to them. The hour might be canonical or uncanonical, it mattered not; they did not stand upon nice points of ecclesiastical regularity or irregularity; they lifted up their voices like at trumpet, and spared not. Every sermon might be their last. Graves were lying open around them; life seemed now not merely a handbreadth but a hairbreadth; death was nearer now than ever; eternity stood out in all its vast reality; souls were felt to be precious; opportunities were no longer to be trifled away; every hour possessed a value beyond the wealth of kingdoms; the world was now a passing, vanishing shadow, and man's days on earth had been cut down from threescore years and ten into the twinkling of an eye!

Oh, how they preached! No polished periods, no learned arguments, no labored paragraphs, chilled their appeals, or rendered their discourses unintelligible. No fear of man, no love of popular applause, no ever-scrupulous dread of strong expressions, no fear of *excitement* or enthusiasm, prevented them from pouring out the whole fervor of their hearts, that yearned with tenderness unutterable over dying souls.

"Old Time," says Vincent:
> seemed to stand at the head of the pulpit, with his great scythe, saying, with a hoarse voice, 'Work while it is called to-day: at night I will mow thee down.' Grim Death seemed to stand at the side of the pulpit, with its sharp arrow, saying, 'Do thou shoot God's arrows, and I will shoot mine.' The grave seemed to lie open at the foot of the pulpit, with dust in her bosom, saying,
>
>> Louden thy cry
>>   To God,
>>   To men,
>> And now fulfill thy trust;
>> Here thou must lie—
>>   Mouth stopped,
>>   Breath gone,
>> And silent in the dust
>
> Ministers had now awakening calls to seriousness and fervor in their ministerial work; to preach on the side and brink of the pit into which thousands were tumbling. Now there is such a vast concourse of people in the churches where these ministers are to be found that they cannot many times come near the pulpit doors for the press, but are forced to climb over the pews to them; and such a face was seen in the assemblies as seldom was seen before in London; such eager looks, such open ears, such greedy attention, as if every word would be eaten which dropped from the mouths of the ministers.

Should We Be Less Earnest?

Thus did they preach, and thus did they hear in those days of terror and death. Men were in earnest then, both in speaking and hearing. There was no coldness, no languor, and no studied oratory. Truly they preached as dying men to dying men. But the question is, SHOULD IT EVER BE OTHERWISE? Should there ever be less fervor in preaching or less eagerness in hearing than there was then? True, life was a *little* shorter then, but that was all. Death and its issues are still the same. Eternity is still the same. The soul is still the same. Salvation is still the same. Only one small element was thrown in then which does not always exist to such an extent; namely, the increased shortness of life. But that was all the difference.

Why then should our preaching be less fervent, our appeals less affectionate, our importunity less urgent? We are a few steps father from the shore of eternity; that is all. Time may be a little longer than it was then, yet only a very little. Its everlasting issues are still as momentous, as unchangeable. Surely it is our UNBELIEF that makes the difference! It is unbelief that makes ministers so cold in their preaching, so slothful in visiting, and so remiss in all their sacred duties. It is unbelief that chills the life and straitens the heart. It is unbelief that makes ministers handle eternal realities with such irreverence. It is unbelief that makes them ascend with so light a step, "that awful place the pulpit," to deal with immortal beings about heaven and hell.

Hear one of Richard Baxter's appeals:

> I have been ready to wonder, when I have heard such weighty things delivered, how people can forbear crying out in the congregation; much more how they can rest till they have gone to their ministers, and learned what they should do. Oh that heaven and hell should work no more upon men! Oh that everlastingness should work no more! Oh how can you forbear when you are alone to think with yourselves what it is to be everlasting in joy or in torment! I wonder that such thoughts do not break your sleep; and that they come not in your mind when you are about your labor! I wonder how you can almost do anything else; how you can have any quietness in your minds; how you can eat, drink, or rest till you have got some ground of everlasting consolations!

> Is that a man or a corpse that is not affected with matters of this moment? That can be readier to sleep than to tremble when he hears how he must stand at the bar of God? Is that a man, or a clod of clay, that can rise or lie down without being deeply affected with his everlasting estate? That can follow his worldly business, and make nothing of the great business of salvation or damnation; and that, when they know it is hard at hand? Truly, Sirs, when I think of the weight of the matter, I wonder at the very best of God's saints upon earth, that they are no better, and do no more in so weighty a case. I wonder at those whom the world accounteth more holy than needs, and scorns for

making too much ado, that they can put off Christ and their souls with so little; that they pour not their souls line very supplication; that they are not more taken up with God; that their thoughts be not more serious in preparation of their accounts. I wonder that they be not a hundred times more strict in their lives, and more laborious and unwearied in striving for the crown than they are.

And for myself, as I am ashamed of my dull and careless heart, and of my slow and unprofitable course of life; so, the Lord knows, I am ashamed of every sermon I preach; when I think what I have been speaking of, and who sent me, and that men's salvation or damnation is so much concerned in it, I am ready to tremble, lest God should judge me as a slighter of His truths and the souls of men, and lest in the best sermon I should be guilty of their blood. Methinks we should not speak a word to men, in matters of such consequence, without tears, or the greatest earnestness that possibly we can; were not we too much guilty of the sin which we reprove it would be so.

We are not in *earnest* either in preaching or in hearing. If we were, could we be so cold, so prayerless, so inconsistent, so slothful, so wordly, so unlike men, whose business is all about eternity? We must be more in earnest, if we would walk in the footsteps of our beloved Lord, or if we would fulfill the vows that are upon us. We must be more in earnest, if we would be less than hypocrites. We must be more in earnest, if we would finish our course with joy, and obtain the crown at the Master's coming. We must work while it is day; THE NIGHT COMETH WHEN NO MAN CAN WORK.

7. Notes

1   From the hymn, "Go Labor; Spend, and Be Spent," in *Hymns by Horatius Bonar, selected and arranged by his son, H.N. Donar (London: Henry Frowde, 1904), pp. 60-61.*

2   T. Christie Innes, in his Introduction to the 1947 Edition of *Words to Winners of Souls (New York: American Tract Society, 1947), p. 1.*

3   Sylvester's Funeral Sermon for Baxter.

The Deeper Life

Robert Murray McCheyne 1813-1843

*With an Introduction
By Lyle W. Dorsett and David P. Setran*

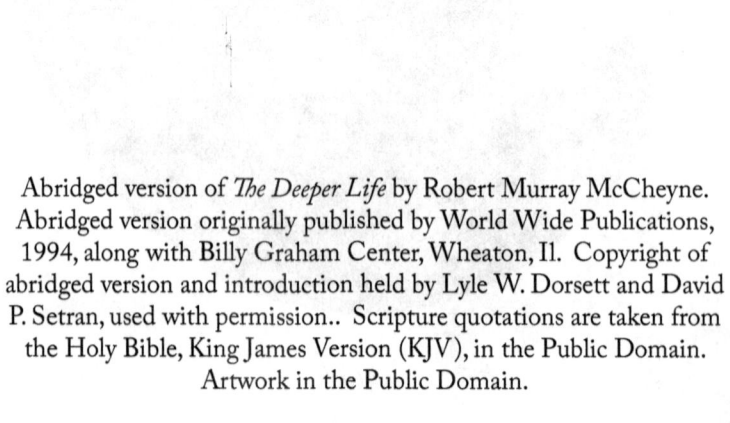

Abridged version of *The Deeper Life* by Robert Murray McCheyne. Abridged version originally published by World Wide Publications, 1994, along with Billy Graham Center, Wheaton, Il. Copyright of abridged version and introduction held by Lyle W. Dorsett and David P. Setran, used with permission.. Scripture quotations are taken from the Holy Bible, King James Version (KJV), in the Public Domain. Artwork in the Public Domain.

Book Chapters

1. Introduction
   By Lyle W. Dorsett and David P. Setran 407
2. Personal Renewal 410
   Reformation in Secret Prayer 416
3. Do What You Can 419
   Doctrine—Do What You Can 419
   These Are Things Which We Can Do 420
   Reasons Why We Should do What We Can 422
   Let Us Answer Objections 423
4. Reasons Why Children Should Fly to Christ Without Delay 425
   Because Life is Very Short 425
   Because Life is Very Uncertain 426
   Most That Are Ever Saved Fly to Christ When Young 427
   Because It Is Happier To Be In Christ Than Out of Christ 428
   The Child Coming To Jesus 431
5. Miscellaneous Quotes (Arranged by Topic) 432
   Evangelism 432
   Suffering 433
   Life in Christ 433
   Bible/Prayer 436
6. Daily Bible Calendar 438
   January 439
   February 441
   March 443
   April 445
   May 447
   June 449
   July 451
   August 453
   September 455

October 457
November 459
December 461

7. Notes 463

1. Introduction
By Lyle W. Dorsett
and David P. Setran

Robert Murray McCheyne was only twenty-nine years old when he died. Despite the brevity of his life, his profound impact for Christ Jesus and His kingdom continues a century and a half later.

McCheyne was born in Edinburgh, Scotland, on May 21, 1813. Although he was raised in a faithful Church of Scotland family, he never experienced the regenerating touch of Christ's Spirit until he was eighteen. Grief over the death of an older brother in 1831 was the impetus for McCheyne's spiritual conversion—a transformation that manifested itself in the confession of sins, sincere repentance, and a deep sense of calling into full-time pastoral and evangelistic ministry.

After studying theology and church history at the University of Edinburgh, McCheyne was ordained in the Church of Scotland. Although the young pastor had only seven and a half years to minister before he died, his sojourn reveals that the quality of a life, rather than its length, is the key to success. During his short pilgrimage, the Reverend McCheyne, pastor of St. Peter's Church, Dundee, led many souls to Christ Jesus and helped countless others know the Lord better and love Him more.

His own life was a striking example of personal holiness. A close associate said of him, "Whether viewed as a son, a brother, friend, or a pastor, often has the remark been made by those who knew him most intimately, that he was the most faultless and attractive exhibition of the true Christian which they had ever seen embodied in a living form."[1]

McCheyne spent a good deal of his time, both personally and in his preaching, studying the disciplines of the Christ-like life. He arose well before the dawn to take time for prayer and Bible reading. His great goal was to be in Christ before being in ministry, allowing his service to be a simple outflow of the cultivation of his spirit within. Of him it was said, "The real secret of his soul's prosperity lay in the daily enlargement of his heart and fellowship with his God. And the river deepened as it flowed on to eternity."[2]

Besides his considerable evangelistic and pastoral ministry, McCheyne continues to help people grow in Christ through his written work, most of which was published and edited posthumously by Andrew A. Bonar, in three volumes: *Memoir and Remains of the Reverend Robert Murray McCheyne* (1844), *Additional Remains of Robert Murray McCheyne* (1846), and *A Basket of Garments* (1848).

The following pages are comprised of excerpts from McCheyne's letters, addresses, sermons and journals. These devotional nuggets have been edifying Christians for over one hundred and fifty years. Equally important is the Bible calendar reprinted at the end of the book. Originally prepared by McCheyne in 1842 for his congregation in Dundee, McCheyne was prompted to arrange this calendar and make it available to his congregation because he knew that many of them had never read the entire Bible. Furthermore, few members of his flock fed daily on God's inspired message. Recognizing that prescribed readings can lead to dead formality, self-righteousness, carelessness, or even a "yoke too heavy to bear," he nevertheless advocated consuming this "daily bread," despite the dangers, because an enormous blessing awaits those who undertake the discipline in a proper spirit. Among the advantages McCheyne noted are these:

> 1. "The entire Bible will be read through in an orderly manner in the course of a year—the Old Testament once, the New Testament and Psalms twice."
>
> 2. "Time will not be wanted in choosing portions to read."
>
> 3. "...all [who join you in this endeavor will] be feeding in the same portion of this green pasture at the same time."[3]

Lyle W. Dorsett
David P. Setran
Wheaton, Illinois, 1994

Robert Murray McCheyne 1813-1843

Note: The excerpts that follow have been taken from the writings of Andrew Bonar, both in his *Memoir and Remains of the Reverend Robert Murray McCheyne* (1881 ed.) and the subsequent *Additional Remains of Robert Murray McCheyne* (1881 ed.).

2. Personal Renewal

Personal Reformation

I am persuaded that I shall obtain the highest amount of present happiness, I shall do the most for God's glory and the good of man, and I shall have the fullest reward in eternity, by maintaining a conscience always washed in Christ's blood, by being filled with the Holy Spirit at all times, and by attaining the most entire likeness to Christ in mind, will, and heart, that is possible for a redeemed sinner to attain to in this world.

I am persuaded that whenever any one from without, or my own heart from within, at any moment, or in any circumstances, contradicts this—if anyone shall insinuate that it is not for my present and eternal happiness, and for God's glory and my usefulness, to maintain a blood-washed conscience, to be entirely filled with the Spirit, and to be fully conformed to the image of Christ in all things—that is the voice of the devil, God's enemy, the enemy of my soul and of all good—the most foolish, wicked, and miserable of all the creatures. See Proverbs 9:17: "Stolen waters are sweet."

1. To maintain a conscience void of offense

I am persuaded that I ought to confess my sins more. I think I ought to confess sin the moment I see it to be sin; whether I am in company, or in study, or even preaching, the soul ought to cast a glance of abhorrence at the sin. If I go on with the duty, leaving the sin unconfessed, I go on with a burdened conscience, and add sin to sin. I think I ought at certain times of the day—my best times—say, after breakfast and after tea—to confess solemnly the sins of the previous hours, and to seek their complete remission.

I find that the devil often makes use of the confession of sin to stir up again the very sin confessed into new exercise, so that I am afraid to dwell upon the confession. I must ask experienced Christians about this. For the present, I think I should strive against this awful abuse of confession, whereby the devil seeks to frighten me away from confessing. I ought to take all methods for seeing the vileness of my sins. I ought to regard myself as a condemned branch of Adam—as partaker of a nature opposite to God from the womb (Psalms 51)—as having a heart full of all wickedness, which pollutes every thought, word, and action, during my whole life, from birth to death.

I ought to confess often the sins of my youth, like David and Paul—my sins before conversion—my sins since conversion—sins against light and knowledge, against love and grace, against each person of the Godhead. I ought to look at my sins in the light of the holy law, in the light of God's countenance, in the light of the cross, in the light of the judgment-seat, in the light of hell, in the light of eternity. I ought to examine my dreams, my floating thoughts, my predilections, my often recurring actions, my habits of thought, feelings, speech, and action—the slanders of my enemies, and the reproof, and even banterings, of my friends—to find out traces of my prevailing sin, matter for confession.

I ought to have a stated day of confession, with fasting—say, once a month. I ought to have a number of scriptures marked, to bring sin to remembrance. I ought to make use of all bodily affliction, domestic trial, frowns of providence on myself, house, parish, church, or country, as calls from God to confess sin. The sins and afflictions of other men should call me to the same.

I ought, on Sabbath evenings, and on communion Sabbath evenings, to be especially careful to confess the sins of holy things. I ought to confess the sins of my confessions—their imperfections, sinful aims, self-righteous tendency, etc.—and to look to Christ as having confessed my sins perfectly over His own sacrifice.

I ought to go to Christ for the forgiveness of each sin. In washing my body, I go over every spot, and wash it out. Should I be less careful in washing my soul? I ought to see the stripe that was made on the back of Jesus by each of my sins. I ought to see the infinite pang thrill through the soul of Jesus equal to an eternity of my hell for my sins, and for all of them. I ought to see that in Christ's blood-shedding there is an infinite over-payment for all my sins. Although Christ did not suffer more than infinite justice demanded, yet He could not suffer at all without laying down an infinite ransom.

I feel, when I have sinned, an immediate reluctance to go to Christ. I am ashamed to go. I feel as if it would do no good to go—

as if it were making Christ a minister of sin, to go straight from the swine-trough to the best robe—and a thousand other excuses; but I am persuaded they are all lies, direct from hell. John argues the opposite way: "If any man sin, we have an advocate with the Father" (1 John 2:1) and a thousand other scriptures are against it. I am sure there is neither peace nor safety from deeper sin, but in going directly to the Lord Jesus Christ. This is God's way of peace and holiness. It is folly to the world and the beclouded heart, but it is *the way*.

I must never think as in too small to need immediate application to the blood of Christ. If I put away a good conscience, concerning faith I made shipwreck. I must never think my sins too great, too aggravated, too presumptuous—as when done on my knees, or in preaching, or by a dying bed, or during dangerous illness—to hinder me from fleeing to Christ. The weight of my sins should act like the weight of a clock: the heavier it is, it makes it go to the faster.

I must not only wash in Christ's blood, but clothe me in Christ's obedience. For every sin of omission in self, I may find a divinely perfect obedience ready for me in Christ. For every sin of commission in self, I may find not only a stripe or a wound in Christ, but also a perfect rendering of the opposite obedience in my place, so that the law is magnified, its curse more than carried, its demand more than answered.

Often the doctrine of Christ for me appears common, well known, having nothing new in it; and I am tempted to pass it by and go to some scripture more taking. This is the devil again—a red-hot lie. Christ for us is ever new, ever glorious. "Unsearchable riches of Christ"—an infinite object, and the only one for a guilty soul. I ought to have a number of scriptures ready, which lead my blind soul directly to Christ, such as Isaiah 45, Romans 3.

2. To be filled with the Holy Spirit

I am persuaded that I ought to study more my own weakness. I ought to have a number of scriptures ready to be meditated on, such as Romans 7, John 15, to convince me that I am a helpless worm.

I am tempted to think that I am now an established Christian, that I have overcome this or that lust so long, that I have got into the habit of the opposite grace, so that there is no fear; I may venture very near the temptation—nearer than other men. This is a lie of Satan. I might as well speak of gunpowder getting by habit of the power of resisting fire, so as not to catch a spark. As long as powder is wet, it resists the spark; but when it becomes dry, it is ready to explode at the first touch. As long as the Spirit dwells in my heart, he deadens me to sin, so that, if lawfully called through temptation, I may reckon upon God carrying me through.

But when the Spirit leaves me, I am like dry gunpowder. Oh for a sense of this!

I am tempted to think that there are some sins for which I have no natural taste, such as strong drink, profane language, etc., so that I need not fear temptation to such sins. This is a lie, a proud, presumptuous lie. The seeds of all sins are in my heart, and perhaps all the more dangerously that I do not see them.

I ought to pray and labor for the deepest sense of my utter weakness and helplessness that ever a sinner was brought to feel. I am helpless in respect of every lust that ever was, or ever will be, in the human heart. I am a worm, a beast, as if it would not be safe for me to renounce all indwelling strength, as if it would be dangerous for me to feel (what is the truth) that there is nothing in me keeping me back from the grossest and vilest sin. This is a delusion of the devil.

My only safety is to know, feel, and confess my helplessness, that I may hang upon the arm of Omnipotence... I daily wish that sin had been rooted out of my heart. I say, "Why did God leave the root of lasciviousness, pride, anger, etc. in my bosom? He hates sin, and I hate it; why did He not take it clean away?" I know many answers to this which completely satisfy my judgment, but still I do not *feel* satisfied. This is wrong. It is right to be weary of the being of sin, but not right to quarrel with my present 'good fight of faith.'

The falls of professors into sin make me tremble. I have been driven away from prayer, and burdened in a fearful manner by hearing or seeing their sin. This is wrong. It is right to tremble, and to make every sin of every professor a lesson of my own helplessness; but it should lead me the more to Christ... If I were more deeply convinced of my utter helplessness, I think I would not be so alarmed when I hear of the falls of other men. I should study those sins in which I am most helpless, in which passion becomes like a whirlwind and I like a straw. No figure of speech can represent my utter want of power to resist the torrent of sin.

I ought to study Christ's omnipotence more: Hebrews 7:25, 1 Thessalonians 5:23, Romans 6:14; 5:9-10, and such scriptures, should be ever before me. Paul's thorn (2 Corinthians 12) is the experience of the great part of my life. It should be ever before me. There are many subsidiary methods of seeking deliverance from sins, which must not be neglected—thus, marriage (1 Corinthians 7:2); fleeing (1 Timothy 6:11; 1 Corinthians 6:18); watch and pray (Matthew 26:41); the word, "It is written, it is written." So Christ defended Himself (Matthew 4). But the main defense is casting myself into the arms of Christ like a helpless child, and beseeching Him to fill me with the Holy Spirit. "This is the victory that overcometh the world, even our faith," (1 John 5:4-5)—a wonderful passage.

I ought to study Christ as a living Savior more—as a Shepherd, carrying the sheep He finds, as a King, reigning in and over the souls He has redeemed, as a Captain, fighting with those who fight with me (Psalms 35)—as one who has engaged to bring me through all temptations and trials, however impossible to flesh and blood.

I am often tempted to say, "How can this Man save us? How can Christ in Heaven deliver me from lusts which I feel raging in me, and nets I feel enclosing me?" This is the father of lies again! "He is able to save unto the uttermost."

I ought to study Christ as an Intercessor. He prayed most for Peter, who was to be most tempted. I am on His breastplate. If I could hear Christ praying for me in the next room, I would not fear a million enemies. Yet the distance makes no difference; He is praying for me!

I ought to study the comforter more—His Godhead, His love, His Almightiness. I have found by experience that nothing sanctifies me so much as meditating on the Comforter, as John 14:16. And yet how seldom I do this! Satan keeps me from it. I am often like those men who said, "They know not if there be any Holy Ghost." I ought never to forget that my body is dwelt in by the third Person of the Godhead. The very thought of this should make me tremble to sin (1 Corinthians 6). I ought to get a high esteem of the happiness of it. I am persuaded that God's happiness is inseparably linked in with His holiness. Holiness and happiness are like light and heat. God never tasted one of the pleasures of sin.

Christ had a body such as I have; yet He never tasted one of the pleasures of sin. The redeemed, through all eternity, will never taste pleasures of sin; yet their happiness is complete. It would be my greatest happiness to be from this moment entirely like them. Every sin is something away from my greatest enjoyment. The devil strives night and day to make me forget this or disbelieve it. He says, "Why should you not enjoy this pleasure as much as Solomon or David? You may go to heaven also." I am persuaded that his is a lie—my true happiness is to go and sin no more.

I ought not to delay parting with sins. Now is God's time. "I made haste and delayed not." I ought not to spare sins because I have long allowed them as infirmities, and others would think it odd if I were to change all at once. What a wretched delusion of Satan that is!

Whatever I see to be sin, I ought from this hour to set my whole soul against it, using all scriptural methods to mortify it—as the Scriptures, special prayer for the Spirit, fasting, watching.

I ought to mark strictly the occasions when I have fallen, and avoid the occasion as much as the sin itself.

Satan often tempts me to go as near to temptations as possible without committing the sin. This is fearful—tempting God and grieving the Holy Ghost. It is a deep-laid plot of Satan.

I ought to flee all temptations, according to Proverbs 4:15, "Avoid it, pass not by it, turn from it, and pass away." Entire conformity to Christ—for the whole law to be written on my heart—I ought stately and solemnly to give my heart to God, to surrender my all into His everlasting arms, according to the prayer (Psalms 31), "Into Thine hand I commit my spirit." I ought to beseech Him not to let any iniquity, secret or presumptuous, have dominion over me, and to fill me with every grace that is in Christ, in the highest degree, that it is possible for the redeemed sinner to receive it, and at all times, till death.

I ought to meditate often on heaven as a world of holiness, where all are holy, where the joy is holy joy, the work holy work; so that without personal holiness, I never can be there. I ought to avoid the appearance of evil. God commands me; and I find that Satan has a singular art in linking the appearance and reality together.

I find that speaking of some sins defiles my mind and leads me into temptation. I find that God forbids even saints to speak of the things that are done of them in secret. I ought to avoid this.

Eve, Achan, David, all fell through the lust of the eye. I should make a covenant with mine, and pray, "Turn away mine eyes from viewing vanity." Satan makes unconverted men like the deaf adder to the sound of the Gospel. I should pray to be made deaf by the Holy Spirit to all that would tempt me to sin.

One of my most frequent occasions of being led into temptation is this—I say it is needful to my office that I listen to this, or look into this, or speak of this. So far this is true; yet I am sure Satan has his part in this argument. I should seek divine direction to settle how far it will be good for my ministry, and how far evil for my soul, that I may avoid the latter.

I am persuaded that nothing is thriving in my soul unless it is growing. "Grow in grace." "Lord increase our faith." "Forgetting the things that are behind." I am persuaded that I ought to be inquiring at God and man what grace I want, and how I may become more like Christ. I ought to strive for more purity, humility, meekness, patience under suffering, love. "Make me Christ-like in all things," should be my constant prayer. "Fill me with the Holy Spirit."

Reformation in Secret Prayer

I ought not to omit any of the parts of prayer—confession, adoration, thanksgiving, petition, and intercession.

There is a fearful tendency to omit *confession*, proceeding from low views of God and His law, slight views of my heart and the sins of my past life. This must be resisted. There is a constant tendency to omit *adoration*, when I forget to whom I am speaking, when I rush heedlessly into the presence of Jehovah, without remembering His awful name and character, when I have little eyesight for His glory, and little admiration of His wonders. "Where are the wise?" I have the native tendency of the heart to omit *giving thanks*. And yet it is specially commanded (Philippians 4:6). Often when the heart is selfish, dead to the salvation of others, I omit *intercession*. And yet it especially is the spirit of the great Advocate, who has the name of Israel always on His heart.

Perhaps every prayer need not have all these; but surely a day should not pass without some space being devoted to each.

I ought to pray before seeing anyone. Often when I sleep long, or meet with others early, and then have family prayer, and breakfast, and forenoon callers, often it is eleven or twelve o'clock before I begin secret prayer. This is a wretched system. It is unscriptural. Christ rose before day, and went into a solitary place. David says, "Early will I seek Thee; Thou shalt early hear my voice." Mary Magdalene came to the sepulcher while yet it was dark. Family prayer loses much of its power and sweetness; and I can do no good to those who come to seek from me. The conscience feels guilty, the soul unfed, the lamp not trimmed. Then, when secret prayer comes, the soul is often out of tune. I feel it is far better to begin with God, to see His face first, to get my soul near Him before it is near another. "When I awake I am still with Thee."

If I have slept too long, or am going on an early journey, or my time is any way shortened, it is best to dress hurriedly, and have a few minutes alone with God, than to give it up for lost.

But, in general, it is best to have at least one hour *alone with God*, before engaging in anything else. At the same time, I must be careful not to reckon communion with God by minutes or hours, or by solitude. I have poured over my Bible, and on my knees for hours, with little or no communion; and my times of solitude have been often times of greatest temptation.

As to *intercession*, I ought daily to intercede for my own family, connections, relatives, and friends; also for my flock—the believers, the awakened, the careless; the sick, the bereaved; the poor, the rich; my elders, Sunday-school teachers, day-school teachers, children tract distributors—that all means may be blessed. Sunday preaching and teaching; visiting of the sick, visiting from house to house; providences, sacraments. I ought daily to intercede briefly for the whole town, the Church of Scotland, all faithful ministers; for vacant congregations, students of divinity, etc.; for dear brethren by name; for missionaries to Jews and Gentiles—and for this end I must read missionary reports regularly, and get acquainted with all that is doing throughout the world. It would stir me up to pray with the map before me. I must have a scheme of prayer, also the names of missionaries marked on the map. I ought to pray at large for the above on Saturday morning and evenign from seven to eight. Perhaps also I might take a different part for different days; only I ought daily to plead for my family and flock. I ought to pray for everyone. "Be carful for nothing, but in *everything*...by prayer and supplication, make your request known unto God."

Often I receive a letter asking to preach, or some such request. I find myself answering before having asked counsel of God. Still oftener a person calls and asks me something, and I do not ask direction. Often I go out to visit a sick person in a hurry, without asking His blessing, which alone can make the visit of any use. I am persuaded that I ought never to do anything without prayer, and, if possible, special secret prayer.

In reading the history of the Church of Scotland, I see how much her troubles and trials have been connected with the salvation of souls and the glory of Christ. I ought to pray far more for our Church, for our leading ministers by name, and for my own clear guidance in the right way, that I may not be led aside, or driven aside, from following Christ. Many difficult questions may be forced on us for which I am not fully prepared, such as the lawfulness of covenants. I should pray much more in peaceful days, that I may be guided rightly when days of trial come.

I ought to spend the best hours of the day in communion with God. It is my noblest and most fruitful employment, and is not to be thrust into any corner. The morning hours, from six to eight, are the most uninterrupted, and should be thus employed, if I can prevent drowsiness. A little time after breakfast might be given to intercession. After tea is my best hour, and that should be solemnly dedicated to God if possible.

I ought not to give up the good old habit of prayer before going to bed; but guard must be kept against sleep: planning what things I am to ask is the best remedy. When I awake in the night, I ought to rise and pray, as David and as John Welsh did.

I ought to read three chapters of the Bible in secret every day, at least.

I ought on Sunday morning to look over all the chapters read through the week, and especially the verses marked. I ought to read in three different places; I ought also to read according to subjects, lives, etc.

3. Do What You Can

"She hath done what she could; she is come aforehand to anoint My body to the burying." –Mark 14:8

Doctrine—Do What You Can

From the Gospel of John (11:2), we learn that this woman was Mary, the sister of Lazarus and Martha. We have already learned that she was an eminent believer: "She sat at the feet of Jesus, and heard His word." Jesus Himself said to her: "Mary hath chosen the good part, which shall not be taken away from her." Now it is interesting to see this same Mary eminent in another way—not only as a *contemplative believer*, but as an *active believer*.

Many seem to think that to be a believer is to have certain feelings and experiences; forgetting all the time that these are but the flowers, and that the fruit must follow. The engrafting of the branch is good, the inflowing of the sap good, but the fruit is the end in view. So faith is good, and peace and joy are good, but holy fruit is the end for which we are saved.

I trust many of you, last Sunday, were like Mary, sitting at the Redeemer's feet, and hearing His word. Now I would persuade you to be like Mary, in *doing what you can for Christ*. If you have been bought with a price, then glorify God in your body and spirit, which are His. I beseech you by the mercies of God.

These Are Things Which We Can Do

1. We Could Love Christ, Pray and Praise More

What this woman did she did to Christ. Jesus had saved her soul, had saved her brother and sister, and she felt that she could not do too much for Him. She brought an alabaster box of ointment, very costly, and broke the box, and poured it on His head. No doubt she loved His disciples—holy John and frank Peter—yet still she loved Christ more. No doubt she loved Christ's poor, and was often kind to them; yet she loved Jesus more.

On His blessed head, that was so soon to be crowned with thorns—on His blessed feet, that were so soon to be pierced with nails—she poured the precious ointment. This is what we should do. If we have been saved by Christ, we could pour out our best affections on Him. It is well to love His disciples, well to love His ministers, well to love His poor, but it is best to love Himself.

We cannot now reach His blessed head, nor anoint His holy feet; but we can fall down at His footstool, and pour out our affections toward Him. It was not the ointment Jesus cared for—what does the King of Glory care for a little ointment?—but it is the loving heart, poured out upon His feet. It is the adoration, praise, love, and prayers of a believer's broken heart, that Christ cares for. The new heart is the alabaster box that Jesus loves.

Oh, brethren could you not do more in this way? Could you not give more time to pouring out your heart to Jesus—breaking the box, and filing the room with the odor of your praise? Could you not pray more than you do to be filled with the Spirit, that the Spirit may be poured down on ministers, and God's people, and on an unconverted world? Jesus loves tears and groans from a broken heart.

2. We Could Live Holier Lives

The Church is thus described in the Song of Solomon: "Who is this that cometh out of the wilderness like pillars of smoke, perfumed with myrrh and frankincense, with all powders of the merchant?" The holiness of the believer is like the most precious perfume. When a holy believer goes through the world, filled with the Spirit, made more than conqueror, the fragrance fills the room; "tis as if an angel shook his wings."

If the world were full of believers, it would be like a bed of spices. But oh, how few believers carry much of the odor of heaven along with them! How many you might be the means of saving, if you live a holy, consistent life, you were evidently a sacrifice bound upon God's altar! Wives might thus, *without the word,* win their husbands, when they see your chaste conversation coupled with fear. Parents might in this way save their children, when they saw you holy and happy. Children have often thus saved their parents. Servants adorn the doctrine of God your Savior in all things; let your light shine before men. The poorest can do this as well as the richest, the youngest as well as the oldest. Oh, there is no argument like a holy life!

3. You Could Seek the Salvation of Others

If you have really been brought to Christ and saved, then you know there is a hell, you know that all the unconverted around you are hastening to it; you know there is a Savior, and that He is stretching out His hands all the day long to sinners.

Could you do no more to save sinners than you do? Do you do all you can? You say you *pray for them*; but is it not hypocrisy to pray and do nothing? Will God hear these prayers? Have you no fears that prayers without labors are only provoking God? You say you cannot speak, you are not learned. Will that excuse stand in the judgment? Does it require much learning to tell fellow-sinners that they are perishing? If their house was on fire, would it require much learning to wake the sleepers?

Begin at home. Could you not do more for the salvation of those at home? If there are children or servants, have you done all you can for them? Have you done all you can to bring the truth before them, to bring them under a living ministry, to get them to pray and give up sin?

Do you do what you can for your neighbors for years together, and see them on the broad way, without warning them? Do you make a full use of tracts giving suitable ones to those that need them? Do you persuade Sunday-breakers to go to the house of God? Do you do anything in Sunday schools? Could you not tell little children the way to be saved? Do you do what you can for the *world*? The field is the world.

4. Feed Christ's Poor

I am far from thinking that the wicked poor should be passed over, but Christ's poor are our brothers and sisters. Do you do what you can for them? In the great day, Christ will say to those on His right hand, "Come ye blessed for I was an hungered, and ye gave Me meat." They stand in the place of Christ. Christ does not any more stand in the need of Mary's ointment, or Martha's hospitality, or the Samaritan's drink of water. He is beyond the reach of these things, and will never need them more. But He has left many of His brothers and sisters behind in this world, some diseased, some lame, some like Lazarus all covered with sores; and He says, "What ye do to them, ye do to me." Do you live plainly, in order to have more to give away? Do you put away vain and gaudy clothes, that you may be able to clothe the naked? Are you thrifty in managing what you have, letting nothing be lost?

Reasons Why We Should do What We Can

1. Christ Has Done What He Could for Us

"What could have been done more to My vineyard, that I have not done in it?" (Isaiah 5:4). He thought nothing too much to do and to suffer for us. While we were yet sinners, Christ died for us. Greater love than this hath no man. *All his life*, between manger at Bethlehem and the cross of Calvary, was spent in labors and infinite sufferings for us. All that we needed to suffer, He suffered; all that we need to obey, He obeyed. All His life in glory He spends for us. He ever liveth to make intercession for us. He is head over all things for us; makes everything in all worlds work together for our good. It is all but incredible that each person of the Godhead has made Himself over to us to be ours. The Father says, "I am thy God;" the Son, "Fear not, for I have redeemed thee;" the Holy Ghost makes us a temple: "I will dwell in them, and walk in them." It is much that we should do all we can for Him, that we should give ourselves up to Him who gave Himself for us?

2. Satan Does All He Can

Sometimes he comes as a lion; Your adversary the devil, as a roaring lion, walks about, seeking whom he may devour; sometimes as a serpent, "as the serpent beguiled Eve;" sometimes as an angel of light. He does all he can to tempt and beguile the saints, leading them away by false teachers, injecting blasphemies and polluted thoughts into their minds, casting fiery darts at their souls, stirring up the world to hate and persecute them, stirring up father and mother against the children, and brother against brother. He does all he can to lead captive wicked men, blinding their minds, not allowing them to listen to the Gospel, steeping them in swinish lusts, leading them into despair. When he knows his time is short, he rages all the more. Oh should we not do all we can, if Satan does all he can?

3. We Have Done All We Could the Other Way

This was one of Paul's great motives for doing all he could: "I thank Christ Jesus our Lord for putting me into the ministry; for I was a blasphemer, and a persecutor, and injurious." He never could forget how he had persecuted the Church of God, and wasted it; and this made him as diligent in building it up, and haling men and women to Christ. He preached the faith which once he destroyed.

So with Peter: "Let us live the rest of our time in the flesh not to the lusts of men, but to the will of God; for the time past of our lives may suffice to have wrought the will of the Gentiles, when we walked in lasciviousness, lusts, excess of wine, revelings, banqueting, and abominable idolatries."

So with John Newton: "How can the old African blasphemer be silent?"

So with many of you. You ran greedily after sin. You were at great pains and cost, and did not spare health, or money, or time, to obtain some sinful gratification. How can you now grudge anything for Christ? Only serve Christ as zealously as you once served the devil.

4. Christ Will Own and Reward What We Do

The labor that Christ blessed is believing labor. It is not words of human wisdom, but words of faith, that God makes arrows. The word of a little maid was blessed in the house of Naaman the Syrian. "Follow me" was made the arrow to pierce the heart of Matthew. It is all one to God to save, whether with many, or with them that have no might. If you would do all you can, the town would be filled with the fragrance. Christ will reward it. He defended Mary's work of love, and said it should be spoken of over all the world, and it will yet be told in the judgment. A cup of cold water He will not pass over. "Well done, good and faithful servant."

5. If You Do Not Do All You Can, How Can You Prove Yourself a Christian?

"Pure religion and undefiled before God the Father is this, To visit the fatherless and widows in their affliction, and to keep oneself unspotted from the world." You are greatly mistaken if you think that to be a Christian is merely to have certain views, and convictions, and spiritual delights. This is all well; but if it leads not to a devoted life, I fear it is all a delusion. If any man be in Christ, he is a new creature.

Let Us Answer Objections

1. "The World Will Mock at Us" – Answer

This is true. They mocked at Mary. They called it waste and extravagance; and yet, Christ said it was well done. SO, if you do what you can, the world will laugh at you, but you will have the smile of Christ. They mocked at Christ when He was full of zeal; they said He was mad and had a devil. They mocked at Paul and said he was mad; and so with all Christ's living members. "Rejoice, inasmuch as ye are partakers of the sufferings of Christ." "If ye suffer with Him, ye shall also reign with Him."

2. "What Can I Do?—I Am a Woman?"

Mary was a woman, yet she did what she could. Mary Magdalene was a woman, and yet she was first at the sepulcher. Phoebe was a woman, yet a support to many, and to Paul also. Dorcas was a woman, yet she made coats and garments for the poor at Joppa. "I am a child." Out of the mouth of babes and sucklings God perfects praise. God has often used children in the conversion of their parents.

3. "I Have Too Little Grace to do Good"

"He that waters others, shall be watered himself." "The liberal soul shall be made fat." "It pleased the Father that in Christ should all fullness dwell." There is a full supply of the Spirit to teach you to pray; a full supply of grace to slay your sins and quicken your graces. If you use opportunities of speaking to others, God will give you plenty. If you give much to God's poor, you shall never want a rich supply. "God is able to make all grace abound toward you; that ye, always having sufficiency in all things, may abound to every good work." "Bring all the tithes unto my storehouse, and prove me now herewith." "Honor the Lord with thy substances, and with the first-fruits of all thine increase: so shall thy barns be filled with plenty, and thy presses shall burst out with new wine."

April 26, 1842

4. Reasons Why Children Should Fly to Christ Without Delay

"O satisfy us early with thy mercy; that we may rejoice and be glad all our days." –Psalms 90:14

The late Countess of Huntingdon was not only rich in this world, but rich in faith, and an heir of the kingdom. When she was about nine years of age she saw the dead body of a little child of her own age carried to the grave. She followed the funeral; and it was there that the Holy Spirit first opened her heart to convince her that she needed a Savior. My dear little children, when you look upon the year that has come to an end, may the Holy Spirit bring you to the same conviction. May the still small voice say in your heart, Flee now from the wrath to come. Fly to the Lord Jesus without delay. "Escape for thy life: look not behind thee."

Because Life is Very Short

"The days of our years are three-score years and ten; and if by reason of strength they be four-score years, yet is their strength labor and sorrow, for it is soon cut off, and we fly away." Even those who live longest, when they come to die, look back on their life as upon a dream. It is "like a sleep." The hours pass rapidly away during sleep; and when you awake, you hardly know that any time has passed. Such is life. It is like "a tale that is told."

You have seen a ship upon the river, when the sailors were all on board, the anchor heaved and the sails spread to the wind, how it glided swiftly past, bounding over the billows. So it is with your days: "They are passed away as the swift ships." Or perhaps you have seen an eagle, when from its nest in the top of the rocks it darts down with quivering wing to seize upon some smaller bird, how swiftly it flies. So it is with your life: it flies "as the eagle hasted to the prey." You have noticed the mist on the brow of the mountain early in the morning, and you have seen, when the sun rose with his warm cheering beams, how soon the mist melted away. And "what is your life? It is even a vapor that appeared for a little time, and then vanished away."

Some of you may have seen how short life is in those around you. "Your fathers, where are they? And the prophets, do they live forever? How many friends have you lying in the grave! Some of you have more friends in the grave than in this world. They were carried away "as with a flood," and we are fast hastening after them. In a little while the church where you sit will be filled with new worshippers—a new voice will lead the psalm—a new man of God fill the pulpit.

It is an absolute certainty that, in a few years, all of you who read this will be lying in the grave. Oh what need, then, to fly to Christ without delay! How great a work you have to do! How short the time you have to do it in! You have to flee from wrath, to come to Christ, to be born again, to receive the Holy Spirit, to be made meet for glory. It is high time that you seek the Lord. The longest lifetime is short enough. Seek conviction of sin and an interest in Christ. "Oh, satisfy me early with Thy mercy, that I may rejoice and be glad all my days."

Because Life is Very Uncertain

Men are like grass: "In the morning, it groweth up and flourisheth: in the evening, it is cut down and withereth." Most men are cut down while they are green. More than one-half fo the human race die before they reach manhood. In the city of Glasgow alone, more than one-half of the people die before the age of twenty. Of most men it may be said, "He cometh forth as a flower, and is cut down." Death is very certain, but the time is very uncertain.

Some may think they shall not die because they are in good health; but you forget that many die in good health by accidents and other causes. Riches and ease and comforts, good food and good clothing, are no safeguards against dying. It is written, "The rich man also died, and was buried." Kind physicians and kind friends cannot keep you from dying. When death comes, he laughs at the efforts of physicians—he tears you from the tenderest arms.

Some think they shall not die because they are not prepared to die. But you forget that most people die unprepared, unconverted, unsaved.

You forget that it is written of the straight gate, "Few there be that find it." Most people lie down in a dark grave, and a darker eternity.

Some of you may think you shall not die because you are young. You forget that one-half of the human race die before they reach manhood. The half of the inhabitants of this place die before they are twenty. Oh, if you had to stand as often as I have beside the dying bed of little children—to see their wild looks and outstretched hands, and to hear their dying cries—you would see how needful it is to fly to Christ now.

It may be your turn next. Are you prepared to die? Have you fled for refuge to Jesus? Have you found forgiveness? "Boast not thyself of tomorrow; for thou knowest not what a day may bring forth."

Most That Are Ever Saved Fly to Christ When Young

It was so in the days of our blessed Savior. Those that were come to years were too wise and prudent to be saved by the blood of the Son of God, and He revealed it to those that were younger and had less wisdom. "I thank Thee, O Father, Lord of heaven and earth, because Thou hast hidden these things from the wise and prudent, and revealed them unto babes. Even so, Father, for so it seemed good in Thy sight." "He gathers the lambs with His arms, and carries them in His bosom." So it has been in almost all times of the revival of religion. If you ask aged Christians, most of them will tell you that they were made anxious about their souls when young.

Oh, what a reason is here for seeking an early inbringing to Christ! If you are not saved in youth, it is likely you never will be. There is a tide in the affairs of souls. There are times which may be called converting times. All holy times are peculiarly converting times. Sunday is the great day for gathering in souls—it is Christ's market-day. It is the great harvest-day of souls. I know there is a generation rising up that would fain trample Sunday beneath their feet: but prize you the day of rest.

The time of affliction is converting time. When God takes away those you love best, and you say, "This is the finger of God," remember it is Christ wanting to get in to save you: open the door and let Him in. The time of the striving of the Holy Spirit is converting time. If you feel your heart pricked in "quench not the Spirit;" "resist not the Holy Ghost;" "grieve not the Holy Spirit of God."

Youth is converting time. "Suffer little children to come unto Me, and forbid them not." Oh, you that are lambs, seek to be gathered with the arm of the Savior, and carried in His gentle bosom. Come to trust under the Savior's wings. "Yet there is room."

Because It Is Happier To Be In Christ Than Out of Christ

Many that read these words are saying in their heart, "It is a dull thing to be religious." Youth is the time for pleasure—the time to eat, drink and be merry; to rise up to play. Now, I know that youth is the time for pleasure; the foot is more elastic then, the eye more full of life, the heart more full of gladness. But that is the very reason why I say youth is the time to fly to Christ. It is far happier to be in Christ than to be out of Christ.

It satisfies the Heart

I never will deny that there are pleasures to be found out of Christ. The song and the dance, and the exciting game, are most engaging to young hearts. But ah! think a moment. Is it not an awful thing to be happy when you are unsaved? Would it not be dreadful to see a man sleeping in a house all on fire? And is it not enough to make one shudder to see you dancing and making merry when God is angry with you every day?

Think again. Are there not infinitely sweeter pleasures to be had in Christ? "Whoso drinketh of this water shall thirst again; but whoso drinketh of the water that I shall give him shall never thirst." "In Thy presence is fullness of joy: at Thy right hand are pleasures for evermore." To be forgiven, to be at peace with God, to have Him for a father, to have Him loving us and smiling on us, to have the Holy Spirit coming into our hearts, and making us holy, this is worth a whole eternity of your pleasures. "A day in Thy courts is better than a thousand." Oh to be "satisfied with favor, and full with the blessing of the Lord!" Your daily bread becomes sweeter. You eat your meat "with gladness and singleness of heart, praising God." Your foot is more light and abounding, for it bears a ransomed body. Your sleep is sweeter tonight, for "so He giveth His beloved sleep." The sun shines more lovingly, and the earth wears a pleasanter smile, because you can say, "My Father made them all."

It Makes You Glad All Your Days

The pleasures of sin are only "for a season;" they do not last. But to be brought to Christ is like the dawning of an eternal day; it spreads the serenity of heaven over all the days of our pilgrimage. In suffering days, what will the world do for you?

"Like vinegar upon niter, so is he that singeth songs to a heavy heart." Believe me there are days at hand when you will "say of laughter, 'It is mad;' and of mirth, 'What doth it?'" But if you fly to Jesus Christ now, He will cheer you in the days of darkness. When the winds are contrary and the waves are high Jesus will draw near, and say, "Be not afraid; it is I." That voice stills the heart in the stormiest hour. When the world reproaches you and casts out your name as evil—when the doors are shut—Jesus will come in, and say, "Peace be unto you." Who can tell the sweetness and the peace whith Jesus gives in such an hour?

One little girl that was early brought to Christ felt this when long confined to a sickbed. "I am not weary of my bed," she said, "for my bed is green, and all that I meet with is perfumed with love to me. The time, night and day, is made sweet to me by the Lord. When it is evening, it is pleasant; and when it is morning, I am refreshed."

Last of all in a dying day, what will the world do for you? The dance and the song, and the merry companion, will then lose all their power to cheer you. Not one jest more; not one smile more. "Oh that you were wise, that you would understand this, and consider your latter end!" But that is the very time when the soul of one in Christ rejoices with a joy unspeakable and full of glory.

"Jesus can make a dying bed softer than downy pillows are." You remember, when Stephen came to die, his gentle breast battered with cruel stones; but he kneeled down and said, "Lord Jesus, receive my spirit." John Newton tells us a Christian, of eight years of age, came home ill of the malady of which he died. His mother asked him if he were afraid to die. "No," said he, "I wish to die, and if it be God's will: that sweet word, 'Sleep in Jesus,' makes me happy when I think on the grave."

"My little children, of whom I travail in birth again till Christ be formed in you," if you would live happy and die happy, come now to the Savior. The door of the ark is wide open. Enter now or it may be never.

Children Called to Christ

Like mist on the mountain,
   Like ships on the sea,

So swiftly the years
   Of our pilgrimage flee;

In the grave of our fathers
   How soon shall we lie!

Dear children, today
   To a Savior fly.

How sweet are the flowerets
   In April and May!

But often the frost makes
   Them wither away.

Like flowers you may fade:
   Are you ready to die?

While "yet there is room,"
   To a Savior fly.

When Samuel was young,
   He first knew the Lord,

He slept in His smile
   And rejoiced in His word:

So most of God's children
   Are early brought nigh:

Oh, seek Him in youth—
   To a Savior fly.

Do you ask me for pleasure?
   Then lean on His breast,

From there the sin-laden
   And weary find rest.

In the valley of death
   You will triumphing cry—

"If this be called dying,
   'Tis pleasant to die!"

The Child Coming To Jesus

Suffer me to come to Jesus,
   Mother, dear, forbid me not;

By His blood from hell He frees us,
   Makes us fair without a spot.

Suffer me, my earthly father,
   At His pierced feet to fall:

Why forbid me? Help me, rather;
   Jesus is my all in all.

Suffer me to run unto Him:
   Gentle sisters, come with me.

Oh, that all I love but knew Him!
   Then my home in heaven would be.

Loving playmates, gay and smiling,
   Bid me not forsake the cross;

Hard to bear is your reviling,
   Yet for Jesus all is dross.

Yes, though all the world have chide me,
   Father, mother, sister, friend—

Jesus never will forbid me!
   Jesus loves me to the end!

Gentle shepherd, on Thy shoulder
   Carry me, a sinful lamb;

Give me faith, and make me bolder,
   Till with Thee in heaven I am

5. Miscellaneous Quotes (Arranged by Topic)

Evangelism

I have often told you that a work of revival in any place almost always begins with the children of God. God pours water first on "him that is thirsty," and then on the dry ground. But how little as "the word of the Lord sounded out from you"! I do not mean that you should have been loud talkers about religious things. But you should have been "living epistles, known and read of all men." If you had day by day the blood of Christ upon your conscience, how many of your friends and neighbors that are going down to hell might have been saying this day, "Thy people shall be my people, and thy God my God"! Think, my beloved friends, that every act of unholiness, of conformity to the world, of selfishness, of whispering and backbiting, is hindering the work of God in the parish, and ruining souls eternally.

As I was walking through the fields, the thought came over me with almost overwhelming power, that everyone of my flock must soon be in heaven or hell. Oh, how I wished that I had a tongue like thunder, that I might make all hear. Or that I had a frame like iron, that I might visit everyone, and say, "Escape for thy life!" Ah, sinners! you little know how I fear that you will lay the blame of your damnation at my door.

Suffering

I hope this affliction will be blessed to me. I always feel much need of God's afflicting hand. In the whirl of active labor there is so little time for watching and for bewailing, and seeking grace to oppose the sins of our ministry, that I always feel it a blessed thing when the Savior takes me aside from the crowd, as he took the blind man out of the town, and removes the veil, and clears away obscuring mists, and by His word and Spirit leads to deeper peace and a holier walk. Ah! There is nothing like a calm look into the eternal world to each us the emptiness of human praise, the sinfulness of self-seeking and vain glory, to teach us the preciousness of Christ, who is called "the tried stone."

You cannot love trouble for its own sake; bitter must always be bitter, and pain must always be pain. God knows you cannot love trouble. Yet for the blessings that it brings, He can make you pray for it. Does trouble work patience in you? Does it lead you to cling closer to the Lord Jesus—to hide deeper in the rock? Does it make you "be still and know that He is God"? Does it make you lie passive in His hand, and know no will but His?

Thus does patience work experience—an experimental acquaintance with Jesus. Does it bring you a fuller taste of His sweetness, so that you know whom you have believed? And does this experience give you further hope of glory—another anchor cast within the veil? And does this hope give you a heart that cannot be ashamed, because you are convinced that God has loved you, and will love you to the end? Ah! then you have got the improvement through trouble, if it has led you thus.

Life in Christ

Observe it is said, "trust in the Lord with all thine heart." When you believe in Jesus for righteousness, you must cast away all your own claims for pardon. Your own righteousness must be filthy rags in your eyes. You must come empty, that you may go away full of Jesus. And just so, when you trust in Jesus for strength, you must cast away all your natural notions of your own strength; you must feel that your own resolutions, and vows, and promises, are as useless to stem the current of your passions, as so many straws would be in streaming the mightiest waterfall. You must feel that your own firmness and manliness of disposition, which as so long been the praise of your friends and boast of your own mind, are as powerless, before the breath of temptation, as a broken reed before the hurricane. You must feel that you wrestle not with flesh and blood, but with spirits of gigantic power, in whose mighty grasp you are feeble as a child. Then, and then only will you come with all your heart to trust in the Lord your strength. When the believer is weakest, then he is the strongest.

When you came to us weary and heavy-laden with guilt, we pointed you to Jesus, for He is the Lord our righteousness. When you come to us again, groaning under the power of indwelling sin, we point you again to Jesus, for He is the Lord our strength. It is the true mark of a false and ignorant physician of bodies, when to every sufferer, whatever be the disease, he applies the same remedy. But it is the true mark of a good and faithful physician of souls, when, to every sick and perishing soul, in every stage of the disease, he brings the one, the only remedy, the only balm in Gilead.

Christ was anointed not only to bind up the broken-hearted, but also to proclaim liberty to the captives. If it be good and wise to direct the poor broken-hearted sinner, who has no way of justifying himself, to Jesus, as his righteousness, it must be just as good and wise to direct the poor believer, growing under the bondage of corruption, having no way to sanctify himself, to look to Jesus as his wisdom, his sanctification, his redemption. Thou hast once looked unto Jesus as thy covenant head, bearing all wrath, fulfilling all righteousness in thy stead, and that gave thee peace. Well, look again to the same Jesus as thy covenant head, obtaining by his merits gifts for men, even the promise of the Father, to shed down all his members; and let that also give thee peace.

"Trust in the Lord with all thine heart." Thou last looked to Jesus on the cross, and that gave thee peace of conscience. Look to Him now upon the throne, and that will give thee purity of heart. I know of but one way in which a branch can be made a leafy, healthy, fruit-bearing branch; and that is by being grafted into the vine and abiding there. And just so I know of but one way in which a believer can be made a holy, happy and fruitful child of God; and that is by believing in Jesus, abiding in Him, walking in Him, being rooted and built up in Him.

Whoever, then, would live a life of persevering holiness, let him keep his eye fixed on the Savior. As long as Peter looked only to the Savior, he walked upon the sea in safety, to go to Jesus. But when he looked around and saw the wind boisterous, he was afraid, and beginning to sink, cried, "Lord, save me!" Just so will it be with you. As long as you look believingly to the Savior, who loved you, and gave Himself for you, so long you may tread the waters of life's troubled sea, and the soles of your feet shall not be wet. But venture to look around upon the winds and waves that threaten you on every hand, and, like Peter, you begin to sink, and cry, "Lord, save me!" How justly, then, may we address to you the Savior's rebuke to Peter: "O thou of little faith, wherefore didst thou doubt?" Look again to the love of the Savior, and behold that love which constrains you to live no more to yourself, but to Him that died for you and rose again.

Look to Christ; for the glorious Son of God so loved lost souls, that He took on Him a body and died for us—bore our curse, and obeyed the law in our place. Look to Him and live. You need no preparation, you need no endeavors, you need no duties, you need no strivings, you only need to look and live.

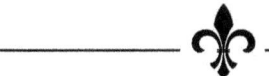

Seek to be made holier everyday; pray, strive, wrestle for the Spirit, to make you like God. Be as much as you can with God. I declare to you that I had rather be one hour with God, than a thousand with the sweetest society on earth or in heaven. All other joys are but streams; God is the fountain: "all my springs are in Thee." Now may the blessings that are on the head of the just be on your head. Be faithful unto death, and Christ will give you a crown of life.

I trust you feel real desire after complete holiness. This is the truest mark of being born again. It is a mark that He has made us meet for the inheritance of the saints in light. If a noble man were to adopt a beggar boy, he would not only feed and clothe him, but educate him, and fit him to move in the sphere into which he was afterwards to be brought; and if you saw this boy filled with a noble spirit, you would say he is meet to be put among the children. So may you be made meet for glory. The farmer does not cut down his wheat till it is ripe. So does the Lord Jesus: He first ripens the soul, then gathers it into His barn.

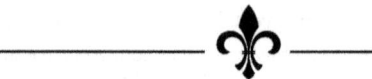

I want my life to be hid with Christ in God. At present there is too much hurry and bustle, and outward working, to allow the calm working of the Spirit on the heart. I seldom get time to meditate, like Isaac, at evening tide, except when I am tired. But the dew comes down when all nature is at rest, when every leaf is still.

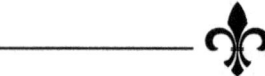

Speak for eternity. Above all things, cultivate your own spirit. A word spoken by you when your conscience is clear and your heart full of God's Spirit, is worth ten thousand words spoken in unbelief and sin. Remember it is God, and not man, that must have the glory. It is not much speaking, but much faith that is needed.

Seek advance of personal holiness. It is for this that the grace of God has appeared to you. For this Jesus died; for this He chose you; for this He converted you—to make you holy men, living epistles of Christ, monuments of what God can do in a sinner's heart. You know what true holiness is. It is Christ in you the hope of glory. Let Him dwell in you, and so all His features will shine in your hearts and faces. Oh, to be like Jesus! This is heaven, wherever it be.

Bible/Prayer

You read your Bible regularly, of course; but do try and understand it, and still more, to feel it. Read more parts than one at a time. For example, if you are reading Genesis, read a Psalm also. If you are reading Matthew, read a small bit of an epistle also.

Turn the Bible into prayer. Thus, if you are reading the first Psalm, spread the Bible on the chair before you, kneel and pray, "Let me not stand in the counsel of the ungodly." This is the best way of knowing the meaning of the Bible, and of learning to pray. In prayer confess your sins by name, going over those of the past day one by one.

Pray for your friends by name. If you love them, surely you will pray for their souls. I know well that there are prayers constantly ascending for you from your own house; and will you pray for them back again? Do this regularly. If you pray sincerely for others, it will make you pray for yourself.

You have hindered God's work by your want of prayer. When God gives grace to souls, it is in answer to the prayers of His children. You will see this on the day of Pentecost. Ezekiel 37:9 shows that in answer to the prayer of a single child of God, God will give grace to a whole valley full of dry and prayerless bones. Where God puts it into the heart of His children to pray, it is certain that He is going to pour down His Spirit in abundance.

"Now, where have been your prayers, O Children of God?" The salvation of those around you depends on your asking. Dear Christians, I often think it strange that ever we should be in heaven, and so many in hell through our soul-destroying carelessness. The good Lord pardon the past, and stir you up for the future. Plead and wrestle with God, showing Him that the cause is His own, and that it is all for His own glory to arise and have mercy upon Zion.

6. Daily Bible Calendar

Jesus prayed "Sanctify them through Thy truth. Thy word is truth," (John 17:17).

The Apostle Paul wrote, "All Scripture is given by inspiration of God, and is profitable for doctrine, for reproof, for correction, for instruction in righteousness; that the man of God may be perfect, thoroughly finished unto all good works," (2 Timothy 3:16-17).

Robert Murray McCheyne said that if you follow this calendar, the entire Bible will be read through completely in the course of a year—the Old Testament once, the New Testament and Psalms twice. He wrote, "I fear many of you never read the whole Bible, and yet it is all equally divine. If we pass over some parts of Scripture, we shall be incomplete Christians."

Part of this introduction and the following calendar were arranged by Robert Murray McCheyne in 1844.

January

"This is my beloved Son, in whom I am well pleased: hear ye Him."

Day	Family Reading	Secret Reading
1	Genesis 1 Matthew 1	Ezra 1 Acts 1
2	Genesis 2 Matthew 2	Ezra 2 Acts 2
3	Genesis 3 Matthew 3	Ezra 3 Acts 3
4	Genesis 4 Matthew 4	Ezra 4 Acts 4
5	Genesis 5 Matthew 5	Ezra 5 Acts 5
6	Genesis 6 Matthew 6	Ezra 6 Acts 6
7	Genesis 7 Matthew 7	Ezra 7 Acts 7
8	Genesis 8 Matthew 8	Ezra 8 Acts 8
9	Genesis 9, 10 Matthew 9	Ezra 9 Acts 9
10	Genesis 11 Matthew 10	Ezra 10 Acts 10
11	Genesis 12 Matthew 11	Nehemiah 1 Acts 11
12	Genesis 13 Matthew 12	Nehemiah 2 Acts 12
13	Genesis 14 Matthew 13	Nehemiah 3 Acts 13
14	Genesis 15 Matthew 14	Nehemiah 4 Acts 14
15	Genesis 16 Matthew 15	Nehemiah 5 Acts 15
16	Genesis 17 Matthew 16	Nehemiah 6 Acts 16
17	Genesis 18 Matthew 17	Nehemiah 7 Acts 17

Day	Family Reading	Secret Reading
18	Genesis 19 Matthew 18	Nehemiah 8 Acts 18
19	Genesis 20 Matthew 19	Nehemiah 9 Acts 19
20	Genesis 21 Matthew 20	Nehemiah 10 Acts 20
21	Genesis 22 Matthew 21	Nehemiah 11 Acts 21
22	Genesis 23 Matthew 22	Nehemiah 12 Acts 22
23	Genesis 24 Matthew 23	Nehemiah 13 Acts 23
24	Genesis 25 Matthew 24	Esther 1 Acts 24
25	Genesis 26 Matthew 25	Esther 2 Acts 25
26	Genesis 27 Matthew 26	Esther 3 Acts 26
27	Genesis 28 Matthew 27	Esther 4 Acts 27
28	Genesis 29 Matthew 28	Esther 5 Acts 28
29	Genesis 30 Mark 1	Esther 6 Romans 1
30	Genesis 31 Mark 2	Esther 7 Romans 2
31	Genesis 32 Mark 3	Esther 8 Romans 3

February

"I have esteemed the words of His mouth more than my necessary food."

Day	Family Reading	Secret Reading
1	Genesis 33 Mark 4	Esther 9, 10 Romans 4
2	Genesis 34 Mark 5	Job 1 Romans 5
3	Genesis 35, 36 Mark 6	Job 2 Romans 6
4	Genesis 37 Mark 7	Job 3 Romans 7
5	Genesis 38 Mark 8	Job 4 Romans 8
6	Genesis 39 Mark 9	Job 5 Romans 9
7	Genesis 40 Mark 10	Job 6 Romans 10
8	Genesis 41 Mark 11	Job 7 Romans 11
9	Genesis 42 Mark 12	Job 8 Romans 12
10	Genesis 43 Mark 13	Job 9 Romans 13
11	Genesis 44 Mark 14	Job 10 Romans 14
12	Genesis 45 Mark 15	Job 11 Romans 15
13	Genesis 46 Mark 16	Job 12 Romans 16
14	Genesis 47 Luke 1:1-38	Job 13 1 Corinthians 1
15	Genesis 48 Luke 1:39-80	Job 14 1 Corinthians 2
16	Genesis 49 Luke 2	Job 15 1 Corinthians 3
17	Genesis 50 Luke 3	Job 16, 17 1 Corinthians 4

Day	Family Reading	Secret Reading
18	Exodus 1 Luke 4	Job 18 1 Corinthians 5
19	Exodus 2 Luke 5	Job 19 1 Corinthians 6
20	Exodus 3 Luke 6	Job 20 1 Corinthians 7
21	Exodus 4 Luke 7	Job 21 1 Corinthians 8
22	Exodus 5 Luke 8	Job 22 1 Corinthians 9
23	Exodus 6 Luke 9	Job 23 1 Corinthians 10
24	Exodus 7 Luke 10	Job 24 1 Corinthians 11
25	Exodus 8 Luke 11	Job 25, 26 1 Corinthians 12
26	Exodus 9 Luke 12	Job 27 1 Corinthians 13
27	Exodus 10 Luke 13	Job 28 1 Corinthians 14
28	Exodus 11, 12:1-21 Luke 14	Job 29 1 Corinthians 15

March

"Mary kept all these things, and pondered them in her heart."

Day	Family Reading	Secret Reading
1	Exodus 12:22-51 Luke 15	Job 30 1 Corinthians 16
2	Exodus 13 Luke 16	Job 31 2 Corinthians 1
3	Exodus 14 Luke 17	Job 32 2 Corinthians 2
4	Exodus 15 Luke 18	Job 33 2 Corinthians 3
5	Exodus 16 Luke 19	Job 34 2 Corinthians 4
6	Exodus 17 Luke 20	Job 35 2 Corinthians 5
7	Exodus 18 Luke 21	Job 36 2 Corinthians 6
8	Exodus 19 Luke 22	Job 37 2 Corinthians 7
9	Exodus 20 Luke 23	Job 38 2 Corinthians 8
10	Exodus 21 Luke 24	Job 39 2 Corinthians 9
11	Exodus 22 John 1	Job 40 2 Corinthians 10
12	Exodus 23 John 2	Job 41 2 Corinthians 11
13	Exodus 24 John 3	Job 42 2 Corinthians 12
14	Exodus 25 John 4	Proverbs 1 2 Corinthians 13
15	Exodus 26 John 5	Proverbs 2 Galatians 1
16	Exodus 27 John 6	Proverbs 3 Galatians 2
17	Exodus 28 John 7	Proverbs 4 Galatians 3

Day	Family Reading	Secret Reading
18	Exodus 29 John 8	Proverbs 5 Galatians 4
19	Exodus 30 John 9	Proverbs 6 Galatians 5
20	Exodus 31 John 10	Proverbs 7 Galatians 6
21	Exodus 32 John 11	Proverbs 8 Ephesians 1
22	Exodus 33 John 12	Proverbs 9 Ephesians 2
23	Exodus 34 John 13	Proverbs 10 Ephesians 3
24	Exodus 35 John 14	Proverbs 11 Ephesians 4
25	Exodus 36 John 15	Proverbs 12 Ephesians 5
26	Exodus 37 John 16	Proverbs 13 Ephesians 6
27	Exodus 38 John 17	Proverbs 14 Philippians 1
28	Exodus 39 John 18	Proverbs 15 Philippians 2
29	Exodus 40 John 19	Proverbs 16 Philippians 3
30	Leviticus 1 John 20	Proverbs 17 Philippians 4
31	Leviticus 2, 3 John 21	Proverbs 18 Colossians 1

April

"O send out Thy light and Thy truth; let them lead me."

Day	Family Reading	Secret Reading
1	Leviticus 4 Psalms 1, 2	Proverbs 19 Colossians 2
2	Leviticus 5 Psalms 3, 4	Proverbs 20 Colossians 3
3	Leviticus 6 Psalms 5, 6	Proverbs 21 Colossians 4
4	Leviticus 7 Psalms 7, 8	Proverbs 22 1 Thessalonians 1
5	Leviticus 8 Psalms 9	Proverbs 23 1 Thessalonians 2
6	Leviticus 9 Psalms 10	Proverbs 24 1 Thessalonians 3
7	Leviticus 10 Psalms 11, 12	Proverbs 25 1 Thessalonians 4
8	Leviticus 11, 12 Psalms 13, 14	Proverbs 26 1 Thessalonians 5
9	Leviticus 13 Psalms 15, 16	Proverbs 27 2 Thessalonians 1
10	Leviticus 14 Psalms 17	Proverbs 28 2 Thessalonians 2
11	Leviticus 15 Psalms 18	Proverbs 29 2 Thessalonians 3
12	Leviticus 16 Psalms 19	Proverbs 30 1 Timothy 1
13	Leviticus 17 Psalms 20, 21	Proverbs 31 1 Timothy 2
14	Leviticus 18 Psalms 22	Ecclesiastes 1 1 Timothy 3
15	Leviticus 19 Psalms 23, 24	Ecclesiastes 2 1 Timothy 4
16	Leviticus 20 Psalms 25	Ecclesiastes 3 1 Timothy 5
17	Leviticus 21 Psalms 26, 27	Ecclesiastes 4 1 Timothy 6

Day	Family Reading	Secret Reading
18	Leviticus 22 Psalms 28, 29	Ecclesiastes 5 2 Timothy 1
19	Leviticus 23 Psalms 30	Ecclesiastes 6 2 Timothy 2
20	Leviticus 24 Psalms 31	Ecclesiastes 7 2 Timothy 3
21	Leviticus 25 Psalms 32	Ecclesiastes 8 2 Timothy 4
22	Leviticus 26 Psalms 33	Ecclesiastes 9 Titus 1
23	Leviticus 27 Psalms 34	Ecclesiastes 10 Titus 2
24	Numbers 1 Psalms 35	Ecclesiastes 11 Titus 3
25	Numbers 2 Psalms 36	Ecclesiastes 12 Philemon 1
26	Numbers 3 Psalms 37	Song of Songs 1 Hebrews 1
27	Numbers 4 Psalms 38	Song of Songs 2 Hebrews 2
28	Numbers 5 Psalms 39	Song of Songs 3 Hebrews 3
29	Numbers 6 Psalms 40, 41	Song of Songs 4 Hebrews 4
30	Numbers 7 Psalms 42, 43	Song of Songs 5 Hebrews 5

May

"From a child thou hast known thy holy Scriptures."

Day	Family Reading	Secret Reading
1	Numbers 8 Psalms 44	Song of Songs 6 Hebrews 6
2	Numbers 9 Psalms 45	Song of Songs 7 Hebrews 7
3	Numbers 10 Psalms 46, 47	Song of Songs 8 Hebrews 8
4	Numbers 11 Psalms 48	Isaiah 1 Hebrews 9
5	Numbers 12, 13 Psalms 49	Isaiah 2 Hebrews 10
6	Numbers 14 Psalms 50	Isaiah 3, 4 Hebrews 11
7	Numbers 15 Psalms 51	Isaiah 5 Hebrews 12
8	Numbers 16 Psalms 52-54	Isaiah 6 Hebrews 13
9	Numbers 17, 18 Psalms 55	Isaiah 7 James 1
10	Numbers 19 Psalms 56, 57	Isaiah 8, 9:1-7 James 2
11	Numbers 20 Psalms 58, 59	Isaiah 9:8-10:4 James 3
12	Numbers 21 Psalms 60, 61	Isaiah 10:5-34 James 4
13	Numbers 22 Psalms 62, 63	Isaiah 11, 12 James 5
14	Numbers 23 Psalms 64, 65	Isaiah 13 1 Peter 1
15	Numbers 24 Psalms 66, 67	Isaiah 14 1 Peter 2
16	Numbers 25 Psalms 68	Isaiah 15 1 Peter 3
17	Numbers 26 Psalms 69	Isaiah 16 1 Peter 4

Day	Family Reading	Secret Reading
18	Numbers 27 Psalms 70, 71	Isaiah 17, 18 1 Peter 5
19	Numbers 28 Psalms 72	Isaiah 19, 20 2 Peter 1
20	Numbers 29 Psalms 73	Isaiah 21 2 Peter 2
21	Numbers 30 Psalms 74	Isaiah 22 2 Peter 3
22	Numbers 31 Psalms 75, 76	Isaiah 23 1 John 1
23	Numbers 32 Psalms 77	Isaiah 24 1 John 2
24	Numbers 33 Psalms 78:1-37	Isaiah 25 1 John 3
25	Numbers 34 Psalms 78:38-72	Isaiah 26 1 John 4
26	Numbers 35 Psalms 79	Isaiah 27 1 John 5
27	Numbers 36 Psalms 80	Isaiah 28 2 John 1
28	Deuteronomy 1 Psalms 81, 82	Isaiah 29 3 John 1
29	Deuteronomy 2 Psalms 83, 84	Isaiah 30 Jude 1
30	Deuteronomy 3 Psalms 85	Isaiah 31 Revelation 1
31	Deuteronomy 4 Psalms 86, 87	Isaiah 32 Revelation 2

June

"Blessed is he that readeth and they that hear."

Day	Family Reading	Secret Reading
1	Deuteronomy 5 Psalms 88	Isaiah 33 Revelation 3
2	Deuteronomy 6 Psalms 89	Isaiah 34 Revelation 4
3	Deuteronomy 7 Psalms 90	Isaiah 35 Revelation 5
4	Deuteronomy 8 Psalms 91	Isaiah 36 Revelation 6
5	Deuteronomy 9 Psalms 92, 93	Isaiah 37 Revelation 7
6	Deuteronomy 10 Psalms 94	Isaiah 38 Revelation 8
7	Deuteronomy 11 Psalms 95, 96	Isaiah 39 Revelation 9
8	Deuteronomy 12 Psalms 97, 98	Isaiah 40 Revelation 10
9	Deuteronomy 13, 14 Psalms 99-101	Isaiah 41 Revelation 11
10	Deuteronomy 15 Psalms 102	Isaiah 42 Revelation 12
11	Deuteronomy 16 Psalms 103	Isaiah 43 Revelation 13
12	Deuteronomy 17 Psalms 104	Isaiah 44 Revelation 14
13	Deuteronomy 18 Psalms 105	Isaiah 45 Revelation 15
14	Deuteronomy 19 Psalms 106	Isaiah 46 Revelation 16
15	Deuteronomy 20 Psalms 107	Isaiah 47 Revelation 17
16	Deuteronomy 21 Psalms 108, 109	Isaiah 48 Revelation 18
17	Deuteronomy 22 Psalms 110, 111	Isaiah 49 Revelation 19

Day	Family Reading	Secret Reading
18	Deuteronomy 23 Psalms 112, 113	Isaiah 50 Revelation 20
19	Deuteronomy 24 Psalms 114, 115	Isaiah 51 Revelation 21
20	Deuteronomy 25 Psalms 116	Isaiah 52 Revelation 22
21	Deuteronomy 26 Psalms 117, 118	Isaiah 53 Matthew 1
22	Deuteronomy 27, 28:1-19 Psalms 119:1-24	Isaiah 54 Matthew 2
23	Deuteronomy 28:20-68 Psalms 119:25-48	Isaiah 55 Matthew 3
24	Deuteronomy 29 Psalms 119:49-72	Isaiah 56 Matthew 4
25	Deuteronomy 30 Psalms 119:73-96	Isaiah 57 Matthew 5
26	Deuteronomy 31 Psalms 119:97-120	Isaiah 58 Matthew 6
27	Deuteronomy 32 Psalms 119:121-144	Isaiah 59 Matthew 7
28	Deuteronomy 33, 34 Psalms 119:145-176	Isaiah 60 Matthew 8
29	Joshua 1 Psalms 120-122	Isaiah 61 Matthew 9
30	Joshua 2 Psalms 123-125	Isaiah 62 Matthew 10

July

"They received the word with all readiness of mind, and searched the Scriptures daily."

Day	Family Reading	Secret Reading
1	Joshua 3 Psalms 126-128	Isaiah 63 Matthew 11
2	Joshua 4 Psalms 129-131	Isaiah 64 Matthew 12
3	Joshua 5, 6:1-5 Psalms 132-134	Isaiah 65 Matthew 13
4	Joshua 6:6-27 Psalms 135, 136	Isaiah 66 Matthew 14
5	Joshua 7 Psalms 137, 138	Jeremiah 1 Matthew 15
6	Joshua 8 Psalms 139	Jeremiah 2 Matthew 16
7	Joshua 9 Psalms 140, 141	Jeremiah 3 Matthew 17
8	Joshua 10 Psalms 142, 143	Jeremiah 4 Matthew 18
9	Joshua 11 Psalms 144	Jeremiah 5 Matthew 19
10	Joshua 12, 13 Psalms 145	Jeremiah 6 Matthew 20
11	Joshua 14, 15 Psalms 146, 147	Jeremiah 7 Matthew 21
12	Joshua 16, 17 Psalms 148	Jeremiah 8 Matthew 22
13	Joshua 18, 19 Psalms 149, 150	Jeremiah 9 Matthew 23
14	Joshua 20, 21 Acts 1	Jeremiah 10 Matthew 24
15	Joshua 22 Acts 2	Jeremiah 11 Matthew 25
16	Joshua 23 Acts 3	Jeremiah 12 Matthew 26
17	Joshua 24 Acts 4	Jeremiah 13 Matthew 27

Day	Family Reading	Secret Reading
18	Judges 1 Acts 5	Jeremiah 14 Matthew 28
19	Judges 2 Acts 6	Jeremiah 15 Mark 1
20	Judges 3 Acts 7	Jeremiah 16 Mark 2
21	Judges 4 Acts 8	Jeremiah 17 Mark 3
22	Judges 5 Acts 9	Jeremiah 18 Mark 4
23	Judges 6 Acts 10	Jeremiah 19 Mark 5
24	Judges 7 Acts 11	Jeremiah 20 Mark 6
25	Judges 8 Acts 12	Jeremiah 21 Mark 7
26	Judges 9 Acts 13	Jeremiah 22 Mark 8
27	Judges 10, 11:1-11 Acts 14	Jeremiah 23 Mark 9
28	Judges 11:12-40 Acts 15	Jeremiah 24 Mark 10
29	Judges 12 Acts 16	Jeremiah 25 Mark 11
30	Judges 13 Acts 17	Jeremiah 26 Mark 12
31	Judges 14 Acts 18	Jeremiah 27 Mark 13

August

"Speak, Lord, for Thy servant heareth."

Day	Family Reading	Secret Reading
1	Judges 15 Acts 19	Jeremiah 28 Mark 14
2	Judges 16 Acts 20	Jeremiah 29 Mark 15
3	Judges 17 Acts 21	Jeremiah 30, 31 Mark 16
4	Judges 18 Acts 22	Jeremiah 32 Psalm 1, 2
5	Judges 19 Acts 23	Jeremiah 33 Psalm 3, 4
6	Judges 20 Acts 24	Jeremiah 34 Psalm 5, 6
7	Judges 21 Acts 25	Jeremiah 35 Psalm 7, 8
8	Ruth 1 Acts 26	Jeremiah 36, 45 Psalm 9
9	Ruth 2 Acts 27	Jeremiah 37 Psalm 10
10	Ruth 3, 4 Acts 28	Jeremiah 38 Psalm 11, 12
11	1 Samuel 1 Romans 1	Jeremiah 39 Psalm 13, 14
12	1 Samuel 2 Romans 2	Jeremiah 40 Psalm 15, 16
13	1 Samuel 3 Romans 3	Jeremiah 41 Psalm 17
14	1 Samuel 4 Romans 4	Jeremiah 42 Psalm 18
15	1 Samuel 5, 6 Romans 5	Jeremiah 43 Psalm 19
16	1 Samuel 7, 8 Romans 6	Jeremiah 44 Psalm 20, 21
17	1 Samuel 9 Romans 7	Jeremiah 46 Psalm 22

Day	Family Reading	Secret Reading
18	1 Samuel 10 Romans 8	Jeremiah 47 Psalm 23, 24
19	1 Samuel 11 Romans 9	Jeremiah 48 Psalm 25
20	1 Samuel 12 Romans 10	Jeremiah 49 Psalm 26, 27
21	1 Samuel 13 Romans 11	Jeremiah 50 Psalm 28, 29
22	1 Samuel 14 Romans 12	Jeremiah 51 Psalm 30
23	1 Samuel 15 Romans 13	Jeremiah 52 Psalm 31
24	1 Samuel 16 Romans 14	Lamentations 1 Psalm 32
25	1 Samuel 17 Romans 15	Lamentations 2 Psalm 33
26	1 Samuel 18 Romans 16	Lamentations 3 Psalm 34
27	1 Samuel 19 1 Corinthians 1	Lamentations 4 Psalm 35
28	1 Samuel 20 1 Corinthians 2	Lamentations 5 Psalm 36
29	1 Samuel 21, 22 1 Corinthians 3	Ezekiel 1 Psalm 37
30	1 Samuel 23 1 Corinthians 4	Ezekiel 2 Psalm 38
31	1 Samuel 24 1 Corinthians 5	Ezekiel 3 Psalm 39

September

"The law of the Lord is perfect, converting the soul."

Day	Family Reading	Secret Reading
1	1 Samuel 25 1 Corinthians 6	Ezekiel 4 Psalm 40, 41
2	1 Samuel 26 1 Corinthians 7	Ezekiel 5 Psalm 42, 43
3	1 Samuel 27 1 Corinthians 8	Ezekiel 6 Psalm 44
4	1 Samuel 28 1 Corinthians 9	Ezekiel 7 Psalm 45
5	1 Samuel 29, 30 1 Corinthians 10	Ezekiel 8 Psalm 46, 47
6	1 Samuel 31 1 Corinthians 11	Ezekiel 9 Psalm 48
7	2 Samuel 1 1 Corinthians 12	Ezekiel 10 Psalm 49
8	2 Samuel 2 1 Corinthians 13	Ezekiel 11 Psalm 50
9	2 Samuel 3 1 Corinthians 14	Ezekiel 12 Psalm 51
10	2 Samuel 4, 5 1 Corinthians 15	Ezekiel 13 Psalm 52-54
11	2 Samuel 6 1 Corinthians 16	Ezekiel 14 Psalm 55
12	2 Samuel 7 2 Corinthians 1	Ezekiel 15 Psalm 56, 57
13	2 Samuel 8, 9 2 Corinthians 2	Ezekiel 16 Psalm 58, 59
14	2 Samuel 10 2 Corinthians 3	Ezekiel 17 Psalm 60, 61
15	2 Samuel 11 2 Corinthians 4	Ezekiel 18 Psalm 62, 63
16	2 Samuel 12 2 Corinthians 5	Ezekiel 19 Psalm 64, 65
17	2 Samuel 13 2 Corinthians 6	Ezekiel 20 Psalm 66, 67

Day	Family Reading	Secret Reading
18	2 Samuel 14 2 Corinthians 7	Ezekiel 21 Psalm 68
19	2 Samuel 15 2 Corinthians 8	Ezekiel 22 Psalm 69
20	2 Samuel 16 2 Corinthians 9	Ezekiel 23 Psalm 70, 71
21	2 Samuel 17 2 Corinthians 10	Ezekiel 24 Psalm 72
22	2 Samuel 18 2 Corinthians 11	Ezekiel 25 Psalm 73
23	2 Samuel 19 2 Corinthians 12	Ezekiel 26 Psalm 74
24	2 Samuel 20 2 Corinthians 13	Ezekiel 27 Psalm 75, 76
25	2 Samuel 21 Galatians 1	Ezekiel 28 Psalm 77
26	2 Samuel 22 Galatians 2	Ezekiel 29 Psalm 78:1-37
27	2 Samuel 23 Galatians 3	Ezekiel 30 Psalm 78:38-72
28	2 Samuel 24 Galatians 4	Ezekiel 31 Psalm 79
29	1 Kings 1 Galatians 5	Ezekiel 32 Psalm 80
30	1 Kings 2 Galatians 6	Ezekiel 33 Psalm 81, 82

October

"O how I love Thy law! It is my meditation all the day."

Day	Family Reading	Secret Reading
1	1 Kings 3 Ephesians 1	Ezekiel 34 Psalm 83, 84
2	1 Kings 4, 5 Ephesians 2	Ezekiel 35 Psalm 85
3	1 Kings 6 Ephesians 3	Ezekiel 36 Psalm 86
4	1 Kings 7 Ephesians 4	Ezekiel 37 Psalm 87, 88
5	1 Kings 8 Ephesians 5	Ezekiel 38 Psalm 89
6	1 Kings 9 Ephesians 6	Ezekiel 39 Psalm 90
7	1 Kings 10 Philippians 1	Ezekiel 40 Psalm 91
8	1 Kings 11 Philippians 2	Ezekiel 41 Psalm 92, 93
9	1 Kings 12 Philippians 3	Ezekiel 42 Psalm 94
10	1 Kings 13 Philippians 4	Ezekiel 43 Psalm 95, 96
11	1 Kings 14 Colossians 1	Ezekiel 44 Psalm 97, 98
12	1 Kings 15 Colossians 2	Ezekiel 45 Psalm 99-101
13	1 Kings 16 Colossians 3	Ezekiel 46 Psalm 102
14	1 Kings 17 Colossians 3	Ezekiel 47 Psalm 103
15	1 Kings 18 1 Thessalonians 1	Ezekiel 48 Psalm 104
16	1 Kings 19 1 Thessalonians 2	Daniel 1 Psalm 105
17	1 Kings 20 1 Thessalonians 3	Daniel 2 Psalm 106

Day	Family Reading	Secret Reading
18	1 Kings 21 1 Thessalonians 4	Daniel 3 Psalm 107
19	1 Kings 22 1 Thessalonians 5	Daniel 4 Psalm 108, 109
20	2 Kings 1 2 Thessalonians 1	Daniel 5 Psalm 110, 111
21	2 Kings 2 2 Thessalonians 2	Daniel 6 Psalm 112, 113
22	2 Kings 3 2 Thessalonians 3	Daniel 7 Psalm 114, 115
23	2 Kings 4 1 Timothy 1	Daniel 8 Psalm 116
24	2 Kings 5 1 Timothy 2	Daniel 9 Psalm 117, 118
25	2 Kings 6 1 Timothy 3	Daniel 10 Psalm 119:1-24
26	2 Kings 7 1 Timothy 4	Daniel 11 Psalm 119:25-48
27	2 Kings 8 1 Timothy 5	Daniel 12 Psalm 119:49-72
28	2 Kings 9 1 Timothy 6	Hosea 1 Psalm 119:73-96
29	2 Kings 10 2 Timothy 1	Hosea 2 Psalm 119:97-120
30	2 Kings 11, 12 2 Timothy 2	Hosea 3, 4 Psalm 119:121-144
31	2 Kings 13 2 Timothy 3	Hosea 5, 6 Psalm 119:145-176

November

"As new-born babes, desire the sincere milk of the word, that ye may grow thereby."

Day	Family Reading	Secret Reading
1	2 Kings 14 / 2 Timothy 4	Hosea 7 / Psalm 120-122
2	2 Kings 15 / Titus 1	Hosea 8 / Psalm 123-125
3	2 Kings 16 / Titus 2	Hosea 9 / Psalm 126-128
4	2 Kings 17 / Titus 3	Hosea 10 / Psalm 129-131
5	2 Kings 18 / Philemon 1	Hosea 11 / Psalm 132-134
6	2 Kings 19 / Hebrews 1	Hosea 12 / Psalm 135-136
7	2 Kings 20 / Hebrews 2	Hosea 13 / Psalm 137-138
8	2 Kings 21 / Hebrews 3	Hosea 14 / Psalm 139
9	2 Kings 22 / Hebrews 4	Joel 1 / Psalm 140, 141
10	2 Kings 23 / Hebrews 5	Joel 2 / Psalm 142
11	2 Kings 24 / Hebrews 6	Joel 3 / Psalm 143
12	2 Kings 25 / Hebrews 7	Amos 1 / Psalm 144
13	1 Chronicles 1, 2 / Hebrews 8	Amos 2 / Psalm 145
14	1 Chronicles 3, 4 / Hebrews 9	Amos 3 / Psalm 146, 147
15	1 Chronicles 5, 6 / Hebrews 10	Amos 4 / Psalm 148-150
16	1 Chronicles 7, 8 / Hebrews 11	Amos 5 / Luke 1:1-38
17	1 Chronicles 9, 10 / Hebrews 12	Amos 6 / Luke 1:39-80

Day	Family Reading	Secret Reading
18	1 Chronicles 11, 12 Hebrews 13	Amos 7 Luke 2
19	1 Chronicles 13, 14 James 1	Amos 8 Luke 3
20	1 Chronicles 15 James 2	Amos 9 Luke 4
21	1 Chronicles 16 James 3	Obadiah 1 Luke 5
22	1 Chronicles 17 James 4	Jonah 1 Luke 6
23	1 Chronicles 18 James 5	Jonah 2 Luke 7
24	1 Chronicles 19, 20 1 Peter 1	Jonah 3 Luke 8
25	1 Chronicles 21 1 Peter 2	Jonah 4 Luke 9
26	1 Chronicles 22 1 Peter 3	Micah 1 Luke 10
27	1 Chronicles 23 1 Peter 4	Micah 2 Luke 11
28	1 Chronicles 24, 25 1 Peter 5	Micah 3 Luke 12
29	1 Chronicles 26, 27 2 Peter 1	Micah 4 Luke 13
30	1 Chronicles 28 2 Peter 2	Micah 5 Luke 14

December

"The law of his God is in his heart; none of his steps shall slide."

Day	Family Reading	Secret Reading
1	1 Chronicles 29 2 Peter 3	Micah 6 Luke 15
2	2 Chronicles 1 1 John 1	Micah 7 Luke 16
3	2 Chronicles 2 1 John 2	Nahum 1 Luke 17
4	2 Chronicles 3, 4 1 John 3	Nahum 2 Luke 18
5	2 Chronicles 5, 6:1-11 1 John 4	Nahum 3 Luke 19
6	2 Chronicles 6:12-42 1 John 5	Habakkuk 1 Luke 20
7	2 Chronicles 7 2 John 1	Habakkuk 2 Luke 21
8	2 Chronicles 8 3 John 1	Habakkuk 3 Luke 22
9	2 Chronicles 9 Jude 1	Zephaniah 1 Luke 23
10	2 Chronicles 10 Revelation 1	Zephaniah 2 Luke 24
11	2 Chronicles 11, 12 Revelation 2	Zephaniah 3 John 1
12	2 Chronicles 13 Revelation 3	Haggai 1 John 2
13	2 Chronicles 14, 15 Revelation 4	Haggai 2 John 3
14	2 Chronicles 16 Revelation 5	Zechariah 1 John 4
15	2 Chronicles 17 Revelation 6	Zechariah 2 John 5
16	2 Chronicles 18 Revelation 7	Zechariah 3 John 6
17	2 Chronicles 19, 20 Revelation 8	Zechariah 4 John 7

Day	Family Reading	Secret Reading
18	2 Chronicles 21 Revelation 9	Zechariah 5 John 8
19	2 Chronicles 22, 23 Revelation 10	Zechariah 6 John 9
20	2 Chronicles 24 Revelation 11	Zechariah 7 John 10
21	2 Chronicles 25 Revelation 12	Zechariah 8 John 11
22	2 Chronicles 26 Revelation 13	Zechariah 9 John 12
23	2 Chronicles 27, 28 Revelation 14	Zechariah 10 John 13
24	2 Chronicles 29 Revelation 15	Zechariah 11 John 14
25	2 Chronicles 30 Revelation 16	Zechariah 12, 13:1 John 15
26	2 Chronicles 31 Revelation 17	Zechariah 13:2-9 John 16
27	2 Chronicles 32 Revelation 18	Zechariah 14 John 17
28	2 Chronicles 33 Revelation 19	Malachi 1 John 18
29	2 Chronicles 34 Revelation 20	Malachi 2 John 19
30	2 Chronicles 35 Revelation 21	Malachi 3 John 20
31	2 Chronicles 36 Revelation 22	Malachi 4 John 21

7. Notes

1   A memorial account of Robert Murray McCheyne's life, written by friend and colleague Rev. J. Roxburgh in Andrew A. Bonar's book, *Memoir and Remains of the Reverend Robert Murray McCheyne (1881 ed.), p. 593.*

2   This quote, by Andrew A. Bonar, is found in his *Memoir and Remains of the Reverend Robert Murray McCheyne (1881 ed.), p. 63.*

3   Andrew A Bonar, *Memoir and Remains of the Reverend Robert Murray McCheyne (1881 ed.), p. 562.*

For more information on the life, ministry and writings of Robert Murray McCheyne see:

Andrew A. Bonar, *Memoir and Remains of the Reverend Robert Murray McCheyne* (1844).

_____, *Additional Remains of the Reverend Robert Murray McCheyne* (1846).

_____, *A Basket of Gragments* (1848).

Alexander Smellie, *Robert Murray McCheyne* (1913).

J.C. Smith, *Robert Murray McCheyne* (1910).

James A. Stewart, *Robert Murray McCheyne* (1963).

Holiness

John Charles Ryle 1813-1900

*With an Introduction
By Tom Phillips*

Abridged version of *Holiness* by John Charles Ryle. Abridged version originally published by World Wide Publications, 1996, along with Billy Graham Center, Wheaton, Il. Copyright of abridged version and introduction held by Tom Phillips, used with permission. Scripture quotations are taken from the Holy Bible, NIV © 1973, 1978, 1984, International Bible Society. Used by Permission of Zondervan Bible Publishers. Artwork in the Public Domain.

Book Chapters

1. Introduction
   By Tom Phillips 468
2. Holiness 471
   What True Holiness Is: 471
3. Without Christ 479
4. Thirst Relieved 484
   The case supposed: Our Lord says, "If any man thirst." 485
   I now pass to the remedy proposed: "If anyone thirst, let him come unto Me and drink." 486
   The promise is held out to all who come to Christ. "Whoever believes on Me, as the Scripture has said, streams of living water will flow from within him." 487
5. Christ is All 492

1. Introduction
By Tom Phillips

When one thinks of the Victorian Age, names like Disraeli, Gladstone, Dickens, or possibly even Spurgeon may come to mind, but not Ryle. Bishop J.C. Ryle served the Lord in ministry in the Church of England for almost the entire length of the Victorian Age. Whether in the rural setting of places like Helmingham or the bustling commercial trade center of Liverpool, his sermons, tracts and other publications had a profound impact on evangelicalism.

John Charles Ryle was born into a family of means on May 10, 1816, in Macclesfield, England. His father was a successful banker, and he enjoyed the benefits of a well-educated upbringing, including attendance at Eton and Christ Church, Oxford. He might well have gone into banking himself and subsequently dabbled in politics had his father not gone bankrupt in 1841.

So instead of a lucrative secular career, Ryle turned to the ministry for his livelihood. He held various rural positions in the Church of England for almost 36 years, leading up to his appointment as the First Bishop of Liverpool in 1880. His appointment (in the official Church of England, all bishop positions were political appointments) was a bit of a surprise. It may well have been a "stop-gap" appointment counting on a short tenure because of his relatively advanced age of 64: but his term lasted 20 years, and he used this very visible platform to great advantage.

By 1880, Liverpool had become a sizable urban sprawl, with its wealthy suburbs, terrace housing and inner-city decay, much the same as today's urban challenge. Although Ryle was committed to all forms of evangelism, his heart beat strongest for mass evangelism in the cities.

He rued the church's inability to meet the spiritual needs of population centers like Liverpool, and as Bishop, he allocated his own resources and those of the church to aggressively reach his see's one million inhabitants with the Gospel.

Much of his immediate influence on Victorian evangelicalism stemmed from his prolific number of tracts. Several million copies of his more than 200 different tracts were distributed in a variety of languages throughout the land. They were comprised of small, manageable sections, as was most of his writing, lending themselves to a variety of formats from one-page sheets to 30-page editions.

Most of his books are collections of the sermons he first delivered during his early years in the rural pulpits of Fawley, Winchester, Helmingham and Stradbroke. His writing style closely follows his preaching style of word/phrase repetition, a compelling sense of urgency, and the use of vivid illustrations. His style was developed out of necessity to keep members of his rural congregations attentive on those hot August Sundays.

His most well known book is *Holiness*, first published in 1877. In a more recent reprint by Centenary, it is eulogized as "a feast, a goldmine, a spur and heart warmer, food, drink, medicine and vitamin tablet, all in one."

Bishop Ryle's desire, and his answer to the issues of his day, was the pursuit of personal revival of Scriptural holiness. As he said,

> I have had a deep conviction for many years that practical holiness and entire self-consecration to God are not sufficiently attended to by modern Christians. The subject of personal godliness has fallen sadly into the background.
>
> Do you want to attain holiness? Then **go to Christ.** Wait for nothing. Wait for nobody. Go and say to Him, in the words of that beautiful hymn.
>
> > "Nothing in my hand I bring. Simply to Thy cross I cling; Naked, flee to Thee for dress; Helpless, look to Thee for grace."
>
> Let us aim at eminent holiness. Let us labor to be unmistakable Christians. Let us so love that all may see that to us the things of God are the first things, and the glory of God the first aim in our lives—to follow

Christ our grand object in time present—to be with Christ our grand desire in time to come.

May it be so for you! We at the Billy Graham Center Institute of Evangelism trust that this devotional booklet may help you make Bishop Ryle's desire a reality in your life.

Tom Phillips

President, International Students, Inc.

Institute of Evangelism Advisory Board

2. Holiness

"...without holiness, no one will see the Lord," Hebrews 12:14

This text opens up a subject of deep importance, that of practical holiness. It suggests a question which demands the attention of all professing Christians. Are we holy? Will we see the Lord?

How does the account stand between God and our souls? In this hurrying, bustling world, let's stand still for a moment and consider the matter of holiness. I believe I could not have chosen a subject more profitable to our souls. It is sobering to hear God's Word saying, "Without holiness, no one will see the Lord," (Hebrews 12:14). By God's help, I will examine what true holiness is and why it is so important. In conclusion, I will try to point out the only way in which holiness can be attained.

What True Holiness Is:

To find out what true, practical holiness is, let's look at the people who God calls holy. A person can go to great lengths and never reach holiness. It is not knowledge: Balaam had that. Nor is it a profession: Judas had that. Nor morality and good outward conduct; the young ruler had that. Yet none of these were holy. A person may have any one of these qualities and yet never see the Lord.

What then is true holiness? This is a tough question. There is plenty of Scripture on the subject, yet it can easily be distorted. So let me try to draw a mental picture of holiness. Only remember that this is an imperfect sketch at best.

Holiness is the habit of being one mind with God and agreeing with God's judgment. This includes hating what He hates and loving what He loves. It means measuring everything by the standard of His Word. This includes striving to be like Jesus. It goes beyond depending on Him, to laboring to have His mind and to be conformed to His image.

Holy people strive to avoid every known sin, and to keep every known commandment. Their minds will be bent toward God, with a hearty desire to do his will. They have a greater fear of displeasing God than the world. They feel what Paul felt, "For in my inner being I delight in God's law," (Romans 7:22).

Holy people's lives will be characterized by meekness, long-suffering, gentleness, patience and self-control. They implement what Jesus warned against, "Be careful, or your hearts will be weighed down with dissipation, drunkenness and the anxieties of life," (Luke 21:34). Also that of Paul "I beat my body and make it my slave so that after I have preached to others, I myself will not be disqualified for the prize," (1 Corinthians 9:27).

The holy life is characterized by giving and kindness. The golden rule is worked out in their lives. They care about others-about their characters, feelings, property, and souls. They abhor all lying, slandering, backbiting, cheating, and dishonesty. What a great condemnation are the words in 1 Corinthians 13 and the Sermon on the Mount when compared to the conduct of many professing Christians.

Holy people show mercy towards others. Their days are productive. They are not content with just staying away from doing harm but will try to do good. They strive to impact their generation, and to lessen the spiritual misery around them. Such was Dorcas in Acts 9:36, who not only purposed and planned to help the poor but did.

Holy people strive after a pure heart. They dread all contamination of spirit and seek to avoid it. They know their hearts are like tinder and will diligently keep clear of the sparks of temptation. Who dares to talk of strength when a man as David can fall?

Holy people fear God. I do not mean the fear of a slave, which is work driven by the fear of punishment. This fear is that of a child, who wishes to please his father because he loves him.

Holy people strive after humility. They desire to esteem all others better than themselves. They see more evil in their own hearts than in any other. They identify with Paul's "I am the chief of all sinners."

Holy people pursue faithfulness in all aspects of life. They are mindful of Paul's words: "Whatever you do, work at it with all your heart, as working for the Lord, not for man," (Colossians 3:23). Holy people aim at doing everything well and are ashamed of mediocre work. Like Daniel, they seek to give no fault against themselves except their faith. They strive to be good spouses, parents and children. They are good bosses, employees, friends, citizens, and neighbors; in both public and private. Holiness is worthless if it does not have this result.

Holy people follow after spiritual mindedness. They strive to set their hearts entirely on things above and to hold things on earth with a loose hand. They don't neglect this present life, but they aim to live with their treasures in heaven. To commune with God through prayer, the Bible and His people are the holy people's chief enjoyments. The value of everything is gauged on how it draws them nearer to God.

These are the main characteristics of a holy life. But I fear my meaning will be mistaken and the description given of holiness will discourage some. I would not willingly make a righteous heart sad or throw a stumbling block in any believer's way. Yet true holiness is a great reality. It is something in a person that can be seen, and felt by those around him. Like light, if it exists, it will show.

I do not say that holiness shuts out indwelling sin. The greatest misery of a holy person is that he carries with him "a body of death." When he would do good, "evil is present with him." The old nature is clogging all his movements, trying to draw him back at every step he takes (Romans 7:21). But not being at peace with indwelling sin is the mark of a holy person. The work of sanctification is like the wall of Jerusalem—the building goes forward even "in times of trouble," (Daniel 9:25).

Holiness does not come to perfection all at once. Sanctification is a progressive and imperfect work. All must have a beginning so we must never despise the small things. The history of great Christians contains many a "but" and "however" before you reach the end. The holiest people have many blemishes and defects. Their life is a continual warfare with sin and the world. Sometimes you see them not overcoming but overcome. The flesh is ever fighting against the spirit. But still, to have a holy character is the heart's desire and prayer of all true Christians. They press towards it. They may not attain it, but they always aim at it.

We need to be ready to make allowance for much stumbling and occasional deadness in professing Christians. Roads have many turns. A person may be truly holy and not perfect. But after every allowance, I cannot see how anyone can be called "holy" who willfully allows himself to sin and is not humbled and ashamed of it. I dare not call anyone "holy" who habitually and willfully does what he knows is wrong.

Such are the leading characteristics of practical holiness. Examine yourselves. Now, let me attempt to show why practical holiness is so important.

Can holiness save us? No. Our purest works are no better than filthy rags when in the light of God's holy law. The white robe Jesus offers must be our only righteousness and the Lamb's book of life our only ticket to heaven. With all our holiness, we are no better than sinners. Our best is stained and tainted with imperfection (Ephesians 2:8-9).

Then why is holiness so important? Why does the Apostle say, "Without it no man shall see the Lord?"

We must be holy because God commands it. Jesus says to His people, "For I tell you that unless your righteousness surpasses that of the Pharisees and the teachers of the law, you will certainly not enter the kingdom of heaven," (Matthew 5:20). Paul tells the Thessalonians, "It is God's will that you should be sanctified," (1 Thessalonians 4:3). And Peter says, " But just as he who called you is holy, so be holy in all you do; for it is written: 'Be holy, because I am holy,'" (1 Peter 1:15-16).

We must be holy because this is the purpose for which Christ came into the world. Paul writes to Titus, "[Jesus Christ] who gave himself for us to redeem us from all wickedness and to purify for himself a people that are his very own, eager to do what is good," (Titus 2:14). So to talk of people being saved from the guilt of sin without being saved from its dominion is to contradict the witness of all scripture. Jesus is a complete Savior. He does not merely take away the guilt of a believer's sin. He breaks its power.

We must be holy because this is the only sound evidence that we have a saving faith in our Lord Jesus Christ. James warns us about dead faith: a faith which goes no further than a profession and has no impact on a person's character (James 2:17). But true faith always shows itself by its fruits. It will work by love, overcome the world and purify the heart. Those who live for the Lord are generally the only people who die in the Lord. If we want to die the death of the righteous, let us seek to live His life.

We must be holy because this is the only proof that we sincerely love the Lord Jesus Christ. He spoke of this in John, "If you love me, you will obey what I command... Whoever has my commandments and obeys them, he is the one who loves me," (John 14:15, 21). It couldn't be clearer, and woe to those who neglect them. It is an unhealthy soul who can think of all that Jesus suffered and yet cling to those sins He suffered for.

We must be holy because this is the only sound evidence that we are true children of God. Children generally look like their parents. It is much the same with the children of God. The Lord Jesus says, "If God were your Father, you would love me, for I came from God and now am here," (John 8:42). If people have no likeness to the Father in heaven, it is vain to talk of their being His children. If we know nothing of holiness, we don't have the Holy Spirit dwelling in us (Romans 8:14). We must show by our lives our family or our sonship is but an empty name.

We must be holy, because this is the way to help others. We don't live in a vacuum. Our lives will either do good or harm to those who see them. They are a silent sermon which all can read. I believe that far more is done for Christ's kingdom by holy living than we are aware of. There is a reality in such living that forces people to think. It carries a weight and influence which nothing else can give. The Judgment Day will prove that many husbands were won "without a word" by a holy life (1 Peter 3:1). You may talk to people about the doctrines of the Gospel and few will listen, still fewer will understand. But your life is an argument that none can escape.

I believe there is much harm done by unholy and inconsistent Christians. Such people are among Satan's best allies. They pull down with their lives what ministers build with their lips. They supply the world a never-ending excuse for remaining as they are because they see Christians' lives that are no different from their own. They are reasons why some view the church as a bunch of hypocrites. Let us take heed lest the blood of souls should be required at our hands. Oh Lord, deliver us from the murder of souls by inconsistency. Oh, for the sake of others, if for no other reason, let us strive to be holy!

We must be holy, because our present comfort depends upon it. We soon forget the close connection between sin and sorrow, holiness and happiness. God has ordered that our well-being and our well-doing are linked together. Our salvation is not from works. But a person will not have an acute sense of assurance so long as he does not strive to live a holy life (1 John 3:19). When the disciples fled from Jesus on that last night, they escaped danger but were miserable. Shortly after, when they confessed Him boldly before men, they were cast into prison and beaten. We are told, "The apostles left the Sanhedrin, rejoicing because they had been counted worthy of suffering disgrace for the Name," (Acts 5:41). He who follows Jesus most fully will always follow Him most comfortably.

Lastly, we must be holy because holiness on earth prepares us to enjoy heaven. Heaven is a holy place, and God is a holy being. Revelation says of heaven, "Nothing impure will ever enter it, nor will anyone who does what is shameful and deceitful, but only those whose names are written in the Lamb's book of life," (Revelation 21:27).

How shall we ever be happy and at home in heaven, if we die unholy? Death works no change. Each will rise again with the same character which he died with. Where will our place be if we are strangers to holiness now?

For a moment suppose that you were allowed to enter heaven without holiness. What would you do? What could you possibly enjoy? Who would you associate with? Their pleasures are not your pleasures, their taste not your taste and their character not your character. How could you possibly be happy, if you were not holy on earth?

Perhaps now, you view Sunday as a burden. You can only spend a small part of it worshipping God. But remember heaven is a never-ending Sabbath. The inhabitants never cease singing the praise of the Lamb. How could an unholy person find pleasure in this?

Could you delight to meet David, Paul, and John after a life spent in doing the very things they spoke against? Would you find much in common with them? Above all, could you rejoice to meet Jesus, the crucified one, face to face after clinging to the sins for which He died? Would you stand before Him with confidence, and join in the cry, "Surely this is our God; we trusted in Him and He saved us," (Isaiah 25:9)? I think these words would get stuck in the unholy person's mouth with shame, and his only desire would be to be cast out.

Heaven would be a miserable place for the unholy. People may vaguely say they hope to go to heaven, but they don't know what they are saying. To reach the holiday of glory, we must pass through the training school of grace. We must be heavenly minded, with heavenly tastes in this present life, or we will never find ourselves in heaven.

Before I go further, here are some words of application. Are you holy, today? Do you know anything of the holiness of which I speak?

These questions ought to make us consider our ways and search our hearts. It should send us to prayer. You may try to put me off by saying that I think too much about these things. But the lost souls in hell do the same. The great question is not what you think and what you feel, but what you do.

You may say that holiness is only possible for the great saints, but that is not what scripture says. First John 3:3 says that every man with hope in Christ purifies himself. It may seem impossible to be that holy and still work in this life. But it can be done. With Christ on your side, nothing is impossible. Christian history is full of examples of ordinary people living a holy life. You may object to the holy life because you would stand out. So it should. Christ's true servants are always unlike the world around them.

With this standard, it seems that very few will be saved. This is precisely what Jesus told us in the Sermon on the Mount. He always said that people must take up their cross and be ready to sacrifice everything if they would be His disciples. Like all other areas of life, that which costs nothing is worth nothing.

I ask another question. Do you feel the importance of holiness as much as you should? I greatly doubt whether it holds the place it deserves in the thoughts of some of the Lord's people. We are apt to overlook the doctrine of growth in grace, and not sufficiently consider how far a person may go in a profession of faith and be dead in God's sight. We had better think more about the churches of Sardis and Laodicea than we do.

I don't want to make an idol of holiness. But I wish sanctification was given more thought. It is sometimes forgotten that God married justification and sanctification. They are distinct and different but one is never without the other. Don't tell me you're justified, unless you have some marks of sanctification. Don't boast of Christ's work for you, unless you can show the Spirit's work in you. Don't think that Christ and the Spirit can ever be divided. Let us try to continually keep this text in view "Follow holiness, without which no man shall see the Lord."

I wish there wasn't such a sensitivity on the subject of holiness in some believers. A person might think it was a dangerous subject, because of how cautiously it is handled. Yet surely when we have exalted Christ as "the way, the truth, and the life," we cannot err in speaking strongly about what should be the character of His people.

I don't say that I am better than other people. But you cannot read the Bible without desiring to see believers more spiritual, more holy, and more heavenly minded. I want to see among believers a clear separation from the world. Is it not true that we need a higher standard of personal holiness? Where is our patience? Where is our zeal? Our love? Our works? Our silver has become dross. Wake up and sleep no more. "Let us lay aside every weight and sin that doth easily beset us."

A word of advice to all who desire to be holy, begin with Christ. You will make no progress until you feel your sin and run to Him. He is the root and beginning of holiness. To His people, Christ is not only wisdom and righteousness but also sanctification. People sometimes try to make themselves holy first, yet they keep becoming worse. As Traill said, "Wisdom out of Christ is damning folly; righteousness out of

Christ is guilt and condemnation; sanctification out of Christ is filth and sin; redemption out of Christ is bondage and slavery."

Do you want to attain holiness? Then go to Christ and wait for nothing or nobody. Don't get ready. Just go and cling to Him. Nothing can be done until we go to Christ. Holiness is His special gift to His people. It is the work He carries on in their hearts by the Spirit. Holiness comes not through genetics, or by the will of the flesh, but from Christ. It is the result of a vital union with Him.

Would you remain holy? Then abide in Christ. He says, "If a man remains in me and I in him, he will bear much fruit; apart from me you can do nothing," (John 15:5). All the fullness dwells in Christ, a full supply for all a believer's wants.

> May we know these things first hand. May we feel the importance of holiness far more than we have. May our years be holy and then they will be happy ones. Whether we live or die, may both be unto the Lord. When He comes for us, may we be found in peace, without spot and blameless.

3. Without Christ

"…you were separate from Christ…" Ephesians 2:12

This text describes the state of the Ephesians before they became Christians. It also describes the state of every unconverted person. There is not a more miserable state. It is bad enough to be without money, health or friends: but to be without Christ is far worse.

The expression "without Christ" is not my own, but was written under the inspiration of the Holy Spirit through Paul. The Ephesians had been buried in idolatry and heathenism. But this he completely passes over. Their former state could be summed up by saying, "At that time you were without Christ," (Ephesians 2:12). Now what does the expression mean?

A person is "without Christ" when he has no head knowledge of Him. Millions are in this condition. They don't know who Christ is or what He has done. Those who have never heard the Gospel come under this description, but they aren't alone. The large percent of the people in your country today have no idea about Christ. Ask them about Jesus Christ and you will be astounded at the gross darkness which covers their minds. You will find that they can tell you no more about Jesus than about Mohammed. About such people, only one thing can be said: They are "without Christ."

Some modern pastors do not take this view. They tell us that all people, however ignorant while they live, shall be taken to heaven when they die by Christ's mercy! Such views cannot be reconciled to God's Word. It is written, "Now this is eternal life: that they may know you, the only true God and Jesus Christ whom you have sent,"

(John 17: 3). It is one of the marks of the wicked that they don't know God (2 Thessalonians 1:8). An unknown Christ is no savior.

What is the state of the heathen after death? How shall the native who never heard the Gospel be judged? These questions we may safely leave alone. We may rest assured that, "Will not the judge of all the earth do right," (Genesis 18:25). But we must not fly in the face of Scripture. According to the Bible, to be ignorant is to be "without Christ."

A person is "without Christ" when he has no heart-faith in Him as his Savior. It is possible to know all about Christ and not put your trust in Him. There are multitudes who can tell you about Christ. They have it engraved in their memories: but that knowledge doesn't change their lives. They put their trust in things other than Christ. They hope to go to heaven because they are moral or religious. But as for an active faith in God's mercy through Christ, they know nothing at all. And of these people it can be said: they are "without Christ."

Some believers tell us that all baptized people are members of Christ by virtue of their baptism. Others say that where there is head knowledge, we have no right to question a person's relationship with Christ. To these views I have only one answer. The Bible says that a person is joined to Christ upon believing. Head knowledge is no proof that we are joined to Christ. The devil knows Christ, but he is not saved. God knows who are His from all eternity. But man knows nothing of anyone's justification until he believes. The question is, "Do you believe?" "Whoever believes in the Son has eternal life, but whoever rejects the Son will not see life, for God's wrath remains on Him," (John 3:36). According to the Bible, to be without faith is to be "Without Christ."

A person is "without Christ" when the Holy Spirit's work cannot be seen in his life. There are myriads of professing Christians who know nothing of a changed heart. They will tell you that they are Christians, go to church somewhat regularly, and they would be offended if their Christianity was doubted. But where is the Holy Spirit seen in their lives? Who is reflected in their tastes and habits? They know nothing of the renewing, sanctifying work of the Holy Spirit. They are yet dead to God. And the only thing to be said is that they are "without Christ."

Few will admit this. The vast majority will tell you that it is extreme to require so much from Christians, and that it is impossible to keep up the high standard in this world. To all this I ask, "What does scripture say?" It is written, "...unless you change and become like little children, you will never enter the kingdom of heaven. You, however, are controlled not by the sinful nature but by the Spirit, if the Spirit of God lives in you," (Matthew 18:3, Romans 8:9). The scripture cannot be broken. To be without the Spirit is to be "without Christ."

These statements may seem severe. But aren't they God's truth as revealed in Scripture? I desire above all things to magnify the riches of God's mercy to sinners. I long to tell all mankind what a wealth of mercy and loving kindness there is laid up in God's heart for all who will seek it. But I cannot find that ignorant, unbelieving, and unconverted people have any apart in Christ! If I am wrong, I shall be grateful to anyone who will show me. But I must stand fast on these positions, lest I be found guilty of handling God's Word deceitfully. I dare not be silent, lest the blood of souls be required at my hands. The person without knowledge, without faith, and without the Holy Spirit is "without Christ."

Another point for consideration is: What is the actual condition of a person "without Christ"?

I can easily imagine someone thinking, "So what if I am without Christ? I am no worse than others. I hope God will be merciful." With God's help, I will show you that you are sadly deceived. "Without Christ" all will not be right but desperately wrong.

For one thing, to be without Christ is to be without God. Paul plainly told the Ephesians this when he ended the sentence which begins, "You are without Christ," with "you are without God in the world." God is the most pure, holy, glorious spiritual being. It is evident that human nature is corrupt, sinful, and defiled. How can any person draw near to God for comfort? How can he look up to Him with confidence and not feel afraid? There must be a mediator between God and man. That mediator is Christ.

Who are you to talk of God's mercy and love separate of Christ? There is no such love and mercy recorded in Scripture. Know that God, outside of Christ, is a consuming fire (Hebrews 12:29). He is rich in mercy, but His mercy is inseparable from the mediation of His beloved Son Jesus It must flow through Him. It is written, "I am the way, the truth and the life. No one comes to the Father except through me," (John 14:6). Without Christ, we are without God.

To be without Christ is to be without peace. Every person has a conscience which must be satisfied before he can be truly happy. As long as this conscience is asleep, he gets along fairly well. But as soon as it wakes up, he begins to think of past sins, present failings, and future judgment. Many things are tried but the only peace giver to a troubled conscience is the blood of Jesus. A clear understanding of Christ's death as the payment of our debt to God and its transference to man when he believes is the grand secret of inward peace. It meets every craving of conscience, answers every accusation and calms every fear. Jesus said, "I have told you these things, so that in me you may have peace. In this world you will have trouble. But take heart! I have overcome the world," (John 16:33). We have peace through the blood of His cross. But "without Christ," we are without peace.

To be without Christ, we are without hope. Almost everyone thinks he has hope. Yet there are so few who can give "reason for the hope" that is in them (1 Peter 3:15). So much hope is nothing better than a vague, empty feeling, which in the hour of death will prove impotent to comfort or to save. There is but one hope that has roots, life and strength. That is the hope which is built on Christ's work on the cross. This hope will stand examination and meet every inquiry. Search it through, and no flaw will be found. All other hopes are worthless. Like summer-dried fountains, they fail people just when they are needed. There is no good hope without Christ, and "without Christ" is to have "no hope" (Ephesians 2:12).

To be without Christ is to be without heaven. Not only is there no entrance into heaven, but without Christ, there could be no happiness in being there. A person without a Savior and Redeemer could never feel at home in heaven. He would feel that he had no lawful right to be there. Amidst pure and holy angels, under the eyes of a pure and holy God, he would bow his head with shame.

Who are you who dreams of a heaven in which Christ has no place? In every Biblical description of heaven, the presence of Christ is one essential feature "In the midst of the throne," says John, "stood a Lamb that was slain," (Revelation 5:6, 22:3, 21:22, 23, 7:17, 19:9). A heaven without Christ would not be the heaven of the Bible. To be without Christ is to be without heaven.

So to be without Christ is to be without life, without strength, without safety, without foundation, without a friend in heaven, and without righteousness.

If this life were all, it would be a waste to trouble yourself with such thoughts. But your conscience tells you that there is a judgment beyond the grave. This subject demands the attention of every one. It lies at the root of our salvation. To be "without Christ" is to be miserable. Now I ask every reader to examine yourself and find out your precise condition. Are you without Christ?

Do not allow life to pass away without some self-examination. You cannot continue as you are. A day must come when everyday living will end. And where will you be then, if you have lived and died without thought about your soul? Oh remember, it is better to be without money, health, and friends, than to be without Christ.

If you have lived without Christ, I invite you to change your course today. Seek the Lord Jesus, while He may be found. He is sitting at God's right hand, able to save everyone who comes to Him. Seek Christ without delay.

If you are Christ's friend, I exhort you to be thankful. Awake to a deeper sense of the infinite mercy of having an Almighty Savior, a home that is eternal, and a Friend that never dies! What a comfort to think that we have in Christ something that we can never loose.

Awake to a deeper sorrow for those who are without Christ. We are often reminded of the many whose physical needs are not being met. Let us help them as we can. But let us never forget that those without Christ are in a worse state. Have we relatives and neighbors without Christ? Let us feel for them, pray for them, strive to share the Gospel with them. Let us be relentless in our efforts to bring them to Christ.

The night comes when none can work. Happy are they who live under the abiding conviction that to be "in Christ" is peace, safety, and happiness; and that to be "without Christ" is to be on the brink of destruction.

4. Thirst Relieved

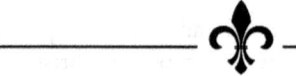

"On the last and greatest day of the festival, Jesus stood and said in a loud voice, "Let anyone who is thirsty come to me and drink. Whoever believes in me, as Scripture has said, rivers of living water will flow from within them." John 7:37-38

This text contains one of Christ's golden sayings. All Scripture is given by the inspiration of God, but some are particularly rich and full. In order to see the whole force and beauty of the text, we must remember its place, time, and occasion.

The PLACE was Jerusalem, the metropolis of Judaism, and the stronghold of the priests and scribes. The OCCASION was the Feast of Tabernacles. The great annual feast in which every Jew who could would go to the temple according to the law. The TIME was "the last day of the feast" when all the ceremonies were drawing to a close. The water, which was drawn from the fountain of Siloam, had been solemnly poured on the altar, and the worshippers were getting ready to leave.

At this critical moment, Jesus "stood" on a prominent place and spoke to the assembled crowds. I don't doubt that He read their hearts and saw their aching consciences and unsatisfied minds. They were leaving with nothing from their blind teachers, and carrying away a barren recollection of pompous actions. He pitied them and cried aloud, "If any man thirst, let him come unto me and drink." I doubt if this was all our Lord said. I suspect this was the beginning of His address, but this was the first sentence on His lips. If anyone wants living, satisfying water, let him come unto ME.

There are three points in this great saying of our Lord to which I direct your attention.

Case Supposed: "If any man thirst."

Remedy Proposed: "Let him come unto Me and drink."

Promise Held Out: "He that believes on Me ... "

Each point concerns us all. I will expound on each one.

The case supposed: Our Lord says, "If any man thirst."

Bodily thirst is notoriously the most painful sensation a person can experience. Ask anyone who has endured extreme thirst and you will find that the testimony is unvarying: there is nothing as unbearable as thirst.

But if bodily thirst is so painful, how much more so is spiritual thirst? Physical suffering is a minor thing, even in this world, compared to the suffering of the mind. To feel the burden of unforgiven sin and not know where to turn for relief; this is the highest degree of pain. It is the pain which drinks up soul and spirit. This is the thirst of which our Lord is speaking. It is a thirst after forgiveness and peace with God. It is the craving of an awakened conscience wanting satisfaction and not knowing where to find it.

This is the thirst which the Jews felt when Peter preached to them on the day of Pentecost. This is the thirst many of the great servants of God seem to have felt when light first shined on their minds. In fact, all of us know this thirst. Living as we do in a dying world, knowing that there is a world beyond the grave, feeling our own depravity and longing for a way out: we feel a "thirst" for a sense of peace with the living God.

Yet nothing proves so conclusively the fallen nature as the common lack of spiritual appetite! The symptom of physical death is the loss of all feeling. There is no clearer sign of dead soul than utter absence of spiritual thirst. For money, power, and pleasure, the vast majority are now intensely thirsting. The competition is fierce and unceasing for these corruptible crowns! But few thirst for eternal life. No wonder the natural person in Scripture is called dead, sleeping, and blind. No wonder that we need a second birth.

Do you feel the burden of sin and long for peace with God? Thank God. A sense of sin is the first stone laid by the Holy Spirit when He builds a Spiritual temple. Light was the first thing called into being in the material creation (Genesis 1:3). Light about our own state is the first work in the new creation. Thirsting soul, His Kingdom is near you. It is not when we begin to feel good about ourselves, but when we feel bad that we take our first steps toward heaven. As Elihu said in the book of

Job, "I have sinned and perverted what is right, but I did not get what I deserved. He redeemed my soul from going down to the pit, and I will live to enjoy the light," (Job 33:27, 28). Don't be ashamed of spiritual thirst. Rather lift your head and pray that God would continue the work He has begun.

I now pass to the remedy proposed: "If anyone thirst, let him come unto Me and drink."

There is a grand simplicity about this little sentence. The literal meanings are plain to a child, yet it is rich in spiritual meaning. It solves a problem which the great philosophers could never solve: "How can one have peace with God?" Christ is the Fountain of living water which God has graciously provided for thirsting souls. From Him flows an abundant stream for all who travel through the wilderness of this world. In Him there is an endless supply of all that people can ever need.

This rich provision Christ has bought for us at the price of His own precious blood. To open this wondrous fountain, He bore our sins in His own body on the cross. He, who knew no sin, was made sin for us that we might be made righteous (1 Peter 2:24, 3:18; 2 Corinthians 5:21). And now He is appointed to be the Giver of living water to those who thirst. It is His office to receive sinners, and His pleasure to give them pardon, life, and peace. The words of the text are a proclamation He makes to all, "If anyone thirst, let him come unto Me and drink."

I offer some caution and advice about the Fountain of living water. If you thirst and want relief you must come to Christ Himself. Going to church and obeying the Ten Commandments is not sufficient. You will only thirst again. You must have personal dealings with Christ; all else in religion is worthless without Him. Christ's hand alone can take the burdens off our backs and give us freedom.

He who thirsts and wants relief must actually come to Christ. It is not enough to intend. The road to Hell is paved with good intentions. What if the prodigal son had been content with saying, "How many hired servants of my father have bread enough, and I perish with hunger! I hope someday to return home." He might have forever remained with the swine. It was when he stood and came to his father that his father ran to meet him. Like him, we must not only "come to ourselves," but we must actually come to Christ. He that thirsts and wants to come to Christ must remember that simple faith is the one thing required. By all means let him come with a penitent, broken, and contrite heart, but faith is the only hand that can carry living water to our lips. It is written, "whoever believes in him shall not perish but have eternal life," (John 3:15-16).

How simple this remedy for thirst appears, yet how hard it is to persuade some people to receive it. Tell them to do something great, and they will try. Tell them to throw away all idea of merit and works and come to Christ as empty sinners, and they will run away with disdain. But, simple as it seems, it is the only cure for man's spiritual disease and the only bridge from earth to heaven. Everyone must drink of this water. For centuries, people have labored to find some other medicine for weary consciences, but they have labored in vain. Thousands, after blistering their hands hewing out "broken cisterns that cannot hold water," (Jeremiah 2:13), have come back to the old Fountain and have confessed in their last moments that in Christ alone, is true peace.

This simple remedy for thirst is the root of all God's greatest servants. They were all people who came to Christ daily by faith. People from all denominations have borne uniform testimony to the value of the Fountain of Life. Separated and contentious as they sometimes were in life, they have been united in their deaths. All have clung to the cross of Christ and gloried in nothing but the precious blood and the Fountain open for all sin.

How thankful we ought to be that we live in a land where the remedy for spiritual thirst is known. We do not realize our great privileges. Turn to the pages of Plato and see how he groped after light like one blindfolded. Read of the human sacrifices in Africa and the self-imposed tortures of the Hindu and remember that these are the result of an unquenched thirst and an unsatisfied desire to get near God.

The promise is held out to all who come to Christ. "Whoever believes on Me, as the Scripture has said, streams of living water will flow from within him."

In everyday life, promises lie at the bottom of nearly all human transactions. The vast majority of people are acting every day on the faith of promises. In fact, promises, faith in them, and actions based on them are the backbone of most of our dealings. But there is one big difference between the promises of man and the promises of God. The promises of man are not always fulfilled. With the best intentions, we cannot always keep our word. The promises of God are certain to be kept. Nothing can prevent His doing what He said. The Bible is full of the miraculous fulfillment of promises. Whatever He promises, He is certain to perform.

Most of our Lord's promises refer specially to the person to whom they are addressed. This promise is somewhat unique for it is a general invitation to all who thirst. It is figurative, and I will try to show what it conveys.

For one thing, I believe our Lord meant that they who come to Him by faith shall receive an abundant supply of everything they can desire for the relief of their souls. The Spirit will give to them a sense of pardon, peace, and hope. My own belief is that whenever a person really comes to Christ by faith, he finds this promise fulfilled. He may have many doubts about his condition, but the newest believer has the river of living water which began to run in his heart when he came to Christ.

But this verse contains more. Those who come to Him by faith will also become a source of blessing to the souls of others. This is an important part of our Lord's promise. Many live and die in the faith who are not aware that they have benefited another soul. But I believe on the Judgment Day, when the secret history of all Christians is revealed, it will show that the full meaning of this promise has never failed. I doubt if there will be a believer who has not been a channel through whom the Spirit has conveyed saving grace. Even the thief on the cross, short as the time was after his repentance, has been a source of blessing to thousands of souls.

Some believers are "rivers of living water" while they live. Their conversations are a means by which the water of life has flowed in the hearts of others. Such were the Apostles who wrote no books and only preached the Word.

Some believers are "rivers of living water" when they die. Their courage in facing the king of terrors, their boldness in painful suffering, their peace on the edge of the grave have set thousands thinking and led hundreds to repent and believe.

Some believers are "rivers of living water" long after their deaths. Their books and writings continue to impact lives long after the hands that wrote them are moldering in the dust. These servants of God probably do more by their books than they did with their words when they were alive.

Finally, some believers are "rivers of living water" by the beauty of their daily conduct and behavior. There are many quiet, gentle, and consistent Christians who exercise a deep influence on those around them. They "win without a word," (1 Peter 3:1). Their love, patience, and unselfishness sow seeds of thought in many minds.

Hold to our Lord's promise and never forget it. Don't think for a moment that your soul is the only soul that will be saved if you come to Christ by faith. You may be the means of bringing many to Christ. You may die without seeing the conversions, but never doubt that few go to heaven alone.

And now let me ask you a question. Have you felt any spiritual thirst? People may go for years attending church and yet never feel their sins. The cares of this world and the love of pleasure choke the good seed every Sunday. Yet I don't give up on anyone, while he is alive. That grand old bell in St. Paul's Cathedral, London, which has announced the hours of so many years, is seldom heard during the business hours. The roar of traffic deadens its sound. But when the daily work is over and quiet reigns, the case is altered. As the bell strikes the night hours, thousands hear it who never heard it during the day.

And so is the case of many in regards to their souls. Now in the rush of everyday life, I fear the voice of your conscience is often stifled. The time may come when you are forced to be still, left with nothing but to examine your soul. In that day, I trust that you will thirst and come to Christ for relief.

But do you feel anything now? Is your conscience awake and working? Are you spiritually thirsting and longing for relief? Then hear the invitation: "If anyone thirst"—no matter who, "If anyone thirst, let him come to Christ and drink." Accept this invitation without delay and wait for nothing and nobody. You might wait until it is too late. The fountain is now open: but it may soon be closed forever. Don't say that you don't know how to come and that you must wait for more light. Will a tired person say that he is too tired to lie down? Oh cast away vain excuses! The fountain is not yet closed. Jesus invites you. It is enough that you feel thirsty and desire to be saved. Come to Christ.

If you have come to Christ and found relief, come nearer still. The closer you are to Christ, the more comfort you will feel. The more you daily live by the Fountain, the more you shall feel in yourself "a spring of water welling up to eternal life," (John 4:14). You will not only bless yourself but the lives of others.

In this evil world, you may not feel comfortable. But remember, you cannot have two heavens. Perfect happiness is yet to come. The devil is not yet bound. When He comes again we will be completely satisfied. We will remember all our journey on which we were led and see the need of everything that happened. Above all, we will wonder how they could have lived so long without Christ, and how we could hesitate in coming to Him.

There is a pass in Scotland called Glencroe, which beautifully illustrates what heaven will be to the souls who come to Christ. The road is long and steep with many little turns. But at the top, there is a stone by the wayside with these simple words inscribed on it "Rest, and be thankful." Those words describe the feeling with which we will enter heaven. We shall cease from our weary journey and sit down in God's kingdom. We will look back on our lives with thankfulness and see the perfect wisdom of every step in the steep ascent by which we were led. We will forget the toil of the upward journey in the glorious rest. In this world, our sense of rest in Christ is feeble and impartial. We hardly seem to taste the living water. But "when I awake, I will be satisfied," (Psalm 17:15). We will drink out of the river of His pleasures and thirst no more.

There is a passage from an old writer which throws some light on these points, so I present it in its entirety. It has done me good, and I think it might benefit others.

> When a person is awakened and asks, "What shall I do to be saved?" (Acts 16:30-31), we have the apostolic answer: "Believe on the Lord Jesus Christ and you shall be saved." This answer is so old that it seems out of date, but it is always fresh and new. It is the only resolution for this case of conscience. No wit of man will ever find a flaw in it, or devise a better answer. This alone can heal the wound of an awakened conscience.
>
> Let this person seek resolution and relief in some masters of the Law. They would say, "Repent and mourn for you sins and leave them: and God will have mercy on you." The poor man responds, "My heart is hard and I cannot repent right. I find my heart more vile than when I was secured in sin." This person knows nothing of Christ's qualifications. His definition of sincere obedience follows: "Obedience is the work of a living man, and sincerity is only in a renewed soul." Sincere obedience is as impossible to a dead sinner as perfect obedience is. The right answer to be given to an awakened sinner is: "Believe on the Lord Jesus Christ and you shall be saved." Tell him who Jesus is and what He has done. Plainly tell him the history and mystery of the Gospel.
>
> If he asks why he should believe on Jesus Christ, tell him that he has an indispensable need for it. For without believing on Him, he must perish eternally.

Tell him of God's gracious offer. Christ and all His redemption. Tell of God's express commandment (1 John 3:23) to believe on Christ's name. Tell him that there is no medium between faith and unbelief, that believing on Jesus for salvation is more pleasing to God than obedience of His law.

If he asks what he is to believe, tell him that he is to believe God's record concerning Christ (1 John 5:10-12). This record is that God gave us eternal life in His Son Jesus Christ: and that all who believe this report in their hearts shall be saved (Romans 10.9-11). He is to believe to be justified (Galatians 2:16).

If he still thinks that believing is hard, this can easily be resolved. Ask him what it is that makes it difficult to believe. Is it unwillingness to be saved? This he will surely deny. Is it a distrust of the truth of the Gospel? This he will dare not. If he says that he cannot believe on Jesus Christ because of the difficulty of faith, you must tell him that believing in Jesus is no work, but a resting on Jesus Christ. You must tell him that this pretense is as unreasonable as if a man, wearied with a journey, should argue "I am so tired that I am not able to lie down."

The poor wearied sinner can never believe on Jesus until he finds he can do nothing for himself. In his first believing, he asks for salvation as a man hopeless and helpless in himself. The Lord will convey faith, joy, and peace by believing.

5. Christ is All

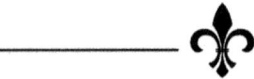

"Set your minds on things above, not on earthly things." Colossians 3:2

These words are few but they contain great things. They are the essence and substance of Christianity. If our hearts accept them, then it is well with our souls. If not, we have much to learn.

I purposely close with a section on this text, because Christ is the mainspring of doctrinal and practical Christianity. A right knowledge of Christ is essential to a right knowledge of sanctification and justification. Those who follow after holiness will make no progress unless Christ has His rightful place. I began with a plain statement about sin, I will now end with a plain statement about Christ. First of all, Christ is all and in all the counsels of God concerning man. There was a time when this earth did not exist and man was unknown. And where was Christ then?

Christ was "with God" and "was God" (John 1:1). He was the beloved Son of the Father (John 17:5, 24; Proverbs 8:23). Even then He was the Savior: "He was chosen before the creation of the world, but was revealed in these last times for your sake" (1 Peter 1:20).

Then this earth was created in its present order. Everything was called into being and made out of chaos. Last of all, man was formed out of the dust of the ground. Where was Christ then?

According to Scripture, "Through Him all things were made; without Him nothing was made that has been made" (John 1:3). Then sin entered the world. Adam and Eve ate the forbidden fruit and fell. They forfeited the friendship of God, and became guilty, helpless, and hopeless sinners. Sin became a barrier between themselves and their holy Father. And where was Christ then?

On that day, He was revealed to our trembling parents as the only hope of salvation. The day they fell, they were told that a Saviour born of a woman would overcome the devil and win for sinful man eternal life (Genesis 3:15). Christ was held up as the true light of the world. By Him all saved souls have entered heaven, and without Him none has ever escaped hell.

Then came a time when the world seemed buried in ignorance of God. The nations had forgotten the God that made them. The great empires had done nothing but spread superstition and idolatry. The poets, historians, and philosophers had only proved that they had no right knowledge of God and that man left to himself, was utterly corrupt (1 Corinthians 1:21). Except for a few despised Jews, the whole world was dead in ignorance and sin.

And what did Christ do then? He left the glory He had from all eternity and came down into the world to provide salvation. He took our nature and was born a man. As a man, He perfectly did the will of God. He suffered on the cross God's wrath for us. He rose again and now sits at God's right hand, waiting until His enemies will be made His footstool. And here He sits, offering salvation to all who will come to Him, interceding for all who believe in Him.

Someday sin will be cast out from this world, and there will be a time of restitution. There will be a new heaven and a new earth, where righteousness dwells and the earth will be full of the knowledge of the Lord (Romans 3:21; 2 Peter 3:13; Isaiah 11:9).

And where will Christ be then? He will be King and Judge. To Him, every knee will bow and every tongue confess that He is Lord. His dominion will be everlasting and His Kingdom will not be destroyed (Matthew 24:30; Revelation 11:15; Psalm 2:8; Philippians 2:10-11). In that day, everyone will be judged according to their works (Revelation 20:13; Daniel 12:2). And He will righteously distribute justice (John 5:22; Matthew 25:32; 2 Corinthians 5:10).

If you don't regard Christ highly, you are not like God. You think it is enough to give Christ a little honor, a little reverence, and a little respect. But in all the eternal counsels of God the Father, Christ is "all." As scripture says, "He who does not honor the Son does not honor the Father, who sent Him" (John 5:23).

Understand that "Christ is all" in the Bible. In both testaments, Christ is found, vaguely at the beginning, more clearly in the middle, and completely at the end, but substantially everywhere. Christ's sacrifice for sinners, His Kingdom, and His future glory are the light we must use to read scripture. Christ's cross and crown are the clues we must use to find our way through scripture mysteries. Some complain that they do not understand the Bible, and the reason is very simple. They do not use the key.

It was Christ to whom Abel looked when he offered a better sacrifice. He showed his knowledge of vicarious sacrifice and his faith in an atonement. It was Christ to whom Abraham looked when he dwelt in tents in the land of promise. He believed that from his family all the nations of the earth should be blessed. By faith he saw Christ's day and was glad (John 8:56).

It was Christ crucified who was set forth in every Old Testament sacrifice. He was the substance of the ceremonial law. The continual shedding of blood, the high priest, the scapegoat, and the day of atonement: all were pictures of Christ and His work.

It was Christ who the prophets spoke of. They saw through tinted lenses. Sometimes they focused on His sufferings, and other times His glory. They did not always make a distinction between His first and second comings. Like two candles in a straight line, they sometimes saw both comings at the same time. But Jesus was the focus of their minds and writings.

It is Christ who fills the New Testament. The Gospels are Christ living and speaking among men. The Acts are Christ preached and proclaimed. The Epistles are Christ explained and exalted. From first to last there is the one name of Jesus Christ.

Ask yourself what the Bible means to you. Is it a book that contains nothing more than good moral precepts and sound advice? Or have you found Christ? If not, you are like the person who studies the solar system without studying the sun, which is the center of it all. No wonder you find your Bible dull!

In another sense, Christ is all in the lives of all true Christians. Don't misunderstand me. I believe that there is perfect harmony in the three persons of the Trinity in bringing anyone to glory. The same three who said at the beginning. "Let us create," said also, "Let us redeem and save," at the same time. Scripture proves that the Trinity decided that Christ should be prominently exalted in the manner of saving souls. Christ's atoning death on the cross is the great cornerstone of salvation. Christ is the only meeting place between God and man.

I want you to clearly understand that in saying, "Christ is all," I do not mean to shut out the work of the Father and the Spirit. What I do mean follows.

Christ is all in a sinner's justification before God. Through Him alone can we have peace with a Holy God. By Him alone can "We have boldness and access with confidence by faith in Him." In Him can God be just and justify the ungodly (Ephesians 3:12; Romans 3:26).

How can any mortal come before God? What can we bring as a plea for acquittal? Our hollow works can do nothing to appease God's righteousness. How can we come before God? We must come in the name of Jesus alone. Our only plea can be, "Christ died on the cross for the ungodly and I trust Him. Christ died for me and I believe on Him." Christ's robe of righteousness is the only robe which can cover us and enable us to stand in heaven without shame. The name of Jesus is the only name by which we can enter through the gate of eternal glory.

Do you believe that you can reach Heaven by hastily saying at the end, "Lord have mercy on me" without Christ? Or do you believe that by living a good life you can pass through heaven's gates? Friends, you are wrong. The blood of Christ is the only mark that can save us from destruction. We must go to heaven as beggars, saved by free grace, simply as believers in Jesus.

Do you want to be saved? To you I say, "Come to Christ and He shall save you. Cast the burden of your soul on Him. Fear not: only believe." In Christ we find redemption, closeness, perfection, and worth..

But Christ is also all in sanctification. I don't undervalue the work of the Spirit, but no one is ever holy until he comes to Christ and is united to Him. Until then his efforts are useless. First you must be joined to Christ, and then you shall be holy. Christ is the great root from which every believer must draw his strength. A believer must not only "receive Christ Jesus the Lord," but "walk in Him and be rooted and built up in Him" (Colossians 2:6-7).

Would you be holy? Then Christ is the Manna you must daily eat and the Rock from which you daily drink. Would you be holy? Then you must be ever looking unto Jesus. Focusing on Him, you will become like Him.

The true way to be strong is to realize our weakness and to let Christ be our all. The true way to grow in grace is to rely on Christ for every minute's need. We should be able to say, "I have been crucified with Christ and I no longer live, but Christ lives in me. The life I live in the body, I live by faith in the Son of God, who loved me and gave Himself for me" (Galatians 2:20).

I pity those who try to be holy without Christ! Your labor is all in vain. You must come to Christ first, and He shall give you His sanctifying Spirit. Learn to say with Paul, "I can do everything through him who gives me strength" (Philippians 4:13).

Christ is all in comforting His people. Saved souls have many sorrows. They have a body weak and frail. They have trials and losses to bear like others, often more. They have the world to oppose, persecutions to endure, and a death to die.

What enables a believer to bear all this? Nothing but the encouragement from being united with Christ (Philippians 2:1). Jesus is the brother born for adversity. He alone can comfort His people. He can be touched with the feeling of their infirmities, for He suffered Himself (Hebrews 4:15). He knows what sorrow and pain are. He knows how to soothe the wounds of the spirit, how to fill up empty hearts and mend broken ones. There is no sympathy like that of Christ. In all our afflictions, He is afflicted. As David once said, "When anxiety was great within me, your consolation brought joy to my soul" (Psalms 94:19).

Oh, you who want unfailing comfort, turn to Christ! In Him alone there is no failure. Every human relationship will bring disappointment but no one was ever disappointed in Christ.

Christ is all also in a Christian's hope in the future. Most people hold some kind of hope for their souls. But the hopes of the majority are nothing but vain fantasies with no solid foundation. Only a sincere Christian can give a reasonable account for the hope that is in him. And what is this hope? It is that Jesus Christ is coming again. He's coming to wipe away every tear and to gather His family that they may be forever with Him. Why is a believer patient? Because he expects his Lord's soon return. He knows that time is short. His treasure is in heaven and his good things are yet to come. Christ is coming and that is enough (Hebrews 10:37). This is a "blessed hope!" (Titus 2:13). Now is the scattering, then the gathering. Now is the time for sowing, then the harvest. Now the cross, then the crown.

One last thing, Christ will be all in Heaven. I don't have much to say on this point because I can't describe things unseen and a world unknown. But I know for sure that all who reach heaven will find that there also, "Christ is all." Jesus will fill the eyes of all who enter glory.

The praise of the Lord Jesus will be the eternal song of all the inhabitants of heaven. They will say, "Worthy is the Lamb who was slain, to receive power and wealth and wisdom and strength and honor and glory and praise!" (Revelation 5:12-13). The service of the Lord Jesus will be the eternal occupation of all the inhabitants of heaven. We will finally serve Him without distraction or weariness. His presence will be the everlasting enjoyment of the inhabitants of heaven. We shall see

His face, hear His voice, and speak with Him as friend with friend. His presence will satisfy all our wants (Psalm 17:15; Revelation 2:44).

What a sweet and glorious home heaven will be to those who have loved Jesus in sincerity! Here we live by faith in Him, and find peace even though we don't see Him. There we will see Him face to face. But how unfit for heaven are those who manifest no saving faith and no real acquaintance with Christ. You give Christ no honor, have no communion with Him, and do not love Him. What could you do in heaven? It would be no place for you. Its joys would be no joys for you. Its employments would be weariness and a burden to your heart. Repent and change before it is too late!

I trust I have shown how deep are the foundations of that little expression, "Christ is all." I have barely scratched the surface of it, yet I have said enough to throw light on the subject. Now I will show the immense importance of the practical conclusions.

Is Christ all? Then learn the utter uselessness of a Christless religion. Too many baptized people practically know nothing about Christ. Their religion consists of a few vague notions and empty expressions. But what do they know practically about Christ? Nothing at all! What experience have they with His work, His blood, and His righteousness? None at all. Yet this is the religion of thousands of people who are called Christians. If this describes you, I warn you that such Christianity will never take you to heaven. It may get you by in the eyes of man, but it will never save your soul. I warn you that all theories about God being merciful without Christ are baseless delusions and empty fantasies. The God of heaven has appointed Christ as the one and only Savior by whom all must be saved. A religion without Christ will never save your soul.

Is Christ all? Then learn the folly of adding anything with Christ in the matter of salvation. There are multitudes of people who profess to honor Christ but in reality do Him great dishonor. They give him a corner of their faith but not the center of their souls. If you have added anything to your faith, then your religion is an offense to God. You are changing God's plan of salvation into one of your own devising. I don't care who teaches it to you, if anything is added to Christ it is wrong.

Is Christ all? Then let all who want to be saved go directly to Christ. There are many who hear of Christ and believe all they are told. But they never seem to get beyond this general acknowledgment. They hope one day to get full benefit of it, but they get no benefits now. If this is you, I warn you that there must be actual faith in Christ or else Christ died in vain as far as you're concerned. Just looking at bread does not satisfy a hungry person. It is not merely knowing and behaving that

Christ is Saviour that saves your soul, unless there are actual transactions between you and Christ.

Hear the advice and act upon it. Stand still no longer. Don't wait for imaginary feelings that never come. Come to Christ as you are. He is the Doctor for sin-sick souls. Talk to Him and tell Him of your wants. Cry to the Lord Jesus for pardon and peace. Don't rest until you have tasted of the Lord's graciousness.

Is Christ all? Let His people deal with Him as if they really believed by leaning on, and trusting Him far more than they already do. Many of the Lord's people live far below their privileges. This is the result of people not making Christ all in all. Now I call on every reader who is a believer to make sure that Christ is really your all in all.

Do you have faith? It is a priceless blessing. But do not make a christ of your faith. Don't rest on it but on Christ. Does the Spirit work in your soul? Thank God for it. But be careful not to make a christ out of the work of the Spirit. Don't rest on the work of the Spirit but on Christ. Have you experienced grace and the inward feelings of religion? Be thankful; thousands have no more religious feelings than a cat or dog. But beware of making a christ of your feelings and sensations! They are uncertain and dependent on our bodies and outward circumstance. Rest only on Christ.

Learn to look more at the great object of faith, Jesus Christ, and to keep your mind dwelling on Him. In doing so, you will see faith, and all the other graces, grow. A skillful archer focuses on the mark, not the arrow.

I fear there is a lot of pride and unbelief still stuck in the hearts of many believers. Few understand how they are indebted to Him. Few can-seem to know the peace, joy, strength, and power to live a godly life which is possible in Christ.

If your conscience convicts you: change your plan and learn to trust Christ more. Christ loves His people to lean on Him, to rest in Him, to call on Him, and to abide in Him. Let us learn and strive to do so more and more. Let us live on, in, and with Christ. In so doing, we shall prove that we fully realize that "Christ is all." Then we shall feel great peace, and attain more of that "holiness without which no man shall see the Lord" (Hebrews 12:14).

Aggressive Christianity

Catherine Booth 1829-1890

With an Introduction
By Lyle W. Dorsett

Abridged version of *Aggressive Christianity* by Catherine Booth. Abridged version originally published by World Wide Publications, 1993, along with Billy Graham Center, Wheaton, Il. Copyright of abridged version and introduction held by Lyle W. Dorsett, used with permission. Scripture quotations are taken from the Holy Bible, King James Version (KJV), in the Public Domain. Artwork in the Public Domain. Taken from *The Short Life of Catherine Booth* by F. de L. Booth-Tucker.

Book Chapters

1. Introduction
   By Lyle W. Dorsett 460
2. Aggressive Christianity..463
   To The Standard of Their Own Religious Life....................................465
   As to Their Duties and Obligations to the World..............................467
3. The World's Need 474
   Our Call to Work for God..475
   We are Called by the Spirit..476
   We Are Called by What He has Done for Us 478
4. Notes..483

1. Introduction
By Lyle W. Dorsett

Raised in a strict English Methodist home where she was encouraged to read the Bible and study Wesleyan hymns daily, Catherine (Kate) Mumford attended worship services regularly and poured considerable energy into the British Christian Temperance movement. All of her religious activity notwithstanding, she had neither inner peace nor assurance of salvation.

In 1845, at age sixteen, Kate Mumford experienced a profound conversion. For some time, this very attractive young woman with slight build, lustrous dark hair, and strikingly beautiful brown eyes, went to bed with her Bible and hymnbook under the pillow. Her fervent prayer was that she might awaken in the morning with a genuine confidence in her salvation. Soon thereafter she woke up one morning, opened her hymnal and read these lines by Charles Wesley:

> My God, I am thine!
> What a comfort divine!
> What a blessing to know
> that my Jesus is mine!

Wesley's words pierced her heart. From that moment on, she was a new creature who gradually knew Jesus Christ better, loved Him more, and grew increasingly burdened to make Him known to others.

Six years later another event changed Kate's life. At a religious gathering in her hometown in Derbyshire, she heard a strong sermon by a twenty-two-year-old preacher named William Booth. Later, the

Catherine Booth 1829-1890 / 461

two of them met socially at a friend's home. Immediately the tall, pale-faced young man with jet-black hair and fiery eyes fell mightily in love with the brilliant, outspoken, and vivacious Kate. She was powerfully drawn to this preacher who was her same age, and soon the two were betrothed and committed to a life of marriage and ministry.

The couple married in 1855, while William served as a traveling evangelist with the New Methodist Connection. In 1861, however, the Methodist leaders in annual conference stripped Booth of his freedom to itinerate as an evangelist. He was told to oversee local congregations and give up the work of evangelism.

When this order was announced from the floor an inflamed Catherine Booth cried, "Never," from the crowded gallery. The devoted wife and mother of four walked out of the conference. Within a few minutes William Booth followed his wife from the meeting hall. Together they vowed to leave the Methodist church and follow God's call to take the Gospel message to England's most impoverished and decadent urban masses.

At age thirty-two, Catherine and William Booth gave up salary and security. On their own, but with a keen sense of the Holy Spirit's guidance, they set out on a pilgrimage that led them into an ambitiously holistic urban ministry. They were determined to tell every drunk, drug addict, prostitute, vagrant, and orphan they could find that Jesus Christ had taken upon Himself the penalty for the sins of everyone who would call upon His name for mercy.

Catherine Booth, like her husband, believed that the earth was embroiled in a mighty spiritual war. Satan had a death grip on the urban poor, but Jesus Christ had come to destroy the work of the evil one. Consequently, Catherine and William set out to break down the gates of hell by telling the captives what Christ Jesus had done for them. Furthermore, they wanted to break the bondage of poverty, addiction, and hopelessness that gripped these helpless city dwellers.

Because of the urgency of the urban crisis, Catherine Booth became an aggressive ally of her husband. She began preaching alongside of William and the men who had joined them. She also invited other women to join the work. By 1878, they founded the Salvation Army. From its ranks, they preached the Good News of the Kingdom of God; and in Jesus Christ's name, they fed the hungry, clothed the poor, housed the widows and orphans, and helped rehabilitate and employ those who had previously been the flotsam and jetsam of society.

The co-founder of the Salvation Army and mother of eight children died in 1890 at the age of sixty-one. During nearly three decades of ministry, God used her to liberate thousands of women and men from the bondage of personal sin and the shackles of urban poverty through an evangelistic organization and holistic ministry that was spreading allover the world.

Catherine Booth also played a key role in establishing the right of women to preach. Furthermore, she helped combat the exploitation of women and children, and she demonstrated that disciples of Jesus Christ could meet the physical needs of people while simultaneously ministering to their lost and broken souls.

Catherine Booth and her husband left the Methodist church because they felt it had grown comfortable and complacent. Indeed, by 1861 many Methodist leaders seemed to be offended by evangelism and appeared to be calloused toward the poor. But Catherine Booth was convinced that she and her husband and all who would join them were commissioned by Christ to proclaim the Good News to the poor. The huddled masses, she believed, comprised a great harvest. What was lacking, however, was an aggressive work force to bundle and bring in the sheaves.

The two messages that follow were preached by Mrs. Booth, as she liked to be addressed, in London in 1880. She agreed to have them published three years later in hopes that indolent Christians would be aroused to go out aggressively into the highways and hedges and compel the perishing masses to come into the Great Feast that God had prepared for them.

These two sermons were originally printed in a little volume of sermons entitled *Aggressive Christianity* (Philadelphia: National Publishing Company for the Promotion of Holiness, 1883). Both messages have been slightly abridged and edited.

Lyle W. Dorsett
Wheaton, Illinois, 1992

2. Aggressive Christianity

"And He said to them, "Go into all the world and preach the gospel to every creature." -Mark 16:15

"So I said, 'Who are You, Lord?' And He said, 'I am Jesus, whom you are persecuting. But rise and stand on your feet; for I have appeared to you for this purpose, to make you a minister and a witness both of the things which you have seen and of the things which I will yet reveal to you. I will deliver you from the Jewish people, as well as from the Gentiles, to whom I now[a] send you, to open their eyes, in order to turn them from darkness to light, and from the power of Satan to God, that they may receive forgiveness of sins and an inheritance among those who are sanctified by faith in Me.'" -Acts 26:15-18

Suppose we could blot out from our minds all knowledge of the history of Christianity from the close of the period described as the Acts of the Apostles; suppose we could detach from our minds all knowledge of the history of Christianity since then, and take the Acts of the Apostles and sit down and calculate what was likely to happen in the world, between then and now. We should have said, if we knew nothing of what has intervened from that time to this, that, no doubt, the world where that spiritual war commenced, would have long since been subjugated to the influence of the Originator and Founder! I say, from reading these Acts, and from observing the spirit which animated the early disciples, and from the way in which everything fell before them, we should have anticipated that ten thousand times greater results would have followed, and, in my judgment, this anticipation would have been perfectly rational and just.

We Christians profess to possess in the Gospel of Christ a mighty lever which, rightly and universally applied, would lift the entire burden of sin and misery from the souls of our fellowmen—a panacea, we believe it to be, for all the moral and spiritual woes of humanity, and in curing their spiritual plagues we should go far to cure their physical plagues also. We all profess to believe this. Christians have professed to believe this for generations gone by, ever since the time of which we have been reading, and yet, look at the world, look at so-called Christian England and America, in this end of the nineteenth century! The great majority of the nations utterly ignoring God, and not even making any pretence of remembering Him one day in a week.

And then, look at the rest of the world. I have frequently been so depressed with this view of things that I have felt as if my heart would break. I don't know how other Christians feel, but I can truly say that "rivers of water do often run down my eyes because men keep not His law," (see Psalm 119:136), and because it seems to me that this dispensation, compared with what God intended it to be, has been, and still is, as great a failure as that which preceded it.

Now, I ask, how is this? I do not for a moment believe that this is in accordance with the purpose of God. Some people have a very convenient way of hiding behind God's purposes, and saying, "Oh! He will do His own will." I wish He did! They say, "You know God's will is done after all." I wish it were! *He* says it is *not* done, and over and over again laments the fact. He wants it to be done, but it is NOT DONE! Again, they say, "It is of no use to stand up and propound theories that are at variance with things as they are." There has been a great deal too much of this, and it has had a very bad effect. The world is in this condition, and yet the Christian church was launched with such purposes, with such promises, and with such prospects, and yet nearly nineteen hundred years have rolled away and here we are. How little has been done, comparatively. What little change has been effected in the habits and dispositions of humankind.

But some of you will say, 'Well, but there is a good deal done." Thank God for that. It would be sad if there were nothing done; but it looks like a drop in the ocean compared with what should have been done. Now I cannot accept any theory which so far reflects upon the love and goodness of God as to make Him to blame for this effeteness of Christianity. And, so far as my influence extends, I will not allow the responsibility and the blame of all this to be rolled back upon God, who so loved the world that He gave His only Son to ignominy and death in order to redeem the world. I do not believe it for a moment.

I believe that the old archenemy has done in this dispensation what he did in former ones—so far circumvented the purposes of God that he has succeeded in bringing about this state of things—in retarding the accomplishment of God's purposes and keeping the world thus largely under his own power and influence. I believe he has succeeded in doing this, as he has succeeded always before, by DECEIVING GOD'S OWN PEOPLE. He has always done so. He has always produced a caricature of God's real thing, and the nearer he can get it to be like the original the more successful his is. He has succeeded in deceiving God's people:

First, AS TO THE STANDARD OF THEIR OWN RELIGIOUS LIFE.

And, *second*, he has succeeded in deceiving them AS TO THEIR DUTIES AND OBLIGATIONS TO THE WORLD.

To The Standard of Their Own Religious Life

He has succeeded, first, in deceiving them as to the standard of their own religious life. He has led the church, nearly as a whole, to receive what I call an Oh-wretched-man-that-I-am religion! He has gotten them to lower the standard which Jesus Christ Himself established in this Book—a standard, not only to be aimed at, but to be attained unto—a standard of victory over sin, the world, the flesh, and the devil, *real, living, reigning, triumphing Christianity*! Satan knew what was the secret of the great success of those early disciples. It was their wholehearted devotion, their absorbing love to Christ, and their utter abnegation of the world. It was their entire absorption in the salvation of their fellowmen and the glory of their God. It was an enthusiastic religion that swallowed them up, and made them willing to become wanderers and vagabonds on the face of the earth-for His sake to dwell in dens and caves, to be torn asunder, and to be persecuted in every form.

It was this degree of devotion before which Satan saw he had no chance. Such people as these, he knew, must ultimately subdue the world. It is not in human nature to stand before that kind of spirit, that amount of love and zeal, and if Christians had only gone on as they began, the glorious prophecy would have been fulfilled. The kingdoms of this world would have become the kingdoms of our Lord and His Christ.

Therefore, the archenemy said, "What must I do? I shall be defeated after all. I shall lose my supremacy as the god of this world. What shall I do? No use to bring in a gigantic system of error, which everybody will see to be error." Oh, dear, no! That has never been Satan's way; but his plan has been to get hold of a good man here and there, who shall creep in, as the Apostle said, unawares, and preach another doctrine, and who shall deceive, if it were possible, the very elect. *And he did it.* He accomplished his design. He gradually lowered the standard of Christian life and character, and though, in every revival, God has raised it again to a certain extent, we have never gotten completely back to the simplicity, purity, and devotion set before us in these Acts of the Apostles and in the Epistles.

And just to the degree that it has approximated thereto, in every age, Satan has encouraged somebody to show that this was too high a standard for human nature, altogether beyond us, and that, therefore, Christians must sit down and just be content to be Oh-wretched-man-that-I-am people to the end of their days. He has deceived the church into a condition that makes one sometimes positively ashamed to hear professing Christians talk: and ashamed, also, that the world should hear them talk. I do not wonder at thoughtful, intelligent men being driven from such Christianity as this. It would have driven me off, if I had not known the *power* of godliness. I believe this kind of Christianity has made more infidels than all the infidel books ever written.

Yes, Satan knew that he must get Christians down from the high pinnacle of wholehearted consecration to God. He knew that he had no chance till he tempted them down from that blessed vantage ground. Therefore, he began to spread those false doctrines, to counteract what John wrote before he died. He saw what was coming, and sounded down the ages: "Little children, let no man deceive you: he that doeth righteousness is righteous, even as He is righteous. He that committeth sin is of the devil; for the devil sinneth from the beginning. For this purpose the Son of God was manifested, that he might destroy the works of the devil," (1 John 3:7-8). Lord, revive that doctrine! Help us afresh to put up the standard!

Oh, the great evil is that dishonest-hearted people, because they feel it condemns them, lower the standard to their miserable experience. I said, when I was young, and I repeat it in my maturer years, that if it sent me to hell I would never pull it down. Oh, that God's people felt like that. There is the glorious standard put before us. The power is proffered, the conditions laid down, and we CAN all attain it if we will; but if we will not-for the sake of the children, and for generations yet unborn—do not let us drag it down, and try to make it meet our little, paltry, circumscribed experience. LET US KEEP IT UP. This is the way to get the world to look at it. Show the world a real, living, self-sacrificing, hardworking, toiling, triumphing religion, and the world will be influenced by it; but anything short of that, they will turn around and spit upon!

As to Their Duties and Obligations to the World

Second, Satan has deceived even those whom he could not succeed in getting to lower the standard of their own lives with respect to their duties and obligations to the world.

I have been reading, of late, the New Testament with special reference to the aggressive spirit of Primitive Christianity, and it is wonderful what floods of light come upon you when you read the Bible with reference to any particular topic on which you are seeking help. When God sees you are panting after the light, in order that you may use it, *He pours it in upon you*. It is an indispensable condition of receiving light that you are willing to follow it. People say they don't see this and that; no, because they do not wish to see. They are not willing to walk in it, and, therefore, they do not get it; but those who are willing to obey shall have all the light they want.

It seems to me that we have come infinitely short of any right and rational idea of the aggressive spirit of the New Testament saints. Satan has gotten Christians to accept what I may call a namby-pamby, kid-gloved kind of system of presenting the Gospel to people. "Will they be so kind as to read this tract or book, or would they not like to hear this popular and eloquent preacher? They will be pleased with him quite apart from religion." That is the sort of half-frightened, timid way of putting the truth before unconverted people, and of talking to them about the salvation of their souls. It seems to me this is utterly antagonistic and repugnant to the spirit of the early saints: "Go ye and preach the Gospel to EVERY CREATURE," and again the same idea—"Unto whom now I send thee." Look what is implied in these commissions.

It seems to me that no people have ever yet fathomed the meaning of these two divine commissions. I believe the Salvation Army has come nearer to it than any people that have ever preceded them. Look at them. Would it ever occur to you that the language meant, "Go and build chapels and churches and invite the people to come in, and if they will not, let them alone." "GO YE." "If you sent your servant to do something for you, and said, "Go and accomplish that piece of business for me," you know what it would involve. You know that he must see certain persons, running about the city to certain offices and banks, and agents, involving a great deal of trouble and sacrifice; but you have nothing to do with that. He is *your servant*. He is employed by you to do that business, and you simply commission him to "go and do it."

What would you think if he went and took an office and sent out a number of circulars inviting your customers or clients to come and wait on his pleasure, and when they chose to come, just to put your business before them? No, you would say, "Ridiculous." Divesting our minds of all conventionalities and traditionalisms, what would the language mean? "Go ye!" "To whom?" "To every creature." "How am I to get to them?" WHERE THEY ARE. "Every creature." There is the extent of your commission. Seek them out; run after them, wherever you find a creature that has a soul—there go and preach my Gospel to him. If I understand it, *that* is the meaning and the spirit of the commission.

And then again, to Paul, he says, "Unto whom now I send thee, to open their eyes, *and* to turn *them* from darkness to light, and *from* the power of Satan unto God." They are asleep—go and wake them up. They do not see their danger. If they did, there would be no necessity for you to run after them. They are *preoccupied*. Open their eyes, and turn them around by your desperate earnestness and moral suasion and moral force. And, oh, what a great deal one man can do for another, it makes me tremble to think! "Turn them from darkness to light, and from the power of Satan unto God." How did Paul understand it? He says, "We persuade men." Do not rest content with just putting it before them, giving them gentle invitations, and then leaving them alone. He ran after them, poor things, and pulled them out of the fire.

Take the bandage off their eyes which Satan has bound round them. Knock, hammer, and burn in, with the fire of the Holy Ghost, your words into their poor, hardened, darkened hearts, until they begin to realize that they are IN DANGER, that there is something amiss. Go after them. If I understand it, that is the spirit of the apostles and of the early Christians; for we read that when they were scattered by persecution, they "went everywhere preaching the Word." The laity, the new converts, the young babes in Christ. It does not mean always in set discourses, and public assemblies, but they went after men and women, like ancient Israel—"every man after his man," to try and win him for Christ.

Some people seem to think that the apostles laid the foundations of all the churches. They are quite mistaken. Churches sprang up where the apostles had never been. The apostles went to visit and organize them after they had sprung up, as the result of the work of the early laymen and women going everywhere and preaching the Word. Oh, may the Lord shower upon us in this day the same spirit!

We should build churches and chapels; we should invite the people to them; but do you think it is consistent with these two commissions, and with many others, that we should rest in this, when three parts of the population utterly ignore our invitations and take no notice whatever of our buildings and of our services? *They will not come to us.* That is an established fact. What is to be done? They have souls. You profess to believe that as much as I do, and that they must live forever. Where are they going? What is to be done? Jesus Christ says, "Go after them."

When all the civil methods have failed; when the genteel invitations have failed; when one man says that he has married a wife, and another that he has bought a yoke of oxen, and another that he has bought a piece of land—then does the Master of the feast say, "The ungrateful wretches, forget about all of them!"? "No!" (see Luke 14:21-24). He says, "Go out into the highways and hedges, and compel them to come in, that my house may be filled. I will have guests, and if you can't get them in by civil measures, use military measures. Go and COMPEL them to come in." It seems to me that we want more of this determined, aggressive spirit. Those of you who are right with God—you want more of this spirit to thrust the truth upon the attention of your fellowmen.

People say that you must be very careful, very judicious. You must not thrust religion down people's throats. Then, I say, you will never get it down. What! Am I to wait till an unconverted, godless man *wants* to be saved before I try to save him? He will never want to be saved till the death rattle is in his throat. What! Am I to let my unconverted friends and acquaintances drift down quietly to damnation, and never tell them about their souls, until they say, "If you please, I want you to preach to me!" Is this anything like the spirit of early Christianity? No. Verily we must *make* them look—tear the bandages off, open their eyes, make them bear it. And if they run away from you in one place, meet them in another, and let them have no peace until they submit to God and get their souls saved.

This is what Christianity *ought* to be doing in this land, and there are plenty of Christians to do it. Why, we might give the world such a time of it that they would get saved in very *self-defense* if we were only up and doing, and determined that they should have no peace in their sins. Where is our zeal for the Lord? We talk of Old Testament saints, but I would we were all like David. "Rivers of water ran down his eyes because men kept not the Law of his God." But you say, "We cannot all hold services." Perhaps not. Go as you like. Go as quietly and softly as the morning dew. Have meetings like the Friends, if you like, ONLY DO IT. Don't let your relatives and friends, and acquaintances die, and their blood be found on your skirts!

I shall never forget the agony depicted on the face of a young lady who once came to see me. My heart went out to her in pity. She told me her story. She said, "I had a proud, ungodly father, and the Lord converted me three years before his death, and, from the very day of my conversion, I felt I ought to talk to him, and plead, and pray with him about his soul, but I could not muster up courage. I kept intending to do it, and intending to do it, until he was taken ill. It was a sudden and serious illness. He lost his mind, and died unsaved." And she said, "I have never smiled since, and I think I never shall any more." Don't be like that. Do it quietly, if you like; privately, if you like: but do it. And do it as if you felt the value of their souls, and as if you intended to save them, if by any possible means in your power it could be done.

I had been speaking in a town, in the west of England, on the subject of *responsibility* of Christians for the salvation of souls. The gentleman with whom I was staying had winced a bit under the truth, and instead of taking it to heart in love, and making it the means of drawing him nearer to God, and enabling him to serve Him better, he said, "I thought you were rather hard on us this morning." I said, "Did you? I should be very sorry to be harder on anybody than the Lord Jesus Christ would be."

He said, "You can push things to extremes, you know. You were talking about seeking souls, and making sacrifices. Now, you are aware that we build the chapels and churches, and pay the ministers, and if the people won't be saved, we can't help it." (I think he had given pretty largely to a chapel in the town.) I said, "It is very heartless and ungrateful of the people, I grant; but, my dear sir, you would not reason thus in any temporal matter. Suppose a plague were to break out in London, and suppose that the Board of Health were to meet and appropriate all the hospitals and public buildings they could get for the treatment of those diseased, and suppose they were to issue proclamations to say that whoever would come to these buildings should be treated free of charge and every care and kindness bestowed on them, and the treatment would certainly cure them.

"But, supposing the people were so blind to their own interests, so indifferent and hardened that they refused to come, and consequently, the plague was increasing and thousands dying, what would you in the provinces say? Would you say, "Well, the Board of Health has done what it could, and if the people will not go to be healed, they deserve to perish; let them alone!" No, you would say, "It is certainly very foolish and wicked of the people, but these men are in a superior position. They understand the matter. They know and are responsible for the consequences. What in the world are they going to do? Let the whole land be depopulated?" No! If the people will not come to them, they must go to the people, and force upon them the means of health, and insist that proper measures should be used for the suppression of the plague." It needed no application. He understood it, and I believe, by the Spirit of God, he was enabled to see his mistake, to take it home, and set to work to do something for perishing souls.

Catherine Booth 1829-1890 | 471

People are preoccupied, and it is for us to go and force it upon their attention. Remember, you can do it. There is some *one soul* that you have more influence with than any other person on earth—some soul, or souls. Are you doing all you can for their salvation? Your relatives, friends, and acquaintances *are* to be rescued. Thank God! we are rescuing the poor people all over the land by thousands. There they are, to be looked at, and talked with, and questioned—people rescued from the depths of sin, degradation, and woe—saved from the worst forms of crime and infamy; and, if He can do that, He can save your genteel friends, if only you will go to them desperately and determinedly. Take them lovingly by the buttonhole, and say, "My dear friends, I never spoke to you closely, carefully, and prayerfully about your soul." Let them see the tears in your eyes; or, if you cannot weep, let them *hear the tears in your voice* and let them realize that you feel their danger, and are in distress for them. God will give His Holy Spirit, and they *will be saved*.

I was going to note that both texts imply opposition—for, He adds, "Lo, I am with you always, even unto the end of the world," (Matthew 28:20). As much as if He had said, "You will have need of my presence. Such aggressive, determined warfare as this will raise all earth and hell against you." And then He says to Paul, "I will be with thee, delivering thee from the people and the Gentiles unto whom I send thee." Why would they need this? Because the Gentiles would soon be up in arms against him, and indeed they were.

Opposition! It is a bad sign for the Christianity of this day that it provokes so little opposition. If there were no other evidence of it's being wrong, I should know it from that. When the church and the world can jog along comfortably together, you may be sure there is something wrong. The world has not altered. Its spirit is exactly the same as it ever was, and if Christians were equally faithful and devoted to the Lord, and separated from the world, living so that their lives were a reproof to all ungodliness, the world would hate them as much as ever it did.

It is the *church* that has altered, not the world. You say, "We should be getting into endless turmoil." Yes! "I came not to bring peace on the earth, but a sword," (see Matthew 10:34). There would be uproar. Yes! And the Acts of the Apostles are full of stories of uproars. One uproar was so great that the Chief Captain had to get Paul over the shoulders of the people, lest he should have been torn in pieces. "What a commotion!" you say, Yes; and, bless God, if we had the like now we should have thousands of sinners saved.

"But," you say, "see what a very undignified position this would bring the Gospel into." That depends on what sort of dignity you mean. You say, "We should always be getting into collision with the powers that be, and with the world, and what very unpleasant consequences would result." Yes, dear friends, there always have been unpleasant consequences to the flesh, when people were following God and doing His will. "But," you say, "wouldn't it be inconsistent with the dignity of the Gospel?" It depends from what standpoint you look at it. It depends upon what really constitutes the dignity of the Gospel.

What does constitute the dignity of the Gospel? Is it human dignity, or is it divine? Is it earthly, or is it heavenly dignity? It was a very undignified thing, looked at humanly, to die on the cross between two thieves. That was the most undignified thing ever done in this world, and yet, looked at on moral and spiritual grounds, it was the grandest spectacle that ever earth or heaven gazed upon, that the inhabitants of heaven gazed upon. And I think that the inhabitants of heaven stood still and looked over the battlements at that glorious, illustrious Sufferer, as He hung there between heaven and earth.

The Pharisees, I know, spat upon the humbled Sufferer, and wagged their heads and said, "He saved others, himself He cannot save." Ah! But He was intent on saving others. That was the dignity of Almighty strength allying itself with human weakness, in order to raise it. It was the dignity of eternal wisdom shrouding itself in human ignorance, in order to enlighten it. It was the dignity of everlasting, unquenchable love, baring its bosom to suffer in the stead of its rebellious creature-man. Ah! It was incarnate God standing in the place of condemned, apostate man—the dignity of love! *love!* LOVE!

Oh, precious Savior! Save us from maligning Thy Gospel and Thy name by clothing it with our paltry notions of earthly dignity, and forgetting the dignity which crowned Thy sacred brow as Thou didst hang upon the cross! That is the dignity for us, and it will never suffer by any gentleman here carrying the Gospel into the back slums or alleys of any town or city in which he lives. That dignity will never suffer by any employer talking lovingly to his servant maid or errand boy, and looking into his eyes with tears of sympathy and love, and trying to bring his soul to Jesus.

That dignity will never suffer, even though you should have to be dragged through the streets with a howling mob at your heels, like Jesus Christ, if you have gone into those streets for the souls of your fellowmen and the glory of God. Though you should be tied to a stake, as were the martyrs of old, and surrounded by laughing and taunting friends and their howling followers—that will be a dignity which shall be crowned in heaven, crowned with everlasting glory. If I understand it, *that* is the dignity of the Gospel—the dignity of love. I do not envy, I do not covet any other. I desire no other—God is my witness—than the dignity of love.

Oh, friends! Will you get this baptism of love! Then you will, like the apostles, be willing to push your limbs into a basket, and be let down by the wall, if need be, or suffer shipwreck, hunger, peril, nakedness, fire, or sword, or even go to the block itself, if thereby you may extend His kingdom and win souls for whom He shed His blood. The Lord fill us with this love and baptize us with this fire. And then the Gospel will arise and become glorious in the earth, and men will believe in us, and in it. They will feel its power, and they will go down under it by thousands, and by the grace of God, they SHALL.

3. The World's Need

"Son, go work today in my vineyard." -Matthew 21:28

"And the Lord said unto the servant, Go out into the highways and hedges, and compel them to come in, that my house may be filled." -Luke 14:23

We might have mentioned other texts teaching the same truth. There are plenty of them, but the general tenor and bearing of the Word of God, especially of the New Testament, is clear. It seems to me that no one can disinterestedly and dispassionately study the New Testament without arriving at the conclusion that there is a fundamental principle underlying the whole. His light and grace is expansive, teaching us that God has, in no case, given His light, His truth, and His grace to any individual soul, without holding that soul responsible for communicating that light and grace to others.

Real Christianity is, in its very nature and essence, aggressive. We get this principle fully exhibited and illustrated in the parables of Jesus Christ. If you will study them, you will find that He has not given us anything to be used merely for ourselves, but that we hold and possess every talent which He has committed to us for the good of others, and for the salvation of the lost. If I understand it, I say this is a fundamental principle of the New Testament.

How wonderfully this principle was exhibited in the lives of the apostles and early Christians! How utterly careless they seemed to be of everything compared with evangelism—this was the first thing with them everywhere! How Paul, at the very threshold, counted nothing else of any consequence, but willingly, cheerfully gave up every other consideration to live for this; and how he speaks of other apostles and helpers in the Gospel who had been nigh unto death, and laid down their necks for the work's sake; and we know how he traveled, worked, prayed, wept, and suffered, bled and died, for this one end.

Also the early Christians, scattered through the persecution, went everywhere preaching the Word. How earnest and zealous they were. Even after the apostolic age, we learn from ecclesiastical history, they would push themselves in everywhere, winning converts, and real, self-denying followers even in kings' courts. They would not be kept out, and could not be put down, and could not be hindered or silenced. "These Christians are everywhere," said one of their bitterest persecutors. Yes, they were instant in season and out of season. They won men and women on every hand, to the vexation and annoyance of those who hated them. Like their Master, they could not be hid; they could not be repressed, so aggressive, so constraining was the spirit which inspired and urged them on.

It becomes a greater puzzle every day to me, coming in contact with individual souls, how people read their Bibles! They do not seem to understand what they read. Well might a Philip or an angel come to them and say, "Understandest thou what thou readest?" Oh, friends, study your New Testament on this question, and you will be alarmed to find to what an awful extent you are your brother's keeper—to what an awful and alarming extent God holds you responsible for the salvation of those around you.

I want to glance, *first*, at OUR CALL TO WORK FOR GOD; and *second*, AT TWO OR THREE INDISPENSABLE QUALIFICATIONS FOR SUCCESSFUL LABOR.

Our Call to Work for God

And, first, as I have just said, we are called by the Word not only in these direct passages, but by the underlying principle running through it all, and laying upon us the *obligation to save the lost*. In fact, the world is cast upon us; we are the *only people who* CAN *save the unconverted*. Oh, I wish I could get this thought thoroughly into your minds. It has been, perhaps, one of the most potent, with respect to any little service I have rendered in the vineyard—the thought that Jesus Christ has nobody else to represent Him here but we Christians. Nobody else to work for Him. These poor people of the world, who are in darkness and ignorance, have nobody else to show them the way of mercy. If we do not, by the power of the Holy Spirit, bind the strong man and take his goods, who is to do it? God has delegated it to us. I say this is an alarming and awful consideration.

We are Called by the Spirit

Second, we are called by the Spirit. The very first aspiration of a newly born soul is to go after some other soul. The very first utterance, after the first burst of praise to God for deliverance from the bondage of sin and death, is a prayer gasped to the throne for some other soul still in darkness. And is not this the legitimate fruit of the Spirit? Is not this what we should expect? I take anyone here, who has been truly saved, to record if the first gushings of his soul, after his own deliverance, were not for somebody else—father, mother, child, brother, sister, friend?

Oh, yes, some of you could not go to sleep until you had written to a distant relative, and poured out your soul in anxious longings for his salvation; you could not take your necessary food until you had spoken or written to somebody in whose soul you were deeply interested. The Spirit began at once to urge you to seek for souls; and so it is frequently the last cry of the Spirit in the believer's soul before it leaves the body.

You have sat beside many a dying saint, and what has been the last prayer? Has it been anything about self, money, family, circumstances? Oh, those things are now all left behind, and the last expressed anxiety has been for some prodigal soul outside the kingdom of God. When the light of eternity comes streaming upon the soul, and its eyes get wide open to the value of souls, it neither hears nor sees anything else! It goes out of time into eternity, praying, as the Redeemer did, for the souls it is leaving behind. This is the first and last utterance of the Spirit in the believer's soul on earth.

Oh, if Christians were only true to the promptings of this blessed Spirit, it would be the prevailing impulse, the first desire and effort all the way through life. It is not God's fault that it is not so.

In personal dealing with souls, no point comes out more frequently than this: nothing which those who have really been converted and become backsliders in heart more frequently confess and bemoan than their unfaithfulness to the urgings of the Spirit with respect to other souls. In fact, backsliding begins here in thousands of instances. Satan gets people to yield to considerations of ease, propriety, being out of season, being injudicious, and so on, and they lose opportunities of dealing with souls, and so the Spirit is grieved and grieved. Oh, what numbers of people have confessed this to me.

A gentleman, in advanced life, said: "When I was a young man, and in my first love, the zeal of the Lord's house so consumed me that I used to neglect my daily business, and could scarcely sleep at night. But alas, that was many years ago." "Was it not better with you then than now?" I asked; and the tears came welling up into his eyes. Oh, yes, the Lord says of him, "I remember thee, the kindness of thy youth, the love of thine espousals, when thou wentest after me in the wilderness, in a land that was not sown: Israel was holiness unto the Lord, and the firstfruits of His increase," (Jeremiah 2:2-3). And, alas, there are many such today. They have it all to do over again. They have to repent and do their first works. They have to come back and get forgiven, and washed, and saved, if they are to go into the kingdom on high, all for lack of systematically and resolutely obeying the urgings of the Holy Spirit toward their fellowmen.

Now, some of you have been hearing about grieving the Spirit, and about being filled with the Spirit; and some of you are puzzled as to how you ought to wait—whether you ought to go on with your lawful avocations and wait. I say, my friends, this is the great point—you must so wait, wherever it may be; so plead and wrestle, and believe, THAT YOU GET IT. Then I care not whether it be in Jerusalem, in the Upper Room, or anywhere else-only, get it.

Don't let us lose the substance in quibbling about the way. Wait in the way congenial to your present circumstances; but, oh, wait for it until you get it, for this is the life of your souls, and the life of many souls, perchance, besides yours. You want this Spirit—the Spirit that yearns over the souls of your fellowmen; to weep over them as you took at them in their sin, and folly, and misery; the Spirit that cannot be satisfied with your own enjoyments or with feeling that YOU are safe, or even that your children are safe; but that yearns over every living soul while there is one left unsaved, and can never rest satisfied until it is brought into the kingdom.

Such are the urgings of the Spirit; and if people would only be obedient to them, they would never lose these urgings. Why, what an anomaly it is! Does it look reasonable, or like God's dealings, that people should begin, like the old man felt when he was young, and instead of waxing stronger, and having this holy zeal and desire increased, get weaker and weaker, and less and less? Does it look like God's way of doing things? Oh, no! This eclipse is through grieving and quenching the Spirit.

Now, my friend, you are called by the Spirit to this work. Obey the call—DO IT. Never mind if it chokes you—do it. Say, "I would rather die in obedience than lie in disobedience." Oh, these everlasting likes and dislikes. "I cannot speak to that person." "I cannot write that letter." "Oh, you don't know what would be the consequences." Never mind the consequences—do it. God will stand between you and the consequences; and, if He lets you suffer, never mind—then suffer; but obey the voice of the Spirit.

There would have been thousands of souls saved if all those who have had these urgings had obeyed them. Where do these urgings come from? Do they come from your own evil hearts? Then you are better than the apostle. Separated from the Spirit that dwells in you, and disunited from Christ, your living Head, you are selfish, devilish. Then where do these urgings come from? Do they come from the devil? Satan, then, would indeed be divided against himself. Where do they come from? It is the Spirit of the living God that is urging you to come out and seek to save the lost.

Will you obey these urgings? Will you give up your reasonings? Will you give up your likes and dislikes and OBEY? If you will, then He will come to you more and more, till, like David, you will feel the interests of His kingdom to be more to you than meat or drink, than silver or gold. Nay, you will become like him who said, "The zeal of Thine house hath eaten me up,"(Psalm 69:9).

We Are Called by What He has Done for Us

But, further, we are called to this work by what He has done for us. And what is that? Oh, you say, I cannot tell. No, no; we shall have to get to heaven first, and then we shall never be able to tell. We shall never be able to cast up that sum, not even for the gratification of the angels. That will remain an unexplored quantity forever, what He has done for us! We shall have to find out what it would have been to have been lost, and what it is to be saved in all its fullness and eternity, before we can tell what He has done for us!

What has He done for us? Oh, if we had a tithe of the love to sinners that He had for us, of His forbearing patience, of His persevering effort, when He followed us day and night, reasoned and reasoned with us, wooed and allured us, what could we not do?

I remember reading, somewhere, the story of a nobleman (Count Zinzendorf) who was, I think, a backslider. He was stopping at some country inn, and he went up into a room in which, over the mantelpiece, there was a very good picture of the crucifixion by a good old master, and under it was written, "I suffered this for thee—what hast thou done for me?" This question went home. It struck deep. He thought, "Yes, what indeed?" He went out into the stables to his horses, to try to get rid of the uncomfortable impression, but he could not forget it. A soft, pathetic voice seemed to follow him, "I suffered this for thee-what hast thou done for me?" At last it broke him down, and he went to his knees. He said, "True. Lord, I have never done anything for Thee, but now I give myself and my all to Thee, to be used in Thy service."

And have you never heard that voice in your soul, as you have been kneeling at the cross? Did you ever gaze upon that illustrious Sufferer, and hear His voice, as you looked back into the paltry past? "What hast Thou done for me?"

Now, there have been, at least, something like 350 people, who have come forward so far in these services, professing to give themselves afresh and fully to Jesus. I am sure, in the main, they have been sincere. They have come for the witness of the Spirit to their adoption, and for power for service. Now, friends, I want to know what this is to come to—what is to be the end of it?

"What are you going to do, brother? What are you going to do?"

And, sister, too. Is it going to die out in sentiment? Is it going to evaporate in sighs and wishings, and end in "I CANNOT"? God forbid!

What are you GOING TO DO? What HAVE you been doing for Him the last week? Ask yourselves. You say, "Well, I have read my Bible more." Very good, so far as it goes. What have you read it for? "Well," you say, "to get to know the Lord's will and to get instruction and comfort." Aye, exactly, but that is all for yourself, you see. "I have prayed a great deal." Very good. I wish everybody would pray. The apostles say all men everywhere ought to pray. "I have been asking the Lord for great things." Very good, praise the Lord; but those are for yourself, mainly. If you have been led out in agonizing supplication for souls, thank God for it, and go on, and, as the apostle says, "Labour thereunto, with all perseverance, praying in the Holy Spirit." But if it has been merely to get all you can for yourself, what profit is that to the Lord?

But you say, "I am bringing up my family." Exactly; so are the worldly people around you, but what for? For God or for yourself? Oh, let us look at these things, friends. I am afraid a great deal of religion is a mere transition of the selfishness of the human heart from the world to religion. I am afraid a great deal of the religion of this day ends in getting all you can and doing as little as you can—like some of your employees. You know the sort, who will do no more than they are forced—just get through, because they are hired. There is a great deal of that kind of service in these days, both toward man and toward God!

Now, friends, what have you been doing for Him—for the promotion of HIS blessed, glorious, saving purposes in the world? What have you been denying yourself for the sake of His kingdom? What labor have you gone through of mind, or heart? How many letters have you written? How many people have you spoken to? How many visits have you made? What self-denying labor have you been doing for Him who has done (as you say) so much for you? What have you been suffering for Him? Have you been trying to do some little measure "for His body's sake, the church" (see Colossians 1:24)?

Have you been carrying the sins and sorrows of the guilty world on your heart before God and pleading with Him for His own Name's sake, to pour out His Spirit upon the ungodly multitudes outside, and to quicken half-asleep professors inside? Have you been subjecting yourself to reproach and contempt—not only from the world, but from halfhearted professors and Pharisees, bearing the cross, enduring the shame of unkind reproaches in living and striving to save them? Oh, what have you been doing, brother and sister?

Come now, friends, I want a practical result. He suffered that for you. He is in heaven interceding for you. Five bleeding wounds He always bears in the presence of His Father, for you. If He were to forget you for a single moment, or cease His intercession, what would happen? What are you doing for Him? He has left you an example that you should follow in His steps. What were they? They were blood-tracked; they were humble steps. They were steps scorned by the world. He was ignored and rejected of men. He had nowhere to lay His head. He carried in His body and in His soul the sorrows and sufferings of all people.

He was a man of sorrows-not His own. He had no reason to be sorrowful. He was the Father's own beloved, and He knew it, but He was a man of sorrows, and acquainted with grief. The griefs of this poor, lost, half-damned world He bore, and they were sometimes so intolerable that they squeezed the blood through His veins. Have you been following in His footsteps, in any measure? He lived not for Himself. He came not to be ministered unto, but to minister, and took upon Him the form of a servant. What are you doing? Oh, my friends, up, up, and be doing. Begin! If you have not begun-begin today. Ask Him to baptize you with His Spirit, and let you begin at once to follow Him in the regeneration of the Spirit. You are called by what He did for you!

Then, you are called by the needs of the world. I have said so much about this at other times that I will not say more now, only I think this is a theme that is never exhausted, and never will be while there are any more sinners to save. Oh, the needs of the world! To me it is an overwhelming, a prodigious thought, that He shed His blood for every soul, and that as He hung there, He saw, under all the vileness, and sin, and ruin of the Fall—the human soul created originally in His own image, and capable of infinite and eternal development and progress. The soul to be rescued, washed, redeemed, saved, sanctified, and glorified—He saw this glorious jewel and He gave HIMSELF for it.

Look at these souls. There is not one of them so mean, or vile, or base, but can be rescued by the power of His Spirit, and by His living, glorious Gospel brought to bear upon them. The Savior, quoting from the Prophets, says, "Ye are gods (and adds) the Scriptures cannot be broken," (see John 10:34,35). He had no such little, mean, insignificant estimate of the worth of human souls as some people have nowadays, who consign whole generations to hell without any bowels of mercy or compassion. Oh, the Lord fill us with the pity of Jesus Christ, who, when He saw the multitudes, wept over them.

Oh, friends, think of one such soul! What is your gold, or houses, or lands—what your respectability, what your reputation, what all the prizes of this world? We talk about it, but who realizes it—who, WHO?—the value of one precious, immortal soul, saved, redeemed, sanctified. Oh, the needs of the world. They are dying, THEY ARE DYING! When people come to me with their fastidious objections, I say, "My friend, all I know is-souls are dying, dying."

If your homes were being decimated by the cholera, you would not be very particular about the means you used to stop it, and if anybody came with objections to the roughness of your methods, you would say, "The people are dying, they are dying," and that would be the end of all argument. I say, they are dying and they ARE TO BE SAVED. Satan is getting them: I want God to have them. Jesus Christ has bought them. He was the propitiation for the sins of the whole world. They belong to Him, and He shall have everyone I can reach, and everyone I can inspire others to reach also.

The world is dying. Do you believe it? You are called by the needs of the world. Begin nearest home if you like, by all means: I have little faith in those people's ministrations who go abroad after others, while their own are perishing at their firesides. Begin at home but do not end there. "Oh, yes," people say, "begin at home," but they end there. You never hear of them anywhere else, and it comes to very little, what they do at home, after all. God has ordained that the two shall go together. Get them saved by all means, but somebody else saved as well.

Set yourself to work for God. Go to Him to ask Him how to do it. Go to Him for the equipment of power, and then begin. Never mind how you tremble. I dare say your trembling will do more good than if you were ever so brave. Never mind the tears. I wish Christians would WEEP the Gospel into people. It would often go deeper than it does. Never mind if you do stammer. They will believe you when it comes from the heart. They will say, "He talked to me very naturally," as a man said, some time ago—wondering that he should be talked to about religion in a natural way. But be careful, no mock feeling, for they will detect it in a minute—yes, "be careful." Go off and pray until you get filled with the Spirit, and then go and let Him work through you. Finney says, "I went and let my heart out on the people."

Get your heart full of the living water and then open the gates and let it flow out. Look them in the face and take hold of them lovingly by the hand and say, "My friend, you are going to everlasting death. If nobody has ever told you till now—I have come to tell you. My friend, you have a precious soul. Is it saved?" They can understand that! Do not begin in a roundabout way, but talk to them straight, "Do you ever think about your precious soul? Are your sins pardoned? Are you ready to die?" Your neighbors, rich and poor, can understand that.

A lady said to my daughter, "I have begun talking to people about their souls in quite a different way to what I used to. I begin asking them if they do not know they are sinners and if they are ready to die, and it produces quite a different effect." For one reason, she has her own heart full of the love and Spirit of God, and that burns her words in. Begin in that way and see what God will do through you; for, of course, I only recognize you as the instrumentality which He has chosen, and those who reflect upon the instrumentality, reflect upon His wisdom. You go and put your hand to the plough and He will give you strength to push it along.

The Lord help you to go home thinking about the lost souls of the world.

4. Notes

For more information on the life and ministry of Catherine Booth see:

Mildred Duff, *Catherine Booth: A Sketch* (1914)

F.De L. Booth Tucker, *The Life of Catherine Booth: The Mother of the Salvation Army* (1892), 2 vols.

Preacher and Prayer

E. M Bounds 1835-1913

*With an Introduction
By Robert E. Coleman*

Abridged version of *Preacher and Prayer* by E. M. Bounds. Abridged version originally published by World Wide Publications, 1993, along with Billy Graham Center, Wheaton, Il. Copyright of abridged version and introduction held by Robert Coleman, used with permission. Scripture quotations are taken from the Holy Bible, King James Version (KJV), in the Public Domain. Artwork in the Public Domain.

Book Chapters

1. Introduction
   By Robert E. Coleman 488
2. Men and Women of Prayer Needed 490
3. Our Sufficiency Is of God 493
4. The Letter Kills 496
5. Tendencies to Be Avoided 499
6. Prayer, the Great Essential 502
7. Much Time Should Be Given to Prayer 505
8. Heart Preparation Necessary 508
9. Unction, the Mark of True Gospel Preaching 511
10. Prayer Marks Spiritual Leadership 514
11. A Praying Pulpit Gives Birth to a Praying Pew 517
12. Notes 520

1. Introduction
By Robert E. Coleman

Shortly before his death, Edward McKendree Bounds wrote a friend: "Pray more and more. You can't pray too much; you may pray too little. The devil will compromise with you to pray as the common standard, on going to bed, and a little prayer in the morning. Hell will be full if we don't do better than that."[1]

These words reflect the consuming burden of Bounds' life. Believing that God works through men, not methods, he became a specialist in prayer. It was said of him, "He talked with God as a man talks with a friend."[2] Hours were spent on his knees every day. Out of this communion came a written legacy that probably has inspired more men and women to pray than any work of his generation.

He was born in Shelby County, Missouri, August, 1835.[3] At the age of twenty-four, he heard the call to preach and entered the Methodist ministry. For many years he pastored churches in Missouri, Tennessee, and Alabama. During the Civil War he served as a chaplain in the Southern Armies. Later he became an editor of *The Christian Advocate*. Growing weary of the liberalizing trends of doctrine in his church, he retired to his home in Washington, Georgia. There he gave the rest of his life to evangelistic work, until his death on August 24, 1913.

Most of his writings were completed during his last years. The manuscripts often were compiled from notes scribbled on backs of old circulars and unused envelopes. Among his published works are expositions on the resurrection, heaven, and Satan. But he is remembered best for his eight volumes on prayer.[4]

The selection that follows is taken from the most familiar work entitled *Power Through Prayer*. Since first appearing in 1907, the book has been reprinted many times by various publishers, and has gone into a number of translations. Because much of the message is addressed to preachers. I have used the name commonly ascribed to it. I trust that reading these pages will cause you, as it has me, to aspire more than ever to become a man of prayer.

Robert E. Coleman

2. Men and Women of Prayer Needed

Study universal holiness of life. Your whole usefulness depends on this, for your sermons last but an hour or two; your life preaches all the week. If Satan can only make a covetous minister a lover of praise, of pleasure, of good eating, he has ruined your ministry. Give yourself to prayer, and get your texts, your thoughts, your words from God. Luther spent his best three hours in prayer.
–Robert Murray McCheyne

We are constantly on a stretch, if not on a strain, to devise new methods, new plans, and new organizations to advance the church and secure enlargement and efficiency for the Gospel. This trend of the day has a tendency to lose sight of the individual or sink the individual in the plan or organization. God's plan is to make much of the man or woman, far more of them than of anything else. People are God's method. The church is looking for better methods; God is looking for better people. "There was a man sent from God whose name was John." The dispensation that heralded and prepared the way for Christ was bound up in that man John. "Unto us a child is born, unto us a son is given," (Isaiah 9:6). The world's salvation comes out of that cradled Son. When Paul appeals to the personal character of the men who rooted the Gospel in the world, he solves the mystery of their success.

The glory and efficiency of the Gospel is staked on the individuals who proclaim it. When God declares that "the eyes of the Lord run to and fro throughout the whole earth, to show Himself strong in the behalf of them whose heart is perfect toward Him," (2 Chronicles 16:9). He declares the necessity of men and women, and His dependence on them as a channel through which to exert His power upon the world.

This vital, urgent truth is one that this age of machinery is apt to forget. The forgetting of it is as baneful on the work of God as would be the striking of the sun from his sphere. Darkness, confusion, and death would ensue.

What the church needs today is not more machinery or better, not new organizations or more and novel methods, but men and women whom the Holy Ghost can use—people of prayer, people mighty in prayer. The Holy Ghost does not know through methods, but through men and women. He does not come on machinery, but on men and women. He does not anoint plans but people—people of prayer.

An eminent historian has said that the accidents of personal character have more to do with the revolutions of nations than either philosophic historians or democratic politicians will allow. This truth has its application in full to the Gospel of Christ; the character and conduct of the followers of Christ can bring the power of Christ into the world, transfiguring nations and individuals. Of the preachers of the Gospel it is eminently true. The character, as well as the fortunes, of the Gospel is committed to the preacher. He makes or mars the message from God to man. The preacher is the golden pipe through which the divine oil flows. The pipe must not only be golden, but open and flawless, that the oil may have a full, unhindered, unwasted flow.

The individual makes the preacher. God must make the individual. The messenger is, if possible, more than the message. The preacher is more than the sermon. The preacher makes the sermon. As the life-giving milk from the mother's bosom is but the mother's life, so all the preacher says is tinctured, impregnated by what the preacher is. The treasure is in earthen vessels, and the taste of the vessel impregnates and may discolor.

The individual, the whole individual, lies behind the sermon. Preaching is not the performance of an hour. It is the outflow of a life. It takes twenty years to make a sermon, because it takes twenty years to make the preacher. The true sermon is a thing of life. The sermon grows because the preacher grows. The sermon is forceful because the preacher is forceful. The sermon is holy because the preacher is holy. The sermon is full of the divine unction because the preacher is full of the divine unction.

The sermon cannot rise in its life-giving forces above the individual. Dead people give out dead sermons, and dead sermons kill. Everything depends on the spiritual character of the preacher.

Under the Jewish dispensation the high priest had inscribed in jeweled letters on a golden frontlet: "Holiness to the Lord." So every preacher in Christ's ministry must be molded into and mastered by this same holy motto. It is a crying shame for the Christian ministry to fall lower in holiness of character and holiness of aim than the Jewish priesthood. Jonathan Edwards said, "I went on with my eager pursuit after more holiness and conformity to Christ. The heaven I desired was a heaven of holiness."

The Gospel of Christ does not move by popular waves. It has no self-propagating power. It moves as the people who have charge of it move.

The preacher must impersonate the Gospel. Its divine, most distinctive features must be embodied in him. The constraining power of love must be in the preacher as a projecting, eccentric, an all-commanding, self-oblivious force. The energy of self-denial must be his being, his heart and blood and bones. He must go forth as a man among men, clothed with humility, abiding in meekness, wise as a serpent, harmless as a dove. He must bear the bonds of a servant with the spirit of a king, a king in high, royal, independent bearing, with the simplicity and sweetness of a child.

Preachers must throw themselves, with all the abandon of a perfect, self-emptying faith and a self-consuming zeal, into their work for the salvation of men and women. Hearty, heroic, compassionate, fearless martyrs must the men and women be who take hold of and shape a generation for God. If they be timid time-servers, place-seekers, if they be people-pleasers or people-fearers, if their faith has a weak hold on God or His Word, if their denial be broken by any phase of self or the world, they cannot take hold of the church nor the world for God.

The preacher's sharpest and strongest preaching should be to himself. His most difficult, delicate, laborious, and thorough work must be with himself. The training of the twelve was the great, difficult, and enduring work of Christ. Preachers are not sermon-makers, but people-makers and saint-makers, and he only is well trained for this business who has made himself a man and a saint.

It is not great talents nor great learning nor great preachers that God needs, but people great in holiness, great in faith, great in love, great in fidelity, great for God—always preaching by holy sermons in the pulpit, by holy lives out of it. These can mold a generation for God!

3. Our Sufficiency Is of God

But above all, he excelled in prayer. The inwardness and weight of his spirit, the reverence and solemnity of his address and behavior, and the fewness and fullness of his words have often struck even strangers with admiration, as they used to reach others with consolation. The most awful, living, reverend frame I ever felt or beheld, I must say, was his prayer. And truly it was a testimony. He knew and lived nearer to the Lord than other men, for they that know Him most reason to approach Him with reverence and fear. –William Penn of George Fox

The sweetest graces, by a slight perversion, may bear the bitterest fruit. The sun gives life, but sunstrokes are death. Preaching is to give life; it may kill. The preacher holds the keys; he may lock as well as unlock.

Preaching is God's great institution for the planting and maturing of spiritual life. When properly executed, its benefits are untold; when wrongly executed, no evil can exceed its damaging results. It is an easy matter to destroy the flock if the shepherd be unwary or the pasture be destroyed, easy to capture the citadel if the watchmen be asleep or the food and water be poisoned.

Invested with such gracious prerogatives, exposed to so great evils, involving so many grave responsibilities, it would be a parody on the shrewdness of the devil and a libel on his character and reputation if he did not bring his master influences to adulterate the preacher and the preaching. In the face of all this, the exclamatory interrogative of Paul, "Who is sufficient for these things?" is never out of order.

Paul says, "Our sufficiency is of God: who also hath made us able ministers of the New Testament: not of the letter, but of the spirit: for the letter kills, but the spirit giveth life," (2 Corinthians 3:5-6). The true ministry is God-touched, God-enabled, and God-made.

The Spirit of God is on the preacher in anointing power; the fruit of the Spirit is in the preacher's heart, the Spirit of God has vitalized this preacher and the Word. This preaching gives life, gives life as the spring gives life; gives life as the resurrection gives life; gives ardent life as the summer gives ardent life; gives fruitful life as the autumn gives fruitful life.

The life-giving preacher is a servant of God, whose heart is ever athirst for God, whose soul is ever following hard after God, whose eye is single to God, and in whom—by the power of God's Spirit—the flesh and the world have been crucified, and this ministry is like the generous flood of a life-giving river.

The preaching that kills is nonspiritual preaching. The ability of the preaching is not from God. Lower sources than God have given to it energy and stimulant. The Spirit is not evident in the preacher nor this preaching. Many kinds of forces may be projected and stimulated by preaching that kills, but they are not spiritual forces. They may resemble spiritual forces, but are only the shadow, the counterfeit; life they may seem to have, but the life is magnetized.

The preaching that kills is the letter. Shapely and orderly it may be, but it is the letter still, the dry, husky letter, the empty, bald shell. The letter may have the germ of life on it, but it has no breath of spring to evoke it. Winter seeds they are, as hard as the winter's soil, as icy as the winter's air, no thawing nor germinating by them.

This letter-preaching has the truth. But even divine truth has no life-giving energy alone-it must be energized by the Spirit, with all God's forces at its back. Truth unquickened by God's Spirit deadens as much as, or more than, error. It may be the truth without admixture; but without the Spirit, its shade and touch are deadly, its light darkness.

Letter-preaching is unctionless, neither mellowed nor oiled by the Spirit. There may be tears, but tears cannot run God's machinery; tears may be but summer's breath on a snow covered iceberg, nothing but surface slush. Feelings and earnestness there may be, but it is the emotion of the actor and the earnestness of the attorney.

The preacher may feel warm from the kindling of his own sparks, be eloquent over his own exegesis, earnest in delivering the product of his own brain. The professor may usurp the place and imitate the fire of the apostle. Brains and nerves may serve the place and feign the work of God's Spirit. By these forces, the letter may glow and sparkle like an illumined text, but the glow and sparkle will be as barren of life as the field sown with pearls. The death-dealing element lies back of the words, back of the sermon, back of the occasion, back of the manner, back of the action.

The great hindrance is in the preacher himself. He has not in himself the mighty life-creating forces. There may be no discount on the preacher's orthodoxy, honesty, cleanness, or earnestness; but somehow the person, the inner person, in the secret places, has never broken down and surrendered to God. The inner life is not a great highway for the transmission of God's message, God's power.

Somehow, self and not God rules in the holy of holies. Somewhere, all unconscious to himself, some spiritual nonconductor has touched the preacher's inner being, and the divine current has been arrested. His inner being has never felt its thorough spiritual bankruptcy, its utter powerlessness. He has never learned to cry out with an ineffable cry of self-despair and self-helplessness till God's power and God's fire comes in and fills, purifies, empowers. Self-esteem, self-ability in some pernicious shape has defamed and violated the temple which should be held sacred for God.

Life-giving preaching costs the preacher much—death to self, crucifixion to the world, the travail of his own soul. Crucified preaching only can give life. Crucified preaching can come only from one who has been crucified.

4. The Letter Kills

During this affliction I was brought to examine my life in relation to eternity closer than I had done when in the enjoyment of health. In this examination relative to the discharge of my duties toward my fellow creatures as a man, a Christian minister, and an officer of the church, I stood approved by my own conscience; but in relation to my Redeemer and Savior the result was different. My returns of gratitude and loving obedience bear no proportion to my obligations for redeeming, preserving, and supporting me through the vicissitudes of life from infancy to old age.

The coldness of my love to Him who first loved me and has done so much for me overwhelmed and confused me; and to complete my unworthy character, I had not only neglected to improve the grace given to the extent of my duty and privilege, but for want of improvement had, while abounding in perplexing care and labor, declined from first zeal and love. I was confounded, humbled myself, implored mercy, and renewed my covenant to strive and devote myself unreservedly to the Lord.
–Bishop McKendree

The preaching that kills may be, and often is, orthodox-dogmatically, inviolably orthodox. We love orthodoxy. It is good. It is the best. It is the clean, clear-cut teaching of God's Word. It defends the trophies won by truth in its conflict with error, the levees which faith has raised against the desolating floods of honest or reckless misbelief or unbelief. But orthodoxy, clear and hard as crystal, suspicious and militant, may be but the letter well-shaped, well-named, and well-learned—the letter which kills. Nothing is so dead as a dead orthodoxy; too dead to speculate, too dead to think, to study, or to pray.

The preaching that kills may have insight and grasp of principles, may be scholarly and critical in taste, may have every detail of the derivation and grammar of the letter, may be able to trim the letter into its perfect pattern, and illuminate it as Plato and Cicero may be illuminated, may study it as a lawyer studies his textbooks to form his brief or to defend his case, and yet be like a frost, a killing frost.

Letter-preaching may be eloquent, enameled with poetry and rhetoric, sprinkled with prayer, spiced with sensation, illuminated by genius, and yet these be but the massive or chaste costly mountings, the rare and beautiful flowers which coffin the corpse. The preaching which kills may be without scholarship, unmarked by any freshness of thought or feeling, clothed in tasteless generalities or vapid specialties, with style irregular, slovenly, savoring neither of closet nor of study, graced neither by thought, expression, or prayer. Under such preaching how wide and utter the desolation! How profound the spiritual death!

This letter-preaching deals with the surface and shadow of things, and not the things themselves. It does not penetrate the inner part. It has no deep insight into, no strong grasp of the hidden life of God's Word. It is true to the outside, but the outside is the hull which must be broken and penetrated for the kernel. The letter may be dressed so as to attract and be fashionable, but the attraction is not toward God nor is the fashion for heaven.

The failure is in the preacher. He has never been in the hands of God like clay in the hands of the potter. He has been busy about the sermon, its thought and finish, its drawing and impressive forces. But the deep things of God have not been sought, studied, fathomed, experienced by him. He has never stood before "the throne high and lifted up," never heard the seraphim song, never seen the vision nor felt the rush of that awful holiness, and cried out in utter abandon and despair under the sense of weakness and guilt, and had his life renewed, his heart touched, purged, inflamed by the live coal from God's altar.

His ministry may draw people to him, to the church, to the form and ceremony; but no true drawings to God, no sweet, holy, divine communion induced. The church has been frescoed but not edified, pleased but not sanctified. Life is suppressed; a chill is on the summer air; the soil is baked. The city of our God becomes the city of the dead; the church a graveyard, not an embattled army. Praise and prayer are stifled; worship is dead. The preacher and the preaching have helped sin, not holiness.

Preaching which kills is prayerless preaching. Without prayer, the preacher creates death, and not life. The preacher who is feeble in prayer is feeble in life-giving forces. The preacher who has retired prayer as a conspicuous and largely prevailing element in his own character has shorn his preaching of its distinctive life-giving power. Professional praying there is and will be, but professional praying helps the preaching do its deadly work. Professional praying chills and kills both preaching and praying.

Much of the lax devotion and lazy, irreverent attitudes in congregational praying are attributable to professional praying in the pulpit. Long, discursive, dry, and inane are the prayers in many pulpits. Without unction or heart, they fall like a killing frost on all the graces of worship. The deader they are the longer they grow. A plea for short praying, live praying, real heart praying, praying by the Holy Spirit—direct, specific, ardent, simple, unctuous in the pulpit—is in order. A school to teach preachers how to pray, as God counts praying, would be more beneficial to true piety, true worship, and true preaching than all theological schools.

Stop! Pause! Consider! Where are we? What are we doing? Preaching to kill? Praying to kill? Praying to God, the great God, the maker of all worlds, the Judge of all men! What reverence, what simplicity, what sincerity, what truth in the inward parts is demanded! How real we must be! How hearty! Prayer to God—the noblest exercise, the loftiest effort of man, the most real thing! Shall we do the real thing, the mightiest thing—prayerful praying, life-creating preaching, bring the mightiest force to bear on heaven and earth and draw on God's exhaustless and open treasure for the need and beggary of man?

5. Tendencies to Be Avoided

Let us often look at Brainerd in the woods of America, pouring out his very soul before God for the perishing heathen, without whose salvation nothing could make him happy. Prayer-secret, fervent, believing prayer— lies at the root of all personal godliness. A competent knowledge of the language where a missionary lives, a mild and winning temper, a heart given up to God in closet religion—these, these are the attainments which, more than all knowledge, or all other gifts, will fit us to become the instruments of God in the great work of human redemption. —Carey's Brotherhood, Serampore, India

There are two extreme tendencies in the ministry. The one is to shut oneself out from involvement with people. The monk, the hermit were illustrations of this. They shut themselves out from people to be more with God. They failed, of course.

Our being with God is of use only as we expend its priceless benefits on men and women. This age, neither with preacher nor with people, is much intent on God. Our hankering is not that way. Some of us shut ourselves to our study; we become students, bookworms, Bible worms, sermon-makers, noted for literature, thought, and sermons. But the people and God, where are they? Out of heart, out of mind. Preachers who are great thinkers, great students, must be the greatest of prayers, or else they will be the greatest of backsliders, heartless professionals, rationalistic, less than the least of preachers in God's estimate.

The other tendency is to thoroughly popularize the ministry. This person is no longer God's man, but a man of affairs, of the people. He prays not, because his mission is to the people. If he can move the people, create an interest, a sensation in favor of religion, an interest in church work—he is satisfied. His personal relation to God is no factor in his work. Prayer has little or no place in his plans.

The disaster and ruin of such a ministry cannot be computed by earthly arithmetic. What the preacher is in prayer to God, for himself, for his people, so is his power for real good to men and women, so is his true fruitfulness, his true fidelity to God, to people—for time, for eternity.

It is impossible for the preacher to keep his spirit in harmony with the divine nature of his high calling without much prayer. That the preacher, by dint of duty and laborious fidelity to the work and routine of the ministry, can keep himself in trim and fitness is a serious mistake. Even sermon-making, incessant and taxing as an art, as a duty, as a work, or as a pleasure, will engross and harden, will estrange the heart, by neglect of prayer, from God. The scientist loses God in nature. The preacher may lose God in his sermon.

Prayer freshens the heart of the preacher, keeps it in tune with God and in sympathy with the people, lifts his ministry out of the chilly air of professionalism, fructifies routine, and moves every wheel with the facility and power of a divine unction.

Mr. Spurgeon says,

> "Of course the preacher is, above all others, distinguished as a man of prayer. He prays as an ordinary Christian, else he were a hypocrite. He prays more than ordinary Christians, else he were disqualified for the office he has undertaken. If you as ministers are not very prayerful, you are to be pitied. If you become lax in sacred devotion, not only will you need to be pitied, but your people also. And the day cometh in which you shall be ashamed and confounded.
>
> "All our libraries and studies are mere emptiness compared with our closets. Our seasons of fasting and prayer at the Tabernacle have been high days indeed; never has heaven's gate stood wider; never have our hearts been nearer the central Glory."

The praying which makes a prayerful ministry is not a little praying put in as we put flavor to give something a pleasant taste, but the praying must be in the body, and form the blood and bones. Prayer is no petty duty, put into a corner; no piecemeal performance made out of the fragments of time which have been snatched from business and other engagements of life—but it means that the best of our time, the heart of our time and strength must be given. It does not mean the closet absorbed in the study or swallowed up in the activities of ministerial duties. But it means the closet first, the study and activities second—both study and activities freshened and made efficient by the closet.

Prayer that affects one's ministry must give tone to one's life. The praying which gives color and bent to character is no pleasant, hurried pastime. It must enter as strongly into the heart and life as Christ's "strong crying and tears" did; must draw out the soul into an agony of desire as Paul's did. It must be an inwrought fire and force like the "effectual, fervent prayer" of James; must be of that quality which, when put into the golden censer and incensed before God, works mighty spiritual throes and revolutions.

Prayer is not a little habit pinned on to us while we were tied to our mother's apron strings. Neither is it a little decent quarter-of-a-minute's grace said over an hour's dinner. Rather, it is a most serious work of our most serious years. It engages more of time and appetite than our longest dinings or richest feasts!

The prayer that makes much of our preaching must be made much of. The character of our praying will determine the character of our preaching. Light praying will make light preaching. Prayer makes preaching strong, gives it unction, and makes it stick. In every ministry weighty for good, prayer has always been a serious business.

The preacher must be preeminently devoted to prayer. The heart must graduate in the school of prayer. In the school of prayer only can the heart learn to preach. No learning can make up for the failure to pray. No earnestness, no diligence, no study, no gifts will supply its lack.

Talking to people for God is a great thing, but talking to God for people is greater still. No one will ever talk well and with real success to people for God who has not learned well how to talk to God for people. More than this, prayerless words in the pulpit and out of it are deadening words.

6. Prayer, the Great Essential

You know the value of prayer: It is precious beyond all price. Never, never neglect it. –Sir Thomas Buxton

Prayer is the first thing, the second thing, the third thing necessary to a minister. Pray, then, my dear brother; pray, pray, pray. –Edward Payson

Prayer, in the preacher's life, in the preacher's study, in the preacher's pulpit, must be a conspicuous, an all-impregnating force, and an all-coloring ingredient. It must play no secondary part, be no mere coating. To the preacher it is given to be with the Lord "all night in prayer," (Luke 6:12). The preacher, to train himself in self-denying prayer, is charged to look to his Master, who, "rising up a great while before day, went out, and departed into a solitary place, and there prayed," (see Mark 1:35).

The preacher's study ought to be a closet, a Bethel, an altar, a vision, and a ladder, that every thought might ascend heavenward ere it went manward; that every part of the sermon might be scented by the air of heaven and made serious, because God was in the study.

As an engine has no power until the cylinders ignite, so preaching, with all its machinery, perfection, and polish, is at a dead standstill, as far as spiritual results are concerned, until prayer has ignited the fuel. The texture, fineness, and strength of the sermon is as so much rubbish unless the mighty impulse of prayer is in it, through it, and behind it.

The preacher must, by prayer, put God in the sermon. The preacher must, by prayer, move God toward the people before he can move the people to God by his words. The preacher must have had audience and ready access to God before he can have access to the people. An open way to God for the preacher is the surest pledge of an open way to the people.

It is necessary to iterate and reiterate that prayer, as a mere habit, as a performance gone through by routine or in a professional way, is a dead and rotten thing. Such praying has no connection with the praying for which we plead. We are stressing true praying, which engages and sets on fire every high element of the preacher's being—prayer which is born of vital oneness with Christ and the fullness of the Holy Ghost, which springs from the deep, overflowing fountains of tender compassion, deathless solicitude for peoples' eternal good; a consuming zeal for the glory of God; a thorough conviction of the preacher's difficult and delicate work and of the imperative need of God's mightiest help. Praying grounded on these solemn and profound convictions is the only true praying. Preaching backed by such praying is the only preaching which sows the seeds of eternal life in human hearts and builds men and women up for heaven.

It is true that there may be popular preaching, pleasant preaching, appealing preaching, preaching of much intellectual, literary, and brainy force, with its measure and form of good, with little or no praying. But the preaching which secures God's end in preaching must be born of prayer from text to application, delivered with the energy and spirit of prayer, followed and made to germinate, and kept in vital force in the hearts of the hearers by the preacher's prayers, long after the occasion has passed.

We may excuse the spiritual poverty of our preaching in many ways, but the true secret will be found in the lack of urgent prayer for God's presence in the power of the Holy Spirit. There are preachers innumerable who can deliver masterful sermons after their order. But their effects are short-lived and do not enter as a factor at all into the regions of the spirit where the fearful war between God and Satan, heaven and hell, is being waged—because they are not made powerfully militant and spiritually victorious by prayer.

The preachers who gain mighty results for God are those who have prevailed in their pleadings with God before venturing to plead with men and women. The preachers who are the mightiest in their closets with God are the mightiest in their pulpits with people.

Preachers are human folks, and are exposed to, and often caught by, the strong driftings of human currents. Praying is spiritual work, and human nature does not like taxing, spiritual work. Human nature wants to sail to heaven under a favoring breeze, a full, smooth sea.

Prayer is humbling work. It abases intellect and pride, crucifies vainglory, and signs our spiritual bankruptcy—and all these are hard for flesh and blood to bear. It is easier not to pray than to bear them. So we come to one of the crying evils of these times, maybe of all times—little or no praying. Little praying is a kind of make-believe, it is salve for the conscience, a farce and a delusion.

The preacher is commissioned to pray as well as to preach. His mission is incomplete if he does not do both well. The preacher may speak with all the eloquence of men and of angels. But unless he can pray with a faith which draws all heaven to his aid, his preaching will be "as sounding brass or a tinkling cymbal" for permanent God-honoring, soul-saving uses.

7. Much Time Should Be Given to Prayer

The great masters and teachers in Christian doctrine have always found in prayer their highest source of illumination. Not to go beyond the limits of the English church, it is recorded of Bishop Andrews that he spent five hours daily on his knees. The greatest practical resolves that have enriched and beautified human life in Christian times have been arrived at in prayer.
—Canon Liddon

While many private prayers, in the nature of things, must be short; while public prayers, as a rule, ought to be short and condensed; while there is ample room for, and value put on, impromptu prayer—yet in our private communions with God time is a feature essential to its value. Much time spent with God is the secret of all-successful praying. Prayer which is felt, as a mighty force is the mediate or immediate product of much time spent with God. Our short prayers owe their point and efficiency to the long ones that have preceded them. The short prevailing prayer cannot be prayed by one who has not prevailed with God in a mightier struggle of long continuance. Jacob's victory of faith could not have been gained without that all-night wrestling.

God's acquaintance is not made by pop calls. God does not bestow His gifts on the casual or hasty comers and goers. Much time with God alone is the secret of knowing Him and of influence with Him. He yields to the persistency of a faith that knows Him. He bestows His richest gifts upon those who declare their desire for, and appreciation of, those gifts by the constancy as well as earnestness of their importunity.

Christ, who in this as well as other things is our Example, spent many whole nights in prayer. His custom was to pray much. He had His habitual place to pray. Many long seasons of praying make up His history and character.

Paul prayed day and night. It took time from very important interests for Daniel to pray three times a day. David's morning, noon, and night praying were doubtless on many occasions very protracted. While we have no specific account of the time these Bible saints spent in prayer, yet the indications are that they consumed much time in prayer, and on some occasions they dedicated themselves to long seasons of prayer.

We would not have anyone think that the value of their prayers is to be measured by the clock. But our purpose is to impress on our minds the necessity of being much alone with God; and that if this feature has not been produced by our faith, then our faith is of a feeble and surface type.

The men and women who have most fully illustrated Christ in their character, and have most powerfully affected the world for Him, have spent so much time with God as to make it a notable feature of their lives. Charles Simeon devoted the hours from four till eight in the morning to God. Mr. Wesley spent two hours daily in prayer. He began at four in the morning. Of him, one who knew him well wrote, "He thought prayer to be more his business than anything else, and I have seen him come out of his closet with a serenity of face next to shining."

John Fletcher stained the walls of his room by the breath of his prayers. Sometimes he would pray all night; always, frequently, and with great earnestness. His whole life was a life of prayer. "I would not rise from my seat," he said, "without lifting my heart to God." His greeting to a friend was always, "Do I meet you praying?"

Luther said, "If I fail to spend two hours in prayer each morning, the devil gets the victory through the day. I have so much business I cannot get on without spending three hours daily in prayer." He had a motto: "He that has prayed well has studied well."

Archbishop Leighton was so much alone with God that he seemed to be in a perpetual meditation. "Prayer and praise were his business and his pleasure," says his biographer. Bishop Ken was so much with God that his soul was said to be God-enamored. He was with God before the clock struck three every morning.

Bishop Asbury said, "I propose to rise at four o'clock as often as I can and spend two hours in prayer and meditation." Samuel Rutherford, the fragrance of whose piety is still rich, rose at three in the morning to meet God in prayer. Joseph Alleine arose at four o'clock for his business of praying till eight. If he heard other tradesmen plying their business before he was up, he would exclaim, "O, how this shames me! Doth not my Master deserve more than theirs?" He who has learned this trade well draws at will, on sight, and with acceptance, of heaven's unfailing bank.

8. Heart Preparation Necessary

For nothing reaches the heart but what is from the heart, or pierces the conscience but what comes from a living conscience. –William Penn

In the morning was more engaged in preparing the head than the heart. This has been frequently my error, and I have always felt the evil of it, especially in prayer. Reform it, then, O Lord! Enlarge my heart, and I shall preach. –Robert Murray McCheyne

A sermon that has more head infused into it than heart will not come home with efficacy to the hearers.
–Richard Cecil

Prayer, with its manifold and many-sided forces, helps the mouth to utter the truth in its fullness and freedom. The preacher is to be prayed for; the preacher is made by prayer. The preacher's mouth is to be prayed for; his mouth is to be opened and filled by prayer. A holy mouth is made by praying, by much praying; a brave mouth is made by praying, by much praying. The church and the world, God and heaven, owe much to Paul's mouth; Paul's mouth owed its power to prayer.

How manifold, illimitable, valuable, and helpful prayer is to the preacher in so many ways, at so many points, in every way! One great value is, it helps his heart.

Praying makes the preacher a heart preacher. Prayer puts the preacher's heart into the preacher's sermon; prayer puts the preacher's sermon into the preacher's heart.

The heart makes the preacher. Men of great hearts are great preachers. Men of bad hearts may do a measure of good, but this is rare. The hireling and the stranger may help the sheep at some points, but it is the good shepherd, with the good shepherd's heart, who will bless the sheep and answer the full measure of the shepherd's place.

We have emphasized sermon preparation until we have lost sight of the important thing to be prepared—the heart. A prepared heart is much better than a prepared sermon. A prepared heart will make a prepared sermon.

Volumes have been written laying down the mechanics and taste of sermon making, until we have become possessed with the idea that this scaffolding is the building. The young preacher has been taught to lay out all his strength on the form, taste, and beauty of his sermon as a mechanical and intellectual product. We have thereby cultivated a vicious taste among the people and raised the clamor for talent instead of grace, eloquence instead of piety, rhetoric instead of revelation, reputation and brilliance instead of holiness. By it we have lost the true idea of preaching, lost preaching power, lost pungent conviction for sin, lost the rich experience and elevated Christian character, lost the authority over consciences and lives which always results from genuine preaching.

It would not do to say that preachers study too much. Some of them do not study at all; others do not study enough. Numbers do not study the right way to show themselves workmen approved of God. But our great lack is not in head culture, but in heart culture; not lack of knowledge, but lack of holiness is our sad and telling defect—not that we know too much, but that we do not meditate on God and His Word and watch and fast and pray enough. The heart is the great hindrance to our preaching. Words pregnant with divine truth find in our hearts nonconductors; arrested, they fall shorn and powerless.

Can ambition, that lusts after praise and place, preach the Gospel of Him who made Himself of no reputation and took on Him the form of a servant? Can the proud, the vain, the egotistical preach the Gospel of Him who was meek and lowly? Can the bad-tempered, passionate, selfish, hard, worldly person preach the system which teems with long-suffering, self-denial, tenderness, which imperatively demands separation from enmity and crucifixion to the world?

Can the hireling official, heartless, perfunctory, preach the Gospel which demands that the shepherd give his life for the sheep? Can the covetous man, who counts salary and money, preach the Gospel till he has gleaned his heart and can say in the spirit of Christ and Paul, phrased in the words of Wesley, "I count it dung and dross; I trample it under my feet; I (yet not I, but the grace of God in me) esteem it just as the mire of the streets, I desire it not, I seek it not"? God's revelation does not need the light of human genius, the polish and strength of human culture, the brilliance of human thought, the force of human brains to adorn or enforce it. But it does demand the simplicity, the docility, humility, and faith of a child's heart.

Our great need is heart preparation. Luther held it as an axiom: "He who has prayed well has studied well." We do not say that people are not to think and use their intellects: but they will use their intellect best who cultivate their heart most. We do not say that preachers should not be students: but we do say that their great study should be the Bible, and he studies the Bible best who has kept his heart with diligence. We do not say that the preacher should not know men and women, but he will be the more adept in human nature who has fathomed the depths and intricacies of his own heart.

We do say that while the channel of preaching is the mind, its fountain is the heart; you may broaden and deepen the channel, but if you do not look well to the purity and depth of the fountain, you will have a dry or polluted channel. We do say that almost any person of common intelligence has sense enough to preach the Gospel, but very few have grace enough to do so. We do say that the one who has struggled with his own heart and conquered it; who has taught it humility, faith, love, truth, mercy, sympathy, courage; who can pour the rich treasures of the heart thus trained, through a strong intellect, all surcharged with the power of the Gospel, on the consciences of his hearers—such a one will be the truest, most successful preacher in the esteem of his Lord.

9. Unction, the Mark of True Gospel Preaching

Speak for eternity. Above all things, cultivate your own Spirit. A word spoken by you when your conscience is clear and your heart full of God's Spirit is worth ten thousand words spoken in unbelief and sin. Remember that God, and not man, must have the glory. If the veil of the world's machinery were lifted off, how much we would find is done in answer to the prayers of God's children. –Robert Murray McCheyne

Unction is that indefinable, indescribable something which an old, renowned Scotch preacher describes thus: "There is sometimes somewhat in preaching that cannot be ascribed either to matter or expression, and cannot be described as to what it is, or from whence it cometh, but with a sweet violence it pierceth into the heart and affections and comes immediately from the Lord; but if there be any way to obtain such a thing, it is by the heavenly disposition of the speaker."

We call it unction. This unction combines with the Word of God, which is "quick and powerful, and sharper than any two-edged sword, piercing even to the dividing asunder of soul and spirit, and of the joints and marrow, and a discerner of the thoughts and intents of the heart," (see Hebrews 4:12). It is this unction which gives the words of the preacher such point, sharpness, and power, and which creates such friction and stir in many a dead congregation.

The same truths may have been told in the strictness of the letter, smooth as human oil could make them; but no signs of life, not a pulse throb; all as peaceful as the grave and as dead. The same preacher in the meanwhile receives a baptism of this unction, the divine Spirit is on him, the letter of the Word has been embellished and fired by this mysterious power, and the throbbings of life begin—life which receives, or life which resists. The unction pervades and convicts the conscience and breaks the heart.

This divine unction is the feature which separates and distinguishes true Gospel preaching from all other methods of presenting the truth, and which creates a wide spiritual chasm between the preacher who has it and the one who has it not. It backs and impregnates revealed truth with all the energy of God.

Unction is simply putting God in His own Word and on His own preacher. By mighty and great prayerfulness, and by continual prayerfulness, it is all potential and personal to the preacher. It inspires and clarifies his intellect, gives insight and grasp and projecting power. It gives to the preacher heart-power, which is greater than head-power; and tenderness, purity, force flow from the heart by it. Enlargement, freedom, fullness of thought, directness and simplicity of utterance are the fruits of this unction.

Often, earnestness is mistaken for this unction. He who has the divine unction will be earnest in the very spiritual nature of things, but there may be a vast deal of earnestness without the least mixture of unction.

Earnestness and unction look alike from some points of view. Earnestness may be readily and without detection substituted or mistaken for unction. It requires a spiritual eye and a spiritual taste to discriminate.

Earnestness may be sincere, serious, ardent, and persevering. It goes at a thing with good will, pursues it with perseverance, and urges it with ardor; puts force in it. But all these forces do not rise higher than the mere human. The *man* is in it—the whole man, with all that he has of will and heart, of brain and genius, of planning and working and talking. He has set himself to some purpose which has mastered him, and he pursues to master it. There may be none of God in it. There may be little of God in it, because there is so much of the man in it. He may present pleas in advocacy of his earnest purpose, which please or touch and move or overwhelm with conviction of their importance. And in all this, earnestness may move along earthly ways, being propelled by human forces only, its altar made by earthly hands and its fire kindled by earthly flames.

It is said of a rather famous preacher of gifts, whose construction of Scripture was to his fancy or purpose, that he "grew very eloquent over his own exegesis." So men grow exceedingly earnest over their own plans or movements. Earnestness may be selfishness simulated.

What of unction? It is the indefinable in preaching which makes it preaching. It is that which distinguishes and separates preaching from all mere human addresses. It is the divine in preaching. It makes the preaching sharp to those who need sharpness. It distills as the dew to those who need to be refreshed. It is well described as:

> A two-edged sword
> Of heavenly temper keen,
> And double were the wounds it made
> Where'er it glanced between.
> 'Twas death to sin; 'twas life
> To all who mourned for sin.
> It kindled and it silenced strife,
> Made war and peace within.

This unction comes to the preacher not in the study, but in the closet. It is heaven's distillation in answer to prayer. It is the sweetest exhalation of the Holy Spirit. It impregnates, suffuses, softens, percolates, cuts, and soothes. It carries the Word like dynamite, like salt, like sugar; makes the Word a soother, an arraigner, a revealer, a searcher. It makes the hearer a culprit or a saint, makes him weep like a child and live like a giant, opens his heart and his purse as gently, yet as strongly, as the spring opens the leaves.

This unction is not the gift of genius. It is not found in the halls of learning. No eloquence can woo it. No industry can win it. No hands of a prelate can confer it. It is the gift of God—the signet for his own messengers. It is heaven's knighthood, given to the chosen true and brave ones who have sought this anointed honor through many an hour of tearful, wrestling prayer.

10. Prayer Marks Spiritual Leadership

Give me one hundred preachers who fear nothing but sin and desire nothing but God, and I care not a straw whether they be clergymen or laymen: such alone will shake the gates of hell and set up the kingdom of heaven on earth. God does nothing but in answer to prayer.
–John Wesley

The apostles knew the necessity and worth of prayer to their ministry. They knew that their high commission as apostles, instead of relieving them from the necessity of prayer, committed them to it by a more urgent need. They were exceedingly jealous else some other important work should exhaust their time and prevent their praying, as they ought. So they appointed others to look after the delicate and engrossing duties of ministering to the poor, that they (the apostles) might, unhindered, "give themselves continually to prayer and to the ministry of the word," (see Acts 6:4). Prayer is put first, and their relation to prayer is put most strongly—"give themselves to it"—making a business of it, surrendering themselves to praying, putting fervor, urgency, perseverance, and time in it.

How holy, apostolic men devoted themselves to this divine work of prayer! "Night and day praying exceedingly," (1 Thessalonians 3:10), says Paul. "We will give ourselves continually to prayer," is the consensus of apostolic devotement. How these New Testament preachers laid themselves out in prayer for God's people! How they put God in full force into their churches by their praying!

These holy apostles did not vainly fancy that they had met their high and solemn duties by delivering faithfully God's Word, but their preaching was made to stick and tell by the ardor and insistence of their praying. Apostolic praying was as taxing, toilsome, and imperative as apostolic preaching. They prayed mightily day and night to bring their people to the highest regions of faith and holiness. They prayed mightier still to hold them to this high spiritual altitude.

The preacher who has never learned in the school of Christ the high and divine art of intercession for his people will never learn the art of preaching, though homiletics be poured into him by the ton, and though he be the most gifted genius in sermon-making and sermon-delivery.

The prayers of apostolic, saintly leaders do much in making saints of those who are not apostles. If the church leaders in after years had been as particular and fervent in praying for their people as the apostles were, the sad, dark times of worldliness and apostasy would not have marred the history, eclipsed the glory, and arrested the advance of the church. Apostolic praying makes apostolic saints, and keeps apostolic times of purity and power in the church.

What loftiness of soul, what purity and elevation of motive, what unselfishness, what self-sacrifice, what exhaustive toil, what ardor of spirit, what divine tact are requisite to be an intercessor for men!

The preacher is to lay himself out in prayer for his people; not that they might be saved, simply, but that they be mightily saved. The apostles laid themselves out in prayer that their saints might be perfect; not that they should have a little relish for the things of God, but that they "might be filled with all the fullness of God," (Ephesians 3:19).

Paul did not rely on his apostolic preaching to secure this end, but "for this cause he bowed his knees to the Father of our Lord Jesus Christ," (see Ephesians 3:14). Epaphras did as much or more by prayer for the Colossian saints than by his preaching. He labored fervently, always in prayer for them, that "they might stand perfect and complete in all the will of God," (see Colossians 4:12).

Preachers are preeminently God's leaders. They are primarily responsible for the condition of the church. They shape its character; give tone and direction to its life.

Much every way depends on these leaders. They shape the times and the institutions. The church is divine, the treasure it encases is heavenly, but it bears the imprint of the human. The treasure is in earthen vessels, and it smacks of the vessel. The church of God makes, or is made by, its leaders. Whether it makes them or is made by them, it will be what its leaders are; spiritual if they are so, secular if they are, conglomerate if its leaders are. Israel's kings gave character to Israel's piety. A church rarely revolts against or rises above the religion of its leaders.

Strongly spiritual leaders, people of holy might, at the lead, are tokens of God's favor. Disaster and weakness follow the wake of feeble or worldly leaders. Israel had fallen low when God gave children to be their princes, and babes to rule over them. Times of spiritual leadership are times of great spiritual prosperity to the church.

Prayer is one of the eminent characteristics of strong spiritual leadership. People of mighty prayer are people of might, and they mold things. Their power with God has the conquering tread.

How can a man preach who does not get his message fresh from God in the closet? How can he preach without having his faith quickened, his vision cleared, and his heart warmed by his closeting with God? Alas, for the pulpit lips which are untouched by this closet flame. Dry and unctionless they will ever be, and truths divine will never come with power from such lips. As far as the real interests of religion are concerned, a pulpit without a closet will always be a barren thing.

A preacher may preach in an official, entertaining, or learned way without prayer; but between this kind of preaching and sowing God's precious seed with holy hands and prayerful, weeping hearts there is an immeasurable distance.

A prayerless ministry is the funeral undertaker for all God's truth and for God's church. He may have the most costly casket and the most beautiful flowers, but it is a funeral, notwithstanding the charming array. A prayerless Christian will never learn God's truth. A prayerless ministry will never be able to teach God's truth. Ages of millennial glory have been lost by a prayerless church. The coming of our Lord has been postponed by a prayerless church. Hell has enlarged herself and filled her dire caves in the presence of the dead service of a prayerless church.

The best, the greatest offering, is an offering of prayer. "Pray without ceasing" is the trumpet call to the preachers of the twentieth century. If the twentieth century will get their texts, their thoughts, their words, their sermons in their closets, the next century will find a new heaven and a new earth. The old sin-stained and sin-eclipsed heaven and earth will pass away under the power of a praying ministry.

11. A Praying Pulpit Gives Birth to a Praying Pew

I judge that my prayer is more than the devil himself; if it were otherwise, Luther would have fared differently long before this. Yet men will not see and acknowledge the great wonders or miracles God works in my behalf if I should neglect prayer but a single day, I should lose a great deal of the fire of faith. –Martin Luther

Only glimpses of the great importance of prayer could the apostles get before Pentecost. But the Spirit's coming and filling on Pentecost elevated prayer to its vital and all-commanding position in the Gospel of Christ. The call of prayer to every saint is now the Spirit's loudest and most exigent call. Sainthood's piety is made, refined, and perfected by prayer. The Gospel moves with slow and timid pace when the saints are not at their prayers early and late and long.

Where are the Christly leaders who can teach the modern saints how to pray and put them at it? Do we know we are raising up a prayerless set of saints? Where are the apostolic leaders who can put God's people to praying? Let them come to the front and do the work, and it will be the greatest work which can be done. An increase of educational facilities and a great increase of monetary strength will be the direst curse to religion if they are not sanctified by more and better praying than we are doing.

More praying will not come as a matter of course. The campaign for the twentieth or thirtieth century fund will not help our praying, but hinder it if we are not careful. Nothing but a specific effort from a praying leadership will avail. The chief ones must lead in the apostolic effort to radiate the vital importance and *fact* of prayer in the heart and life of the church. None but praying leaders can have praying followers. Praying apostles will give birth to praying saints. A praying pulpit will give birth to praying pews.

We do greatly need somebody who can set the saints to this business of praying. We are not a generation of praying saints. Nonpraying saints and a beggarly gang of saints who have neither the ardor, nor the beauty, nor the power of saints. Who will restore this breach? The greatest will he be of reformers and apostles, who can set the church to praying.

We put it as our most sober judgment that the great need of the church in this and all ages is people of such commanding faith, of such unsullied holiness, of such marked spiritual vigor and consuming zeal, that their prayers, faith, lives, and ministry will be of such a radical and aggressive form as to work spiritual revolutions which will restructure individual and church life.

We do not mean people who get up sensational activities by novel devices, nor those who attract by a pleasing entertainment; but people who can stir things, and work revolutions by the preaching of God's Word and by the power of the Holy Ghost—revolutions which change the whole current of things.

Natural ability and educational advantages do not figure as factors in this matter. But capacity for faith, the ability to pray, the power of thorough consecration, the ability of self-littleness, an absolute losing of one's self in God's glory, and an ever-present and insatiable yearning and seeking after all the fullness of God—people who can set the church ablaze for God; not in a noisy, showy way, but with an intense and quiet heat that melts and moves everything for God.

God can work wonders if He can get suitable individuals. Such can work wonders if they will allow God to lead them. The full endowment of the spirit that turned the world upside down would be eminently useful in these latter days. People who can stir things mightily for God, whose spiritual revolutions change the whole aspect of things, are the universal need of the church.

The church has never been without such individuals. They adorn its history. They are the standing miracles of God's blessing on the church. Their example and history are an unfailing inspiration and blessing. An increase in their number and power should be our prayer.

That which has been done in spiritual matters call be' done again, and be better done. This was Christ's view. He said, "Verily, verily, I say unto you, he that believeth on Me, the works that I do shall he do also; and greater works than these shall he do; because I go unto My Father," (John 14:12). The past has not exhausted the possibilities nor the demands for doing great things for God. The church that is dependent on its past history for its miracles of power and grace is a fallen church.

God wants elect individuals out of whom self and the world have been removed by a severe crucifixion, by a bankruptcy which has so totally ruined self and the world that there is neither hope nor desire of recovery; individuals who by this insolvency and crucifixion have turned toward God perfect hearts.

Let us pray ardently that God's promises to answer such prayer may be more than realized.

12. Notes

1   Letter to Homer W. Hodge, written from Washington, Georgia, July 1, 1912, cited in the Foreword to Bounds' book *Satan: His Personality, Power, and Overthrow* (Grand Rapids: Baker, 1963), p. 6.

2   Homer W. Hodge, in his Foreword to Bounds' book *The Reality of Prayer* (New York: Fleming H. Revell, 1924), p. 6.

3   For an excellent biography of this remarkable man, see the warmly written account by Lyle Wesley Dorsett, *E. M. Bounds, Man of Prayer* (Grand Rapids: Zondervan Publishing House, 1991). By any measure, this is the most complete and carefully researched story of Bounds' life and work. The volume also includes extensive excerpts from the writings of Bounds, most of which have not been published before in readily available book form.

4   The books include *Power Through Prayer* (1907), *Purpose in Prayer* (1920), *Bible Men of Prayer* (1921), *The Possibilities of Prayer* (1923), *The Reality of Prayer* (1924), *The Essentials of Prayer* (1925), *The Necessity of Prayer* (1929), and *The Weapon of Prayer* (1931).

I Believe in the Holy Ghost

D. L. Moody 1837-1899

*With an Introduction
By Nathan L. Oates*

Abridged version of teachings found in *Glad Tidings: Sermons and Prayer Meeting Talks* and *Secret Power: The Secret of Success in Christian Life and Work* by D. L. Moody. Abridged version originally published by the Institute of Evangelism Billy Graham Center, 1997, Wheaton, IL. Copyright of abridged version and introduction held by Nathan L. Oates, used with permission. Scripture quotations are taken from the New King James Version (NKJV). Copyright © 1979, 1980, 1982 by Thomas Nelson, Inc. Used by permission. Artwork in the Public Domain.

Book Chapters

1. Introduction
   By Nathan L. Oates 249
2. Honor the Holy Ghost 252
3. Power—Its Source 254
   Identity and Personality 255
   Agent and Instrument 256
   Secret of Efficiency 256
   The Reservoir of Love 258
   The Right Overflow 259
   The Triumph of Hope 260
   The Boon of Liberty 261
4. Power "In" and "Upon" 263
   Power "In" and "Upon" 263
   Praising With One Heart 264
   What Is Needed 266
   The Greatest Weapon 267
   "None of Self" 268
   Spiritual Irrigation 269
   Outflowing Streams 270
   Why Some Fail 271
   Fresh Supplies 272
   Green Fields 273
5. Witnessing In Power 275
   What is the Testimony? 276
   Greater Work 276
   The Sure Guide 278
   The Unerring Guide 278
   An Aid to Memory 279
   Long and Short Sight 279
   The Faithful Friend 280

	The Climax Sin	281
6.	Power Hindered	283
	What It Is Not	283
	Worldly Amusements	283
	What Is Success?	284
	Quench Not	285

1. Introduction
By Nathan L. Oates

The full extent of Dwight L. Moody's impact on the world for the cause of Christ is impossible to measure. There is, however, much evidence of his extraordinary effectiveness. Moody preached to more people than anyone who lived before 1900. Without the aid of microphones or radio, 100,000,000 people heard him proclaim the Gospel. Thousands came to Christ through the powerful ministry of this anointed American evangelist. Moody also established four schools through which hundreds of women and men received inexpensive education and ministry training. These students went throughout the nations spreading the message of Christ. Moody also wrote many inspirational books, which were translated into dozens of languages and dispersed throughout the world. By the time of his death in 1899, missionaries who had come to Christ through Moody's ministry could be found in every continent of the world except Antarctica.

Dwight Lyman Moody was born in Northfield, Massachusetts in 1837. The fifth of nine children raised by his widowed mother, Moody attended only three years of school. Bored with the monotony of farm life, he left home at age seventeen, confident that he could make a name for himself in Boston. The day Moody set out on his own, no one could have imagined that by the end of the century hundreds of millions of people all over the world would not only recognize his name but would regard him as one of the greatest promoters of Christianity of all time.

The transformation of D. L. Moody began in the back of a Boston shoe store when a gentle Sunday school teacher urged him to surrender his life to Jesus Christ. Ironically, the young convert's first application for church membership was denied because of his ignorance of church doctrine and his inability to clearly articulate his thoughts about Christ.

Soon Moody moved to the growing western city of Chicago to pursue a promising career as a shoe salesman. Immediately he became burdened for the souls of the youth in Chicago's slums and began a mission Sunday school. Moody ultimately gave up his lucrative business career, and committed his life to full time ministry with Chicago's Young Men's Christian Association.

Meanwhile Moody had fallen in love with Emma Revell, whom he married August 28, 1862. Graceful and compassionate, wise and devout, Emma had an incalculable influence both on Moody and his ministry.

Next to his conversion and his marriage, the pivotal point in Moody's life was his baptism in the Holy Spirit. After several years of evangelistic ministry which included campaigns throughout the Eastern United States and England, Moody was confronted with his need for the Holy Spirit's anointing by two women who regularly attended his meetings. Prior to this time Moody's ministry proved fruitful. He had planted a church, was elected president of the YMCA, his Sunday school mission was thriving, and he was maintaining a busy speaking schedule. But while his work appeared to be flourishing, the two women had discerned the truth: Moody had been ministering in his own strength to the point of exhaustion. Indeed, he showed signs of impending burnout. What he needed was an outpouring of power from on high.

Months of pleading with God for the fullness of His Spirit finally came to fruition one afternoon in 1872 while Moody walked down a crowded street in New York. Suddenly overwhelmed with an overpowering sense of the presence of God, he rushed to a friend's home and asked for a room where he could be alone. Within the walls of this chamber, the power of God rested so heavily on Moody that he had to ask God to withdraw His hand for fear that he might die. From that moment forward, Moody's ministry possessed unusual power.

Within weeks Moody sailed to Great Britain for another series of evangelistic services where previous meetings had met an unspectacular response. The campaign lasted 27 months, during which a religious awakening comparable only to the Wesley and Whitefield revival swept across the United Kingdom. Moody returned to America in 1875, the most sought-after preacher in the world.

For the remaining years of Moody's life, the Holy Spirit's ministry in the life of believers was a constant theme in every element of his work. He wrote about the Holy Spirit. He preached about the Holy Spirit.

He invited others to teach at his schools and conferences about the Holy Spirit. He wanted all Christians to experience the Spirit-filled life so they could minister through the Holy Spirit's power.

What follows is the central theme of Moody's teaching on the Holy Spirit. Taken from two books of his sermons: *Glad Tidings: Sermons and Prayer Meeting Talks*, (NY 1876) and *Secret Power: The Secret of Success in Christian Life and Work*, (Chicago, 1881), these messages contain the core of Moody's teaching on the baptism of the Spirit and the role of the Spirit in the life and ministry of the believer. I hope that these documents will continue to fulfill Moody's desire for more Christians to seek and surrender to the fullness of the power of God through His Spirit.

Nathan L. Oates
Wheaton, Illinois

2. Honor the Holy Ghost

I remember once when I was first converted I spoke in a Sabbath school, and there seemed to be a great deal of interest and quite a number rose for prayer, and I remember I went out quite rejoiced; but an old man followed me out – I have never seen him since. I never had seen him before and don't even know his name – but he caught hold of my hand and gave me a little bit of advice. I didn't know what he meant at the time, but he said, "Young man, when you speak again, honor the Holy Ghost." I was hastening off to another church to speak, and all the way over it kept ringing in my ears –"Honor the Holy Ghost," and I said to myself, "I wonder what the old man means." I have found out since what he meant, and I think that all that have been to work in the vineyard of the Lord have learnt that lesson that, if we honor Him in our efforts to do good, He will honor us and work through us; but if we don't honor Him, we will surely break down. The only work that is going to stand to eternity is the work done by the Holy Ghost, and not by anyone of us. We may be used as His instruments, but the work that will stand to eternity is that done by the Holy Ghost; and every conversion in these meetings that is not by the power of the Holy Ghost will not stand. There may be impressions that last for a few weeks or months, but then they will pass away like the morning cloud; and I firmly believe that if a man or woman be not converted by the Holy Ghost, we will not see them in Heaven.

Now, I have got a great many letters against that hymn "Come, Holy Spirit, Heavenly Dove," and I hear a great many people complain about our singing that hymn and praying for the Holy Ghost to come. They say He came on the day of Pentecost, and has been here ever since. But when we pray for Him to come, it is that He may anoint us afresh, that He may endow us with fresh power. There is such a thing as a man just having life but not having power, and so when we pray that the Holy Ghost may come upon us with power that we may be anointed, that is a different thing. And a thought I want to call your attention to be this, that God has got a good many children who have just barely got life, but no powers for service. You might say safely, I think, without exaggeration that nineteen out of every twenty of professed Christians are of no earthly account so far as building up Christ's kingdom; but on the contrary they are standing right in the way, and the reason is because they have just got life and have settled down, and have not sought for power. The Holy Ghost coming upon them with power is distinct and separate from conversion. If the Scripture doesn't teach it I am ready to correct it. Let us look and see what God says, and if you will look in the 3rd Chapter of Luke you will see that all these thirty years that Christ had been in Nazareth He had been a son, but now the Holy Ghost comes upon Him for service, and He goes back to Nazareth and finds a place where it is written: "The Spirit of Lord God is upon me because He hath anointed me to preach the good news to the poor. He has sent me to heal the broken hearted, to proclaim liberty to the captive, to recover sight for the blind, and set at liberty them that are bruised. And for three years we find Him preaching the kingdom of God, casting out devils, and raising the dead, while for thirty years that He was at Nazareth, we hear nothing of him. He was a son all the while, but now He is anointed for service; and if the Son of God has got to be anointed, do not His disciples need it, shall we not seek for it, and shall we barely rest with conversion?

3. Power—Its Source

"Without the soul, divinely quickened and inspired. The observances of the grandest ritualism are as worthless as the motions of a galvanized corpse." –Anon.

I quote this sentence, as it leads me at once to the subject under consideration. What is this quickening and inspiration? What is this power needed? From whence its source? I reply: The Holy Spirit of God. I am a full believer in "The Apostles' Creed," and therefore "I believe in the Holy Ghost."

A writer has pointedly asked: "What are our souls without His grace? –as dead as the branch in which the sap does not circulate. What is the church without Him? –as parched and barren as the fields without the dew and rain of heaven."

There has been much inquiry of late on the subject of the Holy Spirit. In this and other lands thousands of persons have been giving attention to the study of this grand theme. I hope it will lead us all to pray for a greater manifestation of His power upon the whole church of God. How much we have dishonored Him in the past! How ignorant of His grace, and love and presence we have been? True, we have heard of Him and read of Him, but we have had little intelligent knowledge of His attributes, His offices, and His relations to us. I fear He has not been to many professed Christians an actual existence, nor is He known to them as a personality of the Godhead.

The first work of the Spirit is to give life: spiritual life. He gives it and He sustains it. If there is no life, there can be no power; Solomon says: "A living dog is better than a dead lion." When the Spirit imparts this life, He does not leave us to droop and die, but constantly fans the flame. He is ever with us. Surely we ought not to be ignorant of His power and His work.

Identity and Personality

In John 6:7, we read: "There are three that bear record in heaven, the Father, the Word, and the Holy Ghost, and these three are one." By the Father is meant the first Person, Christ, the Word is the second, and the Holy Spirit, perfectly fulfilling His own office and work in union with the Father and the Son, is the third. I find clearly presented in my Bible, that the One God who demands my love, service and worship, has there revealed Himself, and that each of those three names of Father, Son and Holy Ghost has personality attached to them. Therefore we find some things ascribed to God as Comforter and Teacher. It has been remarked that the Father plans, the Son executes, and the Holy Spirit applies. But I also believe they plan and work together. The distinction of persons is often noted in Scripture. In Matthew 3:16, 17 we find Jesus submitting to baptism, the Spirit descending upon Him, while the Father's voice of approval is heard saying: "This is my beloved Son, in whom I am well pleased." Again, in John 14:16, we read: "I (i.e. Jesus) will pray the Father, and He will give you another Comforter." Also in Ephesians 2:18: "Through Him (i.e. Christ Jesus) we both (Jews and Gentiles) have access by one Spirit unto the Father." Thus we are taught the distinction of persons in the Godhead, and their inseparable union. From these and other scriptures also we learn the identity and actual existence of the Holy Spirit.

If you ask do I understand what is thus revealed in Scripture, I say "no." But my faith bows down before the inspired Word and I unhesitatingly believe the great things of God when even reason is blinded and the intellect confused.

In addition to the teaching of God's Word, the Holy Spirit in His gracious work in the soul declares His own presence. Through His agency we are "born again," and through His indwelling we possess superhuman power. I believe, and am growing more into this belief, that divine, miraculous creative power resides in the Holy Ghost. Above and beyond all natural law, yet in harmony with it, creation, providence, the divine government, and the up building of the church of God are presided over by the Spirit of God. His ministration is the ministration of life more glorious than the ministration of law (2 Corinthians 3:6-10). And like the Eternal Son, the Eternal Spirit having life in Himself, is working out all things after the counsel of own will, and for the everlasting glory of the Triune Godhead.

The Holy Spirit has all the qualities belonging to a person: the power to understand, to will, to do, to call, and to feel, to love. This cannot be said of a mere influence. He possesses attributes and qualities, which can only be ascribed to a person, as acts and deeds are performed by Him, which cannot be performed by a machine, an influence, or a result. Some people have an idea that the Holy Spirit is an attribute of God, just like mercy—just an influence coming from God...

If we want to honor the Holy Ghost, let us bear in mind that He is one of the Trinity, a personality in the Godhead.

Agent and Instrument

The Holy Spirit is closely identified with the words of the Lord Jesus. "It is the Spirit that quickened; the flesh profited nothing, the words that I speak unto you, they are spirit and they are life." The Gospel proclamation cannot be divorced from the Holy Spirit. Unless He attends the word in power, vain will be the attempt in preaching it. Human eloquence or persuasiveness of speech are the mere trappings of the dead, if the living Spirit be absent; the prophet may preach to the bones in the valley, but it must be the breath from heaven which will cause the slain to live.

In the 3rd Chapter of 1 Peter, it reads, "For Christ also hath once suffered for sins, the just for the unjust, that He might bring us to God, being put to death in the flesh, but quickened by the Spirit."

Here we see that Christ was raised up from the grave by this same Spirit, and the power exercised to raise Christ's dead body must raise our dead souls and quicken them. No other power on earth can quicken a dead soul, but the same power that raised the body of Jesus Christ out of Joseph's sepulcher. And if we want that power to quicken our friends who are dead in sin, we must look to God, and not be looking to man to do it. If we look alone to ministers, if we look alone to Christ's disciples to do this work, we shall be disappointed; but if we look to the Spirit of God and expect it to come from Him and Him alone, then we shall honor the Spirit, and the Spirit will do His work.

Secret of Efficiency

I cannot help but believe there are many Christians who want to be more efficient in the Lord's service, and the object of this book is to take up this subject of the Holy Spirit, that they may see from whom to expect this power. In teaching of Christ, we find the last words recorded in Matthew 28:19, "Go ye, therefore, and teach all nations, baptizing them in the name of the Father, and of the Son, and of the Holy Ghost."

Here we find that the Holy Spirit and the Son are equal with the Father – are one with Him, "teaching them in the name of the Father, and of the Son, and of the Holy Ghost." Christ was now handing His commission over to His apostles. He was going to leave them. His work on earth was finished, and He was now just about ready to take His seat at the right hand of God, and He spoke unto them and said: " All power is given unto me in heaven and in earth." All power, so then He had authority. If Christ was mere man, as some people try to make out, it would have been blasphemy for Him to have said to the disciples, go in His own name, and that of the Holy Ghost, making Himself equal with the Father.

There are three things: All power is given unto me, go, teach all nations. Teach them what? To observe all things. There are a great many people now that are willing to observe what they like about Christ, but the things that they don't like they just dismiss and turn away from. But His commission to His disciples was, "Go, teach all nations to observe all things whatsoever I have commanded you." And what right has a messenger who has been sent of God to change the message? If I had sent a servant to deliver a message, and the servant thought the message didn't sound exactly right – a little harsh – and that servant went and changed the message, I should change servants very quickly; he could not serve me any longer. And when a minister or a messenger of Christ begins to change the message because he thinks it is not exactly what it ought to be, and thinks he is wiser than God, God just dismisses that man.

They haven't taught "all things." They have left out some of the things that Christ has commanded us to teach, because they didn't correspond with man's reason. Now we have to take the Word of God just as it is; and if we are going to take it, we have no authority to take out just what we like, what we think is appropriate, and let dark reason be our guide.

It is the work of the Spirit to impress the heart and seal the preached word. His office is to take of the things of Christ and reveal them unto us.

Some people have got an idea that this is the only dispensation of the Holy Ghost; that He didn't work until Christ was glorified. But Simeon felt the Holy Ghost when he went into the temple. In 2 Peter 1:21, we read: "Holy men of old spoke as they were moved by the Holy Ghost." We find the same Spirit in Genesis as is seen in Revelation. The same Spirit that guided the hand that wrote Exodus inspired also the epistles, and we find the Same Spirit speaking from one end of the Bible to the other. So holy men in all ages have spoken as they were moved by the Holy Ghost.

The Reservoir of Love

We read that the fruit of the Spirit is love. God is love, Christ is love, and we should not be surprised to read about the love of the Spirit. What a blessed attribute is this. May I call it the dome of the temple of the graces. Better still, it is the crown of crowns worn by the Triune God. Human love is a natural emotion, which flows forth towards the object of our affections. But divine love is as high above human love as the heaven is above the earth. The natural man is of the earth, earthy, and however pure his love may be, it is weak and imperfect at best. But the love of God is perfect and entire, wanting nothing. It is as a mighty ocean in its greatness, dwelling with and flowing from the Eternal Spirit.

In Romans 5:5, we read: "And hope maketh not ashamed, because the love of God is shed abroad in our hearts by the Holy Ghost which is given to us." Now if we are co-workers with God, there is one thing we must possess, and that is love. A man may be a very successful lawyer and have no love for his clients, and yet get on very well. A man may be a very successful physician and have no love for his patients, and yet be a very good physician; a man may be a very successful merchant and have no love for his customers, and yet he may do a good business and succeed; but no man can be a coworker with God without love. If our service is mere profession on our part, the quicker we renounce it the better. If a man takes up God's work as he would take up any profession, the sooner he gets out of it the better.

We cannot work for God without love. It is the only tree that can produce fruit on this sin-cursed earth that is acceptable to God. If I have no love for God nor for my fellow man, then I cannot work acceptably. I am like sounding brass and a tinkling cymbal. We are told "the love of God is shed abroad in our hearts by the Holy Ghost." Now, if we have had that love shed abroad in our hearts, we are ready for God's service; if we have not, we are not ready. It is so easy to reach a man when you love him; all barriers are broken down and swept away.

Paul, when writing to Titus (2:2), tells him to be sound in faith, in charity, and in patience. Now in this age, ever since I can remember, the church has been very jealous about men being unsound in the faith. If a man becomes unsound in the faith, they draw their ecclesiastical sword and cut at him; but he may be ever so unsound in love, and they don't say anything. He may be ever so defective in patience; he may be irritable and fretful all the time, but they never deal with him. Now the Bible teaches us, that we are not only to be sound in the faith, but in charity and in patience. I believe God cannot use many of His servants, because they are full of irritability and impatience; they are fretting all the time, from morning until night. God cannot use them; their mouths are sealed; they cannot speak for Jesus Christ, and if they have not love, they cannot work for God. I do not mean love for those that love me; it doesn't take grace to do that; the rudest Hottentot in the world can do that; the greatest heathen that ever lived can do that; the vilest man that ever walked the earth can do that. It doesn't take any grace at all. I did that before I ever became a Christian. Love begets love; hatred begets hatred. Now you know the first impulse of a young convert is to love. Do you remember the day you were converted? Was not your heart full of sweet peace and love?

The Right Overflow

I remember the morning I came out of my room after I had first trusted Christ, and I thought the old sun shone a good deal brighter than it ever had before; I thought that the sun was just smiling upon me, and I walked out upon Boston Common, and I heard the birds in the trees, and I thought that they were all singing a song for me. Do you know I fell in love with the birds? I never cared for them before; it seemed to me that I was in love with all creation. I had not a bitter feeling against any man, and I was ready to take all men to my heart. If a man has not the love of God shed abroad in his heart, he has never been regenerated. If you hear a person get up in prayer-meeting, and he begins to speak and find fault with everybody, you may know that his is not a genuine conversion; that it is counterfeit; it has not the right ring, because the impulse of a converted soul is to love, and not to be getting up and complaining of every one else, and finding fault. But it is hard for us to live in the right atmosphere all the time. Someone comes along and treats us wrongly, perhaps we hate him; we have not attended to the means of grace and kept feeding on the Word of God as we ought; a root of bitterness springs up in our hearts, and perhaps we are not aware of it, but it has come up in our hearts; then we are not qualified to work for God. The love of God is not shed abroad in our hearts, as it ought to be by the Holy Ghost.

But the work of the Holy Ghost is to impart love. Paul could say, "The love of Christ constrained me." He could not help going from town to town and preaching the Gospel. Jeremiah at one time said: "I will speak no more in the Lord's name; I have suffered enough; these people don't like God's word." They lived in a wicked day, as we do now. Infidels were creeping up all around him, who said the word of God was not true; Jeremiah had stood like a wall of fire, confronting them, and he boldly proclaimed that the word of God was true. At last they put him in prison, and he said: "I will keep still; it has cost me too much." But a little while after, you know he could not keep still. His bones caught fire; he had to speak. And when we are so full of the love of God, we are compelled to work for God, and then God blesses us. If, our work is sought to be accomplished by the lash, without any true motive power, it will come to naught.

Now the question comes up, have we the love of God shed abroad in our hearts, and are we holding the truth in love? Some people hold the truth, but in such a cold strem way that it will do no good. Other people want to love everything, and so they give up much of the truth; but we are to hold the truth in love; we are to hold the truth even if we lose all, but we are to hold it in love, and if we do that, the Lord will bless us.

There are a good many people trying to get this love; they are trying to produce it of themselves. But therein all fail. The love implanted deep in our new nature will be spontaneous. I don't have to learn to love my children. I cannot help loving them. I said to a young miss some time ago, in an inquiry meeting, who said that she could not love God; that it was very hard for her to love Him –I said to her, "Is it hard for you to love your mother? Do you have to learn to love your mother?" And she looked up through her tears, and said, "No; I can't help it; that is spontaneous." "Well," I said, "when the Holy Spirit kindles love in your heart, you cannot help loving God; it will be spontaneous." When the Spirit of God comes into your heart and mine, it will be easy to serve God.

The fruit of the Spirit, as you find it in Galatians, begins with love. There are nine graces spoken of in the 6th Chapter and of the nine different graces Paul puts love at the head of the list; love is the first thing – the first in that precious cluster of fruit. Someone has put it in this way: that all the other eight can be put in the word love. Joy is love exulting; peace is love in repose; long suffering is love on trial; gentleness is love in society; goodness is love in action; faith is love on the battlefield; meekness is love at school; and temperance is love in training. So it is love all the way; love at the top; love at the bottom, and all the way along down these graces; and if we only just brought forth the fruit of the Spirit, what a world we would have; there would be no need of any policemen; a man could leave his overcoat around without someone stealing it; men would not have any desire to do evil. Says Paul, "Against such there is no law"; you don't need any law. A man who is full of the Spirit doesn't need to be put under law; doesn't need any policemen to watch him. We could dismiss all our policemen; the lawyers would have to give up practicing law; and the courts would not have any business.

The Triumph of Hope

In Romans 15:13 the apostle says: "Now the God of hope fill you with all joy and peace in believing, that you may abound in hope through the power of the Holy Ghost." The next thing then is hope.

Did you ever notice this, that no man or woman is ever used by God to build up His kingdom with has lost hope? Now, I have been observing this throughout different parts of the country, and whenever I have found a worker in God's vineyard who has lost hope, I have found a man or woman not very useful. Now, just look at these workers. Let your mind go over the past for a moment. Can you think of a man or woman whom God has used to build His kingdom that has lost hope? I don't know of any; I never heard of such a one. It is very important to have hope in the church; and it is the work of the Holy Ghost to impart hope. Let Him come into some of the churches where there have not been any conversions for a few years, and let Him convert a score of people, and see how hopeful the church becomes at once. He imparts hope; a man filled with the Spirit of God will be very hopeful. He will be looking out into the future, and he knows that it is all bright, because the God of all grace is able to do great things. So it is very important that we have hope.

If a man has lost hope, he is out of communion with God; he has not the Spirit of God resting upon him for service; he may be a Son of God, and disheartened so that he cannot be used of God. Do you know there is no place in the Scriptures where it is recorded that God ever used even a discouraged man.

The Boon of Liberty

The next thing the Spirit of God does is to give us liberty. He first imparts love; He next inspires hope, and then gives liberty, and that is about the last thing we have in a good many of our churches at the present day. And I am sorry to say there must be a funeral in a good many churches before there is much work done, we shall have to bury the formalism so deep that it will never have any resurrection. The last thing to be found in many a church is liberty.

If the Gospel happens to be preached, the people criticize, as they would a theatrical performance. It is exactly the same, and many a professed Christian never thinks of listening to what the man of God has to say. It is hard Work to preach to carnally minded critics, but "Where the Spirit of the Lord is, there is liberty."

Very often a woman will hear a hundred good things in a sermon, and there may be one thing that strikes her as a little out of place, and she will go home and sit down to the table and talk right out before her children and magnify that one wrong thing, and not say a word about the hundred good things that were said. That is what people do who criticize.

God does not use men in captivity. The condition of many is like Lazarus when he came out of the sepulcher bound hand and foot. The bandage was not taken off his mouth, and he could not speak. He had life, and if you had said Lazarus was not alive, you would have told a falsehood, because he was raised from the dead. There are a great many people, the moment you talk to them and insinuate they are not doing what they might, they say: "I have life. I am a Christian." Well, you can't deny it, but they are bound hand and foot.

May God snap these fetters and set His children free, that they may have liberty. I believe He comes to set us free, and wants us to work for Him, and speak for Him. How many people would like to get up in a social prayer meeting to say a few words for Christ, but there is such a cold spirit of criticism in the church that they dare not do it. They have not the liberty to do it. If they get up, they are so frightened with these critics that they begin to tremble and sit down. They cannot say anything. Now, that is all wrong. The Spirit of God comes just to give liberty, and wherever you see the Lord's work going on, you will see that Spirit of liberty. People won't be afraid of speaking to one another. And when the meeting is over they will not get their hats and see how quick they can get out of the church, but will begin to shake hands with one another, and there will be liberty there. A good many go to the prayer meeting out of a mere cold sense of duty. They think, "I must attend because I feel it is my duty." They don't think it is a glorious privilege to meet and pray, and to be strengthened, and to help someone else in the wilderness journey.

What we need today is love in our hearts. Don't we want it? Don't we want hope in our lives? Don't we want to be hopeful? Don't we want liberty? Now, all this is the work of the Spirit of God, and let us pray to God daily to give us love, hope, and liberty. We read in Hebrews 10:19: "Having, therefore, brethren, boldness to enter into the holiest by the blood of Jesus." If you will trun to the passage and read the margin it says: "Having, therefore, brethren, liberty to enter into the holiest." We can go into the holiest, having freedom of access, and plead for this love and liberty and glorious hope, that we may not rest until God gives us the power to work for Him.

If I know my own heart today, I would rather die than live as I once did, a mere nominal Christian, and not used by God in building up His kingdom. It seems a poor empty life to live for the sake of self.

Let us seek to be useful. Let us seek to be vessels meet for the Master's use that God, the Holy Spirit, may shine fully through us.

4. Power "In" and "Upon"

You remember that strange, half-involuntary "forty years" of Moses in the "wilderness" of Midian, when he had fled from Egypt. You remember, too, the almost equally strange years of retirement in "Arabia" by Paul, when, if ever, humanly speaking, instant action was needed. And pre-eminently you remember the amazing charge of the ascending Lord to the disciples, "Tarry at Jerusalem." Speaking after the manner of men, one could not have wondered if out-spoken Peter, or fervid James, had said: "Tarry, Lord! How long?" "Tarry, Lord! Is there not a perishing world, groaning for the 'good news?'" "Tarry? Did we hear Thee aright, Lord? Was the word not haste?" Nay, "Being assembled together with them, He commanded them that they should not depart from Jerusalem, but wait for the promise of the Father" (Acts 1:4). –Grosart.

Power "In" and "Upon"

The Holy Spirit dwelling in us is one thing; I think this is clearly brought out in Scripture; and the Holy Spirit upon us for service, is another thing. Now there are only three places we find in Scripture that are dwelling-places for the Holy Ghost.

In the 40th chapter of Exodus, commencing with the 33rd verse, are these words:

"And he (that is, Moses) reared up the court round about the tabernacle and the altar, and set up the hanging of the court gate. So Moses finished the work.

"Then a cloud covered the tent of the congregation, and the glory of the Lord filled the tabernacle.

"And Moses was not able to enter into the tent of the congregation, because the cloud abode thereon, and the glory of the Lord filled the tabernacle."

The moment that Moses finished the work, the moment that the tabernacle was ready, the cloud came, the Shekinah glory came and filled it so that Moses was not able to stand before the presence of the Lord. I believe firmly, that the moment our hearts are emptied of pride and selfishness and ambition and self-seeking, and everything that is contrary to God's law, the Holy Ghost will come and fill every corner of our hearts; but if we are full of pride and conceit, and ambition and self-seeking, and pleasure and the world, there is no room for the Spirit of God; and I believe many a man is praying to God to fill him when he is full already with something else. Before we pray that God would fill us, I believe we ought to pray Him to empty us.

There must be an emptying before there can be a filling; and when the heart is turned upside down, and everything is turned out that is contrary to God, and then the Spirit will come, just as He did in the tabernacle, and fill us with His glory. We read in 2 Chronicles 5:13, 14: "It came even to pass, as the trumpeters and singers were as one to make one sound, to be heard in praising and thanking the Lord, and when they lifted up their voice with the trumpets and cymbals and instruments of music, and praised the Lord, saying, 'For He is good; for His mercy endured forever;' that then the house was filled with a cloud, even the house of the Lord. So that the priests could not stand to minister by reason of the cloud, for the glory of the Lord had filled the house of God."

Praising With One Heart

We find, the very moment that Solomon completed the Temple, when all was finished, they were just praising God with one heart – the choristers and the singers and the ministers were all one; there was not any discord; they were all praising God, and the glory of God came and just filled the Temple as the Tabernacle. Now, as you turn over into the New Testament, you will find, instead of coming to tabernacles and temples, believers are now the temples of the Holy Ghost. When, on the day of Pentecost, before Peter preached that memorable sermon, as they were praying, the Holy Spirit came and came in mighty power. We now pray for the Spirit of God to come, and we sing:

> "Come, Holy Spirit, heavenly Dove,
> With all thy quickening power;
> Kindle a flame of heavenly love
> In these cold heart of ours."

I believe, if we understand it, it is perfectly right; but if we are praying for Him to come out of heaven down to earth again, that is wrong, because He is already here; He has not been out of this earth for 1800 years; He has been in the church, and He is with all believers; the believers in the church are the called out ones; they are called out from the world, and every true believer is a temple for the Holy Ghost to dwell in. In John 14:17 we have the words of Jesus:

> "The Spirit of Truth, whom the world cannot receive, because it sees Him not, neither knows Him; but ye know Him, for He dwells in you."

> "Greater is He that is in you than He that is in the world." If we have the Spirit dwelling in us, He gives us power over the flesh and the world, and over every enemy. "He is dwelling with you, and shall be in you."

Read 1 Corinthians 3:16: "Know ye not that ye are the temple of God, and that the Spirit of God dwells in you?"

There were some men burying an aged saint some time ago, and he was very poor, like many of God's people, poor in this world, but they are very rich, they have all the riches on the other side of life – they have them laid up there where thieves cannot get them, and where sharpers cannot take them away from them, and where moth cannot corrupt – so this aged man was very rich in the other world, and they were just hastening him off to the grave, wanting to get rid of him, when an old minister, who was officiating at the grave, said, "Tread softly, for you are carrying the temple of the Holy Ghost." Whenever you see a believer, you see a temple of the Holy Ghost.

In 1 Corinthians 6:19, 20, we read again: "Know ye not that your body is the temple of the Holy Ghost which is in you, which ye have of God, and ye are not your own? For ye are bought with a price, therefore glorify God in your body and in your spirit, which are God's." Thus are we taught that there is a divine resident in every child of God.

I think it is clearly taught in the Scripture that every believer has the Holy Ghost dwelling in him. He may be quenching the Spirit of God, and he may not glorify God as be should, but if he is a believer on the Lord Jesus Christ, the Holy Ghost dwells in him. But I want to call your attention to another fact. I believe today, that though Christian men and women have the Holy Spirit dwelling in them, yet He is not dwelling within them in power; in other words, God has a great many sons and daughters without power.

What Is Needed

Nine-tenths, at least, of the church members never think of speaking for Christ. If they see a man, perhaps a near relative, just going right down to ruin, going rapidly, they never think of speaking to him about his sinful course and of seeking to win him to Christ. Now certainly there must be something wrong. And yet when you talk with them you find they have faith, and you cannot say they are not children of God; but they have not the power, they have not the liberty, they have not the love that real disciples of Christ should have. A great many people are thinking that we need new measures, that we need new churches, that we need new organs, and that we need new choirs, and all these new things. That is not what the church of God needs today. It is the old power that the apostles had; that is what we want, and if we have that in our churches, there will be new life. Then we will have new ministers – the same old ministers renewed with power filled with the Spirit. I remember when in Chicago many were toiling in the work, and it seemed as though the car of salvation didn't move on, when a minister began to cry out from the very depths of his heart, "Oh, God, put new ministers in every pulpit." On next Monday I heard two or three men stand up and say, "We had a new minister last Sunday—the same old minister, but he had got new power," and I firmly believe that is what we want today all over America. We want new ministers in the pulpit and new people in the pews. We want people quickened by the Spirit of God, and the Spirit corning down and taking possession of the children of God and giving them power.

Then a man filled with the Spirit will know how to use "the sword of the Spirit." If a man is not filled with the Spirit, he will never know how to use the Book. We are told that this is the sword of the Spirit; and what is an army good for that does not know how to use its weapons? Suppose a battle going on, and I were a general and had a hundred thousand men, great, able-bodied men, full of life, but they could not one of them handle a sword, and not one of them knew how to use his rifle, what would that army be good for? Why, one thousand well-drilled men, with good weapons, would rout the whole of them. The reason why the church cannot overcome the enemy is, because she doesn't know how to use the sword of the Spirit. People will get up and try to fight the devil with their experiences, but he doesn't care for that, he will overcome them every time. People are trying to fight the devil with theories and pet ideas, but he will get the victory over them likewise. What we want is to draw the sword of the Spirit. It is that which cuts deeper than anything else.

Turn in your Bibles to Ephesians 6:14: "Stand, therefore, having your loins girt about with truth, and having on the breastplate of righteousness; and your feet shod with the preparation of the Gospel of peace; above all (or over all) taking the shield of faith, wherewith ye shall be able to quench all the fiery darts of the wicked. And take the helmet of salvation and the sword of the Spirit, which is the Word of God."

The Greatest Weapon

The sword of the Spirit is the Word of God, and what we need especially is to be filled with the Spirit, so we shall know how to use the Word. There was a Christian man talking to a skeptic, who was using the Word, and the skeptic said, "I don't believe, Sir, in that Book." But the man went right on and he gave him more of the Word; and the man again remarked, "I don't believe the Word," but he kept giving him more, and at last the man was reached. And the brother added, "When I have proved a good sword which does the work of execution, I would just keep right on using it." That is what we want. Skeptics and infidels may say they don't believe in it. It is not our work to make them believe in it; that is the work of the Spirit. Our work is to give them the Word of God not to preach our theories and our ideas about it, but just to deliver the message as God gives it to us. We read in the Scriptures of the sword of the Lord and Gideon. Suppose Gideon had gone out without the Word, he would have been defeated. But the Lord used Gideon; and I think you find all through the Scriptures, God takes up and uses human instruments. You cannot find, I believe, a case in the Bible where a man is converted without God calling in some human agency using some human instrument; not but what He can do it in His independent sovereignty; there is no doubt about that. Even when by the revealed glory of the Lord Jesus, Saul of Tarsus was smitten to the earth, Ananias was used to open his eyes and lead him into the light of the Gospel. I heard a man once say, if you put a man on a mountain peak, higher than one of the Alpine peaks, God could save him without a human messenger; but that is not His way; that is not His method; but it is "the sword of the Lord and Gideon"; and the Lord and Gideon will do the work; and if we are just willing to let the Lord use us, He will.

"None of Self"

Then you will find all through the Scriptures, when men were filled with the Holy Spirit, they preached Christ and not themselves. They preached Christ and Him crucified. It says in Luke 1:6-7, speaking of Zacharias, the father of John the Baptist:

> "And his father, Zacharias, was filled with the Holy Ghost, and prophesied, saying: Blessed be the Lord God of Israel, for He hath visited and redeemed His people, and hath raised up an horn of salvation for us in the house of His servant David. As He spoke by the mouth of His holy prophets, which have been since the world began."

See, he is talking about the Word. If a man is filled with the Spirit, he will magnify the Word; he will preach the Word, and not himself; he will give this lost world the Word of the living God.

We also find that Simeon, as he came into the Temple and found the young child Jesus there, at once began to quote the Scriptures, for the Spirit was upon him. And when Peter stood up on the day of Pentecost, and preached that wonderful sermon, it is said he was filled with the Holy Ghost, and began to preach the Word to the multitude, and it was the Word that cut them. It was the sword of the Lord and Peter, the same as it was the sword of the Lord and Gideon. And we find it says of Stephen, "They were not able to resist the spirit and wisdom by which he spoke." Why? Because he gave them the Word of God. And we are told that the Holy Ghost came on Stephen, and none could resist his word. And we read, too, that Paul was full of the Holy Spirit, that he preached Christ and Him crucified, and that many people were added to the church. Barnabas was full of faith and the Holy Ghost; and if you will just read and find out what he preached, you will find it was the Word, and many were added to the Lord. So that when a man is full of the Spirit, he begins to preach, not himself, but Christ, as revealed in the Holy Scriptures.

The disciples of Jesus were all filled with the Spirit, and the Word was published; and when the Spirit of God comes down upon the church, and we are anointed, the Word will be published in the streets, in the lanes, and in the alleys; there will not be a dark cellar nor a dark attic, nor a home where the Gospel will not be carried by some loving heart, if the Spirit comes upon God's people in demonstration and in power.

Spiritual Irrigation

It is possible a man may just barely have life and be satisfied, and I think that a great many are in that condition. In the 3rd Chapter of John we find that Nicodemus came to Christ and that he received life. At first this life was feeble. You don't hear of him standing up confessing Christ boldly, and of the Spirit coming upon him in great power, though possessing life through faith in Christ. And then turn to the 4th Chapter of John, and you will find it speaks of the woman coming to the well of Samaria, and Christ held out the cup of salvation to her and she took it and drank, and it became in her "a well of water springing tip into everlasting life." That is better than in the 3rd Chapter of John; here it came down in a flood into her soul; as someone has said, it came down from the throne of God, and like a mighty current carried her back to the throne of God. Water always rises to its level, and if we get the soul, filled with water from the throne of God it will bear us upward its source.

But if you want to get the best class of Christian life portrayed, turn to the 7th Chapter and you will find that it says he that received the Spirit, through trusting in the Lord Jesus, "out of him shall flow rivers of living water." Now there are two ways of digging a well. I remember, when a boy, upon a farm, in New England, they had a well and they put in an old wooden pump, and I used to have to pump the water from that well upon wash-day, and to water the cattle; and I had to pump and pump and pump until my arm got tired, many a time. But they have a better way now; they don't dig down a few feet and brick up the hole and put the pump in, but they go down through the clay and the sand and the rock, and on down until they strike what they call a lower stream, and then it becomes an artesian well, which needs no labor, as the water rises spontaneously from the depths beneath.

Now I think God wants all His children to be a sort of artesian well; not to keep pumping, but to flow right out. Why, haven't you seen ministers in the pulpit just pumping, and pumping and pumping? I have, many a time, and I have had to do it, too. I know how it is. They stand in the pulpit and talk and talk and talk, and the people go to sleep, they can't arouse them. What is the trouble? Why, the living water is not there; they are just pumping when there is no water in the well. You can't get water out of a dry well; you have to get something in the well, or you can't get anything out. I have seen these wooden pumps where you had to pour water into them before you could pump any water out, and so it is with a good many people; you have to get something in them before you can get anything out. People wonder why it is that they have no spiritual power. They stand up and talk in meeting, and don't say anything; they say they haven't anything to say, and you find it out soon enough; they need not state it; but they just talk, because they feel it is a duty, and say nothing.

Now I tell you when the Spirit of God is on us for service, resting upon us, we are anointed, and then we can do great things. "I will pour water on him that is thirsty," says God. Oh, blessed thought – "He that hungers and thirsts after righteousness shall be filled"!

Outflowing Streams

I would like to see someone just full of living water; so full that they couldn't contain it; that they would have to go out and publish the Gospel of the grace of God. When a man gets so full he can't hold any more, then he is just ready for God's service.

When preaching in Chicago, Dr. Gibson remarked in the inquiry meeting, "Now, how can we find out who is thirsty?" Said he, "I was just thinking how we could find out. If a boy should come down the aisle, bringing a good pail of clear water, and a dipper we would soon find out who was thirsty; we would see thirsty men and women reach out for water; but if you should walk down the aisle with an empty bucket, you wouldn't find it out. People would look in and see that there was no water, and say nothing." So said he, "I think that is the reason we are not more blessed in our ministry; we are carrying around empty buckets, and the people see that we have not anything in them, and they don't come forward." I think that there is a good deal of truth in that. People see that we are carrying around empty buckets, and they will not come to us until they are filled. They see we haven't any more than they have. We must have the Spirit of God resting upon us, and then we will have something that gives the victory over the world, the flesh, and the devil; something that gives the victory over our tempers, over our conceits, and over every other evil, and when we can trample these sins under our feet, then people will come to us and say, "How did you get it? I need this power; you have something that I haven't got; I want it." Oh, may God show us this truth. Have we been toiling all night? Let us throw the net on the right side; let us ask God to forgive our sins, and anoint us with power from on high. But remember, He is not going to give this power to an impatient man; He is not going to give it to a selfish man; He will never give it to an ambitious man whose aim is selfish, till first emptied of self; emptied of pride and of all worldly thoughts. Let it be God's glory and not our own that we seek, and when we get to that point, how speedily the Lord will bless us for good. Then will the measure of our blessing be full. Do you know what heaven's measure is? Good measure, pressed down, shaken together, and running over. If we get our hearts filled with the Word of God, how is Satan going to get in? How is the world going to get in, for heaven's measure is good measure, full measure, running over. Have you this fullness? If you have not, then seek it; say by the grace of God you will have it, for it is the Father's good pleasure to give us these things. He wants us to shine down in this world; He wants to lift us up for His work; He wants us to have the power to testify for His Son. He has left us in this world to testify for Him. What did He leave us for? Not to buy and sell and to get gain, but to glorify Christ. How are you going to do it without the Spirit? That is the question. How are you to do it without the power of God?

Why Some Fail

We read in John 20:22: "And when He had said this, He breathed on them, and said unto them, 'Receive ye the Holy Ghost.'"

Then see Luke 24:49: "And, behold, I send the promise of my Father upon you; but tarry ye in the city of Jerusalem until ye be endued with power from on high."

The first passage tells us He had raised those pierced and wounded hands over them and breathed upon them and said, "Receive ye the Holy Ghost." And I haven't a doubt they received it then, but not in such mighty power as afterward when qualified for their work. It was not in fullness that He gave it to them then, but if they had been like a good many now, they would have said, "I have enough now; I am not going to tarry; I am going to work."

Some people seem to think they are losing time if they wait on God for His power, and so away they go and work without unction; they are working without any anointing, they are working without any power. But after Jesus had said "Receive ye the Holy Ghost," and had breathed on them, He said: "Now you tarry in Jerusalem until you be endued with power from on high." Read in Acts 1:8: "But ye shall receive power, after that the Holy Ghost is come upon you."

Now, the Spirit had been given them certainly or they could not have believed, and they could not have taken their stand for God and gone through what they did, and endured the scoffs and frowns of their friends, if they had not been converted by the power of the Holy Ghost. But now just see what Christ said:

> "Ye shall receive power after that the Holy Ghost is come unto you; and ye shall be witnesses unto me both in Jerusalem and in all Judea, and in Samaria, and unto the uttermost parts of the earth."

Then, the Holy Spirit *in* us is one thing, and the Holy Spirit ON us is another; and if these Christians had gone out and went right to preaching then and there, without the power, do you think that scene would have taken place on the day of Pentecost? Don't you think that Peter would have stood up there and beat against the air, while these Jews would have gnashed their teeth and mocked him? But they tarried in Jerusalem; they waited ten days. What! you say. What, the world perishing and men dying! Shall I wait? Do what God tells you. There is no use in running before you are sent; there is no use in attempting to do God's work without God's power. A man working without this unction, a man working without this anointing, a man working without the Holy Ghost upon him, is losing his time after all. So we are not going to lose anything if we tarry till we get this power. That is the object of true service, to wait on God, to tarry until we receive this power for witness bearing. Then we find that on the day of Pentecost, ten days after Jesus Christ was glorified, the Holy Spirit descended in power. Do you think that Peter, James, John, and those apostles doubted it from that very hour. They never doubted it. Perhaps some question the possibility of having the power of God now, and that the Holy Spirit never came afterward in similar manifestation, and will never come again in such power.

Fresh Supplies

Turn to Acts 4:31, and you will find He came a second time, and at a place where they were, so that the earth was shaken, and they were filled with this power. The fact is, we are leaky vessels, and we have to keep right under the fountain all the time to keep full of Christ, and so have a fresh supply.

I believe this is a mistake a great many of us are making; we are trying to do God's work with the grace God gave us ten years ago. We say if it is necessary, we will go on with the same grace. Now, what we want is a fresh supply, a fresh anointing, and fresh power, and if we seek it, and seek it with all our hearts, we will obtain it. The early converts were taught to look for that power. Philip went to Samaria, and news reached Jerusalem that there was a great work being done in Samaria, and many converts: and John and Peter went down, and they laid their hands on them, and they received the Holy Ghost for service. I think that is what we Christians ought to be looking for – the Spirit of God for service – that God may use us mightily in the building up of His church and hastening His glory. In Acts 19 we read of twelve men at Ephesus who, when the inquiry was made if they had received the Holy Ghost since they believed, answered: "We have not so much as heard whether there be any Holy Ghost." I venture to say there are very many, who, if you were to ask them, "Have you received the Holy Ghost since you believed?" would reply, "I don't know what you mean by that." They would be like the twelve men down at Ephesus, who had never understood the peculiar relation of the Spirit to the sons of God in this dispensation. That is the reason men dare not speak to their neighbors about Christ, and the reason why every night so many go away from here that are anxious about their souls, and yet the Christian who sits next to them has not the moral courage to speak to them about Christ and salvation...I firmly believe that the church has just laid this knowledge [of the baptism of the Spirit for service] aside, mislaid it somewhere, and so Christians are without power. Sometimes you can take one hundred members into the church, and they don't add to its power. Now that is all wrong. If they were only anointed by the Spirit of God, there would be great power if one hundred saved ones were added to the church.

Green Fields

When I was out in California, the first time I went down from the Sierra Nevada Mountains and dropped into the Valley of the Sacramento, I was surprised to find on one farm that everything about it was green – all the trees and flowers, everything was blooming, and everything was green and beautiful, and just across the hedge everything was dried up, and there was not a green thing there, and I could not understand it; I made inquiries, and I found that the man that had everything green, irrigated; he just poured the water right on, and he kept everything green, while the fields that were next to his were as dry as Gideon's fleece without a drop of dew; and so it is with a great many in the church today. They are like these farms in California – a dreary desert, everything parched and desolate, and apparently no life in them. They can sit next to a man who is full of the Spirit of God, who is like a green bay tree, and who is bringing forth fruit, and yet they will not seek a similar blessing. Well, why this difference? Because God has poured water on him that was thirsty, that is the difference. One has been seeking this anointing, and he has received it; and when we want this above everything else God will surely give it to us.

The great question before us now is, Do we want it? I remember when I first went to England and gave a Bible reading, I think about the first that I gave in that country, a great many ministers were there, and I didn't know anything about English theology, and I was afraid I should run against their creeds, and I was a little hampered, especially on this very subject, about the gift of the Holy Spirit for service. I remember particularly a Christian minister there who had his head bowed on his hand, and I thought the good man was ashamed of everything I was saying, and of course that troubled me. At the close of my address he took his hat and went away, and then I thought, "Well, I shall never see him again." At the next meeting I looked all around for him and he wasn't there, and at the next meeting I looked again, but he was absent; and I thought my teaching must have given him offense. But a few days after that, at a large noon prayer meeting a man stood up and his face shone as if he had been up in the mountain with God, and I looked at him, and to my great joy it was this brother. He said he was at that Bible reading, and he heard there was such a thing as having fresh power to preach the Gospel; he said he made up his mind that if that was for him he would have it; he said he went home and looked to the Master, and that he never had such a battle with himself in his life. He asked that God would show him the sinfulness of his heart that he knew nothing about, and he just cried mightily to God that he might be emptied of himself and filled with the Spirit, and he said, "God has answered my prayer." I met him in Edinburgh six months from that date, and he told me he had preached the Gospel every night during that time, that he had not preached one sermon but that some remained for conversation, and that he had engagements four months ahead to preach the Gospel every night in different churches. I think you could have fired a cannon ball right through his church and not hit anyone before he got this anointing; but it was not thirty days before the building was full and aisles crowded. He had his bucket filled full of fresh water, and the people found it out and came flocking to him from every quarter. I tell you, you can't get the stream higher than the fountain. What we need very specially is power. There was another man whom I have in my mind, and he said, "I have heart disease, I can't preach more than once a week," so he had a colleague to preach for him and do the visiting. He was an old minister, and couldn't do any visiting. He had heard of this anointing, and he said, "I would like to be anointed for my burial. I would like before I go hence to have just one more privilege to preach the Gospel with power." He prayed that God would fill him with the Spirit. I met him not long after that, and he said, "I have preached on an average eight times a week, and I have had conversions all along." The Spirit came on him. I don't believe that man broke down at first with hard work so much as with using the machinery without oil, without lubrication. It is not the hard work breaks down ministers, but it is the toil of working without power. Oh, that God may anoint his people! Not the ministry alone, but every disciple. Do not suppose pastors are the only laborers needing it. There is not a mother but needs it in her house to regulate her family, just as much as the minister needs it in the pulpit or the Sunday school teacher needs it in his Sunday school. We all need it together, and let us not rest day or night until we possess it; if that is the uppermost thought in our hearts, God will give it to us if we just hunger and thirst for it, and say, "God helping me, I will not rest until endued with power from on high."

5. Witnessing In Power

If we do not have the Spirit of God, it were better to shut the churches, to nail up the doors, to put a black cross on them, and say, "God have mercy on us!" If you ministers have not the Spirit of God, you had better not preach, and you people had better stay at home. I think I speak not too strongly when I say that a church in the land without the Spirit of God is rather a curse than a blessing. If you have not the Spirit of God, Christian worker, remember that you stand in somebody else's way; you are as a tree bearing no fruit standing where another fruitful tree might grow. This is solemn work the Holy Spirit or nothing, and worse than nothing. Death and condemnation to a church that is not yearning after the Spirit, and crying and groaning until the Spirit has wrought mightily in her midst. He is here; He has never gone back since he descended at Pentecost. He is often grieved and vexed, for He is peculiarly jealous and sensitive, and the one sin never forgiven has to do with His blessed person; therefore let us be very tender towards Him, walk humbly before Him, wait on Him very earnestly, and resolve that there should be nothing knowingly continued which should prevent Him dwelling in us, and being with us henceforth and forever. Brethren, peace is unto you and your spirit —*Spurgeon*.

The subject of witness bearing in the power of the Holy Ghost is not sufficiently understood by the church. Until we have more intelligence on this point we are laboring under great disadvantage. Now, if you will take your Bible and turn to John 15:26, you will find these words: "But when the Comforter is come, whom I will send unto you from the Father, even the Spirit of Truth, which proceeded from the Father, He shall testify of me; and ye also shall bear witness, because ye have been with me from the beginning." Here we find what the Spirit is going to do, or what Christ said He would do when He came; namely, that He should testify of Him. And if you will turn over to the 2nd Chapter of Acts, you will find that when Peter stood up on the day of Pentecost, and testified of what Christ had done, the Holy Spirit came down and bore witness to that fact, and men were convicted by hundreds and by thousands. So then man cannot preach effectively of himself. He must have the Spirit of God to give ability, and study God's Word in order to testify according to the mind of the Spirit.

What is the Testimony?

If we keep back the Gospel of Christ and do not bring Christ before the people, then the Spirit has not the opportunity to work. But the moment Peter stood up on the day of Pentecost and bore testimony to this one fact, that Christ died for sin, and that He had been raised again, and ascended into heaven – the Spirit came down to bear witness to the Person and work of Christ. He came down to bear witness to the fact that Christ was in heaven, and if it were not for the Holy Ghost bearing witness to the preaching of the facts of the Gospel, do you think that the church would have lived during these last eighteen centuries? Do you believe that Christ's death; resurrection and ascension would not have been forgotten as soon as His birth, if it had not been for the fact that the Holy Spirit had come? Because it is very clear, that when John made his appearance on the borders of the wilderness, they had forgotten all about the birth of Jesus Christ. Just thirty short years. It was all gone. They had forgotten the story of the shepherds; they had forgotten the wonderful scene that took place in the Temple, when the Son of God was brought into the Temple and the older prophets and prophetesses were there; they had forgotten about the wise men coming to Jerusalem to inquire where He was that was born King of the Jews. That story of His birth seemed to have just faded away; they had forgotten all about it and when John made his appearance on the borders of the wilderness it was brought back to their minds. And if it had not been for the Holy Ghost coming down to bear witness to Christ, to testify of His death and resurrection, these facts would have been forgotten as soon as His birth.

Greater Work

The witness of the Spirit is the witness of power. Jesus said, "The works that I do shall ye do also, and greater works than these shall ye do because I go to the Father." I used to stumble over that. I didn't understand it. I thought, what greater work could any man do than Christ had done? How could anyone raise a dead man, who had been laid away in the sepulcher for days, and who had already begun to trun back to dust; how with a word could he call him forth? But the longer I live the more I am convinced it is a greater thing to influence a man's will;

a man whose will is set against God; to have that will broken and brought into subjection to God's will – or, in other words, it is a greater thing to have power over a living, sinning, God-hating man, than to quicken the dead. He who could create a world could speak a dead soul into life; but I think the greatest miracle this world has ever seen was the miracle at Pentecost.

Here were men who surrounded the apostles, full of prejudice, full of malice, full of bitterness, their hands, as it were, dripping with the blood of the Son of God, and yet an unlettered man, a man whom they detested, a man whom they hated, stands up there and preaches the Gospel, and three thousand of them are immediately convicted and converted, and become disciples of the Lord Jesus Christ, and are willing to lay down their lives for the Son of God. It may have been on that occasion that Stephen was converted, the first martyr, and some of the men who soon after gave up their lives for Christ. This seems to me the greatest miracle this world has ever seen. But Peter did not labor alone; the Spirit of God was with him; hence the marvelous results.

The Jewish law required that there should be two witnesses, and so we find that when Peter preached there was a second witness. Peter testified of Christ and Christ says that when the Holy Spirit comes "He will testify of me." And they both bore witness to the verities of our Lord's incarnation, ministry, death, and resurrection, and the result was that a multitude turned as with one heart unto the Lord. Our failure now is, that preachers ignore the Cross, and veil Christ with sapless sermons and superfine language. They don't just present Him to the people plainly, and that is why I believe, that the Spirit of God doesn't work with power in our churches. What we need is, to preach Christ and present Him to a perishing world. The world can get on very well without you and me, but the world cannot get on without Christ, and therefore we must testify of Him, and the world, I believe, today is just hungering and thirsting for this divine, satisfying portion. Thousands and thousands are sitting in darkness, knowing not of this great Light, but when we begin to preach Christ honestly, faithfully, sincerely and truthfully; holding Him up, not ourselves; exalting Christ and not our theories; presenting Christ and not our opinions; advocating Christ and not some false doctrine; then the Holy Ghost will come and bear witness. He will testify that what we say is true. When He comes He will confirm the Word with signs following. This is one of the strongest proofs that our Gospel is divine; that it is of divine origin; that not only did Christ teach these things, but when leaving the world He said, "He shall glorify me," and "He will testify of me." If you will just look at the 2nd Chapter of Acts – to that wonderful sermon that Peter preached – the 36th verse, you will read these words: "Therefore let all the house of Israel know assuredly that God hath made that same Jesus whom ye crucified, both Lord and Christ." And when Peter said this the Holy Ghost descended upon the people and testified of Christ – bore witness in signal demonstration that all this was true. And again, in the 40th verse, "And with many other words did he testify and exhort saying, Save yourselves from this untoward generation." With many other words did He testify, not only these words that have been recorded, but many other words.

The Sure Guide

Trun to John 16:13, and read: "Howbeit, when He the Spirit of Truth is come, He will guide you into all truth; for He shall not speak of Himself; but whatsoever He shall hear that shall He speak; and He will show you things to come." He will guide you into all truth. Now there is not a truth that we ought to know but the Spirit of God will guide us into it if we will let Him; if we will yield ourselves up to be directed by the Spirit, and let Him lead us, He will guide us into all truth. It would have saved us from a great many dark hours if we had only been willing to let the Spirit of God be our counselor and guide.

Men and women are in total darkness, because they have not been willing to be guided by the Spirit of God. "He shall guide you into all truth. He shall not speak of Himself." He shall speak of the ascended, glorified Christ.

What would be thought of a messenger, entrusted by an absent husband with a message for his wife or another who, on arrival, only talked of himself and his conceits, and ignored both the husband and the message? You would simply call it outrageous. What then must be the crime of the professed teacher who speaks of himself, or some insipid theory, leaving out Christ and His Gospel? If we witness according to the Spirit, we must witness of Jesus.

The Holy Spirit is down here in this dark world to just speak of the Absent One, and He takes the things of Christ and brings them to our mind. He testifies of Christ; He guides us into the truth about Him.

The Unerring Guide

I am told by people who have been over the Alps, that the guide fastens them, if they are going in a dangerous place, right to himself, and he just goes on before; they are fastened to the guide.

And so should the Christian be linked to His unerring Guide, and be safely upheld. Why, if a man was going through the Mammoth Cave, it would be death to him if he strayed away from his guide – if separated from him, he would certainly perish; there are pitfalls in that cave and a bottomless river, and there would be no chance for a man to find his way through that cave without a guide or a light. So there is no chance for us to get through the dark wilderness of this world alone. It is folly for a man or woman to think they can get through this evil world without the light of God's Word and the guidance of the divine Spirit. God sent Him to guide us through this great journey, and if we seek to work independent of Him, we shall stumble into the deep darkness of eternity's night.

An Aid to Memory

It is a great comfort to us to remember that another office of the Spirit is to bring the teaching of Jesus to our remembrance. This was our Lord's promise, "He shall teach you all things, and bring all things to your remembrance" (John 14:26).

How striking that is! I think there are many Christians who have had that experience. They have been testifying, and found that while talking for Christ the Spirit has just brought into mind some of the sayings of the Lord Jesus Christ, and their mind was soon filled with the Word of God. When we have the Spirit resting upon us, we can speak with authority and power, and the Lord will bless our testimony and bless our work. I believe the reason why God makes use of so few in the church is because there is not in them the power that God can use. He is not going to use our ideas, but we must have the Word of God hid in our hearts, and then, the Holy Spirit inflaming us, we will have the testimony, which will be rich, and sweet, and fresh, and the Lord's Word will vindicate itself in blessed results. God wants to use us; God wants to make us channels of blessing; but we are in such a condition He does not use us. That is the trouble, there are so many men who have no testimony for the Lord; if they speak, they speak without saying anything, and if they pray, their prayer is powerless; they do not plead in prayer; their prayer is just a few set phrases that you have heard too often. Now what we want is to be so full of the Word, that the Spirit coming upon us shall bring to mind – bring to our remembrance – the words of the Lord Jesus.

Long and Short Sight

He brings to our mind what God has in store for us. I heard a man, some time ago, speaking about Abraham. He said: "Abraham was not tempted by the well-watered plains of Sodom, for Abraham was what you might call a long-sighted man; he had his eyes set on the city which had foundation – 'whose Builder and Maker is God.'" But Lot was a short-sighted man; and there are many people in the church who are very short-sighted; they only see things right around them they think good. Abraham was long-sighted; he had glimpses of the celestial city. Moses was long-sighted, and he left the palaces of Egypt and identified himself with God's people – poor people, who were slaves; but he had something in view yonder; he could see something God had in store. Again there are some people who are sort of long-sighted and shortsighted, too. I have a friend who has one eye that is longsighted and the other is shortsighted; and I think the church is full of this kind of people. They want one eye for the world and the other for the kingdom of God. Therefore, everything is blurred, one eye is long and the other is short, all is confusion, and they "see men as trees walking." The church is filled with that sort of people. But Stephen was long-sighted; he looked clear into heaven; they couldn't convince him even when he was dying, that Christ had not ascended to heaven. "Look, look yonder," he says, "I see Him over there; He is on the throne, standing at the right hand of God"; and he looked clear into heaven; the world had no temptation for him; he had put the world under his feet. Paul was another of those longsighted men; he had been caught up and seen things unlawful for him to utter; things grand and glorious. I tell you when the Spirit of God is on us the world looks very empty; the world has a very small hold upon us, and we begin to let go our hold of it. When the Spirit of God is on us we will just let go the things of time and lay hold of things eternal. This is the church's need today; we want the Spirit to come in mighty power, and consume all the vile dross there is in us. Oh! that the Spirit of fire may come down and burn everything in us that is contrary to God's blessed Word and will.

In John 14:16, we read of the Comforter. This is the first time He is spoken of as the Comforter. Christ had been their Comforter. God had sent Him to comfort the sorrowing. It was prophesied of Him "The Spirit of the Lord is upon me, because He hath anointed me to preach the Gospel to the poor; He has sent me to heal the brokenhearted." You can't heal the broken-hearted without the Comforter; but the world would not have the first Comforter, and so they rose up and took Him to Calvary and put him to death; but on going away He said, "I will send you another Comforter; you shall not be comfortless; be of good cheer, little flock; it is the Father's good pleasure to give you the kingdom." All these sweet passages are brought to the remembrance of God's people, and they help us to rise out of the fog and mist of this world. Oh, what a comforter is the Holy Spirit of God!

The Faithful Friend

The Holy Spirit tells a man of his faults in order to lead him to a better life. In John 16:8, we read: "He is to reprove the world of sin." Now, there are a class of people who don't like this part of the Spirit's work. Do you know why? Because He convicts them of sin. They don't like that. What they want is someone to speak comforting words and make everything pleasant; keep everything all quiet; tell them there is peace when there is war; tell them it is light when it is dark, and tell them everything is growing better; that the world is getting on amazingly in goodness; that it is growing better all the time; that is the kind of preaching they seek for. Men think they are a great deal better than their fathers were. That suits human nature, for it is full of pride. Men will strut around and say, "Yes, I believe that; the world is improving; I am a good deal better man than father was; my father was too strict; he was one of those old Puritanical men who was so rigid. Oh, we are getting on; we are more liberal; my father wouldn't think of going out riding on Sunday, but we will; we will trample the laws of God under our feet; we are better than our fathers." That is the kind of preaching, which some dearly love, and there are preachers who tickle such itching ears. When you bring the Word of God to bear upon them, and when the Spirit drives it home, then men will say: "I don't like that kind of preaching; I will never go to hear that man again"; and sometimes they will get up and stamp their way out of church before the speaker gets through; they don't like it. But when the Spirit of God is at work he convicts men of sin. "When He comes He will reprove the world of sin, of righteousness and of judgment; of sin" – not because men swear and lie and steal and get drunk and murder – "of sin, because they believe not on me."

The Climax Sin

That is the sin of the world. Why, a great many people think that unbelief is a sort of misfortune, but do not know, if you will allow me the expression, it is the damning sin of the world today; that is what unbelief is, the mother of all sin. There would not be a drunkard walking the streets, if it were not for unbelief; there would not be a harlot walking the streets, if it were not for unbelief; there would not be a murderer, if it was not for unbelief; it is the germ of all sin. Don't think for a moment that it is a misfortune, but just bear in mind it is an awful sin, and may the Holy Spirit convict every reader that unbelief is making God a liar. Many a man has been knocked down on the streets because someone has told him he was a liar. Unbelief is giving God the lie; that is the plain English of it. Some people seem to boast of their unbelief; they seem to think it is quite respectable to be an infidel and doubt God's Word, and they will vainly boast and say, "I have intellectual difficulties; I can't believe." Oh, that the Spirit of God may come and convict men of sin! That is what we need – His convicting power, and I am so thankful that God has not put that into our hands. We have not to convict men; if we had I would get discouraged, give up preaching, and go back to business within the next forty-eight hours. It is my work to preach and hold up the Cross and testify of Christ; but it is His work to convict men of sin and lead them to Christ. One thing I have noticed, that some conversions don't amount to anything; that if a man professes to be converted without conviction of sin, he is one of those stony ground hearers who don't bring forth much fruit. The first little wave of persecution, the first breath of opposition, and the man is back in the world again. Let us pray, dear Christian reader that God may carry on a deep and thorough work, that men may be convicted of sin so that they cannot rest in unbelief. Let us pray God it may be a thorough work in the land. I would a great deal rather see a hundred men thoroughly converted, truly born of God, than to see a thousand professed conversions where the Spirit of God has not convicted of sin. Don't let us cry: "Peace, peace, when there is no peace." Don't go to the man who is living in sin, and tell him all he has to do is to stand right up and profess, without any hatred for sin. Let us ask God first to show every man the plague of his own heart, that the Spirit may convict him of sin. Then will the work in our hands be real, and deep, and abide the fiery trial which will try every man's labor.

Thus far, we have found the work of the Spirit is to impart life, to implant hope, to give liberty, to testify of Christ, to guide us into all truth, to teach us all things, to comfort the believers, and to convict the world of sin.

6. Power Hindered

What It Is Not

I admit there is such a thing as resisting the Spirit of God, and resisting till the Spirit of God has departed; but if the Spirit of God has left any, they will not be troubled about their sins. The very fact that they are troubled shows that the Spirit of God has not left them. If a man is troubled about his sins; it is the work of the Spirit; for Satan never yet told him he was a sinner. Satan makes us believe that we are pretty good that we are good enough without God; safe without Christ, and that we don't need salvation. But when a man wakes up to the fact that he is lost, that he is a sinner, that is the work of the Spirit; and if the Spirit of God had left him, he would not be in that state; and just because men and women want to be Christians, is a sign that the Spirit of God is drawing them.

If resisting the Spirit of God is an unpardonable sin, then we have all committed it, and there is no hope for any of us; for I do not believe there is a minister, or a worker in Christ's vineyard, who has not, some time in his life, resisted the Holy Ghost; who has not some time in his life rejected the Spirit of God. To resist the Holy Ghost is one thing, and to commit that awful sin of blasphemy against the Holy Ghost, is another thing; and we want to take the Scripture and just compare them...

Worldly Amusements

I believe when we bring the church down to the level of the world to reach the world, we are losing all the while and grieving the Spirit of God.

But some say, if we take the standard and lift it up high, it will drive away a great many members from our churches. I believe it, and I think the quicker they are gone the better. The world has come into the church like a flood...

What Is Success?

The Gospel has not lost its power; it is just as powerful today as it ever has been. We don't want any new doctrine. It is still the old Gospel with the old power, the Holy Ghost power; and if the churches will but confess their sins and put them away, and lift the standard instead of pulling it down, and pray to God to lift us all up into a higher and holier life, then the fear of the Lord will come upon the people around us.

It was when Jacob put away strange gods and set his face toward Bethel that the fear of God fell upon the nations around. And when the churches trun towards God, and we cease grieving the Spirit, so that He may work through us, we will then have conversions all the while. Believers will be added to the church daily. It is sad and when you look over Christendom and see how desolate it is, and see how little spiritual life, spiritual power, there is in the church of God today, many of the church members not even wanting this Holy Ghost power. They don't desire it; they want intellectual power; they want to get some man who will just draw; and a choir that will draw not caring whether anyone is saved. With them that is not the question. Only fill the pews, have good society, fashionable people, and dancing; such persons are found one night at the theater and the next night at the opera. They don't like the prayer meetings; they abominate them; if the minister will only lecture and entertain, that would suit them. I said to a man some time ago, "How are you getting on at your church?" "Oh, splendid." "Many conversions?" "Well-well, on that side we are not gelling on so well. But," he said, "we rented all our pews and are able to pay all our running expenses; we are getting on splendidly." That is what the godless call "getting on splendidly"; because they rent the pews, pay the minister, and pay all the running expenses. Conversions! that is a strange thing. There was a man being shown through one of the cathedrals of Europe; he had come in from the country, and one of the men belonging to the cathedral was showing him around, when he inquired, "Do you have many conversions here." "Many what?" "Many conversions here?" "Ah, man, this is not a Wesleyan chapel." The idea of there being conversions there! And you can go into a good many churches, in this country and ask if they have many conversions there, and they would not know what it meant, they are so far away from the Lord; they are not looking for conversions, and don 't expect them.

Quench Not

In 1 Thessalonians, we are told not to quench the Spirit. Now, I am confident the cares of the world are coming in and quenching the Spirit with a great many. They say: "I don't care for the world"; perhaps not the pleasures of the world so much after all as the cares of this life; but they have just let the cares come in and quench the Spirit of God. Anything that comes between me and God – between my soul and God – quenches the Spirit. It may be my family. You may say: "Is there any danger of my loving my family too much?" Not if we love God more; but God must have the first place. If I love my family more than God, then I am quenching the Spirit of God within me; if I love wealth, if I love fame, if I love honor, if I love position, if I love pleasure, if I love self, more than I love God who created and saved me, then I am committing a sin; I am not only grieving the Spirit of God, but quenching Him, and robbing my soul of His power. May we know Him in all His wealth of blessing. This is my prayer for myself – for you. May we heed the words of the grand apostle: "My speech and my preaching was not with enticing words of man's wisdom, but in demonstration of the Spirit, and of power: that your faith should not stand *in the wisdom of men, but in the power of God.*"

Say a Good Word for Jesus

John Watson (Ian Maclaren) 1850-1907

With an Introduction
By Robert E. Coleman

Abridged version of *Beside the Bonnie Brier Bush* by John Watson (Ian Maclaren). Abridged version originally published by World Wide Publications, 1994, along with Billy Graham Center, Wheaton, Il. Copyright of abridged version and introduction held by Robert Coleman, used with permission. Artwork in the Public Domain.

Book Chapters

1. Introduction
   By Robert E. Coleman 566
2. His Mother's Sermon 570
3. The Transformation of Lachlan Campbell 577
   His Bitter Shame 577
   Like As a Father 585
4. Notes 592

1. Introduction
By Robert E. Coleman

Many years ago while in college, I heard the story of a mother's dying admonition to her son, "Speak a good word for Jesus Christ." Most of the erudition of my student days has been forgotten, but the charge left with that trembling young man lingers with me to this day. I trust that his message will never go unheeded. To keep the words fresh in mind, occasionally I slip away from the pressing duties of a busy ministry, close the door, and in the privacy of my office read the story again as the tears fall down.

The account, along with two others gathered in this little volume, appear in a collection of Scottish rural life sketches entitled *Beside the Bonnie Briar Bush*. Few books written in English prose awaken in the reader more tender and profound feelings of pathos.

Since its publication a century ago, nearly a million copies of the book have been sold. However, in recent years, the book has been allowed to go out of print, and copies are now hard to find. The slightly condensed selections reprinted here are adapted from the 1894 edition published in New York by Dodd, Mead and Company. Some words are translated into more familiar language, but the essential dialogue of the stories is preserved in the original Scotch brogue.

The author is John Watson, writing under the pseudonym of Ian Maclaren.[1] A son of pure Scotch stock, he was born in Manningtree, Essex, on November 3, 1850. The family moved to Perth where he attended grammar school. Later he was sent to high school at Sterling. Henry Drummond was a classmate, with whom he developed a lasting friendship.

John Watson (Ian Maclaren) 1850-1907

In 1866 he enrolled at Edinburgh University. After graduation with an M.A., he entered New College and pursued a four-year course for ministry in the Free Church of Scotland. Then to expose himself still further to intellectual inquiry, he spent a semester at Tubingen University in Germany. From an academic point of view, his education was the best that could be given a young man of his day. Yet, judging from his own reflections, he did not feel himself adequately prepared for the calling before him.

Toward the end of 1874 he began his ministerial work as assistant pastor at Barclay Church, Edinburgh. His experience was such a disappointment that he seriously considered leaving the pastorate and studying for the bar. Fortunately, in 1875 the bachelor preacher received a call to the Free Church at Logiealmond, Pershire. In this small parish among the peasants of the Highlands he found the joy of serving the Lord. Some of the happiest years of his life were lived in this humble setting, which is in the "Drumtochty" of *Beside the Bonnie Briar Bush*.

He accepted a call to the wealthy pulpit of the Free St. Matthew's Church, Glasgow, in 1877. During this period he married a lovely girl, giving some success to an otherwise unharmonious ministry. After three years he went to Liverpool to develop a new work in the Sefton Park district, where he remained for the rest of his pastoral life. When he retired twenty-five years later, the congregation was the most influential in the Presbyterian Church in England.

Amid these pressing responsibilities, John Watson did most of his writing. *Beside the Bonnie Briar Bush* was the first and most popular of his twenty-five books. Other titles with much the same folk appeal are *The Days of Auld Lang Syne* (1895), *Kate Carnegie* (1897), and *Church Folks* (1901). Of the theological works under his own name, he is remembered most for his interpretation of the person and teaching of Jesus in *The Mind of the Master* (1896) and *The Life of the Master* (1901). Also of note are his Lyman Beecher Lectures at Yale (1896) published under the title of *The Cure of Souls*.

Indicative of the high esteem in which he was held by his colleagues was his election as moderator of the Church Synod in 1900. Seven years later he was made President of the National Free Church Council. Both Yale University and St. Andrews awarded him honorary degrees. Had he lived a few weeks longer, he would have assumed the principalship of Westminster College, Cambridge.

But on May 6, 1907, he died of a brief illness. The end came in Mt. Pleasant, Iowa, while he was on his third lecture tour in the United States. His body was returned to Liverpool where he was given a public funeral, with burial in Smithdown Cemetery.

During the span of his fifty-seven years, John Watson became one of the best-known ministers of his day. People from all walks of life were drawn to him. One secret of his appeal is reflected in the remark of a visitor to his church:

> He addressed his hearers not from some platform of scholastic thinking and hypothetical experience, but from a homely stable ground, common to him and to them and to the whole world of men and women.[2]

A deeper reason for the attraction may be found in his own statement of purpose in his first sermon at Sefton Park Church:

> I shall not try to astonish you with any display of learning, nor attract you by the mere eloquence of words. But I promise by the grace of God, and according to my ability, to preach the cross of Christ. The cross, as I understand it, combines both the doctrine of forgiveness and the doctrine of holiness, and I trust to be able to show that Christ who is our sacrifice is also our ideal.[3]

This passion to keep the life of Christ in focus was an obsession with Watson. It was so strong that sometimes he seemed to over-emphasize Christ's humanity, an emphasis which has caused some to question his doctrinal correctness. Perhaps he could have been more theologically precise. But at heart he had a sincere and steadfast commitment to the central tenets of evangelical Christianity. The counsel given the lad in "His Mother's Sermon" shines through his ministry.

In a sense, the story is reminiscent of the author's own experience. Though written as fiction, many of the characters resemble people that he knew in his pastorate in Logiealmond. The Margaret Howe of Whinnie Knowe, a mother whose only son died while preparing for the ministry, alludes to a brilliant high school classmate of Watson who died at the age of 21. Even the young man receiving the chain with a pledge of his mother's prayer was probably inspired by a compact which Watson entered into with his mother on her deathbed—he called it "his mother's tryst." This pact proved to be a great bulwark against temptations throughout his life.

Whatever the historical background of the tale, the principal admonition could not be more realistic or more timely. Everyone should be bold to speak up for Jesus. When all is said and done, He is all we have to preach—He is all and in all. There is no other name under heaven whereby people must be saved. Regardless of our particular calling and gift, we should burn with the desire to make Christ known and loved.

It is for this reason that I read again and again the account of the young preacher of Drumtochty, and the stories of the simple people in his parish who taught him lessons he never learned at seminary. Such reading prods me always to keep the priorities of the Gospel in focus. I trust that it will be for you, too, a reminder of our first love.

Robert E. Coleman, 1994

The chapters that follow are from *Beside the Bonnie Brier Bush*. The abridged chapters and sections correspond with the book's chapters and sections. The chapters have been changed from the original publishing of the 1994 abridged edition.

Faith E. Parry, 2014

2. His Mother's Sermon

He was an ingenuous lad, with the callow simplicity of a theological college still untouched, and had arrived on the preceding Monday at the Free Kirk [church] manse with four cartloads of furniture and a maiden aunt. For three days he roamed from room to room in the excitement of house holding, and made suggestions which were received with hilarious contempt; then he shut himself up in his study to prepare the great sermon, and his aunt went about on tiptoe. During meals on Friday he explained casually that his own wish was to preach a simple sermon, and that he would have done so had he been a private individual, but as he had held the MacWhammel scholarship a deliverance was expected by the country. He would be careful and say nothing rash, but it was due to himself to state the present position of theological thought, and he might have to quote once or twice from Ewaid.

His aunt was a saint, with that firm grasp of truth and tender mysticism whose combination is the charm of Scottish piety, and her face was troubled. While the minister was speaking in his boyish complacency, her thoughts were in a room where they had both stood, five years before, by the deathbed of his mother.

He was broken that day, and his sobs shook the bed, for he was his mother's only son and fatherless; and his mother, brave, and faithful to the last, was bidding him farewell.

"Don't grieve like that, John, nor break yir hert [heart], for it's the will of God, and that's a'ways best."

"Here's my watch and chain," placing them beside her son, who would not touch them, nor would lift his head, "and when ye feel the chain about yir neck it will mind ye o' yir mother's arms."

"Ye'ill not forget me, John, I know that well, and I'll never forget ye. I've loved ye here, and I'll love ye yonder, so don't be comfortless."

Then she felt his head and stroked it once more, but he could not look nor speak.

"Ye'ill follow Christ and when He offers ye His cross, ye'ill not refuse it, for He a'ways carries the heavy end Himself. He's guided yir mother a' these years, and been as good as a husband since yir father's death, and He'ill hold me fast to the end. He'ill keep ye too, John, I'll be' watchin' for ye. Ye'ill not fail me," and her poor cold hand that had tended him all his years tightened on his head.

But he could not speak, and her voice was failing fast.

"I cannot see ye now, John, but I know yir there, and I've just one other wish. If God calls ye to the ministry, ye'ill not refuse, an' the first day ye preach in yir own kirk, speak a good word for Jesus Christ, an', John, I'll hear ye that day, though ye'ill not see me, and I'll be satisfied."

A minute after she whispered, "Pray for me," and he cried, "My mother, my mother!"

It was a full prayer, and left nothing unasked of Mary's son.

"John," said his aunt, "your mother is with the Lord," and he saw death for the first time, but it was beautiful with the peace that passeth all understanding.

Five years had passed, crowded with thought and work, and his aunt wondered whether he remembered that last request, or indeed had heard it in his sorrow.

"What are you thinking about, aunt? Are you afraid of my theology?"

"No, John, it's not that, laddie, for I know ye'ill say what ye believe to be true without fear o' man," and she hesitated.

"Come out with it, auntie: you're my only mother now, you know," and the minister put his arm around her, "as well as the kindest, bonniest, goodest auntie ever man had."

Below his student self-conceit he was a good lad, and sound of heart.

"Shame on you, John, to make a fool of an old worn body, but ye'ill not come round me with yir flattery. I know ye too well," and as she caught the likeness in his face, her eyes filled suddenly.

"What's the matter, auntie? Will ye not tell me?"

"Don't be angry wi' me, John, but a'm concerned aboot Sunday, for a've been praying ever since ye were called to Drumtochty that it might be a neat day, and that I might see ye comin' to yir people, laddie wi' the beauty o' the Lord upon ye, according to the old prophecy: 'How beautiful upon the mountains are the feet of him that bringeth good tidings, that publisheth peace,'" and again she stopped.

"Go on auntie, go on," he whispered; "say all that's in yir mind."

"It's not for me to advise ye, who am only a simple old woman, who knows naethin' but her Bible and the catechism, and it's not that a'm feared for the new views, or aboot yir faith, for I a'ways mind that there's mony things the Spirit has still to teach us, know well the man that follows Christ will never lose his way in any thicket. But it's the folk, John, a'm anxious aboot; the flock o' sheep the Lord has given ye to feed for Him."

She could not see his face, but she felt him gently press her hand, and took courage.

"Ye may mind, laddie, that they're not clever and learned like what ye are, but just plain country folk, with his own temptation, an' a' sore troubled wi' many cares o' this world. They'll need a clear word to comfort their herts and show them the way everlasting. Ye'ill say what's right, no doot o' that, and a'body 'ill be pleased wi' ye, but, oh, laddie, be sure ye say a good word for Jesus Christ."

The minister's face whitened, and his arm relaxed. He rose hastily and went to the door, but in going out he gave his aunt an understanding look, such as passes between people who have stood together in a sorrow. The son had not forgotten his mother's request.

The manse garden lies toward the west, and as the minister paced its little square of turf sheltered by fir hedges, the sun was going down behind the Grampians. Black massy clouds had begun to gather in the evening and threatened to obscure the sunset, which was the finest sight a Drumtochty man was ever likely to see and a means of grace to every sensible heart in the glen. But the sun had beat back the clouds on either side, and shot them through with glory, and now between piled billows of light he went along a shining pathway into the Gates of the West. The minister stood still before that spectacle, his face bathed in the golden glory, and then before his eyes the gold deepened into an awful red, and the red passed into shades of violet and green, beyond a painter's hand or the imagination of man. It seemed to him as if a victorious saint had entered through the gates into the city, washed in the blood of the Lamb, and the afterglow of his mother's life fell solemnly on his soul. The last trace of sunset had faded from the hills when the minister came in, and his face was of one who had seen a vision. He asked his aunt to have worship with the servant, for he must be alone in his study.

It was a cheerful room in the daytime with its southern window through which the minister saw the roses touching the very glass and dwarf apple trees lining the garden walks; there was also a western window that he might watch each day close. It was a pleasant room now, when the curtains were drawn and the light of the lamp fell on the books he loved and which bade him welcome. One by one he had arranged the hard-bought treasures of student days in the little bookcase and had planned for himself the sweetest of pleasures, an evening of desultory reading. But his books went out of his mind as he looked at the sermon shining beneath the glare of the lamp and demanding judgment. He had finished its last page with honest pride that afternoon, and had declaimed it, facing the southern window, with a success that amazed himself. His hope was that he might be kept humble, and not called to Edinburgh for at least two years; and now he lifted the sheets with fear. The brilliant opening, with its historical parallel, this review of modern thought reinforced by telling quotations, that trenchant criticism of old-fashioned views would not deliver. For the audience had vanished, and left one careworn, but ever beautiful face, whose gentle eyes were waiting with a yearning look. Twice he crushed the sermon in his hands, and turned to the fire his aunt's care had kindled, and twice he repented and smoothed it out. What else could he say now to the people? And then in the stillness of the room he heard a voice, "Speak a good word for Jesus Christ."

Next minute he was kneeling on the hearth, and pressing the magnum opus, that was to shake Drumtochty, into the heart of the red fire, and he saw, half-smiling and half-weeping, the impressive words "Semitic environment" shrivel up and disappear. As the last black flake fluttered out of sight, the face looked at him again, but this time the sweet brown eyes were full of peace.

It was no masterpiece, but only the crude production of a lad who knew little of letters and nothing of the world. Very likely it would have done neither harm nor good, but it was his best, and he gave it for love's sake, and I suppose there is nothing in a human life so precious to God, neither clever words nor famous deeds, as the sacrifices of love.

The moon flooded his bedroom with silver light, and he felt the presence of his mother. His bed stood ghostly with its white curtains, and he remembered how every night his mother knelt by its side in prayer for him. He is a boy once more, and repeats the Lord's Prayer, then he cries again, "My mother! My mother!" and an indescribable contentment fills his heart.

His prayer next morning was very short, but afterward he stood at the window, for a space, and when he turned, his aunt said:

"Ye will get yir sermon, and it will be worth hearing."

"How did ye know?" But she only smiled. "I heard you pray."

When he shut himself into the study that Saturday morning, his aunt went into the room above, and he knew she had gone to intercede for him.

An hour afterward he was pacing the garden in such anxious thought that he crushed with his foot a rose lying on the path, and then she saw his face suddenly lighten, and he hurried to the house, but first he plucked a bunch of forget-me-nots. In the evening she found them on his sermon.

Two hours later—for still she prayed and watched in faithfulness to mother and son—she observed him come out and wander round the garden in great joy. He lifted up the soiled rose and put it in his coat; he released a butterfly caught in some mesh; he buried his face in fragrant honeysuckle. Then she understood that his heart was full of love, and was sure that it would be well on the morrow.

When the bell began to ring, the minister rose from his knees and went to his aunt's room to be robed, for this was a covenant between them.

His gown was spread out in its black silken glory, but he sat down in despair.

"Auntie, whatever shall we do, for I've forgotten the bands?"

"But I've not forgot them, John, and here are six pair wrought with my own hands, and now sit still and I'll tie them around my laddie's neck."

When she had given the last touch, and he was ready to go, a sudden seriousness fell upon them.

"Kiss me, auntie."

"For your mother, and her God be with you," and then he went through the garden and underneath the honeysuckle and into the kirk, where every Free Churchman in Drumtochty that could get out of bed, and half the Established Kirk, were waiting in expectation.

I sat with his aunt in the minister's pew, and shall always be glad that I was at that service. When winter lies heavy upon the glen I go upon my travels, and in my time have seen religious functions. I have been in Mr. Spurgeon's Tabernacle, where the people wept one minute

John Watson (Ian Maclaren) 1850-1907 / 575

and laughed the next; have heard Canon Liddon in St. Paul's, and the sound of that high, clear voice is still with me, "Awake, awake, put on thy strength, O Zion." I have seen High Mass in St. Peter's, and stood in the dusk of the Duomo at Florence when Padre Agostino thundered against the evils of the day. But I never realized the unseen world as I did that day in the Free Kirk of Drumtochty.

It is impossible to analyze a spiritual effect because it is largely an atmosphere, but certain circumstances assisted. One was instantly prepossessed in favor of a young minister who gave out the second paraphrase at his first service, for it declared his filial reverence and won him the blessing of a cloud of witnesses. No Scottish man can ever sing, "God of our fathers, be the God of their succeeding race," with a dry heart. It satisfied me at once that the minister was of a fine temper when, after a brave attempt to join in, he hid his face and was silent. We thought none the worse of him that he was nervous, and two or three old people who had suspected self-sufficiency took him to their hearts when the minister concluded the Lord's Prayer hurriedly, having omitted two petitions. But we knew it was not nervousness which made him pause for ten seconds after praying for widows and orphans, and in the silence which fell upon us the divine Spirit had free access. His youth commended him, since he was also modest, for every mother had come with an inarticulate prayer that the "puir laddie wud dae wed [poor boy would do well] on his first day, and him only twenty-four."

Texts I can never remember, nor, for that matter, the words of sermons; but the subject was Jesus Christ, and before he had spoken five minutes I was convinced, who am outside dogmas and churches, that Christ was present. The preacher faded from before one's eyes, and there rose the figure of the Nazarene, best lover of every human soul, with a face of tender patience such as Sarto gave the Master in the Church of the Annuziata, and stretching out His hands to old folk and little children as He did, before His death, in Galilee. His voice might be heard any moment, as I have imagined it in my lonely hours by the winter fire or on the solitary hills-soft, low, and sweet, penetrating like music to the secret of the heart, "Come unto me ... and I will give you rest."

During a pause in the sermon I glanced up the church, and saw the same spell held the people. Donald Menzies had long ago been caught into the third heaven, and was now hearing words which it is not lawful to utter. Campbell in his watchtower at the back had closed his eyes, and was praying. The women were weeping quietly, and the rugged faces of our men were subdued and softened, as when the evening sun plays on the granite stone.

But what will stand out forever in my mind was the sight of Margaret Howe. Her face was as white as death, and her wonderful gray eyes were shining through a mist of tears, so that I caught the light in the manse pew. She was thinking of George, and had taken the minister to her heart.

The elders, one by one, gripped the minister's hand in the vestry, and, though plain, homely men, they were the godliest in the glen; but no man spoke save Burnbrae.

"I a' but lost my farm [I just about lost my farm] for the Free Kirk, and I wud have lost ten to be in the Kirk this day."

Donald walked with me homeward, but would only say:

"There was a man sent from God whose name was John." At the cottage he added, "The friend of the bridegroom rejoiced greatly because of the bridegroom's voice."

Beneath the honeysuckle at his garden gate a woman was waiting.

"My name is Marget Howe, and I'm the wife of William Howe of Whinnie Knowe. My only son wes preparin' for the ministry, but God wanted him nearly a year ago. When ye preached the evangel o' Jesus today I heard his voice, and I loved you. Ye have no mother on earth, I hear, and I have no son, and I wanted to say that if ye ever wish to speak to any woman as ye wud to yir mother, come to Whinnie Knowe, an I'll count it one of the Lord's consolations."

His aunt could only meet him in the study, and when he looked on her his lip quivered, for his heart had wrung with one wistful regret.

"Oh, auntie, if she had only been spared to see this day, and her prayers answered."

But his aunt flung her arms around his neck.

"Don't be cast down, laddie, nor be unbelievin'. Yir mother has heard every word, and is satisfied, for ye did it in remembrance o' her and yon [that] was yir mother's sermon."

3. The Transformation of Lachlan Campbell

His Bitter Shame

The Free Kirk people were very proud of their vestry [prayer room] because the Established Church had none, and because it was reasonably supposed to be the smallest in Scotland. When the minister, who touched five feet eleven, and the beadle [church officer], who was three inches taller, assembled for the procession, with the precentor [song leader], a man of fair proportions, there was no waste ground in that room, and any messenger from the church door had to be selected with judgment.

It was eight feet by eight, and consisted largely of two doors and a fireplace, and its chief glory was a portrait of Dr. Chalmers, whose face, dimly seen in the light of the lamp, was a charter of authority, and raised the proceedings to the level of history. Lockers on either side of the mantelpiece contained the church library, which abounded in the lives of Scottish worthies, and was never lightly disturbed.

Where there was neither grate nor door, a narrow board ran along the wall, on which it was simply a point of honor to seat the twelve deacons, who met once a month to raise the Sustentation Fund by modest, heroic sacrifices of hard-working people, and to keep the slates on the church roof in winter. When they had nothing else to do, they talked about the stove which "came out in '43," and, when it was in good humor, would raise the temperature in winter one degree above freezing.

578 / Say a Good Word for Jesus

Seating the court was a work of art, and could only be achieved by the repression of the smaller men, who looked out from the loop-holes of retreat, the projection of bigger men on to their neighbors' knees, and the absolute elimination of Archie Moncur, whose voice made motions on temperance from the lowest depths. Netherton was always the twelfth man to arrive, and nothing could be done till he was safely settled. Only some six inches were reserved at the end of the bench, and he was it full sitter, but he had discovered a trick of sitting sideways and screwing his leg against the opposite wall—that secured the court as well as himself in their places on the principle of a compressed spring. When this operation was completed, Burnbrae used to say to the minister, who sat in the middle on a cane chair before the tiniest of tables—the living was small, and the ministers never grew fat till they left—

"We're fine and comfortable now. Moderator, and ye can begin business as soon as ye like."

As there were only six elders they could sit in state, besides leaving a vacant space for any penitents who came to confess their sins and receive absolution, or some catechumen who wished to be admitted to the Sacrament. Carmichael used to say that a meeting of Session affected his imagination, and would have made an interior for Rembrandt.

On one side of the table sat the men who represented the piety of the district, and on the other a young girl in her loneliness, who wrung her handkerchief in terror of this dreaded spiritual court, and hoped within her heart that no elder would ask her "effectual calling" from the Shorter Catechism. Meanwhile the little lamp, hanging from the ceiling, cast a fitful light on the fresh, tearful face of the girl and the hard, weather-beaten countenances of the elders, composed into a serious gravity not untouched by tenderness. They were little else than laboring men, but no one was elected to that court unless he had given pledges of godliness, and they bore themselves as men who had the charge of souls.

The little Sanhedrin had within it the school of Hillel, which was swayed by mercy, and its Rabbi was Burnbrae; and the school of Shammai, whose rule was inflexible justice, and its Rabbi was Lachlan Campbell. Burnbrae was a big-hearted man, with a fatherly manner, and had a genius for dealing with "young communicants."

"Well, Jessie, the Dominie [preacher] wes tellin' me juist last week that ye did yir work at school grand, and knew yir Bible from end to end."

"It'll not be easy to ask the like o'you questions, but ye mind Abraham, Jessie."

"O'ay!" [oh, yes] and Jessie is all alert, although she is afraid to look up.

"What was the name o' his wife, now?"

"Sarah, an' their son was Isaac."

"That's right, and what aboot Isaac's wife?"

"Isaac married Rebecca, and they had two sons, Jacob and Esau," and the girl takes a shy glance at the honest elder, and begins to feel at home.

"Domsie [preacher's nickname] wasn't far wrong, a' [I] see. But it's not possible ye could tell us the names o' Jacob's sons?—it's maybe not fair to ask such a tough question," knowing all the while that this was a test case of Domsie's.

When Jessie reached Benjamin, Burnbrae could not contain himself.

"It's no use trying to stick Jessie wi' [with] the Bible, neighbors. We'll see what she can dae [do] wi' the Catechism. Yir not the lassie that said the questions from beginning to end without mistak's, are ye?"

Yes, she was, and dared him to come on, for Jessie had forgotten the minister and all the Session.

"The elders would like to hear 'What is the Lord's Supper?'"

"That's it; and Jessie, ma [my] woman, gie's [what is] the 'worthy receiving.'"

Jessie achieves another triumph, and is now ready for anything.

"Ye have the Word well stored in yir mind, lassie, and ye must keep it in yir life, and never forget that Christ's a good Master."

"A'll do my best," and Jessie declared that Burnbrae had been as kind as if she had been "his own bairn [child]," and that she "wasn't feared at all." But her trial is not over: the worst is to come.

Lachlan began where Burnbrae ended, and very soon had Jessie on the rack.

"How old will you be?"

"Euchteen [eighteen] next March."

"And why will you be coming to the Sacrament?"

"My mither [mother] thought it was time," with a threatening of tears as she looked at the face in the corner.

"Ye will maybe tell the Session what has been your 'lawwork' and how long ye have been at Sinai."

"A' dinna know what yir askin'. I was never out o' Drumtochty," and Jessie breaks down utterly.

"A' dinna think, Moderator, we ought to ask such questions," broke in Bumbrae, who could not see a little one put to confusion. "There's a commandment Jessie keeps well, as a' can testify, and that's the fifth, for there's no better daughter in Drumtochty. A' move, Moderator, she get her token."

"It was Dr. John's mark I was trying the girl by," explained Lachlan after Jessie had gone away comforted. "And it is a good mark, oh, yes! and very searching."

Two minutes later the minister pronounced the benediction, as no one had offered any remark in the interval.

It seemed to the elders that Lachlan Campbell dealt harshly with young people and those that had gone astray, but they learned one evening that his justice had at least no partiality. Bumbrae said afterwards that Lachlan "looked like a ghost comin' in at the door," but he sat in silence in the shadow, and no one marked the agony on his face till the end.

"If that is all the business, Moderator, I have to bring a case of discipline before the Session, and ask them to do their duty. It is known to me that a young woman who has been a member of this church has left her home and gone into the far country. There will be no use in summoning her to appear before the Session, for she will never be seen again in this parish. I move that she be cut off from the roll, and her name is"—and Lachlan's voice broke, but in an instant he recovered himself—"her name is Flora Campbell."

The pastor confessed to me that he was stricken dumb, and that Lachlan's ashen face held him with an awful fascination.

It was Burnbrae that first found a voice, and showed that night the fine delicacy of heart that may be hidden behind a plain exterior.

"Moderator, this is a terrible calamity that has befallen our brother, and a'm feelin' as if a' had lost a bairn o' my own, for a sweeter lassie never crossed our kirk door. None o' us want to know what had happened or where she has gone, and not a word of this will cross our lips. Her father's done more than could be expected o' mortal man, and now we have our duty. It's not the way of this Session to cut aff ony member of the flock at a stroke, and we'ill no begin with Flora Campbell. A' move, Moderator, that her case be left to her father and yerself, and our neighbor may depend on it that Flora's name and his own will be mentioned in our prayers every mornin' an' night, till the good Shepherd o' the sheep brings her home."

Burnbrae paused, and then, with tears in his voice—men do not weep in Drumtochy—"With the Lord there is mercy, and with Him is plenteous redemption."

The minister took the old man's arm and led him into the manse, and set him in the big chair by the study fire. "Thank God, Lachlan, we are friends. Tell me about it as if I were your son and Flora's brother."

'The father took a letter out of an inner pocket with a trembling hand, and this is what John Carmichael read by the light of the lamp:

> "DEAR FATHER: When this reaches you I will be in London, and not worthy to cross your door. Do not be always angry with me, and try to forgive me, for you will not be troubled any more by my dancing or dressing. Do not think that I will be blaming you, for you have been a good father to me, and said what you would be considering right, but it is not easy for a man to understand a girl. Oh, if I had had my mother, then she would have understood me, and I would not have crossed you. Forget poor Flora's foolishness, but you will not forget her, and maybe you will still pray for me. Take care of the geraniums for my sake, and give milk to the lamb that you called after me. I will never see you again, in this world or the next, nor my mother ... [here the letter was much blotted]. When I think that there will be no one to look after you, and have the fire burning for you on winter nights, I will be rising to come back. But it is too late, too late! Oh, the disgrace I will be bringing on you in the glen! Your unworthy daughter, FLORA CAMPBELL."

"This is a fiery trial, Lachlan, and I cannot even imagine what you are suffering. But do not despair, for that is not the letter of a bad girl. Perhaps she was impatient, and has been led astray. But Flora is good at heart, and you must not think she is gone forever."

Lachlan groaned, the first moan he had made, and then he tottered to his feet.

"You are very kind, Pastor, and so was Burnbrae, and I will be thankful to you all, but you do not understand. Oh, no! You do not understand." Lachlan caught hold of a chair and looked the minister in the face.

"She has gone, and there will be no coming back. You would not take her name from the roll of the church, and I will not be meddling with that book. But I have blotted out her name from my Bible, where her mother's name is written, and mine. She has wrought confusion in Israel and in an rider's house, and I...I have no daughter. But I loved her; she never knew how I loved her, for her mother would be looking at me from her eyes."

The minister walked with Lachlan to the foot of the hill on which his cottage stood, and after they has shaken hands in silence, he watched the old man's figure in the cold moonlight till he disappeared into the forsaken home, where the fire had gone out on the hearth, and neither love nor hope were waiting for a broken heart.

The railway did not think it worthwhile to come to Drumtochty, and we were cut off from the lowlands by miles of forest, so our manners retained the fashion of the former age. Six elders, besides the minister, knew the tragedy of Flora Campbell, and never opened their lips. Mrs. MacFadyen, who was our newspaper, and understood her duty, refused to pry into this secret. The pity of the glen went out to Lachlan, but no one even looked a question as he sat alone in his pew or came down on a Saturday afternoon to the village shop for his week's provisions. My Drumtochty neighbors would have played an awkward part in a drawing-room, but never have I seen in all wanderings men and women of truer courtesy or tenderer heart.

"It tears my heart just to see him," Mrs. MacFadyen said to me one day, "so bowed an' dejected, him that was that so tidy and firm. His hair's turned white in a month. But least said is soonest mended. It's not right to interfere with another's sorrow. We must just hope that Flora'll soon come back, for if she doesn't, Lachlan'll not be long with us. He's sayin' nothing and a' respect him for't; but anybody can see that his heart is breakin'."

We were helpless till Marget Howe met Lachlan in the shop and read his sorrow at a glance. She went home to Whinnie Knowe in great distress.

"It was awful to see the old man going about wi' a shakin' hand, and speakin' to me about the weather, and a' the time his eyes were sayin', 'Flora, Flora!'"

"Whar do ye:' think the young girl is, Marget?" asked her husband.

"Nobody needs to know, William, an' ye mustn't speak that way, for whatever's come over her, she's dear to Lachlan and to God."

"It's laid on me to visit Lachlan, for a'm thinking our Father didna comfort us withoot expeckin' that we would comfort other folk."

When Marget came round the corner of Lachlan's cottage, she found Flora's plants laid out in the sun, and her father watering them on his knees. One was ready to die, and for it he had made a shelter with his plaid.

He was taken unawares, but in a minute he was leading Marget in with hospitable words.

"It is kind of you to come to an old man's house, Mistress Howe, and it is a very warm day. I am very good at making tea."

Marget was not as other women, and she spoke at once.

"Masiter Campbell, ye will believe that I have come in the love of God, and because we have both been afflicted. I had a son, and he is gone; ye had a daughter, and she is gone. A' know where George is, and am satisfied. Yir sorrow is deeper than mine."

"Would to God that she was lying in the kirk-yard," Lachlan replied. "But I will not speak of her. She is not anything to me this day. See, I will show you what I have done, for she has been a black shame to her name."

He opened the Bible, and there was Flora's name crossed out with wavering strokes, but the ink had run as if it had been mingled with tears.

Marget's heart burned within her at the sight, and perhaps she could hardly make allowance for Lacklan's blood and theology.

"This is what ye have done, and ye let a woman see yir work. Ye are an old man, and in sort' travail, but a' tell ye before God ye have the greater shame. Juist twenty o'age this spring, and her mother dead! No woman to watch over her, and she wandered from the fold, and a' [all] ye can do is to take her out o' yir Bible. Where would we be if our Father had blotted out our names from the Book o' Life when we left His house. But He sent His own Son to seek us, an' a weary road He came. A' tell ye, a man wouldn't leave a sheep to perish as ye have cast off yir ain [own] bairn. Yir worse than Simon the Pharisee, for Mary was no kin to him. Poor Flora, to have such sic [inconsiderate] a father!"

"Who will be telling you that I was a Pharisee?" cried Lachlan, quivering in every limb, and grasping Marget's arm.

"Forgive me, Lachlan, forgive me! It was the thought o' the misguided lassie carried me, for a' didn't come to upbraid ye."

But Lachlan had sunk into a chair and had forgotten her.

"She has the Word, and God has smitten the pride of my heart, for it is Simon that I am. I was hard on my child, and I was hard on the minister. The Lord has laid my name in the dust. She is the scapegoat for my sins, and has gone into the desert. God be merciful to me a sinner!"

And then Marget understood no more, for the rest was in Gaelic: but she heard Flora's name, with another she took to be her mother's, twined together.

So Marget knew it would be well with Lachlan yet, and she wrote this letter:

> "MY DEAR LASSIE: Ye know that I was always yir friend, and I am writing this to say that yir father loves ye more than ever, and is wearing out his heart for the sight o' yir face. Come back, or he'll die thro' want of his bairn. The glen is bright and bonny now, for the purple heather is on the hills, and down below the garden corn, wi' bluebell and poppy flowers between. Nobody 'ill ask ye where ye've been, or anything else; there's not a bairn in the place that's not wearying to see ye. And, Flora, lassie, if there will be such gladness in our wee glen when ye come home, what think ye o' the joy in the Father's House? Start the very minute that ye get this letter. Yir father bids ye come, and I'm writing this in place o' yir mother. MARGARET HOWE."

Marget went out to tend the flowers while Lachlan read the letter, and when he gave it back the address was written in his own hand.

He went as far as the crest of the hill with Marget, and watched her on the way to the post office till she was only a speck upon the road.

When he entered his cottage the shadows were beginning to fall, and he remembered it would soon be night.

"It is in the dark that Flora will be coming, and she must know that her father is waiting for her."

He cleaned and trimmed with anxious hand a lamp that was kept for show, and had never been used. Then he selected from his books Edwards' "Sinners in the Hands of an Angry God," and Coles' "On the Divine Sovereignty," and on them he laid the large family Bible out of which Flora's name had been blotted. This was the stand on which he set the lamp in the window, and every night till Flora returned its light shone down the steep path that ascended to her home, like the Divine Love from the open door of our Father's House.

Like As a Father

It was only by physical force and a free use of personalities that the Kildrummie passengers could be entrained at the Junction, and the Drumtochty men were always the last to capitulate.

They watched the main-line train that had brought them from Muirtown disappear in the distance, and then broke into groups to discuss the cattle sale at leisure, while Peter, the factotum [chieftain] of the little Kildrummie branch, drove his way through their midst with offensive pieces of luggage, and abused them by name without respect of persons.

"It's most aggravatin', Drumsheugh, 'at ye'ill stand there grinnin' at the prices, as if ye were a poor cottar body [farm woman] that had sold her own cow, and us two minutes late. Man, get into yer kerridge [carriage]; he'ill not be fat that buys from you, a'll wager."

"Peter's in an awfu' excitement tonight, neighbor," Drumsheugh would respond after a long pause. "Ye would think he was spokesman to hear him speak," and Drumsheugh settles himself in his seat.

Peter escaped this winged shaft, for he had detected a woman in the remote darkness.

"Woman, what are ye doing there out o' a'body's sicht [out of my sight]? A' near set off without ye."

Then Peter recognized her face, and his manner softened of a sudden.

"Come awa' [awa], lassie, come awa'. A' didna know ye at the moment, but a' heard ye' have been visiting in the south. The third class car is terrible full with the Drumtochty lads. Ye'ill maybe be as handy in our second." And Flora Campbell stepped in unseen.

Between the Junction and Kildrummie, Peter was accustomed to wander along the footboard, collecting tickets and identifying passengers. He was generally in fine trim on the way up, and took ample revenge for the insults of the departure. But it was supposed that Peter had taken Drumsheugh's withering sarcasm to heart, for he attached himself to the second class car that night, and was invisible to the expectant third class till the last moment.

"Ye've had a long journey, Miss Cammil, and ye must be nearly done in. Just ye sit still till the folk get off, and the good wife and me would be prood if ye took a cup o' tea with us afore ye, start home. A'll come for ye as soon a' get the van emptied and ma little choors finished."

Peter hurried up to his cottage in such hot haste that his wife came out in great alarm.

"Na, there's nothing wrong: it's the opposite way this night. Ye mind o' Flora Cammil that left her father, and none o' the Drumtochy folk would say anything about her. Well, she's in the train, and a've asked her up to rest, and she was glad to come, poor thing. So give her a couthy [warm] welcome, woman, and the best in the hoose, for ours'ill be the first roof she'ill be under on her way home."

Our women do not kiss one another like the city ladies; but the motherly grip of Mary Bruce's hand sent a thrill to Flora's heart.

"No a' ca' this [now this is] real kind o' ye, Miss Cammil, to come in without ceremony, and a'd be terrible pleased if ye would do it any time yer traveling. The rail is so fatiguing, but a cup o' tea'ill set ye up," and Mary had Flora in the best chair, and was loading her plate with homely dainties.

Peter would speak of nothing but the new engine that was coming, and was to place the Kildrummie branch beyond ridicule forever. On this great event he continued without intermission, till he parted with Flora on the edge of the pine woods that divided Drumtochty from Kildrummie.

"Good night to ye, Miss Cammil, and thank ye again for yir visit. Bring the old man with ye next time ye're passing, though a'm feared ye've been deafened with the engine."

Flora took Peter's hand, that was callous and rough with the turning of brakes and the coupling of chains.

"It was not your new engine you was thinking about this night, Peter Bruce, but a poor girl that is in trouble. I have not the words, but I will be remembering your house: oh, yes! as long as I live."

Twice Peter stopped on his way home. The first time he slapped his leg and chuckled:

"Say, it was clever o' me: a hale [full] kerridge o' Drumtochty lads, and not one o' them ever had a glint o' her."

At the second stoppage he drew his hand across his eyes.

"Poor lassie, a' hope her father 'ill be kind to her, for she's so broken, and looks more like death than life."

No one can desire a sweeter walk than through a Scottish pine wood in late September, where you breathe the healing resinous air, and the ground is crisp and springy beneath your feet, and gentle animals dart away on every side, and here and there you come on an open space with a pool and a brake of gorse [clearing in the brush]. Many a time on market days Flora had gone singing through these woods, plucking a posy [bunch] of wild flowers and finding a mirror in every pool, as young girls will.

But now she trembled and was afraid. The rustling of the trees in the darkness, the hooting of an owl, the awful purity of the moonlight in the glades, the cold sheen of the water, were to her troubled conscience omens of judgment. Had it not been for the kindness of Peter Bruce, which was a pledge of human forgiveness, there would have been no heart in her to dare that wood. It was with a sob of relief she escaped from the shadow and looked upon the old glen once more, bathed from end to end in the light of the harvest moon. Beneath her ran our little river, spanned by its quaint old bridge. Away on the right the Parish Kirk peeped out from a clump of trees. Halfway up the glen the clachan [inn] lay surrounded by patches of corn, and beyond were the moors, with a shepherd's cottage that held her heart.

Two hours ago squares of light told of warmth and welcome within; but now, as Flora passed one house after another, it seemed as if everyone she knew was dead, and she was forgotten in her misery. Her heart grew cold, and she longed to lie down and die, when she caught the gleam of a lighted window. Someone was living still to know she had repented, and she knelt down among the flowers with her ear to the glass to hear the sound of a human voice.

Archie Moncur had come home late from a far-away job, but he must needs have worship with his sister before they went to bed, and well did he choose the psalm that night. Flora's tears rained upon the mignonette [sweet smelling plant] as the two old people sang:

"When Sion's bondage God turned back,
    As men that dreamed were we,
Then filled with laughter was our mouth,
    Our tongue with melody;"
while fragrance of the flowers went up as incense unto God."

All the way along the glen the last words of the psalm still rang in her ears. "Rejoicing shall return." But as she touched the footpath to her home, courage failed her. Marget had written for her dead mother, but no one could speak with authority for her father. She knew the pride of his religion and his iron principles. If he refused her entrance, then it had been better for her to have died in London.

A turn of the path brought her within sight of the cottage, and her heart came into her mouth, for the kitchen window was a blaze of light. One moment she feared Lachlan might be ill, but in the next she understood, and in the greatness of her joy she ran the rest of the way. When she reached the door, her strength had departed, and she was not able to knock. But there was no need, for the dogs, who never forget nor cast off, were bidding her welcome with short joyous yelps of delight, and she could hear her father feeling for the latch, which for once could not be found, and saying nothing but "Flora, Flora!"

She had made up some kind of speech, but the only word she ever said was "Father," for Lachlan, who had never even kissed her all the days of her youth, clasped her in his arms and sobbed out blessings over her head, while the dogs licked her hands with their soft, kindly tongues.

"It is a pity you have not the Gaelic," Flora said to Marget afterwards. "It is the best of all languages for loving. There are fifty words for 'darling,' and my father would be calling me every one that night I came home."

Lachlan was so carried with joy, and firelight is so hopeful, that he had not seen the signs of sore sickness on Flora's face. But the morning light undeceived him, and he was sadly dashed.

"You will be very tired after your long journey, Flora, and it is good for you to rest. There is a man in the hamlet I am wanting to see, and he will maybe be coming back with me."

When Lachlan reached his place of prayer, he lay on the ground and cried, "Have mercy on me, O Lord, and spare her for Thy servant's sake, and let me not lose her after Thou hast brought her back and hast opened my heart…Take her not till she has seen that I love her…Give me time to do her kindness for the past wherein I oppressed her…O, turn away Thy judgment on my hardness, and let not the child suffer for her father's sins." Then he arose and hastened for the doctor.

It was afternoon before Dr. MacLure could come, but the very sight of his face, which was as the sun in its strength, let light into the room where Lachlan sat at the bedside holding Flora's hand, and making woeful pretense that she was not ill.

"Well, Flora, ye've got back from yir visits, and a' tell ye we've missed ye most terible. A' doubt the south country folk have been feeding ye weel, or maybe it was the town air. It never agrees with me. A'm half choking a' the time a'm in Glasgow, and as for London, there's too many folk to the square yard for health."

All the time he was busy at his work, and no man could do it better or quicker, although the outside of him was not encouraging.

"Lachlan, what are ye traivelling in and out there for with a fan' that would sour milk? What ails ye, man? Ye're surely not imagining Flora's going to leave ye?"

"Lord's sake, it's most provokin' that if a body has a bit o' illness in Drumtochty, their friends take to prophesying death."

Lachlan had crept over to Flora's side, and both were waiting.

"No, no: ye know a' never tell lies like the grand city doctors, and a'll warrant Flora 'ill be in kirk afore November, and hiking up the braes [hills] as hardy as a highland pony by the new year."

Flora puts an arm round her father's neck, and draws down his face to hers, but the doctor is looking another way.

"Dinna vex wi' [don't worry about] medicine; give her plenty o' fresh milk and plenty o' air. There's no living for a doctor with that Drumtochty air. It starts from the Moray Firth and sweeps down Badenoch, and comes over the moor o' Rannoch and across the Grampians. There's the salt o' the sea, and the caller air o' the hills, and the smell o' the heather, and the bloom o' mony [many] a flower in't. If there's no disease in the organs o' the body, a puff o' Drumtochty air would bring back a man from the gates o' death."

"You hef made two hearts glad this day, Dr. MacLure," said Lachlan, outside the door, "and I am calling you Barnabas."

"Ye've called me worst names than that in yir time," and the doctor mounted his horse. "It's done me a world o' good to see Flora in her home again, and I'll give Marget Howe a cry in passing and send her up to have a look, for there's no wiser woman in the glen."

When Marget came, Flora told her the history of her letter.

"It was a beautiful night in London, but I will be thinking that there is no living person caring whether I die or live, and I was considering how I could die, for there is nothing so hopeless as to have no friend in a great city. It is often that I have been alone on the moor, and no man within miles, but I was never lonely. Oh, no! I had plenty of good company. I would sit down beside a burn [stream], and the trout will swim out from below a stone, and the cattle will come to drink, and the muirfowl [pheasant] will be crying to each other, and the sheep will be bleating. Oh, yes! And there are the bees all round, and a string of wild ducks above your head. It is a busy place, a moor; and a safe place too, for there is not one of the animals will hurt you. No, the big highlanders will only look at you and go away to their pasture. But it is weary to be in London and no one to speak a kind word to you, and I will be looking at the crowd that is always passing, and I will not see one kind face, and when I looked in at the lighted windows the people were all sitting round the table, but there was no place for me. Millions and millions of people, and not one to say 'Flora,' and not one sore heart if I died that night.

"Then a strange thing happened, as you will be considering, but it is good to be a Highlander, for we see visions. You maybe know that a wounded deer will try to hide herself, and I crept into the shadow of a church, and wept. Then the people and the noise and the houses passed away like the mist on the hill, and I was walking to the kirk with my father, oh, yes! and I saw you all in your places, and I heard the Psalms, and I could see through the window the green fields and the trees on the edge of the moor. And I saw my home, with the dogs before the door, and the flowers that I planted, and the lamb coming for her milk. and I heard myself singing, And I awoke.

"But there was singing, oh, yes! and beautiful too, for the dark church was open. And this was the hymn:

There is a fountain filled with blood.

"So I went in and sat down at the door. The sermon was on the Prodigal Son, but there is only one word I remember. 'You are not forgotten or cast off,' the preacher said, 'you are missed.' And then he will come back to it again, and it was always 'missed, missed, missed.' Sometime he will say, 'If you had a plant, and you had taken great care of it, and it was stolen, would you not miss it?' And I will be thinking of my geraniums, and saying 'yes' in my heart. And then he will go on. 'If a shepherd was counting his sheep, and there was one short, does he not go out to the hill and seek for it?' and I will see my father coming back with that lamb that lost its mother. My heart was melting within me, but he will still be pleading. 'If a father had a child, and she left her home and lost herself in the wicked city, she will still be remembered in the old house, and her chair will be there,' and I will be seeing my father all alone with the Bible before him, and the dogs will lay their heads on his knee, but there is no Flora.

"So I slipped out into the darkness and cried, 'Father!' but I could not go back, and I knew not what to do. But this was ever in my ear, 'Missed,' and I was wondering if God will be thinking of me. 'Perhaps there may be a sign,' I said, and I went to my room, and I saw the letter. It was not long before I will be in the train, and all the night I held your letter in my hand. And when I was afraid I will read 'Your father loves you more than ever,' and I will say 'This is my warrant.' Oh, yes! And God was very good to me, and I did not want for friends all the way home.

"The English guard noticed me cry, and he will take care of me all the night, and see me off at Muirtown. And this is what he will say as the train was leaving, in his cheery English way, 'Keep up your heart, lass, there's a good time coming.' And Peter Bruce will be waiting for me at the Junction, and a gentle man is Peter Bruce, and Maister Moncur will be singing a psalm to keep up my heart. And I will see the light, and then I will know that the Lord has had mercy upon me. That is all I have to tell you, Marget, for the rest I will be saying to God."

"But there is something I must be telling," said Lachlan, coming in, "and it is not easy."

He brought over the Bible and opened it at the family register where his daughter's name had been erased. Then he laid it down before Flora, and bowed his head on the bed.

"Will you ever be able to forgive your father?"

"Give me the pen, Marget," and Flora wrote for a minute, but Lachlan never moved.

When he lifted his head, this was what he read in a vacant space:

Flora Campbell.
Missed April 1873
Found September 1873
"Her father fell on her neck and kissed her."

4. Notes

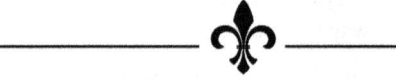

1 The most complete bibliographical information is in W. Robertson Nicoll's 400-page *"Ian Maclaren," Life of the Rev. John Watson* (London: Hodden and Stoughton, 1908). A condensed eulogy by the same author may be found in *Princes of the Church* (London: Hodden and Stoughton, 1921), pp. 204-216. J.B. Pond also has a brief sketch in *Eccentricities of Genius* (New York: Dillingham, 1901), pp. 645, 646; National Dictionary of Bibliography, *1901-1911 Supplement*, Vol XXIII (London: Oxford University Press, 1912), pp. 605-607.

2 W. Robertson Nicoll, *"Ian Maclaren," Life of the Rev. John Watson*, op. cit., p. 92.

3 *Ibid.*, p. 92

Why God Used D.L. Moody

R.A. Torrey 1856-1928

*With an Introduction
By Robert E. Coleman*

Abridged version of *Why God Used D.L. Moody* by R. A. Torrey.
Abridged version originally published by World Wide Publications,
1992, along with Billy Graham Center, Wheaton, Il. Copyright of
abridged version and introduction held by Robert Coleman, used with
permission. Artwork in the Public Domain.

Book Chapters

1. Introduction
   By Robert E. Coleman 596
2. Why God Used D.L. Moody 599
3. A Fully Surrendered Man 601
4. A Man of Prayer 603
5. A Deep and Practical student of the Bible 605
6. A Humble Man 609
7. His Entire Freedom from the Love of Money 612
8. A Consuming Passion for the Salvation of the Lost 614
9. Definitely Endued with Power from on High 619

1. Introduction
By Robert E. Coleman

God delights to confound the world by working powerfully through men considered foolish and weak.

Dwight Lyman Moody was such a person. One of nine children, his father died when he was four years old. The family was raised by a courageous mother in destitute circumstances. Little opportunity was afforded for formal education. What meager religious training he received in a Unitarian Church lacked any evangelical substance. When D. L. at seventeen left home to seek work in Boston, no one would have thought that this restless youth was destined to shake two continents with the gospel of redeeming grace.

The plan of God began to unfold in a shoe store, where Moody found employment. It was April 21, 1855. He was called on by a Sunday school teacher, who with tear-filled eyes told him of the Savior's love and the love Jesus wanted in return. Though the young clerk had heard many great sermons, never had anyone so personally confronted him with the claims of Christ. There in the back of the store he embraced his loving Lord.

Immediately Moody made application to join the Mount Vernon Congregational Church. However, noting his theological ignorance, the examining committee deferred the request. The future renowned evangelist had to wait ten months before being admitted to membership upon reapplication.

Soon afterward Moody moved to Chicago, where he began to prosper as a shoe merchant. Touched by the poor children living in the slums, he went out in the streets to gather boys to attend church. Later he rented a vacant saloon building and started his own mission Sunday school.

One day a teacher came to Moody with the news that he had tuberculosis and had only a short time to live. What made his grief unbearable was the knowledge that not one of his class of girls professed to be saved. Accordingly the enterprising shoe salesman offered to go with the man to visit each member and tell them of their need to make a decision. Within a few days every pupil was converted. The sight of those girls saying good-bye to their dying teacher so moved Mr. Moody that he was led to give up his business pursuits and devote himself entirely to gospel work.

The fact he never received ordination by any ecclesiastical system was no impediment to his calling. His Sunday school grew to be the largest in the city, and out of it a thriving church was organized.

With the outbreak of the Civil War, he joined the Christian Commission. Frequently he visited the troops in the field, as well as those in prison camps. He also became active in the YMCA. Under his leadership the first building of this new organization was erected.

In 1867 Moody took his first trip to Europe, though his evangelistic impact was unspectacular. Following a deeper experience of the Holy Spirit's outpouring in 1871, a new fruitfulness became apparent in his labors. Subsequent trips to England resulted in unprecedented numbers coming to his meetings, with thousands responding to the gospel invitation. By the close of his London campaign in 1875, his fame had spread across the Atlantic, and he returned to America the most sought-after preacher in the world.

Thereafter until his death, Moody held crusades in the largest cities across the United States. People from every rank of society crowded the largest halls of the nation to hear him. His campaigns became front-page news. Wherever he went a spirit of revival lifted the tone of the church and penetrated communities with the savor of righteousness.

His preaching ministry was paralleled by a concern for Christian education. The Northfield Schools were established in 1878, and the Moody Bible Institute in 1889. The numerous Bible conferences which he promoted expressed this interest on a different level. He also was a leader in the World Student Christian Federation and the Student Volunteer Movement, out of which multitudes of young people went as missionaries to the ends of the earth.

Moody was conducting a crusade in Kansas City in 1899 when his physical strength finally failed and he was forced to return to his home at

Northfield. On December 22, with his beloved family by his bedside, he whispered: "God is calling me, and I must go." The chariot was waiting. In a few minutes he answered the heavenly summons.

As few people of his generation, Moody left a spiritual legacy which continues to point this passing world to the things that will endure forever.

Such a life can only be explained by the sovereign grace of God. Yet on the human level, we do well to ponder why it was possible. The following account by one of Moody's closest friends, R. A. Torrey, gives an insight. Though written in 1924, it is still fresh with meaning and challenge.

The qualities seen in Moody's life also can be present in ours. Our gifts and callings may be different, but the source of power is the same for all. In this assurance we can rejoice that God will use anyone willing to be used. Let us hope that reading these pages will help us see more clearly the secret.

Robert E. Coleman, 1973

2. Why God Used D.L. Moody

On February 5, 1837, there was born of poor parents in a humble farmhouse in Northfield, Massachusetts, a little baby who was to become the greatest man, as I believe, of his generation or of his century—Dwight L. Moody. After our great generals, great statesmen, great scientists and great men of letters have passed away and been forgotten, and their work and its helpful influence has come to an end, the work of D. L. Moody will go on and its saving influence continue and increase, bringing blessing not only to every State in the Union but to every nation on earth. Yes, it will continue throughout the ages of eternity.

My subject is "Why God Used D. L. Moody," and I can think of no subject upon which I would rather speak. For I shall not seek to glorify Mr. Moody, but the God who by His grace, His entirely unmerited favor, used him so mightily, and the Christ who saved him by His atoning death and resurrection life, and the Holy Spirit who lived in him and wrought through him and who alone made him the mighty power that he was to this world. Furthermore: I hope to make it clear that the God who used D. L. Moody in his day is just as ready to use you and me, in this day, if we, on our part, do what D. L. Moody did, which was what made it possible for God to so abundantly use him.

The whole secret of why D. L. Moody was such a mightily used man you will find in Psalm 62:11: "God hath spoken once; twice have I heard this; that POWER BELONGETH UNTO GOD." I am glad it does. I am glad that power did not belong to D. L. Moody; I am glad that it did not belong to Charles G. Finney; I am glad that it did not belong to Martin Luther; I am glad that it did not belong to any other Christian man whom God has greatly used in this world's history. Power belongs to God. If D. L. Moody had any power, and he had great power, he got it from God.

But God does not give His power arbitrarily. It is true that He gives it to whomsoever He will, but He wills to give it on certain conditions, which are clearly revealed in His Word; and D. L. Moody met those conditions and God made him the most wonderful preacher of his generation; yes, I think the most wonderful man of his generation.

But how was it that D. L. Moody had that power of God so wonderfully manifested in his life? Pondering this question it seemed to me that there were seven things in the life of D. L. Moody that accounted for God's using him so largely as He did.

3. A Fully Surrendered Man

The first thing that accounts for God's using D. L. Moody so mightily was that *he was a fully surrendered man.* Every ounce of that two-hundred-and-eighty-pound body of his belonged to God; everything he was and everything he had, belonged wholly to God. Now, I am not saying that Mr. Moody was perfect; he was not. If I attempted to, I presume I could point out some defects in his character. It does not occur to me at this moment what they were; but I am confident that I could think of some, if I tried real hard. I have never yet met a perfect man, not one. I have known perfect men in the sense in which the Bible commands us to be perfect, i.e., men who are wholly God's, out-and-out for God, fully surrendered to God, with no will but God's will; but I have never known a man in whom I could not see some defects, some places where he might have been improved. No, Mr. Moody was not a faultless man. If he had any flaws in his character, and he had, I presume I was in a position to know them better than almost any other man, because of my very close association with him in the later years of his life; and furthermore, I suppose that in his latter days he opened his heart to me more fully than to anyone else in the world. I think he told me some things that he told no one else. I presume I knew whatever defects there were in his character as well as anybody. But while I recognized such flaws, nevertheless, I know that he was a man who belonged wholly to God.

The first month I was in Chicago, we were having a talk about something upon which we very widely differed, and Mr. Moody turned to me very frankly and very kindly and said in defense of his own position: "Torrey, if I believed that God wanted me to jump out of that window, I would jump." I believe he would. If he thought God wanted him to do anything he would do it. He belonged wholly, unreservedly, unqualifiedly, entirely, to God.

Henry Varley, a very intimate friend of Mr. Moody in the earlier days of his work, loved to tell how he once said to him: "It remains to be seen what God will do with a man who gives himself up wholly to Him." I am told that when Mr. Henry Varley said that, Mr. Moody said to himself: "Well, I will be that man." And I, for my part, do not think, "it remains to be seen" what God will do with a man who gives himself up wholly to Him. I think it has been seen already in D. L. Moody. If you and I are to be used in our sphere as D. L. Moody was used in his, we must put all that we have and all that we are in the hands of God, for Him to use as He will, to send us where He will, for God to do with us what He will, and we, on our part, to do everything God bids us do. There are thousands and tens of thousands of men and women in Christian work, brilliant men and women, rarely gifted men and women, men and women who are making great sacrifices, men and women who have put all conscious sin out of their lives, yet who, nevertheless, have stopped short of absolute surrender to God, and therefore have stopped short of fullness of power. But Mr. Moody did not stop short of absolute surrender to God; he was a wholly surrendered man, and if you and I are to be used, you and I must be wholly surrendered men and women.

4. A Man of Prayer

The second secret of the great power exhibited in Mr. Moody's life was that *Mr. Moody was in the deepest and most meaningful sense a man of prayer*. People oftentimes say to me: "Well, I went many miles to see and to hear D. L. Moody and he certainly was a wonderful preacher." Yes, D. L. Moody certainly was a wonderful preacher; taking it all in all, the most wonderful preacher I have ever heard, and it was a great privilege to hear him preach as he alone could preach; but out of a very intimate acquaintance with him I wish to testify that he was a far greater prayer than he was preacher. Time and time again, he was confronted by obstacles that seemed insurmountable, but he always knew the way to surmount and to overcome all difficulties. He knew the way to bring to pass anything that needed to be brought to pass. He knew and believed in the deepest depths of his soul that "nothing was too hard for the Lord" and that prayer could do anything that God could do.

Oftentimes Mr. Moody would write me when he was about to undertake some new work, saying: "I am beginning work in such and such a place on such and such a day; I wish you would get the students together for a day of fasting and prayer"; and often I have taken those letters and read them to the students in the lecture room and said: "Mr. Moody wants us to have a day of fasting and prayer, first for God's blessing on our own souls and work, and then for God's blessing on him and his work." Often we were gathered in the lecture room far into the night—sometimes till one, two, three, four or even five o'clock in the morning, crying to God, just because Mr. Moody urged us to wait upon God until we received His blessing. How many men and women I have known whose lives and characters have been transformed by those nights of prayer and who have wrought mighty things in many lands because of those nights of prayer!

One day Mr. Moody drove up to my house at Northfield and said: "Torrey, I want you to take a ride with me." I got into the carriage and we drove out toward Lover's Lane, talking about some great and unexpected difficulties that had arisen in regard to the work in Northfield and Chicago, and in connection with other work that was very dear to him. As we drove along, some black storm clouds lay ahead of us, and then suddenly, as we were talking, it began to rain. He drove the horse into a shed near the entrance to Lover's Lane to shelter the horse, and then laid the reins upon the dashboard and said: "Torrey, pray"; and then, as best I could, I prayed, while he in his heart joined me in prayer. And when my voice was silent he began to pray. Oh, I wish you could have heard that prayer! I shall never forget it, so simple, so trustful, so definite and so direct and so mighty. When the storm was over and we drove back to town, the obstacles had been surmounted, and the work of the schools, and other work that was threatened, went on as it had never gone on before, and it has gone on until this day. As we drove back, Mr. Moody said to me: "Torrey, we will let the other men do the talking and the criticizing, and we will stick to the work that God has given us to do, and let Him take care of the difficulties and answer the criticisms."

On one occasion Mr. Moody said to me in Chicago: "I have just found, to my surprise, that we are twenty thousand dollars behind in our finances for the work here and in Northfield, and we must have that twenty thousand dollars, and I am going to get it by prayer." He did not tell a soul who had the ability to give a penny of the twenty thousand dollars deficit, but looked right to God and said: "I need twenty thousand dollars for my work; send me that money in such a way that I will know it comes straight from Thee." And God heard that prayer. The money came in such a way that it was clear that it came from God, in direct answer to prayer. Yes, D. L. Moody was a man who believed in the God who answers prayer, and not only believed in Him in a theoretical way but believed in Him in a practical way. He was a man who met every difficulty that stood in his way-by prayer. Everything he undertook was backed up by prayer, and in everything, his ultimate dependence was upon God.

5. A Deep and Practical Student of the Bible

The third secret of Mr. Moody's power, or the third reason why God used D. L. Moody, was because *he was a deep and practical student of the Word of God*. Nowadays it is often said of D. L. Moody that he was not a student. I wish to say that he was a student; most emphatically he was a student. He was not a student of psychology; he was not a student of anthropology—I am very sure he would not have known what that word meant; he was not a student of biology; he was not a student of philosophy; he was not even a student of theology, in the technical sense of the term; but he was a student, a profound and practical student of the one Book that is more worth studying than all other books in the world put together; he was a student of the Bible. Every day of his life, I have reason for believing, he arose very early in the morning to study the Word of God, way down to the close of his life. Mr. Moody used to rise about four o'clock in the morning to study the Bible. He would say to me: "If I am going to get in any study, I have got to get up before the other folks get up"; and he would shut himself up in a remote room in his house, alone with his God and his Bible.

I shall never forget the first night I spent in his home. He had invited me to take the superintendency of the Bible Institute and I had already begun my work; I was on my way to some city in the East to preside at the International Christian Workers' Convention. He wrote me saying: "Just as soon as the Convention is over, come up to Northfield." He learned when I was likely to arrive and drove over to South Vernon to meet me. That night he had all the teachers from the Mount Hermon School and from the Northfield Seminary come together at the house to meet me, and to talk over the problems of the two Schools. We talked together far on into the night, and then, after the principals and teachers of the Schools had gone home, Mr. Moody and I talked together about the problems a while longer. It was very late when I got to bed that night, but very early the next morning, about five o'clock, I heard a gentle tap on my door. Then I heard Mr. Moody's voice whispering: 'Torrey, are you up?" I happened to be; I do not always get up at that early hour but I happened to be up that particular morning. He said: "I want you to go somewhere with me," and I went down with him. Then I found out that he had already been up an hour or two in his room studying the Word of God.

Oh, you may talk about power; but, if you neglect the one Book that God has given you as the one instrument through which He imparts and exercises His power, you will not have it. You may read many books and go to many conventions and you may have your all-night prayer meetings to pray for the power of the Holy Ghost; but unless you keep in constant and close association with the one Book, the Bible, you will not have power. And if you ever had power, you will not maintain it except by the daily, earnest, intense study of that Book. *Ninety-nine Christians in every hundred are merely playing at Bible study; and therefore ninety-nine Christians in every hundred are mere weaklings, when they might be giants, both in their Christian life and in their service.*

It was largely because of his thorough knowledge of the Bible, and his practical knowledge of the Bible, that Mr. Moody drew such immense crowds. On "Chicago Day," in October 1893, none of the theatres of Chicago dared to open because it was expected that everybody in Chicago would go on that day to the World's Fair; and, in point of fact, something like four hundred thousand people did pass through the gates of the Fair that day. Everybody in Chicago was expected to be at that end of the city on that day. But Mr. Moody said to me: "Torrey, engage the Central Music Hall and announce meetings from nine o'clock in the morning till six o'clock at night." "Why," I replied, "Mr. Moody, nobody will be at this end of Chicago on that day; not even the theatres dare to open; everybody is going down to Jackson Park to the Fair; we cannot get anybody out on this day." Mr. Moody replied: "You do as you are told"; and I did as I was told and engaged the Central Music Hall for continuous meetings from nine o'clock in the morning till six o'clock at night. But I did it with a heavy heart; I thought there would be poor audiences. I was on the program at noon that day. Being very busy in my office about the details of the campaign, I did not reach the Central Music Hall till almost noon. I thought I would have no trouble in getting in. But when I got almost to the Hall I found to my amazement that not only was it packed but the vestibule was packed and the steps were packed, and there was no getting anywhere near the door; and if I had not gone round and climbed in a back window they would have lost their speaker for that hour. But that would not have been of much importance, for the crowds had not gathered to hear me; it was the magic of Mr. Moody's name that had drawn them. And why did they long to hear Mr. Moody? Because they knew that while he was not versed in many of the philosophies and fads and fancies of the day, he did know the one Book that this old world most longs to know—the Bible.

I shall never forget Moody's last visit to Chicago. The ministers of Chicago had sent me to Cincinnati to invite him to come to Chicago and hold a meeting. In response to the invitation, Mr. Moody said to me: "If you will hire the Auditorium for weekday mornings and afternoons and have meetings at ten in the morning and three in the afternoon, I will go." I replied: "Mr. Moody, you know what a busy city Chicago is, and how impossible it is for business men to get out at ten o'clock in the morning and three in the afternoon on working days. Will you not hold evening meetings and meetings on Sunday?" "No," he replied, "I am afraid if I did, I would interfere with the regular work of the churches."

I went back to Chicago and engaged the Auditorium, which at that time was the building having the largest seating capacity of any building in the city, seating in those days about seven thousand people; I announced weekday meetings, with Mr. Moody as the speaker, at ten o'clock in the mornings and three o'clock in the afternoons. At once protests began to pour in upon me. One of them came from Marshall Field, at that time the business king of Chicago. "Mr. Torrey," Mr. Field wrote, "we business men of Chicago wish to hear Mr. Moody, and you know perfectly well how impossible it is for us to get out at ten o'clock in the morning and three o'clock in the afternoon; have evening meetings." I received many letters of a similar purport and wrote to Mr. Moody urging him to give us evening meetings. But Mr. Moody simply replied: "You do as you are told," and I did as I was told; that is the way I kept my job.

On the first morning of the meetings I went down to the Auditorium about half an hour before the appointed time, but I went with much fear and apprehension; I thought the Auditorium would be nowhere nearly full. When I reached there, to my amazement I found a queue of people four abreast extending from the Congress Street entrance to Wabash Avenue, then a block north on Wabash Avenue, then a break to let traffic through, and then another block, and so on. I went in through the back door, and there were many clamoring for entrance there. When the doors were opened at the appointed time, we had a cordon of twenty policemen to keep back the crowd; but the crowd was so great that it swept the cordon of policemen off their feet and packed eight thousand people into the building before we could get the doors shut. And I think there were as many left on the outside as there were in the building. I do not think that anyone else in the world could have drawn such a crowd at such a time.

Why? Because though Mr. Moody knew little about science, or philosophy, or literature in general, he did know the one Book that this old world is perishing to know and longing to know; and this old world will flock to hear men who know the Bible and preach the Bible as they will flock to hear nothing else on earth.

During all the months of the World's Fair in Chicago, no one could draw such crowds as Mr. Moody. Judging by the papers, one would have thought that the great religious event in Chicago at that time was the World's Congress of Religions. One very gifted man of letters in the East was invited to speak at this Congress. He saw in this invitation the opportunity of his life and prepared his paper, the exact title of which I do not now recall, but it was something along the line of "New Light on the Old Doctrines." He prepared the paper with great care, and then sent it around to his most trusted and gifted friends for criticisms. These men sent it back to him with such emendations, as they had to suggest. Then he rewrote the paper, incorporating as many of the suggestions and criticisms as seemed wise. Then he sent it around for further criticisms. Then he wrote the paper a third time, and had it, as he trusted, perfect. He went on to Chicago to meet this coveted opportunity of speaking at the World's Congress of Religions. It was at eleven o'clock on a Saturday morning (if I remember correctly) that he was to speak. He stood outside the door of the platform waiting for the great moment to arrive, and as the clock struck eleven walked on to the platform to face a magnificent audience of eleven women and two men! But there was not a building anywhere in Chicago that would accommodate the very same day the crowds that would flock to hear Mr. Moody at any hour of the day or night. Oh, men and women, if you wish to get an audience and wish to do that audience some good after you get them, *study*, study, STUDY the one Book, and *preach*, preach, PREACH the one Book, and *teach*, teach, TEACH the one Book, the Bible, the only Book that contains God's Word, and the only Book that has power to gather and hold and bless the crowds for any great length of time.

6. A Humble Man

The fourth reason why God continuously, through so many years, used D. L. Moody was because *he was a humble man*. I think D. L. Moody was the humblest man I ever knew in all my life. He loved to quote the words of another: "Faith gets the most; love works the most; but *humility keeps the most*." He himself had the humility that keeps everything it gets. As I have already said, he was the most humble man I ever knew, i.e., the most humble man when we bear in mind the great things he did, and the praise that was lavished upon him. Oh, how he loved to put himself in the background and put other men in the foreground. How often he would stand on a platform with some of us little fellows seated behind him and as he spoke he would say: "There are better men coming after me." As he said it, he would point back over his shoulder with his thumb to the "little fellows." I do not know how he could believe it, but he really *did* believe that the others that were coming after him were really better than he was. He made no pretense to a humility he did not possess. In his heart of hearts he constantly underestimated himself, and overestimated others. He really believed that God would use other men in a larger measure than he had been used.

Mr. Moody loved to keep himself in the background. At his conventions at Northfield, or anywhere else, he would push the other men to the front and, if he could, have them do all the preaching—McGregor, Campbell Morgan, Andrew Murray, and the rest of them. The only way we could get him to take any part in the program was to get up in the convention and move that we hear D. L. Moody at the next meeting. He continually put himself out of sight.

Oh, how many a man has been full of promise and God has used him, and then the man thought that he was the whole thing and God was compelled to set him aside! I believe more promising workers have gone on the rocks through self-sufficiency and self-esteem than through any other cause. I can look back for forty years, or more, and think of many men who are now wrecks or derelicts who at one time the world thought were going to be something great. But they have disappeared entirely from the public view. Why? Because of overestimation of self. Oh, the men and women who have been put aside because they began to think that they were somebody, that they were "IT," and therefore God was compelled to set them aside.

I remember a man with whom I was closely associated in a great movement in this country. We were having a most successful convention in Buffalo, and he was greatly elated. As we walked down the street together to one of the meetings one day, he said to me: "Torrey, you and I are the most important men in Christian work in this country," or words to that effect. I replied: "John, I am sorry to hear you say that; for as I read my Bible I find man after man who had accomplished great things whom God had to set aside because of his sense of his own importance." And God set that man aside also from that time. I think he is still living, but no one ever hears of him, or has heard of him for years.

God used D. L. Moody, I think, beyond any man of his day; but it made no difference how much God used him, he never was puffed up. One day, speaking to me of a great New York preacher, now dead, Mr. Moody said: "He once did a very foolish thing, the most foolish thing that I ever knew a man, ordinarily so wise as he was, to do. He came up to me at the close of a little talk I had given and said: 'Young man, you have made a great address tonight.'" Then Mr. Moody continued: "How foolish of him to have said that! It almost turned my head." But, thank God, it did not turn his head, and even when pretty much all the ministers in England, Scotland and Ireland, and many of the English bishops were ready to follow D. L. Moody wherever he led, even then it never turned his head one bit. He would get down on his face before God, knowing he was human, and ask God to empty him of all self-sufficiency. And God did.

Oh, men and women! especially young men and young women, perhaps God is beginning to use you; very likely people are saying: "What a wonderful gift he has as a Bible teacher, what power he has as a preacher, for such a young man!" Listen: get down upon your face before God. I believe here lies one of the most dangerous snares of the devil. When the devil cannot discourage a man, he approaches him on another tack, which he knows is far worse in its results; he puffs him up by whispering in his ear: "You are the leading evangelist of the day. You are the man who will sweep everything before you. You are the coming man. You are the D. L. Moody of the day"; and if you listen to him, he will ruin you. The entire shore of the history of Christian workers is strewn with the wrecks of gallant vessels that were full of promise a few years ago, but these men became puffed up and were driven on the rocks by the wild winds of their own raging self-esteem.

7. His Entire Freedom from the Love of Money

The fifth secret of D. L. Moody's continual power and usefulness was *his entire freedom from the love of money*. Mr. Moody might have been a wealthy man, but money had no charms for him. He loved to gather money for God's work; he refused to accumulate money for himself. He told me during the World's Fair that if he had taken, for himself, the royalties on the hymnbooks, which he had published, they would have amounted, at that time, to a million dollars. But Mr. Moody refused to touch the money. He had a perfect right to take it, for he was responsible for the publication of the books and it was his money that went into the publication of the first of them. Mr. Sankey had some hymns that he had taken with him to England and he wished to have them published. He went to a publisher (I think Morgan & Scott) and they declined to publish them, because, as they said, Philip Phillips had recently been over and published a hymnbook and it had not done well. However, Mr. Moody had a little money and he said that he would put it into the publication of these hymns in cheap form; and he did. The hymns had a most remarkable and unexpected sale; they were then published in book form and large profits accrued. The financial results were offered to Mr. Moody, but he refused to touch them. "But," it was urged on him, "the money belongs to you"; but he would not touch it. Mr. Fleming H. Revell was at the time treasurer of the Chicago Avenue Church, commonly known as the Moody Tabernacle. Only the basement of this new church building had been completed, funds having been exhausted. Hearing of the hymnbook situation Mr. Revell suggested, in a letter to friends in London, that the money be given for completion of this building, and it was. Afterwards, so much money came in that it was given, by the committee into whose hands Mr. Moody put the matter, to various Christian enterprises.

In a certain city to which Mr. Moody went in the latter years of his life, and where I went with him, it was publicly announced that Mr. Moody would accept no money whatever for his services. Now, in point of fact, Mr. Moody was dependent, in a measure, upon what was given him at various services; but when this announcement was made, Mr. Moody said nothing, and left that city without a penny's compensation for the hard work he did there; and, I think, he paid his own hotel bill. And yet a minister in that very city came out with an article in a paper, which I read, in which he told a fairy tale of the financial demands that Mr. Moody made upon them, which story I knew personally to be absolutely untrue. Millions of dollars passed into Mr. Moody's hands, *but they passed through*; they did not stick to his fingers.

This is the point at which many an evangelist makes shipwreck, and his great work comes to an untimely end. The love of money on the part of some evangelists has done more to discredit evangelistic work in our day, and to lay many an evangelist on the shelf, than almost any other cause. While I was away on my recent tour I was told by one of the most reliable ministers in one of our eastern cities of a campaign conducted by one who has been greatly used in the past. (Do not imagine, for a moment, that I am speaking of Billy Sunday, for I am not; this same minister spoke in the highest terms of Mr. Sunday and of a campaign, which he conducted in a city where this minister was a pastor.) This evangelist of whom I now speak came to a city for a united evangelistic campaign and was supported by fifty-three churches. The minister who told me about the matter was himself chairman of the Finance Committee. The evangelist showed such a longing for money and so deliberately violated the agreement he had made before coming to the city and so insisted upon money being gathered for him in other ways than he had himself prescribed in the original contract, that this minister threatened to resign from the Finance Committee. He was, however, persuaded to remain to avoid a scandal. "As the total result of the three weeks' campaign there were only twenty-four clear decisions," said my friend; "and after it was over the ministers got together and by a vote with but one dissenting voice, they agreed to send a letter to this evangelist telling him frankly that they were done with him and with his methods of evangelism forever, and that they felt it their duty to warn other cities against him and his methods and the results of his work." Let us lay the lesson to our hearts and take warning in time.

8. A Consuming Passion for the Salvation of the Lost

The sixth reason why God used D. L. Moody was because of *his consuming passion for the salvation of the lost*. Mr. Moody made the resolution, shortly after he himself was saved, that he would never let twenty-four hours pass over his head without speaking to at least one person about his soul. His was a very busy life, and sometimes he would forget his resolution until the last hour, and sometimes he would get out of bed, dress, go out and talk to someone about his soul in order that he might not let one day pass without having definitely told at least one of his fellow-mortals about his need and the Savior who could meet it.

One night Mr. Moody was going home from his place of business. It was very late, and it suddenly occurred to him that he had not spoken to one single person that day about accepting Christ. He said to himself: "Here's a day lost. I have not spoken to anyone today and I shall not see anybody at this late hour." But as he walked up the street he saw a man standing under a lamppost. The man was a perfect stranger to him, though it turned out afterwards the man knew who Mr. Moody was. He stepped up to this stranger and said: "Are you a Christian?" The man replied: "That is none of your business, whether I am a Christian or not. If you were not a sort of a preacher I would knock you into the gutter for your impertinence."

Mr. Moody said a few earnest words and passed on. The next day that man called upon one of Mr. Moody's prominent business friends and said to him: 'That man Moody of yours over on the North Side is doing more harm than he is good. He has got zeal without knowledge. He stepped up to me last night, a perfect stranger, and insulted me. He asked me if I were a Christian, and I told him it was none of his business and if he were not a sort of a preacher I would knock him into the gutter for his impertinence. He is doing more harm than he is good. He has got zeal without knowledge." Mr. Moody's friend sent for him and said: "Moody, you are doing more harm than you are good; you've got zeal without knowledge: you insulted a friend of mine on the street last night. You went up to him, a perfect stranger, and asked him if he were a Christian, and he tells me if you had not been a sort of a preacher he would have knocked you into the gutter for your impertinence. You are doing more harm than you are good; you have got zeal without knowledge."

Mr. Moody went out of that man's office somewhat crestfallen. He wondered if he were not doing more harm than he was good, if he really had zeal without knowledge. (Let me say, in passing, it is far better to have zeal without knowledge than it is to have knowledge without zeal. Some men and women are as full of knowledge as an egg is of meat; they are so deeply versed in Bible truth that they can sit in criticism on the preachers and give the preachers pointers, but they have so little zeal that they do not lead one soul to Christ in a whole year.) Weeks passed by. One night Mr. Moody was in bed when he heard a tremendous pounding at his front door. He jumped out of bed and rushed to the door. He thought the house was on fire. He thought the man would break down the door. He opened the door and there stood this man. He said: "Mr. Moody, I have not had a good night's sleep since that night you spoke to me under the lamppost, and I have come around at this unearthly hour of the night for you to tell me what I have to do to be saved."

Mr. Moody took him in and told him what to do to be saved. Then he accepted Christ, and when the Civil War broke out, he went to the front and laid down his life fighting for his country.

Another night, Mr. Moody got home and had gone to bed before it occurred to him that he had not spoken to a soul that day about accepting Christ. "Well," he said to himself, "it is no good getting up now; there will be nobody on the street at this hour of the night." But he got up, dressed and went to the front door. It was pouring rain. "Oh," he said, "there will be no one out in this pouring rain." Just then he heard the patter of a man's feet as he came down the street, holding an umbrella over his head. Then Mr. Moody darted out and rushed up to the man and said: "May I share the shelter of your umbrella?" "Certainly," the man replied. Then Mr. Moody said: "Have you any shelter in the time of storm?" and preached Jesus to him. Oh, men and women, if we were as full of zeal for the salvation of souls as that, how long would it be before the whole country would be shaken by the power of a mighty, God-sent revival?

One day in Chicago—the day after the elder Carter Harrison was shot, when his body was lying in state in the City Hall—Mr. Moody and I were riding up Randolph Street together in a streetcar right alongside of the City Hall. The car could scarcely get through because of the enormous crowds waiting to get in and view the body of Mayor Harrison. As the car tried to push its way through the crowd, Mr. Moody turned to me and said: "Torrey, what does this mean?" "Why," I said, "Carter Harrison's body lies there in the City Hall and these crowds are waiting to see it." Then he said: "This will never do, to let these crowds get away from us without preaching to them; we must talk to them. You go and hire Hooley's Opera House (which was just opposite the City Hall) for the whole day." I did so. The meetings began at nine o'clock in the morning, and we had one continuous service from that hour until six in the evening, to reach those crowds.

Mr. Moody was a man on fire for God. Not only was he always "on the job" himself but he was always getting others to work as well. He once invited me down to Northfield to spend a month there with the schools, speaking first to one school and then crossing the river to the other. I was obliged to use the ferry a great deal; it was before the present bridge was built at that point. One day he said to me: "Torrey, did you know that that ferryman that ferries you across every day was unconverted?" He did not tell me to speak to him, but I knew what he meant. When some days later it was told him that the ferryman was saved, he was exceedingly happy.

Once, when walking down a certain street in Chicago, Mr. Moody stepped up to a man, a perfect stranger to him, and said: "Sir, are you a Christian?" "You mind your own business," was the reply. Mr. Moody replied: "This is my business." The man said: "Well, then, you must be Moody." Out in Chicago they used to call him in those early days "Crazy Moody," because day and night he was speaking to everybody he got a chance to speak to about being saved. One time he was going to Milwaukee, and in the seat that he had chosen sat a traveling man. Mr. Moody sat down beside him and immediately began to talk with him. "Where are you going?" Mr. Moody asked. When told the name of the town he said: "We will soon be there; we'll have to get down to business at once. Are you saved?" The man said that he was not, and Mr. Moody took out his Bible and there on the train showed him the way of salvation. Then he said: "Now, you must take Christ." The man did; he was converted right there on the train.

Most of you have heard, I presume, the story President Wilson used to tell about D. L. Moody. Ex-President Wilson said that he once went into a barbershop and took a chair next to the one in which D. L. Moody was sitting, though he did not know that Mr. Moody was there. He had not been in the chair very long before, as ex-President Wilson phrased it, he "knew there was a personality in the other chair," and he began to listen to the conversation going on; he heard Mr. Moody tell the barber about the Way of Life, and President Wilson said, "I have never forgotten that scene to this day." When Mr. Moody was gone, he asked the barber who he was; when he was told that it was D. L. Moody, President Wilson said: "It made an impression upon me I have not yet forgotten."

On one occasion in Chicago Mr. Moody saw a little girl standing on the street with a pail in her hand. He went up to her and invited her to his Sunday school, telling her what a pleasant place it was. She promised to go the following Sunday, but she did not do so. Mr. Moody watched for her for weeks, and then one day he saw her on the street again, at some distance from him. He started toward her, but she saw him too and started to run away, Mr. Moody followed her. Down she went one street, Mr. Moody after her; up she went another street, Mr. Moody after her; through an alley, Mr. Moody still following; out on another street, Mr. Moody after her; then she dashed into a saloon and Mr. Moody dashed after her. She ran out the back door and up a flight of stairs, Mr. Moody still following; she dashed into a room, Mr. Moody following; she threw herself under the bed and Mr. Moody reached under the bed and pulled her out by the foot, and led her to Christ.

He found that her mother was a widow who had once seen better circumstances, but had gone down until now she was living over this saloon. She had several children. Mr. Moody led the mother and all the family to Christ. Several of the children were prominent members of the Moody Church until they moved away, and afterwards became prominent in churches elsewhere. This particular child, whom he pulled from underneath the bed, was, when I was the pastor of the Moody Church, the wife of one of the most prominent officers in the church. Only two or three years ago, as I came out of a ticket office in Memphis, Tennessee, a fine looking young man followed me. He said: "Are you not Dr. Torrey?" I said, "Yes." He said: "I am so and so." He was the son of this woman. He was then a traveling man, and an officer in the church where he lived. When Mr. Moody pulled that little child out from under the bed by the foot he was pulling a whole family into the Kingdom of God, and eternity alone will reveal how many succeeding generations he was pulling into the Kingdom of God.

D. L. Moody's consuming passion for souls was not for the souls of those who would be helpful to him in building up his work here or elsewhere; his love for souls knew no class limitations. He was no respecter of persons; it might be an earl or a duke or it might be a colored boy on the street; it was all the same to him; there was a soul to save and he did what lay in his power to save that soul. A friend once told me that the first time he ever heard of Mr. Moody was when Mr. Reynolds of Peoria told him that he once found Mr. Moody sitting in one of the squatters' shanties that used to be in that part of the city toward the lake, which was then called, "The Sands," with a colored boy on his knee, a tallow candle in one hand and a Bible in the other, and Mr. Moody was spelling out the words (for at that time the boy could not read very well) of certain verses of Scripture, in an attempt to lead that colored boy to Christ. Oh, young men and women and all Christian workers, if you and I were on fire for souls like that, how long would it be before we had a revival? Suppose that tonight the fire of God falls and fills our hearts, a burning fire that will send us out all over the country, and across the water to China, Japan, India, and Africa, to tell lost souls the way of salvation!

9. Definitely Endued with Power from on High

The seventh thing that was the secret of why God used D. L. Moody was that *he had a very definite enduement with power from on high, a very clear and definite baptism with the Holy Ghost.* Mr. Moody knew he had "the baptism with the Holy Ghost"; he had no doubt about it. In his early days he was a great hustler; he had a tremendous desire to do something, but he had no real power. He worked very largely in the energy of the flesh. But there were two humble Free Methodist women who used to come over to his meetings in the Y.M.C.A One was "Auntie Cook" and the other Mrs. Snow. (I think her name was not Snow at that time). These two women would come to Mr. Moody at the close of his meetings and say: "We are praying for you." Finally, Mr. Moody became somewhat nettled and said to them one night: "Why are you praying for me? Why don't you pray for the unsaved?" They replied: "We are praying that you may get the power." Mr. Moody did not know what that meant, but he got to thinking about it, and then went to these women and said: "I wish you would tell me what you mean"; and they told him about the definite baptism with the Holy Ghost. Then he asked that he might pray with them and not they merely pray for him.

Auntie Cook once told me of the intense fervor with which Mr. Moody prayed on that occasion. She told me in words that I scarcely dare repeat, though I have never forgotten them. And he not only prayed with them, but he also prayed alone. Not long after, one day on his way to England, he was walking up Wall Street in New York; (Mr. Moody very seldom told this and I almost hesitate to tell it) and in the midst of the bustle and hurry of that city his prayer was answered; the power of God fell upon him as he walked up the street and he had to hurry off to the house of a friend and ask that he might have a room by himself, and in that room he stayed alone for hours; and the Holy Ghost came upon him filling his soul with such joy that at last he had to ask God to withhold His hand, lest he die on the spot from very joy. He went out from that place with the power of the Holy Ghost upon him, and when he got to London (partly through the prayers of a bedridden saint in Mr. Lessey's church), the power of God wrought through him mightily in North London, and hundreds were added to the churches; and that was what led to his being invited over to the wonderful campaign that followed in later years.

Time and again Mr. Moody would come to me and say: "Torrey, I want you to preach on baptism with the Holy Ghost." I do not know how many times he asked me to speak on that subject. Once, when I had been invited to preach in the Fifth Avenue Presbyterian Church, New York (invited at Mr. Moody's suggestion; had it not been for his suggestion the invitation would never have been extended to me), just before I started for New York, Mr. Moody drove up to my house and said: "Torrey, they want you to preach at the Fifth Avenue Presbyterian Church in New York. It is a great, big church, cost a million dollars to build it." Then he continued: "Torrey, I just want to ask one thing of you. I want to tell you what to preach about. You will preach that sermon of yours on 'Ten Reasons Why I Believe the Bible To Be the Word of God' and your sermon on 'The Baptism with the Holy Ghost'?" Time and again, when a call came to me to go off to some church, he would come up to me and say: "Now, Torrey, be sure and preach on the baptism with the Holy Ghost." I do not know how many times he said that to me. Once I asked him: "Mr. Moody, don't you think I have any sermons but those two: 'Ten Reasons Why I Believe the Bible To Be the Word of God' and 'The Baptism with the Holy Ghost'?" "Never mind that," he replied, "you give them those two sermons."

Once he had some teachers at Northfield—fine men, all of them, but they did not believe in a definite baptism with the Holy Ghost for the individual. They believed that every child of God was baptized with the Holy Ghost, and they did not believe in any special baptism with the Holy Ghost for the individual. Mr. Moody came to me and said: "Torrey, will you come up to my house after the meeting tonight and I will get those men to come, and I want you to talk this thing out with them." Of course, I very readily consented, and Mr. Moody and I talked for a long time, but they did not altogether see eye to eye with us. And when they went, Mr. Moody signaled me to remain for a few moments. Mr. Moody sat there with his chin on his breast, as he so often sat when he was in deep thought; then he looked up and said: "Oh, why will they split hairs? Why don't they see that this is just the one thing that they themselves need? They are good teachers, they are wonderful teachers, and I am so glad to have them here; but why will they not see that the baptism with the Holy Ghost is just the one touch that they themselves need?"

I shall never forget the eighth of July 1894, to my dying day. It was the closing day of the Northfield Students' Conference—the gathering of the students from the eastern colleges. Mr. Moody had asked me to preach on Saturday night and Sunday morning on the baptism with the Holy Ghost. On Saturday night I had spoken about "The Baptism with the Holy Ghost: What It Is; What It Does; The Need of It and the Possibility of It." On Sunday morning I spoke on "The Baptism with the Holy Spirit: How to Get It." It was just exactly twelve o'clock when I finished my morning sermon, and I took out my watch and said: "Mr. Moody has invited us all to go up on the mountain at three o'clock this afternoon to pray for the power of the Holy Spirit. It is three hours to three o'clock. Some of you cannot wait three hours. You do not need to wait. Go to your rooms; go out into the woods; go to your tent; go anywhere where you can get alone with God and have this matter out with Him." At three o'clock we all gathered in front of Mr. Moody's mother's house (she was then living), and then began to pass down the lane, through the gate, up on the mountainside. There were four hundred and fifty-six of us in all; I know the number because Paul Moody counted us as we passed through the gate.

After a while Mr. Moody said: "I don't think we need to go any further; let us sit down here." We sat down on stumps and logs and on the ground. Mr. Moody said: "Have any of you students anything to say?" I think about seventy-five of them arose, one after the other, and said: "Mr. Moody, I could not wait till three o'clock; I have been alone with God since the morning service, and I believe I have a right to say that I have been baptized with the Holy Spirit." When these testimonies were over, Mr. Moody said: "Young men, I can't see any reason why we shouldn't kneel down here right now and ask God that the Holy Ghost may fall upon us just as definitely as He fell upon the apostles on the Day of Pentecost. Let us pray." And we did pray, there on the mountainside. As we had gone up the mountainside heavy clouds had been gathering, and just as we began to pray those clouds broke and the raindrops began to fall through the overhanging pines. But there was another cloud that had been gathering over Northfield for ten days, a cloud big with the mercy and grace and power of God; and as we began to pray our prayers seemed to pierce that cloud and the Holy Ghost fell upon us. Men and women that is what we all need—the Baptism with the Holy Ghost.

D.L. Moody.

Light on the Way

J. Wilbur Chapman 1859-1918

Edited with an Introduction By
K. Erik Thoennes

Abridged version of *Light on the Way* by J. Wilbur Chapman. Abridged version originally published by The Institute of Evangelism Wheaton, Il. Copyright of abridged version and introduction held by K. Erik Thoennes, used with permission. Artwork in the Public Domain.

Book Chapters

1. Introduction
   By K. Erik Thonnes 626
2. Light on the Way 631
   The Way 631
   Failure 632
   The Word Incarnate 633
   Our Foundation 634
   Sin 635
   The Greatest Sin 636
   Death 637
   A Suggestion 638
   The Gospel in a Nutshell 639
   Our Guide 640
   A Pledge 641
   Our Deliverer 642
   A Canceled Debt 643
   Repentance 643
   Confession 644
   Forgiveness 645
   Justification 646
   Assurance 647
   Surrender 648
   Personal Work 650
   The End of the Journey 651
   A Final Question 652
3. My Covenant 654
4. Notes 655

1. Introduction
By K. Erik Thoennes

In a letter written by his good friend John Converse, on behalf of the Presbyterian General Assembly, we get an eloquent and comprehensive picture of the life and ministry of J. Wilbur Chapman:

> His work has been a tonic to the preacher and churches of all denominations. It has been an indomitable apologetic for the cross. It has confirmed the faith of the people in the inspiration of Holy Scripture and triumphantly vindicated the truth of the Gospel. Dr. Chapman has shown beyond doubt or question, that the old story needs only to be told with a tongue of flame and a heart of love to win men of all classes and conditions to the Savior of the world. His trumpet has never given an uncertain sound. He has never lowered the standard or struck a false note. We rejoice in what he has done. Our grip on the sword of the Spirit is firmer because he has so well shown what the old blade can do when fearlessly and faithfully driven home.[1]

Born August 30, 1884 in Yale, Illinois, Chapman would no doubt be better known if his mentor did not overshadow him at the beginning of his ministry, D. L. Moody, and at the end by his apprentice, Billy Sunday. With degrees from Lake Forest University and Lane Seminary he had more formal education than any other evangelist of his time, and "'all who knew him attested to Dr. Chapman's brilliance."[2] His writings include over thirty books including a biography of D. L. Moody. Some of his most notable works include *Light on the Way*, *The Secret of a Happy*

Life, The Surrendered Life, Revivals and Missions, The Minister's Handicap, and *Received Ye The Holy Ghost?* He also wrote several hymns and compiled hymnals.

Before Chapman began full time evangelistic work in 1903, he pastored five churches, in which he always fostered a renewed commitment to evangelism. A major earmark of Chapman's ministry was his commitment to the long term strengthening of the local church and its pastor. He determined success by this goal. "We don't want the success of our efforts to be judged by the number of members added to the church at once. Our purpose is to point the city to the church and make it easier for the pastors to do their work."[3] A major element of this commitment was Chapman's willingness to work across denominational lines. "I think we have found that the best interest of the church should be served in my interdenominational work. I do not give a snap of my finger whether you know what denomination I belong to or not. I shall preach the truth. It is the truth which unites us and moves us as a solid army."[4]

Chapman had a significant ministry to pastors. He would usually hold meetings for them whenever he would hold a crusade. At these meetings, he would encourage them and give direct and practical advice. Some excerpts of his meetings were usually printed in the newspapers and were called Chap-o-grams. The following are some of his best that were directed to pastors:

- A preacher who makes his work a profession instead of a passion cannot succeed.

- There may be a reverent criticism of the Bible but the pulpit is no place for it... the average minister has no time to go into it. He must have a positive message for his people. The Gospel of Jesus Christ is what they need to hear.

- Neglect of prayer and Bible study are two reasons for failure in ministry. Without these, no man can really succeed. The preacher should study the Bible not only for sermons, but for the power it lends to his church work.

- Let us have courage and boldness to preach the truth. I am a minister of the Gospel and I am afraid of no man. Have we lost courage and become infused with a man fearing spirit? Tell people that they are lost if they reject God and must go to hell. However, tell it to them with a tear. Never mind if you think it worth your place to preach that way.

Although, Chapman believed in preaching hell unapologetically, his love for the lost always came across clearly when he preached. As a New York reporter observed,

> Yet there were more tears and less of the fear in his sermon then he had advised. The end of the godless, the torture and horror of hell seemed not half so great as the sweetness of the grace and love of God. A stillness that was impressive came over the auditorium as he rose to speak tall and sturdy, he leaned forward over the pulpit and began, and here was no passion, no loudness in his voice, but it reached to every corner. It was as if he were a father pleading with his children.[5]

This dignified fatherly approach typified Chapman's preaching style. He did not depend on emotion or sensationalism. His addresses were never more than twenty minutes and his delivery was more similar to Jonathan Edwards then many of his contemporaries. Another reporter observed; "As the end approached, the meetings seem to grow in sober interest with little of sensationalism."[6] Chapman himself stated at one meeting:

> You men who came here expecting something sensational and smutty will be disappointed. That is not my style. You can deal in plain truth without offending the modesty of a decent man.[7]

Chapman believed that evangelism was every Christian's responsibility. To a group of businessmen he said,

> You have no business dictating letters to a stenographer to whom you have not talked to about Jesus. If you are a Christian, it is your duty to tell your employees about the Savior, to invite them to come to Christ and do all in your power to influence them to Christian living. That means that your treatment of them and your relations with them must be such as to bring them to the Master.[8]

He also believed that evangelism and discipleship begins in the home. As he once wrote in his weekly newspaper article,

> The greatest need of our nation is homes where Christ is honored, where God is loved and where the Bible is studied. What we need today more than anything else is a home where the father is a priest and the mother is a saint. Where the children feel that the home is the

best earthly place this side of heaven. We need homes where the old white-haired man gathers his wife and children around him and reads to them God's Word, sings the good old hymns, prays and sends them to their work with shining faces.[9]

Chapman showed unusual prudence and wisdom when it came to finances. An example of this wise attitude toward money is found in a letter Chapman wrote to John Converse concerning the profits from songbooks. In it he writes, "It is my personal decision I shall not assume any financial interest in the sale of books used in the meetings, either in this country or abroad ... I have no desire for a financial interest in this part of the work as it might cause criticism, possibly hindering the work in other ways."

Like any great evangelist, Chapman had tremendous vision. His vision was never so narrow that it could not see through barriers of class, nationality, denominations, or economic status. In its most basic formulation the life goal of J. Wilbur Chapman was the same as that of his Savior, "to preach the Good News to the poor."

It is the hope and dream of my life that the last years of my evangelistic experience may be devoted to preaching to the poor. I have long dreamed that I might some day when I am sufficiently well known, enter into a city with the cooperation of the pastors, conduct a mission in harmony with the work of the Salvation Army and some other missionary organization and then leave my testimony with the people who are in some way out of sympathy with the church.[10]

A great evangelist has universal and eternal foundations for his ministry. He must be sensitive and responsive to the peculiarities of his age, and some of his methods will change with them. However, his basic message and character will be very similar to all of the great bearers of the Good News throughout history. J. Wilbur Chapman would have been a successful evangelist in any age. His ministry was based on timeless truths. He was committed to building up the church by speaking the truth boldly and lovingly. His preaching was based on solid biblical doctrine, but did not dwell on disputable matters. While innovative in his methods, he avoided extremes in theology, politics, finance, and emotion. J. Wilbur Chapman exhibited the timeless qualities in his life and ministry that would have enabled him to reach the lost in first century Corinth as effectively as he did in twentieth century Chicago.

Perhaps the most important legacy that Chapman leaves is his life, which is a shining example of humble spiritual depth and godliness.

He understood that "some men preach good sermons and live them miserably" and "unless one's message to the unsaved was reinforced by a life surrendered to Christ, one's testimony becomes worthless." Chapman knew that "nothing so much appeals to worldly people as consistency in Christian living,"[11] and if he was to be successful in his one great purpose in life, preaching the Gospel, he must live a life fully surrendered, body, soul, and spirit to the indwelling power of God. He would not allow himself to be one of the many men who are public successes and private failures. His evangelism started with his own personal relationship with God, and he believed that if God is to become real to us we must practice His presence. Chapman maintained this kind of witness until, due to complications from emergency surgery, he went to be with his Savior before the dawn, on Christmas day 1918, at the age of fifty-nine.

The readings that follow are selected from Chapman's book *Light on the Way*. This book shows the clear and uncompromising gospel presentation that exemplified Chapman's preaching. Here he lays out the plan of salvation, the believer's identity in Christ, and helpful teaching for the Christian pilgrimage. It is my hope that reading these selections will point the reader to the source of J. Wilbur Chapman's devoted and holy life. A description of Chapman by one of his seminary classmates best summarizes this ultimate foundation of "The Pastor Evangelist's" legacy. "I counted Dr. Chapman one of the most devoted servants of Christ that I have ever known: a man who walked with God, who proclaimed the gospel with extraordinary power, and who not only preached, but lived in such a way that all who knew him took knowledge of him that he had been with Jesus."[12]

K. Erik Thoennes
Deerfield, Illinois, 1998

2. Light on the Way

The Way
"This is the way, walk ye in it." -Isaiah 30:21

It is to be my privilege to write a series of brief articles under the general title of "Light on the Way." I find the text above referred to be a most satisfactory one with which to start. For in this text God is telling His ancient people that the voice behind them will be saying, "This is the way, walk ye in it." In addition, this voice, when we come to the New Testament dispensation, illustrates what the Spirit of God is doing for sinful and rebellious men who have gone out of the way.

It is the way about which I am to write. There are many ways along which the people of the world have traveled, but they are well described by the wise man who said: "There is a way which seemeth right unto a man, but the end thereof are the ways of death" (Proverbs 14:12). In contrast, with this way, another way is described by him in these words - "But the path of the just is as the shining light, that shineth more and more unto the perfect day" (Proverbs 4:18). The first way starts well, but ends in despair; the second way starts well, and grows brighter and brighter, until in the end it is a perfect day, with a morning, but no evening, for we are safe home in the Father's house.

The way about which I am to write, leads from gloom to glory, from bondage to freedom, from doubt to faith, and from darkness to light. It is best described by Him who said, "I am the way, the truth, and the life. No man cometh unto the Father but by me," (John 14:6). It is my purpose to show how one may accept Christ as a personal Savior, and thus be free from sin's penalty; how he may walk with Him, and come to know the Father; how he may love Him, and come to be like Him. No case is hopeless with such a Savior. No one is too far away for Him to find, and none too weak for Him to strengthen. In the most practical manner I hope to make *"The Way"* plain. Every line is to be written with the hope and prayer that all who read the messages may find them to be a *"Light on the Way"* indeed. As you walk with Him, remember it is only a step at a time. A year of service might dismay you: even a week of effort might make you afraid: sometimes even a day may seem to be almost an impossibility; but who is there among us who could not take a step with Him, and then take another, and still another, until the days would grow into the week, and the weeks into the month? And thus going on, you will have formed the habit of travelling with Him who said, "He that followth me shall not walk in darkness," (John 8:12).

Failure
"Come short of the glory of God." -Romans 3: 23

This is the condition of every life separated from God. We were made for Him, and can never be satisfied until we find Him, nor can our lives be complete until they fit into His plan, and are directed and controlled by His will. It is the sense of coming short that makes life unsatisfactory. It is missing the mark; it is failing to reach the goal; it is the consciousness we have of lacking something, it may be only one thing, which causes us repeatedly to be depressed, and sometimes to feel that life is scarcely worth living.

Such a conviction as described above expresses itself in various ways; generally, the following:

1) *Unrest.* There is no peace for the one who puts God out of his life. "The wicked are like the troubled sea" (Isaiah 57: 20).

2) *Dissatisfaction.* This is felt not only with oneself, but with one's surroundings as well. Put over against this the statement of the Psalmist, "I shall be satisfied, when I awake, with Thy likeness" (Psalm 27:15), and what the Psalmist anticipated may be realized now in Christ.

3) *Frequent failure.* The Apostle Paul once said, "When I would do good, evil is present with me" (Romans 7:21). This is equally true in the present day for a Christian, and especially true of the one who has no hope in Christ. Human nature is too weak to resist the terrific tides of sin and the downward pull of the

law of moral gravitation. But, while this is true, the Apostle Paul also wrote, "I can do all things through Christ which strengtheneth me" (Philippians 4:13).

4) *Consciousness of weakness.* All who have rejected Christ and have turned from God's teachings are conscious more or less of their weakness. It is impressed upon them in everyday living, and is especially apparent when the times of crisis come and the days of testing dawn.

5) *Yielding to the tempter.* In the time of temptation, God alone can provide the way of escape. It is fatal to victorious living to be blind to the way and to resist His aid.

6) *A repeated longing for God.* Whatever men may say with their lips, it is undoubtedly true that repeatedly their heart cry is, "Oh, that I knew where I might find him!" (Job 13:3).

In such a condition, God meets us. He offers us life in His son, in whom we find all that we have lacked by nature, and as the Apostle Paul puts it, we may become "complete in Him" (Colossians 2:10). To resist His calling and to reject His offered mercy is to come short of the glory of God.

The Word Incarnate
"Declared to be the Son of God with power." - Romans 1:4

If anyone denies the Deity of Jesus Christ, they have confronting them a most difficult task, for they are obliged in all fairness to account for Him.

He was not the product of His times, for they were not such as to produce Him; and if they had produced Him, then where is His counterpart?

He was not the product of His race, for the wisdom, which He displayed in His words, and works did not come to Him by inheritance from those who were His earthly ancestors; and if His race had produced Him, why were there not others like Him? Never man spoke like Jesus; when He taught He spoke with authority, and this is according to the testimony of even His foes.

We must consider Christ fairly, because He is a fact of history. He is not a doctrine, a myth, a theory, and an imagination. His is a mighty personality, which has moved the world for more than nineteen centuries, and we must reckon with Him.

We can prove His deity by His teaching. He knew God and man equally well, and He knew the relationship, which they should sustain to each other. His ethical teaching has given the standard for right living for almost two thousand years. Why has He not been surpassed if you count Him only a man and rob Him of His deity. We can prove His deity by the things He did. Not only His miracles—they were great enough—but also what He did with human lives. Match His influence over His followers if you can. No great leader in the world's history has ever equaled Him at this point.

We can also prove His deity by the fact that His absence in the flesh from the immediate presence of His followers has not, during all the intervening centuries, caused their love to abate or their zeal to languish. Having proved His deity, accept Him, follow Him, obey Him, and seek to be like Him.

Our Foundation
"My words shall not pass away." - Matthew 24:35

A sure foundation is a great asset, if a substantial building is to be erected. Since we are building not for time, but for eternity, it behooves us to look well to that upon which we are to build. The Word of God is a sure rock. It has never yet failed. It is an incomparable Book. It converts, strengthens, and guides here, and in the hereafter it will not only be the standard of judgment, but, I doubt not, will be the cause for much rejoicing, because there we shall read its conclusions in completed lives, for what God has promised here shall be perfectly fulfilled there.

1) It is God-breathed, while the best of other books are simply man-made. All other books have but a limited influence over special people. The world's great classics may convey little meaning to the inhabitants of some parts of the earth, the Bible may be translated into every language the world has known and still retain its sweetness.

2) It is life giving. One verse of this Book will reveal Christ, point out the way to God, give strength for weakness, impart joy to the sorrowing heart, and make the dead in sin to live in Him.

3) It is God's Word. There are depths in it you cannot sound, and heights you cannot scale. However, there

are a countless number of truths, which will seem to have been stated just for your heart alone.

4) It is an eternal message. Let us, therefore, wait until eternity dawns for the solution of all its mysteries. Let us remember that irreverent criticism will close its doors, while the touch of love will throw them wide open. Live its principles, and you will know its teachings to be true. Love it, and you will be transformed by its power. Memorize it, and you will be strengthened. Mark it, and you will make all with whom you come in contact know that you have taken hold of God, and that He has laid hold upon you. I have tested its promises, and proved its power; in all lands, I have seen its uplifting influence, to me it is truer, better, dearer than ever before, and I therefore receive it as the authoritative message of God Himself.

Sin

"He will reprove the world of sin." - John 16:8

Sin is a state as well as an act. It is true that sin is any want of conformity to or transgression of the law of God; but to him who boasts of self-righteousness, and does not count himself a sinner, the Word of God speaks, saying: "Thy heart is not right in the sight of God." If the springs of life be wrong, we are guilty before God, and need a Savior.

There are scriptural definitions of sin, which far surpass any statement which man has ever made concerning the subject.

Sin is the transgression of the law (1 John 3:4); that is, it is going contrary to God's law. God's law is His will for our lives. To make one's life parallel with His will is to please Him; to cross His law is not to break it, but to break oneself against it.

All unrighteousness is sin (1 John 5:17). Righteousness is the divine ideal for a human life. Unrighteousness is falling short of the mark. God gives us an ideal, and promises aid to us that we may attain unto it. To resist His assistance and reject His offered help is sin.

To know to do good, and do it not, is sin (see James 4:17). There can be no plea of ignorance before God. We know the right in little things, at least, and inasmuch as we do not live up to what we know or may know, we sin against Him. God's plan for our lives is clearly marked out. His suggestions for right living are plainly made; to refuse His aid is sin.

Unbelief is sin (see John 16:9). There is no act so sharply described or so emphatically defined as this. It is called resistance and rebellion, as if we had fought against God. It is spoken of as rejection, as if we had tried Him, and found Him unnecessary for our living, or considered Him and tossed Him contemptuously aside. Ours is a greater sin than that committed by those who actually nailed Him to the cross on Calvary, for our rejection is in the face of all that He has done and said in the past, and has promised to do for us in the future.

The Greatest Sin
"Of sin, because they believe not on me" - John 16:9

What is the greatest sin in the world? It is not intemperance; it is not lust; it is not dishonesty; it is not a thousand other things, which may be mentioned. *It is unbelief.*

I know it, because He said Himself that the Spirit was to come to "reprove the world of sin, and of righteousness, and of judgment," and then He said, "Of sin, because they believe not on me" (John 16:8,9). Unbelief makes God a liar. He has stated certain great truths in the Bible regarding the past, present, and future life of the individual. He has told us about sin, and its remedy; about His Son, and His love. Faith is giving assent to all He has stated. Unbelief is the rejection of His statements, and counting them either as if they were not worthy of credence, or not of sufficient importance to occupy our time or thought.

Unbelief is a blow at God's Word. Here great principles are stated, marvelous promises made, precious truths offered for the testing. Unbelief is indifference, a sneer, a contemptuous treatment of God's message, an attitude assumed as if it were not worth considering. In other words, unbelief is rejection. However, the Bible is the standard of judgment, and the Book we reject, whatever may be the spirit of our rejection, will one day rise to judge us.

Unbelief is an arraignment of Jesus Christ, and an announcement, either by word, or act, or thought, that the story of the prophets, the account of the journey of the wise men to the star marked cradle, and of His incomparable youth, as well as the story of His great life and the record of His death and resurrection, are not true, or, at least, are not worth our thought. Unbelief is something more: it is refusing to believe in the Lord Himself. When the Day of Judgment dawns, the question of questions will be, not "Were you drunken, or impure" but "What did you do with Jesus?" In addition, your answer to this question will determine your position before God there as your relation to Him in this life determined it here.

Death

"There is but a step between me and death." - 1 Samuel 20: 3

David is flying before the anger of Saul, and comes hurrying into the presence of Jonathan. His face is white; he is momentarily expecting to be overtaken, and he speaks the words of the text above quoted, and in thus describing his own condition, he pictures that of everyone who lives today. Life is exceedingly short at best. The average of human life used to be about fifty years; it is far less now. The first third of these years is spent in childhood, the second third in preparing for life in our training schools, and we have thus only about ten years to get ready for eternity. One-third of this time we are sleeping. So it would be well for us to keep in mind such a scripture: "There is but a step between me and death."

It must not be implied from this, however, that we cannot prepare for eternity in childhood or while getting ready for life in the training schools, for the moment the youngest child intelligently trusts in Christ he or she begins to prepare for eternity.

Great men have given varying definitions of life, but each interprets life from his own standpoint. It would be far better for us to hear what God has to say concerning life. He speaks as follows: "For what is your life? It is even a vapour that appeareth for a little time and then vanisheth away" (James 4:14).

"Behold, Thou hast made my days as an handbreadth" (Psalm 39:5).

"My days are swifter than a weaver's shuttle,
and are spent without hope" (Job 7:6).

"Man is like to vanity; his days are as a shadow
that passeth away" (Psalm 144:4).

"There is but a step between me and death" (1 Samuel 20:3).

There are certain illustrations in life, which make plain to us how uncertain it is, and how necessary it is to be ready for eternity. A minister in the city where I live rose, apparently in the best of health, to preach his sermon; he lifted his hand to lead the people in prayer, and fell dead. A man was seen walking along the streets of a city where we were conducting a mission. He was engaged in eager, earnest conversation with his friend. Apparently, he was in his usual health; he was seen to stagger and fall and they picked him up dead.

Ask, and answer this question: Would you like to meet God as you are? Then remember that possibly you may do so. He who is dishonest, impure, drunken, unbelieving, or sinful may have to face God in a moment, and the time will come when the books shall be opened. There are three books to be opened on the Judgment Day if you continue to reject the Lord Jesus: God's book of record, your own book, in which you have written the story of your life, and the Word of God, the teachings of which you spurned. There are two ways of leaving the world. One is the way of the wicked. Job describes it when he says, "He shall be driven from light into darkness, and chased out of the world," (Job 18:18). The other is the way of the righteous, and is pictured in the death of Samuel, where we are told, "And Samuel died, and all the Israelites were gathered together, and lamented him," (1 Samuel 25:1). Which way do you choose?

I would not like to give the impression that I am urging you to be a Christian lest you should die. I have a far stronger reason; that is, the possibility of life. No one can be at his best in this life unless he lives in harmony with God's will here. However, if life is so uncertain, and death so very near, it is quite necessary that we should give a thought to the future, and order our lives accordingly. If we are right with God, and with His Son here, then when we leave this world death will lose its sting and the grave its victory. Our departure will be but going home to be with Him, and also with those who we have loved and who have gone before.

A Suggestion

"Oh that I knew where I might find Him!" -Job 33:3

The soul of man naturally longs for God. It is quite useless to attempt to satisfy this longing with less than God is. He who aims at anything lower than the knowledge of God will be disappointed and unhappy in the end, if not along the way. Gold will lose its fascination, power its glamour, distinction its charm when times of testing come. But the knowledge of God increases one's strength as time passes on, and is never more to be desired than when the days are long, the nights are dark, the burdens are heavy, and the testing severe. It is cheering to know that what the world counts as greatness may be sought and found by only a few, but that which makes man truly great is within the reach of us all.

It is largely because the way to God is not understood, or by the enemy of our souls is made difficult, that this longing is for so long a time unsatisfied, and the cry after Him so pathetic. Would you find him?

Then Make No Compromise with Sin. This is the point of danger. Minimize sin, and you will be overthrown before you realize your danger; make too little of sin, and you will unconsciously depreciate the only way of escape from its penalty and power.

Lay Aside Your Prejudices. Prejudice is blighting in its influence. Through the clouds of prejudice, the love of God, the cross of Christ, and the best teaching in the entire Bible will lose their power and beauty. For the time being give up your preconceived notions as to what a Christian should or should not be. You may be going quite contrary in your thought to the will and plan of God.

Accept Christ by Faith. That is, take what God's Word says of Him as truth, fulfill His conditions, and follow Him carefully.

Accept the Divine Program for Your Life as outlined in the New Testament. Fill it in as God will give you strength, and you will find that the path of the just as the shining light that shineth more and more unto the perfect day (Proverbs 4:18).

The Gospel in a Nutshell

"For God so loved the world, that He gave His only begotten Son that whosoever believeth in Him should not perish, but have everlasting life." - John 3:16.

Luther well said that this text contained the Gospel in a nutshell. Here is a revelation of God's great love for lost and ruined men, and here is hope for all who have gone out of the way. On the ground of this scripture alone we need have no fear in approaching God, for if He loved us well enough to give us anything, why should we hesitate to come to Him with all our need and sins, and since His gift was His only begotten Son, let us come with boldness unto the throne of grace.

"For God so loved the world." This is inclusive enough for all, for we are a part of the world, and thus the object of His love.

"That He gave His only begotten Son." Here is provision enough for all. The sacrifice was infinite, and the price He paid sufficient to cancel the world's indebtedness on account of sin, and this included all mankind.

"That whosoever believeth in Him." This is definite enough for all, for we are a part of the great company of the "whosoevers," and need only to determine whether we really believe on Him who loved us and gave Himself for us, in order to claim our share in this great blessing.

"Should not perish." By the gift of God's Son, and by means of His death upon Calvary, atonement has been made, the penalty for sin has been paid, and the destroying effects of sin have been overcome.

"Have everlasting life." The wicked have continual existence, but everlasting life is entirely different. Accepting Christ, He becomes our life, we live in Him, He lives in us, we shall never perish, and neither shall any man pluck us out of His hand. It is a good thing to make personal God's precious promises. If you should underscore all the

personal pronouns in the Gospels and Epistles, you would be amazed to see how individualistic is God's message to man. There is no better illustration of this than John 3:16. Write this verse on the flyleaf of your Bible. Only write in your own name as I have written mine. "For God so loved the world, that he gave His only begotten Son that *Wilbur Chapman* believing in Him should not perish, but have everlasting life." As a matter of fact, God's promises are all quite as definite as this. Then why should we fear?

Our Guide
"I am the way, the truth, and the life." - John 14:6

Whatever is lacking in our lives may be found in Christ. He said, "I am the way, the truth, and the life"; and from past experience we have learned that without Him as the way there is nothing but wandering; without Him as the truth, there is nothing but error; without Him as the life, there is nothing but death.

The secret of victory over sin, of recovery from failure, of deliverance in the time of need is the fastening of one's thought upon Him. To be occupied with self is always despair; to be occupied with Christ is never-failing glory. The text clearly indicates that He is the way to God, and the only way: He is not a way, as if there were many; He is the way. In addition, the wonderful thing about Jesus is that, as we know Him, we come to know God. He said, "He that hath seen me hath seen my Father also." When we accept Him, we also find that He is the way to a complete life, and He gives rest and peace in place of our unrest. He makes up to us and to God for our past failure, and shows us a way along which we may walk, and be clothed with strength instead of weakness. He leads us continually into the Father's presence, and ever afterwards battles with us against the tempter, helping us on in the way which grows brighter and brighter until we are safe home with Him.

Take the expression, "I am the way," and whatever your soul longs for, and is for your highest good, add to these words, and you will begin to understand what is your inheritance in Christ.

He is the way:

- *To God* - "No man cometh unto the Father but by me" (John 14:6).
- *To peace* - "He is our peace" (Ephesians 2:14).
- *To rest* - "Take my yoke upon you and learn of me, for I am meek and lowly in heart, and ye shall find rest unto your souls" (Matthew 11:29).
- *To joy* - "That my joy might remain in you, and that your joy might be full" (John 15:11).
- *To power* - "In Him dwelleth all the fullness of the Godhead bodily" (Colossians 2:9).
- *To victory over sin* - "I can do all things through Christ, which strengtheneth me" (Philippians 4:13).
- *To heaven* - For my standing before God throughout eternity is due to His finished work.

A Pledge

"Him that cometh to me I will in no wise cast out," - John 6: 37

This is one of the most comprehensive texts, and at the same time one of the most inclusive. It fitly represents the love and mercy of God for the sinner, and includes all who have gone out of the way. Every word is packed full of meaning.

"*Him.*" That is as broad as the word "whosoever." God is no respecter of persons in the display of His grace. Have you failed in life's struggle? Have you sinned, even according to your own standard of right? Are you heartsick or hopeless? Are you in need of spiritual assistance? Are you dissatisfied with self or the world, Then you are the one to whom He gives His invitation. This pronoun is as broad as the human race.

"*That cometh.*" It is a good thing He did not say, "him that understandeth," and it is equally fortunate for us that He did not say that we must have that in us, which would commend us to the world or to Him. He has so made the promise as to bring us all within the reach of it. No one is excluded.

I have a friend who heard a minister preach from this text. He listened carefully to the statement of truth, and then bowed his head as he said. "I will come." It was the moment of his conversion. For wellnigh forty years, he has been kept by God's power. To come to God is to turn from Sin, to cease trusting in oneself, to yield to His entreaties, to turn squarely about in thinking and in living, and to trust Him not only to save, but also to keep.

"*In no wise cast out.*" Let no great transgression, no oft-repeated failure, no consciousness of an impaired will and an all but blighted life keeps you back from Him. No condition could possibly arise that would make it possible for God to either be indifferent to you as a sinner or turn from you if you came to Him as a seeker after light and life.

Our Deliverer
"*Christ our Passover*" -1 *Corinthians* 5:7

Here is a New Testament text, which requires an Old Testament story for its illumination. The Children of Israel were in bondage in Egypt. However, a way of escape was offered. The paschal lamb had been slain, and its blood sprinkled on the two side posts and the upper doorpost of the houses. Then God said: "I will pass through the land of Egypt this night, and will smite all the first-born in the land of Egypt, both man and beast; and against all the gods of Egypt I will execute judgments: I am the Lord. And the blood shall be to you for a token upon the houses where ye are: and when I see the blood, I will pass over you, and the plague shall not be upon you to destroy you, when I smite the land of Egypt" (Exodus 12:12, 13).

However, the word "Passover" means more than would be understood by casual study. The word is found in Isaiah 31:5 (RV). "As birds hovering, so will Jehovah of hosts protect Jerusalem: He will protect and deliver it. He will pass over and preserve it." In addition, just as the mother bird watches over her young, so God cares for His own people. Therefore, it was that God not only spared His people at the time of Egypt's doom, but also stood on guard, as it were, at every blood marked door, protecting all who were within.

While God's ancient people were in Egypt the paschal lamb was slain; while we were yet in our sins Christ died for our sins; but remember, the shed blood of the Passover lamb was not enough, it must be applied to the doorposts; the death of Christ is not enough for our individual salvation, we must accept Him by faith. When God saw the blood had been applied, the people within the house were secure; when He sees our acceptance of Christ, we who are under the blood are safe. It is Christ who intercedes for us before God, and it is Christ, who is by our side to keep back that which might overthrow us or make us afraid. It was such a conception as this that enabled Paul to say, "For even Christ our Passover is sacrificed for us" (1 Corinthians 5:7).

A Canceled Debt

"Nailing it to His cross" - Colossians 2:14

He would be a presumptuous man, indeed, who would dare to say that he had not sinned. If he has sinned, then there stands against him a penalty for his transgression, and someone must answer for this. Human efforts will fail-it always has failed: but man's extremity is God's opportunity, and where we fail, Christ comes to help. He takes "the handwriting of ordinances that was against us ... out of the way, nailing it to His cross."

So many New Testament texts can only be understood in the light of Old Testament teaching. This is especially true of Colossians 2:14. The text above quoted. In Isaiah 40:2 we read, "For she hath received of the Lord's hand double for all her sins." This does not mean double penalty for her sin, but rather it is an illustration of the old days when one became indebted to another, and a piece of parchment was used on which to write a statement of the obligation. This was indented in the middle, it was then torn in two, half was given to the debtor, and half was kept by the creditor. When the debt was paid the creditor returned to the debtor the half of the parchment in his possession, then the debtor took the two pieces and nailed them to the door, to show to all passers by, and to remind himself that his obligation had been met, and that he was free.

This is what becomes possible when the sinner accepts his Savior. Our sin was against God; human effort could not touch it, but Christ's atonement took it out of the way. Our sin was against society; sorrow failed to right it, but He took it out of the way and nailed it to His cross. When we accept Him as our personal Savior all that He did for us in His death upon the cross avails for us, and all that the cross stands for in the matter of atonement is ours.

Free from the law, oh, happy condition!

Jesus hath bled, and there is remission;

Cursed by the law and bruised by the Fall.

Grace hath redeemed us once for all.

Repentance

"Repentance toward God, and faith toward our Lord Jesus Christ." - Acts 20:21

The Bible puts repentance in a very prominent place in all its teachings as regards personal salvation, and over and over insists upon its absolute necessity. It is not only a great truth, but it is fundamental.

We must be changed in mind and heart before we can enjoy with any degree of satisfaction the presence of God. Repentance is not sorrow for sin. One may be sincerely sorry because of his failure, but continue in the way of the transgressor. Repentance is not remorse on account of sin. One may be in a perfect agony of remorse, and not change his manner of living. Repentance is such sorrow for sin and such remorse on account of sin as would lead the sinner with God's help to turn away from his sins.

In the scriptures, there are two words for repentance. One signifies a change of mind, the other an amendment of life. Repentance and faith go hand in hand, and the divine order seems to be given in the words of the Apostle where he speaks of "repentance toward God, and faith toward our Lord Jesus Christ." I am quite sure that did we turn from sin as God directs, faith in Christ would follow naturally: for sin makes doubt easy and faith difficult. A low estimate of sin makes repentance seem less of an obligation; a deep conviction on account of sin makes repentance of the most sincere sort a positive necessity. Sin felt, sin confessed, sin turned from, is a well-put order in making the subject plain. If repentance is sincere, it will seek to make right the wrongs of the past and when once the path is entered upon, it is a surprise to find how easy the way is to travel. If you would know Christ and be free from the bondage of sin, answer these questions,

- *Are you a sinner?*
- *Are you sorry for the sin that has estranged you from God?*
- *Will you accept the Savior, God's only way of escape from sin and its penalty?*
- *Will you, with His help, turn from your evil ways?*
- *Will you make past wrongs right to the best of your ability?*
- *Will you keep step with Him who always did the will of God?*

If these questions are answered in the affirmative, Then joy unspeakable will be yours.

Confession

"If thou shalt confess with thy mouth the Lord Jesus, and shalt believe in thine heart that God hath raised Him from the dead, thou shalt be saved." - Romans (10:9)

This is like the prescription of a physician. There are two parts to the prescription, namely, belief and confession. Either without the other would prevent our receiving the full blessing of the prescription; both together will enable the most helpless and the most sin-sick to be saved.

If an earthly physician were to leave his prescription for a patient, and because of the whim of that patient the prescription should be sent to the chemist with instructions to leave out one of the ingredients, it would not be strange if the patient should fail to recover. Then why expect relief from sin when confession is withheld.

I once called upon a physician in my parish, and found that he had a sort of belief in Christ, but that he had always declined to confess Him before the world, for the reason that he could not understand why public confession was necessary. Then I told him that if he would truly receive Christ and honestly believe in Him, then confess Him before the world, turn from all known sin, sincerely follow Him, and then take the sacrament of the Lord's Supper, I would agree, if it were possible, to answer for him myself before God if there did not come to him a thrill of joy and satisfaction. I heard his public confession a few days later, and I received him into my church. With my own hands, I gave him the bread and the wine in the Lord's Supper. Walking back from the pew where he sat, and taking my seat at the table, I dropped my head in my hand for a moment, when suddenly I felt a hand upon my head, and I heard a voice speaking. It was the doctor, saying, in a whisper, "The joy has come; it has come." I saw him years afterwards, just before he passed away, and with faith triumphant he said, "It has been brighter and brighter all along the way, and I am just waiting to go on." I bid you take the whole prescription, and take it now. It is your only hope.

Forgiveness
"And their sins and iniquities will I remember no more - Hebrews 10:17

Forgiveness is always to be desired. Whether it is human or divine, it is worthwhile, but the difference between the former and the latter is most striking. We forgive and count the act genuine, but we remember the injury that was done to us, and because of which the forgiveness was asked. God forgives and He forgets our sins. While we may remember them ourselves, they have been blotted out of the book of His remembrance, and because of our acceptance of Christ He will not take them into account again. In the 32nd Psalm, the lesson of forgiveness is taught with David's own experience as an illustration. In the first two verses there are three words used to describe sin in its different forms. This must be kept in mind to appreciate the extent of God's forgiveness to those who seek Him.

"Blessed is he whose *transgression* is forgiven, whose *sin* is covered. Blesses is the man unto whom the Lord imputeth not *iniquity*."

Transgression means lawlessness, rebellion, breaking away from God. Sin means a failure to reach the mark, and inability to please God. *Iniquity* is the depravity of our being, the weakness of our human nature. These are the three roots, which grow up into so many different forms of sin in human lives.

There are also three words in the scripture above quoted, which show how completely God forgives sin.

Transgression is forgiven; this means that it is borne away as the scapegoat bore away Israel's sin.

Sin is covered; that is, it becomes invisible even to God, and is as if it had never been committed.

Iniquity is not imputed; that is, it is not reckoned as if it existed, and is entirely canceled because the debt has been paid. Put these three thoughts together, and you have God's forgiveness of sin. Our sins are carried away; they are erased or annihilated, they are entirely offset by the sacrifice of Christ. When to all these statements you add the words, "And their sins and iniquities will I remember no more," you have the best message that human hearts could ever receive.

Justification
"*Therefore being justified by faith.*" - Romans 5:1

Man's right relation to God was forfeited by sin. Justification has to do with his restoration and complete reconciliation with God. It is much more than pardon. A criminal may be pardoned, but that does not remove the fact of his sin nor stay the awful remorse on account of sin. When God justifies, then man stands before Him as if he never had sinned. Forgiveness is wonderful but it does not equal justification. Forgiveness may be many times repeated; justification is an act of God done once and for all, and never repeated. We grow in grace and in the knowledge of our Lord and Savior Jesus Christ, but we do not grow in justification. Fifty years after we have come into right relations with God we are not more justified than when we first turned to Him. We are justified on the ground of the atoning sacrifice of Jesus and because of His merit. Perfect obedience is required by God, and Christ gave it. This is reckoned to us, and God looks upon us as being in Him.

Faith unites us to Christ and because we are one with Him, we become at one with God. Because the debt of sin has been paid, we stand before God justified; because of our acceptance of a crucified Savior there is perfect harmony between us and God; with all the righteousness of Christ reckoned as ours, we stand before God as if we had not sinned. The first eleven versus of the fifth chapter of Romans give to us the fruit of justification. "We have peace with God." Our rebellion is at an end, we are at enmity no longer: we have access into grace by means of which we appreciate all that is ours in Christ; we have the love of God shed abroad in our hearts; we have strength in place of weakness: we are saved from wrath through Him; we are kept safe in His life, in which we dwell as in a garrison. He loves us with an everlasting love; He holds us with an infinite strength; He is our Father, as such, we may approach Him with boldness.

Assurance

"Verily, verily, I say unto you, He that heareth my word, and believeth on Him that sent me, hath everlasting life, and shall not come into condemnation; but is passed from death unto life." - John 5:24

The ground of assurance for every child of God is found not in his feelings, nor even in some great change, which may have come over him. Feelings may be stirred by influences quite apart from religion, and a most radical change in one's living may be brought about in many different ways. Such foundations are unstable, and structures reared upon them will surely fall. However, there is a sure foundation upon which we may build; it is God's Word. "Heaven and earth may pass away," but this foundation will stand forever.

I once saw Mr. Spurgeon's Bible, and beside John 5:24, written in his own hand, were these are words, "My text." It was the scripture used so frequently by D. L. Moody in leading Christians from Doubting Castle to the full assurance of their acceptance with God. I came to Mr. Moody myself one day, full of doubts and fears, the great evangelist led me to this scripture, and from that day, I have had no doubts.

"Verily, verily." This is like ringing a bell to attract attention. It is like His saying, "Listen! What I am about to say is of eternal importance."

"I say unto you." There is no higher authority. He is speaking who knows man through and through, and who knows what His word can do for those who fully accept Him.

"He that heareth my Word." This is another statement so general as to include all who are in need of divine help. It is hearing and heeding which are here suggested. To hear and not to heed of itself constitutes condemnation.

"And believeth on Him that sent me." That is, believes in the sense of trust, confidence, or such complete acceptance of His word as to apply the truth just to oneself alone, and then to live in the power of it. With this sentence ends man's part of this scripture. Are you quite clear up to this point? Do you accept Him fully? This is not a question of feeling,

but of faith. Then hear the conclusion, for this is God's portion of the promise.

"*Hath everlasting life.*" A present possession, here and now. The gift is yours for the claiming.

"*Shall not come into condemnation.*" The word "condemnation" is literally "judgment." There is no fear of judgment for the trusting soul, for him the Great White Throne need have no terror. God has accepted His Son's sacrifice. He is our substitute. God could not in justice judge my substitute and myself too.

"*Is passed from death unto life.*" Here and now, we are set free from sin's penalty and dominion. You can be quite sure that God will keep His promises. Do you think He would begin breaking them with you? Then stand upon this immovable rock, and trust in Him.

Surrender

> "*I beseech you, therefore, brethren, by the mercies of God, that ye present your bodies a living sacrifice, holy, acceptable unto God which is your reasonable service.*" - Romans 12:1

It is the wholly surrendered life that counts. When God has all there is of us He is able to use us. It is not so much a question of personal ability or fitness, though these cannot be ignored; yet, the secret of power in Christian living is absolute and unconditional surrender to Him. When He is on the throne in our lives, when He holds the key of every door into every part of our nature, when our affection for Him is supreme, and when our desire to do His will is constant, then there is power. So important does the Apostle consider this yielding of ourselves to God to be, that he uses the strongest language when he says, "I beseech you," and he presents to the Roman Christians the best of reasons for the life of complete surrender when he says, "By the mercies of God." If you would realize the force of his statement, it is necessary to go back a little bit in his epistle and find our just what mercies he may have in mind, and they are clearly indicated as follows:

- "*Justification by faith*" (Romans 6:1). Justification is a new relationship towards God with sins pardoned and the righteousness of Christ imputed, with lives made clean every whit by the precious blood of Christ, and with the sinner standing before God as if he had not sinned.

- "*Kept safe in his life*" (Romans 5:10). This is the place of safety for the Christian; with the strong rock upon which we build; with God's arms round about us to keep us from falling; with His wings overspreading us, and with His love filling us, the position is secure indeed. He lives in us, and we live in Him.

- *"Baptized into His death"* (Romans 6:3). This is the strongest way of expressing the fact that, in the thought of God, when Christ died, we who were chosen in Him, died with Him. So that atonement for sin has been made, and every provision for the sinner's escape from the penalty of a broken law has been secured.

- *"Alive, unto God"* (Romans 6:11). If we were crucified with Christ, we were also buried with Christ. The identification is complete. It is also true that in the plan of God we rose with Christ and that we are now in possession of eternal life. Continual existence is one thing, that is for all who have ever lived or who ever will live; Eternal life is the life of the Eternal possessing life for time and eternity.

- *"Deliverance from the self life"* (Romans 7:24; 8:2). The enthronement of self is wretchedness; the yielding to the law of the spirit of the life in Christ Jesus is perfect freedom. When the flesh is in the ascendancy there is failure, when the spiritual life is in control there is power.

- *"No condemnation"* (Romans 8:1). God has accepted our substitute, Jesus Christ. Judgment for sin was passed upon Him, and because we have accepted Him and are in Him, we are free. As far as the Christian is concerned, the judgment for sin is forever settled.

- *"No separation"* (Romans 8: 38,39). There is nothing here or hereafter that can separate us from His love. We shall never perish; neither shall any man pluck us out of His hand.

These are the mercies of God. Because of them, yield yourself to Him. Let Him think with your mind, look with your eyes, love with your heart, lift with your hands, and walk with your feet. Be all and in all to Him. Keep back no part of the price. Then power will be yours, and increasing joy in His service will be your experience.

Personal Work

"He that winneth souls is wise." –Proverbs 11:30

When audiences of Christian people are questioned, it is surprising to find how many came to Christ because of faithful personal work of some friend who was interested in them. As a rule, the one who is unsaved does not consider the sermon preached by the minister to have a personal application for himself. He listens to the most fervent appeal, and goes away still saying, "No man cares for my soul." It is also surprising to find how many people there are in the world who, have never been personally approached on the subject of their individual acceptance of Christ. It is believed that if the members of the church could only be aroused to this work there would be a phenomenal ingathering of such as should be saved. The text above quoted is full of suggestion.

"He." This is another one of the general texts. It is for everybody who will take heed. If we were obliged to turn people to Christ in our own strength we might well hesitate to undertake the work; if we were responsible for their conversion most of us would fail. It is when our weakness is lost in His strength, and when we become possessed of the mind of Christ, and attempt to work in His spirit that we become equipped with power to win others to Him.

"Winneth." This is the right suggestion for personal work. We must not fail here. If one's speech should be charming, and his life should be inconsistent, he would accomplish very little. It is when we are right with God, it is when our public life and our private life agree, it is when we walk in close fellowship with Him, it is when we remind other people of Him that our words count with those who do not know Him, and then it is that we have an argument which the skeptics cannot answer, and because of which the man who has drifted from Christ will yield.

"Souls." Here is the inspiration for our work. If it were a quest for gold, the subject would not be unimportant. If it were a contest for reputation or fame it would be the cause of much enthusiasm; but since it is for souls, who can estimate the importance of the work in the light of what the Lord Jesus said. "What shall it profit a man if he gain the whole world and lose his own soul?" and in that wonderful sentence, He put all the world's wealth, power, and fame on one side of the balance and a single soul on the other side, and the soul of the humblest man is found to be of greater value. It is also an inspiration to know that in presenting the Gospel it works with such transforming power.

"Wise." Wisdom is required if we are to be successful in this work. It is not of necessity wisdom of the schools, although that is not to be despised, but it is that wisdom which comes when Christ is in possession, when the life is controlled by Him, when thought, and speech and action are under His supervision. He is wise who does this work also, because of the satisfaction, which is attached to it. Nothing can equal it. There is joy in three places when a soul is saved - in the worker's heart, in the sinner's heart, and in the presence of the angels of God, which surely must indicate in the heart of God.

How shall we go about this work? Only a few suggestions are necessary. Go whenever the Spirit of God indicates that you should, go in a kindly way, go with a solemn spirit, and go in the power of prayer and faith. There must be a concern back of all our work if it is to be crowned with success, because souls without Christ are lost. Delay is dangerous, because of this fact now is the accepted time, and now is the day of salvation.

The End of the Journey

"Well done, good and faithful servant... enter thou into the joy of thy lord." -Matthew 25:21

Some time we shall finish our journey here upon earth, and if our Lord should delay His coming, we will come to the last day of business, of pleasure, or of service. The end may come sooner than we think. It would be well for us now and again to take account of stock, and see if we have done our work well; if the motive prompting our service has been true; and if we are as God intended we should be as a result of all His teaching and discipline and love. Is our record now, as we would like to have it when the last page is written, and our work on earth is done? It is a good thing to know that the text above quoted reads: "Well done, good and faithful servant." If we were obliged to be successful from man's standpoint, or even from our own, we might well be discouraged, but we may at least have been faithful. Therefore, let us answer the following questions:

With reference to the personal acceptance of Jesus Christ as a Savior, am I quite sure that He is mine and that I am His? If not, then let me accept Him quickly ere it be too late.

As regards my faithful study of His word, have I been true to it? Have I read things into it, which were not intended to be there, have I been disposed to doubt the truth of His statements and the declarations of His word? Have I added to or taken away from it? If so, then let me be forgiven quickly, else what shall I say to Him when I meet Him face to face?

As far as my prayer life is concerned, have I talked to Him intimately and lovingly, telling Him my needs, acquainting Him with my burdens, asking Him for help, and have I believed that if I fulfill the conditions He would keep His promises? If not, then let me seek His pardon quickly, for how can I meet Him, having been faithless here?

With reference to soul winning, have I tried to lead others to Him - my own household, my dear friends, the people by whose side I have toiled, and in whose company I have enjoyed so many hours of social pleasure? Have I allowed those whom I know to drift out into eternity unwarned and unsaved? If so, then what shall I say to Him as I stand in His presence?

Some time is still left to us. We may be faithful if we will. Let us do our best, so that when we see Him we may be prompted to say that with the talents with which we were endowed, the time at our disposal, the equipment we were able to secure, we did the very best we could. Meeting Him thus, I am sure He will say, "Well done, good and faithful servant."

A Final Question
"What shall I do then with Jesus?" -Matthew 27:22

I must make one final appeal to all who have read these messages. I take it for granted that you are an honest seeker after truth, either for yourself or on behalf of another, and I likewise have assumed that you have a sincere desire to know the way, that you may walk in it. Knowledge of the way and a refusal to follow it would but increase your condemnation.

You must do *something* with the Lord Jesus. You cannot be indifferent to Him, for surely in reading these messages you have heard about Him and His power to save. In addition, you will do something with Him. That something will be either an acceptance or a rejection. There is no middle ground.

You must do something with Him, for the question is facing you as an individual. Of all the persons in the world, you alone can determine what your next step is to be. The prayers of others may influence you, the preaching of the word will instruct you, the testimony of friends may help to clear your way; but the final step out of self into Christ and out of darkness into light, you must take.

You cannot ever again be the same after reading these messages through. Your responsibility has immeasurably increased, and there is now before you a wide-open door. Jesus stands at that door beckoning you to enter: stretching forth His nail-marked hands, He would remind you of His death for you upon Calvary; and standing before you in an attitude of earnest pleading, He would not let you forget that He who was once dead is now alive, and waits to be not only your Redeemer and Savior, but your Advocate as well, in the presence of God.

Why not settle the question now, and once and for all determine that, with God's help, you will turn from sin unto Christ, accept Him as your personal Savior who has so clearly been presented in the word of God; believe that you are saved because in His word He has plainly promised it, and in fellowship with Him go forward to a life of ever-increasing joy?

My last work is an earnest plea. Will you not yield to Him now? If so, then make the record here, and keep these messages as a testimony to yourself, to the world, and to God, that you are forever His.

3. My Covenant

——————— ———————

"As many as received *Him to them gave He power to become the sons of God." -John 1:12*

I DO THIS DAY

TURN from my sins unto God,

TRUST in Jesus Christ as my Savior,

RESOLVE by the aid of the Holy Spirit

to obey Christ as my Lord and Master.

Signed _____

Date _____

4. Notes

1. John Converse, writing Chairman of the P.C. USA General on March 12, 1909.
2. Lyle W. Dorsett., *Billy Sunday and the Redemption of Urban America* (Eerdmas, Grand MI, 1991), p. 57.
3. From a newspaper article which appeared in the "Syracuse Post Standard," Thursday, January 18, 1900.
4. *Ibid.*
5. "Syracuse Post Standard," Thursday, January 18, 1900.
6. "North American Philadelphia" article, July 6, 1906.
7. From a sermon text entitled "Judas Iscariot."
8. "Union Post," Saturday, Morning Edition, 1904.
9. "The Kings Business," week of March 20 1901. This was an article Chapman wrote for several weekly newspapers.
10. In a letter to John Converse in 1901.
11. John C. Ramsay, *John Wilbur Chapman: The Man, His Methods and His Message* (Boston: Christopher, 1962), p.77.
12. Ford C. Ottman, *J. Wilbur Chapman, A Biography* (Doubleday Page & Co, New York, 1920), p. 37.

The Laws of Revival

James Burns 1865-1945

*With a Forward
By Tom Phillips*

Abridged version of *The Laws of Revival* by James Burns. Abridged version originally published by World Wide Publications, 1993, along with Billy Graham Center, Wheaton, Il. Copyright of abridged version and introduction held by Tom Phillips, used with permission. Some scripture quotations are taken from the *Holy Bible, New International Version* (NIV) © 1973, 1978, 1984, International Bible Society. Used by permission of Zondervan Bible Publishers. Some scripture quotations are taken from *The Holy Bible, New King James Version* (NKJV) © 1979, 1980, 1982 Thomas Nelson, Inc. Used by permission. Some scripture quotations are taken from *The Living Bible* © 1971. Used by permission of Tyndale House Publishers Inc. All rights reserved. Artwork used by permission of University of Louisville, Archives & Special Collections.

Book Chapters

1. Foreword
   By Tom Phillips 660
2. Introduction 661
3. Revivals 663
   The Law of Progress 663
   The Law of Spiritual Growth 664
   The Law of Periodicity 665
   The Law of Ebbing Tide 666
   The Law of the Fullness of Time 666
   The Law of the Advent of the Prophet 668
   The Law of Awakening 669
   The Law of Variety 674
   The Law of Recoil 675
   The Law of the Theology of Revivals 676
   The Law of the Coming Movement 677

1. Foreword
By Tom Phillips

Periodically in the history of the Christian Church a work is produced which transcends time. *Revivals, Their Laws and Leaders* by James Burns was written in 1909 and last published in 1960.

Though it is out of print, portions of the book, especially the sections on "The Laws of Revival," are so pertinent today that they literally cry out for editing and republishing.

"If my people, who are called by my name, will humble themselves and pray and seek my face and turn from their wicked ways, then will I hear from heaven and will forgive their sin and will heal their land." -2 Chronicles 7:14, NIV

As the above scripture encourages us regarding awakening in our time, so will this booklet. We pray that it will be a tremendous blessing to you in your ministry as you read it.

May an expectation for true spiritual revival come as we sense in reading this wonderful spiritual treatise that the world in which we live today is ripe for a new, profound movement of God's Spirit, perhaps one that has already begun. May you be encouraged.

Tom Phillips
Director of Counseling and Follow-Up
Billy Graham Evangelistic Association

2. Introduction

In Christian history, no phenomenon is clearer than the recurrence of revivals.

At times, a passion for repentance sweeps across specific geographical areas. Many people who had been unaware of the supernatural become keenly aware of it. They are stopped during their jobs as their minds are gripped by a terror of wrongdoing and a fear of coming judgment. Throwing all else aside, they desperately search for a way of salvation.

Having started, these movements spread like wildfire and are seemingly carried in the air. Breaking out in unexpected places, they produce a strange phenomenon and awaken forces that have lain dormant. Mostly, these movements are contained in a local geographic area, but they can spread throughout nations, with incredible results.

Since revivals are a major characteristic of Christianity, a study of church growth and survival would be worthless if it ignored the impact of revivals.

In light of this, we cannot regard revivals as isolated incidents. To interpret the mind and will of God in relation to humanity, we need to look at the permanent elements of human nature and the underlying laws, which shape human history. Such movements witness to us the supremacy of spiritual forces. They reveal the spiritual instincts in humankind that are often clouded by less worthwhile pursuits. They encourage faith by showing God's hand in history and in His guidance of the Church. These movements prove that God is working through His laws, for the salvation of His people and for the world's good.

In a revival, a few, then dozens, then thousands say with David, "Though I walk in the midst of trouble, you will revive me" (Psalm 138:7, NKJV).

3. Revivals

The Law of Progress

We need to acknowledge the part revivals play in God's plan as we take a broader look and see them appear in places outside of the Church. Progress, we see, occurs through revival. Any progress is like the incoming tide. Each wave is a revival, going forward, receding, and being followed by another. To the onlooker it seems as if nothing is gained, but the force behind the ebb and flow is the power of the tide. Therefore, it is with the nations. One will rise and carry human progress to a zenith. Having done so, it falls back, and another replaces it. Thus, the progress of humanity is continued through successive revivals.

The same is true in all realms of human expression. When new discoveries are made, the scientific outlook captivates people's minds and other areas are put on the back burner. However, nothing can totally dominate the mind. The initial force eventually fades. After making its contribution to human knowledge and making life better by its discoveries, the movement gives way and is replaced by another in a different area.

Each outburst has its own characteristics and direction, but its nature is revival. There is an excitement in an area, a gathering of energy to leap forward, and when its strength is spent, it recedes. This is even seen in commerce. Trade depressions are succeeded by trade revivals, and in the world market, there is a constant ebb and flow.

In all this, we can see God's wisdom. Revivals are necessary to push humankind to higher planes. If progress were uniform, with all aspects of life improving at once, advancement would be so slow that life would stagnate. There would be no high hopes, no eager rush forward. Progress would be imperceptible - and men and women, robbed of aspirations, would give up the fight. By the breath of fresh life, God keeps the world active and keeps the heart fresh with hope. In God's purposes, no part of human nature is left unrevived. Each revival is needed for helping human nature. Their order is God's secret; the equilibrium is in His hands. Behind the ebb and flow is the unrelenting tide of His redemptive purposes. He it is who said, "Let all the world look to me for salvation!" (Isaiah 45:22, TLB).

The Law of Spiritual Growth

Revivals are the method by which progress occurs in all other realms of human expression. In light of this, we can approach their recurrence in religion free from bias, and even scorn, which has been popularly considered the right attitude. It is in this area that the word *revival* gains a new intensity, for religion deals with the awesome and immeasurable. It goes deep into men and women's spiritual consciousness. As interesting as other revivals may be, they are shadows when compared with the importance of revivals in the individual and the Church. Though they occur in this mysterious realm, they are not necessarily erratic or arbitrary. The supreme discovery is that nothing is erratic in God's universe. Characteristics common to all revivals may be found.

When we examine revivals in the spiritual life, we are confronted with a mass of interesting material. Revivals are used of God to stimulate individual and corporate spiritual life and to advance spiritual education and progress. They are characterized with the same frequency and fluctuations as revivals in other areas.

First, we discover fluctuations in the common experience of men and women before decisions about Christianity are made. Let us remember back before your conversion. There were times when you were conscious of definite, spiritual influences moving you powerfully to Him. Then there were long periods in which you seemed to have no consciousness of any spiritual pressure. After months--or even years--of spiritual lethargy, the influence would return.

This ebb and flow of spiritual experience is still characteristic in life after conversion. No life is maintained at the same level. The Psalms reveal the varying nature of the divine life in the believer's heart. Caught by the inflowing wave, the writer's heart rejoices in God. Then in the trough of the wave, the Psalmist cries out for help, with his heart in despair. From this, God rescues him. He is then carried forward on a new tide of joy.

This same experience characterizes all Christian church life. The spiritual life within any congregation is never constant. Each church has times of being a spiritual desert, followed by times of awakening and revival. Even in the first century Church, the believers longed for greater manifestations of God's word and power (Acts 4:23-31).

Progress never occurs in an unbroken sequence. The pressure of the Holy Spirit upon the life of an individual and the Church is never uniform. The reason is not difficult to discover. A constant pressure becomes a mere condition of our life. We adjust to it, without its attracting our attention, but a pressure that is occasional and variable captivates our attention. The Holy Spirit demonstrates His sovereignty in nurturing change in us and captivates our interest by varying His influence at different times, for it is by this method that the conscience is reached and the heart is won.

In the influx of the tide, there are not only tiny ripples, but also tumultuous waves and mighty breakers. In the inflowing tide of human spiritual progress, there is the same variety of waves. There are revivals, which affect the individual. There are larger movements, which affect separate congregations, and even larger ones that affect whole geographical areas and spread beyond.

The history of revivals reveals large movements, infrequent in their appearance, but monumental in their character. They change life's conditions and deeply alter the history of the world. In looking at some of these movements, we discover certain laws, which govern their activity. How they work becomes more apparent, the effect more convincing and overpowering. For what is common to all great movements is present in small ones.

The Law of Periodicity

We may assume that revivals are one of the primary methods God uses to fulfill His purposes in the world. These revivals move according to a divine law. There is an orderly sequence in their movements. However, can we discover this sequence? Do revivals recur at definite intervals? Can we forecast their appearance, as astronomers forecast the appearance of a comet? Obviously, this is impossible. The movements cannot be treated as an exact science. Human life does not move with precision. The wills of men and women enter, with all their inconstancy. The unexpected occurs, which changes the course of events. While these cannot stop God's plan, they may retard it.

It is impossible for us to map out with precision the recurrence of revivals. This does not mean that all that pertains to them is hidden away in the unsearchable purposes of God. It is clear that their appearance at specific times is not haphazard. One's spiritual nature is not allowed to stagnate for long periods. Neither do, revivals rush upon men and women at random, without preparation or purpose. A certain law of periodicity is discernible. Even though we cannot prophesy with unerring accuracy their arrival, we can at least know that behind them is divine law and order.

The Law of Ebbing Tide

We find preceding each revival a spiritual desert. During those times, all whose hearts are alienated and are skeptical of the Church's authority break away. In those dark days, unbelief reigns while the enfeebled Church, without the strength to fight back, sits in humiliating impotence.

The Church is not blameless. The loss of hope is due to the loss of spiritual power. The loss of spiritual power is the result of leaving the heart of the Church unprotected against the world. Individually, we see this when our hearts are left in such a state. As the inner fire ceases to glow, the warmth departs. We still act like Christians. In fact, we may even look more spiritual in our effort to cover up our spiritual decay. Since the Spirit is not there, we are only offering lip service to God. The length of relapse will depend upon the character of each person. In some, because of their intense spirituality, the ebb and flow will be faint. In others, the waves will be strong and violent.

In those large movements thrown upon pages of human history, we see these facts magnified. The defection of the individual spreads until it reaches the Church. In the lowered spiritual state, corruption creeps in until finally the whole body is permeated with worldliness. Each generation has its own level of corruption. Thus, it would be wrong to say that revival will not occur because the corruption is not the same as previously. There is ebb and flow, but it is that of a constantly advancing tide. Yet, the extent of the falling away may be great, for the fall has to be measured from the fresh advance, which has been reached. Each age receives the renewed perception of God's standard of righteousness. Each age also develops its own standard of judgment. However, it is according to God's standard that the Church may be condemned for defection.

The Law of the Fullness of Time

The next fact, which the study of revival discloses, is that this time of spiritual deadness has its definite limits. The wave of spiritual progress recedes, but even in receding, it is gathering in power and volume to

James Burns 1865-1945 / 667

return, and to rush further in. God has set a limit to the defection of His Church. When the night is at its darkest, the dawn is on the way.

This next period is characterized by dissatisfaction in many hearts. A period of gloom sets in; a weariness and exhaustion invades the heart. The pleasures of the world no longer satisfy. Thus, men and women turn to God. They realize that, in exchanging heavenly for earthly joys, they have encountered immense loss. Slowly this aching grows, the hearts of people begin to cry out to God. From a faint desire, this multiplies until it becomes a vast human need, until, in its urgency; it seems to beat at the very gates of heaven.

Within the Church, not all have fallen away. Some have mourned its loss of spiritual power and have never stopped earnestly praying for revival. Their prayer seems to go unanswered. It appears as if God has forgotten to be gracious. Gradually, the number of people praying increases. Prayer becomes more urgent and more confident. The condition of the Church becomes apparent. The need increasingly weighs upon the hearts of the devout. The longing for better things becomes an intense pain. People form into prayer groups. They do not cease imploring God to visit the souls of men and women. In many different places, unconnected with each other, this spirit of intercession awakens. With it comes an expectation that will not be denied, a premonition that there are better days ahead.

Times of awakening in the individual mostly occur at times of transition, especially from one stage of development to another. Spiritual awakenings coincide with profound change in the social or political life of the people. The value of this is apparent, since new energies are conserved, and directed into channels, which will lead to true progress.

The twelfth century saw Europe passing out of the Middle Ages. The feudal system was breaking up, and people were gathering in cities. A new sense of corporate life was emerging. Individuals were grouping themselves in wider combinations. Papal absolutism, which had held individuals' minds in subjection, was beginning to lose its grip. It was losing its power because of the growing independence of secular authorities and the irritation growing from newly awakened intelligence. At this time, universities began to spring up. There was a widening of sympathies, due to the Crusades and the ferment of new ideas, thus marking the close of one stage of human development and the beginning of another.

When we come to the next great movement, we stand again at a crisis in human affairs. Europe, which had in the previous period passed from childhood into youth, was in the sixteenth century passing from youth to maturity. Loyalty to the city was giving way to loyalty to the state. Europe was rearranging itself under modern geographical and national divisions. It was the time of the awakening of learning and art. Here again we see one stage of growth completed and a fresh stage beginning.

After the sixteenth century, revivals shifted to the national level, since each nation differed in its stage of development. In addition, at this time, the Reformation had destroyed the unity and the control of Rome. Still, in these more limited movements, revival synchronizes with crises in development.

Thus, we see how at times all things seem to unite and cry out for a revival. The waters are far withdrawn and heaped up, foaming behind the barricade. The times are ripe. The soul of humankind cries out for God. A spirit of intense expectation is present. Once more, the long bitter night has ended; the dawn is at hand.

The Law of the Advent of the Prophet

The next event common to the history of all great revivals is the appearance of a leader. The person sums up in himself or herself the longings of the time and interprets to the generation their inmost needs. When this person speaks, the hearers recognize his or her authority.

In this sense, the leader is recognized not as the creator but as the interpreter of the movement. The burden of the times, which others only faintly feel, becomes an intolerable load. The leader feels God's hand upon him or her and proceeds possessed by the Holy Spirit to be God's agent in leading men and women into new life.

Though the agent and the interpreter, the leader is not a machine. The leader brings into the movement his or her own individuality, and within certain limits defines its characteristics. When we survey the leaders in the world's revivals, we see how wide the selection is, how varied the characters of God's chosen servants. For example, Isaiah and Paul were separated by more than centuries. The same wide difference may be seen in the movements themselves because the characteristics of the movements are marked by their leaders. These characteristics were essential for the success of the movement, because each age has different needs the leader can meet.

Here the differences end. All of these great leaders share an unshakable faith in God, an overwhelming sense of a call to service, a mysterious equipment of spiritual power, and a determination to do the work of God at the expense of life itself.

The Law of Awakening

When these elements of preparation, timing, and leadership fall into place, the awakening occurs. The people that walked in darkness see a great light. They fling off the garments of despair and celebrate life.

In each movement, there is something incalculable. New forces, long preparing under the surface, burst into being. The revival's tide rolls in from an unseen continent and moves with a gathering, unresisting momentum. Yet, while each is individual, there is uniformity.

Each revival is characterized by the extraordinary swiftness with which it spreads. Once the first words of the new message are spoken, mysterious forces arise, like the wind, and carry them from place to place. The revival spreads like an epidemic. It bursts out in places that have not been in contact with other infected places, and individuals are moved in multitudes.

Luther's nailing of the 98 Theses on the church door at Wittenberg seemed to be of little importance, but it was a spark to a dry forest, and the fire that it began has yet to be put out. When Wesley stood up in the open air to address a crowd of illiterate miners, no one knew that it would be the beginning of one of the largest Protestant churches in the world.

The rapidity with which revivals spread is an indication of the silent preparation, which goes on beneath the surface long before the revival itself takes place. It shows how God's Spirit is always active.

Everyone who studies the phenomena of revivals is struck by the similarity of the effects produced upon those who are touched by them. Two of these stand out with startling vividness and are common to all.

First is the deep conviction of sin. In the intense spiritual light, the sin and guilt of the awakened soul stand out in terrifying blackness. Not only are their sins laid bare, but also the convicted see themselves as in a mirror. Every sin, seemingly minor, confronts them. Their sin drags them to judgment. Terror seizes them as the conviction of sin burns like fire. Yet, this terror of the Lord is not the terror of punishment. It is inspired by a sense of having rebelled against God.

Under this agony of conviction, men and women openly confess their sins. Their one intense longing is to cast their sins forever from them, to be brought into reconciliation and peace with God. Even those who are only attracted by curiosity feel the irresistible power dragging them to confession. Some, though totally ignorant of spiritual things, are brought to conversion.

The dulled conscience has permitted many things to creep within the Church's doors. They might not be wrong in themselves, but tend to dull the edge of its spiritual life. When the inner fires cease to glow with love for Christ, there is nothing left to defend the Church from the world. In many cases, divisions arise or worship is reduced to cold formalities. Worldly practices are permitted in order to maintain interest. Although they are condemned by many, there is not the power to eject them. The Church becomes worldly, selfish, and almost Christless.

With a revival, all this is changed. The Church's long defection ends. A new consciousness of sin is awakened in the Church as well as in the individual. There passes over the Church a wave of deep conviction and shame. Then follows a time of reformation, of purging the impurities. It seeks by united prayer and intense zeal to bring to Jesus those who do not know Him. This reformation of the Church is not sudden. The Church absorbs those large masses affected by the revival and fresh life is poured back into the hearts of its members. Actually, the fresh winds of revival may break outside the boundary or walls of the organized church, and become the spiritual fire to ignite the church, and the divine detergent to cleanse and refresh its ministry.

The second characteristic produced by a revival movement is its joy. When the night is passed, and with it the agony of conviction and the grief and terror of sin, there breaks upon the humbled heart the peace of forgiveness. No joy on earth compares with this that awakens in the forgiven heart. People have exhausted language in trying to describe it.

At such times, Isaiah's description of the mountains and hills breaking forth into singing and all the trees of the field clapping their hands does not appear excessive. To those caught in the revival's flood, all the world seems changed. Their hearts are light, and their faces glow.

This joy is not limited to those newly converted. It fills the hearts of those who are already followers of Christ. It sweeps into the Church, making all its worship pulse and glow with spiritual fervor. This is the effect of revival, wherever it appears. It leaves in its wake numberless men and women whose faces glow with a new light and whose hearts throb with an intense and pure joy.

This new gladness characteristically finds an outlet in song. Song is the natural expression of the jubilant heart. It is the escape valve for feelings, which are too exhilarating to remain silent. Most of the great leaders of revival have been poets, and the revival is born along the wings of praise. Singing has been a prominent feature in most revivals.

The conditions for revival are timeless. There are no 20th century shortcuts. In 1904, all Wales was aflame with revival. The nation had drifted far from God, and spiritual conditions were at the lowest. Church attendance was pitiably poor and practices of immorality and sinful indulgence abounded on every hand. Suddenly, through the power of prayer, like an unexpected tornado, the power of God moved in and swept over the land. Churches were crowded with three services every day lasting from 10 a.m. to 12 midnight. Evan Roberts was the human instrument God used to turn the tide of revival.

There was little preaching mostly singing, testimonies, and prayer. There were no hymnbooks, no offerings, no advertising but everybody sang. History records there were more songs composed than sermons delivered. Nothing had ever come over Wales with such mighty, far-reaching results.

Infidels were converted. Drunks, thieves, and thugs by the hundreds were born again. Multitudes of the most respected and socially prominent were converted. Old debts were paid, theaters and pubs closed, and the mules in the mines refused to work, being unused to the transformed attitudes of the workers, nor were they thereafter required to work on the Lord's Day.

Whatever the expression, the gladness itself is never absent. In many, it becomes so extreme that it can be dangerous. Almost every revival is accompanied by outbursts of excitement and by startling physical phenomena.

Outbreaks of physical anguish are followed by outbursts of uncontrollable joy. The effect of these extreme emotions on unstable people is often disastrous. A revival's value is not to be based on these exceptions. Many who are looking for reasons to point a finger at the movement use these cases to justify their criticisms. Those whose minds are fixed on the trivial and hearts are void of spiritual life miss the true impact of the revival on the individual soul.

All revivals affect large masses of the community. They leave a permanent influence for good behind them and create a new era in progress. All revivals start from the bottom. Their leaders are almost entirely of the people. Their greatest influence is on the poor and upon those neglected by the Church. When faith is waning, the Church loses its spirit of sacrifice. It becomes self-seeking. It uses its influence over its members to obtain comfort and ease. Consequently, those masses of the community who are unattractive because of their ignorance and poverty are neglected.

When the news of redeeming love is proclaimed with passionate joy and conviction, the poor are reached. It is the common people who hear it with gladness. They live in poverty, neglected and uncared for by those who ought to give their lives for them. Having found little to satisfy their hunger for love, their hearts are drawn to the message of God's love. Drawn into Christianity, their hearts are uplifted by pure emotion. Their whole lives are changed, and they become an asset to the wealth of a nation. Thus, a revival means the re-creation of large portions of the community, a segment that once seemed to be a deficit to society. In the light of this fact, it would be trite to say that the next revival will be an ethical one. All revivals are ethical. They move, if authentic and sent from above, not merely in the realm of emotion but in the sphere of the conscience and the will. They leave behind them not merely joyful, but changed lives. The chains of addiction are broken. Revivals implant a new set of emotions within the heart. They inspire men and women to develop their characters and enrich their lives through education, self-discipline, and especially prayer.

The effect of a revival upon the Church is no less profound and far-reaching. For while the word *revive* literally means "to bring to life again," the word in its religious context includes the awakening of those who were dead and rejuvenating those who were alive but slumbering.

Every revival exposes the spiritual decay of the Church, with its worldliness and hypocrisy. This spiritual decay seems to move along two distinct lines.

The first tendency is for the doctrine of the Church to lose its power to convict the conscience, convince the mind, or move the heart. After a time of immense theological interest, that interest begins to wane. People's minds are attracted by fresh discoveries in other fields. Thus, theology fails to keep pace with the fresh thought of the age. It is outdated and treated with contempt by other areas of human thought, which are on the cutting edge of progress.

In addition, each age requires a restatement of truth. The truth does not change, but our comprehension of it does. We are taught to see it from new angles and with an altered perspective. Thus, there is the necessity for a new statement, for a reinterpretation of the old words in terms of the new. For words are like coins, of full value fresh from the mint, but capable of being defaced and robbed of their full value. In spiritually dead times, preachers continue to use the old words. Once so full of power, now they have no impact. This is partly because the language has changed, but also because the words have become the mere jargon of the pulpit. Preachers mumble out their clichés that have no impact on the conscience or the heart, because they themselves have ceased to be moved by them.

The Church passes through a period of skepticism. Unbelief chills its vital fires, and hypocrisy leaves its message powerless. With the first pronouncement of the leader's living message, all this passes away. A new aspect of truth is declared, or an old and forgotten truth is restated, and suddenly people's hunger is appeased. They are fed again with the bread of life.

The second tendency in spiritual decay is for worship to become formal. The pulpit exalts ritual until the spirit is crushed. Religion is represented, not as a response of the soul to God, but as a rigid performance of outward observances and ceremonies. Ritual forms of worship, even when elaborate, are not evil in themselves. Some people find their spiritual life enriched by them. They are not dangerous to the general worshiper as long as the spiritual life of the church is intense, and the form is the expression of the spirit. It is when the spiritual fire departs that the danger appears. The form then becomes an end in itself. Strict obedience to it becomes religion and is coldly offered to God in lieu of spiritual worship. At such times, outward observance increases rather than diminishes. The self-righteous are given opportunity to display their zeal, while they impose heavy burdens upon the hearts of the humble and the ignorant. This shift of focus, from inner life to outward observance, divorces religion from morality.

At such a time, the pastorate degenerates. The love of wealth, ease, and power appears. Ministers become the object of scorn to the skeptical and indifferent.

An example of this is the condition of Israel at the time of Christ. When the Israelites returned from the captivity, the rulers of the people turned to the law with passionate devotion. While this devotion remained, the spiritual life of Israel was maintained. No sooner did it diminish than the minute observances of the law became intolerable bondage. Their religion, emptied of its spiritual content, became a worship of externals. So bankrupt of spiritual discernment did the people become that the hypocrite became the popular ideal of the religious person. They had become so dead that they not only failed to recognize the Messiah, but also crucified Him as a heretic.

Christ had lamented over such people "O Jerusalem, Jerusalem, the one who kills the prophets and stones those who are sent to her! How often I wanted to gather your children together, as a hen gathers her chicks under her wings, but you were not willing!" (Matthew 23:37, NKJV).

This despiritualizing of religion, this worship of the form rather than of the spirit, is a constant threat to the Church. However, the moment the first breath of revival touches the heart of the Church, the chains, which bind it, are broken. With a new joy, it returns to simplicity of worship and intense sincerity of life.

The Law of Variety

The appearance of revivals owes nothing to chance; they are a witness to God's sovereignty. Used of God for the progress of the world, they revitalize men and women's lives. They appear at intervals, and at points of crisis in individuals' lives. Although these cannot be delineated with precision, we are able to see regularity in their appearance and, within certain limits, to anticipate their coming. Next, we see that there is sufficient data to conclude that the laws, which govern them, are constant like any other of God's laws. First, we perceive that they come when preparations have been made, when the times are ripe. Next, their appearance is signaled by certain infallible signs, one of which is a growing discontentment in individuals' hearts with corruption and backsliding. With this, comes an intense craving for something better. A growing spirit of expectation that change is coming soon develops. At last, when contributing streams converge at a definite point, there suddenly appears the messenger who speaks for God, and whose voice people instantly recognize and obey.

Another similarity is what occurs when the revival movement is set in motion. When the voice of the leader is heard, vast forces, which seem to have been lying dormant, are awakened. The revival spreads like fire, and huge numbers of people are affected. Wherever it goes, and into whatever heart it enters, it creates an overwhelming realization of sin then confession. With the forgiveness of sin comes a joy that expresses itself in song. The main effect of the revival is felt in the inner life. It awakens new spiritual emotions. It sharpens lives into subjection to the will of God. It brings the Church back to simplicity, sincerity, and a renewed spiritual vitality.

As in all of God's dealings with His creation, there are the elements of the mysterious. No two revivals are identical. While possessing common elements, every expression of each law contains unique characteristics. Each is adapted to the need of the times. It is modified first by the conditions of the age, secondly by nationality, and then by the individual characteristics of its leader. This outward variety is a necessity for success. Were all revivals identical, the majority of the people would remain unaffected. Variety is a source of life. A revival, which affects one nation or people, may have little influence upon another. In many cases where the attempt was made to duplicate a revival's characteristics, the attempt not only failed, but also stirred up irritation and strife.

An illustration of this fact may be discovered in the history of the Reformation in the sixteenth century. That movement, which profoundly affected the Teutonic races, left the Latin races almost unaffected. Its geographical area was so pronounced that it remains, and the chasm, which it created, still separates the Roman Catholics from the Protestants.

Another fact about revival movements is the variety in the character of their appeal. Sometimes that appeal moves in the realm of the affection. Emotional revivals are, of all revivals, the most immediately effective and the least enduring. Sometimes a revival's chief characteristic is theological, emerging in the discovery of some new truth. Each adapts itself to the urgent need of the age, and thus produces the most permanent results. Each wins its way because of its adaptation to the needs of the times and to the temperament of the people. What is effective for one cannot be effective for all.

One other significant fact regarding the variety in revivals is that movement in one direction is often followed by a movement in an opposite one. In religion, as in politics, there are two distinct camps, liberal and conservative. The watchword of the one is Freedom that of the other is Authority. The conflict between the two is constant, but each represents too deep a factor of human life to destroy the other. Thus, a revival, which carries to one extreme, will be followed by a countermovement in the other direction.

Striking as the similar points are in revivals, there are also as many illustrations of variety. The same laws are in each, but as with all the laws of God, there is adaptation and readjustment.

The Law of Recoil

Every revival has a time limit. It has its day, and then it recedes. Luther set the limit to a revival at thirty years, Isaac Taylor at fifty. Rarely does it last beyond a generation. However, in duration two revivals are rarely alike. Because of the variables and their different characters, the extent and duration are varied. The constant factor is that, whatever the size of the wave, it has its limits marked out for it.

Many people are swept into a revival's current by yielding to emotion, while their natures remain unchanged. They cool down and are swept back into the world again. Nothing can be said about the percentage who fall away. Revival movements differ in this also. In revivals where emotions are held in check and the appeal is made to the conscience, the effect is more permanent.

The good effect of a revival runs on long after the surprise and emotion are gone. Yet there comes a time when this seems to end, and the movement falls into decay. It becomes not an influence for good, but for evil. Instead of liberating, it becomes an agent of oppression. Few things in life are more pathetic than how quickly the good gets tarnished or corrupted. Such was the case with the recoil that came after the days of Luther, with its bitterness and rivalries.

In all revival movements, this law of recoil must be recognized in order to be wisely and prayerfully anticipated. A wider knowledge of such movements will prepare the Church for this, and thus its dangers can be minimized. It is the ebb of the wave which falls back, only to gain strength to push further on. When each revival has made its original contribution to the wealth of human experience, it falls back to give place to something else. There is no need to mourn. As Tennyson truthfully said, "The old order changeth, yielding place to new, and God fulfills Himself in many ways, lest one good custom should corrupt the world."

This longing for a fresh movement from God was expressed most succinctly by the Psalmist: "Oh, revive us! Then your people can rejoice in you again" (Psalm 85:6, TLB). We echo that longing when we read of past revivals, then fall to our knees and cry, "Do it again, Lord. Do it again!"

The Law of the Theology of Revivals

It is important for us to know what the great doctrines have been which have awakened people to new life in past centuries.

First, we see that all revivals fall back upon simplicity. They cut through the accumulated doctrines and subtle complexities, until they arrive at some aspect of truth, which has become forgotten or has been buried by tradition.

In perspective, every revival goes back to apostolic times and to the spirit of the early Church. Each attempts to strip the Church and the individual of the heavy burdens imposed in a time of decay, a time when men and women are more intent on *proving* the doctrines of the Church than on living them. Its central effort is to get back to the source of life.

When we analyze the messages in those great days of revival, we see one message, which is never absent, a message that is at the heart of every movement. This is the message of the Cross.

How much we need the focus of the apostle Paul: "But God forbid that I should glory except in the cross of our Lord Jesus Christ, by whom the world has been crucified to me, and I to the world" (Galatians 6:14, NKJV).

In every case where the life of the Church has become powerless, it will be found that the message of the Cross has either been denied or forgotten.

If this is true, and it is, then its value is of the utmost importance. It shows that, whenever men's and women's hearts are profoundly moved, they turn to the Cross for satisfaction, with the same instinct with which a child in need turns to its mother. Redeeming love is the message underlying every great spiritual movement of the Church. Never has there been a spiritual movement in the Christian Church in which Christ has not been realized as the source of life. Every revival is a return to Christ. Each comes from a fresh recognition of His power to save.

In the time of the Reformation, the doctrine of justification by faith had ceased to exist. Ecclesiasticism so dominated people's minds that they were blind to the truth when reading Paul's epistles. This is a curious fact about the human mind, that it has the power only to see what agrees with current opinion. Every age is imprisoned in its own conceptions and has to be set free by the minds, which refuse to be enslaved.

There is a vast difference in the ways people hold the same doctrines. They are held either as supreme, or as of secondary importance. It makes all the difference in the life of the Church when prominence is given to the essential doctrines. The Church is revived when it is brought back to Christ, when it takes up the Cross-again. With the message of salvation burning in its heart, it goes out once again, as its Master did "to seek and to save them that are lost."

In addition, it is a significant fact that no religious system, which rejects the Cross, knows anything of revivals in the same way that Christianity does. Their ranks are recruited from those who become skeptical in the days of depression. They are never flooded with enthusiastic life, nor charged with messages, which move large amounts of people to the knowledge of divine things.

The Law of the Coming Movement

Let us close with a glance into the future. With the help of these stated biblical principles, we will ask what the future has in store. Before we can do this, we must first examine the present condition of the Church and read the signs of our times.

First, no one pretends that all is well with the Church today. When allowance is made for exaggeration, there are enough problems left to arouse deep soul searching. On every side, there is complaint of the Church's loss of spiritual power, the increasing indifference of its people, and a decrease in membership. Where there is not decline, there is a conscious arrest of her influence, and in the world hostility to her claims.

The Church is still active. Never were there more activity and less result. There is abundant energy, but it is not conquering energy conscious of its power, but feverish energy, conscious of its impotence. The message of the pulpit has largely lost its power to convince and the preacher his power to lead to conversion.

When we look beneath the surface, we see much to account for this. We have been passing through an age of commercialism. Never in the history of the world have the hearts of individuals been set with such a passion upon materialism. This has deadened men and women's hearts to the Gospel. However, this is not the sole reason. The Church itself has not escaped from materialism's corruption. It has been allowed to creep in and devitalize the Church's spiritual witness.

A new conscience is arising which is judging the Church by new standards. People are growing conscious of a contradiction between Christ's attitude toward the poor and the attitude of those who profess to be Christians. There is a growing sense of social injustice. Indignation is rising because, in the presence of this, the Church has remained silent-ignoring those who need it the most.

Much of this accusation is undeserved and can be repudiated by individual congregations. However, concerning the Church in general, it is impossible to deny it. Because of this, many are making sacrificial efforts to rectify their attitudes, though they know that the Church is not behind them.

Another reason for the present state of impotence arises because we have gone through an age of theological unrest. Our foundations are shifting. It is an age of transition, and such periods are ones of suffering. This unrest in the area of belief has arisen through the scientific revival, which has characterized this century. The progress has been amazing. However, no area of human thought has been more threatened than theology. The theory of evolution has challenged the completely Christian creed and has demanded a reevaluation of its essential beliefs. Historic research dealing with the Bible has left nothing unexamined, which was once considered too holy to touch.

For many, the result of these changes has been the unsettlement of belief; for others, the loss of their faith. For all, an uncertainty regarding even the most central doctrines has arisen. These changes have introduced into the pulpit insecurity brought about by preachers who were not quite certain of their ground. A tendency to leave many of the disputed doctrines alone and rely upon moral precepts and good living has arisen.

The result is that much, if not all, of the message of Christianity has been silenced. Passion is simulated. Energy is directed toward useless things. People in the pew are unconsciously affected by the absence of certainty, and of intense conviction. Therefore, pulpit and pew are united in a common misgiving. People find it easy to drift from the Church. Their consciences are unaffected by their relapse, because there is not the atmosphere of reality which makes neglecting the Church a sin.

If this is true, then it is a fact, which should awaken the dullest heart concerned about the welfare of the world and his or her own spiritual life. Of course, a weakening Church means that the forces working against the Church are growing stronger. It makes us turn to the future and ask, "What is before us? Is the day of the Church over? Must we live on to see the decline, until it results in death?"

From such questions, we can turn away with a smile. The Church is not on the eve of destruction. It is on the eve of a revival. Like the day that comes when the long night is over, so every revival comes after times of tribulation. Nothing in the world is more certain than this. The question is not "if," but "when." Regarding such a question, it would be impious to speak with authority. It is not for us to know the times, which God has hidden. At the same time, there is much to give us hope.

When we turn to the present social and political conditions, it is not difficult to see that a great revolution is taking place. There is emerging a multitude of the neglected, demanding recognition, justice, and human rights. A new cry is heard today. The cry not only pierces the halls of government, but echoes like a wail in our churches. It is the cry of those who are awakening to a sense of bitter wrong and of social discontent. As crude as their cry may be, it is valid. People are coming to the recognition that the poor and deprived are men and women made in the image of God, thus having value.

All awakenings are dangerous if unattended by spiritual illumination and allowed to grow in hostility to religion. As a rule, today's leaders are often not found in the Church. They are standing outside the Church, accusing it of betraying God. Whether this is true or not is irrelevant, only this pathetic and humiliating fact of history has to be recalled: nearly every great revival has originated outside of the Church. This may not happen today, but in times of degeneracy, the Spirit of Christ is often found outside of the Church. Again, when the Spirit is freshly poured out, it is not the Church, but those outside it who make the first response. Only afterward is the Church awakened.

The Church today appears helpless to cope with its growing responsibilities. The problems are so great that the Church seems to sink under the weight of them. It is the Church's duty, not to solve the problems, but to give an inspiration. It is a flood of new spiritual life that is needed. When the heart is alive, the hardest problem becomes solvable. Love awakes and finds its own channels. It is the Church's coldness that makes problems unsolvable.

The solution is a revival of spiritual religion a new breath, which will pass over the valley of dry bones and make them live. The world is ready for this revival, whether or not the Church is. For the Church, revival means humiliation, a bitter knowledge of unworthiness, and an open and humiliating confession of sin. It comes to scorch before it heals.

This is why revival has been unpopular with many within the Church. It says nothing to them of the power they have learned to love, the ease, or success. It accuses them of sin; it tells them that they are dead. It calls them to forsake all else and follow Christ.

Is the Church today ready to hear that voice? Some doubt it. It is upon the hearts of the few that the agony falls. Revivals are not preceded by the Church becoming aware of the need, but by a few people here and there, who, feeling the need, begin to entreat God for a revival. This sense of need grows into a burden, until the cry becomes an agony. This is the cry, which God cannot deny.

No revival can come from below. All attempts to create a revival fail. Nor can we bring a revival down, since prayer is not the cause of a revival, but the human preparation for one. By prayer, we prepare the soil.

Is there a disposition to pray for revival? Are devout men and women everywhere becoming alarmed, not for the success of the Church, but for the glory of Christ? If not, then the night is not far spent; a deeper darkness is yet to come. For what use would a revival be, if we were not prepared for it? It would pass over us without doing its work. J. Hudson Taylor affirmed this when he wrote, "The spirit of prayer is, in essence, the spirit of revival."

However, there are signs that this burden to pray is being laid upon the souls of men and women. Many are beginning to passionately long for better things and to agonize in prayer. To fail in this is to be a traitor to Christ and to the deepest need of the world around us.

Encouragement that the dawn is near comes from another side. Some have pointed out that we have been passing through an age of criticism, when much of the accepted truth has not been able to stand the test. Most careful onlookers are convinced that the worst is over. The destructive era has ended and the constructive era has begun. A great change has overcome the leaders of science and of thought. There is a new reverence for the spiritual life, and thought has drifted far from the agnostic position.

One of the most significant facts connected with this new movement is the orthodox position. Much has changed, but nothing vital in Christian belief has been lost. The old lives still in the new. With the recognition of the spiritual reality, it is possible to return to that same sense of security of belief, which makes a revival of religion possible. As long as belief was uncertain and those responsible to defend the Church's faith were panic-stricken, this was impossible. With the new confidence, there is also arising a longing for a revived Church.

It is encouraging that this dryness is only local. In other parts of the world, the wave that is subsiding here is flowing in full force. In Asia, Latin America, and Africa, Christianity is spreading rapidly. However, not only there is Christianity growing, but also in Eastern Europe the growth is remarkable.

Of what character will the next revival be? No one can say, but there are certain things that we can hope for; others we may regard with certainty. First, no revival would be worth anything if it excluded those who are alienated from the Church. Whatever the message is, it must bring the people back to their heritage within the Church. It must bring the Church back to the needs of the poor and underprivileged. Such a message will demand a greater sacrifice than the Church has been called to make since its birth. For it was not power and position which won the hearts of the poor and outcast in those days, but it was the Church's poverty and love.

The next revival will move us toward unity, which goes along with the spirit of our age. Denominationalism is breaking down around us. In the face of the complexities of modern life, the cry for unity is heard. All that is needed is the increase of love that comes with revival, to cement those unions already formed.

Whatever form the coming awakening may take, we may be certain that it will bring us back to the essentials. This is the result of every true revival. It cuts through the trappings until it gets to the core of life. It leads men and women back to simplicity. When the heart earnestly seeks God, it takes the shortest route. Above all, it will bring us back to Christ.

The day may be near. Even now, He may be preparing His messenger.

"But who can endure the day of His coming? And who can stand when He appears? For He is, like a refiner's fire and like fuller's soap. He will sit as a refiner and a purifier of silver; He will purify the sons of Levi, and purge them as gold and silver, that they may offer to the Lord an offering in righteousness. Then the offering of Judah and Jerusalem will be pleasant to the Lord, as in the days of old, as in former years. And I will come near you for judgment; I will be a swift witness against sorcerers, against adulterers, against perjurers, against those who exploit wage earners and widows and the fatherless, and against those who turn away an alien–because they do not fear Me,' says the Lord of hosts."

"But to you who fear My name the Sun of Righteousness shall arise with healing in His wings; and you shall go out and grow fat like stall-fed calves." -Malachi 3:2-5; 4:2, NKJV

www.ingramcontent.com/pod-product-compliance
Lightning Source LLC
Chambersburg PA
CBHW071956150426
43194CB00008B/887